THE SEEDS OF THE DIVINE BEGINNING

The Seeds of the Divine Beginning

A Personal Recollection of the
Birth of Higher School on Earth

LINDA L KAPLAN

OREGON HOUSE
2023

Copyright © 2023 Linda L Kaplan.

All rights reserved. No part of this publication may be reproduced, stored in a retrieval system, or transmitted, in any form or by any means, electronic, mechanical, photocopying, recording, or otherwise, without the written prior permission of the author.

ISBN 978-1-7335653-4-9

Book Design by William Bentley

Cover Photo by Engelbert Goethals of a rare double-lotus bloom that appeared in a fountain pond in the gardens of the Fellowship of Friends, Apollo, California in June 2016.

Back Cover Photo by Leonid Novoselov of a painting of the original lodge in August 1971 (see Chapter 40).

Back Cover Photo of the Author by Susan Schofield.

Contents

About This Book .... page *vii*

To the Reader .... *ix*

Dedication .... *xi*

Part I: Before the Beginning 1

Part II: The Beginning 51

Part III: The Middle 285

Part IV: The Beginning of the End 417

Part V: The End 525

Part VI: The Next Beginning 587

Part VII: The Divine Continuance 611

Acknowledgments 615

About This Book

This book was prompted by requests to describe what it was like to participate in the birth of higher school on earth, the Fellowship of Friends. In my attempt to recall my experience of the inception of this school of awakening, which covers a two-year period of my life, I understood profoundly that at best all I could provide was an honest narrative; anyone looking for the truth in these pages will be highly disappointed.

Each person who lived this journey with me may have a different tale to tell, which is as it should be. This book is based on my memory of events as I experienced them, and is written by the person who experienced them — not the person who could later comment or advise on the "errors of my ways."

It is not a simple storytelling. Historical events can be documented, of course, but it is truly the relationships that comprise and inform the experiences of our lives. And to do justice to each experience, one must expand the definition of relationship. It cannot be limited to merely you and me. It needs to include six types of relationship: relationship to higher powers; relationship to time; relationship to the school; relationship to the teacher; relationship to other students; and, perhaps most importantly, relationship to the higher and lower parts of one's being. The way each layer interacts with each other paints a more authentic picture.

In this narrative, some people are referenced by a descriptor but not named, while some others have different names — all in the interests of privacy. Because the story dates back over fifty years, many of the main characters are now deceased. Where full names are given, it is done with permission.

Each person in the story contributed to not only the Fellowship's growth and development, but also to my personal evolution. To them, I am eternally grateful.

Books are like men — the best of them have flaws.
Thank God for the flaws!
                                             Walt Whitman

To the Reader

The effort to tell a tale based on recollection raises a most interesting question: How legitimate is this memory?

What we each recall of a moment we share is colored by the filters of our own mechanics. A recollection is merely an imprint, a result of an internal light source hitting the chemistry of our thinking, feeling, moving, and sensing functions. We remember our thoughts, our emotions, where we were in space and what we heard, smelled, saw, tasted and touched. So real are these remembrances that we can easily miss the point of our lives: these memories do not last because they are products of the human machine. They are not real.

What is to be treasured is the flash of light itself that for some divine reason turned on in that moment to take the snapshot. Although we may study the photos of our past for insights, it is best that we learn to put them down and return to the present. They are not who we are. We are the camera's light, not the developed film. And therein lies the wonder of the great unfolding mystery of our lives.

And so, dear reader, treasure your own experiences. They have been divinely crafted to serve as the breadcrumbs that will take you either to the witch's cage or to your true home. Learn the lessons they reveal as quickly as possible. See who is living your life inside of you, calling itself by your name. Each moment is perfectly designed for you to find your conscious self. Strive to go past the complexity of day-to-day dramas that we imagine are true and real without question. Do not believe the seductive, convincing demand that "I must be me."

You will find that this journey of awakening is a hard ascent for the lower self but a joyous flight for the Higher Self. Cultivate courage, patience, and above all, *trust in the invisible.*

Good luck!

I planted the seed,... but God has been making it grow.
Paul, 1 Corinthians 3:6

*This book is dedicated to those who found the gods and
stayed the course, enduring and transforming suffering to their last breath.
You unshakable ones. You know who you are.*

PART I
Before the Beginning

CHAPTER 1

IT WAS THE summer of 1970. Michael, my new brother-in-law, had just received orders to fight in Vietnam. He was a career officer in the United States Army. Tall and fit, with Clint Eastwood eyes and a John Wayne demeanor, he had understood his duty to his country for years and was ready to go. He and my sister Kathy had met in their sophomore year at UCLA: he was a fraternity man and she was a sorority girl. With her intelligence, deep brown eyes, and long auburn hair, she had zeroed in on his heart. It was a direct hit. Their courtship lasted throughout their college years. Upon graduation, each had received Phi Beta Kappa, the highest collegiate honor, which only confirmed to me that they were perfectly matched.

During that summer the war was raging. Because my sister Kathy understood she might never see her husband again, she took the opportunity of his imminent departure to bring our two families together. We had never gotten together before because Mike and Kathy married in Germany, where he had just been stationed. It was a non-denominational military wedding, we were told; we were shown the pictures. The photo I liked the most was the one with them walking down the aisle. Kathy wore a floor-length white A-line bridal dress. Her long hair was upswept and assembled into symmetrical curls the size of frozen orange-juice cans. A sheer veil draped over her stylish do. Mike's lean, uniformed figure was a good six inches taller than his bride. As he walked proudly by her side under a canopy of military swords, his white-gloved hands gently guided her down the path of seeming danger.

There was another photo, however, that Kathy showed me privately. She was kneeling at the altar. Were my father to have seen that picture, his anger would have spread through our house like an August wildfire fanned by the Santa Ana winds. You see, Mike's family was Catholic and ours was Jewish.

The dislike my father felt for Mike, however, had little to do with the differences in our religious upbringing; it had more to do with a single remark Mike had made to Dad while courting Kathy. I don't remember how the argument began, but when Mike said to my father, "Mr. Kaplan, I do not respect you as a man," whatever bond could have existed between them disintegrated.

That incident, however, not only didn't stop Kathy and Mike from marrying, it may have encouraged the union, as my sister always had a rebellious nature. Dad's sneers, threats, and shouts could never intimidate my sister. She had the same weaponry in her arsenal. Dad had to swallow his pride and get used to the fact that this insolent gentile was now a direct relation.

Our family lived in Los Angeles and Mike's family lived in San Diego. The gathering was to be in San Diego since Mike came from a larger family: two sisters and a brother, who was close to my age. I had just graduated from UCLA and was completing my teaching credential there. Mike's brother, Ron, was attending St. Mary's, a Catholic college in the Bay Area. I had heard Kathy speak of Ron briefly over the years — passing references really, to the fact that he and I shared the same major, English, and that we were both "intellectuals." I was curious about him. But whenever I asked her what he was like, she glared at me, and curtly ended the discussion by saying, "He's GOT a girlfriend." I could not quite understand her concern.

Ours was a family that kept to itself. I never really knew my parents to have close friends. My father was a former boxer, who often introduced himself to people as "Da guy who hadda t'ousand fights and neva won one." His face supported his self-description: a flat, crooked nose; two misshapen ears that looked like pounded chicken cutlets; beady, unfocused eyes; and poorly fit dentures. My mother was a dutiful figure: short, hunched, smiling out of self-defense, with hands neatly folded together even when she was standing. They were two people who limited their experiences to each other. And, oh yes, to the television. That was the common denominator between them. When I grew up, conversations were measured in commercial time: 15-second, 30-second, and, for the most urgent adolescent dilemmas, 60-second spots. As soon as the scheduled program returned to the air, family crises were automatically put on hold. I mention all this to emphasize the stress my parents were under during this trip to San Diego. Not only were they forced, by circumstances, to leave the solace of the 26-inch Zenith for an outing to a gentile's home, they also had to make a deliberate attempt to be sociable.

Mike and Kathy had been staying in a nearby hotel for a week when they first arrived from Germany. Mike then decided to go ahead to San Diego, while Kathy would accompany us in the family car for the 2½ hour drive. Personally, I felt Mike's decision was based more on not having to sit in the same car with my father than on any great desire to be alone with his family.

The trip to San Diego was memorable for me from the start, insofar as I felt lousy. I had cramps, and had to listen to my father's Lecture 237, titled,

"The importance of getting a Ph.D." Like many persons of his generation, Dad had no formal education past the fourth grade, and yet prided himself on his street-smarts, which over the years he had analyzed, categorized, and formulated into a series of free lectures that he generously offered to anyone within ear-range. Bankers and children trapped in cars were his favorite audiences.

When we arrived in San Diego, the lecturing had stopped and the arguing began. My sister had the map to the house, but my father could not (or would not) follow her directions. When the address on the map matched the address on the curb, Dad pulled the car into the driveway and turned off the engine. We had made it. But nobody moved. We sat there as if the drive were the sole purpose of the journey.

Our inertia was interrupted when Betty, Mike's mom, burst out of the house. "They're here!" she exclaimed exuberantly. Mike followed closely behind her. Kathy quickly got out of the car to hug Betty and kiss Mike. Without realizing we were still in the car, Kathy introduced us to Betty. That was our cue to move. Dad got out slowly, came around the car, and shook Betty's hand reluctantly. Mom exited next, smiled weakly, and said hello. I was the last to offer my greeting. I waved.

The rest of Mike's family was waiting inside the house: his father, his brother, and his two sisters. Kathy had positioned herself as the liaison between the two groups. She had just finished introducing everyone to each other as I entered. Kathy turned to me and said, "Linda, I'd like you to meet Ron. Ron, this is my sister Linda."

I extended my hand, and looked into the pale blue eyes of a man who seemed far older than his years. His short-cropped, curly brown hair and neatly trimmed beard befit the image of an intellectual. The smoking pipe held firmly between his lips reinforced this scholarly impression. But something was off: the image seemed too calculated. Here was someone I had looked forward to meeting. I was shocked, however, when my instinct told me, Avoid this guy; he's not what he seems.

After the introductions, we dispersed. The two sisters went outside with Ron, Kathy, and Mike. Betty's husband sat on the couch alone. My parents stood in the living room, as if lost. I followed Betty into the kitchen.

To be polite, I asked if I could help her prepare the meal. "Would you like to make the salad?" she asked. I nodded and smiled. As I tore the leaves off the lettuce, we began to chat. I learned that she had raised four children while maintaining a full-time secretarial job. But what impressed me the most was her appearance. This was a woman who took time for herself. She applied cosmetics — lipstick, pancake makeup, mascara — with a knowledgeable hand. Her curly brown hair clearly indicated she frequented a beauty salon. Her print dress was stylishly cinched by a belt of matching fabric. She wore earrings and fashionable pumps. The feminine yet functional apron underscored her sense of appropriateness. She was a direct contrast to my mother, who wore no makeup, had her hair cut at the barbershop, lounged around the house in pajamas until noon, and thought gourmet cooking was opening two cans instead of one.

Betty was a woman who reflected all that was good about American womanhood of the Fifties. She was the model mother I had seen on TV and could only dream of having. And here I was, working alongside her. For a blissful moment, I felt like the daughter TV's Harriet Nelson and June Cleaver longed for but sadly never had.

She asked me what I was studying at university. I told her I was earning my teaching credential in English and that I had been working as a student teacher that quarter at a special school on campus for kids with learning disorders. When I mentioned that Mario Lanza's son was one child in the class, her eyes lit up. She loved Mario Lanza's singing, she said. In that moment we bonded.

As I continued to describe the teaching techniques I used for these special children, I noticed that Ron had entered the kitchen. I tried to ignore him, as his energy made me nervous. He stood there listening to us, with one hand resting on his hip and the other pressed high against the doorframe. His defiant stance was a prelude to the words that came from his mouth. "If I had a kid," he said, "I would never put him in public school." I looked at him and asked firmly, "And why not?" He went on about how public schools do not teach you to think, but only to regurgitate information. I felt my face heat up and my body tense. My cramps were returning. I could see he was looking for an argument. But a voice inside my head calmly said, "Turn around and slice the cucumber. You don't have energy for this." I kept my mouth shut and let him talk.

Family members passed through the kitchen on the way to the backyard where we were to dine. Mike's youngest sister was helping Kathy gather utensils and napkins for the table setting. His other sister grabbed a broom to sweep the patio. I had no idea where my parents were. After I finished the salad, I walked into the living room. Mike's father was sitting on the couch, alone. I sat next to him and tried to hold a conversation. Each statement I made entered his court like an ace. He made no attempt to volley. He just sat there. It was not a bad place to be, really. For me it was a respite. Unfortunately, it was short lived.

Betty entered the living room. She stood right in front of me, drying her hands with a dish towel, and asked, "Why don't you help Ron with the barbecue?" When I said I knew nothing about barbecues, she countered, "Well, just keep him company then." How could I say, "Sorry, Mum, but your son is not fit for company?" I felt obliged to go.

When I got to the backyard, however, I couldn't find him even though the space was small. A few family members had already gathered around the redwood-plank picnic table and were talking. I went up to the barbecue, which consisted of two red-brick columns connected by a grate that was suspended over a wood burning pit. It was obviously homemade. To the far left of the barbecue I could see Ron behind the garage, splitting wood for kindling.

I approached him. "Hello," I said. He glanced up briefly and reiterated my greeting. I watched the individual muscles in his forearm flex as he chopped the wood with measured strokes. Nice, I thought. He carried the wood to the pit and began to arrange the kindling deliberately. He lit the fire. I then followed him to two chaise lounges whose backs rested against the side of the garage that faced the table. The conversation somehow drifted to a neutral subject: jazz. He asked me if I had ever heard of John Coltrane. I said I had not. He spoke of him with great reverence and authority. I was actually enjoying the conversation. It was not negative. I was even beginning to think he may not be so bad after all.

"Dinner's ready! Come sit down," said Betty, to no one in particular. Ron and I must have spoken longer than I realized.

It was a tight squeeze around the table. Betty sat me next to Ron. Kathy and Betty did most of the talking. I ate quietly. My father started to pick a fight with Mike. Betty quickly tried to neutralize it by criticizing Ron's poor dietary habits. The two sisters began to defend their brothers. Mike's father said nothing. Neither did my mother.

We managed to complete our meals, clear the table, offer our thank-yous, and say goodbye. Halfway home, on I-5, the car blew a tire. My father looked up to the skies and proclaimed it an omen.

CHAPTER 2

Knowing someone who was in Vietnam at that time made the television images of the war frightfully vivid. To ease her stress, Kathy not only wrote Mike long love letters, but also sent him tapes on which she recorded some pretty erotic messages. I never understood why she did this. To me, sending a man sounds of heavy breathing when he bunked with men and only had recourse to prostitutes was neither intelligent nor an act of kindness. But I figured she knew what she was doing. I, too, made an effort to contribute to Mike's wellbeing. What, I reasoned, was the rarest commodity in a war? The answer seemed obvious: humor. So I sent him every joke that appeared on *Laugh-In* each week.

The time passed quickly. Although the jokes grew stale, the passion burned more fervently. I stopped sending him the insipid one-liners, while Kathy was now sending him two tapes filled with libidinous whispers. Kathy was indeed devoted to her man.

As Thanksgiving approached, I thought it would really be nice if I could go to San Diego with Kathy for Christmas. I had never experienced Christmas before, being Jewish. When I asked her if she thought she could swing an invitation for me, she said she didn't think there would be enough room in the house, but she would try. She planned to call Betty on Thanksgiving.

I was in the room when she made that call. I'll never forget the shocked look on Kathy's face one minute into the conversation. Before she could even introduce the subject of Christmas, Betty had said, "Oh, by the way. I spoke with Ron this morning and he wanted me to invite Linda down for Christmas."

* * * *

The late afternoon flight to San Diego was the second time I had been on an airplane. It was a Wednesday, the day before Christmas Eve. During the short trip, Kathy made it quite clear to me that Ron's invitation was sincere, but meaningless. Yes, it was true that he had just broken up with his girlfriend. But, she rationalized, "He asked you to come because he thought you were a nice person. That's all. So get any romantic ideas out of your head."

Why did Ron invite me? Did I really make that great of an impression on him? A sorority type I was not. In fact, my social life was non-existent. I had had three dates during my college years, all of them "blind" and arranged by Kathy from parental pressure. The best physical description I could give of myself was a great "Before shot." Did Ron see past my thick glasses, past my waist-length thick wavy black hair, past my full figure so amply displayed in a size fourteen purple coatdress? Could he detect the real me behind the glasses, the hair, and the matronly apparel? Like the soldier in Hans Christian Andersen's *Tinder Box*, could he get beyond the dog to the real treasure? And even if he could, how much would it matter to me?

As we deplaned, Kathy was the first to spot Ron. I barely recognized him. He still had the beard and pipe, but was dressed more casually in a pale yellow short-sleeved shirt and jeans. And yet, somehow, he seemed completely different, and it had nothing to do with his clothing. It wasn't until he reached out to bear-hug us both that I realized what had changed: his disposition. The reserved cynic was gone and a warm, outgoing young man was now there. I was unprepared for the change in his demeanor. It only increased my anxiety.

As he carried our bags to his car, he updated Kathy about his mother and sisters. When we got into his 1956 two-toned green Chevy, I automatically sat in the back while Kathy sat in the front passenger seat next to him. I looked around for seat belts, but found none. As we entered the freeway on-ramp, Ron gunned the car and the rapid acceleration threw me against the seat. I grabbed onto the door strap to gain my balance. I had to get through the next four days, I thought, and the only way I knew was to be as invisible as I could — and to make sure that Ron and I were never alone together. My anxiety turned to suspicion. I didn't trust him.

* * * *

When we arrived at the house, the early evening dusk had disappeared into darkness. Ron unlocked the front door and moved the bags inside. The Christmas tree was the only source of light illuminating the living room. Despite the dimness, Kathy intuitively found the mistletoe and took advantage of the moment by grabbing Ron and kissing him. It was just a peck on the cheek, really, but it startled me so much that it took several moments before I realized my feet had taken me to the couch. There I sat, alone in the dark, pretending to admire the tree. Kathy and Ron were chatting about Mike; they didn't notice that I had disappeared. I listened to their conversation and heard Ron say that Betty was expected home from work at any moment.

As she entered the door, Betty turned on the lights in the living room. The place instantly became less threatening. After greeting us, she showed us to the bedroom Kathy and I were to share for the next four days.

I unpacked my clothes and put the presents I had purchased for the family under the tree. I liked this custom of Christmas giving, as it made me feel more a part of the family event. I had purchased small gifts for the parents and sisters (coasters, perfume, etc.) that reflected more a polite gesture of appreciation for their hospitality than any particular affection. When it came to Ron, however, I felt I had to buy him a book. I had looked around for the right one, and decided upon a book that meant a great deal to me. It was titled *The Story of Jesus*.

This book documented the twentieth century seer Edgar Cayce's revelation about an esoteric group during Jesus' time named the Essenes. I had privately been studying Edgar Cayce's writings and found them thought-provoking. Why exactly I chose this book of all the many I could have bought remained a puzzle to me. Maybe I wished to engage Ron in an intellectual discussion. Or maybe I wanted to reveal myself to him in a very personal way. Whatever the motive, the gift-wrapped book now rested under the tree.

As the evening progressed, one of Ron's old boyhood pals had arrived to whisk him away to some party. Betty's two teenage daughters had also arrived home by then. They had already eaten and went directly to their rooms after greeting Kathy and me. Betty prepared a light supper for Kathy and me, talking mostly of Mike. I just listened and tried to appear interested, as befit a good guest. We joined her afterwards to wash dishes. By this time, it was close to nine and Betty still needed to prepare her famous apple pie, which she would take to the Christmas Eve party the next evening at the Jansons, who were old friends of the family. Kathy and I retired to our room and prepared for bed. The first day had come to an end.

* * * *

The second day, Christmas Eve, began very early for me. Unlike Kathy, I wasn't used to communal life since I never lived in a sorority house. It was inconceivable for me to appear before strangers in my bathrobe with no makeup and no bra. Privacy was paramount. So I got up around 6 a.m., slowly opening the bedroom door, peaking into the hallway to make sure it was empty, and maneuvering quickly into the bathroom, positioning myself behind the door before closing and locking it. My preparation took an hour.

When I exited the bathroom, to my surprise, the human contents of the house were still slumbering. As I re-entered the bedroom, I sat on my bed and looked at my sister sleeping. It was after seven and I was hoping she would be disturbed by my entrance. She was not. I waited two hours. Sometimes I would lie on the bed. Then get up to search for a book to read. I found nothing. Whoever's bedroom I was using clearly lacked an intellectual capacity. Since I lived in my head, however, I found enough thoughts to entertain me, as I lay prone on the made bed, staring up at the ceiling.

At 9 a.m. I heard the house stirring. Kathy was waking up too, and was surprised to see me dressed and ready for the day. "Weirdo," she remarked. Her assessment of my character was often more a noun than an adjective. For example, she named me Fats, not Fat Person. I got used to it.

THE DIVINE BEGINNING

Kathy surprised me when she put on her bathrobe and immediately headed for the kitchen, not the bathroom. I followed her. There we found Betty, Ron, and his two sisters and father in their bathrobes. And there I was in my street clothes with hair perfectly coifed. Too late to undo it and blend in, I realized.

Standing near the counter, I was offered something called "granola" for breakfast. I had never heard of granola before, let alone eaten it. It looked like some sort of snack, like Cracker Jack. I took the package I was handed, poured a substantial amount into a bowl, and started eating it with my fingers. When Ron handed me a spoon and asked if I wanted milk with it, I realized it was cereal. How would I know this? I was used to Kellogg or Post cereals (Raisin Bran was my favorite). But I had already started eating it. Because I didn't want him to think I didn't know what I was doing, I said, "No, I like it this way." I lied.

I wished I knew about the milk but it was too late. I continued to toss the dry, sweet clumps of grain into my mouth until it became clear to me that I couldn't continue without some liquid, so I stopped without finishing. I could feel Ron's mocking look, as if he could see through my sham of confidence. What would I do with the rest of it? I was taught never to waste food. Here was a Jewish dilemma: finish it to prove to him I know what to do with granola, or leave it, saying I was full. And what would these gentiles do with the remaining granola in my bowl? Do they throw it away or put it back into the cellophane bag? My head swirled with confusion. Here it was before 9:30 in the morning: Already two social missteps. This day was going to be painful.

I turned around to face Kathy and Betty, who were planning their day by the kitchen sink. They'd get dressed and head out to the grocery store and do some other shopping. It was a bonding experience for them, clearly. The sisters had already left the kitchen to prepare for their day. And then there was Ron and me. Basic math revealed I had to speak up, so I said to Betty, "May I go with you shopping?" "Sure," replied Betty politely. And with that I followed them out of the kitchen, leaving Ron with my bowl on the counter.

* * * *

The afternoon's shopping excursion was uneventful for me. I can barely remember where we went or what was purchased. I tagged along with my sister, as had been my habit for my entire life. She was 13 months older than I, and seemed to have a perfect life. Everything she wanted, she got. Friends, sorority, husband, straight A's…you name it. She went after it and it fell into her lap. Or so it seemed to me.

Everything for me was a struggle. I was an average, ordinary person. The boys I was infatuated with ran the other way. Even with Kathy in a sorority, my suggestion she help me pledge was met with, "Sorry, Linda, but my friends don't like big girls." And my mediocrity was only confirmed by my father's oddly placed encouragement while I was in ninth grade. "Honey," he once told me, "you don't have to work so hard to get A's. I know you're just a C student."

* * * *

That evening was the Jansons' party. I was included as part of Betty's family. The elder daughter had a date and couldn't make it. We drove over in one car: Betty, her husband, and Kathy sat in the front; I sat with the apple pie resting on my ample lap in the back with Ron and his younger sister.

The Jansons' home was a scene out of *Redbook* magazine. A holiday wreath hung on the front door; poinsettias lined the entryway; a seven-foot spruce, laden with ornaments, stood tall in the corner of the living room; and the dishes and napkins had Christmas motifs. The fireplace was blazing, and "Jingle Bells" was mirthfully playing on the stereo. No kidding. I was stunned that people actually did this. The whole effect was so contrived that I almost expected Santa Claus to pop out of the closet.

The dinner was equally traditional: baked ham, parsley potatoes, dinner rolls, green beans with onions, and, of course, Betty's apple pie for dessert. The ham was a struggle for me to eat, considering I had only eaten ham once before in my life as part of a Swanson's TV dinner sale that my father could not resist. The TV dinner episode became emblematic of the fall from grace within our Jewish household. Dad's mother kept kosher and Dad had strayed in many ways; but having to choose between a sale and God's ordinance was the ultimate proclamation that we were now living in a no-man's-land of Jewish pseudo-religious tradition: we were Jews that acted like goyim when Grandma — and apparently God — weren't watching. Something in me knew that God could no longer pass over our house without inflicting some painful and debilitating curse on us.

After dinner we gathered around a standup piano while Mrs. Janson played Christmas carols. Kathy and Betty started to sing. Even though I enjoyed singing a great deal, I stood there silently. Kathy encouraged me to join in, announcing to everyone that I had a beautiful voice. My voice was big and operatic, and it often shocked people when the sound came out. Rather than turn carols into arias, I decided simply to whisper the words in tune. That was acceptable.

On the way home, everyone in the car seemed to be talking at once, reminiscing about past Christmases with the Jansons, and laughing about some of the practical jokes Mr. Janson, a jovial fellow, loved to play on his wife. It was easy for me simply to listen since I had no such associations.

When everyone had completed the storylines, a natural silence occurred. After a minute, Betty filled the space by saying, "Gee, Linda, you certainly have been pretty quiet tonight." Kathy immediately answered Betty in my stead, "Oh, Linda's SHY." I'm not sure if she meant it sarcastically, but it put an end to this line of conversation. I sat there, rather pleased that the talk was now centered on Betty's delicious apple pie.

But the attention wasn't completely off me. I felt someone's gaze. Turning my head, I saw Ron smiling at me. I quickly looked the other way, out the window. At that moment, I realized that, like me, he had not participated at all in the conversation. We both had sat quietly, letting the others fill the air with their commentary. For years I survived family life by being the passive observer. It appeared that he was an expert at it, too. Could it be that this was not all we had in common?

CHAPTER 3

It was day three and Christmas morning. Once again, I got up early to shower and dress before the others arose. By the time I got out of the bathroom, the rest of the family had gathered in the living room, still wearing their pajamas and gowns. They were waiting for me to emerge so they could open the Christmas presents.

Betty distributed the gifts. It was clearly the family tradition. I sheepishly sat on the crowded couch with the sisters. I wasn't expecting anything and so was surprised when she handed me a big box. I opened it and was even more surprised to find a flannel nightgown in it. When I looked up to thank her, she blushed noticeably. Apparently, I had received the wrong gift — the nightgown was meant for the younger sister. She then handed me the proper gift, which turned out to be a bottle of cologne. I thanked her and reassured her that she shouldn't feel embarrassed about the mix-up.

The gift distribution stopped. I had been waiting for Betty to unearth that book I had bought Ron. It seemed it was lost under the mounds of Christmas wrapping cluttering the living room. Everyone was focused on their gifts, and I pretended to admire my cologne.

As Betty started to clean up the area, she noticed a package hidden behind the trunk of the tree. She read the attached card out loud, "For Ron from Linda." She handed the wrapped gift to Ron. He smiled at me and everyone watched as he opened it. I began to perspire. This was not the way I thought this moment would go.

I sat on the couch, looking down at my fidgeting hands playing with the cologne bottle I received. Betty looked over Ron's shoulder at the title. *"The Story of Jesus,"* she announced to everyone. My heart raced. I realized I hadn't considered that this private offering, which I had rehearsed many times in my mind, would be given such a public showing.

Then the most unexpected thing occurred: Ron walked over and kissed me on the cheek. Our eyes met and he whispered, "Thank you." Everyone in the room froze like some classical group sculpture, directing their stares with laser-beam intensity on Ron and me. The tension in the room was palpable. To break the spell, Betty jumped up, shouted BREAKFAST IS READY, and disappeared into the kitchen. We all followed after her.

* * * *

The breakfast was delicious: homemade waffles, bacon, coffee, and orange juice. The incident between Ron and me was never mentioned. After breakfast, Betty coordinated the whole cleanup: I helped wash the dishes while Kathy and the younger sister finished cleaning the living room of paper, ribbon, and boxes.

Just as I was folding the kitchen towel, Ron appeared and asked me to come with him. What was I to say? No? Would I be safe? These thoughts fleeted through my head, but curiosity was stronger so I followed him into the bedroom where he was staying. He opened the top drawer of the dresser, pulled out a small, thin book with a black cloth cover, and handed it to me. "This is for you. It's my own copy but it's more important you have it." The name of the book was *The Psychology of Man's Possible Evolution*. The author was P. D. Ouspensky. I had heard of neither.

I thought it was interesting that we each thought of books as gifts, and a bit amused that we were trying to proselytize one another. It seemed to be shades of our first combative encounter in the kitchen. Taking our books with us, we entered the living room and sat on the couch together. I must say, I was more interested in his opinion of the Edgar Cayce book I had given him than I was in reading anything about psychology from a man whose name I found hard to pronounce. I casually perused the pages of my book, while Ron looked more intent as he read from Cayce.

THE DIVINE BEGINNING

After about five minutes I asked him what he thought of the *Story of Jesus*. His remarked stunned me. "What I have read so far is imagination." Before I had a chance to register my feelings, he asked me what I thought of the Ouspensky book. I had nothing to say, since I hadn't read anything particular. I opened the book and quickly tried to catch a phrase or two that would help me form some kind of opinion. Two sentences jumped out: Man does not know himself. First of all, he does not realize that he *actually is a machine*. That last phrase hit me like a sucker punch.

"It hurts to read this," I said quietly, pointing to the italicized phrase.

"Yes," he replied softly, "I know."

I actually said this more to myself than to him. It was as if this Ouspensky had revealed a secret I knew well within some dark recess, but preferred not to contemplate. His statement produced mixed feelings: I felt hurt yet relieved, exposed yet guarded.

I tried to read a little more of the book, which was challenging because, to be honest, it was a bit dry. Ron got up to shower and dress, leaving me on the couch. Clearly the Cayce book was insignificant to him, as he laid it down next to me on the couch, rather than take it with him to place it in the secret drawer in his bedroom. His early and quick dismissal of the Cayce book left me feeling that he expected me to enter his world and refused to meet me half way. I patiently tolerated this inequality, as I figured if I gained something for myself and he didn't, it was his loss, not mine.

It was noon and I was getting hungry. Before I had a chance to think further about lunch, Ron entered the living room and asked, "Would you like to go to the San Diego Zoo this afternoon? If we leave now, we can get some lunch there." I replied yes because this was becoming a real adventure, something I sorely lacked in my life. I gladly put the book down, hoping that this would be the last time I would have to consider his psychological ideas.

* * * *

The San Diego Zoo was huge. We zigzagged in and out of exhibits. We found a hot dog stand by one of the bear enclaves. Ron bought two hot dogs and we went to a park bench. Usually I have a substantial appetite, but I found myself daintily nibbling at the dog in the bun. Ron had even less interest in eating. Instead, he was more interested in discussing these psychological ideas.

"What part in the book did you reach?"

"Are there any ideas you thought were new?"

"Have you ever noticed that people walk around asleep?"

I felt more grilled than the hot dog. Around Ron I was beginning to feel increasingly passive. I could see I liked the attention he was giving me and felt an irresistible urge to please him. I tried to appear intelligent and interested. I told him I had read most of the book, that some of it appeared new, and that there were times when I noticed people were asleep. I knew the answers were trite, yet he continued to respond as if I had similar revelations to his. Behind it all, I didn't understand why he was pursuing me like this.

We walked to the monkey cages. He started to talk about a concept called "body types," using the monkeys in front of us to illustrate this idea. He pointed out how they were of different sizes, although they were all mature adults. I nodded in agreement, but in truth all I could see and would later remember was the size of the male penises.

* * * *

We returned to the house in time for dinner. It was a small dinner because the girls were out with their friends. Betty and Kathy had gone shopping that afternoon but had returned before us. We were four at the table.

During the meal, Betty asked me if I enjoyed the zoo and I replied yes, although I knew her idea of my experience was far from the reality. Ron and I helped to clear the table and wash the dishes. As I left the kitchen, Ron took me aside and said, "I'm going to a party and would like you to come." Sure, why not?

We drove to a suburb of San Diego, and came to a middle-class two-story house. There lived Ron's friend who had gone away to college and was also visiting his parents during the holidays. After exchanging greetings, I learned that we were taking this man with us to an apartment rented by other mutual friends. This is where the party actually was.

As we approached the place, I felt locked in a Star Trek time warp. Here I was, partying with people I had never met before, in an unknown city, and accompanied by a member of the opposite sex. Was I on a date? My social skills were so undeveloped that I had no way to relate to this experience.

We entered the small apartment through the kitchen, where a man and a woman were preparing food. Ron embraced them and introduced me. In the dimly lit living room, I could see four other couples lounging on huge neon-green bean-bag chairs scattered on the brown and yellow shag carpet. No one stood up to greet us as we walked in, but gave us casual welcomes instead.

The first thing I noticed was that the girls wore pants and sweaters; I was the only one wearing a dress. I was uncomfortable sitting on the floor like that, so I sat in a chair next to a dinette table that was pressed against the wall separating the kitchen from the living room. It was an interesting choice of seating: I was clearly the outsider here. My seat not only separated me from them, but also gave me a vantage point from which to observe.

Chips, guacamole, salsa, and beer were passed around. I kept smiling, trying to pick up on the conversation. They were laughing and talking about people whom I did not know. Occasionally someone would ask me how I was doing, and I said fine. Would you like another beer? No thank you, I replied politely.

Ron was smoking a pipe and was describing his pipe collection, which he said he planned to sell. Two of the men gasped and tried to talk him out of it. Ron explained he needed the money and felt he found a good potential buyer. He'd keep one or two of his favorites if he could.

Three hours passed. Then someone whispered something and everyone started to laugh and cheer. A man left the room and returned with a bag of marijuana. Two marijuana cigarettes were rolled and passed around. When it came to me, I kept it moving. One fellow suggested I try it, but I declined. They were laughing at my reluctance, and Ron suggested they leave me alone. The air was thick with smoke.

I was watching people lose control: their words were slurred; their emotions were erratic (two arguments broke out). I was in a bad movie.

Then Ron got up and sat in the chair on the other side of the table. He smiled at me and extended his hand. Automatically I put my hand out to him. He continued to stare at me for a few minutes; his blue eyes were intense. Quietly he said, "Let's go."

I stood up and walked with him to the door. The others were oblivious that we were leaving. We got into the Chevy and drove a distance before Ron pulled the car over to the side of the road. I was unsure of what was happening.

"What are we going to do?" he asked, after a few minutes of silence.

I said nothing because I had no idea what he was talking about.

He continued, "After all, you're in Los Angeles, and I'm in the Bay Area."

"We could write," I suggested lamely, still unclear about what he meant but hoping not to offend him.

We arrived at his home. He turned off the ignition. We sat still for a few moments. And then he reached over to kiss me.

I still felt I was in a movie, but the movie was getting better. We walked arm and arm into the dark living room and stopped in front of my bedroom door. He kissed me once again, said good night, and disappeared down the hall toward his room.

* * * *

Day three blurred its way into day four. I barely slept. Although we had gotten in at 3 a.m., I still arose at six to enter the bathroom to get ready. Emerging fully dressed, I slipped into the bedroom to get the Ouspensky book and headed to the living room to read. The house was quiet. Everyone was asleep. Or so I thought.

Coming down the hall was Ron. He was in his underwear. He sat right next to me, embraced me and said good morning. We started kissing, and before I knew it, we were passionately writhing on the living room floor.

The time warp continued. How could this be happening to me? Could this be love? Had I found my soul mate? A Hollywood girl at heart, I was raised on quick scenarios unfolding irrationally because of studio budget and time constraints. For example, the movie *GI Blues* with Elvis Presley, which I saw in 1960 at the age of eleven, was a little over an hour and a half, and it ended with Elvis and Juliet Prowse deciding to get married after 48 hours of knowing one another. From my limited experience and extensive programming, it seemed possible that this is how real love is born and flourishes.

Before I could contemplate further the profound aspects of my position (quite literally), I heard a scream. Betty was standing over us, rattling off her motherly instructions like a machine gun: "Oh-my-God-Ron-get-your-tail-into-the-bedroom-NOW."

We jumped up and Ron obediently responded, leaving me facing Betty. She went right past me into the kitchen. I headed back into my bedroom. Kathy was in the bathroom using the hair dryer. The two sisters were coming out of their rooms in their pajamas. The house was officially awake.

Breakfast was an exercise in eating. We moved our food-laden utensils to our mouths as rapidly as possible. When it was over, Ron escorted me out the kitchen door to the backyard. He embraced me and continued to speak about Ouspensky and *The Psychology* as he referred to it. He told me about a group of people he had met who were studying these ideas, and he wanted me to finish reading the book he gave me as soon as possible and to let him know what I thought.

As he spoke, he would periodically kiss me. Betty, who was washing dishes, could see us from the kitchen window. I could hear her repeatedly exclaim in anguish, "I'm gonna have a COW! I'm gonna have a COW!" Losing both sons to Jewesses clearly was more inconceivable to her than being the mother of a bovine.

* * * *

Our flight back to LA was to leave at noon. After hoisting our packed bags into the trunk of the Chevy, Ron motioned for me to sit with him on the front porch step. His arm was around my waist, and my head gently lay on his shoulder. He told me he would call me when I arrived back in LA. Everyone else was gathered on the front lawn. Kathy was trying to calm Betty down and would occasionally glare at me in disbelief.

The drive to the airport was remarkably quick. We checked our bags, and Kathy gave Ron a one-armed, half-hearted hug. She said nothing to me until we sat in our seats on the plane. As I finished fastening my seatbelt, she scowled at me and demanded to know, What the hell happened.

Of course, Kathy didn't accept my first reply to her question, even though it was the most honest one. When I said, "I don't know," she rejected it and pushed me into providing an answer that seemed to satisfy her: "I'm in love," I said. With this, she turned away from me as if considering the dire consequences. Then she instructed, "Just don't tell Dad."

CHAPTER 4

I couldn't explain to Kathy what had happened to me during those four days of Christmas because I truly did not understand it myself. All I knew was I felt something miraculous had happened to me. I felt at peace with myself, and very separate from everyone, even from Ron. I had waited all my life to have a real experience, not a virtual one as seen on TV. And now, for the first time, something magical was happening to ME.

When we arrived home, our secret was intact for about an hour. The phone rang and it was Ron calling for me. Immediately, Dad's face registered concern. You see, I rarely got phone calls. I didn't have close friends. I went to university, met some people, but seldom went out. For a man to call me was highly unusual. And for it to be the Gentile Ron, whom we had left three hours earlier, was real cause for alarm.

* * * *

Our phone conversation was centered upon reading as much of Ouspensky as I could and to "verify" the concepts he presented. I promised I would finish *The Psychology*, as we now referred to his Christmas present. At the first opportunity I would look for other books by Ouspensky and by another author named Gurdjieff.

When I returned to UCLA the first week of January, I went directly to its main library, which boasted six million volumes, to search for books by these two Russian authors. I found nothing under Gurdjieff and only one book by Ouspensky, titled *Tertium Organum*.

I checked the book out and began to read it. It was a formidable, intellectual book focusing on space, time, motion, matter, and other general philosophical problems and concepts. I got through it, yet wondered what it had to do with me. I still intended to graduate in six months with a teaching credential in English and Drama and possibly move to either Seattle, Washington or Virginia Beach, Virginia. I longed to be on my own, to have my own car, apartment, dog and bank account. Escaping my parents' home had been my aim since I was thirteen.

But Ron had now entered my life. It was clear that he had become my mentor. Some part of me wanted it to be a short run, really. I often would meet someone, exchange ideas, and then leave them behind. That had been my pattern since high school, and the reason that I had no close friends. I felt that people were episodes in my life, designed to teach me something about myself. Few series had long runs because I rarely found people that interesting. Ron was interesting to me not just because of his ideas, however; I must confess that he was interesting to me because he seemed interested IN me. This was a new adventure, and a romantic one at that. Such episodes were so rare that I could count them on one finger.

The phone calls were getting expensive, so Ron and I started exchanging letters. In one letter, he mentioned that he decided to change his name to Miles, which was his middle name. He included a black-and-white photograph of himself taken in London a year or two earlier. He looked handsome and erudite standing there with a full beard, tousled blond curly hair, his hands in the pockets of his tweed overcoat, and a pipe in his mouth. He looked like Paul Newman playing the role of an Oxford professor. The more I looked at the picture, with Ron (now Miles) gazing directly at me, the more I was falling in love.

* * * *

The evening of February 8, I decided to stay late at UCLA to attend a director's showing of *The Great White Hope* in Macgowan Hall. The film had been released in the fall, and I was studying film as part of my minor degree in

THE DIVINE BEGINNING

Theatre Arts. We watched the film and afterwards Martin Ritt, the director, and Jane Alexander, the female lead, appeared on stage to answer our questions and discuss the social and historical implications of the film. It was a fun evening, even though the Little Theatre was sparsely populated because it was ten o'clock by the time the event ended.

I recall after leaving the hall with classmates that evening how large the moon was in the sky. One fellow said, "The moon is full tomorrow night and there's a total lunar eclipse scheduled for 11:44 p.m. I'm staying up to watch." A chill ran up my spine. I don't know why exactly, but I decided I would not try to watch it.

I took the bus home and got into bed around midnight. I always kept my window open because I liked to hear the sound of the birds chirping before the traffic began its rush on Sunset Boulevard. I slept well that night.

At 5:58 a.m., my eyes popped open. I was startled awake by a strange silence. Within a few seconds I heard a roar like an elephant ready to charge. Then my bed shook back and forth violently. An earthquake! I jumped out of bed and stood in the open doorframe of my closet only two feet away. I watched my bed shake and my full fist taking refuge in the opening of my mouth. Everyone had heard of "The Big One." I had studied Geology at UCLA just to learn more about earthquakes and why they occur. Edgar Cayce also spoke a lot about earthquakes, predicting the occurrence of this Doomsday event to California. Was this it?

After a few minutes, the shaking subsided. I went into the living room and found my parents standing there like little children. A huge, solid wood, floor-to-ceiling bookcase had fallen over from the tremor. All they could do was stare at it, paralyzed. It was such a shocking moment for me. Their personality had been totally stripped away, and they were helpless. I turned to Dad and said, "Help me pick this up." We cleaned up the items and repositioned the furniture. Within an hour, Mom and Dad had returned to their normal identities. This moment we shared, where for the first time in my life I saw them in essence, was never discussed.

* * * *

On February 14, Valentine's Day, I arrived home from morning classes to a surprise. My mother told me that I had received a present. There, on the dining room table, was a long box that clearly contained roses. Next to it was another package the size of a book. She was excited for me, as no one in my family had ever received roses for any occasion. My father always considered such things as wastes of money since flowers die so quickly. Here was a romantic expression that simply brightened my mother's day, even though it wasn't addressed to her.

She quickly offered the attached sealed card that had my name on it and commanded with girlish enthusiasm, "Open it!" Well, I knew who sent it, and was reluctant to open it in front of her because I realized how difficult it would be now to convince her that Miles and I were just friends.

Sure enough, the long-stemmed red roses were from Miles. They were beautiful, yet we had no proper container for them. Improvising, I found a large empty pickle jar, filled it with water, and propped the roses against the inside rim. I placed the bouquet in the middle of the dining table, as that was the only surface large enough in our apartment to support it. I took the other package into my bedroom.

Alone in my room, I sat on my bed and slowly unwrapped the present. It was another book by Ouspensky, titled *The Fourth Way*. As I opened it, I saw that Miles had created a lovely image on the page opposite the title: he had drawn a large circle with my first and middle names flowing into his first and middle names. This was such a lovely personal gift. I scanned the contents and noticed that the format was different from *The Psychology*. Rather than lectures, it contained a series of questions and answers. As I started to skim it, I recognized many of the questions were my own and Ouspensky's answers were surprisingly direct. But more importantly to me, the dialogue was human. This book was what I had been looking for.

When my father arrived home later that afternoon from food shopping, he immediately asked about the roses, and glared at me for a response. I simply repeated my party line: it was only a gesture of friendship. As I started to walk toward my bedroom, my father's voice rose in strength on the subject of gentiles. His anger was so common that I had learned to turn a deaf ear to him. I was accustomed to keeping a low profile with my parents, and they were accustomed to my "introspection" as they liked to call it. Basically, we ignored one another. After the rose incident, they didn't bring up Miles's name and I didn't offer it.

* * * *

I finished reading *The Fourth Way* within two weeks. It was filled with so much information that I could feel my anxiety level rise, for I was trying to reconcile all the other ideas I had had with those of the new system, and they weren't fitting. Would I have to give up everything I thought was true to accept this system? So much of what I considered true the system labeled imagination. I felt shaken to my core.

I had written Miles about this, and his reply was that it was a positive step forward. It meant that I was beginning to see objectively. I didn't like his reply. I had paid dearly for my understandings and beliefs, and I wasn't about to give them up. Something in me was starting to hate this new system. But the strong attraction that I felt toward Miles was increasing and compelling me to move forward.

In the midst of my internal struggle, I received a strange letter from Miles. His tone had changed: there was now a thread of detachment running through it. He said he felt his role was to bring me to the "School," as he now referred to the group, and that I needed to come for a visit so I could meet his teacher. I replied that I could visit him during my spring break in the middle of March.

He wrote back saying he was pleased with that, and ended the letter with the most cryptic sentence I had ever read: "Waiting is good food for separation." I pondered this sentence for hours. What could it mean? Waiting is good, and it is food that needs separating from? Waiting is good food, if you wanted to be separate? Honestly, I couldn't make sense of it. Unlike his other letters, he signed this one simply "Miles" without any expression of affection. I stared at his signature and had a sinking feeling.

His subsequent letter was increasingly dry. Instead of expressions of love, his letter contained descriptions of the school and its activities. They had begun to look for property to purchase and develop. In his next letter he mentioned that Robert had given him a chief feature of grayness. I wasn't sure what that feature meant, but my impulse was to cure him of it so I included jokes in the next letter. I also asked him who Robert was.

In the next letter he wrote that Robert was the name of his teacher and that mentioning him was an error on his part, committed in sleep. I didn't understand the great secrecy, since I was planning on meeting this man very soon anyway.

As spring break approached, I knew I had to tell my parents about the trip to the Bay Area, as I would need a ride to the airport. The news hit hard, and my father yelled emphatically, "You are NOT going!" I looked at him, smiled, and said resolutely, "Oh, yes I am." I was twenty-two years old. My life was just beginning for me. I had money from the residue of college grants and loans and could afford the flight. As it turned out, I could also afford the bus I eventually had to take to the airport.

* * * *

The night before the flight, I had a dream. I was in a dimly lit room with a group of people who were holding hands in a circle. They motioned to me to join them. There was a leader of the group who was tall and thin, with dark hair. He was around thirty years old and stood outside the circle.

As I joined hands with the others, the ring of people started to move clockwise, rotating faster and faster; I could barely keep up and I was getting dizzy. The leader said, "When I say, 'GO,' everyone jump into the inner circle." This inner circle was the empty space at the center; to enter it, you had to pass through a middle circle blowing like a tempest that spun at incredible speeds. Or so it seemed from the vantage point of our circle. To let go of hands that held me and dive into this torrent frightened me.

I trusted this man, however, so when the word was spoken, I leaped into the middle, aiming for this inner circle. I was carried by a wind that arched my body and suddenly suspended it above the others, as if time stood still. I was shocked to see that the others continued to hold hands and to rotate ever so slowly.

The difference in speed between what I experienced in this outer circle and what I saw of it from the middle circle stunned me. What were they waiting for, I thought? There must be some miscommunication, and I didn't know how to convey to the others that the experience of being held by some invisible force was wonderful, not frightening. The leader smiled at me. I saw I had made it to the empty space in the center. It was peaceful and silent. And I was alone.

* * * *

On the plane, I thought about how quickly the last ten weeks passed. I had encountered a Gurdjieff-Spinoza study group at the University Extension. Miles had told me to find out if they practiced "self-remembering," a form of meditation that the school uses.

My experience of the study group was comical. A self-appointed guru had singled me out and asked me if I knew what understanding was. I looked at him and said honestly, "No." He looked at me and replied, "Well, then, you have a question now, don't you?" Everyone smiled and nodded, as if he had just imparted some profound bit of wisdom. I was expecting him to tell me himself; instead, I realized that this guy was using one of the oldest tricks in the teaching trade: If you don't know the answer, throw it back at the kids as another question. This buys you time until you can figure it out yourself. Clearly, I could see this man had nothing to offer me.

During those ten weeks I had also tried to apply the system's ideas to my life. Although Ouspensky seemed at times too harsh in his assessment of people, viewing them as automatons, there were several ideas of his that intrigued me. One was the subject of an adult mentality in early childhood. I had very early memories of childhood.

My first recollection was at the age of nine months. I had crawled to my father, who had just arrived home. He lifted me up into the air, as my mother came to greet him. I estimate my age because this is when my mother had told me I stopped crawling. The image appears in my mind as a nineteenth-century black-and-white photo where the outward surroundings are blurred beyond recognition.

By the age of four, I could recall days at a time. I remember the first time I learned to tie my shoelaces. I had asked my mother what the strings were called. When she said "shoelaces," I remember having this thought: "Oh, so that is what they're called here." It was a strange thought for a toddler to have.

I had always viewed my life with this lens: that I was far older than the people around me. I had never encountered an explanation of this until Ouspensky's comment that he had met some people who could recall the first years of life and that they had what he described as a "ready mind with quite grown-up reactions and a way of looking at people and recognizing them, such as could not be formed in the course of six months of unconscious life."

Another idea was that this knowledge belonged not to himself but came from higher mind. This implied that there was a source of all knowledge, and that there was a connection to it on earth. Once, when I was about seven years old, I asked my father if there was someone in the world who knew everything. He said that was impossible. I looked at him, and didn't tell him my opinion, which was that there had to be someone who knew everything — knew the answers to all the questions, especially why we are here. I felt sure that one day I would find this person.

As the plane landed at the Oakland Airport, I started to imagine what this school was like. The teacher would be tall and venerable, like a wise rabbi. All the women would be thin with long straight hair and no makeup, and would wear jeans and a black sweater. Some would have wire-rimmed glasses. The men would have beards and also be wearing jeans and black sweaters. Of course, I wouldn't fit in. But I would be accepted nonetheless because of Miles.

THE SEEDS OF

Unbuckling my seatbelt, I tried to be aware of myself — be conscious of myself, in the words of Ouspensky. Here I am. Here I am, I repeated to myself. How strange.

CHAPTER 5

It was wonderful seeing Miles again. We kissed, and I felt the emotional connection that appeared to have disappeared was still intact. As he carried my bags to the Chevy, he commented that I had lost weight since we had last seen each other. Yes, it was true that my appetite had left during those ten weeks and that I had dropped about twenty pounds. I thought he would be pleased with my new figure, yet he simply said he wasn't sure how healthy it was for a Venusian type (which he said I was) to lose so much weight, because this type was characterized by cellular bulk. Cellular bulk? Gosh, I always referred to it as fat. What a nice system, I thought, to label it in such non-judgmental terms.

The drive to his apartment was beautiful. I had only been in Northern California once before in my life, and it was foggy. But on this day the sky was blue, the clouds were white and puffy, the air was remarkably fresh, and the sunlight was so bright that the hillsides covered in Irish green simply shouted that spring had arrived. This contrasted sharply with Southern California, where it was dull sky, dull clouds, dull air and dull green twelve months of the year.

When we arrived at his place, which was located in a small suburb of the East Bay known as Pleasant Hill, I realized that it was not in a traditional apartment complex, as I had assumed, but was actually a remodeled basement of a house. The entrance was at the back. We went down several concrete steps, and entered a small kitchen that had a sink, refrigerator, and dinette set. The bathroom — shower, toilet, and sink — was just off the kitchen, separated by a curtain. From the kitchen, we went into the main area that was the size of a large bedroom. There was his bed, a leather recliner, a desk, and shelves filled with books, records, stereo equipment, and his pipe collection.

I saw there was no space for me to sleep, which filled me with concern. I was a virgin. I didn't tell him this, and we hadn't spoken about such arrangements. I didn't know how to bring up the subject, and worse, I didn't know what I wanted to do. I had kept my virginity for twenty-two years because I felt that I wanted to wait until marriage since that was the Good Jewish Girl thing to do. Well, actually, this is what I told the men I met, but the truth was I was scared and didn't know anything about sex. Miles was an attractive and intelligent man with a spiritual drive akin to my own. Could this be the man I had waited for? Should I give myself to him? What should I do?

* * * *

As evening approached, the subject of the sleeping arrangements had yet to be discussed. During a quick dinner, Miles explained to me that there was a meeting in San Francisco that he would attend with his group, and that I had to stay in the apartment since I was not yet a member. He showed me how to use the stereo and mentioned that I might enjoy listening to some jazz records he had, specifically one titled *A Love Supreme* by John Coltrane.

After he left, I thumbed through his records and found the John Coltrane album he suggested I hear. I put on the headphones and concentrated on the sound of the saxophone. I tried to pick up some tune from the music, but could find none. Jazz just sounded like a bunch of random noise to me. I put the headset down and decided to find a book to read instead. There on the shelf was Ouspensky's *The Fourth Way*. I began to reread sections of it, and it helped to improve my state.

When Miles returned late that night he was beaming. The energy he received from his group radiated from him in a lovely gentleness. The combination of his energy and my reading brought me into focus. Here I was, and where I was seemed to be the culmination of a long journey. He was the right man; this was the right place. I knew what to do that night.

* * * *

Losing my virginity was a powerful experience. My body shook violently from the energy coursing through it. Miles looked at me helplessly as I curled into a fetal position. With a trembling voice, I told him I would be fine. But my shaking did not stop. He said he thought we should call a doctor. It appeared to him like I was having a seizure. I had no idea what was happening to me. I just wanted to be left alone. His concern was increasing and his insistence to act confused me further. Then I said, "You'll never know what I'm experiencing." He recoiled.

Getting up from the bed, he went to his chair, prepared his pipe, and put on the headsets to listen to John Coltrane. After fifteen minutes or so, my body came to a rest. I went to him to let him know I was fine. Putting my arms around him, he froze and waved me away.

I knew I had said something hurtful, but didn't understand at the time how deeply I had wounded him. In my own mind, I had given myself up to the man I had chosen to be with, and therefore it didn't matter what I said. He would accept it and we would move on. Sex was an act of commitment, and commitment was a promise that couldn't be broken. I felt safe, which gave me free rein to express myself. When he returned to bed later that night, I was half asleep.

The next morning, Miles arose early to go to work at a pipe shop named the Tinder Box in the Sun Valley mall. I was slow in rising and didn't notice he had already showered, dressed, and eaten breakfast, until he sat on the bed to embrace me and kiss me goodbye. He told me he set out a bowl of granola and a cup of freshly made Kahlua coffee for me on the kitchen table and that he would be back later in the afternoon. There was food in the refrigerator for lunch.

Again, I was to be left alone in the apartment the whole day. I took my time getting ready since I wasn't going anywhere. After showering, I looked in the mirror at my reflection and was startled to see a very different person looking back. The person in the mirror was beautiful to me: silky long black hair, radiant rosy skin, shining deep-blue eyes. Who was this person? I would return to the mirror several times that morning to see if the New Me was still there.

* * * *

When Miles came home from work at five, he was very emotional and said he had a surprise for me. His group decided to have a special meeting that night where friends of members could attend. This meant that I could meet his teacher. Even though I had little idea what the experience would be like, I felt a bit more prepared since I had spent the day reading *The Fourth Way*. Should some of the members ask me a question regarding the Fourth Way system, at least I could answer intelligently.

It was about a ten-minute drive from the apartment to the Alamo Women's Club, where the meeting would be held. We parked the car in the half-paved lot and entered a small, modest building. The main room was dimly lit and seemed even smaller with the thirty or so people who occupied it.

As I looked around the room, I was shocked to see people of different ages and sizes talking in casually formed groups of twos, threes, and fours. Nowhere did I see anyone with a black sweater and jeans and wire-rimmed glasses. Instead, there was a large woman wearing a gaudy print dress standing next to a small bearded man with a pipe and tweed jacket, who was chatting with a big hairy guy whose body shook from silent chuckling. In another corner of the room was a very exotic looking woman with long black hair streaked with gray. Her face was full and round, her complexion dull, and her skin pockmarked. She wore an outfit that resembled an Indian sari. She stared at me as I entered. I immediately looked away as I felt her gaze was too penetrating.

I tried to spot the teacher, and focused on one man standing in a group of four who had graying hair, a beautiful smile, and was the only one wearing a suit and tie. Surely this was the teacher. His age and professorial apparel fit my image of the wise scholar and venerable leader. He appeared courteous as he nodded rhythmically to the words spoken by a tall, younger man with black hair parted on the side.

"There is the teacher," said Miles pointing in the direction of this group of four. As we approached, I smiled at them all, turning my attention more to the man in the suit and tie. Miles began the introduction.

"Robert, I'd like you to meet Linda from Los Angeles."

To my utter surprise, he was addressing the tall young fellow with the black hair.

He gently shook my hand as I looked into his angular face. His sapphire blue eyes were like huge coins. No, I thought. This couldn't be the teacher. He's too young. We stood there looking into each other's eyes for what seemed to be an eternity.

Before I had a chance to speak, Miles led me to the other side of the room to where stacks of chairs were leaning against a wall. Apparently, the meeting was to begin shortly, and the chairs needed to be set up in a circle. I watched Miles and two other men quickly arrange the seating. Everyone went to a seat and I waited until Miles motioned to me.

We sat across from the young teacher. To his right was the large woman with the flower-print dress. Everyone was silent, waiting for him to speak. He gazed down at the floor and slowly raised his head. His face bore a serious expression. His voice was soft and his words were simple and direct. I quickly looked around and noticed I was the only one sitting on the edge of my seat.

CHAPTER 6

Functions of the Human Machine – Four States of Consciousness – The Many 'I's – Imagination – Negative Emotions – Essence – False Personality – Chief Feature – Divided Attention. These were among the topics discussed during that first meeting. A subject would be introduced, followed by brief explanations of what these concepts meant according to the system.

What made this meeting remarkable was not the words themselves, but the way in which they were expressed. Robert measured each word before he uttered it. This was in such sharp contrast to any professor I had ever known: words would flow confidently from them, almost haphazardly, and they almost always would include vocabulary that served to impress. This young teacher had the gift of communicating simply without making you feel inferior.

At one point in that first meeting, his serious face melted into a gentle delight. The subject was the formatory center. The system describes it as an apparatus that can only count to two. It's recognized by opposite thinking, and by its ability to automatically evoke a programmed response. When he introduced this subject, he said, "John Fitzgerald…." The word "Kennedy" popped into my mind. I could observe that something in me had registered this word without any attention on my part. It was automatic. This was my first verification of mechanicality.

Then he turned to the large woman in the flower-print dress sitting next to him and began a short banter.

"Hello."

"Hello."

"How are you?"

"Fine, how are you?"

"Fine. How's your mother?"

"She's fine. And yours?"

"She's fine, too."

A soft energy circulated in the room, intermingled with a few light chuckles, as we each recognized the type of conversation that so frequently engaged us during our day, without thinking. Here were examples from real life that provided the verifications of a system idea. I truly felt like I was in kindergarten. Some of the knowledge I had read appeared daunting and mysterious, like the law of three and hydrogens. Robert did not address these. Instead, he focused on areas that we could immediately recognize as pertaining to ourselves.

During the meeting, he introduced simple practical exercises to help us. One was to look into a person's essence eye, which was the left eye, rather than the person's personality eye, which was the right eye. Essence is gentler, and sharing visual energy in this way would feed the more real part of ourselves.

Another exercise was what he called the "intentional handing exercise," whereby we would hand some object to another person, pause for a moment and make eye contact while the person gripped the object, and then release the object into the person's hand. The aim was to slow movement down long enough to bring more attention to it.

From the beginning it was clear we needed one another to help remind us to be present. What struck me as odd, however, was the unusual assortment of people that were in the room. My mind would wander away from Robert's words as I looked around at how others were viewing his teaching. Some were sitting with their legs and arms tightly crossed. Others sat slumped in their chairs. These were the people I would need to work with, I thought. It was not exactly the kind of people I had in mind. I couldn't find an intellectual among them. How could these people grasp the complexity of the system's ideas? What was in it for them?

* * * *

After the meeting, we stacked the chairs to clear the room so people could once more mingle and chat. I stayed close to Miles's side as he introduced me to the people I hadn't met before the meeting. Many of them left after short conversations, hugging each other goodbye. It was now approaching ten and the room was almost empty. The teacher, who was standing near the door, motioned to Miles to come. I stood watching for a few moments. Miles returned and said, "Robert has invited us to his apartment in Walnut Creek."

Walnut Creek was less than fifteen minutes away by freeway. As I sat in the car en route, I wondered why we were singled out like this. Did the teacher invite others to his apartment? Would we sit and chat for hours? I tried to minimize the feeling of self-importance that this special invitation produced in me. The whole evening had been so unexpected that I just watched to see what would happen next.

When we arrived, we parked the car in a guest slot and accompanied Robert up a flight of stairs to the second story apartment. He unlocked the door and we followed him in. The apartment was small and very neat. He asked me about myself. I told him I had just graduated university and was a high school English teacher. He stood very still with his hands folded politely in front of him as he listened to me explain my profession. The atmosphere around him was so silent that I suddenly recognized I had been speaking too much.

I stopped, and he took a few steps into the living room. There in the middle was a small table with a glass top that held collectibles. It was clear these small items gave him great pleasure. The room was dim and I could not see them properly. We simply stood there, in silence. He was smiling, and I felt the most intimate emotion. It was as if a child had invited us to see their prized possessions. This gesture had touched my heart directly. He then thanked us for coming and kissed us on the forehead goodnight after a warm embrace.

It was such a totally unexpected experience. No profound knowledge or insight had been delivered. It was simply a conscious moment in time that he had captured for me. This was the collectible he prized; this was the gift he shared.

CHAPTER 7

Miles told me I could attend regular meetings with him during that week of March 1971 since I had come a great distance. I learned meetings generally were held in various parts of the Bay Area at members' homes. The next scheduled meeting was in the East Bay, at a lady's house in the Berkeley Hills. Her name was Anna Gold, and Miles explained she was Jewish like me and a former concert pianist. I didn't recall seeing her at the Alamo meeting. I looked forward to meeting her.

Her house was situated above the street on a boulder that jutted out over the narrow sidewalk. A winding stone path led up to the heavy wooden front door. The one-car garage seemed like an afterthought: it was a small shed-like structure that fit into the hillside. When we arrived, many cars lined the street, straddling the pavement. We had to park on the next block and walk the distance.

As we entered, Anna jovially greeted us at the door. She was sturdy with orange feathery hair in gentle curls that embraced her face. Her makeup had a strong foundation that was augmented by rouge, red lipstick and black eyeliner unevenly applied. Her knitted suit fit perfectly, and I learned she had made it herself. Here was indeed a solid person. We moved quickly away from the front door and into the living room, as students were arriving. Many gathered between the large concert piano, which was at one end of the main room, and the bookcases that lined the walls on the other. The empty space in the middle was filled by a circle of chairs.

Just before the meeting began, I was introduced to various members I had not yet met. One particular gentleman was a doctor from Vacaville with affable, sparkling blue eyes, broad chest and a refined sensibility. He had an ease and charm about him. He immediately asked me whether I had decided to join. For the first time I felt pressured. I wasn't sure if I could do what was required of me: leave Los Angeles, move to a strange place with strange people, let alone find money to survive. But more importantly, I reserved the right to decide for myself. I didn't want to join just to be part of a group. This was my search, my decision, my life.

The meeting was structured along the same lines I previously described, with one change: we divided into small groups of six after Robert had taught for 45 minutes. Chairs were rearranged into mini-circles and I was told to join Bonita's group. She was the exotic woman I had seen at that first meeting. I listened to the "angles of thought," as opinions were called, on the subject we were given. I wished to participate as well, so I raised my hand to offer a bit of knowledge from my reading. Bonita looked right at me and said, "You came here to listen not to speak." Her words landed like a punch to my stomach. I sat stunned, trying to assess the situation. Was this just another group with its own brand of intimidation tactics? I felt on the edge of a precipice. Would I make that leap into the inner circle as my dream had predicted?

When the meeting ended, everyone stood up and began to chat. Two women had come to speak with me as if to comfort me after Bonita's comment.

But then the most extraordinary, otherworldly, authentic yet baffling thing occurred.

It was as if the living room ceiling, which was square, suddenly began to rotate above my head like a helicopter propeller. It lifted like a lid separating from a box. A rope appeared that seemed to descend from the light fixture with its source above and beyond this realm of existence. Something in me ascended the rope with lightning speed, rising above the room, the city, the globe, the solar system, the galaxy — as if I was connected to something totally outside this earthly moment. And just as suddenly I returned to the room with this message:

"You have found your family."

I burst into tears.

One of the two women patted my back while the other, whose name I learned was Janet (or Jan) Holmes, looked at me and said, "It's good you can express your emotions like this." I felt totally exposed. And I knew I had to tell Robert I had made my decision.

I moved to the dining area, which was adjacent to the living room, where Robert was standing, talking to another student. I waited. And waited. And waited. My emotions were settling down and my tears were drying up.

Like some poor actor who had wanted to demonstrate an epiphany, but had encountered a lapse in timing because the other actor had not been cued properly, I found myself trying to get my tears to flow again when it was my turn to be with the teacher.

At last, I stepped up to Robert, who looked down at me, smiling. Unlike the others, he wasn't "comforting" me. Instead, he lovingly asked, "Are you happy?" What a strange question I thought, but I replied through my forced tears, "Yeeesssss. I just want you to know I'm joining." He embraced me.

Somehow this profound moment of cosmic consciousness had been reduced to an episode of *I Love Lucy*. Not the way I envisioned establishing my first real connection with the teacher. But then again, when did my life ever follow a script of my choosing?

> *For what you see is but the smallest part*
> *And least proportion of humanity:*
> *I tell you, madam, were the whole frame here,*
> *It is of such a spacious lofty pitch,*
> *Your roof were not sufficient to contain't.*
> William Shakespeare

CHAPTER 8

Miles and I drove home in silence most of the way. I did not share my cosmic experience with him, but did tell him I told Robert I would be joining. Miles was very pleased and said, "I know." Apparently, Robert had spoken to him before we left and had invited us to join him for lunch the next day. Miles mentioned it was a high honor to dine with the teacher, and he said he would take time off from work tomorrow so we could spend the day together.

* * * *

The next morning was sweet, as the sunlight poured its radiance through the kitchen curtains. How its brightness reflected our state! We were a happy couple, greeting the morning from our rapturous embrace, showering together, preparing and eating a light breakfast. I had jumped into the inner circle of my dreams, I thought. What could go wrong?

We drove to a wonderful restaurant in Vacaville named The Nut Tree. After parking, we saw the colorful, full-sized Nut Tree Railroad train with its green, yellow and blue cars filled with smiling, happy children and parents aboard. Once we reached the building that housed the restaurant, we had to maneuver between counters of cookies of all shapes and sizes, candies in bins with the largest circular sucker I'd ever seen — at least two feet in diameter — propped up as a flag announcing to all: Come and Get It! This was a happy place and set the mood for the special lunch we were to have.

THE DIVINE BEGINNING

The entry to the restaurant itself was an elevated, wheelchair accommodating stretch of carpet leading to the reservation desk. Benches lined the wall for those waiting to be seated. There we saw Robert. He was dressed casually in dark corduroy pants and a velour shirt of rich burgundy that hung softly from his broad shoulders. Here was a handsome man.

The hostess led us into the dining area, past a glass enclosure that went straight to the ceiling. Inside this enclosure were exotic birds that perched and flitted joyously. Huge model airplanes hung high over the large main dining area where individual tables were placed. The 20-foot by 20-foot wall that was opposite the entryway was composed of six panes of glass allowing the greenery from the outside garden to add to the ambience of the festive room.

This was a unique place. Rather than being at a small table in the open space, we were taken to a leather booth across from the bird cage that had a striped blue, green and yellow canopy, which lent a sense of privacy to the experience. Robert sat facing us. We were handed large menus.

"The tropical prawns are the best on the menu," said Robert, suggesting that we order it. Miles pointed it out on the menu to me, and I read that the dish included pineapple, mango, orange slices, and wheat berries, which I had never eaten. I saw that there was also tropical chicken. Chicken is more in keeping with my cultural culinary habits (prawns were less familiar to me as they are not kosher). I decided to order the chicken. Miles ordered the prawns.

The waitress came to take our orders and brought with her a basket of the most amazing rolls and butter. The steam from these Kaiser rolls was curling in gray wisps above the rim. Clearly, they were freshly baked.

Robert reached into the basket and removed a roll, broke it open and extended it to me to smell. No one had ever done this before in my life. I inhaled the aroma of warm, comforting bread and smiled back at Robert. It was an act of generous intentionality. I reached for my own roll, tore it apart and applied the sweet butter to the bread's soft insides, watching the yellowness melt. I took a bite and felt like I was tasting Life — my life. I was alive in that moment.

Our plates arrived. It was a beautiful presentation with a lavender orchid positioned next to the fruit, which was laid out in slices on a deep green banana leaf. Robert had me taste one of his prawns: the flesh was sweet, chewy and juicy. My chicken was commonplace. I clearly had chosen the inferior tropical version. It was not willfulness. It was ignorance.

Robert asked me when I was moving up from Los Angeles. I told him I had my degree in English and Theatre Arts and that I will complete my teaching credential in June, that I was enrolled in the Education Department with a fifth year Secondary Education specialty, and that I was also planning to enter the Ph.D. program in English in the fall to get my doctorate.

I looked at him and realized not only was he not impressed, he was waiting for me to answer his question. The fact was I had never even *considered* his question. Mine was a rehearsed response that popped out of my mouth. And now it was irrelevant. Is this really what I was doing? Confusion began to well up in me. How can I answer his question when it hadn't even occurred to me?

He turned to Miles and asked him to speak with Mary Ellen, who I learned was the large woman in the flowered dress, to see if she could mail me meeting notes. He explained, "Mary Ellen works as the post-mistress of Alamo."

The rest of the conversation centered on properties that Miles, Robert and others were visiting along Highway 49. They talked about the King Ranch and whether it would be suitable. Suitable for what, I was not told. Miles offered his opinions and Robert was gently nodding in agreement. I was not included in this conversation since it appeared it was not relevant to me. Instead, I nibbled at my plate, focusing on tasting each bite. Inside, I felt I was at a crossroads. The unknown was coming toward me like a rapidly forming tornado.

That evening Miles and I attended a dinner and jazz concert at the Claremont Hotel in Berkeley. He was very excited to hear Don Ellis, a local jazz trumpeter who was known for his technical abilities. His orchestra had stepped off the platform at one point and distributed themselves around the audience, who were seated at small dining tables.

Being in the midst of this sound produced such a memory for me. I looked around and marveled at how everyone applauded the talent demonstrated by the musicians. I sipped my drink and smiled and tapped to the beat. I pretended to be interested. But my enjoyment was based on Miles's enjoyment, really, because I knew how much he had paid for the tickets. He was happier than I had ever seen him. And this made me happy, too.

* * * *

The next day was Saturday, my last day in the Bay Area. As we settled into our morning routine, Miles asked me if I would like to go for a picnic. I said it sounded like fun, so we drove to Walnut Creek where a special deli provided us with cheeses, meats, and fresh bread. He selected a red wine to go with our lunch.

We were heading to Mount Diablo, meandering through the small town on our way up to the peak. The spring green covered the plots of land. The occasional quaint cottage would appear with fenced areas where a horse could be seen gently grazing. It was so surprising to see an idyllic rural community so near one of the most cosmopolitan cities in America.

As we approached the peak, he pulled the car over by the side of the road. Holding my hand, he helped me maneuver down the grassy hillside. He stopped, unfurled a blanket for me to sit on and said, "Enjoy the view." He climbed up to the car to retrieve the food. There before me was the San Francisco Bay with its blue waters and bridges. It was spectacular. We drank wine, nibbled at the food, and talked about our future.

The plan would be for him to drive down to Los Angeles after I completed my fifth year Education degree in June and bring me up north. "We will probably marry in September," he said casually.

Like watching a 30-minute episode of some television drama, it just seemed to be the statement that suited a romantic occasion. Sure, why not? It makes sense, the way this is unfolding. And yet, something inside realized this was no longer about *my life*. I was now a part of someone else's idea of my life. But there was no resistance in me. My passivity was stunning. After struggling to gain my freedom from a tyrannical father, why am I submitting to someone else so soon?

After the picnic, we strolled around Walnut Creek, hand in hand. Walking into an antique shop, I spotted a lacquered burgundy vase with a portrait of a woman smiling serenely at the viewer. Approximately nine inches in height, the oval-shaped container with narrow aperture was elegant and refined. The color reminded me of Robert in his burgundy velour shirt, and the portrait of this woman with dark hair, I thought, would remind Robert of me.

"I want to buy this as a gift for Robert," I told Miles. He was surprised at my selection, trying to convince me to buy another object that was less feminine. I was firm and laid out the thirty dollars. It was not an inexpensive purchase for me, considering the price of gas was fifteen cents. I watched as the storekeeper wrapped it gently in thin white paper and placed it in a box. I was pleased at the thought of leaving something of myself behind for Robert to place in his home.

* * * *

That night we attended my final meeting before flying out Sunday afternoon. The meeting was at the Alamo Women's Club, the location of my very first meeting.

After listening to Robert teach for thirty minutes, we moved the chairs so that they faced a wall. I was told that tonight was a special night. We would watch Walt Disney's *Alice in Wonderland*.

Someone had set up a 35mm projector, and this animated film appeared on a three-foot-by-three-foot space of the blank wall. The audio was scratchy. When Tweedledum and Tweedledee sang their song, I started to laugh aloud.

I turned to Miles expecting him to be equally delighted but saw him sitting there, stone-faced. He glanced at me as if embarrassed that I laughed. Well, to me it was funny, so when the caterpillar appeared saying "Who are YOU?" I laughed again. This time, everyone was silent except for one other person. I turned and saw this petite lady with short, curly gray hair and delicate features smile at me in the half-darkness. Each time I laughed, she responded like a bird of a similar feather.

After the film, we each took part in stacking the chairs. A few men then set up a long folding table at the other end near the kitchen, and placed a white tablecloth on it. Glasses, plates and utensils were brought out next. The small woman who shared my laughter brought out a sheet cake to place in the middle of the table. We gathered around Robert who stood in the middle. I was standing with Miles to Robert's right, and there in front of me I could read the writing on the cake: Fellowship of Friends.

Robert began to speak.

"Rosemary told me that today we filed our request to become a non-profit religious organization. The name we chose is Fellowship of Friends."

He smiled and we all toasted one another. The white cake with white frosting was delicious.

I helped to bring plates and glasses into the kitchen. An aproned man was standing at the sink washing dishes. I handed him a plate slowly, with intentionality, and looked into his left eye. The man reached out his hand to take the plate and turned quickly to the sink. But I held on because he hadn't looked at me. He got negative. I was surprised at his response. Rosemary, who was the woman who giggled with me during the film, was in the kitchen and explained to him that I was doing the intentional handing exercise, and not to get negative with me.

Rosemary introduced herself to me. I replied, "I'm Linda, Miles's girlfriend from Los Angeles." I told her that I was prepared to join and wondered to whom I should give my payment. She said she would take it and thanked me. I was now a member of the Fellowship of Friends.

Others welcomed me, and I found the women to be friendlier than the men. When the dishes were done, we went into the main room where Miles was speaking with Robert. Robert gently kissed him on the forehead.

I approached and the three of us walked out to the parking lot. I told Robert I had a gift for him in the car. It was a dark night and as Robert opened the box and lifted the vase, the charm of the woman's smile was barely visible. He put it back into the box, kissed me on the forehead, and we departed.

* * * *

The day of the flight had arrived. Miles had prepared a bottle of his homemade Kahlua for me so that I could enjoy this delicious liqueur in my coffee at home. The mood was sweetly loving and affectionate. We left the apartment around noon and decided to stop at a Chinese restaurant for lunch en route to the airport.

We ordered several dishes to share and spoke about the future. We would continue our correspondence and I would still be receiving Mary Ellen's notes, which should hold me in good stead with my inner development until his arrival in LA to transport me up north. He kept reassuring me that all would go well and not to be afraid of my father's reaction. The trepidation I felt about entering this unknown phase of my life was palpable.

At the end of our lunch, the fortune cookies arrived on top of the bill. He offered me first choice and we both cracked the cookies open. He read his aloud and it was a standard Chinese well-wishing of good health and wealth.

When I unfurled my strip of paper and silently read my fortune, I was in shock.

"You will travel for miles."

I read it to him and was surprised he did not react to the double meaning. Instead, he paid the bill and we both stood up to go.

In that moment, I felt the firm grip of Fate's hands envelop my being. Whatever will happen is destined. It was once again clear I had no choice in this matter.

It is written on the gate of heaven: Nothing in existence is more powerful than destiny. And destiny brought you here, to this page, which is part of your ticket — as all things are — to return to God.

Hafiz

CHAPTER 9

Arriving home was like having returned from another planet. I felt like an alien with unusual powers that made me surprisingly immune to the reactions of my parents. I knew now what was important to me, and that was to return to Northern California as soon as I could. The challenge in front of me, however, was surviving the next ten weeks with my parents.

The first surprise I had was that my father actually showed up at the airport to pick me up. He wanted to know, of course, "how it went." I described the beauty of Northern California with its emerald green gently rolling hills, its glistening bay with distant patches of quickly moving fog. I told him I saw the Golden Gate Bridge, which wasn't golden but orange. This was a man who had never been on an airplane in his life. But, of course, this is not what he wanted to know. He wanted to know if I had lost my virginity.

As we entered the apartment, I greeted my mom (she was not a hugger) and then I carried my suitcase to my bedroom and disappeared. The television was on in the living room as usual. As I unpacked, I stopped to put on my favorite record, Simon and Garfunkel's *Bridge Over Troubled Water*. It was their last album together in 1970 that I had, and it seems appropriate esoterically. The music and lyrics always comforted me, like a martini for the underage. Prior to these recent events, my favorite song of theirs had been "I Am a Rock." The lyrics depicted teenage angst, eloquently speaking of solitude, the pseudo-strength one imagines one has in the midst of painful loneliness and estrangement. Basically, it gave voice to the self-pity that I had crafted to perfection over the years.

This stoic approach to life appealed greatly to me ever since I was a child. I felt like almost every person I had met was moving in a different direction from me. I tried to find myself in the reflections of others. Am I like this person or that person? Their interests were not my interests, however. They were focused on the traditional aspects of life: boyfriends, fashion, gossip. I was interested in "Why am I here on earth?" Not the best foundation for friendships, I had discovered.

With the exception of one person. And this occurred in my junior year of high school. She was tall and angular with long, thin brown hair and a maturity beyond her years. Her name was Angel Ann. We met in an English class and started to share our poetry together. This was a very unusual person. She had a streak of independence that I not only admired but envied. She drove her own used car, which her parents had provided to give her the freedom to care for her younger brother. She played musical instruments that were not associated with a rock band: piano, acoustic guitar and zither (which she actually made herself). This was the Sixties, when folk music and rebellion were intertwined.

THE DIVINE BEGINNING

I, on the other hand, was chained to the influence of television and my small bedroom's imaginary world. She was expanding outward into the real world, attending live concerts at the Whisky A Go Go on the Sunset Strip, for example. She took me there once, and I sat upright in my skirt and blouse, legs together, looking at all the thin girls with long blond straight hair wearing colorful prints and bell bottoms, who were leaning closely together chatting with one another over the din of the music. I could feel my awkwardness burning deeply within my psyche. I looked at Angel but she didn't mind a bit that I was wearing a skirt. Angel Ann did not judge me. She enjoyed my company and considered me a friend. My parents liked the fact I had a girlfriend and didn't mind if I stayed out late with her. They trusted her.

She introduced me to Buddhism, the Sufis, and Subud, and other exotic religions as she, too, was exploring the inner meaning of existence. Her grasp of language was stunning, as she painted her poems with skill beyond her years. I felt like we were the Gauguin and Van Gogh of our eleventh-grade class.

And she had connections outside of this small town. Her friendship with our English teacher took us to Royce Hall on the UCLA campus. There we performed in a Busby Berkeley-esque dance number with seven other oddly shaped gals from who-knows-where, trying to actualize the choreography we had learned five hours earlier using hula hoops as part of the routine. When the curtain went up, the audience roared with laughter when they realized we had forgotten everything we were to do and were improvising erratically. Good God. We were horrible. The teacher, who was also enjoying the absurdity of the moment, motioned to us to get off the stage so the film, *The Gold Diggers of 1933*, could begin. I didn't mind the laughter. I had fun. On second thought, truth be told, she and I were more like Abbott and Costello, the fat and skinny comedians.

Then, in our senior year, she mentioned that her family had to move back to Arkansas. I couldn't believe it. Three months before graduation. We wrote to each other weekly for six months; she lived on 44th Street in Little Rock. When she said she was moving back to attend Long Beach State, I was thrilled. I told her I would buy tickets to a concert at UCLA's Royce Hall and treat her. Performing was our favorite group. She said I didn't need to do this, but I insisted, wanting to make the evening special.

During dinner before the concert, I could see she had changed. She was now interested in drugs and sex. When we got back to my apartment after the concert, I knew that would be the last time I would see her. We were going in different directions. She was seeking life experience. I was seeking something not on this level. The live concert was Simon and Garfunkel.

* * * *

Within a week of returning home, I had received Mary Ellen's meeting notes for the first time. Because it was my job to take the stairs from the second to the first floor to retrieve the mail, I could filter its contents before bringing it into the apartment.

The notes read like a script with speakers and dialogue, although mostly Robert did the talking. What was most fun were Harold's cartoons (Harold, Mary Ellen's husband, was a professional cartoonist), which illustrated ideas such as the traits of the chief features, body types, and centers of gravity. He also included small portraits of all the members, which he was able to fit onto a single page. I was surprised to see my face depicted as a cartoon, with square jawline, long wavy black hair, and thick glasses. I studied each person characterized, trying to associate their name with their portrait so that I could recognize who was part of this new family of mine when I returned. This was a far cry from the dry intellectual *Tertium Organum*. The cartoons appealed to the child within me.

I looked forward to these weekly correspondences. Mary Ellen would send me a little note on top of it and I could feel a genuine friendship developing. Letters from Miles were also extracted from the letter box without my parents knowing.

This worked well until Saturday April 10, the first night of Passover.

* * * *

Passover celebrates the exodus of the Jews from slavery in Egypt led by the Prophet Moses. The story begins with Moses commanding the Pharaoh to "Let my people go." He refuses. Then God, through Moses, initiates a series of plagues after each one of the Pharaoh's refusals. The final one (the tenth) was the killing of the first-born child throughout Egypt. God instructs Moses in advance to tell the Jews that the Angel of Death would sweep through the city that night and kill the eldest child within a household, unless that home had an X painted with animal blood on the front door. It worked. The Pharaoh releases the Jews, and the exodus begins.

It's an exciting story. It includes every emotion imaginable: joy, adoration, faith, confusion, doubt, anger. It also includes hunger and thirst, and a few miracles tossed in, such as manna (which the matzo symbolizes) falling from heaven for food and Moses striking a rock with his rod to bring forth water.

THE DIVINE BEGINNING

The most memorable Passover of my life was a family gathering at my father's mother's home in Boyle Heights. She was a strict orthodox Jew. Chickie Bubbie (as grandma was known because she always made chicken dinner when we visited her every Sunday) had a house large enough to accommodate her five children. It had a main floor and an attic and must have been built in the 1920s.

The layout of the house was one long rectangle, and you could literally walk a straight line from the front door through the living room, through the dining room and out the kitchen screen door to the backyard garden. It had seven beds and three bedrooms (one bed was a day bed in the dining room pressed against the left wall below a window with lace curtains). The living room had plastic-covered furniture intended to keep the grandchildren from ruining the shiny, pastel pink-and-green flowered damask fabric. It was a wonderful house for hide-and-seek.

That Passover, the women had sequestered themselves in the kitchen to work their magic to feed 23 Jewish mouths. Besides the food needed for the ceremony, the dinner afterwards was a five-course affair.

We were seated as clans, with each of her five children and their respective offspring clearly ready to compete during the readings. The grandchildren ranged in age from 5 to 16. Because Passover includes having the youngest child ask the question, Why is this night different from any other night?, the pressure was on the youngest who first must know how to read in order to recite well. And that was me.

I could feel the tension in the room when it was time for me to read the question phonetically in Hebrew. If I didn't perform well, my father would not be able to brag about how smart his kids were compared to his millionaire brother's children. I did well, which made my family proud.

After the big dinner, many adults would collapse on the beds and couches. At the age of eight, I honestly thought this keeling over and passing out after filling our bellies was the true meaning of Passover.

Jewish families, I also learned when I was young, were divided into two types when it came to dining: the Chazzer and the Schnorrer. Chazzers, which is Yiddish for pigs, have an incredible ability to eat everything on their plate — and everyone else's. A Schnorrer, which comes from the German "to beg or steal," was used in my family circle to refer to anyone who would drop into an event as long as it had an open bar. I learned this distinction from Dad, who would judgingly point out the distant relatives lingering at the liquor table during an entire event, while we would hover over the banquet table piling on the food once, twice and three times. So we were the Chazzers. I guess it was better to proceed in life as a pig than a beggar.

Now, what does that memory have to do with April 10? Passover observance in our home was an abridged version of the strict religious ceremony just described. That Saturday evening, the table was set with the seder plate of six items: the boiled eggs, the celery root and horseradish for the two types of bitter herbs (maror and chazeret); the honeyed raisins and crushed almonds for charoset (my favorite); a cooked peeled potato; and a chicken bone (instead of the lamb bone because it was cheaper). The requisite salted water was placed in the middle of the table for dipping, to remind us of the bitter tears shed during the Exodus. The three matzos were laid on a separate plate and covered with a dish towel.

It was a four-course meal: chopped chicken liver (mixed with diced hard-boiled egg and schmaltz — rendered chicken fat with sautéed onions — as a binding agent); chicken soup with kneidlach (aka matzo balls); and all the chicken parts and the cooked vegetables used for the soup. And of course, there would be a bottle of Manischewitz Concord Grape Wine for the four mandatory swigs each participant must down during the ceremony.

Since we were not drinkers, a little alcohol impacted us quickly. Basically, by the time we reached the chicken course, we were pretty looped. On that April 10, we began the seder around five, not because the sunset was fast approaching, but because Dad wanted to watch a TV program that started at 7:30.

We rushed through the four questions and the four cups of wine representing redemption. Because we were Ashkenazi (from Eastern Europe), we would always set a place and fill a fifth glass of wine for the Prophet Elijah, whose appearance would herald the coming of the Messiah. This final climactic moment of welcoming Elijah to the table was always performed by my father, who would get up from the table to open the front door, while reciting lines in Hebrew that I never understood. Elijah's invisible spirit would then enter our home. It was considered a blessing upon us. That was the concept.

Why was this night different from any other night? As my Dad stood up to go to the door, suddenly there was a loud knock before he could reach it. We all froze. Who could it be at this hour on a Saturday night, for God's sake? He opened the door and Lo and Behold: it was a Special Delivery Mail carrier for Linda Kaplan. Please sign here.

I got up in shock and signed for a bulging letter that came from Mary Ellen in Alamo, California. The door closed and the wrath of my ancestors channeled through my father's glaring eyes at me.

"Who is this from?!" he demanded.

"Oh, it's just a friend."

I quickly took it to my bedroom and returned to the table.

"Where were we?" I asked sweetly.

Dad announced we were done, took his pants off that he wore only for the occasion and went to lie on the couch in his underwear after turning on the TV. Mom disappeared into the kitchen to do the dishes. I asked if I could help her and she said no, it's fine.

I went to my room, opened the letter and found notes from three meetings. These were the words of Robert that were my manna from heaven. I knew in that moment that I would go the next day to UCLA and open a private post office box on campus to receive Mary Ellen's correspondence.

To me it was simple and clear: my Deliverer had arrived.

A prophet who receives a message has no option, but to deliver it as instructed.

Jewish Tradition

CHAPTER 10

Since I had completed supervised training to teach at the high school level prior to spring break, I was able to apply for substitute teaching jobs in the Los Angeles Unified School District. The aim was to earn money before moving to Northern California. Once I registered, they would call me around 6 a.m. to inform me where I would need to go that day. I had to be ready whether I was called or not, because some of the locations in LA required over an hour of driving.

I learned from a university friend that you needed to know where these schools were so that when they gave you the school's name, you could quickly realize whether or not it was in a good or bad part of LA and whether or not to take it. Good advice. There was, however, no easy way to associate the location by a school name unless you had a printed list. I was unsure how to secure such a list. I had learned from my friend some of the names to avoid, but when the call came that morning I was not prepared for the conversation:

"Are you available to teach today?" the woman asked.

"Yes."

"Very good. Here's the school's name and address. You will check in with Mrs. Snow."

I had no idea what just happened. I had convinced my father the night before to let me drive the only car our family had to my first teaching job, thinking it would be local to Brentwood where we lived. My master teaching classes were at University High School or "Uni." It was upper middle class white kids and it was so close to our apartment that I could walk there.

When Dad learned the address of Garfield High, which was in East LA, he was horrified and refused to let me go alone. He would drive me. We were only six years past the infamous Watts riots. East and South LA were not safe neighborhoods for white folk. I couldn't have been given a worse assignment.

As we got off the freeway and came close to the neighborhood, there was not one white person in sight. The African American "kids" were the size of professional football players. I was only four years older than the seniors I would be teaching. It was frightening. I did convince my father to pull the car over a block away so I could walk to the administration building on my own to check in. He reluctantly agreed, keeping his eye on me all the way. He told me before I exited the car that he would be back at 3:15 SHARP.

When I got into the building, I put on my most serious face and walked down the corridor past the walls of lockers where hovered males and females in ritual mating conversations and gestures. I made it to the door with the word Office on it.

Mrs. Snow was a bespectacled woman with a fast gait and pulled-back dishwater-blond hair. We arrived at the classroom sooner than I had expected. As we entered, the noise from the 18-year-olds milling around "socializing" with one another was unlike anything I had experienced in this setting. Mrs. Snow immediately pointed to a red phone hanging on the wall near the door.

"Use this phone in case of an emergency," she whispered. "It goes to our office. Here's the syllabus. Good luck."

She turned to look at the class and quickly exited, locking the door behind her. That was very strange.

Pretending to be the teacher, I walked over to the board and wrote my name. Turning around I saw no one had taken their seats.

"Please take your seats," I asked politely.

No reaction.

"Class, please take your seats."

THE DIVINE BEGINNING

Again, I was ignored.

I raised my voice this time. "CLASS TAKE YOUR SEATS NOW!"

That worked.

Sort of. The guys didn't sit. They sprawled with outstretched legs in the undersized chairs, their long, muscular arms reaching over the desktops, hands falling at the wrists, fingers dangling. The girls had low-cut blouses and tight skirts, red lipstick on full, voluptuous lips. The clothes these young ladies were wearing could not contain their pubescent hormonal emanations. The intoxication filled the room like invisible catnip to these young lions.

"Open your books to Chapter 3." Some did. Some didn't. One said, "Hey Teach. I forgot my book in my locker." Everyone started laughing. He was clearly the smart, clever one. "Can I go to my locker to get it, Teach?" I knew that game, so I said, "No. Share the book with someone." He then got up, went over to the sexiest girl in the class, and reached his long, muscular arm over her shoulder to hold onto one side of the book, looking down her blouse at the same time. The other boys hooted. One said, "Hey Teach. I need to go to the bathroom." The laughter and noise were beyond anything I had ever encountered. Oh, brother. I was in trouble. What do I do?

So I went to the red telephone. I picked up the receiver and noticed there was no tone. The phone was dead. The laughter and ridicule went off the charts.

I returned to my desk and sat down. At least the kids were locked in and couldn't escape. I let them socialize and I read a book for 45 minutes. This may have been the first time the teacher was the one watching each click of the wall clock, waiting for the period to be over.

At the end of the period, Mrs. Snow returned to unlock the door. This was the worst class in the school, and she knew it. The kids bounded out, and the next crop came in and sat down before the second period bell sounded. The rest of the day was a blur. The course lessons I received to teach them were a joke. We were babysitters at best, prison guards at worst. Five years of college for this.

* * * *

When I arrived home from that experience, there was a deep, unsettling feeling that I had made a big mistake about my career, but had no idea how to fix it. It was no longer, "I will become a High School English Teacher." I now was one, on paper at least. I was instructed to achieve this by my father, who had no education and felt it would provide a suitable income for me for the rest of my life, and so I dutifully followed his request.

My University High teachers training had not been a gloriously satisfying one, albeit much easier than Garfield High. All of the students in the tenth-grade classes looked up to me with a wide-eyed acceptance and programmed respect and that was great. Then there was the senior composition class. All the eighteen-year-old students thought they knew everything and were just passing time before graduation. They judged me as rigid, critical, and demanding. They did everything they could to sabotage my lesson plans, including a strike of silence they had arranged among themselves, blocking my ability to engage them in a dialogue. It was an excruciatingly negative, humiliating experience. On many occasions walking back to my Brentwood apartment, I would be in tears from the day's work.

This profession was beating me up emotionally, and I had barely begun. Still, I needed to make a living, and having my own money to support myself was a strong desire I had had since I was nine. I knew even then that money was power and freedom. I watched my mother wither from disuse and dependency. She had no job. She had no friends. She had no money and was totally reliant on my father for everything. She was stuck. So I told myself, "We all have to do what we have to do. There could be worse ways to make a buck." But the self-doubt was increasing.

* * * *

I had shared the recent teaching experience with Miles in the next letter. His response was for me to substitute whenever I could and not to worry about it.

He also told me that he had a change in his circumstances. He decided to move from Pleasant Hill and quit his job at the Tinder Box in Walnut Creek. He had the opportunity to work with a Fellowship member named Yorgos, a young Greek who had started his own organic apple juice company with another member named Jim. Miles would be the third person, and it looked like he could make good money. He would need to work long hours processing the apples to make the juice. Then he and Yorgos would sell the gallon bottles to local distributors. The apple juice operation was actually in the backyard of Yorgos's home in Vacaville, where he lived with his wife Kerrie. It was a large, old Victorian house on Buck Avenue. The month was May and they were pressing the previous fall's crop.

There was something strangely absent in that letter: he didn't mention where I would be living. I had assumed I would live with him in his apartment and had imagined our relationship picking up where it left off that March. My reply to his "change in circumstances" was to ask him about this. Would I be with him or did he expect me to be on my own? I had about $750 from the leftover grant money from my college education, which at the time was a good amount. I also asked him if he knew which school districts I should apply to for high school teaching in the fall.

He replied within a week: there's plenty of room in the new house for you. He also mentioned that Robert decided to move from his Walnut Creek apartment into the Victorian in Vacaville. There would be six people living in the house: Yorgos and Kerrie, Robert and Jim, and the two of us. He also mentioned that Rosemary, who lived in Vacaville, had told him she would arrange for me to have an interview to teach at Vacaville High School.

Although this reply was satisfying because it was inclusive of me, it raised an instinctive alarm. I had never lived with anyone other than my family. How do I act? Would there be privacy? What type of relationship would I have with Miles with all of these people around? Sex was now on my mind — a lot. What was I getting myself into? Although the road ahead was uncertain, one thing was undeniably clear: I could not stay where I was. The known was a dead zone. The unknown contained unimagined possibilities, whether good or bad.

I could live with that.

*

> *Turn you, and take your journey.*
> *Behold, I have set the land before you: go in and possess*
> *the land, which the LORD swore unto your fathers.*
>
> Moses

PART II
The Beginning

CHAPTER 11

THE DAY HAD arrived. Miles was driving from Vacaville to Brentwood to pick me up and free me from my parental bonds. I had packed my clothes into two medium-sized suitcases and had chosen the books to take. Most were connected to my evolution. The other books I had owned were college texts. I sold these at the UCLA student bookstore for a pittance of the cost of purchase.

All except one: a paperback of Walt Whitman's *Collected Poems*. For some reason I decided to keep it, even though most of the writing seemed rambling and repetitive. The university course I took did not say much about Whitman, other than discuss his controversial and shocking sexual references. These were still the times of the Sixties, a time of sex, drugs, and rock and roll. Sex was on everyone's minds, including staid college professors whose mindset and training had been born in the conservative Fifties, but who now relished their newfound intellectual freedom by revealing sexual innuendoes under the guise of scholarship.

When Miles came to our door, I was surprised how relatively civil my parents were to him. Dad glared at him as he shook his hand and Mom stood behind Dad. I took the suitcases and Miles took the heavy cardboard box of books. Everyone descended the stairs to the awaiting 1956 Chevy parked on Stonehaven Way, the side street of the apartment building, which faced busy Sunset Boulevard. I provided hasty, one-armed hugs and into the car I went, rolling the window down to wave goodbye.

This June day marked the beginning of my adulthood at age 22. At last.

* * * *

As we turned onto the 405 heading north, I could feel an enormous amount of energy building up inside of me. I was bursting with joy and excitement. I began to talk. And talk. And talk. I spoke about work ideas, such as the law of octaves — *do, re, mi, fa, sol, la, si, DO* — whereby each note described the milestones and obstacles contained in any action on this planetary level, from its start ("*do*") to its finish ("*DO*").

"I could feel how I'm sounding the *do* of the rest of my life," I exclaimed, more to myself than to him.

I pointed out the exits that led to my childhood home in Sunland-Tujunga. Like a young child learning to speak, everything I passed evoked a response in me. But Miles was quiet and didn't share my happiness. His face was expressionless. We drove on, leaving the LA basin behind. The Tejon Pass and the purple hue of the majestic Tehachapi Mountains, whose peaks angled sharply up from Highway 5, led into the famous Grapevine Canyon. This divide geographically separates the LA basin from the Central Valley. People recognize it as the point where Southern California ends and Northern California begins. But to me, it represented a powerful milestone in time, the demarcation line between my past and my future.

On our way north, we stopped in a small restaurant for lunch. Standard truck stop décor: vinyl floors, a long counter and swivel stools for single diners, red mock-leather booths with red tabletops, where chrome mini jukeboxes sat between salt-and-pepper and mustard-and-ketchup containers. Good food, good price, and quick service.

As soon as we shimmied into our booth, I realized I needed to use the bathroom so I got up. I walked past several booths and the long counter filled with beefy truck drivers. I could feel their eyes scoping me, beginning with the long hair draped down my back, my big breasts and small waist outlined by the tightness of the top I was wearing, and the round hips and buttocks that filled the light-blue flared denims. I felt very uncomfortable and vulnerable. I knew in that moment that my childhood dream of being an independent woman traveling the country on her own was totally a figment of my imagination. There was danger out there and I was helpless. I needed a man to protect me.

* * * *

We drove on after lunch and Miles announced he was too exhausted to continue. It was best to stop in a motel and finish the drive first thing in the morning. It was then he told me that he had worked the day and night before he drove to LA and that basically he had been up for two days with no sleep. This explained his lack of emotion. He was basically worn out.

We found a very inexpensive place that had a small bathroom and a bed. That was it, really. No natural light to speak of. He fell asleep immediately. I remained full of energy. No TV. Nothing to do. My books were packed so I couldn't read a book. And so, I lay there, waiting for sleep to come to me. It eventually did.

* * * *

THE DIVINE BEGINNING

We got up at sunrise, packed the car, and headed up the highway. The scenery was so lovely. We snaked through spring-green gently rolling hills, passed by filled reservoirs and concrete channels of the California aqueduct, encountered ranching flatlands speckled with grazing animals, which alternated with vast farmlands with perfectly straight rows of cotton, sunflowers, and tomatoes that stretched into the horizon.

When we reached the Bay Area, we skipped the turnoffs we had taken before and headed farther north to Vacaville. The exit read Monte Verde Avenue. We drove to a side street named Buck Avenue. It was the most beautiful, idyllic American street with mature oak trees canopying the narrow two-lane road.

He pulled into the driveway of a two-story Victorian. Here, I thought, was my new home.

As we started unloading the car, a petite woman with short dark hair and bright black eyes appeared, bounding down the wooden porch steps toward us.

"Welcome Linda!" she blurted, embracing me immediately. "I'm Kerrie. We've been looking forward to your arrival."

She introduced me to her husband, Yorgos, who had followed closely behind her. He had twinkling blue eyes, red-apple cheeks and a gentle smile, and stood as tall as his wife. Lovely man, I thought. With his thin blond hair, round wire-rimmed glasses, and plaid shirt and worn jeans, he looked like a working man. This was Miles's business partner.

Behind Yorgos was another man. He was quiet, had a goatee, angular frame, wire-rimmed glasses also, and a playful smile. This was Jim.

For a moment, I felt special because of all this attention and did my best to make a good impression. We all entered the house with my belongings.

Kerrie showed Miles and me where we would be sleeping. It was a separate bedroom that had a wooden floor and a bay window that faced the street. A small double bed was pressed against one wall and a three-shelf wooden bookcase was on the opposite wall. It was quite deluxe I thought, and I was very glad there was a door for privacy since the idea of living with others in the days of communes had me wondering if we all would be sleeping next to each other.

Kerrie and Yorgos had the upstairs room above ours. Jim had a downstairs bedroom. Sounds civilized enough. Even though I was told that Robert also had moved in, there was no sign of him or indication of his lodging.

The kitchen faced the rear of the house. Upon the small back porch was a contraption that I soon learned was the apple press. Miles, Jim and Yorgos began to speak about their business. I followed Kerrie into the kitchen.

It was lunchtime, and Kerrie had been busy preparing the meal. Each burner on the stove had its own pot or pan filled with various vegetarian foods. She had such confidence. It was like watching a conductor cuing each section of the orchestra. She asked if I knew how to cook, and I simply said Yes. I didn't tell her that I usually followed a recipe. That to me was cooking. But watching her, I realized she had an instinctive way of knowing how to season each dish and when the food was done. This I couldn't do without written instructions and a few pictures to illustrate the final result.

By the time we were ready to sit down, Robert had appeared. He was dressed in a green velour shirt and tan corduroy pants. Kerrie said he had been at Rosemary's house that morning. Her home was in Vacaville, too.

I helped to set the long rectangular table in the dining room. The six of us took our seats. Kerrie and Yorgos sat across from each other at the heads of the table. I sat next to Miles who sat next to Yorgos and across from Robert. I was facing Jim who sat next to Robert and Kerrie.

I tried to listen rather than talk. Robert, Yorgos, and Miles were discussing various subjects, among them were the apple juice business and the status of looking for Fellowship property. I was so self-conscious that I ate very little and smiled a lot. I was in the middle of the table, and basically didn't know these people. I had nothing to contribute. Keep smiling, I thought. They're feeding you.

Then Robert complimented Kerrie on the food, which I learned were recipes she had brought back from India, where she and Yorgos had lived for several years. Wow. India. I always imagined I would like to go to India one day, but the thought of living in a foreign country scared me. These people were far more worldly than I was, even though we were the same age, give or take a year. I felt like an unschooled child.

When lunch was over, everyone helped to clear the table, including Robert. The men left the kitchen, and I could hear them talking in another room. The kitchen cooking area was quite tight, and the dishes piled high on a small countertop by the sink.

I stayed with Kerrie, who washed while I dried. She would point to where the dishes belonged and I would carefully, with presence, place them there. As we had finished the last plate, she stunned me with a question.

"Would you like to prepare the dinner for tonight?" Again, I automatically said Yes. But my mind was totally blank. What does this mean? I had no clue. I was willing to participate but needed so much guidance that I didn't even realize how much guidance I needed.

I retired to my room, where I sorted through my clothes and placed them on hangers in the tiny closet. I unpacked my books and arranged them in the bookcase. I then lay down for a nap.

I was awakened around four by a knock on the door. It was Kerrie who wondered if I needed help preparing dinner, which was scheduled for six. I confessed, "I'm not sure what to make." Kerrie graciously offered to help me.

She placed various types of vegetables on the small table next to the screen door of the kitchen. This is how she planned her menus, she said. She mixed and matched, deciding which ones would be served raw, which ones cooked, and which spices to pair with each dish. She had already started the big pot of rice that would accompany the meal. Clearly, she could see I was lost. She lovingly suggested I prepare a dish of broccoli, mushrooms, cheese and bread crumbs. It would be baked in a loaf pan.

As I prepared my small dish, I would periodically ask her if the broccoli pieces were cut to the right size, if the mushrooms needed to be sliced thin or quartered, and if the bread crumbs needed to be mixed together with the vegetables or sprinkled on top. She told me to mix the cheese with the vegetables and sprinkle the bread crumbs on top, which I dutifully did. She said it would only take thirty minutes to cook so we will put it in the oven later.

Close to dinner time, Yorgos showed up, kissed Kerrie on the cheek and asked what's for dinner. She explained and also pointed out my dish that was now in the oven. Everything seemed so caring and positive that I began to relax. I was happy. These people didn't yell, argue, belittle or challenge. These were my people.

Yorgos volunteered to set the table. By six, the men gathered in the dining room, and Kerrie and I brought the dishes to the table. We sat in the same seats we had occupied at lunch.

My small loaf pan seemed miniscule compared to the platters of food that Kerrie had prepared. Jim wondered if it was for one person or if we were to share it. I could feel my blood drain from my face as Miles laughed out loud. I had never heard him laugh like this. Quickly Yorgos countered, "Well, it looks wonderful. We can all take a little."

Although Yorgos's kindness and gentle smile were appreciated, Miles's response shocked me to my core. I was propelled into a state of confusion, not understanding where he and I stood with each other. Why did he not defend me against Jim's snarky observation? Why was Yorgos the man to neutralize the situation? My own childhood family dining had been so contentious that my sister and I learned to time our hunger to the off hours, so that we would not find ourselves at the same table as Dad.

I sat there trying to eat my dinner. The demonstration of my culinary abilities clearly left much to be desired. The conversation continued on other subjects. Struggling to get out of my self-deprecating funk, I looked up at Robert, who reached for my little loaf pan and scooped a small portion onto his plate. After setting it down, he smiled lovingly at me, as if to say, "Good job, Linda." I smiled softly back. As he placed a small amount on his fork to taste, a string appeared that was not part of the cheesy dish. It was a strand of my long black hair. With two fingers, he slowly removed it.

Oh my God! Adrenal heat hit my throat. I wanted to cry.

But Robert looked up from his plate right at me, with the most tender expression. Our eyes met and held. He wasn't laughing at me. He was commiserating with me, as if to say, "What an amusing play this is, yes? Just when you thought it couldn't get worse…." This moment was now our private joke that no one else was sharing. And indeed, no one else had seen him remove it, because they continued to talk and eat obliviously.

For those few seconds, we connected on both a human and conscious level. I felt his love and affection. And I could see that he was familiar with finding oneself in the most humiliating of circumstances that were beyond one's control. That he, too, understood the concept of "the play." He stabilized my state.

This was what I've been looking for my whole life. Here was someone who could pull me back to my Self out of the depths of self-deprecation.

* * * *

After dinner, another chap showed up. He was a shy fellow with red hair named James. We were introduced and I was told that he, too, was a member of the Fellowship. Kerrie followed him outside onto the front porch and they sat together on a little bench under the strong porch light. James had brought his guitar and gently strummed it, creating a beautiful sound in the warmth of the Vacaville summer evening. It was intoxicating and magical, and I was drawn to it. I went outside to join them.

After two songs, another person joined us: Robert. He asked if he could play something. James gave Robert his guitar, and I was amazed at how delightfully Robert strummed it. His voice was lovely. After one song, he returned the guitar to James who continued his serenade. The four of us sat there in the quiet of the night, listening to the music, appreciating each other's sweet company. Robert, the teacher, was not the distant authority figure that night. He was one of us.

When the student is ready the teacher appears.
When the student is truly ready, the teacher disappears.
                                                                        Lao Tzu

CHAPTER 12

The next morning Miles rose early to go with Yorgos to an appointment with a distributor. He had kissed me as he left the bed. Although we hadn't had sex that night, at least he still loved me, I thought.

I could hear everyone bustling but waited until I could make a dash to the bathroom in my nightgown to get ready. When there was a lull, I gathered my toiletries and clothes, making sure they were perfectly positioned in front to hide my breasts. Gently opening my bedroom door, I expected to see the bathroom unoccupied but the door was closed. Someone was using it. I closed my door but kept listening carefully for the sound of a door opening. When I heard it, I once again gathered up my stuff, peeked out my door, but saw the door was closed again. Someone had beaten me to it.

I waited on the bed with my toiletries and clothes on my lap for twenty minutes, listening intently. Then I heard the door open and quickly made my move. Once inside the large bathroom, I placed my items on several counters and got into the shower. That took fifteen minutes since my long thick hair was hard to wash. My makeup took another fifteen minutes. Then someone knocked.

"Yes?"

"Are you almost done?"

"Um. Yes."

This was a lie. I needed thirty more minutes to blow dry my hair in the bathroom because there was no mirror in my bedroom to look into while doing it. After drying my thick hair with a weak hairdryer, I spent another ten to dress and another five to assemble my belongings. As I opened the door, there was Robert standing before me.

"Dear, you need to remember there are others in the house."

"Okay."

I scurried to my bedroom and closed the door behind me, reluctant to come out. By ten o'clock, I emerged and found myself alone. I went into the kitchen and found some granola and milk (yes, I learned something) and sat down to breakfast. The sweetness was comforting.

Having no job and no car, with nothing to do that day, a part of me felt disconnected. I had found friends and was in love, yes? If so, why did I feel so isolated and emotionally vulnerable, so uncertain about the direction of my life? I should be happy since I was now on my own (that is, no longer with my parents), but my state was anxious. Contradictions abounded.

I still had my books, I realized. Rummaging through them, I found Whitman's *Collected Poems*. Poetry was soothing. Maybe I can take a walk, I thought, and find a nice park where I can read, since it was such a lovely June day.

As I went out the door and down Buck Avenue toward the highway, the traffic grew as the sidewalks diminished. I had no idea where I was going. It was an adventure of sorts. After several blocks of careful trekking, I found a commercial space that had a patch of grass with a beautiful oak tree providing sufficient shade on a summer's day. I sat there as passers-by looked curiously at me. It was not exactly secluded and definitely was not a "park," but it was the best I could find.

Opening the book intentionally, I began at the beginning. I never believed in skipping around a book. I always would begin at the beginning, figuring this is how the author intended it to be read. By the second page, I found a short poem titled "Beginning My Studies":

> "Beginning my studies, the first step pleased me so much,
> The mere fact, consciousness — these forms — the power of motion,
> The least insect or animal — the senses — eyesight — love;
> The first step, I say aw'd me and pleas'd me so much,
> I have hardly gone, and hardly wish'd to go, any farther
> But stop and loiter all the time, to sing it in extatic songs."

As I read each word, I was amazed to learn that he, too, once had begun his studies of this cosmic principle — consciousness. He, too, marveled at the forms of life on this planet Earth. I put the book down and looked at the cars moving past me, and the flickering shadows of the tree on the grass.

But then something else occurred, something I was familiar with since childhood but could never explain adequately to anyone. It had been a sacred secret I kept inside.

THE DIVINE BEGINNING

I sensed his *Presence.*

It permeated my heart, as if he invaded my spiritual space. And there was enough room inside for Me. We were there together sharing the moment. What was this? The system had concepts called "self-remembering," even "celestial influences." But it was something more. Was it God? That didn't make sense to me. God was in heaven; this experience was very earthbound, and yet celestial. Again, contradictions.

I continued reading, and he continued to speak to me. He was *there* speaking to *me:* "I witness and wait," "I dote on myself," "Each moment, and whatever happens, thrills me with joy," "There is that in me — I do not know what it is — but it is in me," "Do I contradict myself? Very well, then, I contradict myself; (I am large — I contain multitudes)."

These phrases resonated deeply. I knew that the emotions churning inside of me — the feeling that I was lost and yet found; confused and yet clearheaded; fearful and yet hopeful — were felt as well by him one hundred years earlier.

His last words were especially heartening:

"Failing to fetch me at first, keep encouraged;
Missing me one place, search another;
I stop somewhere, waiting for you."

The afternoon was getting late. I closed the book, got up from the grass, and headed home. I was not alone anymore. Walt was with me.

* * * *

When I arrived at the house, I learned that there would be a meeting at Rosemary's that evening. Kerrie had quickly prepared the rice and vegetables that were her mainstays. It was just Yorgos, Kerrie, Miles and me dining. Jim and Robert were with a few students for an early dinner at the Coffee Tree. (The Coffee Tree I would learn was the local hangout for informal Fellowship gatherings; it was located across from the Nut Tree restaurant along Highway 80.) We ate quickly to make it to the 7 p.m. meeting.

The four of us drove to Rosemary's home in Miles's Chevy. We got there at 6:30, and already cars were parked on the open terrain by her house. She and her husband Donald (simply referred to as Mac) had a commercial walnut orchard and employed a Mexican family to manage the farm, as we would refer to it (as in the children's song, "Old Macdonald Had a Farm"). The immigrants lived in a small cottage behind the barn near the fields.

Walking up the steps, I was impressed by the substantial construct of her home. Stone pillars framed the entrance. The front door was solid wood. When you entered a small hallway, you first passed doors on either side that led to the bedrooms. The spacious lavender living room with deeper purple carpet opened to you almost immediately. On the left in a recessed area was a grand piano couched against a picture window. Directly opposite this space was a stately stone fireplace.

The living room sofas had already been repositioned for the meeting. Mac had placed a beautifully decorated large chair for Robert in front of the hearth. When we arrived, Mac was actively instructing students to arrange the metal chairs to complete a circle. Miles and Yorgos went straight to help, while I followed Kerrie into the kitchen through the entrance near the piano. Kerrie gravitated to the counters where students were arranging the snacks for the break. I just stood there looking at people. I smiled a lot.

At the kitchen table was Rosemary, smoking a cigarette and chatting with Mary Ellen (also smoking) and Harold, puffing on his pipe quietly, and another lady whom I had yet to meet. Rosemary saw me and called me over to introduce us. Her name was Trisha. She had long ash-colored hair and was a Venusian type I was told. Her husband was also in the school and was a Saturnine type.

"Linda," said Rosemary, "I set up an interview with the principal of Vacaville High School for you tomorrow. I've known him for years and praised you, so you should have no problems getting hired."

She handed me the name of the person and the time (noon). I told her I didn't have a car, but she said not to worry because it was close to the Buck House and I could walk. She turned the note over and drew me a street map.

I was so happy. This was what I was waiting for: A real job; a chance to earn my own income and not be dependent on anyone. I couldn't stop thinking about it during the meeting. That little piece of paper returned a sense of dignity to me, and more importantly, a feeling that I was back on track and in control of my life.

※

Parting track'd by arriving,
perpetual payment of perpetual loan.
                                        Walt Whitman

CHAPTER 13

The next morning I slept in, waiting for everyone to leave the house before I got ready. I took my time to shower, apply makeup, and dress. I wanted to be as present and relaxed as I could before the interview. I wore my purple polyester knit coatdress, which actually was the only formal dress I owned. Short-sleeved, with big purple buttons down the front, it gave my figure a more professional, slimming look. Nylons and black pumps completed the ensemble. I allowed myself thirty minutes for the walk. If I'm early, I thought, I could stroll around the grounds familiarizing myself with my new occupational home.

As I approached the front door to leave, I heard someone behind me softly speak.

"Where are you going, Linda?"

It was Robert. Where did he come from?

"I have an interview for a teaching position at Vacaville High School," I replied.

"Well, you look very nice, dear. Tell them you can only work three days a week."

I laughed out loud.

"Robert," I said, shaking my head in disbelief, "there are no permanent teaching positions for only three days a week!"

"Well, you don't know that. Just tell them you can only work three days a week," he insisted.

I said okay. But it wasn't okay. As I walked the route, I kept thinking, "He's my teacher. I must obey him." All teachings have their bad examples: Peter denying Christ was perhaps the most famous. And I did not want to fall into that category.

So there I sat in front of the principal. Lovely man. His hands gently folded on the employment papers that were lying on his desk. We chatted a bit, and he leaned in to listen to me speak about my experiences and qualifications. He seemed pleased, so he extended the pen to me for signature.

Without reaching for it, I blurted out, "I can only work three days a week."

He froze in disbelief. "What?" he said incredulously. "Do you know the job I'm offering you?" His face went from sunny to icy.

"I can only work three days a week," I repeated sheepishly, sounding more like Lucy reusing a lame excuse on Desi.

He stood up and went to the file cabinet, opening the top drawer that was jammed with folders. "See this?" he said. "All of these people want the job I'm offering you."

And for the third time, I repeated my term limits.

We shook hands and I left.

The walk home was longer than the walk arriving. As I entered the house, I saw Robert.

"How did it go dear? Did you get the job?"

I could not believe he would ask me this. Of course, I didn't get the job! Didn't he know this? How could he set me up like this? Why would he do this to me? I had no answers. But I did understand one thing: I did not disobey him.

"No," I replied politely.

"Don't worry dear," he said sweetly. "It will be okay. You'll find something else."

* * * *

I sequestered myself in my room. I had to figure this out, so I went to a work book and pulled out *In Search of the Miraculous*. I needed to understand better how schools worked.

> "The next demand made of members of a group is that they must remember why they came to the group. They came to learn and to work on themselves and to learn and to work not as they understand it themselves but as they are told to. If, therefore, once they are in the group, they begin to feel or to express mistrust toward the teacher, to criticize his actions, to find that they understand better how the group should be conducted and especially if they show lack of external considering in relation to the teacher, lack of respect for him, asperity, impatience, tendency to argument, this at once puts an end to any possibility of work, for work is possible only as long as people remember that they have come to learn and not to teach."

I knew why I came. It was clear to me at a very early age that things were not what they seemed.

The first time I experienced "higher states," as the system calls it, was at the age of ten. It was a Sunday late afternoon at Chickie Bubbie's house. We had eaten our lunch of cheese blintzes, potato latkes, cold beet borscht in a tall glass with a dollop of Knudsen's Sour Cream on top, and challah with schmaltz. It was enough to knock anyone into unconsciousness. After ingesting this fattening fare, we each found our way to one of the beds in her home for a nap.

My bed of choice was the one in the dining room that was pressed against the wall below a large window framed by lace curtains that Bubbie had sewn. I had fallen quickly into a deep sleep. When I awoke, something strange occurred. My ears registered the house was in a profound state of silence. This was highly irregular. I was alert. Upon opening my eyes, my sight immediately focused on the delicate lace curtains that gently filtered the afternoon light.

But it wasn't "me" looking; something else inside of me was using my eyes and ears. It was enraptured by the beauty it saw, the silence it heard. Another something in me was alarmed by the presence of this intruder, who was small and childlike yet very ancient. But the intruder was not bothered by this something else in me. Instead, it continued to gaze at the wonder of sunlight through lace curtains.

Just then my mother said, "Oh, Linda's awake." At that moment, I could feel the intruder smile, indicate wordlessly to hush and not speak of its appearance to anyone. And then it receded. I returned to being the ten-year-old Linda that everyone knew.

I was sad when it departed. It left me with a small grain of truth that would disturb me for years. *This Linda that everyone knew was not really me. She was a phony.* It was not who I really was. But then again, *who was I?*

Try as I might throughout adolescence, I could not locate this personage inside of me. Instead, I found myself manifesting everything I didn't want to be: emotionally volatile, socially awkward, and painfully self-conscious. I felt in the grip of something wild, and longed for that part of me that could silently and serenely behold beauty and bathe in it.

As I began my studies, as Whitman so expressively wrote, it was astounding how truly little I knew of the Real Me. This school and the man leading it I felt were my only hope to find and become that being who visited me in my childhood.

Who is that Invisible One who sees through my eyes and hears through my ears?

Upanishads

CHAPTER 14

The next day set the pattern for those to follow. The morning routine included Miles and Yorgos leaving early to attend to their duties in the apple juice and olive oil business, and Kerrie spending her day with redheaded James. They were obviously good friends.

Jim remained behind with Robert that morning. The teacher gave him the task of painting the back steps leading to the kitchen, and he wished it done by the afternoon.

After instructing him, Robert turned to me. I was expecting an assignment.

"Would you like to go to Rosemary's house with me?"

"Yes!" I replied gleefully, since I hadn't made any other plans. It was my chance to be with him, and I felt honored.

We got into his pale blue and white Volkswagen van. It was very clean outside and inside. Sitting next to Robert, I felt like an innocent child going on a trip with her father. Robert had this effect on one. We pulled out of the driveway heading toward Rosemary's home. Trying to make good use of the time alone with the teacher, I began the conversation:

"Robert, do you know my center of gravity and body type?" I asked.

"Well, you seem to be Venusian. It would appear you may be Queen of Diamonds." The fact he thought I was intellectually centered like Miles supported my picture of myself as being an "Intellectual," which pleased me. I wished him to clarify whether I was a Venusian on the side of Mercury. His reply: "Pretty much centered in Venusian." This did not please me.

I turned to look out my window, appearing to focus on the impressions zipping by. But truthfully, I was beginning to feel insecure in his presence. I was deep into self-deprecation when he spoke.

"Do you see this parking slip under the wiper?"

He pointed to this square paper wildly and noisily flapping in the wind.

"I keep it there because it irritates me. I use it for voluntary suffering," he explained.

I smiled at him in earnest. Wow, I thought. You mean he gets irritated? From the first time we met, he seemed to live in a different world from the one I inhabited. His world was a curiosity to me, and one I longed to live in. How do I get there? In that moment, he pulled me in with him as we each looked at the same object on the windshield. We were together in the Present. It was both a comforting and disarming experience.

Arriving at Rosemary's, I followed Robert up the back steps, which led to the kitchen. Rosemary was at the stove, preparing coffee and scrambled eggs. I helped set the table as she and Robert spoke. The topic had to do with property and Mac, who was making an offer for some land. Rosemary was very knowledgeable about these things and gave Robert her opinion about the price per acre. It seemed like Rosemary and Mac were going to buy some more property. Or so I reasoned.

We sat at the table and the subject changed to my job offer at the high school. Rosemary was not pleased. The principal called her and told her what happened. There was tension at the table. Before I could explain what had occurred from my viewpoint, Robert interceded and told Rosemary that it will be fine and not to worry about Linda. He then changed the subject very quickly.

"Rosemary, do you have a purse you can give Linda so she can throw out this bag she's carrying?"

He picked up my sack. I had made it a year earlier out of a light canvas 100% cotton full-sized laundry bag. I cut it up and made straps out of the material so that the bag slung over my shoulder, draping against my thigh. It was hand embroidered, with a scene of a bird and a tree and a swan and a pond. I had planned to fill in the outlined figures with different colored threads to finish the scene, but I got lazy and quit.

It wasn't until Robert held it up that I saw it as it was: it was filthy. I never washed it. Part of my hippie phase, where making items by hand was the rage, and dirt was prized for its authentic reflection of nature's earthy qualities. This bag also suited my wardrobe: grungy faded light blue bellbottoms and light purple floral form-fitting top, as well as a polyester, empire-waisted, cap-sleeved floral print long dress (what was called a "granny dress") with matching fringed shawl that I had easily made because it required no zipper. These were my costumes of choice. It was a carefree, bohemian look I was after.

Rosemary got up from the table and went into her bedroom. A moment later she appeared with a brown leather handbag that was clearly made in the 1940s. My mother had one just like it. It had a metal latch and a strap long enough for it to be draped over one's forearm. It was flat from disuse, as if it had breathed its last breath and died. It was ugly. She handed it to me.

Then Robert instructed me to take it and throw out my bag. I made a face. It was clear I wasn't happy with the option. His next statement, "Throw it out now," made me realize that keeping it was actually not an option. I emptied my stuff into this bag and walked over to the garbage container next to the sink and tossed the sack into it. Again, I obeyed.

* * * *

The meeting that night was at Anna Gold's home in Berkeley. Miles and I drove together in the Chevy. Robert and Jim had gone with Rosemary. Yorgos and Kerrie had stopped by his parents' home (they lived in Vacaville) before driving to the meeting.

The chairs were already set up by the time we arrived. The meeting format was the same regardless of location: Robert would teach for forty-five minutes, we would break for refreshments and informal conversation for fifteen, and then we would form small groups for another thirty minutes. Robert and Jim would leave just after the intermission and head up the highway to the Coffee Tree, which was open until midnight. Invited students would join them.

But this night would be different.

Robert chose the topics of the four states of consciousness and the four lower functions, reminding us that "consciousness is not functions." We were encouraged to observe our lower functions and to "not express negative emotions." Observation was the first stage of self-remembering, which was the lynchpin of the system. We listened attentively. His expression was serious when he taught, often squinting his eyes and looking upward with slightly bent head as the words gently flowed from his mouth.

After forty-five minutes, Robert rose and disappeared into the kitchen with Rosemary. Some had gathered in the dining room, which was the room to the left of the front entrance, while others stayed to chat in the living room. I moved into the dining room, where the food was laid out on a beautifully pressed white tablecloth: plates of cheeses and crackers, celery and carrots, bean dip and onion dip, and a plate of cookies. On a side table were four opened wine bottles and wine glasses.

Robert and Rosemary entered. They looked elated. He requested everyone gather in the dining room because he had an announcement. We huddled together (there were about thirty of us) in the small space surrounding the table. Robert explained that Mac was on his way with a cake and champagne because "they had accepted our offer." A hoot arose and everyone clapped. I smiled happily, eager to share in the festive atmosphere, and yet having absolutely no clue what they were talking about. I leaned over to Miles and asked, "What does this mean?" He said, "Mac negotiated a price for us to purchase property for the Fellowship."

THE DIVINE BEGINNING

When Mac arrived, others helped him bring in the cake and bottles of champagne. His rosy cheeks and laughing eyes were full of delight. It was clear he scored a victory. Once we had our glasses full of champagne, Robert asked Mac to describe exactly how the negotiations went. We apparently had countered their offer a few times and we settled on $185 per acre. The total acreage was 917. We toasted to the future home of the Fellowship of Friends.

I took my slice of cake and glass of champagne and entered the living room to find a seat. I wanted to know more about what was happening. I learned from several students that in December, Robert had asked for donations to purchase land that would become our main retreat. There we could focus on balancing the three lines of work (work on oneself, work with others, and work for the school).

Many trips around Northern California had occurred in early 1971 to view potential parcels, including that noble-sounding property named the King Ranch. Everyone had been asked to make this "special donation," as it was called, to purchase the land. Robert wanted the property to belong to us all and not to him. The minimum payment was $250, which was considered to be ten times the minimum monthly teaching payment.

"Have you made your Special Donation yet?" someone asked me.

"No," I said. "Who would I give the check to?" I asked.

"Rosemary."

When I finished eating, I took the plate and glass into the kitchen. Others had begun the cleanup. I sat at the little breakfast table in the kitchen and wrote out the check to the Fellowship of Friends for $250. Rosemary, Mac, Robert, and Anna were talking in the dining room. I approached smiling and waited for a small lull in their conversation.

"I would like to make my Special Donation," I said, extending my hand with the check toward Rosemary. Mac was the first to embrace me, laughing. He was the gentleman doctor who had asked me that night at Anna's whether I was going to join. Commitment complete.

In that moment it felt as if I had not only come full circle, but had indeed jumped into that inner space of my dream.

❖

I have joined myself to the land of everlasting,
and it is you who commanded it for me, O my lord.
    Egyptian Texts, Going Forth By Day

CHAPTER 15

The sense that I was in a time warp was deepening. It was stunning to realize that only a week earlier I was taking final exams at UCLA. My new life was now so rich, so full, that mornings, afternoons and evenings each manifested as entirely separate days. It felt like I lived a month in one week.

And yet, the week took so long to live. The calendar charted time for others; it provided no framework to the reality I was living. Time both accelerated and slowed down. How could that be?

Meetings were held in the evenings at students' homes in Vacaville, Walnut Creek, and Berkeley. These north, east, and west points of Northern California formed a magic triangle. Students gathered afterwards at coffee shops along Highway 80 to discuss the latest developments. Robert preferred the Coffee Tree in Vacaville, while others gravitated toward a local Denny's, which had lower prices and more food on the plate.

After the Thursday meeting on June 24, I had spent a Denny's evening with Mary Ellen and Harold and others. We didn't so much gather quickly to eat and disperse as hang out for hours into the night, talking about the Fourth Way system, which we called, "the Work." Endless coffee refills were a must. We used coffee shop clientele as our laboratory rats, studying body types, centers of gravity, chief features — any Fourth Way concept that was able to be verified through observation.

Mary Ellen was very knowledgeable about the Fourth Way. We hit it off. Harold was very quiet but had an impish quality about him; he liked to tease me verbally, and physically poke me to make me giggle. Those late night/early morning sessions were fueled not only by coffee but by the Lunar qualities of being a night owl that Mary Ellen and Harold each possessed. Mary Ellen and others also smoked a lot of cigarettes. It was a common practice among the students. I was not a smoker.

* * * *

That same Thursday night, Miles was spirited away by Robert. I had learned that Robert considered Miles a man number five. This meant that Miles would become a conscious being in this lifetime. Robert also designated Yorgos and Mac as the other men number five in the school. The rest of us were men number four. This meant that although we really wanted to awaken now, our aim to become fully conscious beings wasn't as strong as a man number five's aim, apparently, so complete awakening is not going to happen to us in this lifetime. One couldn't help but feel like a second-class citizen.

I thought I wanted to awaken badly enough, yet I was told that nothing could happen if one didn't have an aim. I had a hard time understanding the concept of aim. What is my aim? I had no idea. From childhood, anything I formulated turned either to ash (earthly desires) or smoke (pipe dreams).

Another student mentioned, "To awaken, you must VALUE self-remembering above all else." I don't think I did. I wanted to be in a relationship, have a steady job, and have friends who liked me.

As I sank more and more into depression, thinking I wasn't a good student and had no right to be in the school, this sweet voice inside me asked, "Well, what is it you like about self-remembering?" That I could answer: It feels good to be present. It feels RIGHT. Whenever I was able to divide my attention, I entered a state that felt more real to me. I liked Ouspensky's description of self-remembering as "the quiet place within." That I understood. "Aim" I did not.

How did I relate to divided attention and self-remembering? The system describes the effort to divide attention and produce self-remembering as a balance of three points that, together, create a pyramid. The first point is you and the second point is what you are observing. You need to include yourself in the picture, so that your attention is both on you as well as the object you are viewing.

A tricky juggle, were it not for the third point that creates the apex of the pyramid. The third point is the impartial Observer that can look at both first and second points simultaneously. Without this apex, self-remembering is not possible. With it, the impartial Observer becomes the seed of development for one's Higher Self. The Observer (Observing 'I') evolves into a Deputy Steward, who is able to watch and recognize one's mechanical manifestations; and later, the Steward, who actually has more capacity to control one's mechanical manifestations so that consciousness can arise.

This psychological pyramid I understood at an early age: I was a movie addict. My father used to get us into the cinema for the Saturday matinee for free by convincing the theater owner that he could teach his son boxing in exchange for the tickets. Dad's con lasted a long time (over a decade), and since each Saturday matinee included a double feature (two movies), I saw an unbelievable number of films.

How is this related to divided attention? Each time I would leave the theater, I felt the camera was following me, filming me in the movie of my life.

The camera was the apex of the pyramid: it captured everything I said, everyone I met, and each action indifferently. It simply recorded it. Watching movies planted within me the seed of this impartial Observer.

My ability to record events as they unfolded was invaluable and critical to my evolution. We were now heading into the last weekend of June 1971, and the purchase of the property will bring exciting changes to our school, I'm sure.

I can hardly wait to see what will happen next.

The future enters into us, in order to transform itself in us, long before it happens.

Rainer Maria Rilke

CHAPTER 16

After that late-night Denny's coffee shop excursion with Mary Ellen and Harold, I got a ride back to the Buck House from another student. Miles made it home before me and had retired. We were still sharing the same bed. It was dark and I tried not to disturb him as I lay down.

In the morning, Miles told me that a student named Helga had invited us to her home on Mount Tamalpais this coming Saturday "so you and I could have some private time together." I did not know this lady but was very grateful for her consideration.

My relationship with Miles had not developed as I had expected, since we were in such a communal situation in the Buck House. A few nights earlier, Robert actually called everyone in the house together and explained he wanted us to sleep on the living room floor in our sleeping bags and not in our individual rooms. He also had us practice hugging one another, first looking into our essence eye with presence. He explained he wanted to encourage affection that nourishes essence, and cautioned us to make certain our embraces "were an end in themselves." They should not have any sexual overtones. He was very clear about this.

* * * *

Around six o'clock that Saturday, we drove to Marin County and wound our way up the mountain. When we arrived at Helga's home, I was surprised to see it was a cocktail party. She graciously welcomed Miles and me, showed us the bedroom we would be using that night, and introduced us to her friends.

THE DIVINE BEGINNING

They were nice people, refined in both manner and appearance. I suddenly felt very out of place.

Miles went directly to the bar to get wine. He was remarkably at ease with everyone there. I sat on the couch and tried to listen to conversation. I smiled a lot. There was laughter and information shared — I couldn't relate to any of this.

I got up and ate some cheese and crackers and looked at the majestic view from her panoramic windows. What do I do? I went back to the couch. I didn't want to appear like the odd one out. It brought up bad memories of high school. I would be invited to a party of my sister's friends, where each girl was paired with a boy at the party. I had no one, and was so uncomfortable that I began to retreat emotionally.

Similarly, in this situation, I tried to listen to one man speak, to be polite, but he was living in a world that I knew nothing about. I said nothing, just nodded occasionally. I could see he was getting uncomfortable around me. He eventually stood up and went to get food as an excuse to move on. Miles, meanwhile, was fitting in so smoothly. He and Helga were enjoying the conversations, laughing and relating to everything that was said.

When the sunset was appearing, we all went to view it. It was beautiful. Dusk followed quickly. Guests left once they realized the time was approaching ten — except one fellow. He lingered with Miles and Helga. The three of them continued their conversation. Miles got up to pour more wine. It was clear the lovely romantic evening I had envisioned and longed for was rapidly becoming another pipe dream. How can I prevent this? Quick, do something!

I yawned and stood up. I looked at Miles and announced I was going to bed. I thought for sure he would get the hint. But no. He, Helga and the other chap bid me good night.

Now what? I was in the bedroom alone. I got ready for bed and lay there, waiting. The clock on the side table moved the hour ahead to eleven. The room was icy cold. I was shivering. I couldn't stay warm. The clock was approaching midnight. Still no sign of Miles.

* * * *

I awoke alone. The clock showed it was 3 a.m. I was in a very present state. I quickly dressed and went into the living to see if anyone was there.

The room was barely lit and unoccupied. But draped over the couch were some clothes. I could hear faint whispers coming from the upstairs bedroom. Immediately I imagined the worst: Miles and Helga were together in bed making love. I had been betrayed.

I could not stay in this house, I thought. What do I do now? I found Miles's car keys and decided to drive down the mountain to a café in Mill Valley. There I would drink coffee and think about my life and what to do next.

I quietly opened the front door. The entire landscape was shrouded in fog. I got into the Chevy and turned the key. It was a manual transmission. Since my father owned a Chevy in the 1950s like this one, I recalled the shifting was an H shape and proceeded to imitate his actions based on my memory. I had never driven a car like this before, so it was quite astonishing that it worked.

The fog was dense. I had no idea where I was going. I followed the sloping road, making turns that seemed to lead down to the valley. My heart was broken. The ache radiated throughout my chest. Tears were flooding my eyes and wetting my cheeks. Fear burned my throat. How could this happen to me? I lost my virginity to *him*. What do I do? Where do I live? Questions spun inside my head. I needed help to figure out my life.

Amidst the pain and confusion, suddenly this voice in my head said, "You must step aside. They have old things to work out."

The apex of the pyramid appeared. I could feel an invisible presence inside the cab of the car, hovering above me. It ignited presence within me. I emotionally let go. A state of calm and reason returned.

Then I saw the strange situation I actually was in: I forgot my purse in my haste to leave, so would be unable to pay for coffee. I was wearing a thin dress on a cold night, which made me look like a hooker. No restaurant would be open in Mill Valley at this hour.

As I continued driving, I reached a crossroads and wasn't sure whether to go up or down. The fog obliterated visibility: I could not read a street sign to see if any name sounded familiar. A house was nearby with a light shining in the front window, so I parked the car in the driveway and knocked on the door. A large dog barked and a man opened it. Luckily, he was nice and I told him the street I was looking for (which fortunately I recalled). It must have been a very odd thing for him to see in the middle of the night. He was quite concerned, but I said I'll be fine and thank you. Sorry to disturb you.

I made all the right turns and found the street. When I pulled into the driveway of Helga's home, I turned off the car and sat there for a few moments. Presence was both in me and around me. I was now smiling. I knew what to do. I would continue as a student in the school and let Helga and Miles resolve their relationship.

As I entered the house, the most bizarre scene greeted me. It was straight out of a Fellini movie. Miles was sitting crouched in a corner, with his head in his hands. Helga was at an easel, painting. The mood was somber. And here I enter, chipper as can be.

Miles got up and sat with me on the couch. We spoke and I shared with him my insight. It must have been strange for both of them. He was afraid, he said, that I had decided to drive back to Los Angeles and that he had caused me to "lose the school." This was never a consideration, and I was surprised he thought this.

It was now approaching dawn. Helga prepared a light meal and we dined together as the sun rose. I hugged Helga, feeling clean in my heart, and Miles and I drove back to the Buck House.

I felt virtuous that I could so easily drop any jealousy. It was a lofty experience for me. Any wounds I suffered seemed to heal quickly. Miles, on the other hand, was still struggling. I felt badly for him, but happy I was no longer involved in this dreamy romance.

That night I decided that my love for him would continue regardless of the outcome between them. I wished them the best.

❖

> *Do not pretend to be what you are not.*
> *God forgives everything except hypocrisy.*
> Meher Baba

CHAPTER 17

In the days that followed, the soundness of the state of presence from that night on the mountain grew thin until the state, with its profound understandings, had evaporated. In its place was the strong feeling of self-sacrifice — the generous gesture of a loving and loyal heart.

Since I had voluntarily "stepped aside" for Miles and Helga to resolve their relationship, I imagined that their play thus would be temporary and quick, and that Miles would remain loyal to me in the end. This assumption was barely a fleeting 'I.' I caught a glimpse of it but it immediately retreated. It did not resurface, so I gave it no mind. He and I were still together, and that's all that mattered to me.

* * * *

Robert said he wanted all of us to move to the newly purchased property over the July 4th weekend. He had requested students pack up and leave their homes to move there. Of course, I had two suitcases, but many had households, so it was not reasonable for them to abandon everything to move to some outpost in the Sierra Foothills. Obeying the teacher had its degrees, it seemed.

On Thursday, July 1st, Robert, Yorgos, Jim, Miles and I went to Helga's home to help her pack her household to move to the property, as we referred to the tract of land we purchased. Robert apparently was interested in some of her furniture, which he felt would bring a little civilization to the place. Yorgos and Jim brought the truck while Miles, Robert and I came in the Chevy.

As I walked into the home that had been the scene of a most intense play several days earlier, I felt remarkably neutral. Helga's young children (two boys) were running around the packed boxes. Yorgos and Jim lifted a beautiful sofa to place in the truck, and I followed them with a box that was not a heavy lift for me. I waited for them to place the sofa in the truck. Robert gave instructions for the furniture's placement, as he peered into the empty space.

I stood at a distance, waiting for them to position the heavy furniture before I handed the box to Jim. As I did so, an overwhelming smell of fresh horse manure radiated out of the empty space. The contradiction of refinement meeting excrement hit me hard. I began to laugh hysterically.

Miles glared at me. I couldn't catch my breath long enough to explain. What amazed me most was that no one else said anything about the stench. Am I the only one to see that we shouldn't put Helga's stuff in this horrible space? I walked back into the living room to grab another box. I took deep breaths to stop the uncontrolled laughter. But as I approached the truck, the undeniable stink hit me in the face. Like a bad case of hiccups, the hysteria was back. Going into the house relieved me of the impressions, and I regained my composure. Once I returned to the truck, however, my laughter exploded like a machine gun. This was not the first time in my life where hair-trigger fits of laughter consumed me over a period of days simply by recollection.

I looked helplessly at Robert and asked through my cackles, "Will I ever be able to control this?" He waved his hand dismissively and said, "Of course, you will." Then he went into the house.

I stood there. The cackles diminished into giggles. If I can control this, I thought, then this is, indeed, a real school.

* * * *

The plan was to leave Friday after lunch to make the journey to this small town named Oregon House. It was in the Sierra Foothills "below the snow and above the fog," as Robert explained at the Thursday evening meeting. Driving instructions were distributed during intermission. Robert wanted everyone to come up that weekend, even if they were not able to move their belongings at that time. He also said, "We will be living here for the rest of our lives."

Depending on location, people were to caravan in groups: the Danville and Walnut Creek group, the San Francisco and Berkeley Group. Those of us in Vacaville would meet at the Coffee Tree for lunch, and go up from there. Our new home was 100 miles away, and we estimated if we had lunch at noon and left by 2 p.m., we could get there by 4 p.m., set things up and prepare dinner for everyone. Apparently, there was a two-story house on the property (a "log cabin") with a kitchen, two bathrooms and two bedrooms. There was enough floor space, aside from these bedrooms, for sleeping accommodations. This was the expectation.

* * * *

Friday July 2nd arrived. Unbeknownst to me, Miles had arranged with Helga to caravan together. She would be driving with her children in a small VW bug, while another student would follow her in the truck that carried her belongings.

The Vacaville group arrived at the Coffee Tree later than expected. The Coffee Tree was crowded, and our lunch took a long time to be served. It was after 4 p.m. by the time we were done. We gathered in the parking lot and made sure everyone understood the directions, since apparently it was tricky.

Miles and I drove together in his Chevy. Robert and Rosemary drove up in his VW van. Don went with Klair, his wife, and their two children. Mac, who was a cardiac physician, was working and couldn't make it. Yorgos, Kerrie and Jim went up earlier that morning.

I had the map and would serve as navigator. But Miles said he knew the way because he had gone up a few months before, when he, Klair, Rosemary and Robert first saw the property. It was raining hard that day, he said. He described how they huddled under the eaves of the house. I asked him about this "log cabin." He chuckled and said, "I told Robert that we should blow it up and start over again."

"Is it that bad?" I asked.

He didn't say anything, but just smiled, knowingly.

* * * *

We drove east on Highway 80 toward Sacramento. Miles knew to take the correct exit that sidestepped the downtown as we headed toward Marysville. Even though that road was named Highway 70, it did not look like any highway I knew. Yes, it was paved. But the road was two-way with narrow lanes that stretched for miles. No homes could be seen from the highway. It was definitely a rural part of Northern California, and it was the farthest north I had ever been in the state. The grasses were golden and the native oak trees with their olive-colored leaves were interspersed among stretches of orchard, farmland, and grazing cattle.

We tried to keep together in a caravan through Marysville, but it was not easy because of the many street signals. Miles and I spoke little. He did say that the route would become more difficult as we left the town; he kept a lookout in the rearview mirror for Helga in her VW. She was behind us.

It was after 7 p.m. The sun was low in the western sky as we drove eastward from Marysville. The road returned to a narrow-lane, two-way highway. Suddenly Miles turned left from the main road into a 76 gas station and stopped. The instructions indicated to make that turn, but it was not an easy road to find. He got out of the Chevy. Helga pulled her VW into the station shortly after and the truck appeared as well. He greeted her with the first smile I had seen on his face all day.

* * * *

Twenty minutes had passed since the gas station. The sun was still above the horizon but the silhouetted hills prevented the sun's rays from reaching us. We turned right onto a road after passing a sign that read Collins Lake. The elevation rapidly increased. This was the Sierra Foothills, and the little town of Oregon House was within a few miles.

Dusk was now upon us. We saw a small grocery store but continued winding our way along what appeared to be the only road in town. As we reached the end of the road, we came upon Robert's VW bus and other students' cars, which were at a standstill. It seemed there was a problem. It was almost dark now. I stayed in the car as Miles spoke with Robert and Yorgos, who stood by the barbed-wire fence entrance to the property. This narrow passage, barely the width of the truck, was our only access point.

Miles returned to the car. He explained that the road was muddy and slick from a nearby natural spring. It would be treacherous, especially for the truck, to maneuver up this path to the main house, but we had no choice. It would be a true test of each car's traction.

As the caravan of cars proceeded past the first challenge – the barbed-wire gate – our focus was on the car ahead of us because, if it got stuck or stalled, our momentum would be lost and our tires mired in the mud. The intensity of the moment was substantial.

We could not be concerned about the cars behind us. We had to press on, regardless. Yorgos was directing traffic, and there was much yelling back

THE DIVINE BEGINNING

and forth, as men communicated their status. A few behind us did get stuck. When a car got stuck, he and a few other students helped the driver to push it along.

Somehow, we made it to a safer stretch of dry land and were able to arrive near the main house, which was on a higher level than the fenced entrance. By now, we were in total darkness. Jim was there with a flashlight. He instructed everyone to take only sleeping bags and other basics to the house for the night; we would unpack in the morning.

As I got out of the car, I looked up and saw the night sky filled with brilliant, glittering stars. The moon was on its way to fullness. The air had a most distinct fragrance: tart like lemon with the sweet, earthy smell of decomposed leaves. It was fresh and clean — delicious, really.

The road to the house was steep and deeply gutted by years of rain runoff. It was very difficult to find my footing. I took the walk carefully, relying on the moon as a source of light. Miles carried both of our sleeping bags, while I carried my smaller suitcase filled with my personal items.

We entered the house. Immediately in front of us was an open kitchen where Kerrie was orchestrating the dinner preparation. Smells of spicy vegetables filled the room. We were guided to the bedroom on the ground floor and told to put our belongings there and then come out for dinner. The room was the size of a single bedroom, perhaps 10 x 12, but it already had stacks of boxes and supplies from students who came earlier. We clearly were the last caravan to arrive.

I took our sleeping bags. Because the room had a light switch and a door for privacy, I quickly positioned our unrolled bags in an unoccupied location between stacks of boxes. I felt I had scored a victory by grabbing this spot.

I entered the living room/kitchen area. It was a large open space, really. Kitchen cabinets that hung from the ceiling hovered over the counters and served as the room divider. The whole area was bustling with activity. Dinner was laid out on the counters. We each took a plate, served ourselves, and sat on the vinyl floor to eat in the dim light, sharing stories of our trek into this western wilderness.

The dishwashing crew, made up primarily of older men, worked until midnight. Yorgos, Robert and Miles were talking in the living room. I decided to get ready for bed since it was late. Near the bedroom was a bathroom and I waited my turn to enter. In my nightgown with my clothes in hand, I scurried out and into the bedroom. The bedroom light was on and students were straggling in to get their belongings for the night. When they left the room, we bid each other Good Night. I felt like I was at a slumber party except for one thing: there I was, alone. The last person to enter the room noticed I had an unoccupied sleeping bag next to me. He asked, "Who is that for?" I said, "Miles." He smiled and asked if I wanted the light turned off. I said, No, I'll wait for Miles.

I waited and waited, just as I had in the bedroom on Mount Tamalpais. Where could he be? Where could he be? I looked at my watch and saw it was 2 a.m. Where else would he sleep? This is his sleeping bag. It baffled me.

I looked down at the shoes I had worn to get me to this place. They were white leather ankle boots. I had purchased them before I left Los Angeles, thinking boots were appropriate protection against the rugged elements. It was naïve. The red dirt ringed the edges of the white leather. Staring at them, I knew deep inside that I would never be able to remove this earthen dye.

I also knew something else. Just as the property's red clay had left its permanent mark on my shoes, so too would it indelibly color what I was and would become.

*

Transformed? Yes, for it is our task to imprint this provisional, perishable earth so deeply, so painfully and passionately in ourselves that its reality shall arise in us again "invisibly." We are the bees of the Invisible. We wildly gather the honey of the visible, in order to store it in the great golden hive of the Invisible.

Rainer Maria Rilke

CHAPTER 18

I awoke around six the next morning refreshed, even though I had gotten only a few hours of sleep. Then I turned to see if anyone had occupied the sleeping bag next to me. No one had. My heart sank.

I arose, gathered my stuff, and was able to use the bathroom quickly. Two students were in the kitchen cooking breakfast: coffee, granola with milk, scrambled eggs, toast, and hashed brown potatoes — a typical American breakfast. We spoke a little and then I took a cup of coffee and stepped outside. There, under a small fig tree near the house, I saw Miles sit up from a double sleeping bag. Next to him was Helga. Her sons' bags were nearby and they were sound asleep.

I looked away quickly, as if to demonstrate I had my composure intact (which I did not). My feet took me in the opposite direction, across the dirt patio to a small pond facing west. From this vantage point I could see the parked cars and the steep ascent we had made in the dark the previous night. It was as if we were in a shipwreck, and the morning revealed what had washed ashore. The cars were facing different directions along the edge of the narrow road.

I had finished my coffee and walked inside the cabin. I asked if I could help and was handed a stack of plates to put on a long table that had been set up against the open kitchen countertop facing the living room. All the countertops were wooden and so terribly deteriorated that towels were placed on top of them to prevent splinters from entering ourselves and our food. Cabinets were without doors, exposing the shelves. Traces of creatures (dead insects and rodent droppings predominately) indicated that they had taken up residence long before we arrived.

I was given metal utensils and napkins and bowls and platters of food to take to the table. I was happy to help as it took my mind off my circumstances. Within ten minutes people showed up for food. Where they came from, I do not know. We each took our filled plates outside to eat. The day was already getting warm as the sun that appeared over the eastern hill behind the house began its crawl across the landscape. I found a rock to sit on and felt fortunate. Most simply sat cross-legged on the dirt. We ate in silence, mostly.

Robert and Yorgos had been speaking about the day's activities by the entrance of the cabin. I had no clue what was in store.

After breakfast, I entered the kitchen to help wash dishes. I was not interested in working outside as I had never done physical work in my life, other than pulling weeds near my house for an elementary school fire-prevention project. Robert was directing people to various chores, which we called "octaves," because each chore — indeed, every human activity — had a beginning, middle, and end and was governed by a cosmic principle called the "law of octaves." Peter Ouspensky describes this concept in his book *The Fourth Way*. Although I had been studying this, referring to a chore as an octave could bring more practical understanding, I thought. One had to be aware of deviations or "intervals," where something could prevent an octave or chore from being completed. We were told to "follow through" with whatever project we were given.

Well, that was theory. Practice turned out to be a very different matter. I was drying dishes and thought I would then help out in the kitchen, preparing lunch. Robert came in, looked straight at me and curled his index finger to say, "Come with me." I set down my towel in the middle of drying a dish.

Someone had unhinged the entry door to the house and rested it against a small boulder near the same fig tree where Miles and Helga had lodged for the night. I was handed a hammer and chisel the size of a screwdriver. My task: remove the caulk to free the panes and set the individual glass squares aside so the wood could be refinished.

Huh? I had no idea what I was to do. I froze and Robert immediately saw my inexperience. He came over and sat next to me to show me what was needed. I watched as he chipped away the caulk, easily freeing the first glass square. And then I tried. Oops. My first hammer stroke cracked the glass.

Robert calmly told me to try again. Still unclear on the method, I positioned the chisel and swung the hammer. Tap. Crack. Robert uttered a soft, "Hmm." He instructed me to stick the chisel in the crevice between the caulk and the wood and give it a gentle touch. I thought I had located that space and held the chisel firmly. But as I lifted the hammer, so too did I lift my hand with the chisel, and the chisel's sharp point came down hard on the glass. Tap. Crack.

We both stared at it in disbelief. I tried the next one, finding it difficult to discern the white caulk from the white paint on the wood, not only because of the identical color, but also because the sweat on my nose was causing my thick glasses to slip, which affected my vision. With great intention, I guided the hammer to the head of the chisel and gave it a quick tap, but nothing was removed. I tried again with more force. Tap. Crack. At this point, Robert gave up on me.

"Well, we will just need to buy new glass," he said.

As we stood up, Robert noticed David, a large, thickly bearded gentle bear-like man, assemble three students to help him clear junk that previous owners had left on the property. This was his assignment. Robert turned to me and said, "Go with David."

A flatbed truck with wooden railings appeared at the top of the drive. I got into the cab next to David, who was driving, and the others got in the back. We drove slowly down the eroded ribbon of a road, bouncing up and down and back and forth, trying to avoid the haphazardly parked cars. It was a wild ride.

He located a wide footpath between the shrubs that was large enough for the truck, and brought it to a stop next to a huge pile of man-made debris. As we jumped out, David stopped us before going further.

"Be careful not to touch the poison oak," he cautioned.

He showed us how to recognize the plant by its three-leaf configuration.

Ahead of us was the carcass of an old car and various wood and metal objects randomly scattered. David moved slowly toward the main pile, and a young fellow, who was Trisha's teenage son, accompanied him. David would point to a heavy object, and the teenager and another male student carried it to the truck.

I grabbed the only shovel, thinking that would be my method of removal. But when I approached the pile, I saw there was nothing there that could be collected using a shovel. Basically, the shovel was useless. After about an hour, most of the junk was on the truck except the rusted car frame.

As I watched the sweat pour off people's faces, I said, "This is hard work." They stopped and stared at me.

One person responded sarcastically, "What are YOU talking about?"

David quietly chuckled. It was then I saw my shadow: I had been standing there, leaning on the shovel, the entire time. I hadn't done any work at all. All I was doing was watching them, as if it were a television show.

* * * *

Lunch was served. Big bowls of salad and platters of sandwiches piled high. Water coolers were filled with lemon and water. Robert had requested the children wait until the adults were served first. This request was shocking for the mothers, who were accustomed to feeding their offspring before serving themselves. A few women spoke negatively about it. The children, on the other hand, were playing a game to see who could be the last person in line. It was such a strong verification to see the pull of a mother's instinct. The term the system uses for this is "feminine dominance."

I was not involved in this identification. I was involved in my own. Miles was sitting near Helga and her young children. He and I hadn't even spoken since we drove up together. What was going on with us? Why did he treat me like this?

The way Miles and Helga interacted with others revealed that others knew something I didn't know about them. Students were not surprised. In fact, they accepted them as a couple. My heart hurt badly. But I had to continue and keep my emotions hidden from others.

* * * *

After lunch, Robert assigned octaves to each of us. Mine was to work with a Russian student named Nadia. She was a Lunar type, which, according to the body types described by Rodney Collin, had "cool, instinctive certainty" and was the "midmost point of femininity." She was petite and had a wiry frame.

Our task: repair the log cabin's living room vinyl floor. The cold winters and hot summers took its toll on the tiles; they were worn so badly that the wood under them was exposed. We were to patch the floor using spare tiles someone had found nearby.

Nadia gave me direction.

"You put glue on. I position the tile."

Okay. Having never done this before, I slathered adhesive with the brush I had been given as if I were applying mayonnaise to a salami sandwich. I wanted to be sure the tile would stick firmly. But the glue was oozing on all sides when Nadia placed it down. I thought Nadia was pressing the tile too hard, causing this to happen, so I suggested she try not to push it so much. She glared at me. It was clear to me that Nadia couldn't position it correctly. It was clear to Nadia that I was putting too much glue on, which caused the tile to wiggle in place. With each application and placement, the negative tension was escalating between us. I blamed her; she blamed me.

Just then Robert passed by. He stopped to look at the job we were doing. Then he said, "You two work well together," and walked away.

We both smiled at him as he made this statement, but inside I thought, "Could he not see that the opposite was true? And he calls himself a conscious being?"

A few minutes later, Nadia stood up.

"I can't work with you!" she announced, and left me with the glue pot.

I tried to do both tasks and found that I had been placing too much glue on the tile. Even though I adjusted the amounts, my hand and eye coordination were sorely lacking. All the tiles I placed were crooked. But I "followed through" and the task was done.

* * * *

Before dinner, Robert decided he wanted all of us to go to the top of a mountain on our property to view the sunset. He had been exploring the land with Yorgos at some point during the day and had discovered a beautiful lush meadow on the northern side of the 917 acres.

There were only eight of us that went: Miles and Helga; Robert, Jim and Yorgos; myself and two young men. Others were either cooking or hiding. As we got out of the cars, Robert pointed to some large rocks that had perfectly formed holes drilled into them. He explained that, according to Yorgos, they were made by the Indians who had lived here centuries before and used these bored holes to grind acorns that fell from the overhanging old oak trees. The Indians made bread from the flour. We marveled.

THE DIVINE BEGINNING

We began the march across the broad meadow. Grass was still green, which was very unusual because it was July and the temperature that day was in the high 90s. My eyes took in this serene view of a meadow salted with white wildflowers. Oak trees stood at guard on either side as if to honor the majesty of this natural wonder.

Feet were not my favorite form of transportation. After walking a few minutes, I was ready to stop. But we had barely started. The others seemed to glide on the grass. My legs were like unsteady stilts as I tried to keep up with Miles and Helga, but it was difficult.

The beautiful meadow was deceptive. It was on an incline and the reason for its lushness was soon evident: it was the site of a natural spring. Not only was it muddy, trying to suck the shoes off our feet, but the long green grass proved slippery. I struggled to make it. I was trailing farther and farther behind. Suddenly, I lost my footing and fell face down in the bog. I started to cry.

A voice inside my head spoke firmly to me.

"You'll never forget this, right?" it said. "So SHUT UP."

That sobered me quickly. I guess I'm getting what I came for, I thought: conscious moments.

Robert heard my cries and turned to direct Jim to help me. He was sweet as he lifted me up by my arm. My face and clothes were muddy. But worse, I was humiliated.

We eventually reached the top of the hill for a view of the sunset. We spread out so each could see the sun slowly decline in the sky below the distant mountain. Robert looked straight ahead as did everyone. He spoke to Yorgos, who turned to each of us and said, "Robert asks that we behold the sunset in silence."

Once the sun set, I was ready to leave, thinking we had accomplished our aim. But everyone stood there staring where the sun had been. This went on for minutes. I was getting antsy. So instead of looking at the sky, I looked at others looking at the sky. It was a part of me that was confrontational, disrespectful, and impatient. Everyone else seemed to be experiencing the profundity of this moment. I wasn't. I was hungry and wanted dinner.

It was dusk when we got to the farmhouse. Dinner was awaiting Robert's arrival. I was hoping to be able to speak with Miles about our relationship, but he was either with Helga or Robert. After dinner, he approached me and said he wanted to talk.

We went outside. The moon was almost full. In the moonlight, I looked into his blue eyes as he told me his plan.

"I want to be with Helga, and I want to be with you. I will alternate sleeping with you and sleeping with her."

It was an odd arrangement, but I was willing to do anything to finally be with him. So I agreed.

"Will we be together tonight?" I asked, which seemed reasonable since he was with her last night.

He said, "Yes. Meet me upstairs. I first have to talk with Helga."

We returned to the living room, and I watched him sit next to Helga to speak. I'm not sure what he told her, but I was happy that he would be back in my arms.

As I entered the upstairs room, a single bare light bulb was the only source of illumination. I lay out our sleeping bags. It was hotter than downstairs, but a window was open to ventilate the space. I used the upstairs bathroom, which had no door; someone, however, had tacked a blanket at the top of the doorframe to create a semblance of privacy. It was a functional space, at best. A 25-watt bulb shed a weak light over the small one-foot-wide sink with a mirror overhead. The sink had no counter for my lotions. A toilet was across from the sink and a shower consisted of a drain and spigot protruding from the wall. The mud on my body had dried, but I wanted to be fresh for him, so I took a mock shower. The water barely trickled over my selected body parts.

I decided to leave the light on for him. As I lay down in my thick, polyester sleeping bag, I felt something on my face. It was a bug. I swatted it. And then another came. And another. I had taken my glasses off to sleep, but found them quickly. Focusing, I could see what appeared to be a hundred earwigs scrambling across the floor. They had infested the kitchen (which is how I learned their name). I guess they moved upstairs at night. I pulled the sleeping bag around my face with only my nostrils exposed, hoping the bugs would not crawl inside them. It was sweltering, but I didn't want to leave, thinking Miles would be up shortly. It mattered that much to me to be here for him.

Despite the fearful thoughts of infestation, I found myself drifting into sleep, bringing to a close the first full day at this newfound home.

*You delight in what vanishes
and are busy with your desires as the one
with a wet dream is deluded by pleasure in sleep.*

Ibn Arabi

CHAPTER 19

It was Sunday morning on the Fourth of July. I was awakened by a student who came upstairs to use the bathroom. My emotions suddenly were a boiling concoction. The brew was composed of anger for having to sleep in such a dirty, hot, insect-infested space; betrayal for having been lied to again; and physical pain from a broken heart. I could hear everything going on in the bathroom, which somehow reflected how exposed I was beginning to feel. I always could hide in my bedroom or bathroom at home, but here, there was no place to hide.

When he left the bathroom, I quickly entered, making as much noise as I could to indicate someone was inside in case anyone else wanted to use it. I was in a hurry. It took me about twenty minutes to get ready, since the breakfast odors were wafting up the stairs, and I knew breakfast was a short-lived affair. I rolled up the sleeping bags and left them there (the bugs were gone with the morning light). I descended the stairs quickly, not only because I was hungry, but more importantly, I wanted to know where Miles was.

I filled my plate with food and took it outside to join the others. There he was balancing his empty plate on his knees, smiling and talking with Robert. A feeling of falling behind overwhelmed me. I was late to everything, out of place. Alone. I wanted to cry again but focused on each bite of food instead, trying to get the morsels down.

When breakfast was over, students seemed to scatter. A few landed in the kitchen to wash up. I placed my plate and utensils down on the counter and went upstairs to retrieve the sleeping bags and to store them in the downstairs room where I had spent the first night. As I stacked the bags with the others, I couldn't hold it in any longer. I found a spot behind some boxes near the back wall and started to sob.

"Who's in here?" said a woman's voice loudly. I ignored her.

"Come out now!" she demanded.

I obeyed. It was Rosemary.

"What's wrong with you? What happened?"

I truly didn't want to tell her. I was not accustomed to sharing my pain with anyone, even my own mother. But then again, my mother was nothing like Rosemary.

"Come with me," she commanded. "We're gonna take a walk and talk."

I followed her outside, and we climbed up above the house through the shrubs. The ascent was steep but Rosemary led the way. She had the most beautiful lavender suede boots I had ever seen, and her delicate frame belied her militant stride. She was a powerhouse. And she took no prisoners.

I told her about Miles and Helga and what he told me last night. It all gushed out, and with each statement I made, she would shake her head and utter, "Oh my!" "You said THAT?" "He did WHAT?" And finally, "You know NOTHING about men."

She started to tell me that strange things were happening that weekend. Don had fallen in love with Doris, despite the fact he was married to Klair. Kerrie was sleeping around with this redhead James that I had seen in the Buck House quietly strumming his guitar. There were all these triangle relationships occurring.

Her advice to me was to speak with Robert. According to Rosemary, he needed to know what was going on. I didn't know how to talk with him. She said, "Just go up to him." Since she was closer to Robert than I was, her advice carried some weight.

When we came down the hill, I saw Robert and approached him.

"Robert, I need to tell you something," I stated.

"Yes, dear?" he replied, guiding me by my elbow to a secluded spot behind the house.

I began to tell him about Miles and Helga, and tears started to flow from my eyes. This sad story opened up a flood gate. The Play of Linda and Miles and Helga I was describing to him began to take on a life of its own. Something in me felt empowered and vindicated as I spun the tale. The lines were being drawn in this play of mine; the good guys and bad guys had been given their appropriately colored hats. And yet something else in me knew this was a fabrication; it wasn't the truth. The truth was we were each suffering and no one was at fault. Yet the small voice that contained this precious insight was drowned out by the melodrama of the moment.

Robert interrupted me as I was getting to the juicy part about last night. He reached in his pocket and handed me a clean white handkerchief. Then he gently said, "Try to remember your Self in this moment."

That was not the response I thought he'd give. I thought he would say, "Wow! Let me speak to that Miles! Don't worry Linda. I'll fix it."

THE DIVINE BEGINNING

Robert kissed me on the forehead and told me to keep the handkerchief. I guess that was it. I turned to go and saw several others standing in line for him. Robert was a busy man.

Rosemary was right there in the front of the house awaiting news.

"Well, what did he say?" she asked.

"He told me to remember myself."

"That's it?"

"Yes."

I could see she was frustrated. Rosemary had two teenage daughters, and I felt her protective motherly instincts toward me. Still, Robert was the teacher, and the higher part of me — the part that wanted to awaken — was grateful for his simple yet clear advice. It echoed my reading of Ouspensky: "The moment you suffer, try to remember yourself."

It was so easy to read, but so hard to remember, and even more difficult to do. I wanted to find that quiet space inside and live there consciously forever. I thought that place would be above all pain. It didn't seem possible to locate it in that moment. The play I found myself in had its strong pull. My lower functions (intellectual, emotional, moving and instinctive) were fully immersed, and I couldn't loosen the glue of identification that had me stuck within the confines of my machine.

After we spoke, Rosemary went into the house to help with lunch, and I decided to do something about my state. What did I do? I sat on the rock in front of the house where I first dined. I made an effort to divide my attention, using the expression, "Here I am. How strange." I pictured an invisible camera above me that saw Linda sitting on the rock next to the house, with her feet resting on the dirt, looking at the pond. For a brief moment — a flash, really — I felt relief. The many 'I's that bombarded my brain and the fire that lodged in my heart were gone. I had found that Quiet Place Within. I was present.

What I understood in that moment was that even though I had no control over this soap opera, I did have control over my ability to change my state of consciousness. My state and my circumstances were independent of one another. They existed on different levels, just as the clouds hover over the earth. With this realization, a smile came on my face. So this is what it means that *consciousness is not functions*. It was an important verification.

As I sat there on the rock, a few of the children were singing around the pond, "This land is your land, this land is my land…this land was made for you and me." The sounds of the voices were enchanting and helped to further elevate my state. I watched a young boy running toward me saying, "Look at me! Look at me!" It was Helga's five-year-old son. His golden hair, bright blue eyes, and sweet face made me smile even more, but I decided not to give in to his command. I wanted to preserve my state of presence. He then approached me with a grin, stood in front of me with his hands on my knees. I bent forward to stroke his lovely head. And then he punched me in the face.

A swarm of negativity flew up inside of me. I wanted to retaliate but stopped, realizing that would be wrong. Rosemary had just come out of the kitchen and apparently had watched the whole thing.

"All he wants is your attention. He's a child, so give it to him," she said.

I couldn't. I didn't know how to be with little children. Wanting attention was false personality, I thought. How could this be essence? I sat there confused and pained at my inability to understand.

Clearly, I had so much to learn.

* * * *

We were eating lunch when the truck arrived. Robert motioned to some students to help unload the supplies. It took several men to carry the heavy roll of vinyl flooring, in addition to pieces of lumber. Work began immediately. Sounds of saws and hammers filled the air. I carried dishes into the kitchen for washing, but that had become a work zone. The rotting wood counters were being replaced and doors put on cabinets. We quickly covered bowls with wet towels to preserve the leftovers, but Robert instructed us to throw the food out. This upset a number of women, who muttered, He's wasting so much food. It challenged their values.

I found myself watching the talents of men who were able to measure, trim, and place our new floor down so fast. Remembering the effort it took me to install a single vinyl tile (was it only yesterday?) simply added to my admiration.

How quickly the results of those efforts were covered over was shocking. It gave me a sense of how important it was not to identify with an effort. No one will ever know what lies beneath, I thought. But those tiles I placed had a purpose that was not known yesterday. Their sole function was to level the floor so that something new could be added. Those tiles played their part.

They were the foundation for something better. It was a poetic notion that penetrated deeply.

❧

> *The Lord has awakened in us a great longing for that sweet experience of His presence within; but it is by daily growth that we acquire it; it is by walking that we grow, and it is by forward efforts we walk, so as to be able at last to attain it.*
>
> Augustine

CHAPTER 20

Monday morning began with the loud, ominous, aching groans of non-humankind creatures. I slept Sunday night alone in the downstairs storage room and easily slipped into the bathroom to throw on clothes before going outside to see where the sounds were coming from. There, only yards from the front door, were cattle. They were huge. The children and a few men were playing cowboy roundup, twirling towels to guide the beasts in a certain direction, which of course these animals resisted. It was quite charming, ridiculous, and frightening — all at the same time.

Robert was standing by the chimney watching the event unfold. The men managed with some pushing of hide to move the lead steer away from the patio and up the mountainside where the herd belonged. Robert turned to Yorgos and asked him to find out who the owners were and request they keep their cattle away from our land.

Students were energized. During breakfast, the conversation covered various topics. We began to refer to the property as the Ranch, as it seemed to be cattle country. Some students were talking about octaves that, in their estimation, needed to be done that day. I decided I would wash the breakfast dishes with two other students, not knowing what else to do but wanting to be useful.

After the round-up and breakfast, Robert got in a car with Jim and left. They both returned two hours later wearing cowboy hats and jeans. It was a funny sight to see Robert walking up the hill to the house in a white Stetson, a cream-colored long-sleeved shirt, and brand-new dark blue jeans. Jim chose a black Stetson. He already had the dirty jeans and broken-in cowboy boots (Robert opted out of this fashion choice, apparently).

As they arrived on the scene, it reminded me of the television show *Laramie* from my childhood: there was a tall Saturnine man in white and his sidekick was a short, sinewy Mercurial type who liked to wear black leather jackets and gloves. The image of Robert and Jim left one feeling that we were playing characters in a production that still only had a working title.

Two students, who had gone into Marysville early that morning to buy building supplies, had discovered thick foam pads that we could use under our sleeping bags. When they returned late morning and showed us what they had found, everyone wanted one. Robert thought the pads were a good idea, so we placed an order and the big truck went down again to pick them up. Robert wanted the pads to be the same size, so they could be easily stacked when not in use. He asked two students to clean the upstairs room, where I had slept, and build a huge wooden frame for them. This room would now be used for storage, which freed the downstairs bedroom space. Robert said the downstairs room would now become a library.

* * * *

After lunch the heat from the sun was becoming increasingly more difficult to bear. I had finished the lunch dishes and thought it was time for a well-deserved break. I went outside to find company in the shade, but was shocked to discover that the students who had just eaten lunch outside had all disappeared. Where were they? I knew they weren't in the house.

I turned around and encountered the beckoning index finger of Robert. He was clearly addressing me since no one else was there. Following him into the house, he led me to the new library area. A student was already constructing the wall-size bookcase that would be attached to the ceiling and floor. I was stunned to see how quickly he was measuring, sawing, placing and hammering it into place.

Robert then handed me a can of paint and a brush and told me to paint the shelves. I had never painted anything in my life. The carpenter showed me how to hold the brush, insert the paint, and stroke the wood evenly. It actually was fun, even though the room was stifling hot.

When Robert came back to inspect my work, he said I was doing a good job, which incentivized me. My strokes were getting more deliberate (another way of saying slower). The carpenter recognized this and kindly suggested that I let him finish. I resisted at first, but then I understood he could do this faster and Robert wanted it done. So I gave in to his request.

THE DIVINE BEGINNING

Just as I went outside, I saw a group of students in bathing suits and towels coming up the path. Something odd hit me when I saw them laughing joyfully because they had found a way to cool off in the hundred-degree temperature. I realized they were acting like this place was a resort. That never had occurred to me. This was a School for Conscious Development, and obeying the teacher and serving Celestial Influence (which the Fourth Way calls C Influence or Influence C) was paramount. It wasn't judgment of their actions, as much as a curiosity to me how we could all be sharing the same experience differently.

I listened to them describing a beautiful river and lake with a waterfall that had the cleanest water around. It was close by, they said, and concealed from public view from the road. This sounded good to me since I was very hot. But something in me couldn't just leave like that, since there was so much more work to do.

As we were speaking, the truck was clanking up the hill with our new deluxe bed gear. We stood in line to get our pads off the truck. When I paid for my foam pad, I also was handed a marker to write my name on it: L-I-N-D-A. We carted our pads upstairs to the wooden frame that had just been constructed. Two fellows took mine from me to place it on the stack.

I helped Kerrie with dinner that evening. The long table was set up with the big bowls of cooked vegetables and brown rice. As I settled in to eat, my mind skipped ahead to the post-dinner activities. Basically, the question of the night was: will I have sex with Miles? It seemed to be my turn, yes? Do I approach him to ask?

He and Helga were together and it seemed awkward to just go up to him, especially with her kids around her. I waited and waited. It was getting clearer that I would have to sleep alone again that night. It was late and the house was still suffocatingly hot, so I decided to get my new pad from upstairs to take it outside to sleep under the moon and stars.

I arrived upstairs and turned the light on (a new brighter bulb was now in place), but I couldn't find my pad. I searched each one for my name and found it was near the bottom of the stack. I tried to pull on it, but discovered that these foam pads stuck together like adhesive. I would have to take each one off first to reach mine, but they were stacked almost to the ceiling.

I returned downstairs to see if anyone could help me. I found a male student who would, and we both went upstairs. Another male student had arrived to retrieve his own, so the two of them managed to dislodge mine from the bottom of the pile. This was an interesting lesson, I thought. Next time I would wait for others to stack theirs in the morning so I could put mine on top.

I dragged my pad outside under the fig tree. No one had yet claimed the spot. Going back to get my sleeping bag, I saw Miles was alone. I approached him.

"Have you decided who you will sleep with tonight?" I asked.

He smiled at me, and looked directly into my eyes.

"Helga."

Without thinking, I hugged and kissed him and went into the storage room to retrieve my items. What else could I do?

As I unfurled my sleeping bag, I wondered why this wasn't going according to plan. I felt helpless, hurt, embarrassed and confused, and yet, somehow not angry. There was always this part in me that, like a phoenix, could rise from the ashes. It separately looked on and refused to defend itself. It just accepted things without a fight. All I could do was wait. Perhaps things would be different tomorrow, I reasoned.

Snuggling in my bag on the firm pad, I lay back and appreciated the comfort. There were no rocks to disturb me now.

The creatures of the neighborhood were actively communicating: the cadent clicks of the crickets, the soft hoots of the owl, the yipping chorus of the coyotes. The blue light of the moon softly illuminated the branches of the little fig tree that canopied me. The stars had settled into their seasonal positions. A gentle breeze travelled down the hill, bringing the earthy fragrance of cattle droppings upon sweet grasses to my nose.

This wilderness was so far from Los Angeles. And yet, it was oddly agreeable. I had found my true home, you see, such as it was. I knew in my heart why I was in this School of Awakening and that I had Celestial Influence to guide me, whom I had known since childhood.

What I could see about this moment in my life was that, although I may have travelled for miles, as the fortune cookie said, I wasn't in the school for Miles. Somehow, I had earned the right to be here.

❧

O children of thought, you have earned the right
to own the mystery hidden from eternity. Now accept it.
                                                    Gnostic Gospels

CHAPTER 21

The next morning, I heard commotion, but decided to roll over and pretend to still be asleep. My goal was to get my pad to the top of the heap, remember? When I thought everyone was up and I could smell the breakfast, I arose. Carting my pad up the stairs, I saw two guys with theirs as well, and I asked if they would help me to put mine on top.

One of them said, "Well, Linda, I don't think we can promise that." I left it with them since I couldn't reach the top of the stack by myself, and they were fellow students. Surely, they would be externally considerate (a Fourth Way concept that meant they would be nice to me in an authentic, understanding way). I used the upstairs bathroom to change, and they were gone when I came out. I checked my pad and saw not only did they put theirs on top of mine, but they added a few more from others. It was clearly intentional. I felt like a kid bullied.

* * * *

The breakfast menu was unusual because Kerrie had been trying to convince Robert to become a vegetarian without milk products. Robert, we learned, was born in Little Rock, Arkansas, where gravy and biscuits, grits, bacon and eggs and strong coffee were the staples of the morning. Robert wanted real eggs, but she told Robert she would teach Jan to make scrambled tofu, instead. I watched Jan as she was finishing the dish in a big cast-iron skillet.

Robert saw me standing there, and turned to me.

"Linda, I want you to learn how to make this for me."

Jan stirred with intentional strokes that kept the finely crumbled tofu from spilling on the stove top. I marveled. She was clearly a skilled cook with two kids and a husband. The tofu was colored yellow from turmeric (a spice) and had plenty of salt and pepper. Jan had added chopped scallions too. She explained to me how she did it, and I just listened. It went in one ear and out the other, as my mother used to say. Deep down I hoped Robert would forget his request.

We watched Robert taste the tofu scrambled "eggs" on his plate, and he proclaimed them, in a hesitating way, to be Good. Kerrie was delighted. I tasted them on my plate and thought they tasted like a sponge that had been grated, sautéed with butter and mixed with onions, salt and pepper. I chuckled. Here was a food with a non-existence feature, like the Venusian body type. How funny. How awful. I picked out and chewed the scallions, ate the toasted bread, and drank the black coffee. I was still hungry. Then I realized if I volunteered to help make lunch, I could raid the pantry. That would become my octave for the day.

* * * *

It was just after lunch when the strange little man appeared on the dirt patio. Robert told Miles to speak with him. We watched Miles and this fellow go toward the west-facing side of the patio to the small pond with its overhanging willow tree. They talked for about five minutes, and then the man squatted at the pond's edge and took out a test tube to fill it with the pond water. When he was done, he shook Miles's hand, got into his truck, and drove down the hill.

"Robert," said Miles, "the man is from the county, and is concerned that too many people are sharing the house, and that the septic system with the two bathrooms won't accommodate this many people. It's against code, and there's a fine we will have to pay if we don't change things. He said he will come back in a week to test the pond water again, which would contain sewage if the system were overloaded. If that's the case, we need to pay the fine."

As they headed toward the cabin, Miles and Robert continued their conversation. A plan was brewing. Miles went inside while Robert asked us all to gather around on the patio. He explained that Miles will be sealing the toilet lids with the sign, "DO NOT USE." We were not to use them for a week.

"What are we supposed to do when we need to use the toilet?" asked a concerned mother.

He didn't reply. It was not only obvious that now we would need to go outside in the bushes to do our business, but also that Robert did not want to know about it. Robert then instructed us to begin taking Bucket Showers. The upstairs and the downstairs showers would each have a metal bucket for us to use. We were allowed only two buckets of water per shower, one to wash and one to rinse.

We started to look for other sources of water for bathing. This was easier for those who clung to the hippie way of life. These women didn't wear make-up, so removing it was not an issue. Unwashed hair and clothes were not only acceptable, but more of a preference, since it did not require an effort. We were each beginning to smell a bit.

The appearance of that little man changed the way we lived. To do our most basic functions would require us to go further into the hills to sleep so that we could be "empty," as it were, in the morning before coming down for breakfast. I was not interested in doing this. There were too many wild animals around. Instead, I clung to the cabin for refuge.

* * * *

That night after dinner, Miles came up to me. He said some of them were going to a little water hole near the entrance to our property now and asked if I wanted to come. We would be "skinny dipping." I knew this meant swimming nude in front of others. I didn't care; I was excited to go because he would be back in my arms. So I smiled and said, Sure!

We drove on the swampy road to this secret location. The car held five of us: three men and two women.

"What is this place?" I asked.

Miles replied, "It's the entrance to the Richards Ranch, who are our neighbors."

When we arrived, everyone quickly disrobed and got into the water except me. The moon, which would reach its fullness in two days, was already a bright beacon for us, and I was uncomfortable being so exposed. Miles had easily gone in and was with the others when he realized I wasn't there yet. He returned to get me.

"Come on in," he urged. "It's a bit slippery at first, but in the middle of the pond it's wonderful."

I took off my clothes behind a small shrub. I could see a bemused look on his face. Here was another "virgin moment" for me, and he was relishing it.

Being totally naked left me with a mixed feeling of freedom and fear. I put one foot down into the water and immediately felt this oozy, mucky substance between my toes. The other foot felt the same. This was disgusting.

Miles took my hands to guide me. As I submerged into the water, the slimy vegetation at the bottom got thicker, and my large breasts floated to the surface like volleyballs. Gosh, I had no idea they could do that.

He embraced me, and we kissed, and he said he would stay with me, and not to worry. Miles got excited. This was the best romance I had had in a week for sure.

When we returned that night, we went upstairs to make love. It was surprisingly quick and he left. There was no caressing, no connection. It felt cold.

Lesson: The heart is not a genital.

*Have nothing to do with a man that can blow
hot and cold with the same breath.*

Aesop

CHAPTER 22

The next morning was heating up rapidly. Someone announced it would be over 100 degrees Fahrenheit.

After placing my pad on the stack, I heard footsteps coming up the stairs, and I immediately went into the bathroom to wash and change. I couldn't hold it any longer, so I slipped the sign off the toilet seat. The water was the color of French's mustard. I wasn't the first one with that idea. I guess they thought that if they didn't flush, they were keeping the exercise.

After helping with the breakfast dishes, I went into the new library and decided I would quietly read a work book, as it always brought a sense of balance to me. I was still feeling a bit sick to my stomach from the previous evening's rendezvous. Dirt was all around us, and it seemed to penetrate my heart and mind.

I pulled *In Search of the Miraculous* from the shelf and started studying triads. I had brought with me a notebook from Los Angeles — a diary really — and started to map out the interactions between the three of us in terms of first (active) force, second (passive) force, and third (invisible) force. From my experience, analyzing a highly emotional situation always could reveal the objective truth to three burning questions: "What the hell was going on?" "Why was it happening to me?" and "What was going to happen next?"

Just as I was unearthing a key to the Miles-Helga-Linda Love Triangle Mystery, I felt a tap on my back. There was that beckoning finger. I followed Robert outside near the end of the dirt patio where six students sat on a log with burlap bags between them. Kerrie and Yorgos were giving instructions.

Apparently, Yorgos had brought up sacks of freshly picked almonds from Vacaville. The task was to release the almonds from their shells by hand and put them in a bag. Robert joined us. He explained our efforts would save us money since these almonds were free.

I took the first one. This is what an almond looks like? It had a furry soft coat. I was shown how to remove it and how to pry open the shell with my fingers. I couldn't manage it. Yorgos sat next to me and said he would help me by removing the coat and then hand it to me to unshell. I looked at others who seemed to do this with ease.

My fingers began to bleed. Tears were forming. Robert, who sat on my right, leaned over and whispered, "You lose your good work easily."

I was crushed. I felt like a battering ram had swung and hit my chest with enough force to topple a ten-story building. The tears dripped and my mouth quivered. I was stuck there. I couldn't leave, but I also couldn't accomplish the task. I was a failure. Perhaps I'm not Fourth Way school material after all. Where was I to go now? What was I to do? An internal darkness that had plagued me since childhood began to consume me.

Robert then said, "I didn't mean THE work." He tried to soften his observation, but it didn't help. I was in such a tender space inside. The pain of all that was occurring to me spread like a tsunami.

"It's okay," he said gently to reassure me, and handed me his white handkerchief for the second time in as many days. "You don't need to do this. You can go." I stood up and went back to the library. My books would comfort me, I thought. But it didn't work. I was an emotional mess.

* * * *

Rooms were shifting inside the house. Walls were torn down and new ones constructed. Robert was communicating his plans to key students like Miles and Yorgos and Don. I was not a part of this discussion. I was more interested in washing my underwear.

The boot room was a narrow passage with its own entry on the north side of the house. An old washing machine and dryer were on the right, and a large horizontal food freezer was on the left. A huge wooden bin was built next to the washing machine, where we would dump our dirty clothes. This left little space to pass when someone entered with dirty boots. Basically, the laundry octave was a task fraught with friction: trying to keep the clothes clean when the floor was getting dirtier with each entering and exiting student only served to raise the level of identification. It was a thankless job, and I pitied the person assigned to it.

The washing machine was going non-stop despite the edicts not to flush toilets and to take bucket showers. This made no sense, of course. But for us, logic was a luxury.

We soon discovered that everyone's underwear looked alike. It was so difficult to find the true owner, that Robert came up with a solution: each of us was to put our name on our clothes — shirts, pants, socks, underwear — in indelible marker. Robert had someone with good penmanship take his clothes and inscribe R-O-B-E-R-T in large letters on the top of his jockey shorts and on his shirt tails.

Robert had gone in to pick up his laundered clothes when he spotted one of my panties, which I was inscribing my name upon. The garment was old and torn.

Rosemary had just entered the boot room. Robert turned to her.

"Rosemary, can you take Linda shopping tomorrow and buy her some underwear?" he requested.

I was embarrassed, but in a strange way grateful. I definitely needed help in this area. Rosemary was going to Vacaville the next morning, and apparently now so was I.

What he didn't know was that I was raised with hand-me-downs: bras from my sister, panties from my mother. Clothes never fit properly. They were generally too small. I didn't know how to look for clothes; childhood shopping experiences were traumatic. I was taken to the women's section at the age of eleven because of my mature figure. Anything I bought was scrutinized by my father, the accountant, for being overpriced. He was a product of the 1929 Great Depression. So I basically avoided buying clothes for myself and just wore whatever I was given until they shredded themselves on me.

My poor panties, I thought. Not even they can hide in this place. Robert sees all.

*

> *People also have two kinds of capacity:*
> *they always have the ability to awaken to themselves*
> *in an instant, while there is the constant need to*
> *refine themselves through gradual practices as well.*
> — So Sahn

CHAPTER 23

It was daybreak when we left for Vacaville. Rosemary said she wanted to get an early start since she had a lot to do in Vacaville, and taking me shopping was now added to her long list.

I made sure to take my bucket shower before leaving. Bubbie called these "sitz baths," where you just address the most odorous parts of the anatomy. I was hoping I would get a chance to take a real shower at Rosemary's home later in the day. All this was up to Rose's schedule, of course.

Leaving the simple, rough environment of the ranch, and heading on a highway with its long stretches of asphalt and zooming cars, left me disoriented and passive. I was clearly along for the ride. We spoke about various topics, among them Robert. It was interesting to hear how she saw him.

"Robert needs a friend," she shared.

He was my teacher, and to me, he was the Great Source of All Objective Knowledge that I had been looking for since childhood. To her, or so it seemed, he was a young man of 32 who was awake and who was entrusted with a difficult task: to build a school of awakening.

"Take a look at students with tramp features who don't pull their own weight," she commented.

I was just beginning to understand chief features, and tramp had characteristics of having too much relativity, not paying bills, wanting something for nothing, not understanding what to value, etc. Mary Ellen's husband Harold had given us wonderful, simple cartoons of each feature associated with a body type.

Here's the idea. Since there were seven body types (Lunar, Venusian, Mercurial, Saturnine, Martial, Jovial, and Solar), there were also seven features, respectively (willfulness, non-existence, power, dominance, fear, vanity, and naïveté). Body types, with their corresponding features, were mapped on the enneagram (a Fourth Way symbol). These features and types also correlated with specific glands in the human machine that served as receptors for planetary influences. Microcosmos man represented the solar system, which demonstrated the ancient concept, "as above, so below." We studied these ideas at each meeting, learning to recognize them in ourselves and others. I thoroughly enjoyed this knowledge and thought it was something I could readily master.

She continued, "We need to help him as much as we can. He needs support and good advice."

That was my goal too — to support him. Giving him advice, though, I would leave to Rosemary, since she appeared to me to be incredibly wise in the ways of the world. She was 49 and I was only 22.

As she was driving, she asked me to reach into her purse for a cigarette and lighter. It was the first time I had ever touched a cigarette. I pulled one out of the box and handed it to her. She then asked me to light it. I had never touched a lighter, so didn't know how to ignite the flame. She told me to hold it and use my thumb to stroke the little wheel quickly. It worked!

I positioned it for her, and she took a long draft and then exhaled a pencil-thin stream of directed smoke through her daintily pursed lips. She continued talking about the school and how much work needs to be done to run a ranch.

"We have to plant an orchard now if we want fruit in a couple of years. I told Robert this, and he ignored me. Robert doesn't have a clue."

She had a walnut orchard and understood agriculture. Robert was a city-boy from the Bay Area.

"But before that, we need a water supply and irrigation."

She went on to describe the need for seasonal planning and not just "sticking seeds in the ground and praying for rain." She told me that in January, Robert had decided to start a garden at her place so that we could practice raising our own vegetables. He had Don design it, she said, with a perfectly attired scarecrow, a la the Nut Tree, which was where Don worked as the Art Director.

"And now who's tending it? No one," she commented, rhetorically.

I had seen the fallow furrows near the driveway of her home that Robert had apparently designated as the location for the garden and had wondered about its history.

"It's tramp. Again, another abandoned octave," she observed.

Her perceptions were very interesting to me. I was amazed at how critical she was, and yet I didn't doubt for one moment her devotion and loyalty to Robert. She didn't hesitate to correct the teacher. She had chutzpah.

* * * *

When we arrived at Macy's, she took me upstairs to the lingerie department and asked me my size. I had no idea. She and a sales lady determined the approximate number and handed me quite a few to try on over my own underwear. I went to the dressing room and came out with several to buy.

Rosemary said, "I'm only paying for one."

The price was far more than fifty cents each, which was the price my father said we were allowed to spend. I couldn't believe you could pay five dollars for a single pair of panties. She picked out the prettiest lavender panty with a little pansy appliqué.

"Here. We'll buy this."

I had never owned such a delicate, truly feminine undergarment. Suddenly the bride's ditty of "something old, something new, something borrowed, something blue," played in my head. The words only fueled my desire for Miles, resurrecting the hope that he would somehow keep his promise about our autumn nuptials, and that I could soon show him my pretty panties.

* * * *

We got back to Rosemary's house in time for lunch. Her two daughters were there. The younger was already preparing fried sliced eggplant coated in this delicious bread crumb mix labeled Panko. The elder focused on the vegetable salad with chicken chunks. Rose pulled a unique, triangular bottle of salad dressing from the crowded side door of the refrigerator. It was Girard's Champagne, and she announced it to be the "best dressing you can buy."

As we ate our lunch, the girls caught Rosemary up with all the latest news. The younger daughter and her boyfriend was the first topic. I listened to the "he said/she said," coordinating my laughter with the girls, as she would announce her triumphant stance when he tried to manipulate her into doing something. I was amazed at her ability to understand men at her young age. Rose delighted in this.

Then they spoke about their father. Mac had a history of girlfriends, apparently. One was a lady named Annabella, a Fellowship student, who was a Rolfer. Mac was a trained Rolfer in addition to being a cardiologist. Rose and her daughters were "being Rolfed," as the expression went, and talked about their Rolfing sessions.

I asked about this and Rose explained. Essentially, Ida Rolf was a woman in Big Sur who had developed a technique of body work, whereby she would use her forefinger knuckle, as well as her elbow, to break the connective tissue in the body. It would release memory and bring one back to a natural physical as well as psychological state. People are known to grow an inch after these treatments because of the readjustment of this tissue.

"When you see people hunched over, for example," explained one daughter, "it's because they have suffered emotional trauma, and the tissue grows in such a way that this type of posture can become permanent."

"Bad posture also messes with your organs," added the other, "repositioning them. When the tissue is broken, the organs can spring back to their normal positions."

Robert had this treatment with Annabella, too. Robert also was a bit enamored of Annabella, according to Rosemary. Rose thought Annabella was a seductress.

As soon as lunch was over, Rosemary lit a cigarette and offered her pack to the girls, who each took one. It was clear they were not regular smokers like their mom. I refused, not only because it was considered an evil in my family, but also because I had no idea how to smoke and preferred not to appear stupid.

The elder daughter shared another bit of news: Mac had been talking to some of their Vacaville friends about the school, adding, "I heard three of them are having prospective student meetings."

Rose said she knew about this and that was one reason she came down. Tonight was the third meeting.

"We will see who joins. Linda, it will be good for you to meet them," advised Rosemary.

Great reason for a shower.

* * * *

When we arrived at the place, there were three of them lined up to be introduced: two men and a woman. It was our custom to hug in greeting.

I embraced the first man and looked at him in his left (essence) eye. I did the same with the other man. Then I approached the woman. She was short of stature with delicately layered light-brown hair. I could feel her reticence when I approached her to hug, and recognized that she had fear, which is a feature of a Martial type. As I enfolded this petite lady in my warm Venusian arms, I turned to Rose and said, "She's soft for a Martial!"

The woman was appalled. She clicked her tongue, rolled her eyes, and gasped several times to demonstrate how utterly offended she was by my comment. She reacted as if I said she was an alien from another planet — a Martian. Then I realized she may not have understood her meeting about body types.

It turned out that this woman was an old friend of Mac and Rosemary. She had a twelve-year-old daughter named Joy. The four of us, I learned, would travel to the ranch together the next morning. The woman's name was Marie.

That which God has given you is something
chosen only for the chosen among the elect.
Al-Junayd

CHAPTER 24

After a hearty breakfast at the Coffee Tree, we headed east on Highway 80 toward the ranch. It was around ten o'clock on a Saturday, so the traffic was light. I sat in the back with Joy. Rosemary drove and Marie took the passenger seat. Both ladies were smoking and talking. I tried to engage Joy in a conversation, but she was having none of it. Joy was a little Martial type as well, with freckles that peppered the bridge of her nose.

I tried to listen to what Rose and Marie were saying, but the engine noise muffled most of the words. I was left to take in impressions of the farmlands that we passed on the 70/99 cutoff. To a certain extent I felt left out of adult conversation, and observed how I was acting like the kid next to me, who looked out the window as if aching to jump overboard into the scenery she passed; anywhere but in this car with these people, she must have thought. It was obvious that Joy was being dragged by her mother to this unknown place. It's tough to be twelve.

As we turned onto Marysville Road off Highway 20, Rose swiveled her head around quickly to me but addressed Marie when she said, "Linda's a school teacher. Maybe she can teach Joy."

It was a strange non sequitur. Where did that come from? It made me wonder what the two of them had been talking about and what they were scheming that obviously would involve me.

Few words were spoken as we entered Rice's Crossing Road, the main road (and only road) leading to the ranch. Driving up the narrow incline to the house, Rosemary pulled over and stopped the engine. We all got out. It was strangely quiet; few cars were around and there was a definite absence of people (or so it appeared). This must have seemed very strange to Marie and Joy.

Rosemary told me to go ahead with Marie and show her the house. Rose instructed Joy to help her carry items from the car. Perhaps Rosemary wanted to talk with Joy privately.

As Marie and I came upon the dirt patio, I was talking to her, explaining the house and where we would eat and sleep. She was looking not at me, however, but at a man standing by the small pond, tossing bread crumbs to the two ducks swimming there.

She observed, "It's so nice that this school accepts mentally disturbed people."

I turned to see this man staring at the pond, head down. I didn't recognize him — until I read the letters on his shirttail: R-O-B-E-R-T.

"That's the teacher," I said, chuckling.

Marie's eyes widened; it was clear she was in shock. I could almost hear her thought processes plummet and fry as if a raw egg had been dropped into a hot skillet. But without skipping a step, she silently continued with me into the house. Her self-control and impeccable demeanor were impressive.

* * * *

Marie, Joy and Rosemary gravitated to the kitchen to help with dinner. I gravitated outside toward three guys, who were chatting under the canopy of a yellow-flowered and wonderfully fragrant tree that was positioned in the middle of the front patio.

One of the fellows was David. I thought they were talking about the Work, so was eager to join them. They welcomed me and offered me a cigarette and beer that they had purchased from the local store. I took a "cold one," even though I never liked the bitterness of beer. It was, however, amazingly refreshing on this hot day.

We sat for a while in silence. Then I began to share my knowledge of the Fourth Way with these guys who apparently hadn't bathed in a few days.

"I've read Ouspensky's *The Psychology of Man's Possible Evolution, The Fourth Way,* and *In Search of the Miraculous,*" I offered, "and particularly enjoyed Rodney Collin's *The Theory of Celestial Influence,* which describes the Six Processes and Human Types."

Excited about how practical these theories can be, I began to point out the nature of Worlds 12, 24, 48 and 96 as it applied to man. I waited for one of them to exchange insights with me. The redheaded, scruffy-looking one on the Martial side of the enneagram slowly rolled a cigarette as he spoke.

"I just finished readin' Mickey Mouse and Donald Duck's adventures, but before that I was really into Superman for a while. I've read all of Batman, too."

The guys started laughing. Was that how I sounded to them? I thought it was important to study the system and apply it. I wanted to let them know I was worthy of being in the school because I was on top of my reading assignments and working on developing Observing 'I.'

These guys were the farthest thing from the intellectuals that would comprise my Fourth Way school. And yet, I was struck by their easy-going manner. They weren't negative and didn't walk away from me, as Nadia did. They showed me something about myself, and I was grateful for that. I laughed, too. They appreciated I could laugh at myself, I guess. We became good friends.

* * * *

As the heat of the day began to wane, people were showing up. It was around five o'clock when Miles, Yorgos and Kerrie came with groceries for the weekend. They also brought in large (three feet by two feet), dark burgundy pillows with intricate designs that we would use to sit on for inside dining.

It was a very interesting style from the East that both Yorgos and Kerrie were encouraging. Kerrie would be preparing a middle-eastern dish for Saturday night for all of us to experience. Yorgos described how a large pan of food will be placed in the middle of the circle of pillows, and we will use the fingers from our right hand to put food into our mouths. Keep in mind, we were still taking bucket showers, so the thought of abandoning cutlery in favor of ancient practices of eating with our fingers made me wince.

A special item had also arrived that day. It was a maple-wood, three-sectioned stereo hi-fi console that had once belonged to Robert's mother. The center section housed the record player and the side sections held the albums. It took several men to carry it carefully into the house. Robert told them to place it in the corner of the main room against a wall and to remove a lamp so they could plug the phonograph into the electrical socket. The light in the room now was dimmer since the arrival of the console because there were no more sockets to plug in the lamp. Remember, this was originally a log cabin and may have been built before electricity.

Robert had also requested his albums, which were an interesting assortment from Bob Dylan classics to *Arthur Fiedler and the Boston Pops Plays Country Western*. These two genres reflected Robert's pre-school interests and essence.

* * * *

Robert wanted us to have a meeting before dinner was served, so we set our new pretty pillows in a circle as well as chairs for Robert, Mary Ellen, Rosemary, Anna and Bonita. We spoke about how to distinguish between essence and personality and how to observe the many 'I's.

To help us, Robert introduced a new challenge: not to say the word "really." If we hear another person saying this word, we are to "photograph" them by moving our forearms up and down with extended hand in front of us. The motion resembled the raising of a railroad crossing gate, although it was supposed to represent a camera shutter.

He also announced that he would like us to think of a new name for our property and welcomed suggestions.

During the good householder portion of the meeting, which was always at the start of the meeting, people were asked to volunteer for octaves for the weekend, since we were expecting around fifty people. I volunteered to make breakfast on Saturday morning. There was a cook book on the library shelf that had a recipe for barley buns, and Kerrie had said she bought barley flour on her shopping trip.

I had made challah (Jewish egg bread) for my family a few times and thought it would be fun to offer this. Another reason for volunteering was to have a chance to impress Miles with my cooking skills.

My many 'I's' were swarming in my head. I still couldn't get him out of my mind.

※

What are you doing, O human soul, what are you doing?
Why are you seized by so many distractions?
How great is man's knowledge when he does not even grasp himself?
Aelred of Rievaulx

CHAPTER 25

The next morning, I arose early to prepare my barley buns. I assembled the ingredients and pulled out the big bowl I would use to mix the dough. With the cookbook in front of me, I carefully multiplied the amounts to accommodate fifty people. Then I realized I needed a bigger bowl. Or three.

I was shaping the barley buns on two baking sheets. They each held nine buns. That's 18 buns. The house only had a single oven with two racks and the baking time was 40 minutes. By 7 a.m. people were looking for food. I kept telling people how good they are going to be with butter soaking into them, reminiscent of the Nut Tree rolls, and to be patient. By 9:30 they could wait no longer. Coffee was available, and Rose jumped in to prepare some eggs for Robert. Others grabbed bowls and filled them with granola and milk. Robert took me aside.

"You wasted others' time. Fifty people waited almost two hours. That's one hundred hours lost. In the future, multiply your actions by one hundred."

His message was clear: if everyone acted like me — keeping people waiting — where would we be as a school?

It was approaching lunch time when my buns were done. No one ate them. Instead of impressing Miles, I was reinforcing the fact that a cook I was not.

* * * *

Yes, I wasn't a cook. Yet, the kitchen was where the food was that I could nibble on, and it certainly was better than working outside in the burning rays of the sun, hauling hardware or digging ditches. So I joined Kerrie in the preparation of the Middle Eastern fare.

It was the late afternoon when Kerrie told me she was going to teach me how to make chapatis. They were like a small tortilla from India. She prepared the dough and then did something extraordinary.

THE DIVINE BEGINNING

On this blistering July day, she built a little fire in the fireplace of the house. The fireplace's opening was very small (about two feet wide) and all she needed, she said, were a few pieces of wood and some stones. She then formed the dough into a ball and used the side of a drinking glass to roll it out into a perfect four-inch circle. She handed me another glass, and the two of us started preparing these chapatis. She then built the fire and threw a chapati on top of a stone. After a minute or so, she flipped it. They were done.

"Do you think you can do this?" she asked.

"I can try," I replied.

The pancakes were easy, and I felt a small bit of dignity return. This was fun, I thought. Kerrie continued to work her magic in the kitchen. Yorgos came in with his rosy cheeks and smiling eyes and felt so happy to have this opportunity to share his Eastern experiences with everyone.

* * * *

The colorful cushions were arranged in three big circles, and several platters were placed in the middle. I chose to sit with Yorgos. Kerrie and Robert were in another circle. We were all taught how to lean in and take a chapati to scoop some of the food and to use our right hand to gather the couscous and place it into our mouths. This was not as easy as it sounds. After a few attempts, couscous was all over the floor. It was a mess. We clearly were cowboys, not Indians. We quickly asked for plates and spoons. I could see Yorgos was frustrated and disappointed, although he didn't express it.

We cleared the dishes and swept the floor because, apparently, the evening had a little entertainment planned. We were told to stand to the side to create space in the middle of the room.

Music (it sounded like a polka) was put on the stereo, and Helga appeared with a Saturn gentleman whom I had recognized from my prospective student meeting in Alamo. His name was John Graham. He was a professional dancer and a friend of Helga (she introduced him to the Fellowship).

Helga's colorful folk outfit looked like it came from Germany. It was a white cap sleeve blouse under a jumper with a full skirt of red, white and black accents. Her hair had a ribbon in it and her face was radiant. She and John pranced and twirled along the inside of the circle of friends with such lightness and expertise. She looked happy. Miles was beaming.

Although I was jealous of her abilities, since I felt like such a failure that day, I thoroughly enjoyed the beauty of her movements. I looked around the room for Robert and found him standing in a small recess in the corner behind several students. He looked like a small, shy boy who had found himself at his parents' party. We hooted and clapped when they exited. Once the music stopped, I looked for Robert, but he had disappeared.

A few of us washed the dishes in the dim light. Others had scattered the cushions into the darkest corners of the room. Beer had been served with the dinner, and some students were still drinking. I saw males and females sitting, talking, and touching. They began to recline as lights were extinguished. I was trying to make out who they were and what was going on. No, I thought. Not in public. But yes, students had paired off, and the sex energy that had been circulating that night was now being released and exchanged in a very intimate way.

Miles had left earlier with Helga before this erotic descent had begun.

I was once again left alone. I took my foam pad and sleeping bag out to the fig tree. Another long, unpredictable day had ended.

True pleasure consists in the consciousness of inward purity.
Lewis Carroll

CHAPTER 26

The strength of the early morning sun's rays purified the spaces in the house. What I had witnessed the previous night was now a dark memory. A new day had begun with new possibilities.

The breakfast of granola with milk and scrambled eggs with toast, hashed brown potatoes and coffee, which remained our standard breakfast, was now eaten to the accompaniment of Arthur Fiedler's Boston Pops Orchestra and his Country Western song stylings. Chet Atkins was featured on the album with his guitar. The solo electric guitar pickings and a full orchestra keeping the beat was bizarre to say the least. But Robert adored it. I was more a Barbra Streisand fan, and country music seemed very hokey and primitive to me. But Robert insisted the record player be on Repeat mode. The dozen songs would become background music to our daily activities.

On that particular morning, as we were ready to go to our assigned octaves, Robert came up to me and, without saying a word, indicated he wanted me to follow him. We both went into the library room. He closed the door behind him.

The music could still be heard through the door. Without looking at me, he took my right hand. And then the most astonishing thing happened: we started swing dancing. He twirled me under his arm, and we swayed side to side to the beat. At times he held both my hands and then would let one drop. I knew these movements well, as this was dancing to me as I grew up in the Fifties. He never made eye contact and he retained a stoic expression. He looked past me. Yet I couldn't take my eyes off of him, and my smile was as bright as my state.

The music lasted about two minutes. When it stopped, Robert put his two hands together reverently and bowed to me. He then walked out and closed the door behind him. I was left in a state of pure delight, like a little girl who received her first kiss from the handsomest boy in the school.

* * * *

After lunch, many students returned to the Bay Area or Vacaville. There was talk that the next evening we would have a meeting in Vacaville at the home of Rosemary and Mac. It was clear that coming up to the ranch was a bit of a hardship for many students. To accommodate them, those of us at the ranch would travel to meetings that were held in the various homes in the Bay Area. Those living in the Bay would then come up to the ranch on the weekends. There was a distinct feeling that we were the Residents and they were the Weekenders. An interesting mental divide was forming.

Rosemary left the ranch with Marie and Joy. Robert joined her, occupying the space I had taken.

Once the Weekenders were gone, the Residents came out on the patio to enjoy the late afternoon. They sat in the Director's chairs that had been reserved for meetings. With Robert's absence, there was this huge psychological exhalation: the teacher had left. We can all relax now.

We spoke for hours, laughing and joking, smoking and eating whatever leftovers were from lunch or in the refrigerator. No one was there to cook dinner for us. Mary Ellen and Harold were living in his recreational vehicle, or RV, which he used to travel to Lake Tahoe to make caricatures of people in the casinos. Neither of them slept under trees or had to contend with bucket showers and flagged toilets. Mary Ellen's 16-year-old daughter joined them.

Then there was this fellow named Alden , a lanky type that was tall like a Saturn yet passive like a Lunar, and easily approachable. I had heard he was intellectually centered, and he appeared that way as he was fond of his pipe, like Miles. He had an RV that Bonita shared. I wasn't sure whether David, who was Bonita's husband, was also included in this accommodation, but I assumed so. Bonita's daughter was also part of this family. These people joined the school having known each other previously, I discovered. They were very comfortable with each other — a little too comfortable with each other, I felt. Sometimes old friends breed old habits.

I was the new kid on the block. I listened to Mary Ellen speak about Robert. She spoke about his weaknesses as a machine, mainly. His Saturn dominance, his ignorance and naïveté. Harold would stoke his pipe, nodding occasionally in agreement. Bonita would wheeze in fits of convulsive laughter at Mary Ellen's verbal caricatures. What distinguished their opinion of Robert from Rosemary's? I did not get a sense that they felt he needed help or that they were there to support him. Their comments were not constructive, but were mean-spirited. It made them all appear superior to Robert. And it made me uncomfortable.

But being of a practical nature, I needed to find a ride to Vacaville. I sat listening to them, hoping they wouldn't turn their spotlight on my weaknesses, too, before I could find out who would be going, how they would travel, when they were leaving, and if there was a place for me.

When there was a lull in the conversation, I made my request.

"Is anyone going to Vacaville tomorrow? And if so, can I get a ride?"

I felt like the runt in the litter, dependent on the more powerful dogs in the pack for tidbits from the bowl. They ignored my question and resumed their exchange of opinions about various students.

Hours passed. The sunset was beautiful: an expanse of pomegranate, mango, and banana colors streaked against a darkening blue sky. As nighttime began to descend, they started to disperse to their sleeping accommodations. I felt lost and left behind — until David turned to me quietly before he left and said, "I'll take you. I'm leaving around eleven."

David, the gentle bear, had adopted me as one of his cubs. He rarely spoke and just listened to the ladies' gossip, without either participating or distancing himself. He had a knack for avoiding confrontation. I could see I had lot to learn from him.

*Let the quiet, the long enduring better mind,
with understanding, teach thee.*

Zoroaster

CHAPTER 27

We didn't quite leave at eleven. Venusians are slow to rise, and I realized that Mary Ellen (who asked us to call her Meg, which was not only a nickname but her initials), David, and Bonita were all Venusians. I, too, shared this body type. Eleven was breakfast: a bowl of granola and milk.

After breakfast, we sat around the patio of the house. No one was in a hurry. In fact, past noon, Bonita said she was going to the Lake to wash her hair, and others thought it was a grand idea. Apparently, this had been her practice for bathing. I made a point of not losing sight of my newly found pack so I grabbed my toiletries and accompanied them.

We left the property and headed east toward a place known as Lake Francis. It was about fifteen minutes away. The beach was empty. Bonita, without hesitation, disrobed her colorful sarong and swam slowly to the depth of the lake. Her daughter accompanied her, bringing the bottle of shampoo. I didn't fully undress, but went out as well to wash my thick long hair.

What fun! To dip your head back and wait a few seconds for the hair to fully absorb the water, then to scrub the scalp while your feet are sometimes treading water to stay afloat was a delightful challenge. I made it back to the shore, and then saw all of the suds that didn't dissipate. They floated like meringue atop the water. Something in me thought, "Uh oh. This isn't right." But I left it at that.

There was a bathroom at the Lake, and I chose to use it to dress and apply makeup for the day. When I came out, Meg and Harold had driven on in their large American-made car, and Bonita and Alden were getting into his smaller sedan. David and Bonita's daughter were left, and the three of us piled into David's Volkswagen Beetle.

It was three o'clock by the time we left Oregon House for Vacaville.

* * * *

David was a safe driver. He drove the speed limit, while other cars zipped by. He sat comfortably in the driver's seat, although there was about an inch from his stomach to the steering wheel. It was a tight fit. He didn't smoke cigarettes, which was nice. The teenager sat in back. Sprawling sideways on the seat, she was busy creating a necklace out of beads.

I learned that David was the second student who joined the school (the order was: first Bonita, then David, then Meg). They held honorable positions, like the Founding Fathers of the American Revolution. I thought I would take the opportunity to learn from David how he met the school. I was surprised how much he was willing to share.

"Bonita was always finding people interested in esoteric ideas. She had formed a group with Jim and they were studying Edgar Cayce."

"You're kidding!" I exclaimed. "I was into Cayce big time, too! Wow!"

I told him a bit about how I gave Miles the *Story of Jesus* book when we first met. He continued.

"I wasn't into that kind of thing. But I knew it made her happy. So on New Year's Eve, 1969, she got invited to a masquerade party with some of her friends. She liked to dress up in exotic clothes and went as a belly dancer with a snake around her."

"A real snake?" I asked astoundingly.

Even now I'm not sure if he was telling me the truth, but knowing how Bonita liked to appear intriguing, that would not have surprised me.

"She came home late and I was already asleep. The next morning, she was telling me about this man she had met, who had some interesting ideas. She liked him, she said. Well, I wasn't interested at all. Just another man with interesting ideas, I thought. I was more interested in watching the football games."

I laughed and told him I was into watching the January 1st college football games, too. It was part of my New Year's Day ritual with my family. The TV was on from early morning to late at night watching the Pasadena Rose Parade, then the College Rose Bowl Championship, then the Sugar Bowl Championship, then the Orange Bowl Championship. We flipped channels a lot in our house on January 1st.

"She told me that this guy gave her his number and said, 'Call me tomorrow.' When she called him that morning, I heard her say, 'Hello. This is Bonita, the woman you met at the party last night. Is this a good time to call?' "

David started to chuckle and his belly rhythmically jumped up and down as he was recalling the moment.

"When she hung up, she told me he wanted to meet her again, and they arranged a time. She also told me that this man said he was watching a football game when she called. I looked at her and said, 'THIS man I want to meet.' "

* * * *

We arrived in Vacaville around 7:30 after stopping for a bite to eat. The meeting was to begin at eight, and Robert insisted on promptness. Meg and Harold were there, as were Bonita and Alden.

And then I spotted Miles. We hadn't had a chance to speak for a long time (or so it seemed). That nagging feeling of uncertainty plagued me emotionally. It was like a lingering virus that had found a comforting home in my heart.

I tried to approach him, but he was smiling and talking with various students. I couldn't find an opportune moment.

THE DIVINE BEGINNING

We were told to take our seats, as the meeting was about to begin. Approximately forty people gathered in the lavender living room. Five chairs were lined up against the fireplace; those were reserved for Robert and the usual Older Students. The rest of us sat in the audience.

Robert would wait until we were all quiet before he would speak. He announced that the name of the property was chosen: Via Del Sol, which meant Way of the Sun.

I'm not sure who had suggested it, nor had I been asked to vote, but that was often how things were done. Decisions were made, and we were informed afterwards. Though a new name came into being, it did not change the other references we had for the place: the ranch and the farm. Even Robert showed his preference for the latter by using it during meetings. I liked the new name, as it seemed more meaningful and esoteric.

Next, Robert welcomed the new students. They stood up when their name was announced by the student who had brought them to the Fellowship. Rosemary introduced Marie, since this was her first formal meeting with the teacher. Most people had met her already at Via Del Sol, but to be introduced in this way was considered a tradition.

Robert added, "Please do your best to reach out to people you know who may have a magnetic center."

A magnetic center is a Fourth Way idea as defined by Ouspensky. The concept has to do with types of influences to which a man may be subject. Life pursuits are Influences A (material influences such as the desire for money or family). When a man's interests in esoteric ideas build, he accumulates B influences, which are conscious in origin, such as religion, art, etc., but become mechanical over time. It is this accumulation that forms the magnetic center. C Influence is conscious in origin and in action and can only be transmitted directly and orally. C Influence requires a conscious teacher in a group setting. This is the basis of a Fourth Way school.

Robert then began the meeting with his customary request.

"Does anyone have a question?"

Several hands were raised simultaneously. He chose someone from the Bay Area.

"I have a question about the word exercise. When we photograph someone for saying 'really,' we are more focused on listening for that word than on understanding what the person is really [hands started flying to photograph this speaker]. Sorry…what the person is trying to say."

Robert replied, "That is an 'I' that does not like the exercise. When a person speaks to another, they are exchanging mechanical rolls or tapes. No one is listening. That is not the case here."

I was surprised how Robert gave the person, who was clearly complaining, the benefit of the doubt. In fact, he gave ALL of us the benefit of the doubt.

Several other questions were asked, and Robert's responses never strayed from self-remembering, the non-expression of negative emotions, and not identifying. The focus was always the same, regardless of question. It seemed to me that some questions were designed to challenge his authority and did not come from a sincere place inside the student. It was an interesting dynamic between teacher and student. But there was one question that did surprise me that night.

"I have a question about the use of sex."

Robert paused for a long while, squinting his eyes and looking up, as if he were contemplating where to begin. Then he spoke.

"This is a long subject," he began. "There are some people here who will not give of themselves sexually unless it is a full-rounded experience. There are some in tramp who will give to several people. When a woman gives herself and the other will not contribute, the man takes the finest from her."

This last sentence hit me like a thunderbolt. It penetrated deeply, opening up my ears and eyes. I was present in that moment. He continued.

"The Self is not the body. The body is not the Self. The emotional center in man wants to give itself to all women. The emotional center in woman wants to give itself to all men. The astral body can arrive with or without abstinence. Humans frequently have sex from personality, 'proving' something from sex. A *man* or *woman* [he emphasized these words] does not have to prove anything."

He paused for a moment to let this sink in. Then he added:

"A teacher cannot make a decision for anybody. Each person is on their own here. Christ said, 'Love one another, as I have loved you.'"

Someone then asked, "Where do sex and love meet?"

He replied, "There is no answer. Whatever is right for you. There is no pattern."

This response was not what I wanted to hear. I had no idea what was right for me. Who decides this for me? How do I know? I felt like I was without an emotional compass. It was scary.

Another related question came.

"Are love and sex from two different centers?"

He paused once more. When he spoke, he was quite emphatic.

"*Real* love can only be *conscious* love; that is, a state awake in a person."

Someone spoke without being called on.

"Once, in a flash, I thought I felt consciousness I never felt before — a sense of oneness, universality, uniting me with all humanity, and a sense of complete independence, too."

Robert replied, "The words are right — and people can flash. And that *state* is not those *words*. 'It' starts talking like that when the Self is present. It is the lower eating the higher. Words try to think *they* are the state."

A hand was raised. "When the self is present, is full communication between people possible?"

Robert answered immediately.

"When that state is present, just about the best words bring it down. It is possible to maintain the state and communicate. The *right* words, however, can bring it up."

* * * *

The first part of the meeting was over. We stood up to get refreshments in the kitchen and to mingle and chat among friends. As I went to get some food, Rosemary approached me and said, "Robert wants to talk with you." Adrenaline hit my heart. My first thought (or 'I') was What did I do wrong?

Robert kissed my left cheek.

"Dear," he said, "I would like you to collect teaching payments from students. This will be your third-line octave. Please speak with Rosemary. She will show you how."

Robert then left with Jim to go to the Coffee Tree.

I considered it an honor to serve C Influence in this way. Third line of work was work for the school. We were told that first line of work — personal efforts on oneself — is where a person starts. Second line of work — working with other students — was the next step in one's evolution. And third line was an honor, as it requires self-sacrifice and a certain understanding of the aims of the organization. It showed an advanced level of being. Or at least this is what I understood from my readings.

I went up to Rose, and she handed me a piece of paper and envelope.

"Do you have a pencil?" she asked.

"No," I replied. She pulled open a drawer and handed me a pencil.

"You are to ask students for their teaching payments before the meeting. When Robert is ready to leave for the Coffee Tree, you are to hand him the money in an envelope with the names and amounts written on this piece of paper."

I felt grateful that I had been found worthy to be assigned an area of school responsibility.

※

There are those who seek knowledge for the sake of knowledge;
    that is Curiosity.
There are those who seek knowledge to be known by others; that is Vanity.
There are those who seek knowledge in order to serve; that is Love.
Bernard of Clairvaux

CHAPTER 28

The drive back to Via Del Sol was enchanting once we made the turnoff from Highway 20 toward Oregon House. The moonlight, which was the only light available except for headlights, was still strong and illuminated the rural vegetation. The oaks were large and dark and seemed to hunker down to sleep in the night. But a special shrub, the manzanita, lived among the oaks and had a magical quality to it: in the moonlight their leaves glowed with the color of oxidized copper, giving off a blue-green luminescence. It was as if these humble shrubs that were considered ugly by day, with their dull leaves and gnarled, scabby brick-red trunks and branches, came alive at night to serve a noble purpose. Their unexpected radiance transformed them into bright lampposts along the way.

Self-deprecation is a deadly thing. Darkness and depression come from some hidden source to drive away any ascending possibility. This I had verified many times in my life. Like the manzanita during the day, I, too, hid among the tall oaks. But the indigenous manzanita — unappreciated expressions of organic life on earth to the sophisticated man — became a constant reminder that it is in the darkest hours that we truly shine.

※ ※ ※ ※

We had arrived back around 2 a.m., and I was pretty tired. The first person I saw in the morning was Yorgos on the patio with a shovel in his hand. I went up to Yorgos to ask him what he was doing, and he said we now have some

THE DIVINE BEGINNING

chickens and a rooster, and he was building a cage under the house for their safety at night. I was amazed at how busy he was so early that morning. It was then that I realized I hadn't seen him at the Vacaville meeting.

I also realized I didn't see Robert or Jim around for breakfast. Someone said they stayed overnight in Vacaville and would be up later in the day. This pretty much made us rudderless.

Trisha was there with her three teenagers and husband. She was in charge of making lunch: sandwiches and salad. Trisha was also Venusian, and her sandwiches were ample and luscious. I went in to help her, since digging ditches or chicken attending was not yet on my resume.

After lunch I joined the gang and went to the swimming hole for the first time. Why not? It was hot and the water sounded so inviting.

Instead, Bonita and Alden, who also had driven back the previous night, decided to go to the Lake. I did not know why they wouldn't want to be with the rest of us.

I got a ride with a couple of moving-centered guys to the magical place everyone else spoke about. Instead of turning right at the end of Rice's Crossing Road, which would have taken us to Lake Francis, we turned left. I hadn't seen a river with a waterfall at all along Marysville Road and was intrigued by where this water oasis was located.

Just before the small bridge, we pulled into a narrow, recessed space along the road. As I got out of the car, I saw a little path descend straight down into what appeared to be a thicket of trees and underbrush.

Holy cow! This is steep! I can't do this.

I was wearing my bathing suit, flip flops and had my towel wrapped around me. I took a step down this incline and began to slip. Others ran down it. Now I know, I thought, why Bonita and Alden chose the Lake.

I held onto the bushes for dear life. Tears came to my eyes. I was so scared. I couldn't continue or turn back. Someone realized my predicament and encouraged me to keep going, promising me a paradise on earth. As soon as the path leveled out, that person left me standing in front of a dark, deep waterhole with laughing figures bobbing up and down, splashing each other. There, to the right, was the fifteen-foot cliff with the waterfall. The agility of everyone astounded me. Some were even naked.

I entered the water and it was amazingly refreshing. It was clean and cold, unlike the Richards Ranch experience with its muddy, slippery bottom. There were people not in the Fellowship, too, who joined us. They seemed to be locals and were friendly. Some suggested I take my suit off. I wasn't quite ready for that, although Trisha had no problem with it. She was a nature woman. I was still the city girl.

We must have spent two hours there because when we returned to the house, it was late afternoon and Robert, Jim, and Yorgos were on the patio. They looked right at us as we came upon them with wet hair and damp clothes. Robert wasn't smiling. I felt ashamed that I had given in to this "resort mentality," as I had referred to it.

I went inside the house to change clothes. There was a clothesline hidden behind the house where I hung my wet bathing suit and towel.

When I went to enter the house, Jim came up to me.

"Robert asked me to tell you that you are now assigned to the laundry octave."

* * * *

Dinner was ready, and I took my full plate and sat on one of the pillows in the living room. Just as I was about to take the first bite, Robert came up to me and handed me a note.

"Dear, would you please clean the garbage bin."

"Now?" I asked, with my mouth full of the first bite.

He nodded yes.

Someone had built this wooden unit with two front doors that hid two big garbage cans. The unit had two metal round lids on the top; we would lift the right lid to dispose of our uneaten food, and the left lid to throw away any paper products. It was obvious that the top hadn't been cleaned in a while. So I abandoned my plate on the floor and found some cleaning materials and started scrubbing.

The effort to respond to the teacher's request brought me into a higher state, as I focused on the task at hand. I was calm and serene and there was a smile on my face. How strange, I thought. I was happy cleaning gunk off of metal lids even though my dinner was getting cold.

In the midst of my task, Robert came up to me and presented me with another note.

"You accept your tasks selflessly."

This encouraging compliment strengthened my state. When the unit was sparkling, I sat back down to eat my cold dinner alone, since most people had finished and were placing their plates in the sink to be washed. Even though there was some commotion in the kitchen, I continued eating.

A message was communicated to us that Robert wanted an impromptu meeting in thirty minutes after the dishes were washed. We were only about fifteen students, so it was a small group, but Robert definitely had something to convey to us all.

He looked stern as he began to speak.

"If a person signs up for something, say cleaning up, and an 'I' doesn't want to do it, it is a lack of 'will.' Three or four students have a problem with willfulness. There are standards to a teaching. When people don't meet those standards, it is negative 'I's in control.

"A teacher is here to get a person to his own Self. What can he do with two selves?"

He paused before continuing. It was clear he wanted this to penetrate.

"A fast student places 'to be or not to be' ahead of everything. We are lucky to be together. Some nights are heavy, and that is the way it is. This is the master game for tonight. We don't know how large our group will grow. More and more the miracle of what we share will grow. We are at a higher level than humanity. We represent the pineal gland of the organism of humanity. We are trying to become conscious."

I looked around the room. Some students were not looking at Robert, but were looking down at the floor as he spoke; their eyes were glazed. He continued.

"Regarding faster students, do not be eaten by slower students. There are some fast students among the new people. Go at your own pace — as fast and as best as you can. Also, fast students: *Do not be eaten by fast students who are asleep.*"

He emphasized this last phrase. It penetrated deeply. There were older students that seemed to have a ranking in the school, like Meg and Bonita, and you could tell by their behavior and attitude that they considered themselves better and more advanced than the rest of us. He was speaking not only to this arrogant posturing, but also to a self-deprecating posturing of the rest of us. Both postures fed one another. Something in me recognized this, but something else (another group of 'I's?) did not want either woman's criticism or judgment directed at me. I wanted them to like me and think well of me as a student. It was a tough position to be in, and I was unsure what to do.

Then this thought (or 'I'?) entered my head: Who was the fastest student? I looked around the room and suddenly realized something extraordinary. It was Robert. The teacher was the fastest student.

THE SEEDS OF

From that point on, I knew it would always be best to follow his lead.

❖

It is easy for a man to find associates in wickedness;
the road is smooth, and the number of such men abound.
But the immortal Gods have placed the sweat on the brow
before virtue: long and steep is the path that leads to it,
and rough at first; but when the summit is reached,
then it is easy, however difficult it may have been.

Hesiod

CHAPTER 29

The next morning the chickens and little red rooster were pecking their way around the patio. Yorgos had enticed the children to feed them in the morning, and they were delighted to see how quickly these clucking birds would rush to find their share of grain.

Robert had finished his breakfast and came onto the patio just as the little red rooster had mounted one of the hens. He kicked the rooster off of the hen before consummation had occurred. The rooster wasn't hurt, but instead ruffled its feathers as if dusting off its overcoat before crowing several times, Cock-a-doodle-doo! Or in English: "How DARE he?" The hens immediately responded with a loud, unison cackling.

The gossiping had started. "Gertrude, did you see what that man did to Little Red? I declare!" "Oh yes! These humans think they own the yard!"

At one meeting, Robert had spoken to us about what he called "hen feature" and "rooster posture." Hen feature was the tendency that women have to gossip. Rooster posture was the machine's way of making itself appear bigger and self-important. We were told not to place our hands on our hips or behind our heads, as these positions puff us up, expanding the size of the machine. Robert had advised us to "stay small." We first heard this idea in the Bay Area, and it seemed so far removed from any direct verification for any of us — until we bought Via Del Sol and populated it with chickens.

This is how we learned our lessons.

* * * *

The laundry octave gave me an excuse to grab a book and read on the patio during wash and dry cycles. I would position myself on my favorite boulder, shaded by the honey locust tree, and read sections from *The Theory of*

Celestial Influence about the cycle of civilizations. When the machines would sound, indicating their jobs were done, I would set the book aside and work as quickly as I could to fold the clothes and put the next batch in the washer so I could return to my reading.

I was engrossed in a section on The Age of the Conquest of Time when Robert appeared. He sat near me with a book in hand. He asked me what I was reading and I told him.

"I started from the back of that book and read forward but didn't finish it," he said.

I was surprised at his response, assuming he must have mastered all the texts long before he started the Fellowship. The first part began with the Structure of the Universe and the Absolute, which I found fascinating. It wasn't that difficult to understand as Collin presented it.

I asked him what he was reading.

"*The Fourth Way.*"

"Haven't you read that before?"

"My higher centers haven't read it yet."

Again, I was surprised by his response. Then I observed that my intellectual center, a lower function, was digesting this material. Not my Higher Self.

How can one be present and read at the same time? How does one do that? It mystified me.

Robert then changed the subject.

"I need you to start making teaching payments beginning in August. I'm supporting Yorgos and Miles, too, and I would like to be able to continue to support you, but the school is drowning."

Teaching payments were $20 a month. I told him I understood, and it would be my pleasure to do this. He smiled lovingly at me, which was unusual to see.

"Thank you," he softly said.

We continued reading our respective books. And then he added:

"I also would like you to be Rolfed. It's an authentic experience. Speak with Annabella."

I agreed, but realized that this would wipe me out financially, since the ten Rolfing sessions cost $500 total.

The school year was months away and substitute teaching wasn't an option. I hadn't planned on this. I had to figure out a way to make money fast.

* * * *

It was about 4 p.m. when I saw Bonita and her daughter having fun mixing dough on the kitchen counter. They invited me to join them, and I said, "Sure," since I was between laundry cycles.

It was then that I learned Bonita made her living as a professional masseuse.

"You mix dough well," she observed. "Although your hands are small, they are strong. You could become a good masseuse with a little training."

That profession never occurred to me. But here was an opportunity to make some money. We talked further and she said she would give me a massage so I can understand how to do it, and then I could give her a massage to show my skills.

At this point, I was willing to try anything to earn money to stay in the school. It was that important.

※

I knew without a doubt I had found what I had been searching for my whole life, perhaps lifetimes. I was groping in the dark, but I had seen a glimpse, a light, a possibility.

Milarepa

CHAPTER 30

Where was Miles?

When I awoke that morning, Miles and Helga were there having breakfast. I was stunned to see them. I hadn't realized how wonderful their absence had been for me. I actually had hours where I totally forgot my emotional predicament. Just seeing them at the breakfast table, scooping food onto their plates, with smiles on their faces, made me imagine what intimate relations they privately were experiencing together. This was supposed to be me. I was supposed to be smiling and happy with the man, not her. A rush of emotions and 'I's paralyzed me. I lost my appetite, but didn't want to appear as if something was wrong. So I put food on my plate and sat alone in the corner playing with it until everyone else had finished and left.

I went into the sanctuary of the boot room to begin my laundry octave for the day. My head was buzzing with 'I's: Miles said he would spend time with me, but is he still interested in that? Is there any way we could still be together? Is there any way I could turn this around and win back his heart?

"Linda, could you maybe wash my jeans now?" pleaded a male student. "I know I'm supposed to put it on the bottom of the pile, but I only have two pair and both are dirty."

"Sure," I said smiling.

"You're the best!" he said, giving me a kiss on the cheek.

I threw his stuff in with the other heavy items.

Where were they? Where are the kids?

"Linda, did you wash my clothes yet?" asked Alden.

"Actually, I did, Alden." I handed him his folded clothes.

"Great!"

I went outside with a book during the cycles. After about an hour, someone's shadow appeared over me. It was Miles.

"We need to talk," he said.

I took the book with me for solace, and we walked over to the embankment on the left side of the small pond with its weeping willow. We both sat down at the edge, overlooking the expanse of sky toward the western hills, just as we had once reclined on Mount Diablo, where he had mentioned we would get married in the fall.

A palpable silence sat between us. Although he used the word "We," it was "He" who had something to say.

"I know I told you that I would be with you and Helga. But I've chosen to be with Helga."

These words were no longer wispy thoughts that flew through my head; their utterance made them concrete and their weight sank my heart.

I looked into his eyes and tried to smile to let him know that I was strong and could survive without him. And then he said the words that would shatter me.

"It's just that Helga satisfies me more sexually than you do."

I immediately turned away. He placed his hand on my shoulder to console me, but I had already turned to stone. He stood up and left me there.

I stared like a sphinx at the horizon. All thoughts and feelings evaporated. I couldn't feel my body, except for a burning, tingling sensation that penetrated my forehead.

And then it appeared: That old being I had encountered at Bubbie's house as a child, who had stared in wonderment at the lace curtains. It was now looking out of my eyes. It was calm and solid, and remarkably HERE.

I sat still for what seemed a long time, not wanting to disturb it. Despite my best efforts, I lost hold of the state, and it slipped underneath an ocean of overwhelming self-pity.

* * * *

Robert surprised us all when he said he wanted to have a picnic that afternoon at Lake Francis. Apparently, he had heard of this place and thought it would be a nice way to cool off in the hundred-degree heat. My view about a school not being a resort was suddenly challenged by his request. You mean it's okay? School rules were not ironclad, it seemed, and are difficult to interpret.

Sandwiches were made, and we arrived in different cars at different times. Bonita and her daughter were already enjoying the water when I arrived in a packed car of other students. Some decided to swim and had their suits on. I was one of them. Robert and Jim were there early, too, as were Miles and Helga, who sat together on their own large beach towel.

When I saw Miles and Helga, I ran past them into the lake and began to swim as hard as I could. My heart was beating and something in me wanted to appear as an accomplished swimmer. I had learned to swim at the age of five and participated in racing competitions by ten. After Miles's comment, it was a desperate attempt to be good at something.

I was a considerable distance from shore when I experienced the first foot cramp. How strange it was. This had never happened to me before. I stopped in the deep water, attempting to rub that foot when the other foot cramped as well. I couldn't move my legs. I went under.

And then the most extraordinary thing happened. I heard a giggle in my ear. Its source materialized there briefly as an ethereal cherubic being, wielding a bow and arrows, two of which it had launched to hit both arches. I did not conjure this vision. It simply was.

Again, an external presence manifested, just as it had on Mount Tamalpais that foggy night. It had appeared to inform me they had created this situation and seemed to take delight in the predicament. Why would they do this to me?

I felt a hand pull me up and drag me. It was Miles. When I surfaced, he said bitingly, "Robert told me, 'Miles, Linda needs help.' Why did you do such a stupid thing?"

I was given a towel and sat on the sand alone, shivering as I stared at the lake. No one came up to me. It was almost like I was a piece of paper that someone had picked up and put in the trash so everything could return to normal, so that the "beautiful day at the lake" could continue. It was a public display of humiliation and failure.

* * * *

No one had said a word to me in the car. Apparently, it was no big deal to them. When we returned to the house, I quickly changed and decided I needed to be alone, so I took a walk, not knowing exactly where I was going.

I went past the lined-up cars that hugged the edge of the narrow, washed-out road and the weather-beaten barn that stood on the left. At the road's end, I found a walking path that led me up a hill but in a northern direction, away from the house. It was unknown territory for me. I would stop periodically, turn around, and look at the landscape to familiarize myself with the path I would take to return to the house. This helped quell my fear of getting lost.

The view was pristine, with its gentle rolling hills of dense foliage and silent nature. The footpath was barely one-person wide and the incline was easy enough for me to manage. At a certain point I started to look for a place to sit, and found a small spot on the slope between two large pine trees. Their needles had created a natural soft cushion. It was there I sat.

Looking over the land, I tried to take stock of what I was going through. It was not a thinking process, but more a communing process to connect with those hovering Divine Guardians — or whatever you want to call them, angels, gods, C Influence — that I had felt since childhood. They ruled my life. They alone knew the reasons for my situation.

I had to empty my mind of the many 'I's. I found myself in a tender emotional state, and as I divided my attention, a deep understanding came to me, which later I would transcribe poetically.

> "Little Alice come to Earth,
> Resting on a seat of needles,
> Hears the giggle up in Heaven,
> Grinning from the Cheshire Cat:
> Yes, you're shrinking Little Alice,
> Little one you're growing smaller.
> See the mountains, broad and high,
> See the trees tickle upward
> As their fingers play with air.
> See your mass amid such masses.
> Yes, you're shrinking Little Alice.

> Little one you're growing smaller.
> Why, says Alice, must I grow small?
> The Cheshire whispers in a smile:
> It is necessary to be little
> Before you can be big."

I found my way back to the house with not only a greater understanding of why each day contained such friction, but perhaps more importantly, a profound trust in the play.

❖

> *I have a fairy by my side*
> *Which says I must not sleep.*
> *When once in pain I loudly cried*
> *It said, "You must not weep."*
> *If, full of mirth, I smile and grin,*
> *It says, "You must not laugh."*
> *When once I wished to drink some gin*
> *It said, "You must not quaff."*
> *When once a meal I wished to taste*
> *It said, "You must not bite."*
> *When to the wars I went in haste*
> *It said, "You must not fight."*
> *"What may I do?" at length I cried,*
> *Tired of the painful task.*
> *The fairy quietly replied,*
> *And said, "You must not ask."*
> *Moral: "You mustn't."*
>
> Lewis Carroll

CHAPTER 31

Midmorning of the next day, the county inspector returned to communicate his findings. Miles spoke with him briefly. We all watched and had no idea what to expect.

We got used to doing it Indian style (or what we assumed the North American Indians did), including trying leaves to clean ourselves. One student accidently used that three-leaf poisonous oak, which left him with a spreading rash in his hidden places. He twitched a lot, as I recall.

Miles went up to Robert to give him the lab results. I tried to eavesdrop. "There was absolutely no proof of bacteria that would shut us down."

Smiling, Miles also said the inspector couldn't understand this. We did, of course. No one flushed.

Although the toilet ban was lifted, Robert still wanted us to preserve water and continue to use the two-bucket technique for bathing. I recall Anna protesting considerably. He gave her and a few other older ladies an exception to the rule.

The truth be told, I discovered that I could actually take a quick shower without anyone knowing. How? Since it took a long time to fill the bucket with running water, instead of filling the bucket, I actually used the stream of water to wash my hair. I then shut the water off to lather. And, rather than fill the second bucket, I turned the water back on to rinse.

No one knew what one did in the shower, I reasoned. I did feel a little guilty but justified it by the sheer fact of the density of my long hair that required far more water than Anna's.

* * * *

The house hadn't changed its basic floor plan. The kitchen had a small white refrigerator for food storage and a single wall-unit chrome oven for baking. A makeshift barbecue was set up outside in the dirt with store-bought bricks, a hole in the ground to hold the charcoal, and a grate. Kerrie and Yorgos suggested to Robert that we construct a cooler (a refrigerated large pantry) in the back of the house to keep the quantities of food we needed preserved for more than a weekend. Robert understood and the construction began quickly. A portable air conditioner was placed in the back of this walk-in structure. Shelves were constructed.

To prepare for the Weekenders, Kerrie bought food in bulk from the local farmers. I accompanied her to the little town of Hallwood to locate a farmer with a commercial peach grove. She was able to negotiate a good price for seconds — those peaches that had minor imperfections and were not sellable to markets. But as soon as she casually mentioned we were from a church, they gave her two free boxes. She was a savvy business woman. When we got back to the house, she was delighted to see her boxes of peaches positioned on the slanted shelves of the new cooler.

* * * *

There was such a coming and going at Via Del Sol that weekend that no one could keep track of attendance. Prospective student meetings had been held in Berkeley, Vacaville, and Walnut Creek during the week, resulting in new students who would appear suddenly. Simple introductions were made, with the casual "hug-unto-itself" greeting. Laura and Clark, Sally, Thomas, Helen, Short Jane and Tall Jane, among them. Hippies and professionals, single mothers and married women without their husbands, attractive people and homely people coming together with a common interest: to learn how to be more awake.

That was the ideal, democratic view of the group of new friends. The actual interpersonal experience was a bit different: people made fun of other people who were not like them. Don, for example, climbed through the dirt and brush wearing a short-sleeve shirt, crisply creased trousers, and laced-up wingtip shoes with socks. This was laughable to the hippie types. For them, Birkenstocks were the common foot attire of the day, which often exposed dull toe nails that hadn't been clipped for months. The refined, cultured city people like Anna found that disgusting and did not engage much with these folk.

I encountered a certain pigeon-holing of my own, when one student looked at me and asked, in front of others, "Are you Jewish?" I said, "Yes, of course." "Say something in Jewish," he begged. No one had ever asked me to do this before, but again, I wanted to fit in so I began to act out a New York Jewish accent. They all began to laugh. Then I realized I was being teased. But by this time, it was too late to stop. I had been stamped.

There was a delicate distinction between laughing at someone and finding humor in the absurdity of the machine's antics. During Saturday's lunch preparation, Anna had bounded out of the kitchen screaming at the top of her lungs, "I can't take it anymore! I can't take it anymore!"

We all gathered around, like the little hens, to inquire what had caused her to erupt like this. It turned out she was mixing the big bowl of salad when she found several live earwigs crawling over the greens. Rosemary tried to console her. Robert came and wrapped his long arms around her five-foot, three-inch Jovial frame and told her it was fine, she didn't need to do this anymore. But most found it amusing, as it was a demonstration of the queen-of-hearts type — the emotional part of the emotional center. It reminded everyone of the Red Queen in *Alice in Wonderland,* who yelled, "Off with their heads!" Anna had been stamped, too.

* * * *

It's so hard to see someone as they are and to have someone truly see you. I was not the Jewish girl. I was not Miles's girlfriend from LA. To be honest, I didn't know exactly who I was, but I knew I wasn't these descriptors.

We often spoke about false personality, true personality, and essence. Essence we studied as those functions of the human machine — the emotional, intellectual, moving and instinctive — that were empty containers at birth, and would later be filled with personalities (the many 'I's). Center of gravity basically meant that one function's container was larger or more predominant than the others. You could describe this as the tendency to manifest more from one part of one's machine. Hence, if you exhibited emotional reactions more than intellectual, instinctive or moving, you were probably emotionally centered.

True personality was that part that was interested in evolution. False personality was everything else that was not yours, but was programmed by parents or society, such as morality, opinions and judgments. How do we know the difference between essence and true and false personality?

Ouspensky said, "Start by realizing that it is all false personality, and then try to find out what is not." Upon reading this, my first reaction was, Am I ALL false personality? That much? This was a frightening thing to consider, especially if you are trying to find out who you are.

We had a discussion after dinner one evening on this subject.

"I think it's more like peeling an onion," offered one Venusian male. "You peel the thin, transparent layers back until you come to the center."

Another student commented, "But, if you keep peeling in this way, you end up with nothing left."

It was at this point I added, "What would that nothing feel like? Do I float away? Do I become a vegetable?"

They burst out laughing. I was being serious, until the irony registered.

I knew that my internal space was still dark, and that I could only describe each area of this vast house named Linda by haphazardly bumping into its contents. Ah, this is the bed so it must be the bedroom; or this is the stove so it must be the kitchen. How is it that humans are so blind internally and consider that acceptable?

The point was, we were all guessing what being a fully awakened conscious being would be like. It is an unknown world, and it is scary to think this is what we are after. How we learn to see our true Selves was the great mystery. Would it hurt? Could we bear it?

* * * *

After lunch I needed to use the bathroom, and the downstairs bathroom line was forming quickly so I went upstairs. The blanket-door was still there and

I wasn't sure if anyone was using the facility, so I knocked on the door frame before entering.

I heard two knocks back. I waited a full minute. I heard nothing at all and I thought, Oh, it must be a Lunar type. They were renowned for their quietness. I thought about all the Lunars around and then figured, for some reason, it must be the sweet, shy Lunar boy of eight named Stevie. He and I had a nice, playful connection.

"Stevie, come out!" I coaxed. "Come on out now. I need to use the bathroom."

Silence.

"I know you're in there, Stevie."

Silence.

But it wasn't ordinary silence. Suddenly, I was present, as if I were hit by a powerful burst of conscious energy that went right through the fabric of the makeshift door.

Oh gosh. Robert's in there.

I was certain of this. I wanted to run, but I couldn't. My feet were pinned to the floor. He knows it's me. All I could do was stand there and wait for the inevitable to emerge.

Robert exited, looking past me with a tight, stoic expression.

I went in and looked at myself in the mirror. This was not just a simple, silly moment, I realized. This moment revealed a part of me that took delight in teasing. I had stamped Stevie as a Lunar. I, too, had this problem, just like those who liked to make fun of my Jewishness. This part was not innocent, and I was forced to see it in myself.

It was a profound understanding of school work. Each embarrassing incident in front of Robert was a gift precisely because it illuminated my internal world, and showed that this was how one awakens. One sees what one is not ("the machine") by the teacher's light. That's the process.

Now I only had to endure it.

❖

> *Each Teacher reveals the truth in his own special way*
> *and then he disappears.*
>
> Attar

CHAPTER 32

Over that weekend I was given an addition to my third-line responsibility: I was now to collect money for the cost of food over the weekend from the Weekenders. The total price for two days of meals was $5. Miles and Yorgos were exempt. Those of us who were Residents were expected to pull their weight during the full week and were not charged.

I kept my list and envelope and writing implement with me in case I ran into a visitor. Anna hadn't paid me for that weekend, and when I saw her enter her little VW bug to drive back to Berkeley, I ran down the hill after her. She stopped the car, rolled down the window, and came up with the five dollars. She simply had forgotten.

Apparently, Robert was watching my dedicated effort, for when I got back up the hill, he thanked me for taking care of this octave for him. I smiled at him and said, "You're welcome."

He then asked me to collect money for some shovels, since we only had two. The price was five dollars. I looked in my own wallet and found six dollars and change. I immediately could feel resistance, but I took the five out, put it in the envelope, and wrote my name down as the first person on the list.

Robert saw this and asked how much I had left. I told him and he pointed upward saying, "That was a test." It hadn't occurred to me that there were tests like this. To me it just was the right thing to do. Then I realized, well of course a school has tests. How could it be otherwise?

* * * *

The meeting on Monday night was at Anna's in Berkeley. I had left the ranch in the afternoon with Meg and Harold and several other students. It was nice to leave the windless high heat of the ranch and go to the coolness of the Bay.

Meg and Harold never drove directly to any destination. In fact, they would stop every hour or so to get some food and coffee at such eateries as Denny's or Sambo's (Denny's competitor in California). We finally arrived in Berkeley at 7:58 with two minutes to spare. The meeting started at eight.

Robert had insisted that meetings begin on time, which was a challenge for some who had to travel longer distances, had just come from work, had children to attend to, or, as was more often the case, had tramp features.

It was a small meeting, actually. There were about twenty students who had gathered. We sat in a circle in Anna's living room. Anna's big, heavy oak door would loudly click, indicating the lock disengaged to let a straggler in, and then click again as we heard the door securely close. We waited for them to be seated. It was past eight when Robert spoke.

"The Self is outside time. To get *out of time,* one first must be *on time.* Try to arrive at least five minutes before the meeting begins."

He paused.

"Being on time is an act of external consideration."

He paused again.

"When we struggle as members of this group to become aware and awake, we will benefit from the help of C Influence. It is never easy to 'Be' the knowledge. This requires self-remembering. C Influence eliminates people who take it for granted."

There was silence. Robert's tone carried weight.

"Everybody's life has been designed by higher forces to meet this teaching. Everybody is playing a part in this teaching. No independent action comes from me. I have not played this role before."

I looked at Robert. In that instance I perceived that the man sitting before me – this "Robert Burton, Teacher" – was not who he actually was. Before an 'I' could quickly label him a fake, however, I was able to catch a glimpse of the *being* playing this role. I saw his courage in imparting information that seemed "other worldly."

Just as I recognized him earlier as the fastest student, I remembered that he was also growing and evolving. The role may be flawed, but the *conscious being* was not, and I could relate to it. I always felt this artificiality about my own life: that I was playing the role of Linda Kaplan, will all its strengths and weaknesses and uncontrollable manifestations. The real me – the conscious being – was housed (or more accurately, imprisoned) in this role. It was my heartfelt desire to get to this essential core of me and free it.

Robert stopped speaking for a long while. I looked at him, and it was as if he was contemplating whether or not to share information with us. Finally, he spoke.

"C Influence is arranging suffering for you in order for you to separate. The Self eats negative emotions." Then he paused and carefully, quietly uttered, *"C Influence is working openly with each of you to awaken you."*

This last statement struck me. It was what I had experienced but dared not express. Just as soon as I heard it, something astounding occurred.

The big, heavy oak door flew open with a gust of wind that howled like a special effect from a *King Lear* production on Broadway. Everyone in the room froze.

I sat there with a big grin on my face, almost ready to laugh. An 'I' entered my head: "Why so dramatic?" I felt like I was at a séance. The howling wind and moving of a seemingly immovable object was like an amateur demonstration intended to convince the doubting Thomases in the room.

But I did not need this theatrical device. I had already verified C Influence. My verification was direct and invisible and unquestionable.

* * * *

After the small groups ended, I learned that Meg and Harold decided to drive back in the morning so I needed to find a way to the ranch that night. The only person going was Kerrie. She had loaded the van with boxes of food supplies from her Berkeley shopping, and I would have to sit among them she said, which I was willing to do. She was with redheaded James, who graciously offered to give me his "shotgun seat" in the front.

When we arrived back around 3 a.m., the house was dark and the silence was unusually deep. James took a flashlight from the van and turned the dim lights on in the boot room, the kitchen, and the living room. No one was around. He returned and the three of us carried the foodstuffs inside and placed them on the racks in the cooler.

James and Kerrie got back into the van to park it and disappeared together into the night. I dragged my sleeping bag and pad under the fig tree. As I lay there exhausted, the fragrance of the meeting remained within my heart, bringing a smile to my face. It was a full day, and I quickly fell asleep.

It is not to all men the Gods give a sight of themselves.
Homer

CHAPTER 33

The next morning Yorgos told us what had happened. In the middle of the night, either a coyote or a mountain lion had ripped through the chicken pen that he had built under the house annex and had eaten all the chickens. I was in shock, considering I was sleeping nearby. I didn't hear anything, so it must have occurred before we got back. Yorgos didn't hear the commotion either, he said. Perhaps it was because he was sleeping in an abandoned metal water tank up the hill, which he was in the process of converting into his own livable space.

With the chickens now gone, there was a feeling that this Via Del Sol enterprise was taking a step backwards. The wonderful enthusiasm we felt that first weekend was quickly diminishing. All for one and one for all was replaced with a feeling of abandonment. The city folk (the Weekenders) stayed in the city, and the Residents were setting their own rules of survival. The Sierra Foothills were a tougher place to civilize than anyone had imagined.

Meanwhile, we kept the place as clean as we could. We used brooms to sweep and sponges to wipe. We unfurled rolls of amber-colored fly paper and hung them from the low ceiling. They quickly filled with black dots of dead flies. We lounged about, feeding ourselves, smoking cigarettes, and talking about the Work. The more I read, the more I relished sharing my personal observations and intellectual discoveries with others. Mastering the Fourth Way gave me a sense of accomplishment and worth. But it was all for a good cause, I reasoned. I viewed it as second line of work.

Robert didn't return that day. No one knew where he was. Kerrie prepared the meals, we played music we wanted to hear on Robert's stereo, and I manned the laundry octave since dirty clothes were a constant.

* * * *

After dinner, Bonita turned to me and said, "Let's go upstairs. I will teach you massage."

I followed her upstairs where she had also stored her massage table. I was surprised to see it was set up already. The light was dim. I stood there not knowing what to do since I'd never had a massage before. I thought she would massage me through my clothes. When she told me to take off all of my clothes and to get on the table face down, she chuckled that wheezy laugh of hers as she saw the shocked look of confusion on my face. But I obeyed. She then covered me with a sheet except for my back.

I waited. I could hear her taking deep breaths. Then she touched my spine beginning at the neck. She put pressure on the spaces between each vertebra with her thumbs. She moved slowly and intentionally.

The massage took an hour, although it seemed much longer. When it was done, I was relaxed and ready to go to bed. As I began to dress, she told me that it was my turn to massage her. Uh, okay. I wasn't expecting this, but I guess a bargain was a bargain.

She disrobed, mounted the table, and instructed me. Her body was dense, not mushy like mine. I immediately understood the difference between an instinctive body type and an emotional one.

She told me to think of the body in four parts and to move from one part to the other without taking a hand off of her body. I was always to have contact with her so that a current could be maintained between us. At one point, I went into imagination (I wanted it to be over) and she immediately called me out on it. "You're in imagination," she said. I was amazed she could tell. "Try to be present with each movement," she advised.

Although I hadn't finished with the third part of her body, she said it was fine and I could stop. She could tell that I was tired and that my energy for self-remembering was not there. I thanked her for taking the time to teach me. I also asked her how much she thought I could charge for giving an hour massage. She said five dollars. She then told me she charges a lot more, of course.

As I got into my sleeping bag that night, I thought, what a successful day this has been! I had learned something new. I fell asleep contented.

* * * *

It was now mid-week and still no sign of Robert. We had our chores, ate our meals, and a few found creative expressions to address basic needs. I learned at breakfast that no one went to Lake Francis anymore because, apparently, Bonita and crew had been caught body washing and told not to come back, as it polluted the waters.

In response to the shower situation, one fellow decided to build his own outdoor shower behind the house. He found some wooden planks and constructed the platform, put up a metal pipe vertically, then horizontally and hooked it up to a nearby water source. He figured all this out himself. Of course, you had to bathe naked out in the open in front of everyone. He was happy to demonstrate to us all how wonderful it was to use. He encouraged everyone to follow his example. I declined, although one or two others took him up on it. It was curious how I was becoming accustomed to seeing naked people.

* * * *

It was late afternoon when I was done with the laundry that had piled up over the weekend. Although people went to the city, they left their dirty ranch clothes in the bin. As I was folding the last load, the boot room door opened and Robert and Jim walked in.

I had never seen Robert like this before. The look on his face was dark and sad. I greeted them, and Robert walked through without acknowledging me. Jim lingered a bit, and I asked him where they were. What happened?

"We drove to Mendocino. All Robert could say was, 'They are all asleep.'"

"But he knew this, yes?" I asked him.

"He knew this, but this time he saw this, I guess. It was depressing for him."

Robert called to Jim, who immediately left me there so he could attend to Robert.

At dinner that evening, I could hear Yorgos explain to Robert what had occurred to the chickens. He asked Robert if he could buy more chickens and told him he would guarantee the structure would be stronger than before.

Robert called Jim over and the three of them discussed expanding the operation. The idea was to convert part of the barn so it could house a hundred chicks, which later would grow into chickens that we could slaughter to feed us all. This would save us money in the long run, Robert reasoned. I watched Yorgos's face and it didn't register as a positive suggestion. Robert was thinking on a much larger scale. Jim would do more research in the morning with Yorgos.

It was nice to have Robert back. Without him, there was a type of stagnation occurring. Something still was missing, however. We tried to alter the house to accommodate a more civilized living experience, but there was just so much that we could do. Some students had artistic design skills, like Don, but we needed someone with expertise in architecture and construction.

Perhaps that person was in the wings, waiting to make his entrance.

✥

Without the assistance of the Divine Being, I cannot succeed. With that assistance, I cannot fail.

Abraham Lincoln

CHAPTER 34

Before breakfast, Robert asked to have the fly paper streamers removed. I was glad about this since they were not only unsightly, but it was easy to back up against one and catch your hair in it.

Robert turned to Jim and whispered something. Jim left and returned within thirty minutes with a flyswatter, which he handed to Robert. I watched Robert with uncanny accuracy aim at a fly and dispatch it with a perfect backhand. Jim handed me a few sheets from a roll of paper towels he was carrying. The two of us followed Robert around the house capturing and disposing of the fly carcasses. The delight Robert took in practicing his tennis skills cheered me up. It looked like he was having fun. He shared his secret of success with me.

"Wait until the fly lands. Position the swatter over it, but don't strike. Once the fly stops moving, then swat it. The reason this works is because the fly's instinctive center has fallen asleep and believes it is out of danger."

* * * *

Late morning, I decided to take a walk down to the barn to see what was occurring with Jim and Yorgos and the deluxe chicken coop.

"How's it going?" I asked Jim, who was standing there with his utility belt strapped to his hips, making him look like a gunslinger: hammers that hung like revolvers, screwdrivers that fit neatly into leather loops like bullets, and pouches for the nails and screws. His mustache and goatee, his long brown hair touching his shoulders, his off-white straw cowboy hat with its sweat marks and dust, and his worn jeans and broken-in cowboy boots made a distinct impression. But it was the characteristic way he put his weight on one leg — that swagger, that lean of his — that made me realize we sure are in the Wild, Wild, West.

"It's goin'," he said. Then he returned to help Yorgos position a long board to complete the wooden frame so the chicken wire could be hammered into place. I just stood there watching as Jim pulled out his Stanley tape measure to mark where to cut the next board. It was about sixteen feet. This is a large structure, I thought.

At that point, it was getting a little weird for me to just stand and watch, so I left to go up to lunch. I asked them if they were coming, and they both said No. They had to finish it first because Robert wanted to leave after lunch to go with them to get the baby chicks.

After lunch, I learned that Kerrie was heading down to the Bay Area to do another shopping run for the weekend, and she asked me to be in charge of dinner preparation that night. I agreed as long as I knew exactly what to prepare. She handed me a piece of paper with the menu as we walked into the cooler. I smiled because I could see she understood my nature, and she was sweet enough to accommodate it.

A work idea immediately entered my head: external consideration. It was a difficult concept for me to grasp. It meant to place yourself in someone else's shoes, so you can give them what they need rather than give them what you think they should have. She was externally considerate of me in the moment, by letting me write down exactly the amounts and the timing so that I could succeed with the menu and cooking. I was excited about this opportunity.

By late afternoon I was fully engaged in the food preparation. Few students were around and the quietness of the kitchen area allowed me to focus. Robert had taken the big truck with Trisha's sixteen-year-old son, and Jim, Yorgos, and Klair, who had experience with chickens apparently (I had seen her often feed the chickens we previously had in the yard). Kerrie went with three other students to Berkeley.

At one point I decided to take a break and went outside with a snack of figs and nuts. David was there speaking with a few students. I listened in and was shocked to hear them talk about the moon that was new in the early morning hours.

"You mean full moon," I corrected.

"No, it's a new moon."

How was that possible? Then it hit me. It had only been two weeks ago that Miles and I first arrived at Via Del Sol, not a month ago. Again, proof that I was living in a time warp.

"We're planning on going to Lake Francis at the peak of the new moon and swim. The stars will be amazing," said Clark.

"I thought we couldn't go there," I questioned.

The response was: no one will know because it will be dark.

They planned to skinny dip. Was I interested in coming along? I told them I'd think about it.

* * * *

Dinner was at eight and no sign of Robert and friends. Nine o'clock came and nothing. Ten o'clock and the food was now, shall we say, past prime. I was tired, impatient, and a bit angry that they were late to dinner after I had made such an effort. What could be taking them so long? They left eight hours ago. These 'I's were circulating faster and faster until a froth of negativity drove me to shut off the kitchen light with the food uncovered on the table so the flies could get to them. Serves them right. I'm going to bed.

As I got into my sleeping bag next to the fig tree and nestled down in the dark, I heard a rumble and looked out to see in the distance the thin beam of headlights growing ever larger. As the truck made its way up the hill in the pitch black of a new moon, I heard animal sounds of a Baa-aa-aa, Moooo, and Ba-uh-aa-uh. What the hell?

I turned away from the sound and pulled the bag over my head, trying to be invisibly asleep. I could hear Robert's voice giving directions. The Ba-uh-aa-uh grew louder until it sounded like it was right next to me. It was. Robert had told Jim to tie the goat to the fig tree.

"Robert wants you to get up and fix dinner," said Jim.

It was so ridiculous a situation that I got up with a chuckle. I could see the part of me that was angry was still huddled in the sleeping bag, refusing to move. Another part of me — the part that understood I was in a conscious school — went into the kitchen.

The food on the table was inedible so I threw it out. I made sandwiches instead, which seemed to be acceptable to all. Robert was excited like a child as he was describing how he could buy a baby calf (oh yes, the momma cow came with a calf) for only ten dollars.

I looked at Klair, who was a more practical, outdoor type, stare straight ahead with pursed lips. She knew about taking care of animals in the same way that Rosemary knew about orchards. Her silent words were loud and clear: where are we going to put them? Who's going to feed them and milk the mother cow? The chicks were ordered and would come the next day (or so), and would now have to share the barn with four-legged mammals. It seemed that who would care for them regularly was still to be determined.

* * * *

By the time I had finished washing dishes that night and listening to the tales of the great animal purchase, it was past one o'clock in the morning. The students who had spoken to me about the new moon swim were assembling. The idea was to be there at 2:15 a.m., which was the peak of the new moon. I resisted until David approached me.

"Come with us, Linda. Believe me, you will never forget this."

There was no need for a bathing suit, I was told, only a towel. Six of us got into a car and turned right at Rice's Crossing Road toward Lake Francis. We drove to the entrance and parked a distance so as not to draw attention to our escapade. With flashlights in hand, we made our way to the lakeside.

I looked straight up in the cloudless night sky and saw the Milky Way, not as a smear of white film veiling the stars, but as a being of depth and complexity with various colors and shapes throbbing together. David undressed and I undressed to join the others, who had already entered the dark water.

As we moved together toward the middle of the lake, the most magical sight appeared: the dazzling intensity of this starry world above reflected equally on the still surface of the black lake. We were swimming in stars that seemed to penetrate the waters. My little speck of human kind had been swallowed up by the enormous scope of celestial existence, as if I were released from my physical form and suspended in the middle of the universe. I could feel my body melt into the cool liquid, leaving behind an internal state of pure presence. It was almost more than I could bear.

David whispered, "Do you see what I mean?"

I softly replied, "Yes."

We remained there for a while, away from the others who were talking and making waves. It was wonderful to be with David, who understood the power of silence.

When we arrived back at the house, it was past four in the morning. Just as David had promised, that mystical night would stay with me forever.

❖

Illuminated in your infinite peace, a billion stars go spinning through the night, blazing high above your head.
But in you is the presence that will be, when all the stars are dead.

Rainer Maria Rilke

CHAPTER 35

I slept late that morning. By the time I roused, the farmhouse was almost empty.

"Where is everybody?" I asked a lady student, who was joining me in an informal breakfast of granola and milk and coffee.

"Robert and others are already down at the barn. Everyone wants to see the new animals, especially the calf."

I was less interested, having already met the goat face to face. Still, I was curious about the activity at the barn, so I headed down the hill once I finished eating. As I approached, I could hear the loud whacking of the hammers. Robert was standing there cuing like a conductor, pointing to areas for the small paddocks that needed to be built to separate the sheep from the goats and cows. Klair was standing next to Robert, giving him advice.

The atmosphere was more like visiting a petting zoo than a working farm. The children were tapping the cow on the sides and stroking the sheep. The goat was ignored. They were cautioned about the little calf because the mother was protective. I was surprised to see Nadia involved; apparently, she had experience with farm animals. She was clearly emotional about them.

THE DIVINE BEGINNING

But it was Klair who was calm, focused, and the apparent new octave leader. She showed Robert how the cow would be milked, which apparently wasn't easy. You needed a special touch for the milk to squirt out of the teat. She told Robert that buckets and milking stools needed to be purchased, as well as storage containers known as crocks to hold the milk. Cleanliness was a must. A schedule also needed to be set up so that the milking could occur twelve hours after the calf was fed, and that the calf needed to be isolated from the mother cow if we wanted to have milk for ourselves. This meant constructing a separate space for the calf.

It turns out that ten dollars was not cheap after all.

* * * *

By lunchtime the cow crew had been determined. It sounded interesting to me at first until I learned that the milking began at 5 a.m. No, thank you. I'll stick to kitchen chores.

One thing that did come up at lunch was the fact that it was not easy to communicate to others at the barn that lunch was ready. As it turned out, one student had with him a big shell that I had seen for sale at the Nut Tree. It was called a "conch," and he had adapted it so that it could be played like a trumpet. He gave Robert a demonstration, which enthralled him. The sound could be heard quite a distance. It reminded me of the Jewish shofer that cantors play during high services. Because the student was good at other things, Robert asked him to teach someone from the kitchen to blow it. Then Robert looked at me and walked away.

One or two students tried it first, but it wasn't successful. I asked if I could try it, and the fellow handed it to me reluctantly. He showed me how to purse my lips and blow from my diaphragm. It definitely wasn't easy, but I was challenged by this. We worked on it for about an hour or so until a true note came out when I blew. I eventually got good at it so that, too, was added to my list of octaves.

* * * *

Late afternoon had come, and for some reason Robert wanted us all to join him in the Big Meadow. Because this was the place of the infamous bog, I wasn't excited to go. It was a long walk directly from the house, so most of us piled into cars to make the bumpy ride to this location. There were a few who decided to hike. We parked the cars and began to walk through these high, dry weeds known as foxtails. Foxtails had thorns that we always referred to as stickers in Southern California, and they embedded themselves in our clothing.

Robert stopped. He removed his socks and handed them to Jim, who in turn handed one to me. We were to remove these burrs, which wasn't easy because they broke off into smaller pieces. I had my own problems with them in my socks, but had to take care of Robert's first. Jim took Robert's sock from my hand and quickly plucked out the spurs since his technique was quicker. He handed the socks to Robert who put them back on.

We moved on to a gate that was tied with a knotted twine rope to the barbed wire fence. Short Jane, who was a Martial type with freckles across her nose, was with her young son. She took out a pocket knife she had and slipped it under the rope. With a quick upward motion of her hand, the knife not only cut the rope but also somehow cut Robert's arm. Robert began to bleed profusely.

She was horrified. We watched as Robert stumbled back, but instead of collapsing, he quietly and intentionally, as if in slow motion, put the other arm behind him and lay down on the ground. Jim immediately went to his side to apply a tourniquet with his kerchief. I was standing over Robert, as were several others, and I saw his face go gray. Robert lay there speaking softly to Jim. When his color returned, I was shocked to see him stand up.

"I was stabbed in the back as a child in school," he explained, "and the machine recalled this traumatic event. I decided to lie down and wait for it to pass. It is better to bend in order not to break."

The wound was not deep or serious enough to require a trip to the emergency room. Some students went ahead to bring the cars. Dusk was approaching rapidly.

As I went to enter the car behind Robert's, I looked ahead and saw Robert moving slowly toward the passenger side of his vehicle. Headlights were on him, but it wasn't exactly Robert I saw.

Instead, it was an old man with pure white hair, not a young man with dark hair. I blinked my eyes quickly. *Who is that?* And then the figure entered the car.

I sat in the passenger seat, perplexed. One moment I saw Robert, and the next moment I saw someone who was not the Robert I knew. What did I just witness? I know what I saw, but how was it that I saw this? Did time move forward in some uncanny way? Was I looking at Robert in the future? That old man was as alive as the young man.

I could never speak about this to anyone. It was an inexplicable experience. And yet, something inside of me knew that one day I would meet this old man, whose name was Robert Burton. It was simply a matter of time.

❧

> *A child appeared before me in the light.*
> *I continued looking at him as he became an old man*
> *And then he changed again, becoming like a young man.*
> *I did not understand what I was seeing.*
> Gnostic Gospels, The Secret Book of John

CHAPTER 36

Don and Doris arrived from Vacaville after breakfast and drove past the lined-up cars, onto the edge of the house patio, and continued up the hill's steep incline leading to Yorgos's water tank hut. No one had done this before. It was like watching someone break a barrier, opening up the West to settlers. Apparently, he had been working on a new design for a living structure: a large tent on an elevated wooden platform with an extended deck area.

Having had a father who couldn't put a bicycle together for me that he bought in pieces since it was cheaper than an assembled one, I could not fathom how a man could magically turn a drawing into a living space. Don had purchased planks of wood and had arranged for a larger vehicle to deliver them to the site, which he had staked out earlier between majestic oak trees. The truck, however, had to negotiate between the thick brush of manzanita and poison oak surrounding the area above the farmhouse. It was exciting to watch the truck with its heavy load negotiate the difficult passage. Some of us bet it wouldn't make it. We were wrong.

At lunch, Don spoke with Robert about the design and invited him to visit when it was done. Robert was interested in the tents as a more civilized housing arrangement. The construction continued after lunch, and the basic platform was completed and the tent pitched by late afternoon. Robert and several of us went up to see it.

The tent was large with gently sloping sides and awning-type openings over the clear plastic windows. Don had brought two director chairs with him to place on the deck. The land immediately surrounding the tent area was grazed clean by years of cattle roaming. He had found the perfect location.

Robert was delighted by these prospects and said he wanted each student to invest in a tent. As we went back to the house, my mind was calculating personal finances. There were tents of various sizes and costs. I decided to go deluxe myself and bought the double for $50, hoping that one day soon I would have a love interest. Don would arrange for the purchases on Monday when he returned to Vacaville.

* * * *

All afternoon I kept thinking about the tent and the status of my finances. If I bought the size of the tent I had ordered, it would leave me with just enough money for the Rolfing treatments, but little else. Robert hadn't said anything to me about this since his first request and I hoped he had forgotten.

At dinner he approached me.

"Have you contacted Annabella yet about your Rolfing?"

I replied that I hadn't and he insisted that I follow through.

"Ask Rosemary to help you set up your first treatment."

It was like being caught by your parents, who reminded you to do your chores just as you were going out with friends for the evening. I wasn't interested in getting Rolfed, especially when Robert would speak of it in these terms: "I was hit by a semi-truck and that wasn't as painful as being Rolfed."

Oh, great. What an inspiring analogy to incentivize me to drop a load of cash.

If I have to pay the five hundred dollars, I thought, I have to start hustling. So that night I asked Bonita if I could borrow her massage table sometime to give massages. She was fine with this, she said, as long as she wasn't using it. Now all I needed were willing customers who were able to pay.

* * * *

The next morning, I arose early to scout out my tent site. I had seen a lovely level area near Don and Doris and was hoping to secure that spot. Unfortunately, I wasn't the only one with that idea. Someone beat me to it. In fact, there were a number of students wandering the slope, picking out their new properties. It was like the Oklahoma land rush. Well, not exactly on that scale, but there was definitely an instinctive scurrying going on.

I knew I didn't want to go too far up the hill into the heavily wooded terrain, with its dense brush of manzanita and poison oak, so I tried to make do with any cleared space closest to the farmhouse. I found an area that was near a rusted barbed wire fence line that had once effectively held back the cattle, but had fallen into disrepair. This would be the perfect landmark for my new abode, I thought. The earth was rocky and uneven though, and not exactly ideal for a tent. In a way, it was like wanting to live in Beverly Hills like Don and Doris but having to settle for the San Fernando Valley. I spoke with a fellow who would be my neighbor, and he told me he would help me pluck the bigger rocks, level the earth, and pitch the tent once the tents arrived.

Contenting myself with a small piece of earth, I happily went down to have breakfast. Seeing Robert, I approached him to say I had found my tent spot and mentioned it had a fenced area around it.

"Take it down," he said without hesitation.

His response confused me. Sure, it wasn't a white picket fence but it would help me know which tent was mine. What's wrong with that?

"Take it down after lunch." He saw my perplexity. "Have Clark help you. This is the instinctive center that wants to isolate you from others."

How could I be isolated in this openly communal atmosphere? But because he was my teacher, I obeyed.

As it turned out, no one would challenge my tent turf because it was on a slight incline, rocky, and hedged by two gnarly manzanita bushes. Beautiful it was not. And yet it would be my domain, the first place in my life I could call my own.

* * * *

Sunday afternoon I left Via Del Sol with Rosemary. She was heading home to Vacaville to prepare her house for Monday's meeting there, and I told her I was happy to help. We spoke about Rolfing and Annabella and she told me to ask Annabella at the meeting, since she knew she would be attending.

I had yet to meet this mysterious lady and already felt a little intimidated by her from what I heard. She was a doctor and had her own home in the Oakland hills. I had never met a woman doctor before and she seemed like someone who was worlds away from everything I was: accomplished, independent, with paramours galore.

Rose's younger daughter was there when we arrived, practicing her piano. Her boyfriend drove up in his refurbished antique Ford truck that he proudly displayed. He whisked her away. Her elder daughter, who played the violin, had a renowned violin teacher in Berkeley with a lesson scheduled on Tuesday. The plan was for me to drive down to the Bay Area Tuesday morning with them and for me to have my first Rolfing with Annabella during the lesson.

After lunch, I helped Rose with the dusting and vacuuming. They were always my favorite chores back home. I liked to handle objects, dusting them with care, polishing if needed to a shine. The vacuum was a Kirby. It was a top of the line, industrial-strength machine, and using it was like driving a car before power steering was invented. It took full body strength to lean into it with both hands on the stick. The noise was loud enough to muffle my

Streisand songs. I could mechanically vocalize both sides of any album. I was having a blast.

When I was done with the living room, I went into the kitchen to help Rose prepare some snacks for the meeting's intermission. The wall phone rang and it was Jim asking Rose to meet Robert for an early Coffee Tree dinner. I was not invited. I was relying on Rose to feed me. I guess the snacks would be my dinner.

* * * *

After Rose left, I showered and dressed, and went into the living room, where the record player was located. Looking through the albums, I discovered they were mostly classical music with a little bit of pop. There was a Shirley Bassey album. She sang the theme song from James Bonds' *Goldfinger* and her voice was big and powerful like mine. Her voice packed a punch (she was what my father called a "belter"). Classical music was still a foreign language to me. Bach, Beethoven, Brahms — all instrumentals. I was looking for voice and found some opera. I put a few albums on to see if I could hit the notes. I was having fun when I heard the first cars pull into the driveway for the meeting. I immediately turned the record player off and assumed my position as hostess of the house.

I opened the front door and students from the Bay Area came in. We hugged each other and I told them to put their jackets in the bedroom to the left. It was a strange feeling to pretend to be the homeowner, especially when I opened the door and there was Mac. We both laughed at the fact that I was welcoming him into his own home. He told me that I didn't need to open the door to everyone now that he was home. People could just enter on their own. I guess I was playing the role of the housewives I saw on television as a child.

I went into the kitchen and pulled out my envelope, piece of paper, and pencil. I was now on the lookout for delinquent accounts. As students began to come in, I was able to collect several payments before the meeting. Rose and Robert had arrived. And then in strolled Annabella.

She went right up to Robert. She was a dark-haired, black-eyed petite Mercurial type with excellent posture. Her self-confidence was larger than her frame, which made her seem a foot taller. Robert almost blushed as she approached him. He kissed her cheek and the two talked face to face. An energy field seemed to encircle them, preventing the rest of us from approaching. It was curious to observe. I was hoping to find a moment to be introduced, but that wasn't going to happen.

After the meeting, I had to put my little money envelope together to hand off to Robert, as he left quickly with Jim. Apparently, Annabella had been invited to the Coffee Tree, but for some reason she told Robert she couldn't go. I felt there was a bit of headstrongness in the way she declined the invitation twice. Robert looked a little disappointed after the two of them had spoken. She then turned to Mac. It was clear the two were flirting with each other. It was Mac who called me over.

"Linda, I'd like you to meet Annabella," he said with a glint in his eye.

We exchanged greetings, and then I found my opening.

"Annabella, Robert wanted me to get Rolfed as soon as possible. I was wondering if it would be possible to have my first one tomorrow since I'll be in the Bay Area."

She looked into her purse and took out a business card. Flipping it over, she wrote down the name and address of a coffee shop.

"Meet me here at 1 p.m."

I agreed, having actually no idea how that was going to occur.

⁂

You have the plan provided for every moment.
Rumi

CHAPTER 37

Finding myself between the Martial Rosemary and the Mercurial Annabella required a great deal of patience and finesse. I had mentioned to Rose that Annabella wished me to meet her at an Oakland café at 1 p.m. Was this possible? Clearly, I was making a demand for her to accommodate me. She said she could drop me off at the café on the way to the violin teacher. She could pick me up after the lesson at 3 p.m. at the same corner. We both assumed I'd meet Annabella, who would take me to get Rolfed, and then return me to the café.

As we left Vacaville, I was looking at my watch frequently, hoping I wasn't going to miss my chance to connect with this Rolfer. We arrived in Oakland at noon. Rose left me off at an intersection with a five-way stop and I had to figure out which direction to go. Well, I had an hour, I thought. I asked a person where this café was and they pointed the way.

I ordered a coffee, even though I wished I could order a lunch, but lack of money precluded this. At one o'clock Annabella showed up. She described Rolfing to me and the ten one-hour treatments. Then she asked me for the $500. I had a check book and wrote her a check.

"When will I be able to get my first treatment?" I asked.

"Not today. When will you be in Oakland next? I have my office here."

I had no idea. I told her I didn't have a car and lived at Via Del Sol. She thought about this for a few moments.

"Thursday's meeting is going to be at my house in Oakland. Can you get there at three? I can give you the treatment before the meeting."

I told her I will do my best to find a way. She gave me the address and then she looked at her watch.

"I have another appointment and have to go." She gave me a quick hug and departed.

I stayed at the café for another hour or so. Three cups of coffee sipped slowly was about as much as I could take. I paid the bill and walked out, trying to find stores to browse. At 3 p.m. I positioned myself at the corner where Rose had left me. She finally appeared and I jumped in the car.

"The violin lesson is still going on," she explained, "but I didn't want you to wait here in this neighborhood for long. Did you get your session?"

I explained the situation and heard Rose exhale loudly, as if to say, "typical." Whatever it was between Annabella and Rose ran deep.

We drove to the elegant home of this venerable violin maestro. His studio was dark wood with eight-paned windows. Light filtered through the leaves and branches of the old oak trees into the room in the gentlest way. It matched the gentility of the homeowners. His wife was old-school, too, graciously and warmly welcoming me, asking if I would like something to drink while we waited for the lesson to be finished. I declined and she quietly exited, stage left.

After the lesson, we drove back to Vacaville for a home-cooked meal with "the girls," as Rose referred to us. It was clear to me that the day was as it should be. I did not accomplish what I had set out to do, but that was because it was not in my hands. Relying so much on others is an interesting triad.

I can only hope that it leads me to where I want to go, and that I can accomplish the task Robert has given me.

❖

Do not fear to progress slowly, fear only to stand still.
                                                                Confucius

CHAPTER 38

I shared the elder daughter's bedroom, using the shag carpet as my foam pad under my sleeping bag. My sleeping bag was as necessary as a toothbrush. With it, I was able to stay anywhere there was a roof and a floor and a welcome.

The morning's breakfast fare was a surprise to me, but traditional for the family: hot blueberry pancakes with real maple syrup, bacon, and hot coffee. The smells of savory meat mingling with hot sugar and coffee made me happy. The pancakes were Rosemary's specialty, and she prepared them in a cast iron skillet. The elder daughter cooked the bacon and the younger prepared the coffee. I set the table.

As we sat down to eat, Rosemary asked me which work books I was reading.

"Collin's *The Theory of Celestial Influence* and Berman's book on endocrinology," I replied.

"Too complicated for me," was her response. She paused a moment.

"What did you learn?"

I began to explain how Berman's book and his work on the glands of the human body helped me to better understand the concept of body types, as Collin presented them in his book. It explains how glands are like receivers for planetary influences. I tried to correlate Berman's presentation with that of Collin on body type.

"I can't understand why you're not using your college education. You're smart, you know."

I said nothing. No, I thought, my sister was the smart one. Every time we fought as children, Dad would hold court as judge, whereby he would instruct us to plead our case. Kathy had a knack for impassioned, detailed rhetoric. I just focused on the simple truth of who got hit first (that would be me). She would win the case. Dad labeled her the Philadelphia Lawyer. I would then get hit with the paddle on my tushie, but because she would giggle at my punishment, she, too, would often get whacked. Dad was an impartial dispenser of justice.

After breakfast, the daughters had chores caring for their horses. Rosemary encouraged me to help out. I told them that I loved horses as a child and that I rode a quarter horse at the age of four. I made it sound like I was an expert equestrian, which I was not.

The actual story was that a friend of my father put me on the horse and then the horse took off. Everyone screamed as I flopped about on the huge saddle, holding on to the horn screaming, "Whoa! Whoa!", which was what I learned to say by watching television cowboy shows. It didn't work, obviously, because the Whoa was uttered by a four-year-old. It was an uncontrollable, frightening situation. An adult mentality inside of me, however, kicked in: I began to analyze my predicament. I reasoned, based on what I knew of my surroundings, that the horse was going toward the freeway. The most appropriate action, therefore, was to jump off before a truck hit the horse (and me) or worse: the horse took me far away from my family and I was never found again. So I dismounted and landed with open mouth in a pile of mud and horse droppings. Dad was right there. He soon brought a hose to rinse my mouth out. Yes, I was fine. I had a mild sore neck, but I faked the degree of soreness so I could watch television that night as a treat for my heroism.

The girls decided to go riding and wondered if I was interested. Sure, I said. The younger took her smaller horse that looked like a cross between a pony and a Palomino. I suddenly saw it perfectly suited her Jovial-Lunar body type: it was rounded and blond, just like her.

The elder daughter saddled her chestnut thoroughbred. With its long legs, it was an equine mirror of her. She was a Saturnine type. How interesting.

"Linda, you can ride Billy," said the elder.

Billy was part thoroughbred and part quarter horse.

"He's tricky to ride — always wants to do what he wants — so you have to ride him with a tight rein," she warned.

I felt I could handle it. It was good to sit on a horse again. The three of us were walking the horses on the main road of the family walnut orchard. The elder urged her thoroughbred to trot, and Billy decided to keep pace. As we approached a turn in the road that led to the house, Billy's ears suddenly pointed backwards toward me. Uh oh, I thought. That was not a good sign. It meant he was checking me out. And sure enough, having checked me out, he took off at a fast gallop. The girls let out a scream.

He was a devilish, Mercurial horse, running just under the large, fully leafed branches of the twenty-foot-high walnut trees. I held on with my legs, tightly embracing the saddle, ducking each branch as it rapidly came toward me. He's trying to knock me off! This was my childhood experience all over again. Where's he taking me? And then I saw, right ahead of me, that the road ended in a drainage ditch. He's going to stop abruptly there, and I'm going to go flying over his head.

Like hell I am. I yanked the reins back with adult force and repeatedly commanded WHOA!!!

He stopped just shy of the edge.

The girls rode up and Rosemary, who had watched the whole thing unfold from the kitchen window, ran outside.

"You could have killed yourself!" she said. Her concern was tinged with anger.

"It's fine, Rose," I replied, smiling.

A different part of me had emerged. This dangerous situation evoked a focus and confidence I had not known. The child with no arm strength and a weak voice, who was unable to handle a runaway horse, was replaced by an adult whose strength and commanding voice could contain the power of a beast with a mind of its own.

That experience had profound implications. This is the nature of evolution: whatever I cannot master now, I will be able to master in time, as long as I have the courage to face it, hold on tight, and not let it control me.

When man lacks wisdom, his mind is always restless and his senses are wild horses dragging the driver this way and that.

Upanishads

CHAPTER 39

I arrived at Annabella's home around 2:30 in the afternoon, expecting her to be there, even though our appointment was at three. She was not. So I sat on a stone ledge near the entry way, waiting for someone to appear. Ten minutes later, a lovely young woman showed up with a door key in her hand.

"Hello," she said. "Can I help you?"

I explained I was here to see Annabella for a treatment before the meeting. The fact I mentioned the meeting made her smile.

"I'm Vicki, her roommate. I'm also in the Fellowship. Come in."

Her figure was evenly proportioned. Her straight chestnut hair was perfectly cut and fell into its proper place when she moved. Chestnut eyes to match the chestnut hair were set in a creamy taupe skin. She was refined, and I wished I looked like her.

"I didn't realize Annabella had a roommate," I said casually. I thought Annabella was an independent woman, remember? Well, maybe she wasn't the person I imagined.

"Oh, yes, there are several of us living here. We're all in the school."

I was taken aback. I hadn't seen her at the Vacaville meetings or at Via Del Sol. And yet, she said she's in the school. It was like living in a four-bedroom home and discovering there was another annex filled with an extended family you never met.

The house was large with high beige ceilings and a sunken living room. A fireplace and twelve-foot glass windows that framed magnificent views of the lush green foliage of the Berkeley Hills gave the home a modern, airy, natural feel.

Vicki told me to make myself comfortable.

"I just came home to change clothes before I go out. I have plans for the evening," she explained, as she turned to enter her room.

The fact she was a student was a surprise, yet it was a greater shock that her plans for the evening did not include the meeting. What else could be more important? I couldn't fathom it.

I hadn't brought a magazine or book with me, and Vogue was not on her coffee table. So I sat on the couch that faced the fireplace. I checked my watch frequently.

Annabella entered just as Vicki was ready to leave. They spoke briefly in the kitchen. I sat watching.

"Hello, Linda. Let me set the room up first," Annabella said as she stepped into the living room.

"Okay," I replied, remaining seated.

When she ushered me into the room, there was a bed instead of a massage table. How odd, I thought. She told me to lie down on my back with just my underwear on. Staring at the ceiling, I wondered what was about to happen to me. I heard that it hurt.

She began with my shoulder area, pressing with the knuckle of her index finger, which had a huge callous on it from her work. She placed it near my collar bone and began to press. She kept pressing. She didn't stop. Her knuckle went deeper than I thought was possible — it was actually *under* the bone. Did it hurt? Yes. But it was such a foreign pain that somehow, through my wincing, I was able to withstand it. My curiosity was stronger than the discomfort.

She would periodically check with me, asking if I was all right. Of course, she stopped pressing when she asked, and of course, I was all right in that moment.

Then she began with my mouth.

She placed her fingers along the top gum line, pressing upwards toward the cheekbone. It was such an unexpected thing to do that something in me was examining her action as if studying it from the inside out. Her fingers went up, and up, and up, as if she was trying to break through the gum to touch the bone. The pain was sharp and invasive. I'm paying someone to torture me, I thought.

She worked on my feet and my legs and my belly button next. When she was done, I sat upright.

She then told me, "This first hour is a general treatment. We will go deeper next time."

I stared in disbelief. She laughed, as if she could now check off my reaction as a sign of her success. Everyone she touched, I'm sure, could not imagine how it could get more invasive. Only she knew what was to come.

She left me alone to dress and use the adjoining bathroom. Looking in the mirror, I could not believe what I saw.

My collar bone was clearly delineated like I had never seen it before. My face was refigured also. Like a mountain ridge magically rising above amorphous clouds, cheekbones appeared above my cheeks. Where did they come from? My psychology was altered, too. A childlike vulnerability that was not afraid had now made its appearance. It was quiet inside. It was a simple, content state.

After dressing, I went into the kitchen area. Annabella was standing over the stove, preparing something for us to eat. She started to talk about Robert and his diet.

"If he decides to go vegetarian, he's going to get a distended stomach."

She was referencing Kerrie's influence on him. I had no idea what a distended stomach was, but it sounded dangerous.

She continued to describe the right kind of diet he should be eating, while I deliberately inserted food into my mouth, hoping she wouldn't start questioning my eating habits. I personally had no idea what I should be eating. I ate whatever was put in front of me, basically, in large quantities. In my case, beggars can't be choosers.

* * * *

Students started to arrive, and I immediately saw Miles. The delicate state I was experiencing suddenly evaporated. A feeling of self-deprecation overwhelmed me, questioning my self-worth. I almost always had this experience whenever I saw him. I stared at him, as the 'I's began to wonder if there was any chance that our relationship could be saved, if the promises made could be kept. After Rolfing, I felt like a new person. Maybe he would recognize this and want me now.

This dark state was a strange mixture of sadness and wakefulness. The sadness was the never-ending longing for an imagined outcome that could never materialize, and the wakefulness came from that small bit of hope, which was like sunlight breaking through the clouds.

This time, I could see it was becoming predictable and was a bad habit. I looked away from him and sat quietly in the corner of the room, waiting for the meeting to begin.

* * * *

Robert faced the rows of students flanked by the usual lineup: Jim, Rosemary, Meg, and Mac. The meeting began with good householder.

Yorgos spoke about the need for students to help with the chicken octave. Two students raised their hands. Klair spoke about the need for students to help with the animal octave. One student raised her hand. Kerrie spoke about the need for students to help with the kitchen octave, specifically washing the dinner dishes on Saturday night. No one raised their hand. I wasn't interested since I was helping to cook. Linda, you could help, said an 'I' inside my head. But my hand wouldn't lift to volunteer the rest of my body. Then slowly, Miles's hand went up.

"This is why Miles is a man number five," said Robert. "He does what needs to be done."

I felt awful, like realizing you missed your bus ride home. The opportunity had passed.

Robert began to speak of super efforts.

"When you're tired and feel you have done your best, make another try with intensity and continue hard work. The person who continuously works hard at self-remembering eighteen hours a day will be the one to become conscious."

Listening to Robert, it seemed not only unimaginable, but almost a ridiculous request. Who could ever self-remember for eighteen hours straight?

Robert had introduced an exercise called the "looking exercise," whereby you moved your eyes every few seconds to a different impression without evoking internal 'I's about them. So let's say, your eyes land on a lamp. You are to look at the lamp and at yourself looking at the lamp without evoking a thought about the lamp or the fact you are looking at the lamp. This is the practice of divided attention. Then you would move your eyes to the next object in the room while holding this level of presence.

I couldn't do it. Each time my gaze moved to the table that held the lamp, I would lose my divided attention, and thoughts or 'I's would flood into my head. I eventually gave this exercise up. The looking exercise reminded me of the circus performers who juggle plates on sticks. Inevitably, the plates dropped with a loud crash.

It could have been a disheartening meeting, but it wasn't. Although I couldn't do what Robert was instructing, I remembered Billy the horse and the feeling of mastering what was hopeless eighteen years earlier. This teaching had the tools to help me, without a doubt. To awaken, one must want it badly enough for a long, long time.

I knew I wanted it badly enough. I just needed a load of perseverance and patience. What other choice do I have?

❖

Continue, because you must.
Johann Goethe

CHAPTER 40

I slept all the way to Via Del Sol, getting a ride with a few students after the meeting. We arrived in the dark around three in the morning.

It was a slow start to Friday morning. Robert hadn't returned, and we once again took our time. Somehow cows were milked, chickens were fed, the laundry was washed, and a few students would leave for the skinny-dipping river run to cool off after lunch. It was now the end of July. Via Del Sol was not yet a month old.

In the afternoon I decided to take a walk, and when I returned, I saw Alden at the edge of the patio facing the house. He sat on a stool with a canvas and easel in front of him. When I approached him from the back, I watched as he applied paint to this image of the rustic log cabin before him.

He turned to smile at me, with a pipe dangling from his mouth.

"I had no idea you could paint," I said to him.

"Oh yes," he replied, nonchalantly.

It was funny, I thought, how the normal chitchat one would have with people one encountered, asking them questions about themselves, just did not seem appropriate to students in the school. I actually knew little about anyone here.

I watched as he applied the olive color to the leaves on the canvas of the giant oak tree next to the cabin.

"Are you going to add the two big oaks in the back that hang over the cabin? They are missing from your painting."

"No."

"Why?"

"This is more artistically balanced."

I thought it was odd that he was painting what he wanted to see, not what he saw. But I let it go.

"Harold was out here doing a few sketches. Did you see them?" Alden asked.

"No," I said.

"He sketches in about thirty minutes. I prefer to take my time," he stated, as he continued to dab a little brown here and there.

I had the distinct impression that Alden was trying to be an artist, like I wanted to be a writer. It was the idea that was so appealing.

He placed his brushes and other items into a wooden case after about fifteen minutes. I asked him whether the painting was done.

"No, it's a work-in-progress," he replied.

He folded his easel and went back to his RV.

* * * *

After he left, I remained on the patio. The experience I just shared with Alden churned up a memory of sorts that contained valuable insight. I waited for the thoughts to emerge.

It took several minutes before I realized what this moment with Alden reminded me of: the Norman Rockwell painting of Norman Rockwell painting Norman Rockwell painting. It was referred to as the "Triple Portrait," and I remember it well from *The Saturday Evening Post* magazine article about the American artist. Rockwell is sitting on a stool in front of his easel that held the portrait he is painting. But instead of looking at the portrait, he is leaning over to the side to look into a full-length mirror of himself at his features, which he is trying to capture accurately. His painting depicts him in this position.

The curious thing to me when I first saw the "Triple Portrait" was: Who is capturing this entire scene from behind the seated Rockwell? The actual artist is not shown in the painting. He is invisible. It is this invisible artist who imprinted the moment on canvas. He is in the position of the silent observer. He exists outside of the picture.

I recalled that in his book *Tertium Organum,* Ouspensky described what he termed Space-Sense and Time-Sense and different dimensions. First dimension was a point. Second dimension was that point moving on a surface and creating a line. Third dimension was that line moving on a plane, creating a solid (e.g., a square becoming a cube, a triangle becoming a pyramid). Then the fourth dimension was that solid as it moved through time. Or so he wrote and so I read.

Ouspensky's writings all made sense to me intellectually because it seemed logical, but I could not imagine exactly how it worked. So I sat in a chair on the patio and gave my thoughts free rein.

By standing behind Alden, watching him paint, I was in the position of the invisible artist who witnessed a fourth dimensional "object," so to speak — Alden painting the cabin on canvas at that point in time. If I press that "object" into my memory for safe-keeping through self-remembering, however, I have captured and locked it into a timeless eternity.

Robert said that we are trying to be outside of time. What could possibly be outside of time? Perhaps the astral body, the soul, the spirit — whatever you want to call it. It, alone, is invisible and not part of the physical world of the third dimension, or even the fourth dimension of time. It functions in the third dimension, has access to the fourth dimension, but exists in another dimension — one that is timeless. What would that dimension be?

Are there truly higher dimensions, and if so, *can we actually experience them now?*

That thought led to another puzzling question: When I die and leave this body, how will I be able move through space and see without physical eyes?

I looked at the weeping willow and the pond in front of me and tried to imagine seeing them without having physical eyes. The photo of the "Triple Portrait" came to me. Memories are like snapshots that often include ourselves in them.

For example, when I review the memory of the first time I met Miles, I can see Linda extending her hand to him with Kathy to the right and Dad and Mom behind Linda. There is no audio. It is a single picture in my mind. But where is the vantage point of the cameraman, the invisible observer? It is positioned about a foot above Linda, looking down upon her. This image does not appear through Linda's physical eyes, as she sees the scene. She's just a figure in the scene; she is not the cameraman that captured this scene, this object in time, as memory. Who or what is this cameraman? *Could it be my astral body levitating above the physical body and taking the photo? Could this observer be Me in a higher dimension?*

This track of thinking gave me my first sense that what is intrinsic in me not only is independent of my body, but can survive death and has properties of its own about which I know virtually nothing. The fact that this part does not need the body deepened my understanding that consciousness is not functions. It also made me contemplate that immortality may not merely be wishful thinking or a hoped-for fantasy. It may actually be a *future reality of me.*

❖

> *If there is no divine dimension to what we are doing,*
> *then whatever we do is merely killing time. On the other hand,*
> *if the presence of God overlaps simultaneously with whatever*
> *we are doing, then anything we work on performs eternity.*
> Bahauddin

CHAPTER 41

Kerrie hadn't returned yet from Berkeley with the food supplies for the weekend. Friday evening was approaching quickly, and about six students came into the kitchen looking for dinner. I was still in charge of the kitchen since Rosemary, Jan, and Trisha were gone as well. I looked into the cooler room and all I could find was a head of cabbage. What could I do with a head of cabbage, I wondered. We had milk from the cow. Perhaps I could make cream of cabbage soup. That sounded good.

I pictured it in my head. I took a stock pot and filled it with milk and placed the head of cabbage in the pot. I turned the heat on and waited until it boiled. I looked into the pot several times and couldn't understand why the cabbage leaves didn't soften and fall into the milk. Surely this would happen. I added salt and pepper to taste and watched the pot. The milk began to boil, so I turned the heat down to a simmer.

Several students came in and I told them to come back in thirty minutes. The soup will be ready by then, I was sure. When they returned, however, the head was still intact, and I had no choice but to serve them the soup. I grabbed the ladle and started placing the milk into their bowls.

"What is this?!" asked one student, belligerently.

"Cream of cabbage soup!" I blurted out. An explosive fire had built up inside of me fueled by frustration, embarrassment, and anger. Who was I angry at? The cabbage head that stubbornly refused to cooperate.

My heated words apparently hit them in the stomach as I watched each student recoil. Some pursed their lips in a desperate attempt to remove the smile from their mouths. Others extended their bowl timidly and looked away when it was their turn to receive the white liquid from the ladle, which pummeled the hard, uncooked yellow head of the vegetable violently against the sides of the pot in search of the remaining milk.

After serving about six customers, the sound of a van backing up toward the house was heard. The bowls were quickly placed on the counter, and the students ran out to greet Kerrie, helping her carry the most wonderful palettes of fresh food into the cooler.

I quickly poured the remaining milk down the drain and dumped the willful cabbage head that was the source of my humiliation into the organic garbage bin, where it belonged.

We all gathered around the kitchen counter happily slicing fresh-baked San Francisco sourdough bread, slathering it with soft cheese and piling on tomato and avocado slices garnished with alfalfa sprouts. Dinner never tasted so good.

* * * *

Saturday morning started slowly. As I was eating my first spoonful of granola, Clark came into the kitchen. He and Laura always seemed to brighten my day. He was a Jovial type and she was a Mercurial — maximum attraction according to the enneagram and body type information.

Clark went into the cooler, but instead of bringing back granola, he had in his hand four bulbs of garlic. He started to peel the garlic and pop the cloves into his mouth. I was shocked.

"What are you doing?" I asked him.

"I'm coming down with a cold and Laura told me to eat some garlic."

He finished the two bulbs, but the third one was difficult to get down. Because Clark was a Yoga teacher, he was disciplined. He got the third one down and then started on the fourth but couldn't do it. The smell of garlic was now mixing with my granola and milk; I had to go outside to finish my breakfast.

By this time, others had entered the kitchen. They too left quickly. The whole kitchen was reeking of garlic.

Laura was coming down the hill from where they both slept at night. We greeted each other, and then she went in to see Clark.

"Clark, what did you do?!" I could hear her asking.

"I could only eat three cloves."

Looking at the counter, Laura said: "Clark, you ate THREE BULBS! THIS is a clove," she explained, holding up a sample.

He started to laugh and then tried to kiss her. She pushed him away giggling at his silliness and ran out of the house. He chased her and grabbed her.

Their playfulness was such fun to watch. But then something happened to me. It was like a black cloud that came out of nowhere. I became painfully sad, and a deep longing that had existed since childhood overwhelmed me. I was suddenly dumbfounded by what I saw. How did they establish this loving relationship? How do you do that? I had no idea.

Just as these 'I's began to circulate, I turned and saw cars ascending the road in the distance. Students were arriving for the weekend. There were Robert and Jim in their cowboy hats, striding toward the house. Don and Doris were behind them, too, and Rosemary. They must have driven in a caravan of cars. And then I saw Miles and Helga. I immediately got up and went into the house.

Moving quickly past the odorous kitchen, I went to the upstairs bathroom and closed the door. On the left of the sink was a window that had a bird's-eye view of the front patio. I felt safe at this perch. I watched as Robert, Jim, Rosemary, and Miles and Helga stood together speaking about some important and timely topic. Robert smiled at some news. I wished I had the sound on for this film, but the subject was nothing I could ascertain. Something was going on.

A knock on the door frame dislodged me from the room. I passed the student who wanted to use the toilet and went directly downstairs into the kitchen. I wanted to look busy when Robert entered the house. Kerrie had appeared and began to rub cut lemons on the wooden counters. This trick did wonders for the strong garlic smell. She asked if I was available to help with lunch. I immediately said, Yes.

As I was slicing tomatoes, Robert entered with the entourage. They stopped near the fireplace and Robert began to explain how he wanted the new architect to remodel the living space. New architect?

As I listened to the course of the conversation, I would learn that Helga had an old friend from Marin who was an architect, and he and his wife had magnetic centers. Robert wanted these people to receive the three prospective student meetings as soon as possible.

Robert and Jim had walked away with Don and Doris to another part of the house. I used my peripheral vision to see Miles and Helga talking and planning. That pain in my heart hadn't subsided; in fact, it surged, bringing tears to my eyes. Today was July 31, 1971. Tomorrow was the first day of August. What would the new month bring?

* * * *

Sunday morning, I arose late from my sleeping bag and when I entered the house, students were already eating breakfast. It was a classic American Sunday brunch with scrambled eggs, hash browns, pancakes, toast and coffee. I went directly to the buffet and grabbed a plate and piled food on it while still in my nightgown. My appetite had been increasing of late, and I recognized that emptiness. It was emotional.

Robert saw me eating. He handed Jim his finished plate and rose from his director's chair. He came up to me.

"Make sure you dress before eating."

I immediately left my plate and started to get up. He then kindly added.

"It's fine for now, but in the future."

I hadn't realized until he gave me this photograph that different buffers had dropped. Buffers were described as psychological devices that prevented us from seeing something about ourselves. Removing them can be disturbing and painful. How did I suddenly go from being such a prude to walking around with just a nightgown in public? The Linda from San Diego and the Linda at Via Del Sol were two different Linda's. How did I become this Linda?

After showering and dressing, I went outside where Robert was sitting in his director's chair. There were Meg and Harold, Rosemary and Anna, Don and Doris, Miles and Helga, Alden and Bonita, as well as David. We sat casually with the teacher. It was not a meeting exactly. Robert was speaking quietly to Meg, who sat next to him. Then his soft voice rose to address everyone.

"We will be a large school, attracting people from around the world."

His eyes narrowed and his mouth was set firmly. That tilt of the head upward gave the impression that he was receiving information from some higher source. He continued.

"You will come to understand that joining the school so early is a privilege." He paused for a long while. We all looked at him waiting for more information.

"There are people who are not born yet that will be part of our school."

I looked around and saw some people were not as riveted as I was. Robert's comments were quite astounding to consider. Why? Because we were just a bunch of local people. In fact, I guess you could say I was the first "foreign student," having joined outside of the Bay Area. How could we possibly be global? We are not organized at all. And if we were, who would be interested in what we are doing when there are so many other groups out there?

Almost as if Robert were reading my mind, he added, "Please do your best to find people who may be interested in joining." Then he spoke about this architect that Helga had found. Others began to speak about people they knew who might be interested.

I sat there, listening. No one I had encountered in my life exhibited magnetic center qualities. I wanted to help the school grow, yet I realized that bringing someone in may not be my contribution. I would have to be content with that.

※

> *The question, O me! so sad, recurring —*
> *What good amid these, O me, O life?*
> *Answer. That you are here — that life exists and identity,*
> *That the powerful play goes on, and you may contribute a verse.*
> Walt Whitman

CHAPTER 42

I stayed at Via Del Sol that first week of August, having found a certain rhythm to my days. Talk had begun about prospective student meetings and those who were in the process of joining. It was as if we were planting seeds to see if some would grow. We would give the water of knowledge and, combined with the fertilizer of personal sufferings, some may recognize their dilemma, while others may choose to content themselves with the angst or pleasure of living one's life in sleep. This seemed to be the inner meaning of the Parable of the Sower in the Bible.

I was so looking forward to the weekend since that was when the tents were scheduled to arrive. Finally, I would have my own place to put my books and other things that were still stored upstairs in the house.

When Don arrived Saturday morning with the tents, I immediately went up to him to secure mine. It was in a large flat cellophane package and surprisingly heavy. I took it to my site and found the fellow who said he would help me nearby. He had just put up his own tent.

"Where are the ropes and spikes?" he asked.

"Huh?" I replied, having no idea what he meant.

"Linda," he said, shaking his head in disbelief, "you need ropes and spikes to secure the tent."

I explained that this is all I got from Don. He assured me that there were other parts, and I watched him lope down the hill to the house to find them. What did I know about camping? The only time I went camping as a child was with the Girl Scouts. Some parents brought tents with them; mine did not. Instead, my mother, who was the Girl Scout leader for our troop, told us to find our own spots under the stars. My sister gravitated toward other girls, leaving me alone. They grouped their bags together, like a slumber party. There was no room for me there, she said. So I found a wonderful spot between two trees. They started to giggle. I had no idea why. I noticed there were some holes in the ground but figured I could just cover them with my bag. What I didn't know until the morning was that I placed my bag over several ant hills. They were crawling all over me by dawn.

He returned with additional cellophane packages. He measured out the site with his feet and tossed the big rocks outside the perimeter. It was a rocky place, and there were still smaller stones in the dirt.

"Do you want to remove them by hand? That might take some time."

I told him that it would be fine as it is. I was in a hurry. He wanted me to know that I would feel the pebbles through the plastic floor of the tent.

"I plan to use my foam pad under my sleeping bag, so it should be fine," I repeated. What I didn't realize until later was that I would feel the stones with every step of my bare feet.

The tent was not an easy thing to put up since the land was on a slight slope. We both worked together. I would hold the rope on one side while he positioned the opposing spike. We laughed a bit whenever it was off-balance and we had to redo it. Eventually, the olive-green tent stood. I was home.

After lunch I brought my box of books and foam pad with sleeping bag to the tent. No more would I have to sleep under the fig tree.

* * * *

I heard rustling outside my tent as the morning light illuminated the olive fabric. It was Sunday morning, and the little tent neighborhood was rousing. I checked my watch. It was 7:30 a.m., and I wasn't ready to start, so I rolled over and fell back to sleep.

When I arose at 9:30, it was unusually quiet. I quickly dressed and descended the hill to the house. Breakfast was over, so I went into the cooler for my customary granola and milk and took the bowl outside to eat.

I joined a few who were just finishing their breakfast and entered the conversation about tent sites. One of these was Meg's teenage daughter. She was tall for her age of sixteen, with straight blond hair and almond eyes. Her figure was athletic, and it was strange to think of her as Meg's daughter since it was virtually impossible to trace a mutual ancestry just by looking at them. I took a liking to her for some reason. Perhaps it was that she seemed so independent and iconoclastic.

"I have a pup tent behind the barn," she explained. "I'm not spending that kind of money on a fancy tent."

"Does Robert have a tent?" I asked.

"I heard that he picked a spot high on the hill and wants a deck built like Don and Doris," said one student.

"Jim and Yorgos are helping to build it," said another.

We sat there watching others, as there didn't seem to be a group octave for the morning. Then Meg's daughter turned to me and asked if I wanted to see her tent.

"Sure," I replied.

After washing my bowl and cup, we headed down the hill. There, in the bushes behind the barn, was an army surplus tent for one. We crawled inside and sat on her sleeping bag. It was as rustic as could be: no flooring like my tent, only dirt. She had a small box of belongings. I then realized she had almost no wardrobe: I only recall her wearing a short-sleeved beige cotton blouse and beige pants. We spoke a bit and then exited.

Standing outside, she pulled out her cigarettes and lighter.

"Want one?" she asked.

I told her I never smoked before.

"Go ahead and try one."

She slapped the pack to dislodge a single cigarette and I reached out to pull it free. I placed it in my mouth. She used her Bic lighter to light it, but the burning tip went out. She shook her head and laughed.

"No, you have to inhale when I light it."

So she tried again and I inhaled. Immediately I started to choke, and again she laughed.

"I'm not good at this," I said apologetically.

"There's always a first time," she said encouragingly.

She lit her own and showed me how to inhale, hold the breath for a moment, and then blow the smoke out. I followed suit.

Dizziness hit me hard, so, to regain my balance, I reached for the nearest thing to steady me: the tent. Her reflexes were keen, as she grabbed my other arm and pulled me upright before my full body weight landed on her little abode.

We sat on the ground with legs crossed swami style, finishing our cigarettes. I tried to imitate the nonchalant gestures: the relaxed positioning of the fingers as they formed a letter "C" and the extended arm over the leg. I looked Cool, like the James Dean poster on my bedroom wall showing his cigarette dangling from those sexy lips.

I remember my parents pounding into our heads never to start smoking since it was an addiction they struggled with before I was born. They called it a "dirty habit." I felt thrilled by my disobedience and free of their chains on me.

Rebellion at twenty-two was empowering.

*
> *The root of every act of rebellion, every appetite and every moment of heedlessness is satisfaction with one's lower self.*
>
> Ibn 'Ata' Allah

CHAPTER 43

The lazy days of summer continued. Robert tried to find enough students to organize a work octave at the start of the week. Because the heat was still intense during the daytime, it proved challenging, since the local watering holes were calling many to a refreshing skinny dip.

The Residents were becoming more and more rustic. The men were growing unkempt beards and the women were dressing skimpily. Cleanliness was a hard standard to maintain, both for the house and for our bodies. I had been skipping showers, and Robert mentioned at an evening meeting that we each should maintain our daily hygiene. I got the message.

One of the improvements to the house that second week of August was a new carpet for the living room. Watching the men lay plywood on the vinyl floor that we had covered only a week or so earlier left me with a strange feeling: the old, crooked tiles I had put down that first week are now part of some archeological site, burying my experience and conscious moments under *two* layers of time past. We were moving so fast that I felt I was part of some cosmic time machine.

The absence of a tangible love interest, and my chosen habit of coping with emotional pain, resulted in additional cellular bulk. I was getting fat while my pocketbook, on the other hand, was getting thin. I needed to search for those massage customers if I was going to stay financially afloat. I mentioned to Bonita that I wanted to start giving massages, and she suggested I give one to Jan, who had asked her for one. Jan took a look at my hands and commented, "They are small." "They are strong," corrected Bonita. That was a great sales pitch, and I appreciated it.

Jan and I had arranged a time in the late afternoon, and I got a male student to help me set up the massage table outside under a large oak not far from my tent site. I borrowed some oil from Bonita. As I worked my way down Jan's spine, I suddenly experienced a tremendous release of her energy coursing through my fingers. It woke me up. I told Jan and she said that was the location of her pain. After the treatment, she told me she felt much better. I realized I may actually have a talent here. She paid me the five dollars, and I asked her if she would spread the word to others who may be interested in a massage. She agreed to help me.

Word did spread, and my next customer that week was Marie. She was shyer than Jan, who was a Yoga instructor and accustomed to body work. Marie wanted to go to a secluded spot, which made lugging the massage table a challenge. No one would help me that day, so I had to explain to Marie that the both of us would have to carry it into the woods. We picked a place well behind the barn and into the thickets. The issue, of course, was that I needed to find flat ground at least the size of the table to stabilize it. We found an opening and Marie and I set it up.

The time was late afternoon. The heat was still oppressive, so I removed all of my clothes except my panties, being confident that our location was secluded. Marie quickly disrobed as well and placed her naked body on a sheet I used to separate her flesh from the leather covering, which was hot. I placed another sheet over the parts of the body I wasn't massaging. It was a quiet day, with the birds chirping and the insects humming in the background. I was now in a meditative, intentionally moving zone as I brought presence to each touch of her muscles and spine, applying the right amount of pressure to relieve her stress.

Fifteen minutes had passed, and I was moving to a different part of her body when I first heard a distant rumble. It grew louder, and the noise was mixed with voices. Who could that be? We were in such a remote place, we thought.

Emerging from behind a large clump of manzanita bushes was a truck with men standing in the back and Yorgos behind the wheel. I continued as if I didn't see them, hoping they would drive away as soon as possible. But they didn't. They stopped and stared.

At dinner that evening, I went up to Yorgos.

"What were you doing in that truck?" I asked him pointedly.

He chuckled. "What were you doing?"

I was giving a massage, I explained. I thought it was obvious.

"Well," he said, "I was showing them possible tent sites. We got a better view than we thought we would," he said laughingly.

Once again it was clear there was no place to hide.

* * * *

I would be lying if I said I didn't think about and yearn for Miles still. It was a strange topic for me. Some 'I's would wish for our lives to be intertwined in a loving relationship, growing stronger and deeper with each passing day; other 'I's were grateful that he was gone from my life and with Helga now. Such mixed emotions concealed a real and deep truth: Not only did I have no control over my life, I had no idea why things were unfolding as they were. I desperately wanted to *understand the why of events*. That was a greater source of burning than the pain of lost love or the rage of betrayal.

I remember as a child watching a Hollywood movie of the Greek hero Jason and the Argonauts. He was going through his trials and tribulations while the gods watched overhead, commenting with focused interest. Even in John Milton's *Paradise Lost*, God speaks with Jesus and describes exactly what Satan will do, but cautions Christ not to worry. Why? He explains to Jesus that He already wrote *Paradise Regained* so "All's Well That End's Well." Paradise Lost had to play out so Paradise Regained could occur.

The separation of earthly drama and heavenly intervention was what fascinated me. I wanted to be the one in Heaven with full knowledge of what was happening and why it was needed.

One of my favorite Jewish jokes was that of the rabbi who played golf on the Sabbath. From Heaven, Moses sees the breaking of the law and speaks to God about it. "Do something," implores Moses. God looks at the man and with a single nod says, "It is done." The Rabbi steps up to the first tee, swings and hits a hole in one. "What!" cries out Moses to God, "I thought you would punish him!" God answers. "I did." Moses replies, "He hit a hole in one!" God, in His wisdom, explains, "Yes...But who can he tell?"

To help me understand a more heavenly explanation, I turned to the work books to find some objective perspective. As I understood from my readings, according to Gurdjieff and Ouspensky, the universe is governed by laws, primarily the law of three and the law of octaves. Could I apply this to what is happening to me? That is, could I make the theoretical, practical?

After dinner I would lie on my sleeping bag inside my tent, positioning the beam of my red plastic flashlight on the pages of my canvas-covered three-ring binder, and map out the law of octaves as it pertained to my current situation.

Do — December 1970: First meet Miles/Start of the Octave
Re — January 1971: Correspond with Miles
Mi — February 1971: Study work books
MI-FA INTERVAL
Fa — March 1971: Meet Robert and decide to join the Fellowship
Sol — April 1971: Return to LA
La — May 1971: Prepare to move North
Si — June 1971: Move North/change in Miles's attitude
SI-DO INTERVAL
Do — July 1971: Breakup

It seemed to map out nicely, which made me feel that what happened was God's plan for me.

Then I would focus on the law of three, which also is referred to as triads or processes. It states that at any given moment there is a neutral force, a passive force, and an active force that combine to produce a given result. Any matter can assume any type of force in relation to the other two. This meant that I can be the neutral, passive, or active force in any given moment.

I wrote down how the three of us manifested in different scenes of our play together. I continued to do this each night. As an example, when I would approach Miles, I would be the active force and he would be the passive force. Helga was a neutral force that eventually would determine the outcome. I must confess, however, that sometimes I had to imagine the rationale behind an action or nonaction just to make my triad work. I was certainly a novice at this.

Logic brings order and can be exceedingly soothing to a machine with many 'I's. Controlling one's behavior was the method to becoming less of a machine, according to my readings: before one can awaken, it was said, one's centers must be balanced to minimize or eliminate wrong work. This was the theory.

But after a few months in this school of awakening, it was only when my world fell apart that consciousness entered the equation. I didn't want to be a balanced machine. I wanted to be free of the machine. That meant separating the conscious being from the machine.

How does one do that?

※

Gods are fighting for us, whose responsibility we are.
Plato

CHAPTER 44

The influx of the Weekenders began that Saturday in mid-August. New students were appearing at Via Del Sol in the late afternoon. A couple from Vacaville were introduced to Robert by Mac and Rosemary. His occupation was a water and irrigation specialist, which Robert was delighted to hear. She was a Jovial type and an elementary school teacher. Their attire made it clear to me that they both were mid-Western Americans: he wore black pants and a white short-sleeved shirt with a pocket for pencils; she wore a colorful blouse and coordinated floral pants.

But the big news of the day was the arrival of the Architect. His lean body indicated he was moving centered. His wife was exotic with her colorful fabrics and darker skin. Her face was small and delicate. I was told she was a friend of Helga, although their connection was unknown to me. They had also brought another person, a short Venusian man with thick black hair and beady eyes. His name was Bill.

The house was bustling by early Saturday evening. The sun still had time to set since it was midsummer. Food preparation had begun in earnest, with Jan, Rosemary, and Kerrie leading the charge. The menu was vegetarian. Robert had wanted Jan to prepare a cheese sauce that he liked to put over the broccoli to make it edible for him. Anna was there as well, squeezing herself between the ladies as she made her way to the small refrigerator to store the aluminum-wrapped roast beef that would be her little dog Pepper's dinner.

I stood in the middle of the room looking at the bustle in the kitchen to the left and trying to listen to Robert's conversation with the Architect to the right that included Miles and Helga.

Robert began to tell the Architect what he wanted, beginning with opening up the living room, removing the counter that separated the kitchen and living room, and replacing the west wall with windows. A main post was in the middle of the room, and Robert insisted it needed to be removed. The Architect laughed and said it was impossible — that post was essential to the structural integrity of the building. Robert repeated his request.

"Robert," the Architect replied, "it's holding up the roof."

Robert had a serious look on his face.

"We will start in the morning," he said before walking away.

End of conversation.

* * * *

When I came down from my tent Sunday morning, men were ripping out all three sides of the u-shaped kitchen's countertops, including their attachments to the floor. Portable tables had been set outside to accommodate lunch preparations. Robert was standing next to the Architect, Don the designer, and Miles. Don had made a sketch of the new plans, and they were studying it on a makeshift design table (two sawhorses and a piece of plywood) that had been set up outside of the house.

The air was thick with sawdust as I worked my way to the cooler to fetch some granola. I stayed there munching until my stomach called for some liquid. A big urn was always available during the workday for coffee, so I grabbed a cup. Everywhere I stood I was herded off by construction. The kitchen counters now would be lining the area in a two-sided L shape, with one-side surrounding the refrigerator and stove and the shorter side with the sink in the middle. This opened up the kitchen area to the living room, which was Robert's request. It was a nifty design, but the absence of that extra countertop for food preparation clearly lacked practicality.

Because the outside of the house remained the same, no one would know that the kitchen had been altered or that, in fact, the farmhouse had changed in any way. It was clear that Robert was trying to improve our living situation as quickly as possible, especially since new students were arriving every day and summer would soon be over. There was a tension I felt between the Architect and Don the designer, both of whom tried to be helpful and positive when around Robert, but seemed not to understand the language of Robert's vision and so had different approaches.

THE DIVINE BEGINNING

The truth was no one understood Robert's vision. It seemed as if he was making it up as he went along. The lack of properly designed plans was testing the professionals. Vision-Design-Construction seemed to be the correct three notes in a building octave (*do-re-mi*). But Robert wanted to skip the second note and go from Vision to Construction.

This young teacher, I felt, definitely had a sense of urgency and yet he was never in a hurry. It was an odd thing to see. Here was a man who knew the *sense of time*. As for the rest of us, we were content to take the familiar roads, which took longer and were more secure. The triad had been set up. Robert was the first, or active, force; Don and the Architect were the second, or denying, forces. But who was the third, invisible force that could resolve the two to produce the required result?

I had no idea. At this point, all I could do was observe how things unfolded. Accurate analysis would have to be done in hindsight.

* * * *

Monday morning revealed that Don and the Architect had returned to work in Vacaville and Marin, respectively, while their families, whom they brought, remained at Via Del Sol. This meant the second forces in the construction octave were removed and the third force, apparently, had never appeared. Renovation would have to wait.

That fellow Bill, however, had decided to stay.

The new kitchen counters were nice to see, greeting one in the morning. Anna was there with her little dog, whose round black eyes looked up to her with hungry anticipation. She opened the refrigerator door to prepare the pot roast breakfast for Pepper, but the aluminum wrapping only held a piece of meat the size of a tablespoon.

"WHAT!" screamed Anna.

She showed all who were there the lack of beef and started to interrogate everyone she saw. While she was questioning some students, Bill entered and went right to the fridge, bending over to reach the shelf that had held the roast. Anna who was savvy, noticed this, and quickly yelled, "YOU!" She had found her culprit.

I listened to the conversation. It was better than television. According to Bill, the vegetarian diet was boring to him and he saw the beef and felt it was his for the taking since it didn't have a name on it. Anna couldn't replace the eaten food so she turned and left him there, with little Pepper following closely at her heels. The other students watching with me made comments like: "It's his tramp feature;" "No, he's got a greed feature;" "It's vanity: why does he think he's special?"

Bill irritated everyone. He came to be known as the student with seven chief features.

⁂

We are entirely made up of bits and pieces,
woven together so diversely and so shapelessly
that each one of them pulls its own way at every moment.
                                                            Michel de Montaigne

CHAPTER 45

Tuesday's meeting was at Rosemary's house in Vacaville. I got a ride with Klair. It was just the two of us and I sat in the passenger seat. She was not a talkative sort, and I kept dozing off. Just as we passed Davis, I closed my eyes. She thwacked me with her hand to wake me up. It worked.

Klair took me to Rosemary's house before going to her own. I had my sleeping bag with me, my toiletries and a change of clothes for the meeting. I was so glad to be in a real home. Rose was there and so was her elder daughter. It was late afternoon and my plan was to groom myself before the meeting.

I used the girls' bathroom, with its dark evergreen walls and mustard-colored basin, and started to shave my legs with a Norelco electric razor that I owned. My skin was thin, and razor blades had nicked me badly so this was something I'd used for years. The problem was it took a long time to remove the stubble on my legs. The shaver was meant for a man's face, not a woman's large legs.

Just as I finished one leg and started on the other, the electricity in the house went off. A moment of irritation arose until I realized the light *inside* of me went on. I started to laugh. I could *sense* the gods' Giggle in Heaven, once again: they had pulled the plug leaving me with one hairy leg to stand on.

I emerged from the bathroom to see what the situation was and Rosemary said it may take longer for the lights to go on, so we should prepare the room with candles for the meeting.

"Mac's coming early since he's leading the meeting. I'll have him check it out," she offered casually.

"Not Robert?" I asked, a bit disappointed, although not entirely surprised. It was not unusual for us not to know where the teacher was or what he was doing. He had a magical way of showing up and disappearing.

"Robert is not coming. He's chosen some students to lead meetings when he's not around."

"Like who?"

"Mac, Miles, Meg, Yorgos, and Richard. That's what I was told."

I knew four of the five well, but not the fifth.

"Why Richard?"

"I don't know," she replied. "Both he and Mac work at Kaiser hospital. He's a doctor, too. Richard enjoys classical music like Mac. He's a good householder." She left it at that.

I could recognize Richard was a Venusian type — medium height, brown hair, cellular bulk, and a non-existence feature — but because I never had a conversation with him, I couldn't tell you what made him tick. Although he was quiet, he seemed to me to have a traditional, conservative way of looking at the world. I had seen Richard with his wife Alice, who was a tall Lunar type, at Via Del Sol with three of their children during the summer (Stevie was one of them). Richard was clearly the breadwinner, while Alice was the homemaker.

After this short talk, we returned to our duties. Rosemary handed me candles to place on the fireplace mantel and side tables. We lit them, but the room was still dark as the meeting time approached.

Mac arrived late, and had to make do with the dim lighting. He had no thoughts about checking the electricity, saying it wasn't up to him, but up to the utility company. Rose let it go.

There were about twenty-five of us gathered, a surprisingly large crowd. Perhaps others expected Robert, too. We took our seats, and waited for Mac, who appeared relaxed and comfortable in this role, to start the meeting.

"Are there any questions?"

A student from Vacaville raised her hand. "How can we see body types?"

He stood up and asked us to rearrange the chairs in the room. Mac had the idea to line up students in the front as they represented the body types of the enneagram: Pure Lunar, Lunar-Venusian, Pure Venusian, Venusian-Mercury, Pure Mercury, Mercury-Saturn, Pure Saturn, Saturn-Mars, Pure Mars, Mars-Jovial, Pure Jovial, Jovial-Lunar. We skipped the Solar type because it was so rare, we were told. It was the "Snow White" type and no one had seen one before.

I was selected to stand as Pure Venusian. It seemed fun to be chosen, although I didn't consider myself this type exactly. Mac began with the Pure Lunar type, and asked what the strengths and weaknesses are. Someone raised their hand and said, "Cool, instinctive certainty." Another said, "Midmost point of femininity." And weaknesses? The same students responded with: "Stubborn." "Lunatic." Mac skipped the mixed type of Lunar-Venusian, and went straight to me.

"Linda represents the Pure Venusian type. What are the weaknesses?"
"Tramp."
"Non-existence."
"Sloppy."
"Lazy."
My shoulders slumped as if I had taken each comment as a physical blow.
"Strengths?" asked Mac.
Silence.
Then a loud voice came from the dark.
"They're GOOD COOKS!"
It was Rosemary's.

In my case, I thought that was a generous observation, but more importantly I understood how Mars and Venus types are maximum attraction: Rose, who was Pure Martial, was a warrior — faithful and protective. Mac didn't have the nerve to put her up on stage to represent her type nor to take the stage himself as a classic Jovial.

When we finished the cycle of types, Mac decided to end the meeting. It was the harmonious thing to do.

* * * *

Breakfast Wednesday morning at Rose's home was leisurely and late. It was more of a brunch than a breakfast. Rose and her daughters and I sat at the table, with our plates of scrambled eggs, bacon, toast with butter and jam and coffee. After an hour of discussing the job that Mac did leading the meeting the previous night, the rear kitchen door opened. There was Trisha. She had her blond hair pulled back into a pony tail and wore a blouse and baggy shorts. Her Venusian type and Rose's Martial made them good friends. She joined the discussion.

"Did you see how Mac tried to humiliate Linda?" commented Rose.

I said nothing. It was an odd observation because I didn't see him putting me down, exactly.

"You set that straight, Rose," said Trisha in support.

More coffee was poured and Trisha passed around her cigarettes. When the Marlboro soft pack came to me, I pulled out a cigarette. Rosemary stared at me.

"Since when do you smoke?" she inquired.

"Oh, I just started," I replied. She frowned in disappointment. Something in me was pleased by her disapproval since I felt like I was breaking free of a psychological constraint, although the intensity of her heated glare almost gave me sunburn.

The talk changed to activities of the day. The younger daughter was going to sew a new outfit (she apparently was a talented seamstress), and had brought out a beautiful pink wool fabric. It wasn't enough material to make a suit, she explained.

"Perhaps Linda would like it," said Rose.

I had no idea how to sew, but I accepted it. It was so soft and pretty.

Trisha had left her husband and son behind at Via Del Sol to come down to Vacaville for the day. I hadn't figured out their marital relationship. They seemed mismatched to me. She was loose and bubbly and he was stiff and stoic.

"I have a job I'm looking into to make some money," said Trisha. She explained it was as a model for an established artist at a place near the Milk Farm restaurant in Dixon.

Rose scowled but said nothing. The girls congratulated Trisha on her independence and creativity.

She had errands to run, she said, and gave everyone a quick hug before departing.

When she left, Rose turned to me.

"Trisha's got a tramp feature. It drives me crazy."

She went on to say that the building Trisha was describing in Dixon had a bad reputation. It had been a "house of ill repute" in the past. Whether the experience Trisha encountered would match her expectations was questionable. Rose was concerned for her.

It was almost noon. We girls pitched in to do the dishes. Rose retired to her bedroom.

It was a quiet afternoon. I picked up a book to read after the girls had left the house. Rose finally came out just before three.

"Mac is coming over to give me a Rolfing," she explained.

Within five minutes he arrived, and they both went into one of the girl's rooms. I remained in the living room reading. I could hear them talking and heard her groaning. It lasted about an hour. He emerged and simply walked out of the house. She remained there for twenty minutes before the door opened. She passed me without a word and went straight to her room. She didn't come out that evening nor did the girls return home for dinner. I made myself a large salad around six, finishing it off with a cigarette from a pack that was left on the kitchen table. The smoke buzzed inside my head. I was enjoying the sensation of the slight high and the opportunity to practice my style.

Out of boredom I went outside to enjoy the sunset. I could see the sliver of the moon as its newness was approaching within a few days. I wanted another cigarette but decided not to push it since it wasn't my pack and I didn't have enough money or opportunity to buy one. After the sunset colors faded and the darkness consumed the sky, I retired to the younger daughter's room, since she was spending the night with her boyfriend.

Heaviness hung over the house.

* * * *

When I arose in the morning, I expected Rose to be in the kitchen, but the house was still. My hunger forced me to cook a breakfast of scrambled eggs and toast. I found the coffee and made a pot, hoping that the aroma would rouse Rose, but it did not.

At about ten I knocked on her door. She told me to enter so I did cautiously. There she was, still in bed. I had never seen her master bedroom before. It was large and had a long dresser of drawers with a rectangular mirror above it. The wallpaper was a soothing pattern of delicate flowers and the floor-to-ceiling drapes were dark heavy fabric, blocking out the day.

"Pull open the drapes," she softly instructed.

I did so, which let in the rays of light, gently filtering through the branches of an ancient oak that hugged the house. It was a serene energy, but it somehow didn't match Rose's disposition. She was clearly bothered.

"I can make you some breakfast — scrambled eggs, toast and coffee," I offered.

"That would be nice," she replied.

I left the room, closing the door behind me. I found a tray below the kitchen counter and noticed that next to it was a small vase. I went outside to cut a rose. This will change her mood, I thought.

When I brought the tray of food, she smiled and said, "This is nice. Thank you."

I sat on the side of her bed, watching her eat and saying nothing. Her appetite wasn't good, as she only ate a few bites.

"Can you bring my cigarettes in from the kitchen table? I left them there," she said.

I did, hoping she didn't notice I had taken one. She lit the cigarette and I asked if I could have one. She handed the pack to me.

After I lit up, she began to speak.

"Mac thinks he's such a great Rolfer. He isn't. I told him he doesn't press hard enough. He kept pressing harder and harder. But I kept telling him it still wasn't doing the trick."

A few more puffs. Her eyes teared up, as she explained Mac said he was getting an apartment with his girlfriend.

I had seen this woman at a meeting, but didn't know until now that this was his girlfriend. She was a Mercurial type (maximum attraction): short black hair whose curls framed an oval face. She had a nice figure but was clearly much younger (closer to my age, it seemed). This was the pain Rosemary was feeling.

There truly was nothing I could say to Rose that would help her suffering go away. I knew this suffering, for hadn't I, too, just experienced it? It is a spear that stabs into the core of your being, and the impalement you carry with you as you proceed through your day. But unlike me, Rose had decades with Mac and had children. She had to appear strong. The fact that she exposed herself to me like this, and that I was able to be there for her as she had been there for me in the log cabin's storage room that one night, was a great gift and honor.

The bonds of true friendship can only be forged in fire.

❧

Should not this ancient pain at last produce in us
More fruit? Is it not time that our loving
Freed us from our beloved and we, trembling, endured;
As the arrow endures the string that, gathered to leap forth,
It may be more than itself. For staying is nowhere.

Rainer Maria Rilke

CHAPTER 46

We returned to Via Del Sol on Friday afternoon for the weekend. When I went up to my tent, it was comforting to see my books stacked on the uneven tent floor. I rolled out my sleeping bag on the foam pad and rested there for an hour or so. It was quiet and the solitude penetrated.

I began to think about self-remembering. In Vacaville I was reading the *The Psychology of Man's Possible Evolution* again and could not quite understand a basic concept: self-remembering can be measured by frequency, duration, and depth. These three characteristics seemed to be the formula for a timeless higher dimensional existence.

Frequency is remembering to be present often. Duration is connecting each moment of self-remembering together so that consciousness can last. Regarding depth, Ouspensky was vague about it, saying, "of what one is conscious, which can vary in a man." What did that mean? How does consciousness go deeper? This I couldn't figure out.

"Linda. You in there?" came a voice outside the tent.

"Yes," I replied.

I stood up and unzipped the flap. It was Jim.

"Robert wondered where you were. He wants you to come down and help Kerrie with dinner."

I put on my socks and laced up my sneakers and followed him down the hill to the house.

When I entered the kitchen, Kerrie was slicing large zucchinis length wise. She greeted me with her sunny smile.

"Hi. Here, take this knife."

She handed me the implement and told me to slice the zukes in half and use a spoon to gut the flesh, placing it into a nearby bowl. She turned her attention to stirring the large hot skillet that contained onions, carrots, and garlic simmering on the stove. She added the zucchini meat from the bowl. The delicious warm aromas were filling the kitchen air.

"My mother just joined," she said as she stirred the mixture. "She came up with me. Marie is showing her around. They've been friends for a long time."

It's always curious to learn who mothered or fathered a friend. I imagined her to be perky like Kerrie. When she appeared, she was clearly a passive Venusian type: thick, beautiful brown hair cut just below the chin and rolled up at the ends, soft eyes and lips, and an hour-glass figure that reflected a nurturing, gentle essence. As she stood next to Marie, for the first time I could feel the non-existence of the Venusian type. She spoke briefly, yet had no opinions of her own, and her desire to be accepted was a large motivating factor in her life, as her eyes looked for approval. She was a stark contrast to Kerrie, who had a competency and confidence that left others in the dust.

Kerrie's mother and Marie decided to help us prepare dinner, and within fifteen minutes Jan and Anna had joined in the fun. We were elbow to elbow, slicing, dicing, stirring, and mixing. When the zucchini boats were in the oven, Kerrie turned to me.

"Would you like to make the couscous?" she asked, adding, "It's easy to do."

I said Sure. She wiped the large iron skillet and told me to melt the butter, pour in the couscous and keep stirring until done. With each motion of the spoon, tiny grains of couscous were spilling out of the pan and onto the stove top. I focused my eyes on the stroke to keep the couscous inside the skillet but my hand wouldn't obey. Kerrie was talking with her mother and when she thought the couscous was cooked, she turned around to find half of it on the stove. She was speechless.

Jan was there and said she would work with this. She told me not to worry about it, which I thought was kind of her. I had a severe bout of inner considering. Jan said I could watch her make it, which I did. How she kept the grains from abandoning ship perplexed me. The couscous rose to the rim of the pan and stayed there as the grains fluffed up. How did she do that?

Dinner was ready and I went outside to blow the conch, calling all to eat. The children set the table. Don had brought up white ceramic plates and cutlery that Robert had asked him to order from the Nut Tree. The days of eating couscous with our fingers were now a distant memory. Western civilization was returning to us, slowly.

After dinner, Robert asked all of us to gather in the living room, including the children, who were helping with the dishes. I looked around and mechanically counted the number of people. We were thirty.

Candles were distributed to each of us. Jim, Miles, and Yorgos used their lighters to ignite each wick. Robert asked that the electric lights be turned off. There we stood with candles dimly illuminating our faces.

Solemnly, Robert said, "We are born alone and we die alone. Each person will awaken individually according to their fate. Everyone calculate the year you will be 65 years old."

The children needed help with the math.

"Does everyone know the year?" he asked. "When we reach the year of your 65th birthday, state your first name and blow out your candle."

Robert intoned the years with a slow cadence: 1971. 1972. 1973. Because we all were so young (the average age of the membership I was told was mid-twenties), it seemed like a silly demonstration at first — until Robert said, "1986."

"Anna," she said, blowing out her candle. Her light went out.

"Rosemary." Her light went out.

My date was 2014. It seemed like a number only, until it came.

"Linda." With one exhalation, my light went out.

Several people extinguished their flames simultaneously as their dates were called. It seemed all candles were out but Robert kept counting, "2021. 2022. 2023."

I looked around and saw only one left.

"2024," said Robert.

"Joy." Her light went out.

It was Marie's twelve-year old daughter. Hers was the final candle.

We all stood there silently in the dark, as the reality of our mortality penetrated deeply. Minutes passed. The lapse of time was hard to endure as the experience sent alarm throughout the machine. That small experiment revealed death still to be a concept only. It was the universal bogeyman hiding under the bed. Surely, he wouldn't find ME.

When the electricity was turned on, our inner light faded, as we quickly returned to speech, which eased the dis-ease we felt from the prospect of our demise.

The memory of that night, however, was imprinted forever, and my life's path — the journey to light not darkness — felt more firmly set now. The year 2014 was not a random number but a demarcation line of sorts. It was fast approaching with each passing day.

*

Phantasy of My Mind, where shall we go?
Take me away, far away, and out of this sad, sad world.
Across the swollen sea, on the Eternal Road where I may wander
And Look
And Feel
And Smell
And Taste
And Hear
And Breathe
My Last Breath
For I am destined to die.

Linda Lee Kaplan
written at the age of 17

CHAPTER 47

An opaque light filtered through the plastic window of my tent at 6 a.m., replacing the usually crisp and clear morning rays. As I unzipped the opening and stuck my head out to look up, I saw a still powder-blue sky with popcorn-shaped clouds held in a humid suspension. The mugginess infused itself into my state. The neighborhood crickets were mute and even the woodpeckers seemed depressed and refused to sing. It's August Summer not October Autumn, I thought. What is this? I am not prepared for an abrupt change in weather. Those thoughts disappeared as instinctive needs propelled me down the hill to the house.

Students were eating breakfast outside and my timing was perfect. I made it into the bathroom without having to wait. After a few minutes, there was a knock on the door. I wasn't ready to emerge so I ignored it. After a few more minutes, a second knock on the door. This person must truly be in a hurry, I thought. I popped in the shower. My Bucket Shower was getting longer each day. I figured everyone was cheating so what did it matter?

The third knock on the door. I was dressing. When I finished, I opened the door only to find Robert standing there.

Oops.

He looked right past me (through me actually) and closed the door behind him.

I went to the kitchen for my granola, milk and coffee and took it outside to join others. Robert emerged from the house and with that little wiggle of his index finger, called me over.

"When you are done with breakfast, go to Miles and Helga's tent and let them know it is supposed to rain so they should be sure to zip up their tent."

Huh?

This made no sense to me. First of all, it wasn't raining as far as I was concerned. Second of all, where the hell was their tent? I had no idea but it meant I had to ask others, which sounded weird. Everyone of course knew about the love triangle. Why does Linda want to know where their tent is? Is she going to spy on them? Even though it was clearly an emotional setup, I did what I was told.

"Does anyone know where Miles and Helga's tent is? I have a message to give them from Robert."

Some students stared at me with that all-knowing glare of judgment and then simply shrugged ignorance.

"It's between the house and the barn to the left," offered Clark. "Poke around the bushes and you'll find it."

Oh, great. I started trekking through the manzanitas, dodging the poison oak. I figured if I looked a little higher than the shrubs, I might see the top of the tent. It worked.

As I approached, I thought how funny the whole scenario was, like I was playing the part of the jilted lover. Cue Linda, stage left.

Standing next to the tent, I cleared my throat and said, "Miles. I have a message from Robert."

I could hear Miles and Helga quietly talking inside the large tent. Instead of Miles stepping out, however, it was Helga.

"Hello," she said sweetly.

"Hi. Robert wanted me to tell you that it may be raining soon and to be sure you zip up the tent."

"Okay. Thank you," she replied politely.

Having delivered the absurd message, I immediately turned to leave. I wanted to be jealous of Helga but she was so nice to me that it was hard to hate her. Miles, on the other hand, didn't even want to face me. Wow. How strange that it had come to this.

As I maneuvered through the brush toward the house, an 'I' in my head said: "So this is how August was meant to be."

Another voice answered: "August is illusion."

*

The world does not move through time as if it were a straight line. Instead, time moves through and within us, in endless spirals.

Shams

CHAPTER 48

As we were approaching the end of the month, renewed focus was placed on finding people with magnetic centers and introducing them to the Fellowship. One couple surprisingly was from Oregon House. Meg and Harold were to give them their prospective student meetings. The Fellowship's series of three prospective student meetings were based on key ideas from Ouspensky's five lectures and Rodney Collin's description of body types.

THE DIVINE BEGINNING

I was invited to attend the second one, which was on the functions, or centers, of the human machine.

We drove to the home of Jeff and Annette. They lived in a sprawling ranch-style house on the road to Lake Francis. Jeff was tall and slim with round wire-rimmed glasses. He seemed smart and accomplished. Annette was blond and shorter with a lovely oval face and bright smile.

After introductions, we sat down at their large oak dining table. Apparently, they had a number of children, and this space was filled with assorted toys, lush plants lining the window sill, and painted ceramic plates filled with assorted snacks such as nuts, dates, cut vegetables, sliced bread and butter, and cheeses.

Meg sat at the head of the table. She brought her own ashtray since she was a chain smoker. I sat across from the couple. Meg took out the deck of playing cards that was used to teach this aspect of the Fourth Way system. According to ancient tradition, playing cards were secretly used to pass down the esoteric map of the human cosmos from generation to generation.

She first lined up the kings facing away from her so that everyone at the table could see them. These four suits represented the four distinct functions, or brains, of the human machine: diamonds were the intellectual center; hearts were the emotional center; spades, the moving center; and clubs, the instinctive center. Then she put the appropriate queens and jacks under each king. Playing cards laid out in this way reinforced Ouspensky's presentation of the division of centers that appeared in the *The Psychology of Man's Possible Evolution.*

I had studied these concepts not only in the *The Psychology* and *The Theory of Celestial Influence,* but also from Harold's drawings. I was not sure whether I was there to contribute or to listen, so I started by listening. I figured if Meg wanted me to speak, she would ask.

She used Robert's banter when describing the formatory apparatus of the jack of diamonds ("Hello, how are you?"). She also focused on the degrees of attention that characterized each level within the centers: the mechanical part, or jacks, had little or no attention; the emotional part, or queens, had attention held by the subject; and the intellectual part, or kings, had attention focused by one's own will and effort.

We concluded the meeting after an hour or so and asked them if they were interested in the third meeting. Because they said they were, that meeting was scheduled for the next day. The meeting would be on body types and I was not invited to attend.

Looking at Jeff and Annette and their pleasant demeanor and interest, it seemed clear that they were going to join. We would not know the outcome until after the third meeting. It was at that time that monthly membership payments were discussed, so if a person truly valued these ideas and the opportunity to work within a school of awakening, the decision to join would be an easy one to make.

* * * *

That afternoon as I entered the house, several students were hovering around the bathroom door, actively expressing their frustrations.

"What's going on?" I asked.

"Bill has been in the bathroom for over an hour and we can't use it."

I could understand their frustration. I also was a bit glad that I wasn't their target since I've already received what I considered my quota of photographs for restroom loitering from the teacher.

When Bill finally emerged, the bathtub was draining. Holy cow! *He took a bath?!*

"Why did you take a bath?" I asked him, pointing out that we were all asked to conserve water (yes, I know I wasn't the perfect example myself, but his obvious disregard for the task lessened my guilt of minor rule-breaking).

He raised his pant leg and showed me a cut across his calf.

"This is from rusty barbed wire!" he exclaimed. His story was he was wandering around the property and tripped over the curled and pointy metal, entangling himself in it. I couldn't quite picture what exactly happened to produce the wound. He continued to rant about getting gangrene if he didn't soak the poison out and how everyone would be responsible if he died. His reasoning was perplexing and extreme. It was like he was living on another planet. But that was Bill.

* * * *

The Tuesday night meeting was held at Richard's home in Walnut Creek. It was a surprise to see. It was the most common-looking ranch-style house, with neither elegance nor pzazz — not what I would expect from a doctor. But as I entered, I learned it had five bedrooms and four bathrooms for his many children. That made more sense. When I looked at Richard and Alice, they were middle-class folk to me in their approach to life. My idea of how a doctor and his wife live needs to be reassessed. Not all of them are dripping with money, apparently.

The meeting was in a wood-paneled room, and when I entered, there were Robert and Meg talking to the couple from Oregon House. It was good to see they had indeed joined the school. They were introduced at the start of the meeting after good householder tasks were assigned, as was the custom. Another couple from the Bay Area had also joined, so our numbers were growing with each passing week. It was the last day of August.

Robert had mentioned that the coming weekend, September 4, would be a day of silence at the ranch and that the Sunday meeting would be mandatory. He wanted as many students there as possible.

"In silence, the moving center will start to speak and negative 'I's will come and try to blame people," he warned. Robert also reminded us to watch for imitation in the moving center.

"Observe how if someone reaches for a glass at the table, others will suddenly do the same. It is mechanical and *happens* to one."

Someone asked a question about essence.

"The Self is already there and you say it grows from essence. Is this a contradiction?"

Robert paused before speaking.

"No, the Self is there and is asleep. As it wakes up, it grows out of essence. It has many names: the Self, Third Eye, Cosmic Consciousness, Satori, Astral Body, Higher Mental and Higher Emotional."

Another question: "Is essence where creativity is?"

Robert's response: "Essence is creative, for sure, like artists, musicians, etc. True creativity belongs to the Self, which is not a word. It must be something mute that is using the human body as an instrument to create. For Beethoven and Mozart — creativity *happened* to them. That is mechanical creativity. They had no Third Eye observing. People may react negatively to this information."

Another question: "Could you talk more about voluntary suffering?"

"Switch your watch from the usual wrist to the other one," Robert replied. "This will be irritating and uncomfortable and give you something to transform. It is a little game at first, finding these alarm clocks that produce a small amount of intentional suffering to awaken us. Generally, we are too lazy to find these for ourselves and C Influence has to arrange them for us."

After several more examples were given of voluntary suffering, Robert stood up to leave the room, signaling that the first half of the meeting had come to a close. Mac then had us count off from one to six, starting with the first row of students to the last row. This numbering method determined which small group you would join in the second half. After the break with refreshments, the chairs were rearranged into six small circles. Mac went around appointing a leader of the group. He chose me to lead my small group.

I sat with my legs crossed and my hands folded just as Robert does. Then I asked, "Does anyone have a question?"

I waited for a response and no one said anything. Meanwhile, I could hear Meg's group chatting away. Suddenly I realized the five other people in my group were Lunars, a quiet and passive type. Oh, boy. I felt I was back teaching high school. Now what?

"Does anyone have any thoughts about what Robert said?" I was improvising.

Again, silence. Some students started to look at their shoes. One had a pained, serious look on his face as he gazed upward searching for that elusive profound question that would pinpoint the greatest mystery of the universe.

Like that episode of teaching in East LA, I began to look at my watch. Finally, Mac gave the call: "Let's end now."

I grabbed my purse and found a ride back to Via Del Sol.

*

Be silent or let thy words be worth more than silence.
Pythagoras

CHAPTER 49

It was customary after a Tuesday meeting in the Bay Area to sleep in late since caravans of students arrived back around 3 a.m. It was September 1, and the bright, almost full moon in the night sky was accompanying us on our return home. I was in the back seat dozing off during the ride from the Coffee Tree, where we had our midnight hamburgers and fries. I was hoping to catch a glimpse of Robert and Jim, but they had already left before we got to the restaurant. A few students, who were finishing up their meals, had seen them and were able to tell us this.

We pulled up to the house, which was the debarkation point after the Tuesday meeting trips. Everyone quickly scattered to their tents like little ants. With my red plastic flashlight in hand, I located the now well-worn path to my tent. After pulling the zipper down to open the flap, I quickly stripped and collapsed on top of the bag.

Although I was exhausted, suddenly I was wide awake. My dozing in the car must have refreshed an accumulator (what the system describes as a vessel that holds energy, like a tank for gas). I started to think about essence and personality and Robert's description of its connection to the Self. How could that be? I thought essence was part of the framework of one's centers and that personality was the content that fills the structure. Essence was a function, that is, part of the makeup of the machine. But could it also be a state? An interesting thought to ponder.

As the many 'I's contemplated the enigma, after almost an hour I was lulled into the first state of consciousness. And with that, my long day came to an end.

* * * *

When I arose in the late morning and descended the hill to the house, I expected lunch. It was quiet, however, so I went to the bathroom and took my time. I had a bad habit of lip syncing in the mirror and I must have gone through the entire flip side of Streisand's *Funny Girl* album. When I emerged, there he was: Robert.

He went in and started to close the door but stopped and called me over.

"C Influence is using you as friction against me," he said.

He had a strange look on his face. He wasn't upset or angry nor was he blaming me; instead, it was a bemused look that had a barely perceptible gentle grin attached to it. His eyes were soft. Could he also know about how the gods deliver their friction, their Giggle in Heaven? It would seem so since he was the teacher, but Robert was always so serious that I had a hard time reading him.

* * * *

After a late lunch, Robert decided to hold an impromptu meeting in the house living room. It was Wednesday and there were only fifteen students assembled, most of whom lived at the ranch.

We placed chairs in a circle and Robert began to speak about transforming suffering. I thought for sure he would speak about his friction with me and how he was transforming it. I braced myself for humiliation.

"This morning I stood up and hit my pot on the head."

HUH?

He started again, "This morning I stood up and hit my pot on the head."

It was clearly wrong but nobody laughed. How could a conscious being make a mistake like this?

Then Robert said, "I mean I hit my head on the pot — the hanging flower pot." That grin I had seen earlier expanded into the sweetest smile. It was the first time I had seen it at a meeting.

He continued.

"Even though it's a full moon I can no longer blame it on the moon. I've been a bit silly for over a month."

What? I had never seen a silly side to Robert. The stern teacher I knew was suddenly replaced by a shy, simple child. We, too, were transported to this gentle childlike state and a light chuckle from all present could be heard. We sat there with him, enjoying this wonderful moment. And then it hit me: *This is the state of essence!*

Robert decided to end the meeting. As we each stood up to put our chairs away, I kept my eyes on Robert, hoping this would be a new beginning for us all. The school was too serious for my taste. I kept attracting the most ridiculous scenarios that made me burst out laughing at times, and I stuck out like a sore thumb. Maybe a little lightness from the emotional center will infuse itself into our daily lives with Robert leading the way, I thought. Fingers crossed.

Just then Robert turned around and the smile had melted like frozen ice cream on hot pavement. There was that serious look again.

His gray Saturnine disposition put a wall between us. I studied him almost as much as I studied myself. Why? Because, somehow, I felt our destinies were connected. Robert had reached an internal, spiritual development beyond mine and I wanted to be where he was. What I could see about him was that he was both student and teacher. He was one of us, trying to figure it out as he went along. And yet, he knew where the student ended and the teacher began. Robert was ever-obedient to the task he was given by the gods: help these people awaken. I observed also that others viewed him as the Man with All the Answers. To me, he was the man who knew which questions were relevant and which were a waste of time. At this point, that was enough for me.

Still the seriousness continued to mystify me. What was bothering him? What was his inner world like? All I could do was wait, watch and be there if he needed me.

*Man is most nearly himself when he
achieves the seriousness of a child at play.*
Heraclitus

CHAPTER 50

Students began to show up Friday for the weekend. Robert expressed his desire to have a meeting at seven to be followed by dinner. We were told that the silence would begin the next morning, September 4. I still wasn't sure how we'd get anything done without words. I assumed we'd learn more about what he had in mind at the meeting.

At 7 p.m., we gathered in the living room. The floor space was limited and it was crowded with Residents and Weekenders, some sitting in chairs and others sitting cross-legged on the carpet. We were all interested to learn what the rules were regarding our weekend of silence.

Robert began to speak.

"Silence will reveal leaks in energy. The machine uses humor and laughter to waste sex energy that is reserved for self-remembering. Because of this, the silence exercise this weekend will also include a no-laughing exercise."

My first thought was, Oh, great. My desire for more emotional lightness was now squashed.

A hand rose. "How will we communicate with each other?"

Robert hesitated before replying, as if he hadn't considered this.

"It is fine to write brief notes of instruction. We will provide small notepads." He turned to Jim and asked him to go to the store early in the morning to purchase some.

"Be careful to limit this type of communication," he continued, "so that it does not become unnecessary writing instead of unnecessary talking."

Another hand.

"Do we have to be in silence if we leave the property, like going to the Oregon House store?"

"No, this would be formatory thinking. The exercise is only within the property limits."

A third hand rose from a married lady.

"At what time on Sunday is the exercise over?"

Robert pondered the question before speaking.

"When you retire."

She continued. "What if you are with another student? Is it okay to talk in bed?"

Robert looked up with that pained expression on his face. He chose not to answer her.

Robert's lack of response made me chuckle inside. The silence exercise has now begun, I thought. Robert did not always address a student's question. This is what I meant about Robert knowing which questions were irrelevant. If you asked too many questions like these, he would ignore you.

Robert turned the meeting over to Kerrie who coordinated good householder tasks for the weekend's dining. The meeting ended after all assignments were made so that we could have dinner.

The discussions continued while we were eating, nonetheless. It seemed some had prepared in advance to manage the status quo of their relationships and octaves by purchasing their own notebooks (not notepads). Others had practiced their gestures. What was not calculated for were any new scenarios that C Influence could arrange to test our ability to adhere to the exercises.

* * * *

Saturday morning breakfast was eerily quiet. Notepads were placed on the stereo cabinet with a little box next to them that read Cost of Notepad 25 cents. They were small (about 3" x 5"). How could one hold a conversation with this?

I was blessed, however, with a wide range of facial expressions. I could still point and mime. Because of these qualities, I decided to pass on the notepads.

Solitary chores would be my focus for the day, such as laundry, vacuuming, etc. This would enable me to look active while adhering to the exercises. As these aims were being formulated, I felt a tap on my shoulder. It was Clark. He was scribbling a message in his notepad.

"The donkey needs to be moved. I need help."

As I read this, his bright jovial eyes opened wide and his head nodded with expectation indicating, You will help me, yes?

I shrugged as if to say, Sure, I guess so.

And with that we were off to the barn.

On the way down the hill, I realized I didn't even know we owned a donkey. I must confess after the petting zoo experience of the first cows, I did everything I could to avoid the place. It meant hard physical work and I wasn't interested. Why did we need to move the donkey? Then I recalled overhearing Klair, who was in charge of the animal husbandry, tell Robert that the young calf needed to be weaned and separated from its mother. We didn't have enough pens to hold the animals, she explained. Perhaps moving the donkey meant creating space for the calf.

When we arrived at the barn, we went to the south side and there I saw three wooden pens that had been constructed to house the animals. I had no idea that these enclosures were there. Such an interesting place this is. It continually changed shape, with new structures sprouting up unexpectedly.

We approached the pen that housed the donkey. It was a large double space with a gate that separated one side from the other. Clark pointed to a smaller single pen, indicating this was where we needed to put the donkey. He went to a post that had a large hook from which hung a bridle. He took the bridle and pointed to the donkey. Through a series of gestures, he indicated we were to bridle the donkey and lead it into the pen.

Sounded simple enough, I thought. We approached the donkey, who stood perfectly still with its head lowered. Then Clark did something totally unexpected. He handed me the bridle.

"Go ahead Linda. Put it on the donkey," he mimed.

I had never bridled an animal before, but then again, how difficult could it be? I'd watched enough Westerns, rode enough horses, and loved to draw them as a kid.

I looked at the loops and straps and bit and figured it was best to work from top to bottom, so I took each loop and inserted the ears into them. The bridle hung over the donkey's face and the bit hit the bridge of its nose, which was at least six inches from its mouth. Hmm. This isn't right, I thought. I turned to Clark to ask his opinion but he had his back to me. Then I saw his body convulsing.

When he turned around, his face was red and his lips were pursed, with tears streaming from his squinting eyes. Oh no! This was going to trigger my hysteria. I put a serious look on my face and tried again. This time I found another, bigger loop in the bridle and thought maybe that was the one for the ear. Two other loops mysteriously appeared and were hanging lopsided down the other side. We both started convulsing.

Clark regained his composure and took over. He pointed to the bit indicating we should perhaps start from the bottom up. He tried to fit it into the donkey's mouth, but was met with great resistance. The donkey's lips wouldn't part at first, but with some pressing, its mouth opened. The donkey immediately spit it out. Clark motioned to me to put it in and I was having nothing to do with inserting a piece of metal into that beast. Clark tried again with the same result.

As Clark looked at the bit to position it before a third attempt, the donkey stared right into my eyes. He had no notepad or gesture but his communication was loud and clear.

"And they call me an ass."

I burst out laughing. Then Clark lost it. We both took some deep breaths to contain ourselves. At that point Clark hung up the bridle and took a rope from the barn. His idea was to wrap the rope around the donkey's neck and lead it into the pen. Once tied, he pulled. The donkey refused to budge. He handed me the rope and he pushed the animal from behind while I tugged from the front. We must have spent thirty more minutes coaxing the animal. Finally, the beast moved and I pulled it forward into the pen. Mission accomplished.

Although we broke the laughing exercise, Clark and I had made a silent promise never to speak about this incident, keeping our ineptitude a secret.

A larger realization was growing inside of me, however. I was beginning to understand that failure and embarrassment were somehow scripted and had the power to release huge amounts of energy that could, like a laser beam, sear consciousness into the moments of my life.

A new attitude was forming: Embrace the ridiculous.

* * * *

By Sunday morning we pretty much figured out who suffered from unnecessary writing. Bill won the prize. He had a stenographer's notebook and expected everyone to stand still while he wrote several pages of script that were designed to communicate something. Once done, he handed the tablet to the person to read. It was filled with so many 'I's that were designed to elicit an equal number of 'I's in the reader. Most of us recognized it as a trap and avoided Bill like the plague. There were a few who enjoyed engaging with him. It gave them something to do.

Robert would occasionally scribble a sentence of instruction to students in charge of completing octaves. You were not given much of an opportunity to respond. He did not share his pencil with you.

After Sunday dinner and chores, it was a relief that the Weekend of Silence had come to an end. It was frustrating, far from the monkish meditation of monasteries where harmony reigned and life was simple, or so I imagined.

The Fourth Way is not a monastery, I thought. It occurs in life and involves normal activities such as social interactions using our mouths and brains. Silence didn't allow me to express myself. My intellectual mind was swarming with 48 hours of unexpressed 'I's. I didn't expect this deluge. I couldn't stop the intense anger welling up in me. All I could do was observe that I had a real problem with the negative 'I's circulating. So I did the only thing I could to relieve the stress: I retired to my tent, lay down, and talked myself to sleep.

Words are many.
If you don't stop them, they won't stop.
Lao Tzu

CHAPTER 51

Monday morning a crisp breeze blew through the netting of my zippered door flap, waking me up. The air outside was refreshing, but inside I felt like I had an emotional hangover. The negative 'I's from the night before left a bad taste in my mouth, and worse than that, I felt guilty that I had expressed them. The feeling was more, Oy, what I did, what I said.

The only balm I knew that could soothe my psychological discomfort was a work book. I reached out and pulled *The Fourth Way* from the stack. I realized that all I could do last night to stop the onslaught of negative 'I's was to observe them. I looked up that work idea and came upon a diagram accompanied by Ouspensky's description.

"In this system the word 'I' can be spoken of in five ways, on five different levels."

I didn't remember reading this sentence before.

He then goes on to list them: the Many 'I's, Observing 'I,' Deputy Steward, Steward and Master. The Many 'I's is the state of man outside the Work. This is the nature of human beings as stimulus-response machines, totally controlled by circumstances. When one decides to work on oneself, a specialized group forms that is interested in pursuing awakening. This group of 'I's is referred to as Observing 'I.' The third level, Deputy Steward, appears when there is control over some of the 'I's. Steward is the level of complete control over the 'I's. Master appears outside of the many 'I's and has a Time-Body.

I had no idea what Time-Body meant. Who is this Master that appears outside of the many 'I's? How does it form? This Master is a mystery to me.

Where am I in my evolution? It seems I'm at the level of Observing 'I.' The next stage is developing Deputy Steward. How would I possibly recognize this level inside of me? What would it be like to develop will in relation to the many 'I's? I still couldn't control my hysterical laughing. I was entering into the unknown here. Hopefully Robert will be able to tell me.

* * * *

I was expecting to find my fellow students as relieved as I was that the Weekend of Silence was over. As I walked into the house for lunch, however, there was a big buzz about Robert. I listened in on the conversation.

"Apparently, Robert is still in silence."

Huh?! What does that mean for the rest of us?

"Yeah," said one student. "But I also heard it was his choice and we don't have to do it."

I spoke up. "How will he teach?"

A discussion followed. Some heard he will write notes that Jim will read to others. But that means you can't just go up to Robert and ask him a question or get help from him privately. I was confused. I needed him to talk to me. The Wall of Seriousness now has become the Wall of Silence.

Now what will I do?

* * * *

Tuesday's meeting was in Berkeley at Anna's home, and I was able to get a ride to the Bay Area early that morning in the food van. Kerrie was still in charge of buying supplies to feed us all, but this time we were accompanied by the son of the Architect. He had decided to stay at Via Del Sol while the rest of his family returned to Marin during the week. With olive skin and shoulder-length black hair, which he liked to keep in place with a folded yellow and green bandana tied around his head, he had the long, slender limbs of his father and the swarthiness of his mother. His bright smile, dancing eyes, and positive mood made him a pleasure to be around. He and Kerrie appeared to have a good friendship. Although he was a teenager, he appeared much older.

It was wonderful to be in the fog and breeze of the Bay Area after the heat of Oregon House. The plan was to place the orders in several Berkeley health food stores and then pick up the food the next day. I wasn't sure where they were staying overnight, but I assumed it was with the Architect's family. As for me, I had arranged another ride home with students who had left the ranch after us. Someone in that car was staying in the Bay Area so there would be space for me to return.

Getting the van parked along the narrow streets of Berkeley was quite a challenge. The Architect's son had his learner's permit so he could drive with Kerrie, who served as the licensed driver. This is the customary way California kids learn to drive at an early age. It was a bit comical to watch him, under the direction of Kerrie, straddle the curb with the van. I should have gotten out of the car beforehand, since the passenger seat now was elevated and the descent was a bit steep. I managed to hop out. I only mention it because this unusual situation did produce a spark of presence (it was one of those "embrace the ridiculous" moments that I was beginning to appreciate and harvest).

When we entered Anna's home at 7:30, I noticed Robert, Jim, and Yorgos standing in the corner near the piano. Jim was holding papers and talking to Yorgos. It was strange to see this since Jim was generally quiet and supportive, especially with Robert around. Robert was looking at Jim with his customary seriousness.

We took our seats and directed our attention at Robert, expecting him to speak. Instead, Yorgos, who sat next to him, began the meeting.

"Robert remains silent indefinitely. He will present angles of thought by writing them out for us and having someone read them at meetings. I will read them tonight."

And with that introduction, Yorgos spoke the teacher's words.

"People cannot move on unless I leave a vacancy. Meher Baba died on December 31, 1969. On that date this teaching began. This teaching is to replace that one. Meher Baba did not speak to his students for forty years. Sometimes a teacher has to do certain things for certain purposes. By being silent on Saturday, September 4, at the farm, people felt something finer."

I certainly didn't feel something finer, I thought. I felt negative.

Yorgos continued reading.

"The 'I's may storm because the teaching is not their idea of it."

I was stunned. Robert just spoke to my problem. How did he know?

"For some students, I will be with them when I pass through the physical body, and you will know it as literally as you know sun and water."

I knew the quality of presence like I knew the sun and water. But as for the future of my life, I was in a deep fog.

Yorgos paused. The next comments were unrelated to the previous ones.

"We need shocks. They disturb our sleep. A student leaving the teaching often becomes a form of payment for a student entering. For those who knew them, they might begin to see this with Sarah Steinfield being a payment for Annette — and Phil Beckerstone being payment for Jeff."

I didn't remember Sarah. I do recall Phil, though. He was at my prospective meetings in Alamo. He was the one snoozing. No big surprise, I thought.

Robert tried to take questions, but the effort to respond in writing was too cumbersome. The formal part of the meeting ended early. We had refreshments, reconvened with good householder announcements, and then divided into small groups.

As we drove home, everyone in the car voiced their opinions about this change in the teaching. Some thought it was weird that Robert associated this teaching with Meher Baba's, as if he were trying to make a connection to a famous guru. One person even said that Meher Baba died January 31st 1969, meaning Robert got his facts wrong so there couldn't possibly be a connection. Others thought his silence was to produce more friction for us. Another expressed his view that Robert was elevating himself above us artificially, making it more difficult for us to connect with him.

I listened, but thought something was missing in all these opinions. Somehow the key was in Robert's comment that the many 'I's have an imaginary picture of the school. From day one this was true for me. None of these people were the students I imagined would be candidates for awakening. Robert was not my idea of the teacher (remember, I thought Don was the teacher). Dashed expectations were the norm for me. I've had abundant experience with this. I knew what to do because I knew what I had found: be grateful, readjust my thinking, and hold on for dear life.

Life is a balance of holding on and letting go.
Rumi

CHAPTER 52

The angle of the sun had changed. September is not March nor is it July. Nature produces muted colors in California during this time of year, not the bright reds, oranges and yellows I've seen in pictures of the East Coast. The Irish spring grass of Vacaville in March is long gone, as is the freshly unfurled young leaves of oaks — September has turned the terrain from a cheerful lime green to a pale golden color with trees of dark olive. The land has lost its youthful hope of fruitful possibilities. Autumn reveals what is.

It was also the season of preparation. I awoke Wednesday midmorning with the thoughts of making money. My teaching payment of $20 for September left me with barely enough for a Denny's hamburger on the Tuesday night meeting ride home. Patterns had already been set, and I was looking for massage customers. The only problem was I had not yet bought my own massage oil as Bonita had requested. I hoped she would let me use her supply just one more time.

Wednesday lunch brought the residents together. There was Bonita with her long, gray-streaked black hair damp from the late-morning swim. She wore a colorful sarong and her bright smile made her approachable.

"Bonita, I was wondering if I could borrow some massage oil."

She looked sharply into my eyes. "I told you to buy your own," she responded.

I explained I hadn't had a chance yet, but had every intention of doing so. In reality, the logistics of securing the oil were challenging for me, having no transportation and barely any money.

She suddenly softened and said Okay adding, "I have it in my tent. Meet me there at three."

I didn't realize she had her own tent. She was a truly enigmatic character. She was married to David, living with Alden, but had her own private space as well. The confines of the structured family that had been my foundation for relationships were relaxed by the Sixties. The sexual revolution was a time of experimentation, and we were in the midst of it.

The hike up the hill to her tent was strenuous since it was the high heat of the afternoon. It was easily in the 90-degree range, which was odd for this time of year. I called out her name and she told me to enter. She was lying on bedding in her sarong. I was surprised how fetid the air was inside.

"The bottle is in the corner," she said, pointing to a little Chinese-style table that held various bottles and the incense that was burning slowly.

"Come, lie down next to me," she instructed.

I did so, thinking we would just be together and talk like girlfriends. She took a deep breath and asked me how I enjoyed giving massages. I told her it was interesting locating pockets of energy that needed release. I didn't know I had this ability. She turned to her side and started to massage my arms slowly, with presence. She stopped, smiling lovingly. I then reciprocated, hoping to show her how I had learned to touch intentionally. She then placed her hand on my breast and turned her head to kiss me on the lips.

I pulled back immediately without thought. Her deep, wheezy laugh filled the tent. As she turned away from me, she said, "You can leave now."

The strangest thing was I didn't want to leave. I didn't want to kiss her either. Instead, I wanted to get to know her better, to learn from her if I could. I didn't judge her or myself. As I walked down the hill, I wondered why she would even think I was interested in women. I actually didn't know I wasn't sexually attracted to women until then. Although it was an unexpected encounter, I saw something about myself. That was all that mattered.

* * * *

Rosemary was sitting outside, sipping on her cigarette. Her apron indicated she was taking a smoking break from dinner preparations. I sat down next to her and asked for a cigarette. She handed me the pack and the Bic lighter.

We sat quietly for a few minutes, inhaling and exhaling. I asked her if she was interested in a massage. Instead, she offered another suggestion.

"Why don't you look for a job in Marysville? There's a bookstore, a Hallmark gift shop — I'm sure they could use someone like you."

She said she was going into town tomorrow morning and could drop me off on the main street. She explained that, in her day, it was customary to go from shop to shop announcing one's availability and inquiring if there was a position open.

"I'm leaving at 9 a.m. Make sure you wear a dress." With that comment, she put out her cigarette, stood up and went back into the kitchen.

* * * *

Wearing the purple coatdress and heels, I walked into the Hallmark Cards store on D Street. The shop had just opened for the day and I was their first customer. Or so they thought.

"Hello. I was wondering if you had a job opening?" I asked.

The lady who approached me turned to the man behind the counter. She was wearing a pink cotton shirtdress with a narrow belt and a flared calf-length skirt, a conservative professional outfit for this time of year — if you were in Kansas. The gentleman behind the counter also was appropriately attired for a restrained town: short-sleeved starched and perfectly pressed white shirt with a narrow black tie, a narrow black belt, and relaxed black trousers. These clearly were not hippies. Now I know why Rosemary insisted I wear my dress. The granny dress and bellbottoms with colorful tops and socks and sneakers that constituted my daily outfits clearly were inappropriate in this place.

Nonetheless, he respectfully responded by saying, "Not at this time, but if you want to leave your name and phone number, we can call you if something is available."

Phone number? I had a name but no phone number. Panic seized me. What do I do?

"Thank you," I said politely and immediately turned around and left.

I walked down this quaint street and decided to just window shop. Without a phone number, what was the point? Across from the Hallmark Cards store was a candy shop. I walked in and pretended to be a customer instead of an unemployed person. My friendly personality engaged the counter clerk who was happy to tell me about the store. Clearly, I wasn't a Marysville resident to her. I learned that the sweets were all handmade and that the shop had been there for decades. She offered me a sample and I happily took it. I hadn't eaten chocolate in months. Oh, my goodness! I made an attempt to hide the exquisiteness of the sugary taste as it coated my tongue and teeth. I told her I would think about it and that it was good to know about this shop. We parted ways.

Next, I went to the bookstore. Browsing the shelves, it became clear that, with all the cowboy and Western-themed titles, indeed, I was not in Los Angeles anymore. I couldn't find a work book or even a book of poetry.

When Rose picked me up at the designated corner at the prearranged time, she asked how it went. I looked at her and was surprised how hopeful she looked. Didn't she understand that these are different times? I don't live in town. I don't own a car. I don't have access to a telephone. It was an exercise in futility. But I didn't have the heart to tell her, so I simply answered, "Nothing was available at this time."

"Well, you tried," she said. "It was good that you tried."

The drive back to Via Del Sol felt longer than usual. I looked out the window like I did as a vulnerable and clueless child of ten. Here I was at twenty-two. I knew she was trying to help me and could feel her frustration with me. At a young age, however, I secretly knew I was a late bloomer. Still, it was hard to accept.

Bob Dylan's lyrics looped in my head: "How does it feel to be on your own, a complete unknown, like a rolling stone?" Dylan's words rang true but needed revision, in my case: "How does it feel to be totally dependent on other people within a school of awakening?" I wanted to be able to support myself and help others, but felt incapable of doing this.

Staring at the distant horizon, with its golden hills and black dots of cattle, I was beginning to slip into that dark comfort zone of self-pity when a word mysteriously and firmly popped into my head: Patience.

This would be my mantra, I resolved.

❖

> *In some quiet hour when they were sociably together,*
> *Faith, Love and Hope felt an urge to fashion something new;*
> *they set to work together and created a lovable new quality,*
> *a higher kind of Pandora: Patience.*
>
> Johann Goethe

CHAPTER 53

After breakfast on Friday, Meg appeared with a stack of papers. She had been working on a newsletter titled *Via Del Sol Journal*. It contained notes from Robert and meeting excerpts. Volume I Issue 1 recorded the previous week's meetings. Each edition was 25 cents, and a month's worth would be 75 cents. I was impressed at how Meg could type a page that had two columns. I wondered how she did that.

Lunchtime drew a larger crowd as the Weekenders were arriving. The Architect came not only with his family, but also with his design plans for the remodeling of the house. He showed them to Robert, and it appeared Robert had definite views on the new vision.

Robert's habit was to write on anything available. He would scribble a few words on a corner of a page, wait to hear your response, and then find a blank space to address your comment. If one were to look at the paper afterwards, it was a series of words and sentences scattered on the page at different angles that made no sense whatsoever when read left to right or top to bottom, since the context was stripped away. It could only be understood in that moment.

I kept my apron on long after the dishes were done, pretending I was taking a break so I could eavesdrop on Robert as much as I could. I longed to be included in the discussion, but was not because I had nothing to do with that project. It made sense to me that I was excluded, of course, but my curiosity remained strong.

I stepped outside to have a cigarette. Although Robert asked that we not gossip, it was the main way we accessed news about the happenings of the school. One thing I did learn that day was that the Architect's son desired to live in a teepee. He had been appearing more and more like an Indian scout from Western movies. In addition to his long hair and bandana, he started to walk around without a shirt and had a Bowie knife in a holder that was strapped around his waist.

"Where is the teepee going to go?" I asked the student who shared the news with me.

"Up the hill past your tent. He's looking for someone to help him. I think Clark may know something about teepees. Maybe I'll hook them up."

"Why is he doing this?" I inquired.

THE DIVINE BEGINNING

"Why not?" replied the student. "I think it's cool. After all, Indians originally owned this land. He's going back to the roots. You know, more essence, less personality."

He looked at the quizzical expression on my face.

"He has a right to do this," he asserted. With that the student left me there to finish the cigarette I pawned from him.

I found it curious how up the hill would be a teepee while down the hill was a log cabin that Robert was trying to pull out of the nineteenth century. Here was a student clinging to the past while the teacher was trying to pull us into the future. I softly chuckled as I put out my cigarette. This reminds me of trying to get that donkey to move, I thought. Gentle reins weren't enough to pull it forward. A rope was needed around the neck. Still, something else felt a little odd to me. It was the first inkling I had that we were not all on the same boat.

* * * *

That night as I lay in my tent, I pondered how a student could think that someone had a right to do his own thing. This is not how a school of any sort works. After my experience in Watts, it was a particularly sensitive area. Obedience and respect were keys to learning and growing. That was my training and understanding. But society was changing. We were in a new decade, and the last decade — the Sixties — was a time of invention when we were all encouraged to reimagine ourselves.

The Beatles, for instance, were from Liverpool and dressed as natty schoolboys with uniform clothes and bowl-cut hairstyles; then they were part of Sgt. Pepper's band, with its colorful military attire from some imaginary land; and now they dress as followers of an Indian guru, with long hair and scraggly beards, oversized cotton shirts, beaded necklaces, sandals and loose stringed pants. When I heard the Beatles broke up, I fell out of love with them because they had somehow lost their innocence, like my high school friend. I had moved on.

As for myself, I remember once attending the Renaissance Pleasure Faire in the San Fernando Valley, where young people dressed as knights and damsels, and fortune-tellers and palm readers plied their wares. How was I dressed? Not like that. I wasn't interested in reimagining myself. I didn't want to add to my layers of identity or exchange one for another. I wanted to get down to the nitty gritty of who and what I truly was. The thought was scary because it required exposing myself, with all of its mechanics, to someone who understood the human machine. I needed a teacher to shine the light on the good and the bad.

I could see also that, by all appearances, the Fellowship of Friends could be viewed as a group, a commune, a Renaissance Faire. This is what it looked like from outside. It was subject to interpretation. But for me it was a Fourth Way school with conscious influence. I had verified the gods before I met the school. *It was a presence I could feel.* And I had verified Robert as a conscious teacher. When I looked into Robert's eyes, he looked back at me with presence and his presence ignited my own. That was enough for me.

I kept the depth of my connection to the gods a secret, as I had when I was that child on the daybed in Bubbie's house. Not everyone wanted to acknowledge this connection, let alone talk about it. Robert was the one to remind us. That was a large part of his role. He would often tell the story of the Zen Master who would point the way for his followers, and admonish those who focused on his finger rather than the horizon. I was shocked by how many fellow students kept focusing on Robert's finger — how long it was, how crooked, how it needed a manicure. It was as if they hadn't recognized the difference between sleep and awakening, and the urgency and horror of their situation.

But these were my comrades, my friends, for now. We all do our best, don't we?

❧

Why am I reaching again for the brushes?
When I paint you, God, nothing happens.
But I can choose to feel you.
Rainer Maria Rilke

CHAPTER 54

When I arrived for breakfast Saturday morning, Robert, Don, and the Architect were discussing the blueprints once again. This was supposed to be a work weekend on the house, but it seemed we hadn't moved from Friday morning's discussion. Don, in his soft tone and pleasant disposition, tried to communicate gently to Robert that the design from the Architect included a thorough analysis of the engineering limitations of the building, and that Robert's plans would cave in the entire building. I felt I was watching a rerun. Robert's expression was pained.

I left with my bowl of cereal. Sitting outside, I pondered the triad of the situation. Don and the Architect were now the Active (First) force, and Robert was put in the position of Denying/Passive (Second) force to their plans. From Robert's viewpoint, they were the Denying force. Where was the

Invisible (Third) force? Not to be found. The work books describe such a situation as an impasse. Then I remembered my mantra: Patience. Wait and see. I was curious how Robert would get this donkey into the pen.

* * * *

The meeting that night began with Mac reading Robert's notes.

"Eventually people here all have the same aim: to be or not to be, that IS the question."

Suddenly a hand rose. Robert acknowledged the student to speak.

"I think a periodic review of one's aim can be worthwhile — to channel energy in a direction."

Usually, people would raise their hand to ask Robert a question. But this was a statement, not a question. In fact, it was an opinion. It was odd.

Robert wrote on his notepad for Mac to read.

"The aim of the group is to wake up. People here are capable of waking up."

Another hand went up.

"So you mean we can do nothing, as if we're in a river where the course is set?"

Robert paused for a moment, looking up. He then wrote.

"In the full meaning of the word, C Influence does *EVERYTHING* here, including conception."

This clearly was a hard idea to digest for many, especially for the successful professionals in the room. I had no problem with this idea since I had come to terms with my own helplessness.

A person seated on the floor raised his hand, keeping a perplexed look on his face.

"If we have no free will, where is responsibility?"

Robert penned his reply: "A conscious Egyptian priest once said, 'We are slaves to the Deity.' Avoid using words like Morality and Responsibility."

He would write, hand the page to Mac to read, and then take it back for his next thoughts. This is how he taught in silence.

"Free will comes with the death of the physical body and the existence of the Astral Body. Walt Whitman said, 'The best of me when no longer visible.'"

"Contradictory magnetic centers occur when certain groups of 'I's move in a different direction at the expense of the Self."

I wondered if he was talking about the teepee. He would address what was going on without naming names. But his observations were definitely pointed.

"Also, people with contradictory magnetic centers want evolution, but on their own terms. Missing opportunities to work here on weekends shows one is being distracted by life."

He finished writing and handed the page with his notes to Mac, who read this last statement, while Robert looked directly at the student who asked the question about responsibility.

"C Influence guides my hand as it writes, as it does your question."

With that, the meeting ended.

* * * *

It was a late Saturday night since we all celebrated a student's birthday after the meeting. I made it to my tent past midnight.

Coming down the hill to the house Sunday morning, I could hear the sounds of construction growing louder. Jim and Miles were carrying material out the front door and piling it in the back of the flatbed truck that was parked at the edge of the patio. Inside was Robert directing another student with a sledge hammer to pound down the southern wall of the living room. The Architect was trying to map what was happening in front of him to the blueprints in his hand. It was clear the triad had shifted. The impasse had been bridged.

The natural light illuminated the living room. The old windows had small panes, and there had been more wood than glass. The new design I was told would have large windows that could open to let in air. The wall had to be reconstructed also because the outdoor boards were rotting, and the wall had to be propped up from the outside with beams.

I asked if I could help in some way and was handed a broom and large pan. I was so happy to sweep up debris that had fallen on the floor. This was exciting to me. We were transforming this ancient relic of a house into something habitable. I still had no idea what the finished house would look like, not being privileged to view the plans, but I wanted to be part of its rebirth.

After lunch, another truck had arrived with the windows, and Robert wished everyone to work as late as necessary to install them and complete the wall. This meant those students who had planned to return to the Bay Area to prepare for the Monday work day in life had to reconsider their options. That sense of life responsibility was strong, and the workforce diminished noticeably by 4 p.m. Even the Architect left.

A handful of students remained to complete the framing of the southern wall and the insertion of the windows. It was well past sundown. I offered to help, but my reputation for imprecise hammer work had already become the thing of legend. Instead, Robert directed me again toward the kitchen to assist with preparing the late dinner.

As we sat there in the living room with our dinner plates, gazing at the transformation, something stood out to me: the main post in the living room. It stuck out like a sore thumb, as it blocked the view we had worked so hard to free up. Its fate would soon be revealed. I felt sure that when the Architect returned the following weekend, he would be in for a surprise. Robert was following a grander plan than could be captured on a piece of paper.

> *But Solomon was building his own house thirteen years, and he finished all his house…And there were windows in three rows, and light was against light in three ranks. And all the doors and posts were square.*
>
> I Kings

CHAPTER 55

The work continued Monday morning on the southern wall. As soon as the stores opened, a few guys went to town with the truck to pick up the necessary materials. This included sheetrock (a new word to me) that needed to be nailed to the frame, plus paint, tape, and spackle, which was a paste used to seal holes and make the surface smooth for painting. I had never before thought about what went into a wall, so this was quite an education.

Jim was working closely with Miles on the wall. After taking measurements and trimming the sheetrock outside, they carried each sheet in and hammered them in place. Then I watched Jim tape the seams of the wall. He saw me standing there and called me over.

"Linda, you can help me by spackling. Let me show you how."

I looked over to Miles, expecting him to smile, but he made a face of disapproval. Jim, on the other hand, was like a brother to me, and I was so grateful he thought I could do a physical task. Women were generally asked to nurture children and animals and cook meals. Men, on the other hand, did the heavy lifting, as the men liked to describe it, such as construction work. No one questioned this.

I watched him apply the spackle. Jim handed me the tool called a "spackle knife," which was like a thin-bladed butter knife that was malleable enough to spread the paste evenly. I applied a little too much the first application, so he took the knife to show me how just a little goes a long way. This reminded me of that first task I had with Nadia, spreading glue on the vinyl tiles, at which I had failed miserably. I saw this as an opportunity to do it better.

He left me alone to work on it and when he returned, he inspected it and pronounced the work Good. A warm, positive feeling of accomplishment filled me. It uplifted my state.

Robert was standing there, communicating with Rosemary. My guess was that they were talking about what color to paint the wall. He was scribbling, of course, so I had no idea what the final determination would be. He called me over. Thinking he wanted my opinion (which would have been lavender), I waited for him to compose his message:

"Have you scheduled your next Rolfing with Annabella?"

"No."

"Please follow up."

With that he walked away.

His three little words blew my mind. The calm state of satisfaction I felt a moment earlier was suddenly destroyed by a swarm of screaming, negative 'I's. How am I supposed to do that? Annabella has yet to show up at the ranch. Why does Robert do this? His simple requests require so much effort. I want to obey him, but this is impossible. Couldn't he see this? I have no car. I have no phone. Why did he push my buttons like this when I was in such a good mood?

During lunch, I went up to Rosemary to tell her what Robert requested me to do, hoping she would commiserate with me. Instead, she mentioned that one of her daughters had a Rolfing scheduled at their home and maybe Annabella could fit me in.

"I'm leaving at 7 a.m. for Vacaville," she said, "There's room in the car for you."

I hadn't planned on leaving the ranch so early in the week. Those of us living at Via Del Sol would make the one-day journey to the Bay Area, arriving just in time for the Tuesday meeting and then leave immediately afterwards. We didn't have the incentive to hang around the Bay mainly because we didn't have the money to spend on shopping or sightseeing. We would eat lunch at the ranch and bring food for dinner, which we would consume in the car just before the meeting.

Not knowing how or when I would eat on Tuesday freaked me out. There was that time when Robert pulled Rose away for dinner and I was left alone to fend for myself. That cold metallic rush of fear started to circulate inside of me. There was nothing to say or do, as I was not in the position to dictate my preference to anyone. Once again, I was just along for the ride.

* * * *

Each night in my tent, as the events of the day replayed themselves in my mind, I would study them.

I could see I had a wide swing of emotions that day. One moment, I was elated that I had accomplished a physical task, and then, within a few minutes, I was thrown into a hornet's nest of 'I's. There I was, expecting Robert to include me, and instead I was told to do something that made my life difficult and uncertain. I had no control over my external or internal worlds. I was a living and breathing example of a stimulus-response machine. Why do I have to keep verifying this? Isn't once enough? When am I going to find that Quiet Place Within and simply live there?

I was sinking into a depression, when the urge to pee overcame me. It was well past midnight. I slipped on my sneakers and unzipped the tent opening, flashlight in hand. The September night was cool and fresh. After relieving myself, I realized I hadn't seen the moon that night. It must be the new moon. The stars of the Milky Way stared down at me and I stared back at them for what seemed to be a long while. They must know what tomorrow will bring, I thought, for they must have seen it all before.

The night's chill compelled me to return to my tent. The alarm had been set for 5:45 a.m. Tomorrow is now today, and it will be a long one.

> *Ah! my Beloved, fill the Cup that clears*
> *To-day of past Regrets and future Fears*
> *To-morrow? — Why, To-morrow I may be*
> *Myself with Yesterday's Sev'n Thousand Years.*
> Omar Khayyam

CHAPTER 56

Rose was strict about the 7 a.m. Monday morning departure. She had told me once about her first meeting with Robert. They were to meet at a restaurant in Sausalito and she was five minutes late. Robert was waiting outside and chastised her for her tardiness. He told her to always arrive five minutes early and not have the teacher wait for her. It was then that he said, "You must be *on time* to be *outside of time*."

I had hit the snooze button and arose at six. My customary Venusian pace forced me to grab figs, dates, and nuts from the cooler for breakfast instead of the normal granola and coffee. I got in the back of the car and slept all the way to Vacaville while Rosemary and her daughter sat in the front talking.

We stopped at the supermarket for supplies. I didn't buy anything for myself, but simply followed Rosemary around, pushing her cart for her. We pulled into her driveway, and I unloaded the car as she went to retrieve the mail from the box in front of the house.

When she entered the kitchen, she was giggling with delight.

"Linda, look at this!" she said, handing me a letter.

It was from the Vacaville School District and was addressed to me but with her last name and her house number on it.

"I guess you are now one of my daughters," she said with a broad grin. "Open it up. What does it say?"

I looked at the beautiful script on the envelope that clearly misnamed me. It was a perfect example of a C Influence shock: the timing was impeccable, it made no sense, and it woke me up in that moment to the chatter of 'I's inside my head that tried to explain the shock away. "How could this happen? This was not my last name. They knew my real name was Kaplan from my job application and college transcripts. Yes, I did use Rosemary's address but I didn't ask for them to reply."

I handed the letter to Rose to read.

"It says you are qualified to be a substitute teacher for the Vacaville School District. There's a number here for you to call the night before so you can let them know you are available to teach the following day. Now you can make some money in your profession," she said, thrilled at my new prospects.

I was a bit stunned. This would have been ideal if I still lived in Vacaville. But I now live at Via Del Sol. I was on a highway going north, not south. I felt like a past and future life had collided inside of me: the past was the full-time teaching job I aspired to but lost only three months ago, and the future was this tempting possibility that would have been ideal for that Linda Kaplan, English Teacher. But where was she to be found now?

In those three months, I had been transformed. It was a messy transformation, more like the rough, makeshift renovation of the log cabin I just left than a beautifully planned remodeling. Indeed, I was the Oregon House farmhouse, a true work-in-progress. What a metaphor of evolution.

I smiled at Rose and said nothing during lunch, trying to hide the pain of my shattered dreams. How could I explain to her that this opportunity applied to someone else with the name Linda, not me. Her last name added, I guess, was as fitting a name as any.

* * * *

There's an old Jewish joke. A man went to the doctor complaining about pain in his shoulder. After sympathetically listening, the doctor suddenly stomped on the patient's foot. The man screamed in pain, wondering why the doctor would do such a thing. The doctor then asked him, "So…how does your shoulder feel?" He replied, "Much better, thank you."

Annabella's Rolfing session at Rose's house focused on my feet. My emotional angst of disappointment and confusion earlier that morning evaporated like fog under a scorching sun when she applied her callused knuckle to the connective tissue between my toes and inside my arches. I had wondered why Robert wanted me to get Rolfed and now I understood.

There's a Fourth Way idea of distinguishing between necessary and unnecessary suffering. Rolfing was real suffering because it produced a higher state. Perhaps the confusion about "what to do with my life" was too large a subject to deal with, and was a problem with no immediate solution. It only produced depression and anxiety.

Although I could articulate this insight, I still could not stop the onslaught of troublesome 'I's. Sure, there was the concept of separation from identification with the many 'I's using divided attention and self-remembering. But those were just words to me now. All my attempts to separate, divide attention, and self-remember were futile. I wasn't good at it. So the torment continued.

I was hoping the meeting that night would help me understand how to be the Master of my internal world.

* * * *

The Tuesday Berkeley meeting was at Anna's house. It was a familiar civilized place to be with students, and yet the ghosts of old Linda lingered there. In the living room I saw myself with Miles when I first came up from Los Angeles. In the dining room I could see that tearful moment with Robert when I deeply understood I needed the school and would become a member. It seemed as if that occurred years ago. Who was this Linda now? Where was Miles now? These 'I's plagued me. They poisoned my brain like a disease.

The meeting was about to begin so we took our seats. Richard read from Robert's notes. Among the highlights was Robert's announcement that we were purchasing a four-year-old 20-foot by 60-foot mobile home that would house the children. Parents would pay $78 a month plus utilities.

Robert stopped Richard from speaking and began to write something, which Richard then had to read.

"Notice Richard just put his finger to his mouth when he read that parents will pay monthly."

Robert was pointing out to us all that Richard's machine was buffering the news with the subtle gesture of covering his mouth. I once overheard Robert point out to a student that the machine will cover its mouth instead of its ears when it doesn't want to hear something because it is a less obvious gesture. Robert's photograph to Richard made everyone in the room stiffen. No one wanted to be used as a bad example in public.

Richard continued to read the notes, which included Robert's comment about leaving several students at the ranch to complete an octave. Immediately I realized both Miles and Jim were missing. I started to think about them. Then I was thinking about the farmhouse renovation. I was only half-listening, as the subjects ranged from parents with children and the right use of sex energy to how to handle life families. These didn't apply to me so I didn't give them much attention. Then Robert wrote, "Are there any questions?"

Suddenly I raised my hand. I wasn't expecting to do this, but a question entered my head quickly.

"You said C Influence does everything. Do they control our moments of self-remembering?"

"Yes."

I was shocked. The implications were enormous. If they control our presence, they also by default control our sleep. That means they control our consciousness *and* functions. What is it we do? What does it mean to make an effort? How can we become our own Master when they control everything?

This time it was a one-word response that blew my mind. The only thing I was sure of was that this simple acknowledgment of how the gods work would take years to verify and a lifetime to accept.

❖

Behind what we achieve is a god, who doesn't take credit.
Michel de Montaigne

CHAPTER 57

The refreshments after the meeting were enough to fill my stomach and quell my fear of starvation. I hitched a ride back to Via Del Sol with four other residents, and I slept with my purse as a pillow positioned against the backseat window.

In the darkness of the new moon, the car pulled up to the farmhouse at 3 a.m. We were all sleepy children after the long drive, and it was customary for us to use the house's bathroom before heading up to our tents. But as I entered, I was stunned awake. The support post in the living room was gone.

No one else had noticed it. I stood there, staring at what was absent, when the last student exiting the bathroom said, "Linda, it's your turn."

After using the toilet and washing my face, I returned to that spot in the living room. Everyone else had left. A special energy filled the area. I smiled, thinking: Behold the handiwork of the gods. The stage was now set for the next chapter of this renovation play. The characters were somewhere in the wings, awaiting their cue.

* * * *

Wednesday morning began at noon with lunch. Robert had stayed in the Bay Area, and still no one had mentioned the absence of the post.

I was actually surprised how few students were around. David was there, as it was his turn to stay at the ranch instead of attending the meeting. After lunch I joined him outside with Trisha's son, who liked to hang out with David. I told them about the new mobile home for the children that would be coming up this weekend. David looked at me concerned.

"What age range?" he asked.

I hadn't thought of this, but I could tell he was thinking of both Trisha's son and Bonita's daughter who were teenagers. There were about twenty kids of varying age who came occasionally and others who stayed regularly at the ranch. The age range was about six to sixteen.

"I'm sure there would be adult supervision," I replied, although as I mentioned, I hadn't truly paid attention to this since it had nothing to do with me.

He puffed on his pipe for a while as I told him about my question and Robert's reply. I wondered how he viewed the effort to self-remember. His round checks lifted into this wonderful smile.

Looking up philosophically he said, "When you see a bird pulling a worm out of the ground, you can safely say you see a bird pulling a worm out of the ground."

Huh?

This was as enigmatic to me as the sound of one hand clapping, which I never understood. Because I looked puzzled, both men started to laugh at me. How simple, I thought. This is David. He's not caught up in Teaching the

Fourth Way system. But then, how could he be in a Fourth Way school if he doesn't know the teachings and doesn't use work language like Essence, Personality and Self-Remembering?

We sat there for a while watching the chickens peck the dirt. Then Trisha's son asked to borrow David's VW bug. A discussion followed during which David turned to me to ask if I knew how to drive a stick shift. I told him I didn't, although I did manage to drive Miles's Chevy with its H transmission. That was a fluke.

"I can teach you if you like. Let's go now."

He stood up and I followed, leaving the teenager behind. We got in the VW beetle, which was parked near the barn. We drove down Rice's Crossing Road, heading in the direction of Lake Francis, which was the outer eastern perimeter of my known world of Oregon House. He continued through the town of Dobbins. The road was two-way and the landscape had quickly changed. The oaks and manzanita gave way to tall pine. We were rapidly climbing into the mountains along this narrow lane with a drop to the valley floor of several hundred feet. The expansive view of dense forest was majestic.

We passed a huge dam, which the sign announced was named Bullards Bar. The road now cut through the forest. David stopped the car on a paved side road and turned the engine off.

"Okay. Let's switch seats."

As I sat on the warm driver's seat, he pointed to the three pedals, indicating which one was the gas, which was the brake and which was the clutch.

"You'll use your right foot for the gas and brake pedals and your left foot for the clutch. Okay. Try them out."

I applied pressure to the gas and the clutch and the brake, to get a feel for them. Unlike the brake, the clutch went straight to the floorboard without resistance. I was surprised.

"Now, let's practice shifting. There are four gears and a reverse. You have to step on the clutch before you can shift into a gear. Try it out."

This was fun. I got the concept right away.

"Good. Put it in first gear. Now step on the clutch and turn the engine on. Release the clutch and give it some gas slowly."

I did as he directed, but the car suddenly lurched and died.

"That's okay," he said kindly. "It takes practice." He used his hand to show me how to ease up on the clutch while pressing the gas pedal down. It was an opposite movement that required coordination. It reminded me of the old circus trick of patting your head with one hand and rubbing your tummy at the same time with the other. I tried again and the car moved forward, but the more gas I applied, the louder the noise from the engine. David quickly said, "Shift into second." I totally forgot how to do this. Panicking, I stomped on the brake and the engine died again.

It took a great deal of David's patience, but never did he yell at me or call me stupid. He was kind. After about thirty minutes of instruction, I was able to shift gears to accelerate and to come to a stop.

I asked him about the speeds for each of the gears so I could coordinate the shifting more smoothly. It was, I reasoned, a much more mathematical approach. I would need to look down at the speedometer, however, which would take my eyes off the road. But David had a different approach. "Just listen to the car. It will tell you when to shift," he said.

I hadn't realized the sound of the engine actually modulated from low to high. This machine had its own language and would communicate its needs to me. What an interesting thought. It was a crescendo that said, "I can't take it anymore, time for a change."

When I retired that night, I reviewed the highlights of my day. I saw the afternoon's driving lessons produced a simple, clear awareness. I had to focus my attention with my moving center (shifting gears and using the pedals), with my senses from the instinctive center (listening to the engine's sound variances), and with my intellectual center (registering the speeds on the dial).

Ouspensky said self-remembering needs focused attention in at least three centers, so by definition I think I was remembering myself. Was this a correct effort to self-remember? It didn't feel like that was my aim. My aim was to learn to drive a stick shift. This required me to follow David's instructions in the moment — indeed, from moment to moment. I simply was *present* watching my machine interact with another machine.

Could this be what David was trying to tell me about the bird and the worm?

❖

That is most difficult which seems easiest:
to be present to what is before you.
                                          Johann Goethe

CHAPTER 58

The next day at the ranch was active, as the land was being remolded to accommodate the mobile home for children. A tractor was rented to scrape the surface level, and to create a path so the trailer could be moved into place. Manzanita, oaks, digger pines, and poison oak were removed and pushed into huge piles alongside the new access road.

Everything I describe about the workers' activities I learned second-hand on Thursday. I hadn't yet ventured to the site. I preferred to stay close to the house, working in the kitchen and cleaning the boot room where the laundry was done. I would blow the conch to alert the workers that meals were ready for consumption. But that was as far outside as I went that day.

Robert had arrived on Friday afternoon and immediately went to see the new trailer, which was now in place. When I learned of this, I didn't want to miss seeing Robert's reactions to the new addition, so I decided to leave the comfort of the house and asked someone to point out the direction to me.

I was told to take a small path below the barn, which apparently led to the site. The path was not well-worn, and I was guessing whether I, indeed, was heading toward the teacher or away from him and into the denser landscape. This trek proved not to be an easy one for me.

Some of the first words I recall as a child were "pavement" and "grass" in that order (as in, Stay on the pavement and Stay off the grass). I was used to walking on flat sidewalks not rocks and loose dirt. The terrain was also a descent from the barn so with each step I was slipping and sliding. I had to tread carefully, which required me to focus my attention on the dirt beneath my feet not the path ahead. It occurred to me to use my sense of hearing to navigate, since work was still being done to clear the land. As the sounds grew louder, I finally arrived at the open area. There it was: the trailer, with Robert, Jim, Miles, Yorgos, and others gathered.

I approached and stood with the crowd of students, most of whom were parents. Like the time we went to see the sunset in silence, I stood there observing, but after twenty seconds or so I was done. I couldn't relate to this event, but only wanted to be around Robert. I missed his energy as it helped me to *be here* wherever that Here was. The teacher was honey to my buzzing bee.

Jim left Robert's side and came up to me.

"Robert wants to talk to you."

Me? A chill ran through me.

I followed Jim and stood next to Robert, who had already written the message, which he handed to me to read: "You will teach the children here."

I smiled and nodded, as if this was perfectly logical and acceptable and that I was 100% on board with his request. Inside, however, the many 'I's were screaming: "Me? I can't teach young kids. I'm qualified only for high schoolers. What do I teach them? The grades would range from 1 to 11. You cannot create a single curriculum for all. Doesn't he know this?"

I felt lost and confused, but was more afraid of denying my teacher. My only hope was that he would forget his request and it would disappear underneath all the other octaves he was trying to accomplish.

At dinner that evening, I heard some of the discussion regarding the separation of child from parent. The kids actually thought it was cool and the parents were mortified. Robert's solution, as I understood it, was to create a schedule whereby two parents would sleep in the trailer with the kids in shifts.

At the Tuesday Berkeley meeting, Robert mentioned in his notes that children were in the many 'I's more than adults and that women especially were subject to satellite feature, which means their worlds revolved around husbands and children like a moon to a planet. It was mechanical and part of the nature of existence.

Still, it was painful for them to hear, but one thing I had learned about difficult subjects was that they hurt precisely because they had a grain of truth in them. Remember when I told Miles that it hurt to read that we are machines? It's not easy to bear the truth. Robert encourages us simply to record an idea until we can verify it. He enjoyed quoting Walt Whitman's advice to approach any new subject with "neither preference nor denial."

False personality buffers grains of truth with landmines whose charges trigger negative emotions like Fourth of July rockets when those grains are stepped on. Telling women how to parent their children was such a landscape. I was grateful I didn't have anything to do with it so it was easy for me to sit back and watch the fireworks.

Wait a minute. If he truly meant I was to be their teacher, I'd be thrown in the middle of this war zone. Oh, pretty please I hope he forgets. Then I remembered the same wishful thinking I had had regarding getting Rolfed. Robert may not pester, but he certainly doesn't forget. Down deep I knew this task was inevitable, but I certainly wasn't going to remind him of it any time soon.

*

Men and women run away from every goal, whether worldly or spiritual, because they overestimate the initial task. The proper way is a bit at a time.

Rumi

CHAPTER 59

Saturday had arrived, and the players had assembled to view the structural changes to the living room. The morning light gently streamed through the new windows with its soft energy. Standing where the missing post had been were Robert, the Architect, and Don.

With my apron on, I moved within ear range and heard the Architect say, while shaking his head in disbelief, "The only thing holding this roof up must be C Influence."

Robert smiled as did Don. I, too, enjoyed the moment, especially as it confirmed the feelings I had had regarding this play — that it was designed to help a student verify that the gods do everything. In that moment, I felt we were all on the same boat. It was comforting.

As this was a work-octave weekend (described as Third Line of Work), the other focus in the house was to replace the oven. That small, wall-unit chrome oven was gone, and a new stove range (top burners with a built-in oven) was installed. I hadn't realized how nostalgic I would be to see the old oven go, as it represented a key lesson in my evolution: to multiply any action by the number of people it would affect. A new scene was being set. I wondered what the next lessons would be for me in this kitchen.

* * * *

The Saturday night meeting was before dinner and after sunset. The living room had been cleared and swept as we gathered around Robert, Meg, Rosemary, and Miles, who had seats in the front. Other chairs were also provided for those who couldn't sit on the floor, like Doris, Don, and Anna.

Meg was asked to describe a situation that preceded one of Robert's comments.

"A student was sitting on the stairs, eyes closed, as another student massaged him. Robert asked what was going on and the student left the room," said Meg.

She then read Robert's comments.

"People will stone you if you do not identify with them, even here. Another student stoned me because I did not share in their identification. Higher centers are not identified. It is weakness to tolerate somebody's identification. Why? Because then you are supporting their sleep. When to help? When someone sincerely needs it. From what little I know of the student's situation, there was delight in the physical body going on. 'To everything there is a season,' and this wasn't the time."

Meg continued to read from Robert's notes on other subjects.

"A student should love no one more than his teacher. Why is this so? A teacher is light in the midst of darkness. To love the other more is to love the lower more than the higher. This love takes a *real student* – one on the Way. Also, a teacher loves nothing more than his students – including his physical family.

"Sex represents union, or unity, on a physical level. It is also one area where the person is aware of another person as well as himself. Non-mechanical union – a true union – is a private experience, a marriage within – an immaculate conception. Intellectual and emotional centers produce a conscious child, the Third Eye. When people try to raise an ideal child, it is a deviation and a buffer from raising their own child within them. Yet both can be had, although few try for the inner child."

When Meg finished, Robert scribbled on his piece of paper, "Are there any questions?"

A hand went up and the question was, "What is meant by men and women having to go against nature?"

Robert wrote his sentences immediately, pausing occasionally to allow Meg to read.

"A male is a male machine. A female is a female machine. All must go against their body type and sex to reach higher centers; this is going against nature. Do not take ideas singularly; use relativity. If too many find out the secret to awakening, they will try to reach higher centers and the social structure would collapse. Consciousness is also designed into the machine.

"Ouspensky said it takes a *Man* or a *Woman* to control negative emotions. Humor is usually useless; however, sometimes there has to be humor. People, at a certain stage of their development, can hear the truth only in the form of a lie, and humor is quite often that. Humor is usually aimed at someone."

Robert looked up before continuing. "We are near the end of an octave. Allow for more difficulties than usual."

With that the meeting ended.

At dinner everyone was talking about the next weekend, which was a getaway weekend to a place known as Coastways Ranch. This news confused me. Why are we leaving Via Del Sol at this time to go on a retreat when Robert was pushing us so hard to continue work here? When I asked, no one could fully explain it. I was told that the ranch off Highway 1 was owned by a student named Mary C., who was a wealthy city planner. I hadn't seen her at meetings or Via Del Sol, so didn't know her. This apparently was the second time the group went to this place, having gone there in May over the Memorial Day weekend.

People were in a good mood during dinner with the prospects of what could best be described as a vacation. I smiled as they spoke about the place. It sounded great with its cool ocean breezes, acres of farmland, and the refined complex of living quarters where we all would be staying. It would be wonderful to sleep in a real bed, I thought.

But just as I took my last bite of food, it happened. I overheard someone mention that it was on the previous trip there that Miles and Helga first hooked up. I froze. With the half-chewed morsel still in my mouth, my throat constricted and it took great effort to swallow. I was in a state of shock.

I stood up and went to the kitchen to stack my plate with the others in the sink. Holding back tears, I went into the boot room and took my supplies and flashlight up to my tent. Unzipping the opening, I stepped inside and slowly undressed. I slipped into my nightgown, lay down, and pulled the sleeping bag around my throat. Tears formed and flowed silently down my cheeks in the darkness.

Why was I weeping so? It wasn't as if I didn't know that Miles and Helga were a couple. Was it self-pity? That could be, but it felt like something deeper.

The strangest image popped into my head: the old stove. I missed it. And Miles in a bizarre way reminded me of the old stove. The old stove was a tool for my conscious development, as much as Miles had been. But I didn't so much miss him as I felt betrayed. Who had betrayed me? Suddenly I knew. It wasn't Miles. *It was C Influence.*

The dam of deep emotions broke and I sobbed uncontrollably. The gods set me up. They've done this my whole life. They give me things that I believe in and then rip them out of the walls of my heart. How can you trust gods who betray you? In less than a year, the Linda who had charted her life course to be a high school teacher, to support herself financially, to find love and a fulfilling, faithful relationship was gone. I kept asking myself, where is this Linda? I deeply longed for her return. It was that Linda, with all of her dreams for the future, that I missed most of all.

※

O living always – always dying!
O the burials of me, past and present!
O me, while I stride ahead, material, visible, imperious as ever!

THE DIVINE BEGINNING

O me, what I was for years, now dead, (I lament not — I am content;)
O to disengage myself from those corpses of me, which I turn and look at, where I cast them!
To pass on, (O living! Always living!) and leave the corpses behind!

Walt Whitman

CHAPTER 60

Before Robert left that Sunday for the Bay Area, he informed me he wanted me to focus on teaching the children, beginning tomorrow. He wasted no time with his request.

Monday morning after breakfast I went down to the children's house to speak with the mothers there regarding the best course of study. As I arrived, the children were running around, laughing, hitting each other with sticks and stones, and being generally unruly. It reminded me a bit of *Lord of the Flies,* which had been a popular book of the time that documented a group of unsupervised children on a deserted island who had turned to barbarism.

The two mothers on duty were Alice, who was a passive type and the wife of Richard, and Tall Jane, a Saturn-Mars with a chief feature of fear. There were 22 kids: one five-year-old, two six-year-olds, one eight-year-old, one ten-year-old, four eleven-year-olds, four fourteen-year-olds, three fifteen-year-olds and six sixteen-year-olds.

I introduced my qualifications to Alice and Tall Jane, explaining I had a high school teaching credential. What is it that they wished me to teach?

Tall Jane was most interested in her eight-year-old learning math and reading.

When I was in high school, I had volunteered to teach elementary school kids how to read. They threw me into a class room after school with a ten-year-old. My initial glee that I was helping a little kid suddenly turned into despair. I was ill-equipped, without text books, educational materials or verbal instructions. I had no idea what to do and was embarrassed and saddened as I looked at the frustration in the poor boy's face. I quit volunteering that day and vowed to get my degree in high school English and Drama instead. When it came to math, forget about it. Numbers had never been my strong suit.

After learning there were no teaching materials at the children's house, such as books or paper and pencils, I found myself negotiating with Tall Jane and Alice, explaining that since the majority was older kids, perhaps I could teach Chaucer. It had wonderful stories, and the language was the foundation for modern English. Alice was a bit more accepting than Tall Jane, who looked crestfallen at my suggestion. I held my ground and they accepted my approach. We agreed that I should begin at 2 p.m.

* * * *

At 2 p.m., with book in hand, I entered the trailer. I told the kids to gather around and announced I would be their teacher for the day.

"We are going to study Chaucer. He lived FIVE HUNDRED years ago and wrote a series of wonderful stories titled *Canterbury Tales*."

I was expecting a reaction such as *Wow! Five hundred years ago!* Instead, I got silence. I continued.

"Each tale spoke about the people of his times, the Knight, the Squire, and the Miller. Chaucer wrote in Middle English, which was the language of his day. Let me read you some Middle English. Even though it sounds weird, it is the foundation of the language we speak now."

I cleared my throat and began.

> "Whan that Aprill with his shoures soote
> The droghte of March hath perced to the roote,
> And bathed every veyne in swich licour
> Of which vertu engendred is the flour;
> Whan Zephirus eek with his sweete breeth
> Inspired hath in every hold and heath
> The tender croppes, and the yonge sonne
> Hath in the Ram his half cours yronne,
> And smale foweles make melodye,
> That slepen al the nyght with open ye
> (So priketh hem nature in hir corages)
> Thanne longen folk to goon on pilgrimages."

At this point I stopped to translate. I noticed I had lost my audience.

"So basically, it says that in April, when it rains a bunch and waters the plants that were dried out from the drought of March, everyone yearned to go on a pilgrimage. Do you understand?"

"What's a pilgrimage?" asked an eleven-year-old.

"It's when you leave your home and decide to go on a long journey for a religious reason, usually. Okay now. Would you like to hear more?"

Some of the boys started hitting each other in the back of the room. The youngest ones had wide-eyed innocent looks of confusion.

THE DIVINE BEGINNING

I panicked. It was time to entertain, I thought. The television program I was offering was clearly boring.

"How about I read a naughty story from the Miller's Tale? But you have to promise you won't tell your mothers."

That got their attention. The pummeling kids stopped what they were doing.

"The Miller's name was John and he was old and ugly. He had a beautiful young wife named Alisoun. To make some money, John rents two rooms in his house to two young dudes named Nicholas and Absolon, who both like Alisoun and want to find a way to be with her. Nicholas decides to trick John the Miller by telling him he had a terrible dream of the end of the world, like Noah's flood. He convinces John to prepare for the flood by sleeping that night in a big tub on top of his house so he can float away when the flood comes. John believes him and when he falls asleep that night, Nicholas takes Alisoun away with him."

I couldn't believe they were listening to me.

"So this other dude, Absolon, is at the window that same night, begging Alisoun to kiss him. So let's listen to what happens.

> "This Absolon gan wype his nouth ful drie.
> Derk was the nyght as pich, or as the cole,
> And at the window out she putte hir hole,
> And Absolon, hym fil no bet ne wers,
> But with his mouth he kiste hir naked ers
> Ful savourly, er he were war of this.
> Abake he stirte, and thought it was amys,
> For wel he wiste a woman hath no berd.
> He felte a thing al rough and long yherd
> And seyde, 'Fye! Allas! What have I do?'
> 'Tehee!' quod she, and clapte the window to,
> And Absolon gooth forth a sory pas.

"Now, can anyone tell me what just happened?"

They looked perplexed and disappointed.

"Okay, let's take it a sentence at a time." I began to translate each line.

"The dude Absolon, wiped his mouth dry in anticipation of kissing the beautiful Alisoun. Since the night was as dark as pitch or coal (meaning, it was so dark that he couldn't see anything), she sticks her bottom out the window instead of her face, and Absolon, with his mouth, kisses her ass with passion (thinking it was her lips), but he suddenly pulls back and realizes something was horribly wrong. 'Wait a minute,' he says, 'A woman doesn't have a beard.'"

At that, the older boys got it, and uttered such words as Yuck and Ewww, while the look of horror was pasted on the young ones' faces.

Oops.

It was only then that I realized that the kids would report back to their mothers in answer to "What did you learn today, dear?" Fie. Alas. I'm in trouble.

"Okay kids, enough for the day."

And with that, the first instruction of Fellowship children came to an end.

The life so short, the craft so long to learn,
The attempt so hard, so sharp the conquering.
Geoffrey Chaucer

CHAPTER 61

I found a way to the Berkeley meeting that Tuesday. It was the end of September. As I was sitting in the passenger seat during the drive to the Bay Area, an 'I' whispered: "September. You were going to get married to Miles in September, remember?" I chuckled, shaking my head at the absurdity of the thought. Just another dashed dream to record.

"What's so funny?" asked the driver.

"Oh, nothing," I replied, trying to change the subject by pointing out the enormous number of World War II battleships positioned in the waters near the Carquinez Bridge. Someone in the car mentioned they were "mothballed," a new term for me that meant they were in storage there as part of the Pacific fleet. What made it such a strange impression was that the ships were so numerous and that the whole scene strangely lacked a sense of scale; it was as if I was looking at toy ships in a child's bathtub.

When we arrived at Anna's house, there were more cars than usual lining the narrow Oxford Street. It was clear the Fellowship was expanding. Every meeting had new faces. As was the custom, the meeting began with the introduction of new students. Each would stand up as their name was announced often by the person bringing them to the school. This meeting had four: Gordon and Susan, and Doug and Colleen.

Robert, who was still in silence, had announced a new meeting schedule. A regular meeting for all members would be on Tuesdays at Anna's while additional optional meetings would be held in Vacaville at Don's home, and at Via Del Sol, all with a pre-arranged topic. Perhaps this was the new octave Robert had mentioned.

Someone questioned the meetings at Via Del Sol, whether it meant we did not have to come up on weekends. It was a bit confusing because Robert did not lead optional meetings; he led required meetings. Robert, however, did not keep to any schedule. He would show up on weekends unannounced and lead a meeting at Via Del Sol, optional or not.

His written reply to the question seemed obvious to me. "It's best to come up on weekends. It is third line of work." He went on to explain that it helps some students overcome what "it" wants and what "it" doesn't want. Clearly many of the Bay Area folk felt the strong want of ready access to indoor plumbing, I thought.

Robert went on with this topic.

"Meher Baba said that there is nothing higher than obedience. 'I' am obedient to higher forces — and that doesn't mean it is easy. Willfulness sometimes pretends to be will, which is incorrect crystallization. The group is in its best position and will get stronger. Problems are for students who are not on the Way."

A hand went up.

"The farm seems far from simple. It's chaotic at times."

Robert looked directly at the student and replied, "The many 'I's don't have knowledge of the whole. We have two houses now in only three months! Notice how practical we are. I take care of being before knowledge in my personal life."

That student continued with his questioning, "Can level of being change without knowledge?"

Robert answered, "Yes. We are all changing and we will continue to change. The next octave, however, will focus on knowledge. That is why we are having more meetings each week. Common sense is useful relativity and is not in a book. It is in you. That is then your Being. It IS you."

The subject of being, I realized, was a bit abstract, like the concept of one's Master. It was difficult to see these "changes in being" that Robert was speaking about.

He must have read my mind in that moment, when he added, "What bothers you now will not bother you later. Why? Because level of being will change. Use common sense: taste your food, make your bed. The farm is a good place to have problems."

Someone then asked a question that made me perk up my ears.

"Is C Influence both benevolent and demonic?"

Robert replied, "Yes, the latter to wake up higher centers."

I was still grappling with being set up by the gods. It reminded me of that cartoon that appears every autumn in the newspaper. Here's old Charlie Brown, trying to kick a football that is held by Lucy. She has a wicked sense of humor, while he is shy and passive and trustworthy. Each year he believes her when she says she'll hold the football as he runs to kick it. And each year, she lifts the ball from the spot at the last moment, causing him to do a somersault and land on his back with a thud.

I woke up from my association just as Robert concluded the meeting by stating, "Do not become paranoid by my silence. It is better than ever. Flowers are silent. You love me and are sometimes insensitive to one another. We will end now, loves. Hope we all have a good time at Coastways."

I noticed that since Robert entered silence, he was much softer and, dare I say, affectionate in his approach to us. I could see changes in him, but I had yet to see them in myself. Instead of becoming a unity, most of the time I felt like I was falling apart. I didn't like what I was seeing. It wasn't my picture of myself, and all the signs of my incompetency and ignorance were almost unbearable to witness. Is this change or decline? Who knew awakening would be this painful.

Do I contradict myself?
Very well, then, I contradict myself;
(I am large — I contain multitudes).
Walt Whitman

CHAPTER 62

Wednesday morning started late as usual, but at lunch I was surprised to find Robert had returned as well last night. In the evening, he called us together for an unscheduled meeting. One of the questions was on buffers. Robert mentioned that people, when rid of false personality, are simple and quiet, like nature. The many 'I's that night were plaguing me, however, and it was hard to imagine being quiet as a flower, as Robert had described his own silent state.

I felt like I was in a fog on Thursday as well. Something was bothering me, and I couldn't figure out what it was. It was a feeling of foreboding, a dread. There were no 'I's associated with it that I could observe. I went to bed puzzled, hoping that this feeling would be gone in the morning.

* * * *

I slept soundly that night. When I awoke, I felt clearheaded — for about five seconds. Then the cloud that hovered in the darkness overnight descended quickly and penetrated my being. It was so heavy that I lay there immobile for a period of time, as I dipped in and out of first state.

I finally came down from my tent around 8 a.m. I had expected to see a host of students busy with breakfast and coordinating the students and cars for the trip to Coastways Ranch. Instead, it was quiet and the house was empty. How strange.

I went to get some granola and milk and sat outside to eat, believing that students would appear at any moment, but no one showed. What was going on? Did everyone leave without me? The thought of this triggered the flow of fear inside.

Just as tears began to pool, I heard distant voices. Three students were coming up the hill from the barn, carrying milk buckets. I quickly composed myself and greeted them with a smile.

"What are you doing here?" one of them asked.

Apparently, they were selected as the caretakers during the weekend retreat. Everyone had left around 6 a.m., including Robert. We spoke, and I learned there was one last carload of students preparing to leave at 9 a.m. If I hurried, I may be able to join them.

I quickly went to my tent and grabbed clean underwear and a dress to stuff into my suitcase. I almost forgot my sundries and was grateful that the 'I' appeared in time. Then I stopped. I looked at my sleeping bag. I had been in the habit of taking it with me whenever there was an overnight, but remembered this ranch had beds so decided to leave it behind.

The car had driven up to the patio area to load belongings and some food for the drive. There were four students. The driver was a male student. I barely knew him, as was the case with the three ladies. He had been told of my need to go with them. None of them were happy, as it meant three of us would be squeezed in the back seat. I sat in the middle, grateful that they consented.

Conversations circulated, snacks were passed around, but the urge to use the bathroom forced us to make a pit stop at a Denny's in Fairfield. The smell of hamburgers and French fries overpowered the driver, and we lingered for a late lunch. Food arrived rather quickly since the lunch crowd was gone. The maps were laid out on the table as we ate.

"I still think we should avoid San Francisco and connect with Highway 1 by taking 680 to 17 and Santa Cruz," said the lady student who brought the maps. "Then we can go up north on Highway 1 and avoid the San Francisco tolls."

The male student thought for a moment and then said, "The instructions we have are through San Francisco, but I like the idea of saving money." And so, the route was determined.

It was nice not to go through the city. The 680 highway was more visually appealing. The emotional dread, like my place in the car, also took a back seat, allowing me to look at the impressions of golden hills and quiet farmland that had just been harvested.

It was midafternoon by the time we reached Santa Cruz. As we drove north, I caught glimpses of waves crashing on the beach. Their beauty made me smile.

"Turn right on Finney Creek," said the student with the driving instructions, which had been passed out, I learned, at the Tuesday meeting.

The driver followed these directions. The road was wide and long and clearly agricultural. We continued for what seemed like a long time.

"There's supposed to be the ranch house complex nearby." No buildings were visible, however. Acres of rolling rows of plants ready for harvest stretched beyond eyesight.

"These are Brussel sprouts," said one of the ladies.

I had never seen how Brussel sprouts grow. In fact, I don't think I had ever eaten a Brussel sprout. The plant had a main trunk with limbs sticking out from all sides laden with green golf-ball-sized growths, which were the Brussel sprouts. How bizarre.

Tension arose in the car as everyone except me weighed in on our current predicament: Where are we? I think we're lost. Turn here. No, turn around. Wait a minute. The instructions are backwards. We came from the south not the north. That shouldn't matter once we are on the main road.

Somehow, we found the correct side road that led past the fields toward a major building complex. We were all tired, yet relieved. It was past five. We recognized some of the cars and knew we had finally arrived at our destination.

I followed them into the main house, leaving our belongings in the car. It was beautiful inside, with color-coordinated walls, old books on dark wood shelves, matching furniture, knick-knacks, and perfectly placed oil paintings.

THE DIVINE BEGINNING

I felt like I was in a fancy hotel. I saw Rosemary, Jan, Mac, Anna, and Marie crowded on couches in the main room, busy with planning the meals and the weekend schedule.

I stood there with the other four as they asked about sleeping quarters. Rosemary in her direct way blurted out, "You are all late. All the beds are taken." Someone reminded her there were other buildings in the complex that had some beds that were used for farm workers. We could go there, but it required a short drive.

Just then I heard the door open behind me. I quickly turned to look. The source of my dread hit me like a tornado. It was Miles and Helga. This is where they began their relationship, while I sat dreaming in Los Angeles of my wedding day. It was more than a simple 'I' that plagued me. It was a frozen moment in time and space from the past that collided with full impact into the present moment. I was stunned. This dread didn't want to leave me. It wanted me to give it my full attention so that I could lapse into self-pity. The waves of sadness rose and tried to overpower me.

In defense, I returned to the conversation regarding lodging and dutifully followed my fellow travelers to the furthest outpost of the property. As we entered this small building, someone else was in the bedroom area already and had claimed one of the so-called beds. It was actually an army cot with a blanket and pillow. I couldn't believe it. No mattress.

Set up again! I started to laugh. The others glared at me, wondering what was so funny. I tried to explain the Fancy Hotel Meets Army Barracks title of this recent episode of my life, but they didn't get it. Oh, well.

We returned to the main house for an informal dinner as more students kept showing up throughout the evening. Where they slept was anyone's guess. When I returned to my quarters at the end of the long day, my bunk mates (two of the women from the ride) were complaining about the inequality of the circumstances. They learned that accommodations had previously been determined, not by arrival time, but by a ranking devised by a few Older Students, apparently.

I was just happy that I wasn't sleeping in a cold tent on a foam pad. I was elevated from the ground at least, and it was a slightly better situation than how I began that morning.

As the lights were turned off in the bedroom, I began to review the day's events in my mind. The beauty of the mental images — the white foam on the crest of the ocean waves, the deep green of living plants, the restful space of a well-appointed living room — wrestled with the thoughts of betrayal, envy, and self-deprecation. Do I indulge in the dark emotions or do I relish the loveliness of these new surroundings?

The question became too philosophical for me to resolve that night. I knew, however, that it would be waiting for me to answer in the morning.

❖

My own thoughts are struggling against me.
Why am I drawn to the bait?

Petrarch

CHAPTER 63

I was surprised how well I slept on the army cot. My tendency to grab the bathroom first surprisingly hadn't manifested. The other ladies were up before me and had begun their morning rituals. They were dressed and out while I still remained in bed.

By the time I had showered, dressed and left the room, the car I had taken with the others to arrive at this overnight place was gone. But that was fine with me. It was about nine in the morning and the day was simply gorgeous. The smell of the distant salt ocean mixed with rich soil and green vegetables. The earth around me was so happy I could feel it smile. My mood became joyous and childlike.

Instead of lamenting my abandonment, I was ready for a trek to the main house. With a general sense of direction, I began to take the road to see where it would lead. I couldn't believe how eager I was for this adventure. Who is *this* Linda? I always had a fear of getting lost, but this Linda didn't. She was bold and confident.

Walking along the path, I noticed a large, white-fenced area with luscious grass inside. Perhaps this would be a short-cut, I thought. So I climbed the fence and hopped onto the soft terrain, with the aim of cutting across at a tangent. Happy as a lark was I. As I proceeded along, something caught my eye: to the far right near the distant fence post, I saw a large black boulder.

It began to move.

I froze. What is this? As it took quicker steps toward me, I saw its horns. It was a big black bull.

Run!

Reversing my steps, I hopped back over the fence to safety.

Was I afraid? Not so much. The bull came toward me out of curiosity and I wasn't hurt. But I had an adventure! What fun!

I went around the fence line talking to the bull, who found the juicy green grass more interesting than my friendly dialogue. Then, at the end of the post where the bull first stood, I saw a bicycle leaning against the wooden slats of the fence.

Oh! I could ride this to the main house, I thought. I loved riding my bike when I was young. I can do this!

The bike, which was designed for a man with its high bar down the center, required me to swing my leg over the seat to mount. I pushed off and found the balance to ride, but the dirt footpath I was following was downhill and I accelerated quickly. I tried to slow down by backpedaling, which was the braking system of my childhood bike, but it didn't have this. Oh no! How do I stop this? Oh, no!

Like my childhood runaway horse episode, I decided to jump off but, in this case, the bike seat stabbed me in the butt before I could make a clean escape. OW!

I got up slowly, rubbing my backside. After the pain subsided enough to walk without a waddle, I decided to accompany the bike to the complex. My bruised butt would be a secret between us.

* * * *

I entered the main house where I knew the kitchen was, and there I saw Robert sitting on a couch surrounded by students. He had a book in his hand. I approached slowly and listened.

"This is a picture of Hitler, who has a lunatic chief feature," he said. "His essence is dead."

Robert had covered Hitler's right eye, which is the personality side, to expose his left eye, which is the essence side. We each crowded around and peered over Robert's shoulder to see what Robert was indicating. When it was my turn, something shocking happened. Hitler's left eye jumped out at me, like a horror movie. It was Evil Eye and it scared me! I started to cry uncontrollably.

"Marie, can you take her away and help her?" instructed Robert. He added, "She is identified with being Jewish."

No, I wasn't. Being Jewish never entered my mind. I was surprised he said that. I thought he would know where I was psychologically. Apparently, he didn't. But then again, neither did I. I was just a kid who had seen the bogeyman.

Once I regained my composure, I caught a glimpse of Miles, who was one of those in the room. His facial expression was not one of concern. It was of judgment. Robert stood up and others dispersed to their respective octaves. It was strange to stand there without being assigned one. Just when that gloomy feeling of isolation tried to rise up, a friendly face appeared.

"Would you like to help us prepare lunch?" it asked. It was Tall Jane. What a kind gesture. I nodded and followed her into the kitchen. I was told to set the utensils, plates and glasses out on the table for lunch. The emotional thunderstorm had passed, and the bright internal sun with its reflected rays lovingly embraced each impression I saw with startling clarity. I was quiet inside and able to focus on the task at hand without words. The Self had emerged.

* * * *

Sunday morning included a meeting after breakfast. Robert had mentioned briefly that after our vacation (yes, this was the word he used), we would work with the two exercises of silence and no laughter at Via Del Sol. The silence would last a few days, but the no-laughter exercise would continue indefinitely.

He explained, "We can be joyful inside, but let's not laugh out loud. The most interesting observation is that 'it' laughs, not you. And this happens, just as there may be rain tomorrow or there may not be. Laughter is mechanical."

Someone asked, "Can we never laugh or be gay?"

Robert replied, "Inner joy will replace laughter. This exercise is designed to wake up higher centers and gain control of personality."

Robert then spoke about what he called "mute presence."

"How many have muteness that sees objects without words?"

Remembering my brief higher state the day before, I raised my hand and looked around. I was the only one. I quickly lowered it when I heard one student snicker in judgment. Perhaps he was thinking of my tear burst.

"That is the Self. It is not a word. It *is*. When you observe an object, such as this vase of flowers, look for three forces: The mute Self, the object, and the word Flowers. The Self will allow personality to speak and use the intellectual center to express what it wants to communicate."

When the meeting was over, I sat on the living room sofa for a while thinking about this mute, higher state. It was so fleeting, like a tease from the gods, like a preview of coming attractions. Once again, I found myself surrounded by my customary rainbow of sensitive feelings. A scowl, a snicker from others — all tried to induce inner considering and challenge my verifications. But then I realized they don't know what I'm experiencing inside. How private is our internal world. How individual this journey.

That weekend, the dread I had felt for days prior to the trip resolved itself. Whatever went on between Miles and Helga was then; this is now. The Coastways Ranch was innocent and did not participate in my imaginary associations. It became clear that as long as I could keep observing like this, my work will proceed. Perhaps the change I was looking for was simply the continuous process of uncovering what is unchangeable. What an interesting thought.

❦

Apart from the pulling and hauling
Stands what I am,
Stands amused, complacent, compassionating, idle, unitary…
Both in and out of the game and watching and wondering at it.
Walt Whitman

CHAPTER 64

I didn't return to Via Del Sol as I had planned after the retreat weekend. Annabella had approached me late afternoon Sunday to remind me I needed to have another Rolfing. She would be available Tuesday early afternoon, if that was okay. I agreed, although I had no idea how this would happen.

I remembered that the Tuesday meeting was scheduled at Anna's house in Berkeley. I spoke with Rosemary and she said I could stay with her in Vacaville on Monday and Tuesday, but not on Sunday evening. She was planning on staying with Anna Sunday night in Berkeley and then would be driving back to Vacaville on Monday.

She suggested I speak with Don because he needed to return to work in Vacaville Monday morning, and perhaps I could stay at his home. I did, and he agreed to take me with him. Rose could then pick me up on Monday from his home. On Tuesday, Rose could drop me off on that corner in Oakland where Annabella would once again meet me for lunch at that little café. After the treatment, I would then drive with Annabella to the Berkeley meeting and find a ride back to Via Del Sol, perhaps with the food truck.

Sounded like a good plan.

* * * *

On the Sunday evening drive north, I sat in the backseat of Don's car. Doris sat next to him. They quietly chatted. She giggled at times, and I could feel the teenage-like romantic connection between them. An 'I' arose in me wondering how these old people got to be In Love when my youthful desires remained unrequited. I let that 'I' go as it was beginning to depress me.

When we arrived at his home, Doris remained in the car while Don opened the door and helped me with my personal belongings. The home had muted lighting when he turned on the switches. I followed him as he showed me the bedroom where I would sleep. He then handed me clean sheets and showed me the bathroom and which towels I could use. Don had also said I could do laundry if I had some and showed me the washer and dryer.

We then went into the kitchen.

"Feel free to make anything you want," he generously said.

There were eggs, bacon, Nut Tree breads, butter, coffee, orange juice, wonderful cutlery and white plates and cloth napkins. The home was compartmentalized, and each area had its own color that harmoniously flowed from one room to the next. It was clearly a home created by someone with an artistic nature.

I thanked him for his generosity. He then left to drive Doris home.

I was alone when I awoke in the morning. I don't recall hearing Don return that evening, but preferred to assume he had. I slept exceedingly well. It was a real bed with mattress. The hot shower was luxurious, as the water pressure was sufficient to cover my entire body without having to turn around to accommodate a weak spray. The soap was creamy and fragrant. The towels were large and soft.

I decided to make scrambled eggs and bacon with toast and jam and coffee for breakfast. Denny's specialized in three-egg omelets so that was my aim. Taking a cereal bowl down from the cupboard, I cracked the first egg, and then the second. Then I cracked the third. Something unexpected happened. Instead of a raw egg flowing into the bowl, I was shocked to discover they were each hard boiled. I froze in place.

What do I do with hard-boiled eggs? I slowly removed the pieces of hard shell and saw this thin translucent membrane clinging to the soft white egg flesh. Something in me was processing what I was witnessing. There was *meaning* in it. What could it be?

Then I recalled reading something regarding the difference between personality and essence and how Ouspensky used the analogy of a shell. I stopped in my breakfast preparation and started to look for a work book. On the bookshelf was *The Fourth Way*. As I skimmed the chapters I found the passage.

"Personality is too heavy, too strong; it surrounds essence like a shell, so nothing can reach it directly, everything has to pass through personality. Essence cannot grow in these conditions, but if personality becomes more transparent, impressions and external influences will penetrate through it and reach essence, and then essence will begin to grow."

I returned to my breakfast preparation, pondering what I had just read. An understanding of what happened to me at the Coastways Ranch began to percolate within. I felt childlike, unprotected suddenly — from feeling playful to feeling terrified. Something was somehow stripped away. There was meaning in this egg: it somehow mirrored my psychological condition, but I was not sure yet in what way. I had to be content with a puzzle, for now.

* * * *

The afternoon passed slowly. I hadn't heard from Rosemary. I was alone in the house and realized I didn't have her phone number. Her house was too long a walk, unlike Kerrie and Yorgos's home, which was around the corner from Don's. I was stuck.

At 5 o'clock, Don came home and was surprised to see me. He tried to reach Rosemary, but was unsuccessful. Around six, the phone rang. It was Rosemary saying her younger daughter would pick me up and that they were preparing dinner now. He seemed relieved that he didn't need to prepare dinner for me.

That evening, it was just us girls, and the female energy flowed as we passed the bowls of salad, chicken and rice between us. I was happy to be with them. I had nothing to offer in terms of conversation since it revolved around men, and my sad tales of Miles were sorely out of date. I just nodded in agreement, laughing at the witty put-downs. I puffed on the cigarette I was able to secure as the pack of Marlboros was also passed around.

Here we were, four strong women who were so much smarter than the men who were insensitive and uncaring. As I prepared for bed, I could tell that something in me felt empowered. It was definitely a better feeling than the awkwardness and uncertainty that had circulated within me a few days earlier. As I closed my eyes, the image of the hard-boiled egg suddenly appeared. What did that *mean*? No answer came as sleep enveloped me.

* * * *

Tuesday morning Rose and I headed out to the Bay Area after coffee and toast. I was hoping that Annabella remembered our appointment at the restaurant. If not, I'd be stuck.

"Here's five dollars," said Rose as I opened the car door at the designated corner in Oakland. I was stunned that she gave me this. It would allow me to have lunch. I thanked her and proceeded to the café.

Sitting at the table with a menu was a profound moment for me. With the five dollars I could order a hamburger, fries and a Coke, with change left over. Looking around the café, I felt like a normal person. I told the waitress I was waiting for a friend. My watch said noon, but I figured Annabella would be arriving soon, since she was a professional and a student, so punctuality was not only a must, but an exercise.

Twelve-thirty came. No Annabella. I was getting quite hungry. I asked the waitress where the pay phone was and she pointed. I still had Annabella's business card and with a dime in hand, I dropped it into the slot, while positioning the phone receiver between my chin and shoulder. Slowly entering the number on the rotary-dial, I took a deep breath. Ring…ring…ring. No answer. I hung up the phone and waited to hear the rattle of the dime falling into the coin bin. There it was…with an additional quarter and nickel. I smiled. Good fortune.

I went back to my table and sat down, thinking I would try again in fifteen minutes. Just as that thought entered my mind, Annabella walked into the café. Waving to her, she quickly approached and we embraced. She immediately apologized for her lateness.

"Couldn't find parking," she said. "Did you order?"

No, I replied. The waitress came over and Annabella ordered a salad. I ordered the burger and fries. Annabella's face showed disappointment.

"This is not good for you," she said, staring at my plate as she unfolded her paper napkin.

What did I know about what food was good for me? Going to a restaurant in my college days always meant you ordered a burger, fries and Coke. It was mechanical. I hadn't considered any other menu item before. How interesting.

After lunch, we drove a short distance to her office. When we arrived, she led me to her session room and left me there to disrobe for the Rolfing. The light was dimmed and the room had a soft, soothing green color. There were no windows. It was a box enclosed with a bed in the middle. I took the position of lying on my back just as she entered.

She began on my hips and proceeded down my legs. The pain was excruciating. Suddenly a powerful, masculine voice within me growled, "Stop it!" and kicked her. She adeptly jumped out of the way. I was watching this part of me react with such violence that I felt embarrassed. Where did that come from? I had no idea I had this Thing inside of me. I had caught a glimpse of its face psychologically, and it reminded me of the devil in the movie *Rosemary's*

Baby. Annabella had disturbed a part of me that had slumbered within some deep, inaccessible part of my being. It was scary.

"Let's try something else," she said, asking me to turn over.

She worked on my shoulder blades, digging between the bone and muscle. She was tearing away the connective tissue that clung stubbornly to my frame. As it disengaged, an overwhelming sadness encompassed my heart. It was almost more than I could bear. I wanted to cry but couldn't. No mental images arose; instead, some ancient emotion was being released, and I had no idea what it was or from where it came. I just knew it was a part of me, too.

After a while she stopped and said, "Take your time," which indicated the session was over.

Wakefulness filled me as I sat up. Was this state the Intruder that had emerged at Bubbie's house? It was looking through my eyes, but somehow It also felt more like Me. The room was unrecognizable to It, however, as if It had been transported suddenly into this space from some alternate universe. It had no idea where It was. Then It looked down at my body and saw my long hair covering my breasts.

"I have long hair now," It uttered in wonder.

It was enthralled by the flowing hair and startled to see each brown strand and the way the hair curled at the ends. The locks were soft and luxurious. Beauty made It smile. It was happy. When Annabella entered, It repeated the discovery to her. She stared at me, turned around and left the room.

It quickly receded. In Its place was the personality of the twenty-two-year-old Linda, who tried to minimize the experience when Annabella re-entered. It was more important to appear Normal. Having a higher state was not something a student should experience at this point in one's evolution. Higher states were reserved for the teacher.

As I sat in Annabella's car on the way to the meeting, looking out the window without saying much, I pondered the events of the last week. I had been on an unexpected psychological roller coaster. I met a monster, a frightened child, and another Linda from a parallel universe. What else is lying inside of me?

I guess you never know what you'll find when you crack an egg.

O you who travel around who are in your egg, may you make me hale even as you make yourself hale; may you release me, may you loosen me.

Egyptian Coffin Texts

CHAPTER 65

During the Tuesday night meeting it was hard to focus on Robert's teaching. The treatment that triggered an extreme range of emotions left me exhausted. It was so strange to sit there like a lump and just have nothing inside of me that could process the knowledge. In fact, on the way home, I was too tired to go into the Coffee Tree, but chose, instead, to lie down in the back seat of the car and sleep.

My state Wednesday morning was equally dull. It was the first time that I could recall having such a struggle with the second state, let alone the third. Bundled up, I tottered down the hill late morning only to find the bathroom already had a line, so I went upstairs to use the facility. No one liked using that one because the lighting was poor, the toilet slow to flush, and the shower flow a single stream that at times reduced itself to a dribble. These inconveniences were small compared to the pressure from others to vacate the lower bathroom within four minutes.

As soon as I got to the top of the stairs and turned left, however, something was different. A pay phone had been installed on the wall outside the bathroom door. When did that happen? How weird. After performing my morning rituals, I went downstairs and asked the first person I saw about the pay phone.

"Robert mentioned it was being installed at the meeting last night," was the written reply.

My facial expression communicated, "Oh, that's right." I smiled to ease the distress of realizing how deeply asleep I had been. How could I go from such a powerful third state of consciousness at Annabella's session to such deep sleep in just a few hours? It was clear whatever I thought I had gained was not mine to possess. It was disheartening.

I proceeded outside and saw Robert sitting alone on the patio in his director's chair. He was watching a student grill chicken on the outside pit. Here was my chance to ask him for help. I approached him and handed him a note.

"Robert, I have a question," it read.

His face tightened and he indicated for me to pull up a chair beside him.

I began to write, "My brain is like mush and I'm trying to remember myself but find it almost impossible." Once I showed him this sentence, he handed me back my notebook, thinking he wanted me to continue to write. I scribbled, "I don't know what's going on. I try taking in impressions, but…"

He put his hand on my arm to stop my flow of 'I's. With his own pad he began to write. Immediately after he handed me his note, he looked away, indicating no further discussion was needed. He wrote:

"Sometimes we get weary. Keep separating and a capacity to deal with the many 'I's will emerge. The 'I's most probably will always be there, but what deals with them — separation — will get stronger."

His answer seemed vague to me. I never truly understood that word Separation. I was looking for some astute analysis that would provide the exact diagnosis of my mechanical problem, that is, some causal behavior that I could learn to control. Was it a feature? A body type limitation? A center-of-gravity manifestation? What do I do to return to the level of presence I had achieved previously? Instead of telling me why sleep was happening and how to fix it, he basically was saying, "Hang in there, Linda."

So I just sat with him in silence, watching the student in charge of lunch flip the chicken parts. At first the 'I's continued to bombard me with their urgency, but in the comforting presence of Robert, these thoughts diminished in intensity.

I don't know if I succeeded in separating from the many 'I's. All I know was the sound of the sizzle of the grill, the sight of smoke plumes rising, the attentiveness of the cook to the task at hand superseded my personal concerns of evolution. I guess you could say all those 'I's that plagued me were for now put on the back burner.

* * * *

Rosemary, who had stayed in Vacaville on Wednesday morning, showed up after lunch. As I sat smoking a cigarette on the patio between dishwashing shifts, she approached me, letter in hand.

"This came to my address. It's for you."

I looked at the envelope and immediately recognized its strong handwriting. It was from my father.

The business-sized envelope was bulging with its contents. I had to destroy the envelope completely to release the twelve pages of single-spaced writing on both sides. As I began to read, I could hear the droning, castigating, pleading, and threatening voice of my father. It was a classic example of his stream of unconscious lectures that I had been subject to throughout my life. The themes flowed from how much he loved me, how he felt he failed me as a father, how he promised me a car, a trip to

Europe – anything if I would return home. Then the pages took a dark turn: if I didn't call him to assure him I was well, he would send a deprogrammer out to kidnap me and free me from the evil cult that had commandeered my innocence.

The threat of outside intervention was a real thing. I had heard about it just before I left Southern California, where a man had been hired by distraught parents to invade hippy sanctuaries to abduct their runaway young adult children. Once found, the children would be taken to an undisclosed place and psychologically broken down until they rejected cult behavior and were able to embrace the wholesome values of society once again. They would be returned to their families after renouncing the cult leader and asking their parents' forgiveness. I wouldn't put it past my father to do something this crazy.

Rose gestured to me as if to say, "Well, what did he write?"

I wrote down the headlines only and her scribbled reply was, "You better call him now." I had reminded her that we were in a vow of silence until Thursday night, but she photographed me for being formatory.

I took the letter, went upstairs to the pay phone, and inserted a dime to call the operator.

"Operator, I would like to make a collect call." I gave her the phone number, and knew my father, who always answered the phone, would accept the charges. Fear gripped my throat as I waited to hear his voice.

"Hello."

I took a deep breath. "Hi Dad. It's Linda. I got your letter."

"Linndaaaa!" he said with melodramatic surprise.

"Dad, I just called to tell you that you were not a failure as a father."

He laughed. "I know that, honey," he replied.

What?

"I read the letter and you said you felt like a failure."

"Yeah, I just did that so you'd call. So how are you?"

Oh my God. He conned me.

"I'm fine."

A few moments of silence and then a statement that stunned me.

"Well, I hope ta God ya haven't changed your personality."

I shook my head in amazement. We were clearly on different planets. It was almost ludicrous how little he knew me.

"No, I'm fine. Well, I just wanted to call. That's all. Take care."

As I went to hang up, I could hear him calling out, "Linda WAIT!" I couldn't wait. I had my own life to live.

❖

> *You wait, little girl, on an empty stage*
> *For fate to turn the light on.*
> *Your life, little girl, is an empty page*
> *That men would want to write on.*
>   from *The Sound of Music*

CHAPTER 66

Wednesday evening after dinner Rosemary asked how the call went. I simply replied, "Fine." The emotions toward my life family were complicated and not something I wanted to put down in writing.

Thursday had finally arrived, and the no-talking exercise was about to come to an end for everyone except Robert. The two exercises of not laughing and not talking removed much of the enjoyment from social interactions. It was odd to see how few people were around this week, unless they were cooking or eating or washing up or tending to the animals.

Apparently at Tuesday's meeting Robert had revised the new schedule he had recently presented. The Tuesday meeting, which was the regular, mandatory meeting in the Bay Area, remained. All other meetings were optional.

The issue, however, was that the majority of students were now in the Bay Area and they had full-time jobs. The hardships of life at the farm were too much for a cosmopolitan type. Robert observed that the farm is hard on false personality because it reveals lies and reduces a person to the simplicity of existence. So, to accommodate those who disliked the farm, Robert decided to expand the Thursday study group beyond Don's home in Vacaville to include Berkeley at Anna's and Via Del Sol. In this way, he explained, the teaching could still occupy a prominent place in our lives during the week.

That Thursday night we had the first study group at Via Del Sol before dinner. Robert was in attendance. It was early October, and the evenings were getting cooler. Yorgos had built a small fire in the fireplace. We gathered around Robert in the living room.

 Good householder came first. Among the topics were the new pay phone and teaching payments. Robert had asked me to mention that everyone would be expected to give a full month of payments beginning November 1. People were lagging behind and I had spent a lot of energy chasing after people. Robert had told me privately that this was due to tramp feature in students and asked me to be persistent when I collect funds. He suggested I remind students that "Payment was a principle in schools," according to Ouspensky.

After good householder, Jim read Robert's first note.

"Bill has sold his VW so that we can buy an old 1954 school bus that will seat 17 people to transport us around the property."

I looked at Bill, expecting to see him smile with pride for his generosity, but instead saw he wasn't too happy about it. I found that strange. Something was up, but I let it go.

Yorgos initiated the formal meeting by asking on Robert's behalf, "Does anyone have a question?"

It was good to see Jeff and Annette there, and especially delightful when Annette raised her hand to ask the first question. She was usually passive, allowing her Saturnine husband to be the dominant one, even though she clearly had some Mercurial in her body type.

"Could you explain a foggy state, where colors seem to lose their brightness?"

I was shocked. This was my question earlier to Robert, in so many words.

Robert wrote, "That is being in the waking or second state. When one is in the waking state, one only knows that one is in it when one gets out of it."

Harold was asked to toss a quarter into the fireplace. We were all silent. One could feel the change of energy in the room.

"That act produced the third state of consciousness. The Self became awake. Some of you are only twenty years old, and will remember this fifty years from now, when you're seventy," wrote Robert.

"The way to the Self is through the king of hearts," he continued, "the intellectual part of the emotional center. It is the seat of the magnetic center and the seed of the Self. A person is less disturbed and over-emotional when the male — the king of hearts — is in control. The emotional part — the queen of hearts — reacts by crying, exploding, etc. When you control the negative emotions, you control the queen of hearts through the king of hearts, by what are called 'reins.' "

A new fellow raised his hand.

"Then we should step on the queen of hearts to keep it down?"

Robert replied, "Don't step on anything. It is a tender center, the queen of hearts."

I smiled at his comment. The queen of hearts was viewed as the carrier of a plague, and anyone who was branded with this center of gravity was treated as a pariah.

He continued, "All five centers are *mechanical:* sex center, intellectual center, emotional center, moving and instinctive centers. Higher mental and higher emotional alone are real."

Robert then paused.

"Annette may begin to see a little of herself in Linda Kaplan."

What does that mean? She doesn't look anything like me.

He then added, "Balance is attempting to have the right center in control."

Immediately I took this last angle personally. I felt out of control most of the time and sought his help to straighten me out. I truly believed that Robert, as teacher, was there to point out my weaknesses and my sleep so that I could better understand the workings of my machine. The Fourth Way said knowledge leads to understanding, which, in turn, results in being and will. I wanted will. Since childhood I've desperately searched for the balance and control he mentioned, but had no idea how to attain it. That is why I needed a teacher.

In the midst of my ponderings, Robert leaned forward and looked at each of us.

"I do not take your good hearts for granted. I see all of your goodness and the nice things you do for people."

That shocked me. This teacher doesn't focus on weaknesses. He sees goodness. A part of me was grateful that he was so loving while another was suspect: How am I to master the machine to achieve balance and attain will if he disregards my weaknesses?

* * * *

Dinner was served after the meeting, and I decided to sit next to Annette to see if she understood Robert's observation about our similarities. I remembered Robert saying Sarah (whom Annette didn't know) was payment for her. Payment was a concept I briefly heard about, where a student's departure from the school was designed by C Influence so that someone else could come who had a stronger connection to the Work and could pass the interval of difficulties that were not possible for the student who left. Sarah didn't resemble Annette either, so that definition I just provided was equally mysterious to me.

Perhaps it was the fact we both had asked Robert the same question. I told her I was having trouble with self-remembering, too, and began to explain my experience. She listened with a sweet interest and invited me to her home the next day for afternoon tea. I explained I had no car and she told me not to worry. She'll pick me up around three.

I slept well that night, thinking of my new friend. The heart longs for validation, and if I could learn something about myself from Annette, it would make this dark place of self-ignorance more bearable.

※

> *The Soul, when it sees a trace of its kindred reality,*
> *is delighted and thrilled and returns to itself*
> *and remembers itself.*
>
> Plotinus

CHAPTER 67

There was a joy in me when I arose at 6 a.m. I made it down the hill early to prepare breakfast. The downstairs bathroom was free and it didn't take me long to exit. Kerrie was not in the kitchen that Friday morning, and the breakfast assignment had me in charge of cooking the scrambled eggs, laying out the granola, fruit, milk, and slices of toast. I became good at taking the big metal coffee urn and filling it with water and placing the right amount of canned coffee grounds in the basket. Making coffee was always the first thing to do since it could take an hour or so for that red light to go on indicating it's ready. I got compliments about the taste of the coffee I made.

I didn't mention to anyone my conversation with Annette and the fact she would come to whisk me away with her for tea in her home. Yorgos was working before sunrise with a few students to prepare a winter garden. I had yet to see Robert. His entrances were always so quiet that he moved through the cabin like a spirit. I tried to remain invisible so I wouldn't attract an octave from Robert that would prevent me from slipping away in the afternoon.

After eating, I went directly to washing breakfast dishes, and continued with the lunch preparations. Whenever I saw Robert appear, I quickly disappeared into the cooler. From my experience, as long as one had an octave, Robert would rarely reassign one. He was often on the lookout for students who were idle.

After lunch I had a game plan. If I met Annette by the barn area, I could intercept her and jump in her car without her looking for me in the kitchen, which could initiate questioning from Robert. So I carefully slipped away and proceeded down to the barn around 2:30 p.m. My plan involved hiding out there until three. I climbed the stacks of hay that were stored to feed the animals. I had found different places to hide around the property, and the hay perch was one of my favorites.

Why did I hide? It was a habit I had had since childhood. Sometimes I wanted to disappear and not be found. But since joining the school, I used it as a way to sort through my dilemmas and commune with C Influence, hoping they would instruct me how to proceed. Since that solo car ride on Mount Tamalpais, I longed for their wisdom to flow to me. I tried to keep still and simply allow the environment around me to be what it was. Perhaps then they would visit.

Just as I entered this quiet state, Jim came in. He didn't see me because I was so high up. I watched him as he sorted through the tools in a wooden basket. I could feel my sex energy flow as I watched him move about.

It was a curious phenomenon that had been occurring for months now since I didn't have a sex partner. Whenever I tried to self-remember, and had reached that higher state, I would find myself hotly attracted to men. I could see their essence, and the beauty of their bodies enraptured me. It felt like love, and I would become obsessed. Jim had been on my radar for quite some time. But since he was Robert's sidekick, clearly there was no time to interact romantically. Although we did have a sound platonic friendship (more like brother and sister), I couldn't shake that curiosity of what it would be like to touch him and make love.

I pulled myself out of this fantasy long enough to realize it was five minutes to three. Jim was still there and I was in a bit of a dilemma: Do I stay where I am and risk missing Annette? Or do I come off my perch, revealing my secret hiding place to Jim? I looked at my Timex watch and nervously counted down the minutes. Come on, Jim. Get out of there!

But he lingered.

I began to make my move off the hay pile. How embarrassing. He was startled to see me. He voiced the obvious question.

"What are you doing up there?"

What could I say?

"Oh, I just thought I'd go up there." Yes, that's what came out of my mouth.

I quickly exited the barn. It was 3:03 and there was Annette in her car coming up the narrow road toward me. I flagged her down, hopped in the passenger seat, and we sped away.

* * *

Before we arrived at her house, Annette needed to pick up her kids from school. Apparently, the oldest ones (a boy and a girl) went to school in Nevada City and were delivered via school bus near her home. When I asked where Nevada City was, Annette looked at me in disbelief.

"It's about thirty miles from here," she said, pointing in the eastern direction while we waited in her station wagon for the school bus. She described it as a lovely town built during the gold rush days. It had little boutique shops and stores that sold handmade jewelry. It sounded enchanting, but I had no idea how I could find my way there. When you live at Via Del Sol, the focus is on developing the property, not exploring the local towns to window shop.

"Perhaps we can go there together someday," she offered, as if reading my mind.

It was enough of a general statement to warm my heart. I could imagine us together shopping for clothes and jewelry. Of course, I had no money to buy anything, but trying on things didn't cost a cent, and the pleasure that excursion would give me would be priceless. I smiled thinking about the possibility of strengthening our bond as girlfriends.

At that moment the school bus arrived, and the kids hopped into the car. Change of subject.

Once in her home, we all gravitated toward the kitchen area, with its large table and smells of prepared snacks for the children. They grabbed the granola cookies that she had freshly baked and went to the fridge to pair them with cold, unpasteurized milk.

The kids took their snacks outside, leaving the two of us alone at the kitchen table. Annette offered me milk, but I said tea would be fine. Some remaining cookies were on a plate in front of me and I couldn't resist having one. It was warm and sweet and comforting.

We settled in to talk. She wanted to know more about me and I pretty much gave her my standard statements of birth location, education, and goals, which by now were pretty obsolete. I asked her about her question to Robert, wondering how she experienced that foggy state, and longing to unlock the mystery of her internal world, hoping I could better understand my own.

Instead, she grabbed the plate of cookies, went to the oven to refill it, while telling me how she and Jeff met and that he was a successful real estate agent. I became irritated that she totally ignored my question.

As I listened to stories of her external life, something hit me hard. It was a memory of a date I had had in college, where I was so uncomfortable that all I could do was talk about how great my sister was. The sex energy from this guy made me extremely nervous. I rarely went out on dates you see. That one was set up by my parents (he was a son of a business acquaintance of my father). Was Annette that uncomfortable around me? Why would she be inner considering me? What was she buffering?

Just then, the teenage son came in to grab more cookies. The two daughters appeared and they fought over the last ones. I watched Annette mediate between them, offering different options of compromise.

As we returned to our conversation, it was nearing five o'clock and Jeff entered the room from work. He was pleased to see me, and he sat down to join the conversation. He had questions about work ideas, such as feature and body type characteristics. I offered what I knew, and he wanted to discuss further observations he had made about the mechanics of the human machine. I looked over at Annette occasionally, and the beams of adoration radiated from her eyes toward her spouse. She was definitely in love.

It was now approaching dinner time, and Jeff offered to drive me home. I sat in the passenger seat listening to him express his other ideas of the Work. I thanked him for the ride and went directly up the hill to help with dinner preparations. No one had noticed my absence.

I felt a bit frustrated and disappointed that Annette never revealed to me what initiated her question to Robert. I was hoping to find out how we were similar through conversation. It didn't happen that way. She seemed too engaged and absorbed in her husband and children, without any intellectual curiosity of her own. Her life was so different from mine. What Robert saw about us remained a mystery to me.

❖

> *Many of the faults you see in others are your own nature reflected in them. We are mirrors to one another.*
>
> Rumi

CHAPTER 68

Saturday was a busy day, as the Weekenders came up from the Bay with new members. Introductions included hugs, and it was always interesting to observe how some people were receptive to it and others were not in the beginning. It was a clue to body type. Meg observed that the planet Saturn had rings, and when trying to hug a new Saturnine student, there was a reluctance to embrace the middle section. They kept you at arm's length and appeared aloof. Hugging was no problem for the Venusian type. The middle for them was like a Twinkie, with its soft creamy center. I could relate to this myself. I enjoyed melting into the arms of someone.

The highlight of the day was the evening's screening of Charlie Chaplin's *The Gold Rush*. I was familiar with this classic since my film studies at UCLA. One of the scenes had Chaplin eating a boot — shoelaces and all — that he had boiled in a pot like a piece of beef. He was surviving winter in a cabin and had to resort to this because of severe hunger. What many people don't know is that the boot was made of licorice, which is a highly effective laxative. Needless to say, Chaplin had a great incentive to complete the scene in one take.

Someone from the Bay Area brought the 16mm projector with the film reel and set up the machine toward the back of the living room. Anyone who has ever used this type of projector, with its two reels (one with the film and the other empty), knows that the threading of the film around the multitude of various-sized sprockets is like finding your way through a complex corn maze. I was grateful no one asked me to help. I failed at it once when substitute teaching, and a moving-centered boy in class stepped up to figure it out quickly. It was a bit humiliating. The Vacaville student, who was herself a teacher, watched the men fiddle unsuccessfully until she boldly took hold of the celluloid and masterfully showed them how to do it within a few minutes.

We had been told prior to viewing that the purpose of the screening was to control laughter. This immediately reminded me of my prospective student meeting when Disney's *Alice in Wonderland* was shown, and Rose and I couldn't control our giggling. I had clearly failed that test. So internally I shifted gears and tried not to find anything funny at all about this movie. I focused on the Great Depression, which the film predated by a few years, and that helped to bring a seriousness and gloom to my thoughts. I counseled myself that there's nothing funny about poverty and hunger. It worked.

After the film, we removed the projector and rearranged our seating to form a circle. The good householder portion of the meeting was dispensed with and Robert began by commenting on the viewing.

"The control of laughter was good," he wrote.

Richard raised his hand and immediately offered, "Robert, it also seemed to be sad in parts."

"That is right. It is life," responded Robert. He paused for a moment and added, tangentially, "Please try to use my name as little as possible. 'I' don't like to hear it. It is not me."

This produced a smile on my face. I understood this about him early on, and was glad he mentioned it as a reminder.

"How many students have verified C Influence is a reality?"

I immediately raised my hand. Looking around, I saw only a few others doing so.

"Help is given in the amount it is appreciated and valued."

It was clear his comment was in reference to C Influence's assistance.

"Everything here is fated. My words are never my own. Even now, C Influence controls all of us to wake us up."

He paused and looked up, as if waiting for the next page to turn in the script. He then added, "People are interested in evolution on their own terms. They would like the teaching to be their idea of it."

A hand went up: "What about other groups who are studying the same things we are?"

He quickly replied, "If you think that anyone in life is on the same path, you don't yet know what you have met here. There are people who could be here but do not have luck — good fate. Remember, Ouspensky said you must have luck to meet a teaching. It is only possible to become conscious in this present life by fate. Some people may become conscious in this present life or in the next life. Gurdjieff reminded us that we are all equally beggars."

He stopped and smiled at us.

"We will end now. I hope you know I love you more now, even though I do not speak."

The meeting itself was short because of the movie. It was late by the time I made it to my tent that night. As I scooted down into my sleeping bag, the film from that day's conscious moments replayed in my mind. When recalling parts of the movie, I suddenly chuckled at the juxtaposition of the Linda comfortably seated in the theatre arts hall at UCLA watching the Little Tramp in a log cabin that was a stage set and the Linda watching the film in a real log cabin in the wilderness.

How amazing that in less than a year, I have become like the Little Tramp with barely anything of my own. We certainly are all equally beggars.

> Remember that you are an actor in a drama, of such kind
> as the author pleases to make it. If short, of a short one;
> if long, of a long one. If it be his pleasure you should act
> a poor man, a cripple, a governor, or a private person,
> see that you act it naturally. For this is your business,
> to act well the character assigned you; to choose it is another's.
>
> Epictetus

CHAPTER 69

Several students were speaking excitedly at Sunday breakfast about a strange sound they heard in the middle of the night.

"No, it was more like a loud groan than a laugh," said one student.

"I heard a crazy laugh more like a cackle than a groan," contradicted another.

"Could it be an animal?" inquired another.

"None I know of," was the reply.

I asked them where this sound was coming from and they said near the top of the mountain. Did I hear it? No, I told them. I had slept soundly.

The conversation continued and everyone who came down from the hill for breakfast was polled. It seemed more like the Japanese movie *Rashomon*, where an incident happened and four witnesses each had totally different stories about what had occurred.

Students' emotional reactions were interesting to see. Some students were scared, others curious, and a few wanted to hunt this strange man down. All, however, were convinced it was an utterance from a human and not an animal. In fact, a name had been given to the mysterious stranger on our property: The Laughing Man.

As soon as I heard this name, the irony of the timing immediately hit me. Here we were with a no-laughing exercise, and the gods bring a wild, elusive character hidden in the night to taunt us. You can't make this stuff up. How funny.

This was the headline news of the day. Robert learned of this mysterious stranger and suggested that it may be best to sleep in the farmhouse instead of the tents if people felt threatened. As it sounded like an option rather than a task, I decided to return to my tent that night. I figured if the Laughing Man had ill intentions and chased someone from the hilltop, I would be awakened in time to make it down to safety.

I slept well again that night, undisturbed.

* * * *

The topic of conversation at Monday's breakfast was once again the Laughing Man. He had made a second appearance and now others claimed they heard him. Robert decided to hold an impromptu meeting after breakfast. I thought for sure he would gather the troops together and address how best to protect the fort. Instead, his message came as a surprise.

"Separate: As a source of friction and health we will stop making coffee in the farmhouse until December first and at that time another decision will be made to continue or not. It will produce negativity, which is a source of food for the Self to come into existence. If you wish to make coffee in your tent, it is your privilege. It would be best to end the habit."

I could feel negativity and confusion enter my machine. Where, it asked, did THAT come from? He seemed to be ignoring the real threat.

Robert continued.

"People do not drink coffee or smoke cigarettes. They drink a habit and smoke a habit. The drinking of coffee and the smoking of cigarettes is a buffer. It keeps filling time to avoid the helplessness of being unable to cope with the simplicity of existence."

I didn't realize that my coffee drinking, which I often paired with a cigarette, was a buffer. I just knew I used it to take a break from working sometimes. Sitting down outside didn't seem like I was buffering the simplicity of existence. In fact, I thought I was enjoying the moment. What was I doing wrong? Was I actually asleep while smoking and drinking? Was Robert going to ban cigarettes, too? I was listening intently to see if he would clarify further. Instead, he gave us another shock.

"We will also give up eating meat this week."

Okay. I guess we are working on depriving the instinctive center of its pleasures. What was most important to me was to obey my teacher so I was willing to give up my coffee for tea and my essence chicken for non-existent tofu.

I could see many students shifting in their seats. They were clearly uncomfortable. I looked over at Meg, one of the original members, thinking for sure she would support Robert in his direction. She sat back and looked up at the ceiling with a smile on her face. Perhaps she already was told about it so it wasn't a surprise. Harold, on the other hand, was focusing on his pipe as he tamped the tobacco in the bowl. He seemed nonchalant about the task. They were both big meat eaters and coffee drinkers, so I wasn't sure how they would handle this. They pretty much operated separately from the rest of us. They didn't live in a tent, they lived in a trailer. Since Robert gave permission for those in a tent to make coffee, it probably would extend to them.

* * * *

After the meeting, Robert decided to leave for the Bay Area. My guess was he stopped at the Nut Tree for lunch (I wondered if the Tropical Prawns were considered meat). Meanwhile, I was informed that Tuesday I was scheduled to remain at Via Del Sol as one of the caretakers, which meant I would miss the Berkeley meeting at Anna's. This was actually fine with me, since money was still an issue and venturing outside of the farm always cost money.

We ate salad for lunch and I placed hot water in the coffee urn without the coffee grounds so we could have enough liquid for tea. The tea had a bit of a coffee aroma (even though I thought I had cleaned the vessel well enough), but that was alright for me. I had an 'I' that questioned whether or not drinking this tainted water was tantamount to cheating. I let that 'I' go.

In the afternoon, I went upstairs to retrieve some storage supplies, and as I reached the top of the landing, I saw Bill on the pay phone. I stopped in my tracks. His conversation was alarming.

"Yeah, they took the bus. I tried to get money, but they wanted me to donate it. Yeah, I'm still hanging around. This place is a deal. I get free food and lodging, and there are young naked girls around."

He started to laugh in an evil way. For the first time since we got the laughing exercise, I could see that laughter is not innocent. It was horrifying.

He hung up, turned around and saw me there. With his head lowered, he passed me and descended the staircase. I stood there stunned.

Then these words entered my head: Teaching Payment. I remembered he hadn't paid October, so I quickly went down the stairs. He was nowhere to be found. Going outside, I saw him walking down the hill. I ran after him, calling his name. He stopped and faced me.

"Bill, you still need to make your October teaching payment," I said.

"Oh, well, I'll give it to you by end of week," was his reply.

"No," I answered firmly. "Empty your pockets."

He stared at me. I restated my demand. He handed me a few dollars and coins, explaining this was all the money he had. I didn't care. The thought that he would take advantage of C Influence's teaching like this was not only unacceptable to me, it was unforgiveable. I counted the money and let him know that the remaining amount would be due by the end of the week.

Bill entered his car and drove away. His appearance at Via Del Sol would undoubtedly be short-lived. Whatever good intentions he pretended to have quickly disclosed themselves as deceit.

> *This pickpocket self keeps stealing conscious life by saying, "Tomorrow, day after tomorrow." All your conscious life is only today, not another day. Do not believe the promise of this cheater.*
>
> Rumi

CHAPTER 70

Tuesday breakfast was scrambled tofu with onions and paprika, toast, granola, and an assortment of nuts, dates and raisins. Milk was always in abundance because of the cows. Klair, our master husbandry lady, churned some fresh butter, which was an amazing treat on the toast. Sandwiches usually were made for those going into the Bay Area. Cashew butter was the spread of choice, and cheddar that was sliced from big blocks was the only other alternative. Sometimes the cheese crumbled, but using mayonnaise as mortar helped the cheese to stick to the bread and not fall out with the first bite. There also was plenty of fruit to add to the lunch bags.

Four of us were the only ones remaining at Via Del Sol by the afternoon. I was glad to see David, whom I hadn't spoken with for quite a while. The other two were Nadia, who was tending the animals, and the Architect's son. Something was definitely different about him. There was a swagger in his step and a glint in his eyes.

I asked David about it. He chuckled. I waited. He quietly smoked his pipe looking into the distant horizon. Thinking he had forgotten my question, I took a few puffs of my cigarette and moved on with my thoughts. About five minutes later, with his eyes inspecting the tobacco in his pipe, he quietly said, "He's spending time with Kerrie now."

I knew that, having gone to Berkeley with them both. It took a considerable while for me to register what he meant.

"You mean they're having sex?"

He chuckled again at my naïveté, but he did not confirm or deny my perception. I didn't know what else to say since my relationship with David was not founded upon gossip. He was not the talkative type. So I decided to let it go and be the observer like David.

As the evening came, we gathered together for an informal dinner in the kitchen. The Architect's son expressed his desire to stand post again with a shotgun he had. Where he found this gun, I had no clue. He was now the man who would protect us apparently. Nadia was strongly opposed to this, expressing something to the effect that he could accidentally kill any of us in the middle of the night. She was thinking about the students returning from the Bay Area. Good point. David, on the other hand, tried once to reason with him, but then let it go when the youngster insisted it was for everyone's safety.

As for me, I had no opinion about an effective method of eliminating an intangible threat. After all, I hadn't heard the Laughing Man, so hadn't verified his existence. Instead of engaging in talk past sunset, I decided to return to my tent, considering it to be the safest location of all since it was between a rock (the Laughing Man's apparent abode on the hilltop) and a hard place (the youngster's armed lookout behind a boulder near the farmhouse).

No noise of laughter or shotgun blast was heard throughout the night. The new moon mysteriously hid from sight, and the Milky Way alone made itself known across the pitch-black sky. I awoke with the sun's first rays, having survived the imaginary.

※

> *When morning comes you will see*
> *to whom you made love in the black of night.*
> Rumi

CHAPTER 71

Kerrie showed up Wednesday afternoon from her Berkeley run with a host of vegetables and fruits. She once again took command of the kitchen. I watched as the Architect's son came into the farmhouse. He apparently had retired at sunrise to his teepee and just arose. His long hair was ruffled. He threw his long and slender arm around her neck and kissed her cheek. She smiled in reserved delight without looking at him.

I was still observing relationships because they simply perplexed me. How do you find a mate? What is the dance? Who leads and who follows? Is it a waltz, where the partners mirror one another in perfect, graceful movement? Or a jitterbug, whereby each does his own wild steps and then reaches out to the other to let gravity take its course in their partnership? What a mystery. How and when did these two simultaneously give consent to cross the line? These thoughts filled my head as Kerrie stood before me with a knife.

"Can you slice the eggplants lengthwise?"

"Sure," I said, slightly startled, as I emerged from the depths of my ruminations.

The menu was stuffed eggplant with tomatoes, mushrooms, and breadcrumbs, and Middle-Eastern couscous with raisins and spices. As dinner time was approaching, it was surprising how few students there were on the property. About eight students came to eat. It was a quiet evening. Afterwards, a few of us sat outside in the coolness of the night, looking up at the stars, smoking cigarettes, sharing news of the Tuesday meeting, and listening all the while for sounds of the Laughing Man.

* * * *

Thursday was a strangely quiet day as well. Usually, Robert and Jim would have come back from the Bay, as well as Meg and Harold. We were supposed to have the Thursday Study Group in the evening, and I assumed Yorgos, who just returned from Vacaville, now would be leading it.

As we gathered in the living room for the meeting before dinner, I positioned myself across from Yorgos. His usual rosy cheeks were pallid, which caused me to wonder how he was doing. He had been working hard outside to tend the winter garden. Then it hit me. Kerrie was sitting next to him and the Architect's son was sitting next to her.

The meeting began with good householder, then proceeded to the usual "Does someone have a question?" and followed by "Are there angles of thought?" But I couldn't concentrate at all on this discourse. I was focused on what was going on behind the scenes. Did Yorgos know about this affair? He lived in his makeshift metal cabin near the water tank, and the youngster's teepee was not so far away. All sorts of imagination filled my head. Before I knew it, the meeting was over.

I went into the kitchen to help with dinner preparation. As I put the plates, utensils and napkins on the table, I could see in the corner of the room Yorgos and Kerrie talking. It was a serious discussion. Yorgos left first, and then Kerrie. The youngster was nowhere to be found. None of them stayed for dinner.

After a quick meal, I positioned myself near the sink as the dirty plates were brought in and stacked. Slowly I moved the rag to wash and rinse each plate, contemplating the tension I had witnessed between Yorgos and Kerrie. The person assigned to drying asked me to hurry up as I handed her the plate. Three students entered, laughing, and I could hear the names of Yorgos,

Kerrie, and the Architect's son spoken. It had become a source of gossip, and it felt cruel since I had just gone through something so similar. Yorgos was the rejected lover in this instance — a role I had just played — and I felt his pain. In the back of my mind, I wondered if others also had been gossiping about me during my plight.

What was so curious was how I was more disturbed about this love triangle than my own. As I lay in my tent that night, memories of arriving in Vacaville from Los Angeles only months earlier flooded my mind. The loving, stable couple who greeted me had found themselves on this seemingly downward path. They represented hope to me when my own desires and expectations went up in smoke. But things were not as they appeared, and each sudden shift in circumstances continued to blindside me. What existed beneath façades of affection was so complex and disturbing that my emotional compass malfunctioned and I felt lost inside of myself.

All I ever wanted was to love and be loved. It was that simple. The love I saw and experienced appeared imaginary and fleeting — and worse, unattainable. Was I fated not to know the warmth, comfort and consistency of such devotion?

This last thought had sunk my heart into such deep sorrow that I cried myself to sleep that night.

Someday, my sweet Hafiz, All the nonsense in your brain will dry up, like a stagnant pool of water beneath the sun.
　　　　　　　　　　　　　　　　　　　　　The teacher of Hafiz

CHAPTER 72

It was so good to see Robert and Jim on Friday after lunch. They were walking up the hill slowly with Meg and Harold. Meg was telling Robert something, and at one point, Robert stopped in his tracks and covered his face with his hands, shaking his head in disbelief. Jim had to look away and I could see him suppressing a convulsing laugh. Meg was known for her sense of humor, and it was equally comical to consider telling Robert a joke during a no-laughing exercise. My curiosity, of course, was heightened, and I hoped to hear what was so funny.

Whether or not Robert was made aware of the youngster's Tuesday night escapade with the shotgun, I did not know. There was always a respectful space given to the teacher. The only ones who could easily bridge it were Meg and Rosemary. A student could always approach Robert if their concern was serious, but one had to be careful not to provide him with information that could be construed as gossip.

By dinner time, most of the students from the Bay Area arrived. The living room was becoming crowded, and I tried my best to position myself as close to Robert and Jim as I could so that I could hear the joke that Meg told him. Robert requested that Yorgos sit next to him, which caused me to have additional 'I's about Yorgos's predicament, and whether he would share it with Robert.

I must admit that these new topics of interest and my curiosity helped to ease the old identification with seeing Miles and Helga. The heart is tender and sore when poked. Sometimes I fall into the pit of self-pity, with its justifiable set of 'I's, and other times I can see the whole situation objectively, rising above the button-pushing. It's truly an emotional roller coaster, and I have no idea where I will find myself. Remember Yourself in Times of Trial were often just words to me, having little power in action. It was like someone tellimg me to lose ten pounds NOW while smells of hot pizza tantalize my nostrils.

Usually after dinner most people disappeared, but that night the living room was abuzz with coordinating accommodations for new students who didn't have their own tents. Also, there were more dishes than normal, and only two of us signed up to wash and dry. I was happy to see Alden float in and offer to help.

It occurred to me that Alden may know what happened to Meg. After washing all the glasses and before beginning the plates, I said I was taking a cigarette break and wondered if Alden would join me. He happily agreed, and we both went outside.

After a few puffs in silence, I broached the subject. I told him I saw Meg tell Robert something that was amusing. Did he know what it could be? He almost started to laugh and told me the tale.

"Meg and Harold went to a Jack-in-the-Box in Marysville on Thursday night and she ordered a burger."

"NO!" I gasped. It was clear they both were struggling with the no-meat exercise.

"Yeah. When she entered their trailer to eat it," he continued, suppressing a giggle, "Meg took a big bite and saw that the meat patty was missing."

We both tried to muffle our laughter.

"Robert then told her, 'Next time, try not to have the gods work so hard.'"

* * * *

Saturday morning, I awoke refreshed and pondered the story of Meg and the burger. Here she was, one of the oldest students, and she had blatantly disregarded a task given to her by her teacher. When the gods reprimanded her, did she hide it from Robert? No. She openly shared the story with him. There was a lesson here for me. My tendency would have been to sneak around him, feel guilty when the gods photographed me directly, and not share my weakness with anyone out of shame. I understood from this event that it was vital I not hide my mechanics from Robert. He was there to help me, not to judge me. What that meant to me was to be willing and able to receive his photographs, which could be fiercely penetrating, but were designed to produce the third state and strengthen my own will.

I was looking forward to the meeting that evening. Meg sat next to Robert and, once good householder was done, he indicated she should tell the story of the burger. Having heard it already, I focused my attention on Robert to see his response and he clearly took delight in the tale. A light energy radiated throughout the living room.

He leaned forward, as Jim read his note.

"When a person does things that are questionable, the reason I may ask about it is you are trying to attach your will to mine, and what you are doing is not my will. This is the lower eating the higher."

A student raised her hand. "Can you further explain how the lower eats the higher?"

"If the teacher is eaten, it is a crime. It is one of the ways C Influence works. Crime can make other students who see it stronger and who then do not make the same mistake."

Immediately I thought about lessons — learning from other's mistakes as well as my own. He continued.

"One area where a student eats the teacher is when the student wastes the teacher's work — for example, not doing a task. A teacher is intended to be drawn from, but not eaten. 'Never did the eagle stoop so low as to listen to the blackbirds.' That is the Self listening to the many 'I's. The lower cannot see the higher. This is a law."

There was a pause before the next question.

"I cannot see the benefit of learning about the ray of creation or the table of hydrogens when we are studying ourselves."

"Different types here need different food," replied Robert. "Also, as buffers are removed, knowledge is necessary to replace the buffers. Much knowledge brings relativity to the scale of our existence. It shows us how small we are. In addition, Ouspensky didn't receive this knowledge until he was in the teaching for about twenty years. Perhaps in twenty years we will find it more useful."

"Does the Self choose the next role, or is it ordered by higher forces?" asked someone.

"A guess, it would be the latter," responded Robert.

A new student asked a simple question: "Why is C Influence?"

Robert's countenance brightened and his response was equally simple: "It enjoys existence."

He paused for quite a while. The energy in the room lightened, and a sense that something higher was now invisibly sharing the space with us was evident to me.

"Isn't it nice we have a farm after all the looking we did? We will end now, loves."

❖

Time may come when men with Angels may participate.
John Milton

CHAPTER 73

Sunday morning the news was circulated that we would have another meeting that night. Each day would bring its own agenda, a schedule that was only known in advance to the gods, or so it seemed. This unpredictable way of living kept everyone on their toes.

Additionally, I overheard a brief discussion about a new living room carpet, one that was of a higher quality than the one that was, a month or so ago, laid down. It was true how quickly the dirty boots had ground the red clay into the tight fibers of carpet. The evening's dim lighting obscured the filth. It was the morning light that made it apparent. Considering, however, that many students here still didn't wash daily, the current carpet seemed to fit the low standards we residents were keeping.

I was surprised to see the Weekenders remain past lunch. Then I learned that Monday was a holiday. I had no idea what holiday it was. In fact, I barely remembered who the President of the United States was. Having spent my entire life with the TV news blaring in our living space on a daily basis, I was stunned to realize how cut off from the world I had become.

The meeting that night was crowded, with most of us sitting cross-legged on the carpet. Robert began with a positive greeting to all.

"By the size of the group tonight, we can see people can afford to have something for their Selves. Ouspensky formulated that a person has to be able to afford to study in this existence. It is a holiday weekend and some people can gain something extra for themselves tonight."

Then the shock.

"We will not speak until next Monday morning, November 1, except those who have dealings in life."

No laughter, no meat, and now no talk.

"Try to use only seven notes per day. Music is okay."

Seven notes. Well, he didn't say how short those notes must be.

"It is a pleasure to see certain students hold their work under any circumstances."

This statement gave me incentive to be listed among the "certain" students. Having just come from a university environment, I still strived to be considered at the top of my class, even though I rarely was.

"The group is quieter. Have all noticed this? Both women and men try to avoid unnecessary talk. For women, the reason they speak unnecessarily is because they are emotionally centered and become excited over unimportant things.

"It is a miracle that 25 people live in the same house with relative harmony. The key is not expressing negative emotions. We are a family.

"On the farm, be sure your clothes are clean. What they look like is secondary. All people here should shower at least five times a week. Daily is best. It is common sense. A shower is a catalyst for positive emotions. Also, make it quick! Our farm eventually will have the cleanliness of a monastery. We have been here only three and a half months and already have accomplished much. We are fortunate we share something that is above money."

It seemed Robert was preparing us for the new carpet and higher standards. Then came another surprise.

"Let's start calling each other by our middle names for self-remembering and confusion purposes. Those without middle names, or who are already using them, can pick a tasteful substitute. When I put my left hand on my right wrist, please give me your new name."

And another task.

"We will stop saying the word, 'get.' Please add this to the list of words to avoid: really, very, a lot, and now get."

Robert concluded the meeting with this final change:

"We will name our farmhouse the Lincoln Lodge in honor of Abraham Lincoln. Like it? He likes it, too. Let us end now. I love you, and won't let you down."

* * * *

Monday morning, I arrived in the living room of the Lincoln Lodge and was shocked to see only about ten students. It was funny how with each silence exercise, students found places to hide. Or so it seemed to me.

John Graham was a Weekender who rarely came to the property because he worked in the Bay Area teaching dance, I had been told. He and I were at that same prospective student meeting in Alamo. I was delighted to see him. He was scrounging around the kitchen for breakfast so I went to help him. I then realized I didn't know his middle name. Taking pen in hand, I wrote down the question. Just as I had finished, I looked up to hand him my note and he had done exactly the same thing. We looked at each other's note and almost fell over in muffled laughter. We had the same middle name: Lee.

I quickly scribbled on my note pad: Funny. You don't look like a Lee.

He wrote back: Neither do you!

We are so different (John is a moving-centered Saturn gentleman and I am an emotionally centered Venusian lady), yet the name made us the same. It totally robbed us of an identity we took for granted. It also bonded us together in an unexpected way. We continued to share our joke with others who also found delight in it.

> *What in endlessly anxious hands one used to be, to be this no more, and even one's own name to lay aside, like a broken toy.*
>
> Rainer Maria Rilke

CHAPTER 74

Tuesday was the Berkeley meeting, and I secured a round-trip ride in the morning with farm residents. This was the perfect way to go to a Bay Area meeting for me. No need to find someone to take me home, no embarrassment when someone says, "Hey! I'm hungry, let's stop at this restaurant," when I knew I couldn't afford a meal.

The good thing about working in the kitchen was I could pack what I wanted from the pantry for my day's food supply. In addition to the three cheese sandwiches and two apples, I put three handfuls of dates and nuts in Saran Wrap. The issue would be what to drink. We didn't have a Coke machine at Via Del Sol, so I had to go without a beverage unless there was a water fountain somewhere or we stopped at a roadside burger joint (there was a great one in a little town named East Nicolaus off Highway 99 that served fresh banana shakes, which were a real luxury). Somehow, we all made do.

We knew this meeting would be in silence for all, and I had no idea how we would arrange it in Anna's home. When we arrived and I entered the living room, the answer was right in front of me: a blackboard. Mac and Miles were positioning it in front of the big window that faced the street. Then someone suggested they put it in front of the piano on the opposite side of the room.

I just stood there watching the moving center's animation of the many 'I's each person had and waited until the more active type succeeded in having their way. I was betting on Miles. To my surprise, Yorgos entered the triad, and his quiet nature neutralized the Martial of Mac and the Mercurial of Miles. Near the piano it was. I secured a seat against the right wall as close to the board as I could since I was quite nearsighted.

Robert had arrived with Jim and something strange was occurring. He was communicating with Jim using some type of hand gesture the way deaf people do. Only it wasn't that system. I knew this because I had studied it briefly at university as part of a linguistics course. It was fascinating to watch. Jim was taking Robert's comments and serving as his scribe by writing them down on paper to share with others. How interesting, I thought. I had wondered whether Robert would use the blackboard to pen his response. Guess not.

The meeting began with Robert's observation about the silence exercise.

"You can see people lose energy through unnecessary talk. The word exercise and silence exercise are psychological exercises we use to wake up. They can only come from the efforts of higher centers and Work 'I's. This exercise will continue until Sunday, November 1st."

Students raised their hands when Robert asked if there were any questions. He chose a lady student, who stood and took chalk in hand to write it on the board. Her script was beautiful. I wondered if she was a school teacher.

"How can we work on feminine dominance within a relationship?"

Robert had previously addressed this subject in relation to women and children, so I was eager to hear his thoughts.

"Men should avoid putting negative 'I's on their wives. It takes responsibility off their shoulders and makes the ladies carry the weight. It is not being a man. Negative 'I's are a poison, and both mates can poison one another.

"Ladies entering or leaving Saturn have a feature of dominating men. If that is the case, please work on letting the man make the decisions and work on not caring what happens to your wishes."

Quickly a hand went up from a Saturnine man. "What about a wife putting negative 'I's on a man?" I could feel a defensive energy in the room. Feminine dominance was a touchy subject.

"A man should use the same advice as was given to women," answered Robert. "It is objective advice and refers to higher centers and trueness in a human, whether male or female. Personally, I try to find opportunities to obey another person."

The wife of a student in the room raised her hand and was given the chalk.

"When a student or love becomes berating, and refuses photographs, how does one help? Remain silent? Walk away?"

Robert's response: "Yes. Remain silent or walk away. Also, change the subject, listen to music, take in impressions — try to hold your work."

Robert indicated it was fine for others to offer angles of thought.

One student approached the blackboard to offer the following.

"On men expressing negativity: Often it helps them to hear other angles of thought, at the same time strengthening the woman who gives other angles."

I did not understand this.

He passed the chalk to another Saturnine male, who wrote:

"Loved one may find another to play the same game, a chance that must be taken. Save yourself first. Help only when possible. Otherwise, you may be eaten."

Again, this was unclear to me.

Then Robert signaled his message to Jim, who took the chalk.

"Notice there are different sets of 'I's at a meeting for some of you, and other sets of 'I's away from the meeting and away from the group's influence."

That I understood. It was such a practical observation based on what was going on in the moment in the room. It brought me back to myself. I was amazed and delighted that Robert could so quickly address the obvious. I could also see how difficult it was for ideas to be formulated that were based on past behavior. Those were vague, clumsy and complicated.

I fled from the Spinoza teacher because I wanted to go beyond intellectualizing the Work. I wanted to pierce the present. And to do that, it was imperative to have someone who was already there, waiting for me.

❧

> Long I thought that knowledge alone would suffice me.
> All the while it is the present only.
>
> Walt Whitman

CHAPTER 75

The roundtrip home cost me 75 cents because of a new task from Robert. Previously, those of us without cars and few resources were able to ride for free. The task, which stated that drivers must charge each person at least this amount, was designed to curtail tramp feature (wanting something for nothing). Although it cut into my finances, I was glad to pay it, since doing so would help me work on this weakness.

The other thing mentioned at the meeting was the use of special socks Robert purchased for walking on the new carpet. The socks had been distributed over the weekend, and some of the residents started to use them inside their work boots immediately, which soiled them and ultimately the new carpet. The socks were meant more as slippers, and Robert, it seemed to me, was tired of having to invest money in floor covering. It was the third solution in as many months.

Wednesday after lunch the carpet was installed. Two men from the company in Marysville that sold us the carpet came to do the work. I couldn't believe how efficient and quick they were. I was used to students who carried a hammer and nails and appeared to be competent, but had no real trade experience. I was watching these people from afar and the technique impressed me. They decided to use the old carpet instead of a pad under the new carpet. They said it would save us money since the old carpet was thin enough and still intact. Once that was determined, they quickly laid out the new carpet, cutting it expertly to fit each corner. Within two hours it was done.

I had my new socks ready, and when my feet landed on the thicker brick-red carpet it was like standing on a marshmallow. In my childhood, wall-to-wall carpeting was considered the height of elegance. Wood and vinyl flooring were more rustic and artificial, and we judged our neighbors by our choices. Here was the first sign of luxury, and it was emotionally uplifting.

Because the rest of the log cabin remained as it was, the new impression provided a glimmer of hope in me that perhaps one day, we would be living in a beautiful place, and not this makeshift shack, with its assortment of creatures that took it upon themselves to share our food and lodging. I mention this because of what happened to me the previous week, before the silence exercise.

As I was preparing the sandwiches for our lunch (avocado, tomato, and alfalfa sprouts on freshly baked whole wheat bread), I went into the cooler to grab the avocados and noticed unusual markings on them, like someone had taken a tiny metal rake and scored the outside leathery black skin, exposing the light-green flesh.

"What's this?" I asked Kerrie as I pointed to the grooves.

"Oh, they're teeth marks. The mice bit into this. I'll have Yorgos work on setting traps."

She took the avocado from my hand and carved away the nibbled part.

"Here, use this," she instructed, handing me the remaining piece.

I was stunned at her nonchalance. I shuddered to think what else they were crawling on and sampling. She noticed an immediate resistance in me to take it from her hand, so she told me to bring just those avocados that were spared.

As I entered the cooler, a fearful state overtook me. This friendly place that I had considered a goodie box full of all sorts of food for me to eat whenever I wanted, suddenly was like entering the bowels of some beast. It was now a dark and cold place, where unseen varmints were lurking, waiting for me to leave so they could indulge. I hurriedly went to the crate of avocados and inspected them closely. I found that only a few were intact. I gathered those and returned to the kitchen.

Quietly I focused on removing the avocado flesh and building the sandwiches. Kerrie saw I was rattled. She must have found it rather amusing that these little creatures had such an effect on this LA Girl.

But something else had upset me, which I couldn't quite pinpoint. After months of living in this place, I had grown accustomed to insects and wild animals. Why was I suddenly so freaked out? It was hard to shake, this unsettled feeling. Somehow, I sensed there was a message in it for me. What could it be?

That night I couldn't sleep; I was still disturbed by my inability to figure it out. My intellectual center was strong, and emotionally I could recognize symbols in my daily life. But this eluded me, and I didn't know why. One thing I did know: the cooler would never be the same.

※

The lower self is like a thief who sneaks into your house at night to steal whatever is valuable and worthwhile. Turn on the light. The thief, who is a coward, will then run out. How do we turn on the light? Through the practice of remembrance.

Sufi Wisdom

CHAPTER 76

I was eager for Saturday, October 30 to arrive because the silence exercise officially ended at the evening meeting. Communication had become cumbersome and laborious. During Tuesday's meeting, one student requested he be relieved from printing Robert's messages on the blackboard because it was taking too much time and his script was difficult to read. Robert instructed him to continue because his slowness was irritating everyone.

"Where there is irritation and separation occurring, the knowledge has a better chance of going directly to higher centers," explained Robert.

Saturday was a beautiful autumn day. The weather was temperate, and the light of the sun brought out the red-gold of the new carpet. I left the kitchen to grab a smoke outside when Robert approached me. He handed me a note.

"We will close the kitchen tomorrow. Fast for 24 hours. Monday breakfast menu: scrambled eggs with garlic and onions, biscuits with country gravy, and potato salad. Have the children help you cook."

I almost burst out laughing. You gotta be kidding, I thought. This is not how you break a fast. You drink liquids only and then proceed with vegetables and easy to digest food. Any hippie worthy of his B Influence studies knew this. I tried to communicate my suggestion to him with a note, but he waved my comments aside. He left me standing there.

End of conversation.

* * * *

News of the fast circulated fast. It was met with shock (What?), disbelief (No Way), confusion (But That's My Octave!) — basically, a range of emotions that didn't include acceptance, gratitude or understanding. Some students even decided to leave earlier than usual to avoid being under this edict. I guess when a person decides to fast, it's considered his choice. When a teacher gives it as a task, it's felt as deprivation and imposition.

Saturday evening's meeting was scheduled for 7 p.m. I was working in the kitchen, helping to prepare a more than ample dinner to tide us over for 24 hours. When I took off my apron to sit for the meeting, I was delighted to see a projector positioned.

After a brief good householder, a short movie on Walt Whitman was shown. It was not a documentary as much as a series of still photographs of him that had been put on film. An accompanying commentary was played on a tape recorder that included the voice of Walt reading from his poem "America." Apparently, this recording was made in 1890, two years before he completed his task. Whether or not it was actually Walt was questioned by some students. The words were almost inaudible, but the strength of the solid, simple American voice and its deliberate cadence penetrated my heart. Here he was and here I am, ages hence.

The focus of the meeting was to share observations on the silence exercise.

"It's easier to ask people to do things with notes. It doesn't seem to come from Me," a timid Lunar observed.

Another person asked, "The moving center tried to communicate. If we are observing these acts, are we out of mechanical parts?"

The teacher replied, "Yes. It is easier not to be identified in silence. That is a valuable observation."

Kerrie commented, "The moving center is more alive than the intellectual center."

The teacher smiled and wrote, "An 'I' just said, 'Kerrie, you spoke!' Some 'I's don't know that the exercise is over. How many are experiencing this?"

Most of us raised our hands.

"Some instinctive-moving acts are bad. Let's go over them."

We discussed how the moving center communicates unnecessarily, such as when we say yes and our heads nod up and down.

"Each 'I' is a different person. Then, who are you? Consciousness is not functions. Later you will be grateful that you are none of the lower centers."

The subject changed to the first open meeting scheduled the following Tuesday in Berkeley. In preparation, Robert laid out certain rules. He asked us to sit on the rug during this meeting.

"It is necessary to be uncomfortable in an esoteric teaching, so don't worry about new students' comfort, or your own."

He also mentioned not to give prospective students his name and not to invite them if they have worked with a teacher named Alex Horn.

Because this last statement was a bit mysterious to me, I asked Meg about it after the meeting and she told me Alex Horn was Robert's teacher. There's some cosmic law apparently that a student must not pull away his teacher's students to form his own group. It is regarded as the lower (a student) trying to eat the work of the higher (his teacher), and therefore represents a criminal act.

Although it was an interesting concept to me, I felt it was more a gracious gesture on Robert's part that he would be careful not to do this to his teacher, out of respect. Cosmic laws of conscious schools I simply had to register. How can one possibly verify them?

> *You must apply yourself with patience to mastering the observance of the law, for then you will experience the removal of the veil from knowledge.*
> Al-Jilani

CHAPTER 77

Sunday was Halloween, and the morning was met with slumber. No need to arise, since the kitchen was closed. I rolled over and slept as late as I could. It was after 9 a.m. when I donned my jeans and top and headed down the hill to the Lodge.

It was eerily quiet. The Lodge was the wheel of our social existence and the kitchen was its hub. Never before was this so apparent. I wandered through the living room, kitchen, and small library and found only one person. We greeted each other and I asked where everyone was. He informed me most left for the Bay Area. Others were tending the animals. The rest, who knows?

We decided to walk down to the barn and check it out.

"I wonder if they need help with the animals?" I asked no one in particular. It was an offering expressed more out of curiosity than from any willingness to assist. However insincere it was, good intentions always made me feel like a strong student especially when I felt uncomfortably adrift without something to do.

Just as the words came out of my mouth, Klair and Nadia appeared from the barn, each grasping a handle of a large container of fresh cow's milk, sharing the load, as they synchronized their steps toward the Lodge.

"Why don't you ask them?" my companion said. So I did, expecting them to say, "No thank you. We have it." Instead, Klair suggested I help Nadia carry the heavy milk crock up the hill to the kitchen.

THE DIVINE BEGINNING

Both Klair and Nadia were diminutive ladies (instinctive-moving Lunars) and I was a fleshy Venusian with arms that showed no sign of musculature. They set the container down and Klair stepped away to attend to the new calf. Here I was again, paired with Nadia. I placed my hand inside the right-side handle and waited for Nadia to do the same with the left-side handle. We both lifted on cue. The weight of the liquid, however, was beyond anything I had imagined. It was so heavy that I couldn't bear my end properly and some milk spilled. Nadia glared at me; she was clearly livid. We proceeded to climb the rutted dirt road, which proved even more challenging to maintaining balance. It was slow going.

Finally, Nadia turned to my companion, who lagged behind, and asked if he could step in to replace me. Nadia and he climbed the hill in perfect unison and it was clear she was relieved he was there. I was left in the middle of the road, not knowing whether to go up or down. A wave of self-deprecation quickly arose, which determined the direction. I headed down hill, looking for a place to hide.

* * * *

It was late and darkness had fallen. The kids were waiting for me in the Lodge. The head chef had boiled a kettle full of Idaho potatoes for the salad and it was placed on one of the long tables in the living room. Our assignment was to remove the skins and put the peelings in a big bowl to give to the animals in the morning. The earthy smell was intoxicating and made my mouth water. I handed potatoes to each child and guided them in their task. The eldest one taunted me by eating some of the cooked potato, exclaiming how delicious it was and that I was forbidden to eat it by Robert. Some of the others imitated him. I played along instead of becoming upset and didn't break my task.

As I crawled into my sleeping bag that night, I thought about how the day was filled with ups and downs, successes and failures. I didn't eat the potato. But I didn't help my fellow students either. Being a good student was important to me, and yet I didn't know what that truly meant. How can the gods keep me in the school when I'm clearly pretty useless at physical tasks? That question was my last thought as I drifted off to sleep.

* * * *

I had been wandering for a long while in a desolate part of the country, without food or water. In the distance I saw a two-story house and approached it, hoping for help. As I knocked on the door, a beautiful child peeked out the window from inside, smiling at the arrival of this stranger. The door opened and a woman appeared.

"May I help you?" she asked.

"Hello. Yes. I'm wondering if you have something for me to eat and drink. I've been traveling for a long while. I have no money to pay you, but am willing to work for it," I said.

She bid me follow her and as I entered, I was stunned to see the house was a large open-spaced building, not a cozy little home. Many people were there, busy with different tasks in silence. It was an active scene.

"What is this place?" I inquired.

Instead of a reply she smiled lovingly and opened a door to a dining area with long tables, where many were either beginning or ending their meals.

"You can eat first," she said.

I sat down and food and drink were brought to me. I could not understand how this woman trusted me. When I had finished, she returned and led me to another room filled with small booths where persons were communicating to others on the other side of a glass divider. It looked like a prison setup for visitors to communicate with inmates, but without the phones.

"You are to sit on one side of the glass partition and give aid to the person on the other side."

I felt totally unqualified for the job. What did she mean by aid? What did I know? What advice could I possibly give?

She felt my concern and with the kindest look said, "Do not worry. All you have to do to help is to listen."

The person who came to talk to me was clearly distraught. I just sat there silently listening as she revealed a wealth of suffering and confusion. When she was done, she thanked me profusely, as if I had given her the salve that would heal all her wounds and bring clarity to her life.

The woman returned to tell me I had earned my meal.

"You are welcome to stay here."

In that moment I awoke in the dark. I reached for my red plastic flashlight and Timex watch to see that it was four in the morning. Shutting off the light, I stared up into the blackness of the tent ceiling, hoping that the meaning of the dream would magically reveal itself.

It did not, at first. As I quietly lay there, my mind become still, and I was thrust into the third state.

The meaning was clear. I was in the right place in my life. I was here, now. That's all I could say. What I couldn't say was what the next day would bring and whether I would be up to the tasks assigned to me to serve the school, the teacher, and my fellow students.

To the servant of God, every place is the right place, and every time is the right time.
St. Catherine of Siena

CHAPTER 78

The Monday breakfast had begun. I was amazed how many students showed up to indulge in the sumptuous buffet on the long table. I took a plate and watched my hand pile the creamy potato salad, heap two servings of scrambled eggs cooked with garlic and onions, grab a couple of biscuits, and pour the gravy over them. Taking my plate outside and balancing it on my knees, a small voice inside instructed me, Don't Eat This. It was going against my training to consume such rich food after a fast. But the urges countered with, "It looks so good and I'm hungry and Robert is eating it and he's a conscious being. He must know it's fine."

After several bites, I looked up and saw Clark and Laura stay away from it, only drinking water. But I couldn't stop. I continued until the plate was clean. And then I went back for two more biscuits and jam with some tea.

After a cigarette, which I smoked mainly to give me time to digest the meal, I went into the kitchen to dry the remaining dishes, as the dream had inspired me to quietly serve and be useful.

It was a tranquil fall day. The exodus to the Bay Area had begun by noon. I had arranged a ride to Berkeley on Tuesday after lunch for the first of the open meetings. Mac was scheduled to lead it in Anna's home. I was looking forward to participating and decided to spend the afternoon in my tent, studying the work books in preparation. Instead, I took a long nap.

Around dinner time I went down to the Lodge to freshen up and was surprised to see a normal dinner had been served. I still could feel the breakfast. The dinner, however, was too good to pass up, especially with the camaraderie of fellow students. Afterwards, I skipped assisting with the cleanup and went straight up the hill to bury my head in the work books. After thirty minutes or so, I was ready to retire, and sleep quickly descended upon me.

* * * *

A wave of nausea and acute pain woke me up. It was 2 a.m., and I stumbled out of my tent to relieve myself. The November full moon illumined my options, and, looking around, I went to the back of the tent to vomit, hoping that would take care of the matter.

I returned to the sack, but the matter was not over. The bowels continued to rumble and roar and sharp pains streaked across my abdomen like lightning strikes. I hurriedly unzipped the tent and walked to the side and squatted. The eruption was loud and the mess smelly and elevated. It was unacceptable to leave it in such plain sight so I tried to find a rock that would cover it up. Most of the large rocks had been removed so I picked up several small ones. I hoped no one would step in it in the morning, as this was one of the narrow paths between tents that was taken to reach the Lodge. Thoughts of someone sliding on it and falling entered my mind, only adding to my agony.

Again, I returned to bed, and again…and again, and again the urges forced me outdoors. On the second trip I had spotted a cow patty or pie that I thought would absorb my releases — and if not, I could pretend that it was a cow, not a human, that had defecated so. This explanation helped to ease both my mental and bodily distress. The evidence will be well hidden, I reasoned, so no one will ever know the true offender.

* * * *

Dawn's dim light heralded the end of my internal woes. I was exhausted. By the time I arrived at the Lodge it was 10 a.m. The timing was ideal since it was between breakfast and lunch service. My body forbade any thought of food. It just wanted to be left alone.

But that was not to be. Robert entered the room and walked straight up to me.

"Can you prepare some scrambled eggs for me, dear?"

My stomach roiled and I replied, with a most pained expression, "Robert, why do we always have to EAT?! That's all we do here. It's nothing but food, food, food," and so forth and so on. Tears rolled down my cheeks, and in the midst of my angst, he did an about-face and asked Helga, who was near the kitchen counter.

"Yes, Robert," she simply said.

How humiliating! Not only had he asked the woman who could satisfy a man better than I could apparently, but even more horrific, I refused a task from the teacher. I recalled the first time I read about Peter and Christ's final moments and thought, "I would never deny Christ." Well, there I was, denying my teacher. I thought for sure my membership in the school had just been revoked.

Feeling weak, dejected, and worthless, I sat in the corner of the room to gather myself. A few minutes had passed when two students near me began arguing.

"I tell you I heard it last night!" said the first male student. "It clearly was not human."

"I think I heard it too. It was around 3 a.m., right?"

"Yes! It was like several loud roars. Then silence. Then it began all over again." He paused as he pondered the source of the sound. The answer to the mystery came to him in a flash: "I bet it was the Laughing Man!"

"Oh God! He's back!"

"Let's ask Linda. It was near her tent."

As I overheard their argument, my humiliation and horror had turned to mortification. When they questioned me about hearing any sounds during the night, I stared at them and slowly shook my head, hoping my usually animated face that never could hide a lie didn't manifest to reveal that I was their Laughing Man. It was difficult for them to believe I slept through the noise since their tents were within fifty feet or so of mine. They questioned me several times, but they finally let it go, changing the topic of conversation. I was off the hook. I only prayed they wouldn't come upon the proof of such foulness and accuse me of desecrating the sacred grounds.

* * * *

Tuesday had finally arrived, but the long Monday still lingered within me.

My ride to Berkeley was with Klair and her mini-entourage. We left after lunch, with a stop in Vacaville, where Klair had lived prior to moving to the farm. When my stomach issues continued, it was clear I needed to rest. She told me I could stay at her home (the one she had with Don) and put me in one of the day beds. Then she left to run errands. When she came back, I couldn't move, so she determined I was to remain there and miss the meeting. She would come back for me afterwards.

But before she left, she introduced me to her dog, a black-and-white Boston terrier. It was surprising that I hadn't encountered this dog before on any of my previous visits. As I tried to rest, the dog sat by my bedside, demanding attention by snorting loudly. I told it to leave, but to no avail. It was the kind of dog that responds to any command you give it with enthusiastic tail wagging and deafness. It was a constant irritant that after an hour I simply had to accept.

As I lay there, the extent of my exhaustion penetrated deeply into my bones. It stripped me of all intellectual capabilities and I realized I was in no condition to contribute any personal insights or knowledge at the open meeting. Basically, I couldn't think straight. But I could observe. What I observed was that my instinctive center dominated all other centers in my machine. It was a simple observation. Not feeling social (emotional center), not formulating sentences correctly (intellectual center), not wanting to move (moving center). It was a verification that the instinctive center was the mind behind the workings of the machine, as Ouspensky wrote. What can one do? One is held hostage in sickness, imprisoned in the machine, and forced to co-habit with a one-brained being.

When Klair returned, I found myself in darkness. I had fallen asleep soon after the observations with no lights on in the house as evening came. Klair shook me awake and told me to start moving. Others were in the car ready to head up to the farm, and I must not keep them waiting.

I felt like I missed the party. This was the only time I could participate in the open meetings (attendance was by invitation only), and I regretted my lack of control. It was not the first time this had happened to me. I longed for discipline, but had no idea how to combat that part of me that clearly had its own agenda.

> *Why do the demons wish to commit acts of gluttony, impurity, avarice, wrath, resentment, and the other evil passions in us? Here is the reason — that the spirit in this way should become dull and consequently rendered unfit to pray.*
>
> Philokalia, Evagrios the Solitary

CHAPTER 79

Wednesday was a recovery day. As I approached the Lodge in the morning, I felt lighter and my clothes were definitely looser. I had wondered if anyone else noticed how thin I was. As the year was drawing to a close, there was a desperate need in me to see change in myself, whether internal or external. Measuring progress was a sure sign of validation of efforts.

Toward evening, Yorgos approached me with an invitation to attend the second open meeting he was leading in Vacaville at Mac's home. I couldn't understand why Mac didn't lead this one in his own home, while Yorgos could have travelled to the Bay Area to lead the meeting there. This seemed more logical. Regardless of my opinion, I was grateful I wouldn't miss an opportunity to share my knowledge and understanding at this open meeting.

All I needed was to find a round-trip ride, which was easier said than done. I did learn that Rosemary was leaving early Thursday morning, but wouldn't return until Saturday. She was told I was looking and came up to me.

"You can help me prepare the house for the meeting. Besides, I want to talk to you," she stated, commandingly.

Rosemary was so firm in her utterances that every direction from her was assumed to be a done deal as soon as the words came out. That was her Martial type in action. She encouraged me to take extra clothes and said her younger girl would be staying with her boyfriend so her bed would be available. I had no idea what she wanted to talk to me about, and this was the only thing that had me hesitate. I was hopelessly attracted to her company, however. Then I remembered Venus and Mars types are maximum attraction.

We left around 2 p.m. Heading down highway 20 toward Marysville, Rosemary broke the silence and asked:

"How is your money holding up?"

That was the subject.

I explained I had a few steady massage customers and was able to make enough to pay teaching donations and provide for necessities. Of course, "necessities" was a general term that actually meant soap, shampoo and toothpaste. Clothes, food and shelter were not necessities to me since the school provided them, for the most part. I was never into fashion so I wore whatever I had until clothes became threadbare.

She questioned me about my plans, advised me not to waste my talents, cautioned me not to allow the tramp of the farm to turn me into a hippie. As I listened, puffing on a borrowed Marlboro, staring pensively out the window, I suddenly realized her viewpoints mirrored our present path on the road: that long stretch of Highway 20 with its two straight and narrow lanes that shot through farmlands, going in opposite directions.

That was how I felt, being yanked between two different roads. Rose's route was so civilized and orderly and filled with propriety and logic. But back at the ranch, it was a trek that was so chaotic and coarse — a life that was more a part of a primitive past than any cultured future — and yet this rough life fed essence in an inexplicable way. That was its draw.

Which way to go? All I knew was Rose's approach had no light. To me, it was a dark closet filled with plastic everythings. The school had light and was an open space with little to sustain the outward person but fresh air for essence to breathe.

As these and other thoughts circulated, we entered her driveway. Rosemary turned off the ignition. She paused before informing me that she had arranged for me to substitute teach tomorrow. They would call me at 6 a.m. to let me know which school I would be assigned.

The play was determined. Or so it seemed.

* * * *

The meeting that night was a blur. Imagination ran amok inside my head regarding the teaching job Friday morning. Questions abounded such as transportation to and from the school, what the subject would be, what grade and age group, whether I looked presentable, would I remember how to act? More than that, however, was the persistent pull between pursuing a normal life, with its structured hours that tapped into my longing for order, and the deeper gravitation toward returning to the farm where I learned to be happy surviving on subsistence.

A large crowd attended the open meeting, and beverages and snacks were offered afterwards so that we could mingle with the interested prospective students. Yorgos's face was rosy and happy. He was truly a beautiful social being as he welcomed people he had never met before. I envied his ease, which I had never mastered while at university. When you feel like an outsider, it's hard to connect with others.

I kept myself busy in the kitchen washing the plates and glasses that were brought in and talking to friends about the meeting. I had learned that Robert was in Vacaville dining at the Coffee Tree with Jim and a couple of other students.

I was tired and waiting for the right moment to sneak into the front bedroom to retire. Tomorrow would be a busy, exciting day of teaching so a good rest was imperative. The house became quiet around eleven. By midnight I was fast asleep.

* * * *

The morning light filtered onto my face to awaken me. It was quiet and for a few moments I was happy. Suddenly, time announced itself and I bolted upright. It was Friday. And the clock read 8:45 a.m.

I jumped into my clothes and went straight to Rosemary's bedroom off the kitchen. I knocked on her closed door. I heard her stir and when she came out, I told her the time and asked her if she had heard the phone ring at 6 a.m. She simply said, No. Why?

I was distraught and reminded her about the phone call for the job. She hadn't remembered. Then she put the blame on me.

"Why didn't you hear the phone?" she asked, accusatorily.

"Why, you ask? I was in the front room and the phone was in the kitchen," I responded, defensively.

She suggested I call them. I insisted first of all that it was too late and second of all, she was the one who knew whom to contact.

This interaction between us continued, with the urgency and confusion rising to a boiling point. Suddenly Robert, in his bathrobe, entered the kitchen. He had slept in another bedroom.

We began to explain to him what the commotion was about. He took the pencil hanging from a string by the calendar near the wall phone. He wrote simply: Let it go.

I read the three words as if they were a suggestion about how to handle the issue at hand. It was, however, no suggestion. It was a command. And I ignored it.

Rose and I continued our heated discussion. Rosemary tried to reason with Robert, as if he didn't understand the great import of this missed opportunity and the need to rectify the problem. Robert stepped between us and, with that pencil, gave his reply: he slowly drew a line under these three words. Rosemary continued talking. He turned and walked away.

I froze in shock.

All 'I's disappeared.

I could do nothing.

I stood silently, staring at the three words.

I was stripped of everything except the present moment.

That was the play. The job was imaginary. The state was not.

❦

In the end, we return to a wordless beholding.
                                        Johann Goethe

CHAPTER 80

Rosemary did not return to the ranch that weekend as expected. She was my ride so I was stuck in Vacaville. It was not a bad thing, however. For whatever reason, I lacked incentive to take my life by the reins. I was passive to external events, and often just went with the flow. My role seemed to be that of a fly on the wall.

Sunday morning breakfast, Rosemary prepared her blueberry pancakes for Robert, Jim and me. The discussion centered on a town named Carmel and a place known as Esalen. What I was able to learn was that Mac had taken his Rolfing courses with Dr. Ida Rolf, who gave classes at Esalen, which was a famous hub of B Influence. Robert wondered if any of these people would be interested in joining our group. Could Mac set up a meeting with the heads of Esalen? Rosemary would speak with Mac.

Meanwhile, Rose had mentioned a dear friend of hers who lived in Carmel that may also have a magnetic center. Her name was Sheila.

"You'll like her," said Rosemary to Robert.

He quickly wrote, "Can you arrange a meeting with her, too?"

A nod from Rose indicated it was as good as done.

The three of them stood up from the table, continuing the conversation about Carmel and Esalen. Since I was totally unfamiliar with this part of northern California and felt I couldn't contribute anything, I cleared the plates and began washing dishes. I tried to listen to the conversation, but the thought of merging a B Influence group with the Fellowship not only distracted me but deeply disturbed me.

It reminded me of that Gurdjieff-Spinoza group I had met at UCLA. This year, 1971, was the Year of Hope, as Miles had written in that copy of the *The Psychology* he gave to me less than a year ago. We had found a school of conscious development. Why is Robert even considering this? I had found what I was looking for and now it seems it was changing its form. I was scared. Would I have to start all over again? I had given up so much.

These thoughts filled me with dread. As I was slowly wiping a plate that I had already dried several times over, Robert suddenly appeared to my right, positioning himself as dishwasher. I was stunned at how his hands moved at lightning speed without a hint of frantic energy. Plates, knives, forks, spoons, cups, saucers, pans and pots landed in the drying area. I couldn't keep up.

I giggled and told him to slow down. He didn't respond to my request, but continued with the task at hand. I was having fun marveling at his abilities when I realized that the dread that had entrapped me so had dissipated like a dense fog in the warm rays of the rising sun. In its place was a lightness, a buoyancy. I was present like a little child watching her father's hidden talent of juggling four balls in the air. He pulled me out of a dark psychological tunnel. My heart knew he would be there for me and would never abandon my quest to awaken.

* * * *

After the breakfast, Rosemary, Robert and Jim left the house for the day. It was curious to me how I was left behind without a comment from anyone. I felt abandoned, with nothing to do and nowhere to go. I went through my normal routine of record playing and reading to pass the time. I even went out to visit the animals behind the barn. I tried to be present rather than allow boredom or self-pity to enter, but my inner state was descending into that dark and dank root cellar known as depression.

Hunger appeared in the early afternoon. I found some leftovers in the refrigerator and made a sandwich and salad, hoping that would help. It didn't.

Rosemary came home around 5 p.m. without the teacher and Jim. She asked me what I was doing and I told her I was studying the work books. That seemed to satisfy her. Then she told me she was going to Carmel Monday morning for a few days. She didn't mention Robert, Jim or Mac, but I assumed they would be joining her.

Sunday was a quiet day with Rose's two daughters floating in and out of the house. Robert and Jim appeared briefly, and Rose insisted that her younger daughter play a complicated piece on the piano for the teacher. It was clear Rose was proud of her accomplishments, but she was a bit stubborn and refused. She was a Lunar type, and they were known for their willfulness.

Regardless, Rosemary's Martial drive made her perform the Bach composition. It was exciting to watch her fingers fly across the keys. Then, at one point I could see her hands shake from inner considering, and she lost her way. She had to begin again. It happened several times until she finally announced she was done with the concert.

Robert listened and gave her respect. It was an awkward moment for her, as she was keen on perfection. She left the house shortly afterward with her sister.

Dinner time came, and Robert wrote on the calendar, "Let's go to the Nut Tree. My treat." Rose and I were standing beside him, but he turned to her only. She took her purse and followed him outside to the waiting car.

Once again, I was left alone to fend for myself.

* * * *

Early Monday morning, Rosemary surprised me by entering my dark bedroom.

"Time to wake up," she announced. "You received a call to substitute teach."

I reached for my glasses, first glancing at the time (it was 5:50) before reading the slip of paper she handed me. It said Youth Services Vacaville High School.

"You're to go to the Vacaville High School main office by 7:45 a.m. and they'll take you to the classroom."

Because her home was a distance from the school, she said she would drive me there, but couldn't pick me up due to her trip to Carmel. She gave me Don's phone number since he worked nearby at the Nut Tree. He could drive me back, she said.

Realizing my two-hour leisurely primping wouldn't fit the situation, I hurriedly grabbed my good-luck purple coatdress with matching heels and decided to put my long hair up into a bun rather than wash it to save time. Rose said I looked nice. We arrived at the main office a minute before the given time.

I greeted the registrar, gave her my name, and showed her my driver's license for verification. We walked across the street toward a separate building that seemed designed for storage. That impression it turned out was fitting, since these were the Problem Kids that had been weeded out from the main population of budding students.

Her tone was deliberately soft and appropriately compassionate as she described the categories of troubled youth: pregnant teenage girls; disruptive boys who smoked cigarettes, disrespected teachers, and failed in their coursework; and those who could not fit in socially because of mild psychological disorders such as low I.Q. I knew kids like these in high school, and they were good kids with tough lives. The registrar was a bit too condescending for my taste, but I ignored these thoughts since I had a job to do and needed to appear like an adult.

As we entered, I saw five small separate classrooms, each one large enough to hold no more than a dozen kids. She led me to the last room at the end of the hallway. Most of the kids were facing forward, while a few turned around to see who their teacher would be for the day. I stood straight to strike an authoritative stance and placed a friendly smile on my face to communicate I was stern but approachable. It was all designed to hide the fact that I had no idea what I was doing.

The registrar left me after explaining that the kids had an assigned book to read. In other words, they knew what they were to do, while I didn't know what I was to do. I felt solace in the wisdom I gained from my education training from UCLA: substituting was glorified babysitting. Keep them quietly in their chairs for an hour and try not to allow disruption.

Grabbing the white chalk, I wrote my name on the blackboard, sat in the chair behind the desk, and placed my purse in the large bottom drawer. Three books were on the desk: a dictionary, a grammar book, and a book of short stories.

Just as I settled in reading a short story, a young lady entered the room and went straight up to me.

"You have a phone call," she said.

Me?

I quickly followed her wondering who could possibly be calling me.

We arrived at the registration office. Rosemary was on the line.

"I'm locking up because the girls are staying with friends for the night. I forgot to tell you where the spare key is. It's outside under the kitchen mat."

It was like my mother had called me, which was a stark reminder that I was not that much older than the kids in the room. When I returned, some were giggling. I ignored that, figuring they had a private joke that was nothing but silliness and had little if anything to do with me. I found two Venusian girls who were soft enough to approach. We spoke a bit about the stories they were reading, and I tried to impart whatever scholarly guidance I could, making me feel as if I was earning my paycheck. This class was a half-day session, so by noon I was done for the day.

Feeling carefree with the knowledge that a paycheck should be available soon, I decided to walk toward the Nut Tree along Monte Vista Avenue. It was a couple of miles and I had the afternoon free, enjoying the muted light of the November sun. Along the way I saw a McDonald's and thought it would be nice to eat a hamburger and fries. As I entered, I checked my wallet to see how much I could spend. When you have little money, you tend to know what's in your pocket. My memory was $5.37. But my wallet was empty. My change was there but the five-dollar bill was gone.

How could this be? I checked through my purse, and then it hit me. I replayed the scenes of putting my purse in the drawer and leaving it there when I went to the registration office. That was the joke from the giggling kids. They stole it.

Not only did my hunger pangs increase as I approached the Nut Tree, so did my imagination. I was thinking how wonderful it would be if Don asked whether I had had lunch and then treated me to a meal. Maybe the Tropical Prawns. The memory of the sweet smell of the buttered roll hit me, too. I was salivating. But why would he ask me this since now it was 3:30? Oh, well, that's not going to happen. Best not to have any expectations.

Then I replayed how stupid I was not to take my purse with me. I could see the shock that someone would want to talk to me completely obliterated common sense in the moment. I was caught in the 'I's trying to figure out who it could be rather than protecting my personal property. It's called "sleep" and "identification."

When I finally arrived at the Nut Tree restaurant, I went up to the woman at the reservation desk and told her I was here to see the Art Director. She was most pleasant and told me simply to go up the stairs inside the restaurant to his office. I didn't recall seeing a staircase when I dined with Robert. I couldn't find it at first, and asked a waitress. She pointed to the side wall where a discreet wooden staircase led to office space that seemed to float from the ceiling. It was on the same level as the hanging airplanes and displays, and from the office's large windows, you could see the entire dining room. It was magical, as if the gods were looking down upon everyone.

Don greeted me with a handshake and introduced me to his colleagues, who were happy to meet me, they said. The positive energy in the room uplifted my spirits. I hadn't realized how rare it was for me to be surrounded by nice people who were interested in me. Students were nice, or at least I thought they should be and forgave them easily when negativity was expressed. Or at least I thought I did.

Don left the office to take me back to Rosemary's house. As he dropped me off, he asked how the teaching went, and I simply said Fine. I couldn't tell him what actually happened and that I was broke. It was better to keep my dignity than to beg.

Entering the house through the kitchen, I went directly to the cupboards. All I could find was a half-full box of crackers. The pancake mix was gone and there was no cereal. In the refrigerator, the remaining leftovers were spoiled and only condiments were on the shelf. I took the box of crackers and ate each one slowly, savoring the taste and enjoying the crunch.

As I sat at the table finishing the snack, my eyes landed on Rosemary's bedroom door, which was off the kitchen. Knowing I was alone, I was enticed to enter. Although I had been there once before, I realized I had not fully taken in the impressions inside. I was more focused on Rosemary that day, who was suffering.

The empty room was filled with emanations of activities from the past. I could feel their traces, and it made me sad in a way. I went to the heavy drapes and touched them. They were made of a plush forest-green velveteen fabric that hung heavily from the metal rods over the windows at the end of the room. They were halfway open and served to frame the most glorious sight. A small orchard was outside, and the sunlight wove its gentle rays through the limbs, putting spotlights on brilliant balls of Christmas red that hung like ornaments from the branches. What fruit could they be? Perhaps Red Delicious apples!

Immediately I left the bedroom, went through the living room to the front door and down the stone steps. The orchard must be to the left, I reasoned. There it was! But the fruit was not apple. It was pomegranate.

I gathered several, reaching high up to the ripest ones. I went around the house and passed the garage with its open door that revealed a burlap bag with the word Walnuts on it. It was loaded. I went back to the kitchen for a bowl and filled it with the nuts. In a drawer I found a nutcracker.

While putting these fruits together, I felt like a child from a fairy tale. Goldilocks came to mind. Intellectually I knew I had only 37 cents in my pocket, but my heart unexpectedly soared with joy. I was present and so were the gods and there was food to eat. I wasn't going to starve and I wasn't alone. True, it was a new standard of financial rock bottom. But the good news was, once you hit this rock bottom, the only way out is up.

❧

Don't talk to me about trouble and trial —
I am too busy with my blessings.
                                    Walt Whitman

PART III
The Middle

CHAPTER 81

THE NEXT DAY was Tuesday. I had lingered in bed the whole morning, trying to ignore the emptiness in my stomach. As I drifted once again to sleep, I was suddenly awakened by the sound of a car pulling into the driveway. It was almost noon.

Quickly I threw on my clothes and entered the kitchen. There was Rosemary carrying a bag of groceries.

"Go outside and help me bring in the bags," she directed.

I could not believe it. With a smile on my face, I chose the heaviest bags first, balancing each on an ample hip and placing them down on the counter. With an about-face I went for the others. She had about a dozen bags in all, filled with supplies.

Handing items to her, she knew exactly where to place the vegetables, fruits, juices, breads, meats, cheeses, cans and boxes. The pantry, refrigerator and freezer were now full.

"Did you have lunch?" she asked.

No, I replied. I didn't dare tell her about my hardship the previous day.

"Well, let's eat."

With great ease, she assembled foods for a quick omelet, handed me the loaf of sliced bread for toast, and heated the water for coffee. Within fifteen minutes we were dining.

I asked her about her trip to Carmel. She explained that Mac had gone ahead and arranged for Robert to meet Mac's friends at Esalen in Big Sur, but Robert decided he wanted them to come to Vacaville and for Mac to host them for dinner at the Nut Tree. Robert would not join them for dinner, but Mac could bring them to the house afterward where Robert would meet them briefly.

"When would this occur?" I asked.

"Tonight. I came back to straighten up the house."

"Let me help you," I said, grateful for the chance to pay my way.

A slight smile crossed her face briefly before she lit the cigarette. She offered me one, and I was surprised how wonderful was the first inhalation since I hadn't smoked for a number of days. It went right to my head and gave me a boost of energy. I enjoyed the buzz.

The prospect of Robert coming to the house that evening was exciting. At least I would see him. But were we to dine together? Or would he once again whisk Rosemary off to the Coffee Tree for dinner, leaving me alone. As if reading my mind, Rosemary proceeded to fill me in on the next scene of the play.

"Mac is bringing Sheila up from Carmel later today. She's staying with us and will prepare dinner for Robert here tonight."

Her response only increased anxiety. I suddenly tensed up, since this was now a different triad. Would I be included? Or would I have to retreat to the bedroom? In that moment I did not know where I stood with the teacher.

The afternoon passed quickly. Rosemary focused on preparing the bedrooms and bathrooms for guests, while I dusted and vacuumed the living room. It was approaching mid-November and darkness came early.

Just as the sun had set around five, Mac walked into the kitchen accompanied by the most beautiful and mysterious woman I had ever met. Sheila was of average height and wore crème raw silk pants and an ivory silk shirt with collars that were perfectly pressed. Her short, ethereal hair was platinum and her nails were painted with the palest shade of pink ice. Her mouth was set firmly and her gaze was contained. She was someone who suffered no fools, I thought. I wondered if she would like me.

Mac introduced us and then Rosemary showed Sheila to her room, leaving me with him in the kitchen. He asked me how things were going, and I told him I was doing substitute teaching. His response was, Great!

In that moment, I realized I had misrepresented something. Was this lying? It was not Great, you see. It was Awful. But it satisfied his desire to know about my life. It was so much like Meg's repartee with Robert about formatory mind. A glimpse of observing something mechanical in me was quickly interrupted when Rose and Sheila re-entered the kitchen.

Mac looked down at his watch.

"I need to go. I don't want to be late," he said, rushing out the door.

The dinner with the Esalen people was scheduled for six-thirty at the Nut Tree. His quick departure, however, seemed more connected to avoiding Rosemary than being late. It was another lie. It was clear there were still issues between them.

Sheila and Rosemary donned aprons and began preparing the dinner. It was to be Sheila's Shrimp Curry, which according to Rose was her famous dish, on a bed of white rice with broccoli. Rosemary directed me to use a special tablecloth and matching napkins from one of the cabinet drawers. She had bought some flowers also and asked me to arrange a nice bouquet.

Meanwhile, the rice was cooking and Sheila was preparing the broccoli. She used a paring knife to shave the stems in such a way that the dense outer stalk was peeled back to reveal a tender, light green part of the vegetable. I had never seen anyone do this before.

The dinner was scheduled for seven. The rice was cooking and the broccoli was ready to drop into boiling water. There was a good half-hour before Sheila needed to complete the meal. The actual shrimp took only a few minutes apparently. The three of us went to our rooms to prepare. When I exited the bathroom, I was surprised to see Sheila sitting on the living room carpet with her items scattered about her. I politely asked if she needed help with anything.

"I'm about to fly to London, but Robert wants me to postpone my flight," she said, with her passport and papers in hand.

"Who does he think he is?" she added. "I'm tired of men telling me what to do."

I smiled. Oh, yes, I certainly knew those 'I's. But I was not in any position to discuss this with her. Although she was not a student, it was clear to me that her life was about to change, and it had little to do with Robert Burton. I was so familiar with redirections from the Powers That Be that I could wholeheartedly sympathize with her.

I asked her how she and Rosemary knew each other.

"Our husbands were in medical school together in Texas. We've known each other for 25 years."

Being 22, I couldn't imagine knowing someone that long and still keeping in touch. She and her husband divorced and he remarried. Looking at Sheila, I could sense the suffering and humiliation she must have endured. It was so similar to Rosemary's current play, and mine as well. My heart opened up to her.

Robert and Jim arrived ten minutes before seven. Robert was so thrilled to see Sheila. I had not seen him so emotional about a student. She stood her ground by the stove, opening a pouch of powder, which she added to the pan.

He signed to Jim, who was Robert's voice.

"What's in the pouch?" asked Robert.

"Spices," she replied, simply.

"What kind of spices?"

"Coriander, mustard, cumin, black pepper, turmeric, chili powder, salt, cayenne, ginger with sugar, and pressed garlic."

Many of these were new to me.

"What are you doing now?" he inquired.

"Making a paste with red wine vinegar."

"Look how she cooks the spices first!" he exclaimed in wonder, like a small child watching snow fall for the first time. In American cooking, spices are sprinkled on top like an afterthought once the food is cooked, but never heated separately like this. It was a revelation and a far cry from the vegetarian food we had been eating at the farm.

Sheila said nothing as she kept stirring the paste so it would not burn. She placed the paste in a separate bowl and turned her attention to chopped onions, which she fried in the pan with olive oil. I stood there, near the stove, expecting to be told to sit down or move away. But I wasn't. I just watched in the same state of wonder, having no idea what she would do next.

After adding the paste to the browned onions, she asked Robert to hand her the bottle of Harvey's Bristol Cream Sherry that was on the counter. Sherry?

She poured directly from the bottle without a measuring cup! Then there was syrup from Major Gray's Chutney and a pint of sour cream. As it cooked, she added a white mixture that Robert asked about. It was half-and-half with corn starch designed to thicken the sauce.

Finally, she added the shrimp.

While the shrimp cooked, I turned to finish setting the table. Rosemary and Sheila assembled the dish and we sat to eat. Jim was on Robert's left while Sheila was on Robert's right. Rosemary and I sat facing them.

The first bite astounded me. I had never tasted such a blend of flavors: the chutney was sweet and fruity; the sauce was hot and tangy without assaulting my tongue. The shrimp was soft yet chewy with a hint of a salty sea. I wished I could tell you the conversation, but my focus was on the food. Each bite was a blessing. Twenty-four hours earlier I was dining on walnuts and pomegranate seeds that barely dented the cavern of my stomach. Now I was dining like royalty. I wished a second helping, but I dared not ask.

At a certain point, I raised my head and paid attention to Robert's conversation with Sheila. He had a way of addressing her indirectly, letting Rosemary know that he asked Sheila to postpone her trip to London. I looked directly at Sheila who appeared stoic; although she kept silent, there was a definite downturn of her mouth. Were it not for our conversation, I would have missed the subtlety of her displeasure.

Dinner had ended, and we were cleaning up when Mac entered the house with the three Esalen visitors. We met in the dim light of the living room. I stood there between Rosemary and Sheila, while Mac introduced two men and a lady to Robert.

I had never seen the teacher like this. He extended his hand slowly, like a shy child who was just learning to shake in greeting. Although he smiled, he was visibly uncomfortable. Basically, he seemed not to know what to do or how to act. Mac was the epitome of joviality, smiling happily that these friends of his were finally meeting his teacher, a conscious being. Robert was not anyone's idea of a conscious being. There was no demonstration of a mastery of functions or open gaze of conscious light. It was actually the opposite. Robert could barely look at them.

The leader was a Martial type. He was well dressed in a beige cashmere sweater over a striped shirt. His tan pants were pressed. He appeared to be a fortyish professional with money, and he had an ease of speech that reminded me of Mac. They were similar, and I could see why they were friends.

But this man looked right past me and spoke to everyone else, focusing his attention mainly on Robert, as if he were sizing him up. He made me feel inadequate; he seemed to pride himself on what he had while it was clear I had nothing. Robert never made me feel like that. What was Robert seeing? Why was he so uncomfortable? I could not tell you.

They left relatively quickly since they had a long drive ahead. Mac returned after escorting them back to their car.

"Well, Robert, what do you think?" asked Mac.

"Are they interested in joining us?" Robert inquired.

"Actually, they thought we should join them," Mac said, chuckling.

"We'll let it go."

Mac was shocked. He tried to reason with Robert, explaining that these people had great connections with many notable, refined people with strong magnetic centers. Just as Robert had instructed me to Let It Go when I missed the substitute teaching opportunity, he repeated it once more to Mac and then he left the room.

Although I could commiserate with Mac's feeling of frustration, I was greatly relieved. My fear that what I had found, a school of awakening, could be diluted with a potpourri of B Influences was unfounded. That was where we had come from. Robert at least had a sense of where we were *not* going. Where we were going was anyone's guess.

Refrain from trying to win other people's approval and admiration. You are taking a higher road.

Epictetus

CHAPTER 82

Rosemary and I returned Thursday morning to Via Del Sol. On the ride there, we spoke of various subjects, from Miles and Mac to prospective students joining the school after the open meeting series, the tramp feature that abounds at the farm, and Robert's interest in Carmel.

I asked her if she knew where Robert was going with the school.

She paused before answering.

"Sheila made quite an impression on him."

Immediately I could feel a little bit of jealousy enter. I wanted to make an impression on Robert, too. I could not possibly be as refined as Sheila. These were the 'I's, but something else inside of me knew that this line of thought was taking me down a dark hole of self-pity. I could feel it. My salvation that pulled me up was a curiosity that wondered what he saw in her. Of course, I didn't put it that way.

"How so?" I simply asked.

"Robert needs help with his wardrobe," was her surprising reply.

I chuckled audibly. Who doesn't?

As we approached the foothills, the weather had dramatically changed. Vacaville was sunny with a bit of cloudiness when we left, but no rain had reached the ground. The skies were now pewter gray and the roads were wet. By the time we fueled up at the 76 gas station, the air had turned uncomfortably cold.

When we made the turn into Oregon House, it was as if we arrived at a different place on earth. What was this place? And it became even stranger when we drove up to the Lincoln Lodge for lunch. It was so rough and rustic. Patches of white clung to the hillside, and the rain had left pockets of mud that needed to be negotiated with each step. Had it been days or months since I was last here? Time had lost its structure; once again, I had been caught in a time warp.

THE DIVINE BEGINNING

Once we entered the Lodge, however, a feeling of familiarity returned. Flames were blazing in the fireplace and heat radiated from the wood burning stove near the bathroom. Instinctively I gravitated to the front of the fireplace, where Laura and Clark also huddled for warmth. It was so good to see them.

We embraced each other in welcome. Then Clark turned to me and asked, "Did your tent survive?"

"What do you mean?" I asked anxiously.

"We had a snowstorm through the night and many tents collapsed. You may want to check yours."

I had totally forgotten about my tent, and the fact that my precious books remained inside. It was a punch to the gut. After lunch, I made it up the hill and was at first a bit disoriented. Where was my tent? I walked around the area and then realized my tent was partially collapsed, and hence, unrecognizable.

I tried to prop it up so I could find the opening. Once the flap was unzipped, I entered, crawling to the spot of my dear books. Most had plastic covers with a few pages slightly damp. The greatest damage was to my favorite work book, *The Fourth Way*, which had been inscribed by Miles, representing the hopeful love that, only nine months earlier, was so strong. I cradled it in my hands, like a dear friend that had been abandoned and abused. It was now wet and dirty. How fitting. The symbolism was not lost on me.

As I walked down the hill, turning my back on that first place I had called my own, it was clear the tent was part of a stage set that no longer fit my current play. So quickly had that set become ephemeral. It had brought me far, I thought, beyond anything I could have imagined. The tent and the book had played their part.

That night I slept in the Lodge near the stove. With the tent destroyed, once again, I was a sojourner, living out of a suitcase. The refrain from Bob Dylan began to repeat in my head: "With no direction home, like a complete unknown, like a rolling stone."

This time, however, it was a bit different. Rather than feeling despair from this change in my play, I felt exhilarated and curious, as my fate was clearly in the hands of the gods, who were transporting me daily from one internal and external location to another. Planning had become futile.

That was the lesson of the year for me: Submit to the moment and accept what may be.

༷

When you meet a force greater than you, submit.
Homer

CHAPTER 83

I awoke Friday morning to discover I was not the only student to abandon a tent for the Lodge. Old friends had found sanctuary in the corners of the living room, while new students, who had been introduced at the Thursday evening meeting, had to adjust to grabbing space where they could on the carpet. This was our lifestyle at the farm. You roll out your sleeping bag, close your eyes, and awake in the morning only to discover complete strangers sleeping next to you.

I had intentionally positioned myself near the stove rather than the fireplace so that I could slip into the bathroom first thing in the morning, which I was able to do. When I had opened the door to exit, once again Robert was standing there. But this time he didn't photograph me. Instead, he gave me a copy of a *Scientific American* article that Yorgos, who had led the meeting the prior night, referenced.

It was about the February earthquake that I had lived through this year, and the way the Pacific Plate and Continental Plate meet on the West Coast. Robert had mentioned that C Influence indicated the Fall of California would occur with a large earthquake. As I had mentioned, this was not news to those of us raised in California or even Edgar Cayce, who lived in Virginia. It was a commonly held belief that it was inevitable.

"Dear, could you please read this article and let me know if you find something particularly interesting to share," requested Robert.

I felt flattered that the teacher would ask this of me since Yorgos had already seemed to have reviewed it. Perhaps Robert felt he needed a more intellectual person to scour the material.

It was dry stuff. Primitive diagrams, technical terminologies abounded with no correlation to mystical prophecy. After lunch I approached Robert with my findings.

"It describes how the Continental Plate overrides the Pacific plate, pushing it down, thereby creating a trench. Should the San Andreas Fault experience a shift, it could push the Pacific Plate down abruptly so that a great tsunami would inundate California. That's the gist of it."

I tried to explain each diagram further, but he wasn't interested in my findings. He already understood the basic idea and was not willing to dive deeper into the drawings. But to spend a few minutes with him was worth the forty-five minutes I spent reading the material. It felt good to be validated.

There was also a special study group that had formed while I was in Vacaville that was reading the *The Theory of Celestial Influence*. It was actually led by a student from Vacaville, unbeknownst to me. That afternoon Miles approached me with a message from Robert.

"Robert wants you to join this study group. Speak with the leader."

He walked away. I was stunned how his physical closeness shocked my system. I could feel adrenaline surging in my chest. What was that? Is it identification? Why do I still have these intense feelings about him? Finding that precious book in my tent with his handwritten notation in it, and then seeing this person who bore no resemblance to the person who wrote such a loving inscription, hit me hard. Although we spent almost no time together now since he and Helga were a couple, it was clear he avoided me as much as possible. I was still vulnerable around him and feelings of inadequacy lingered like the aftermath from a natural disaster.

I felt ruined in his presence.

❖

O humankind, why do you set your hearts there where our sharing cannot have a part?

Dante

CHAPTER 84

The leader of the study group I was to join hadn't arrived until Saturday lunchtime because of his Monday through Friday job. He and I hadn't actually spoken before. When I approached him to let him know Robert's request, I assumed he'd be happy to receive my input.

"I've already read the book, from the front to the back," I said, excitedly. "I made notes and am eager to share them with everyone."

It was funny how he hesitated. It was not the reaction I expected.

"We are beginning with the Six Processes," he said firmly.

"Okay," I replied. I waited for more instructions, but they didn't come. He walked away.

I watched as he mingled with others in the living room, smiling at their responses and easily engaging in conversation. What did I do? What did I say? Why did he react like this? Those thoughts crowded my mind, and I felt blind and helpless, once again. I can't understand people's reactions to me.

I would have retired to my tent to study alone after this encounter, but alas, my tent was no longer an option. I decided instead to go to the small library, which I knew was rarely used by students. I sat on the floor and opened my limp copy of the *The Theory of Celestial Influence*. I began rereading the chapters on the Six Processes. That seemed to be my reading assignment.

Reading always served to calm me down and help me to focus on something other than emotional turmoil. It was my drink of choice. But this time it didn't work. My emotional center was still pained by rejection, and the deluge of hurt feelings drown any intelligent insights. All I could do was observe the swarm of negative 'I's that tried to engulf me, which settled me down.

Observing 'I' had become my new refuge.

* * * *

That evening we had our Saturday meeting. After the good householder segment (asking who can wash dishes after the dinner), Robert began with an amusing observation.

"Isn't it odd that everyone shows up at meal times and meetings? The land absorbs us like a trifle."

Eight new students who joined from the open meetings were introduced.

Robert paused for what seemed to be a long time. Then, looking up at the ceiling with thoughtful eyes, he signaled his comment to Jim.

"This is the one-year anniversary of our first group that joined from an open meeting."

That must have been the meeting when Miles joined, I thought. It was just before Thanksgiving.

"We have 76 students in the teaching now. Last Christmas we had 27.

"It is something personal — to be in an esoteric teaching for a year. The amount of work each student has done is large and good.

"To arrive at the king of hearts — the intellectual part of the emotional center — one has to have developed the queen of hearts, the emotional part of the emotional center. All people in this teaching have their king and queen of hearts working."

That was good to hear. The queen of hearts was often maligned, since negative emotions issued from it. But it seemed to have value, and I was curious to see if Robert pursued it further.

"Emotions as they are," he continued, "can become negative. It requires will to prevent this. When you are with someone who is expressing negativity, try to hold your work by remaining neutral. From one angle, instinctive emotions may be connected with sensations such as pleasure or pain."

Robert's thoughts were coming in these small packages of two or three sentences, with ample pauses in between. He would express them in a matter-of-fact way, as if he had received his insights from above in that moment. They penetrated easily, making them memorable and quotable. We were being spoon-fed.

A new student raised her hand.

"Why do we say 'angle of thought'?"

Robert replied, "We try to view the subject from many angles. Many angles bring relativity."

We listened to Robert describe how the system has existed for thousands of years.

"If information comes that is confusing or meaningless, wait. In time, with work on being, the words will return and a new understanding will come. The words do not change. The perceiver does."

Another new student eagerly raised his hand.

"Why does it sound so complicated? We are hypnotized and should wake up. What is so complicated about that?"

"Humans are complex machines to study," said Robert. "Our level of awareness is not a static quality of our being. It changes from moment to moment."

Once again, Robert quickly switched topics.

"Part of the ranch will be sold to give us operating capital. This will leave us about 700 acres or so. We will buy one to ten acres in Big Sur and have a home in Tahoe. The availability of different environments is good to keep people in emotional parts of centers. It also helps to keep people out of patterns."

He addressed the question I posed to Rosemary on Thursday. So this is what he's doing, I thought. More questions arose in me. Wouldn't this spread us out unevenly? And where was I to end up? Would I have to move away from the farm? I tried to support myself, and when I first arrived in Vacaville from Los Angeles only five months ago, I had to sacrifice this to move to the farm. Things now reversed themselves. Is it here? No, it's there. Is it there? No, it's here.

Well, not to worry. There is no rush. I guess where I will land will reveal itself once the parcel of the property is sold.

* * * *

Sunday morning after breakfast, Rosemary approached me with news. Robert wanted me to stay in Vacaville with a married couple. Who? The man who was running the study group and his wife.

Where did this directive come from? I had no idea how this conversation with Robert even occurred. No one was sharing insights about my life and circumstances with me. I wondered if anyone told the guy this. I don't think he likes me.

After lunch, the man let me know they would be leaving for Vacaville at 2 p.m. I was to travel with them. I brought my books, clothes and sleeping bag to the Lodge and waited. He arrived at the appointed time and helped me with my things. His wife was sitting in the car's passenger seat.

Her smile was bright and welcoming. I could feel distance from him. I sat quietly in the back as we left the property and headed toward Vacaville. There was little conversation. They spoke briefly about dinner, and she mentioned there was enough food in the fridge.

I had never been to their home before. It's fun to look at people and imagine what kind of home they have. As I was designing their home in my mind, I was shocked to see we drove past the normal Vacaville exit of Monte Vista, past the Coffee Tree and Nut Tree. He took the third exit and went under the overpass. I thought, Is this still Vacaville? Their home was definitely not walking distance to Vacaville High. Indeed, it was on the other side of Highway 80. I don't have a car. How would this work?

We pulled into the driveway of their small tract home. It was clean and orderly. I was told they did not have bedroom space for me and hoped it would be fine for me to sleep on the couch in the living room.

"Actually," I said, "I brought my sleeping bag. I'm used to sleeping on the floor."

He was a bit alarmed and turned to go into the kitchen, leaving her to address me.

"We have nice sheets and the couch is comfortable."

I insisted I was fine, mostly because I was uncomfortable finding myself in this situation, where I'm imposing on someone. This was not my idea.

They disappeared into their bedroom. I could hear the shower running and assumed they were washing off the dust from Via Del Sol. I remained in the living room, checking out the books in the bookcase. Professional books, cook books, novels and a few work books. I desperately wanted to bury myself in a magazine, but none could be found. Neither was there a television in the room nor music wafting through the house. After the sound of insects and birds that served as background music at the farm, the silence in their home penetrated painfully. It felt sterile and yet my state had been elevated. Here I am. How strange.

After I used the bathroom to freshen up, I entered the kitchen to see if I could help. The lady of the house gave me the napkins and showed me where the glassware and utensils were.

As we sat down to eat, I was impressed by the civility of their evening meal. Napkins were in laps and water in designated water glasses. The meal was simple, with meat, vegetables and potatoes. A simple dessert of ice cream followed. It was clear that this family was raised like Miles's mother, prim and proper with a wholesome 1950s lifestyle.

The wife engaged me in conversation, asking about my teaching experience so far in Vacaville. I kept it brief, letting her know about Rosemary's efforts to secure a permanent position for me, and why at this time I was hoping for substitute teaching to make ends meet rather than a full-time job.

"I want to stay flexible so that if Robert moves to Carmel or Tahoe, I can relocate," I said by way of explanation. I knew that being around Robert was key to my conscious evolution. I thought for sure they would nod in agreement. Instead, they offered no reply.

"Are there many schools nearby?" I asked to continue the conversation.

The wife mentioned several schools in the Vacaville area, and then the husband asked, "How are you going to arrive at your job?"

"I thought I'd walk," I said, remembering what I did in LA at University High.

They both looked at each other.

"Perhaps you can use my bicycle," said the wife. "Do you ride?"

I hesitated, not knowing if the bike was one from my childhood or one from the encounter with the bull.

"Yes," I said softly. "Can I look at it tonight?"

After dinner and dishes, we went into the garage to check out the bike. It was a blush pink and the absence of a crossbar indicated it was for a girl. But there were the dreaded brake levers attached to the handlebars.

I found myself blurting out the obvious.

"How do these brakes work?"

The guy stood there stunned. The female owner of the bike easily answered.

"The right-hand lever stops the rear brake and the left-hand lever stops the front brake."

"Oh, right," I said nodding to indicate I had simply forgotten. But the fact was, I not only never knew this, I had no idea how to know when to use which lever. Clearly it would require coordination and an analytical ability to assess the terrain to know whether the back or front brakes needed to be employed.

We returned to the living room and bid each other good night.

I rolled out my sleeping bag and placed it on the floor. After washing up, I returned and snuggled inside. But something was different in this home. It felt wrong to be lying here, so I decided to try the couch. A zipper around the perimeter allowed the bag to be opened like a blanket. The plushness of the cushions was like a loving hug, and within minutes I fell asleep.

* * * *

The wife entered the living room and found me on the couch. It was morning. I grabbed my glasses and saw her smile.

"Good morning. Did you sleep well?" she inquired.

"Good morning. Yes, thank you," I replied.

As she went into the kitchen, I hastened to fold up my sleeping bag, gather my toiletries, and enter the bathroom. I felt as if she caught me unawares. What other unexpected things would the day hold, I wondered.

When I emerged, they were at the table having breakfast. He had a pleasant look on his face. It was nice to see.

"How did you sleep?" he asked.

"Fine, thank you."

"What plans do you have for the day?"

"I might study the Six Processes," I said, not knowing what else to say, since I clearly had no pressing engagements.

"That sounds nice," he replied, as he took a bite of his toast.

"I may also take a ride on the bike to find my bearings. Thank you for letting me use it. I truly appreciate it."

The wife smiled.

I volunteered to wash the dishes. She showed me where to put the dishes and utensils. As they went off to work, I ventured into the garage and approached the bike. Mounting it, I pushed down on the pedals and along the straight street I went. What an adventure! I had no idea where I was going since I didn't have a street map. I tried both handbrakes at once and abruptly came to a halt. The highway was before me. I found that I was unwilling to pedal further. Instead, I turned around and returned to their home.

This about-face shocked me. Why couldn't I proceed? I had time on my hands. The reason was there was no destination. I was fooling myself. Vacaville was a dead end. The town was as distant and irrelevant as Los Angeles had become. These were no longer options for me. It was not to be found here.

Why would Robert suggest this? Did he not know Vacaville was no longer on the map for me? The aim of having me find work and live a normal life was a pleasant thought only. My life goals disintegrated the moment he requested I not take that job at the high school. This frustration was carried in my heart and hidden from other students, who went about their lives responsibly. In a way I envied them. From the outside, it must look as if I were irresponsible. I felt instead as if I were a race horse chomping on a bit in the starting stall, watching and waiting for the bell to ring and the gates to open. The waiting was becoming more and more difficult.

> *Do you have the patience to wait until your mud settles and the water is clear? Can you remain unmoving until the right action arises by itself?*
>
> Lao-Tzu

CHAPTER 85

I sat in the backseat of the sedan next to Trisha's daughter as we headed toward the farm. It was early Wednesday morning. This ride had been arranged the night before.

Tuesday afternoon, the Vacaville couple with whom I was staying both sat on the living room couch, hands folded in their laps as neatly as their napkins. The lady spoke softly, proceeding cautiously as if anticipating explosions from a psychological mine field.

"We want you to know how much we like you and wish you well." She paused. "We've discussed it." Another pause. "And realized that this arrangement will not work for us."

She continued talking, and I could see neither of them actually looked at me. It was a planned speech and she was the designated deliverer. The awkwardness had a core of fear. They were expecting a queen-of-hearts outburst of dramatic emotion from me. That did not happen.

Instead, a broad smile spanned my face. My eyes were clear, warm and loving, as I was present to these two people — these two friends — who were put into such an awkward position. They looked beautiful to me, as the serene afternoon light of a late fall day bathed their faces in soft pastels. I had already come to the same conclusion hours before, and I felt badly that they were asked to take care of such a grown child.

When I simply agreed to all they had said, they were shocked awake. Fear was gone and an emotional relief allowed us to connect in the moment. They could have said, "REALLY?" and I would not have photographed them, because it was the correct word. No self-pity, no blame, no rationales. It simply was the right reading of the script. The right thing to do. The right way to be.

That night, as I lay on their couch, I understood why the gods brought me to Vacaville. It was to experience this simple state. It was so clean and unencumbered, and its emergence had no cause that I could determine. I did not Self-Remember it into existence. It just appeared without effort. But I recognized it: it was the same state that came to me that night driving lost on Mount Tamalpais, when I knew Miles and Helga were fated to be together. These two experiences of higher centers were connected now. It was a new internal roadmap.

* * * *

The banter in the car between mother and daughter continued. Since it did not involve me, I quietly took in the farmland after we passed through Marysville, gazing at the bare trees and straw grass of depleted November. I tried to hold on to the state that I had reached in Vacaville, but even looking at the autumn impressions produced 'I's, and the state became Linda.

When we arrived at the Lodge, I took my belongings and carried them to the upstairs storage area. My foam pad was there on the bottom. I was both shocked and delighted. I had left it in the tent because it was soaking wet. Someone had retrieved it, dried it out in the sunlight, and put it on the stack. Perhaps it was Clark, I thought. He would do something like that. But as I looked closely, I saw the name LINDA was now in red marker, not black. This was a new pad.

I went downstairs and asked around and learned that Robert had someone buy additional pads for those who lost theirs in the storm. I was so surprised there was one with my name on it. When I mentioned it, the person said, "Robert treated a few people."

No one had approached me for payment, so I assumed I was one of those gifted. More than having the pad, however, was having the knowledge that Robert kept me in mind even though he was distant and out of sight. I needed help and he knew it.

Trisha and I agreed to meet in the kitchen for lunch preparation. I suddenly realized we were approaching Thanksgiving (it was next week), and I hadn't heard anything about the celebration. It was difficult to keep track of what month it was, let alone what day.

"Anybody know if we're having Thanksgiving?" I asked the small crew.

Trisha was at the stove and said, "Robert said we'd have it here."

"When did he say that?" I asked, a bit surprised that she heard this directly from Robert.

"At the meeting last night."

I was in shock. I didn't know there was a meeting in Vacaville on Tuesday. Why wasn't I there? Why didn't that couple let me know? Why weren't they there?

Gone was that wonderful sense of inclusion. Why did this bother me? I could feel the school was moving fast and I didn't want to be left behind. The possibility that I could lose what I had found scared me, once again.

"Did he say anything else?" I asked.

Without looking up, Trisha replied, "No," as she continued to stir the pot on the stove. I knew I could read about the meeting in Meg's *Via Del Sol Journal,* but I also knew that not everything was conveyed. She was the editor. You had to have been at the meetings to receive all the information, not rely on someone else to select what was pertinent to you. I even noticed sometimes Meg had the dates wrong. How could you rely on information when the dates were wrong?

Trisha lifted the heavy pot to the wooden table top and winced in pain. I went over to rub her shoulder and could feel a huge knot of muscle. Suddenly I saw an opportunity to make some money.

"I could give you a full massage after lunch if you like," I said.

"That sounds great," she replied, smiling.

Bingo.

I had to be creative to find a location because it was approaching winter and the outdoors were not an option. We agreed to meet at 3 p.m. upstairs behind the rack of foam pads. No one would be there we figured in midafternoon, and we were right. Since I didn't own my own table, we grabbed some foam pads so she could lie upon them at a height to accommodate my work. I kept my clothes on and she was under towels. I borrowed some olive oil from the kitchen (Bonita had told me about this trick). Something in me was thrilled to be sneaking around like this making money, while others were doing third line of work for the school.

I had learned from my Rolfing experiences that the body stores information and deposits it in different parts. Organs, muscles, nerves house our earthly history. I discovered that I had an ability to tap into the lives of other people by touching their bodies, often revealing what they were hiding. I can't explain it exactly other than likening it to a TV signal: my fingers served as the receiver and my emotional center registered images and emotions on a screen inside my head.

The moment I touched her, I saw something. As I worked that shoulder knot, the tension was related to her marriage. A picture of her husband appeared to me. He was a slim, moving type who seemed inaccessible emotionally. Although she retained a cheerful attitude with others, deep down she was disturbed. Much of her behavior began to make sense to me.

Just as I was focusing on her body and sensing the source of her tension, a piece of a puzzle emerged that stunned me. A new image appeared and I was in it. I had totally forgotten an encounter with her husband that had occurred two months earlier.

He was sitting near the entrance to the Lodge one afternoon with his leg propped up. He called me over and, smiling, began to engage me in conversation. It was so out of character for him. The words came out of his mouth in an indirect way. What was he saying? He asked if I was open to experimenting. With what? Then I realized he was hitting on me. But he's married, I thought. Affairs outside of marriage were not something I would consider, although obviously it was occurring. A mixture of emotions filled me: confusion, flattery, fear. Smiling in self-defense, I shook my head and fled from him. Who was the next person I saw? Robert, the teacher. I told him what just happened. With a most serious face he said softly, "I will speak with him."

It was not my intent to have Robert do anything about it, but Robert's quick reaction informed me that this was unacceptable. How Robert worked with so many students acting badly was a great mystery to me. His focus was on guiding us to self-remembering, but he also had to deal with our lower functions running wild. I did not envy his role.

* * * *

Even though Trisha was my customer, her massage had opened up wounds inside of me for which I was unprepared. Looking for love and finding disappointment all around plagued me unendingly. I needed to escape, and there was only one place I knew where I could go without anyone finding me. It was the little shed above the small fig tree. Tools were stored there, and it was the end of the work day. I knew I would be alone.

I sat on top of a crate, focusing on dividing my attention. Here am I, How strange, I repeated to myself until my focus on the present moment stilled my functions. My surroundings appeared as they were: the raw wood of the shed, the shelves filled with hammers, saws, buckets of nails and screws, sandpapers of different grades — everything for the handyman.

My goal was to connect my king of hearts to the gods, calling upon them to answer me, for I had, as Mr. Gurdjieff described it, a Burning Question. Actually, I had a burning subject: finding love in this life. I had been struggling over the past month with being attracted to a particular male student. My sex center's radar was turned on day and night, constantly scanning for my Prince Charming.

Sitting calmly, I began:

Q: What is my role?
A: Waiting.
Q: Will I receive in the end?
A: Perhaps.
Q: Why perhaps?
A: It does not matter if you and he are one.
Q: Why?
A: Because that is not important. What is important is how well you play your role.

Suddenly the door opens. It's him.

"What are you doing here?" he asked.

Shocked, I blurted out, "Oh, I'm looking for something." I visibly winced at the stupidity of my response. He shook his head in bewilderment and walked out. I returned to my efforts to conjure up the gods.

Q: Why is it so easy to fall in love?
A: You have learned in your last relationship that you do not need a man; you have learned this well. What is important also is the idea that suffering is food for consciousness. Did it matter that you and Miles did not last? What mattered was the way in which you used the moments of suffering. That you two are no longer lovers is incidental. You have not learned the lesson of waiting.

These words were not actually said but felt. It was a strange communication, like mental telepathy. Suffering, Transformation, Waiting were the concepts. Patience is the last thing I wanted to hear, but it kept returning like a broken record. I had forgotten it was to be my mantra, but the power of life's desires kept pushing it aside. Waiting is hard work. It requires putting a cork into all the longings, urges and drives of the human machine. It requires will. And I simply didn't have that yet. Frustration and anger were building up inside of me.

Just then I heard a scampering and, looking up, saw a tiny mouse scurry across the top plank. He stopped as he sensed something other than himself in the environment. I sat as still as I could. Time seemed to pass slowly, as I measured my breaths so the noise from my inhalation and exhalation did not cause him to run. I wanted to become invisible to him. We both waited, suspended. What will he do next? He seemed to relax after a few minutes and somehow found a kernel between two jars to chew. Resting on his haunches, he rolled the food around in his tiny hands, attacking all sides of it with his teeth. He was happy. I was happy, too, just watching him and pleased that he had not detected me and he felt safe.

I wanted him to stay because his world relieved me of thoughts of my own. But it didn't last. He moved on through a tiny crack in the boards. Who knows what troubles plague him? Although my longings for a man remained, I felt a momentary relief from the burning subject that was perpetually removing me from my higher world.

Oh, to be like a tiny, quiet mouse, content with a morsel.

Each morsel is the link that chains you to the ground.
Rumi

CHAPTER 86

The weekend was approaching fast. The chores of cooking, cleaning, laundry, etc. were becoming more and more mundane without Robert around. They were becoming mechanical. Robert's extended silence led him to communicate through notes and not teach directly at meetings. He's stepped aside now, as Miles and Yorgos have taken on the role of teacher, predominately.

Because of this, I see Robert more and more as an enigma: his state of awakening is like the silent sun that shines on the growing plants that are his students; its position and substance remain unknown to those who receive its radiance. I miss the friendship that was developing before we bought the property. It was short-lived. Now I had to contend with a new sadness and longing, like a child in a big family yearning for the daily, personal embrace of his father.

Saturday morning, I went upstairs to use the bathroom instead of waiting in the long line downstairs. I was thinking about the struggles with my sexual attraction to every new man that joined.

As Thanksgiving approached, the recurring lament that began with my sister's simple comment last Thanksgiving Day — saying Miles (aka Ronnie) wanted to invite me to Christmas in San Diego — and its ultimate, tragic fate of abandonment – resurfaced and continued to fill my head and heart with pangs of forlorn love.

While mulling the myriad of emotions on the subject, I gazed into the mirror in front of me as I washed my hands in the sink. Poor Linda, I thought. So lonely, so scorned.

In that moment, the impulse to peer out of the open window next to the mirror came from nowhere, as if someone had pushed my head to the left, saying, Look at this. And, there it was: Miles outside on the patio, approaching Helga with loving, open arms. I watched as they joyously embraced and kissed.

Are you kidding me? I burst out laughing. For me to behold this encounter in that exact moment given the thoughts in my mind was so perfectly timed and staged that I could hear the orchestral accompaniment, heavy on the weeping violins.

Their rendezvous could have been a scene out of my mother's favorite soap opera, *As the World Turns*. I then recalled coming home on the bus from university one day, finding my mother beside herself in sorrow. I had never seen her cry like that before. What was it, Mom? One of the main characters on the show had died. She was inconsolable.

For the first time, I felt I understood the school. I was in a conscious soap opera! The gods were in the business of button-pushing. It was my job not to fall for it.

* * * *

My mood that evening had changed considerably. I had been given a new understanding of a basic Fourth Way concept: learning the difference between necessary and unnecessary suffering. The missing piece in the triad of being was will. I had to develop the discipline not to fall prey to the many 'I's that endlessly talked about my circumstances. How to do this would depend on how much self-remembering could be brought to the moment. It sounds simple, but I'm discovering it isn't easy. Gurdjieff taught that a different 'I' manifests automatically with each breath. The button-pushing is continuous, and the urge to indulge is strong.

As we assembled the chairs in the living room of the Lodge for the meeting that night, I looked at Miles and Helga with new eyes. They were living their lives as their roles dictated, and I was living mine. I felt free from the identification that dragged me down.

Yorgos led the meeting. It was lovely to see him in this role. His calm demeanor and soft delivery allowed the knowledge to penetrate more deeply.

After good householder, he chose a student whom I had yet to meet (probably from the Bay Area) to offer the first question.

"Can we have some examples of the negative half of the moving center?"

Yorgos paused in thought before offering his angle.

"One angle is it has to do with preservation. The negative half of the moving center will look both ways before crossing the street."

Jan Holmes, who teaches yoga, raised her hand.

"There is a position called 'sponge' or 'corpse,' where yoga students lie flat on the floor with arms extended and eyes closed in a relaxed posture. When it is announced that the exercise is over, almost all the students raise their arms to cover the body."

Yorgos also mentioned that if you tap on the chicks' pen, they all react exactly the same way at the same time.

It was a quiet, slow meeting. We sat there waiting for someone to pose another question. Since none were forthcoming, Yorgos ended the meeting early so we could have dinner.

My heart was calm in the presence of Miles and Helga. I could observe old 'I's that banged on my mental door, hoping with each knock they had found the button allowing them inside. Nope. Not this time.

Had I reached a new level of being? It felt like it. The thought of this helped me to sleep soundly that night.

The breeze at dawn has secrets to tell you,
Don't go back to sleep,
You must ask for what you really want,
Don't go back to sleep,
The door is round and open where the two worlds touch,
Don't go back to sleep.

Rumi

CHAPTER 87

Sunday moved into Monday with such ease that it would seem no one had a place to go other than where they were. This was the week of Thanksgiving, the first big holiday since we moved to Via Del Sol, if you don't count Labor Day in September, which was hardly noticeable up here. Most of the Weekenders stayed instead of rushing back to the Bay Area to work. I realized many must have taken the week off.

We began the week with an out-of-patterns Monday meeting. The dynamic duo of Miles and Yorgos were in charge of the meeting, with Miles taking the lead. The first task at hand was to set up the work octaves for the upcoming Thanksgiving celebration on Thursday. Many were anticipated to come, and how the single oven would pump out roasted turkeys that would feed close to 100 people was a mystery to me.

In my family of four, my father consistently increased the turkey poundage each year from 16 to 18 to 21 to 24 to 28. When I was about sixteen years old, the turkey of all turkeys was carried into the house: it was a huge tom turkey, not a smaller hen, and it weighed a whopping 34 pounds. "It was such a deal," bragged Dad. "The guy just gave it to me for free." We all rejoiced at the thought of leftovers for weeks.

Poor Mom. She had the task of stuffing it and rubbing it with butter, but she soon discovered why it was free. When she tried to put it in the oven, the door wouldn't close. She yelled at Dad, and of course, we girls joined in as back-up singers. It took over 12 hours to cook, and we ate whatever parts clearly were not raw and were not pieces of fat. It was a strange Thanksgiving memory of greed that left us hungrier than in previous feasts.

Back to the meeting. Rosemary spoke up and offered the cooking solution: she would coordinate with the other ladies — such as Jan, Alice, Marie, and Anna — to bring roasted turkeys up from their homes in Vacaville and the Bay Area. The rest of us living here full time would prepare the side dishes such as stuffing, potatoes, green beans, and cranberry sauce. Some also would bring the traditional pies. Mac and Don offered to supply the wine.

Now that the food decisions were out of the way, the meeting began with Miles asking if anyone had a question or a topic. His was a more commanding presence than Yorgos and the meeting flowed with a cadence.

First question.

"Because of the chemical changes in the body from self-remembering, wouldn't it be important to study the table of hydrogens?"

Miles responded.

"Study of the hydrogens involves detailed work. It will be studied in the future. In order to study them, people will have to be at a certain level to understand it. Also, study at any time is good if one just hears the words."

I raised my hand. He looked at me, paused, and then continued speaking.

"A student of Ouspensky and Orage wrote a treatise on levels of human consciousness that has some lengthy explanations of the hydrogen octaves.

This writer is what life calls a 'hard scientist' and was attracted to the system because it said everything must be verified."

He paused once more, and my hand went up. Once again, he looked at me and continued.

"To study the third level of consciousness is difficult — to find a person at that level who could be studied is difficult."

I wasn't sure what he meant by the "third level of consciousness," having not read this treatise. Was he speaking about someone who was a man number five, such as Robert? I was confused.

I raised my hand a third time and Miles called on another student who posed the following question.

"Does self-remembering lead to chemical changes or vice versa?"

Miles replied, "It is both. It is not one thing. It is an either/or question."

I raised my hand. He looked at me. No one else's hand was raised. He then said, "Linda."

I stood to give my angle, which was the meeting custom for those students who spoke, except for the meeting leader, who remained seated.

"As I understand it, moments of self-remembering are accumulative. It's more like a spiral that rises gradually than distinct steps. In any given moment, we can be closer or farther than we want. We are not completely asleep or completely awake, but somewhere in between. But just these moments require work all the time. It's a struggle and sometimes it works and sometimes it doesn't."

As I sat down, I had a strange experience. That was not the angle I had planned to give when I raised my hand. These words suddenly came out of my mouth, and I was as much a listener as a speaker. Where did they come from?

Another question was asked, which was more practical.

"We can do without 'really,' 'very' and 'a lot,' but 'get' is harder to find a substitute for. Any suggestions?"

Miles replied, "You can make sentences without adverbs, but not without a verb. 'Really,' 'very' and 'a lot' are adverbs; 'get' is a verb. It is interesting to see in such a short time what has been done here with the word 'get.' Some people say the word 'obtain' in place of 'get' for everything. In time, a higher level will be present that will rearrange the words before they come out. Instead of replacing 'I'll get by' with 'I'll obtain by,' in time a person can learn to say 'I will manage.' If the exercise is to make speech more conscious, a person will try to use the exercise for its intended purpose, and not use the same word as a substitute each time."

Yorgos added, "In order to progress, something has to be left behind and be replaced by something higher. What is left behind is your idea of things. The person operating at the level of objective knowledge does not have his idea of anything. Be present. What is, is."

A question came from a farm resident.

"What about meeting farm expenses?"

"Your job, as I see it," answered Yorgos, "is to stay awake. One of the reasons we're not good householders may be that we are identified with our own situations. A person who is studying to wake up is asked to detach inwardly from the results of their actions. The aim is to wake up; there is no higher aim. Meher Baba said, 'Don't worry, be happy, do your best.' Worry is a sign of identification. The Shakers have a saying: 'Do your work as if you had a thousand years to do it, and also do your work as if you will die tomorrow.' "

At that point, the meeting ended. I felt uplifted by Yorgos's angles. He was so encouraging and focused that I was proud to call him my friend. His level of being was clearly higher than mine, and I was grateful I could learn from him.

* * * *

While eating dinner, a student next to me said, "I enjoyed your angle about the spiral. It had relativity, and just to hear someone else say 'sometimes it works, and sometimes it doesn't' is a relief."

I smiled at him, and said nothing. I could not take credit for this angle. I could not share this with him. What occurred was so bizarre that it challenged many concepts I had about my own intelligence and understanding. There's the concept of a play and a script, but this experience of having something else use my machine as its own mouthpiece caught me off guard.

Could it be that no original thought comes from us, that this effort of formulation, where one grapples with expressing one's heartfelt suffering and understanding, is an illusion, too? What is that part in me that feels this is the most important thing: to express oneself clearly to others and have them understand one?

A glimpse of the gods putting words in my mouth came to me in that moment. There was no mental process on my part when I offered that angle. I had become their conduit. It was so unexpected that they would reveal themselves to me in such a simple way. Who could I share this with, without them thinking I was boasting I was special or imagining the gods worked through me in this intimate way that was only reserved for Robert, a conscious being?

This revelation was so personal that I kept it a secret for now. I was ready to share it should the opportunity arise, as I knew this experience was part of our evolution and didn't belong to me.

We are all on the same journey, aren't we?

❦

Great changes and shifts occur in me that I cannot describe,
but they are very real. Ways open.
A fragrance from the divine comes through.
No one sees this, but it is the most profound event in my life.

Bahauddin

CHAPTER 88

When I arose at dawn on Tuesday morning, I was excited by the prospect of seeing the teacher in Vacaville, for he was scheduled to lead the meeting in his own mute yet articulate way. I secured a ride with Rosemary and we left by eight, arriving at her home after buying groceries. She still seemed somehow in communication with Robert, so I took the opportunity to ask her about his whereabouts.

"He's been in Carmel," she replied. "I'm meeting him and Sheila for lunch at noon at the Nut Tree."

Her phrasing made it clear I was not invited and that once again, I would fend for myself, scrounging around her kitchen to piece together a decent meal. I am not complaining but merely expressing a preference for his company. I was grateful to have a roof over my head and food in the refrigerator.

When we entered the house, I was given the task of putting the food away. Rosemary took a shower and prepared for her date. She left at 11:30 to make sure she didn't keep the teacher waiting. She explained it was not easy for her to be on time, but she had embraced this as a personal exercise.

My lunch consisted of a small green salad and a sliced ham-and-cheese sandwich. The desire for a cigarette was strong, so I went into her bedroom to see if there was an open pack of Marlboros. To my surprise, it was laying on top of her long dresser next to some old framed photos.

One particularly beautiful frame caught my eye. It was ornate silver with swirls of vine tendrils and buds of flowers. It was a bit tarnished and heavy to hold. I could feel its authenticity from a bygone era. These words were inscribed: "Rosemary is for Remembrance." I recalled from my university studies that this was part of Ophelia's soliloquy in Hamlet. How appropriate, I thought. The photo showed this stern child with thick hair and freckles wearing a simple dress to indicate gender. She stared back at me. It was Rosemary around the age of four. That Take No Prisoners look that I knew so well was deeply rooted within her Martial essence.

I counted the number of cigarettes in the pack and hoped that the absence of one wouldn't be missed. The first puff always sent a shiver through my system. The second puff let me relax. I sat at the kitchen table enjoying the solitude and the buzz.

After extinguishing the cigarette in an ashtray, I went to the sink to rinse it out to remove the evidence of my actions. I returned to the table to relax and muse about the day as it was unfolding, when a sudden impulse to MOVE came from nowhere. The clock said two. I quickly grabbed a dust cloth and began cleaning the living room furniture. I can't tell you where the impetus to do this came from, but it was as if it were a theatrical cue that was delivered with urgency.

Within minutes of entering the living room, I heard the kitchen door open. Rosemary returned, I thought. But I was wrong. It was Miles and Helga with her two young sons. Why are they here? I greeted them. They had bags of food and I guess they thought they would use her kitchen to make lunch.

Another impulse came that said LEAVE. I went back into the living room to continue dusting. The kids were playing loudly. Helga was trying to keep them quiet while preparing lunch. A few more minutes had passed when, once again, I could hear the kitchen door open. Rosemary had returned. The scene was set.

The boys were chasing each other around the kitchen and Rosemary's voice could be heard over the din.

I walked in to see what was occurring. I stood there with my rag and furniture polish. There were Robert, Sheila and Jim. Rosemary told Helga and Miles they were not to come to her home with these children again. They were to leave now. They quickly packed their food bags and exited. Rose looked at me and told Robert how well I was caring for her home in her absence. He smiled and nodded in agreement.

I was dumbstruck. I could not take credit for any of this. Had I not received the mysterious instructions to Quick! Grab the rag and go into the living room, I would have been found out as a thief, pilfering her cigarettes and invading her privacy. I felt so sorry for Miles and Helga. They were set up by the gods. I knew this as fact. For what reason was theirs to discover.

* * * *

After Helga and Miles left, Robert had taken Rosemary aside once she calmed down and scribbled something to her on his notepad. It was clearly a photograph. She tried to explain her actions, but Robert's index finger rose in the air to stop her from proceeding. He wrote something quickly and then went to his room to rest. Rosemary followed by retiring to her room. Sheila went to the guest bathroom to freshen up. Jim explained to me that he would be driving her back to Carmel, per her request. Apparently, her resistance was still a bit intact. Within fifteen minutes, I was left alone, once again, in the kitchen. The time was almost three, and I felt it was best to take the opportunity to rest as well. It had already been a long day.

I awoke to the sounds of chairs being assembled in the living room. Holy cow! It was six o'clock! I grabbed my toiletries and headed to the bathroom for a shower. Some knocks on the door occurred while I was applying makeup, but I just had to ignore them. After emerging, the living room had filled with students. It was almost seven. The meeting was to begin at 7:30.

This was a large meeting. Friends I hadn't seen for a while were there: Meg and Harold, Bonita and Alden, Mac, Anna, and Richard and Alice. Kerrie was there, too. One big surprise was to see Jeff and Annette. I hadn't seen them on the farm for quite a while, although they lived in Oregon House. Annette looked radiant and it was beautiful to see the sweetness in her face.

The meeting began. Robert's presence filled the room. All eyes were on him as we waited for his opening remarks. Sitting next to him was Rosemary. He wrote something on his notepad to her and we could hear her reply, "She made it." He had Anna stand up to show her beautiful knit suit. Rose read from the notes.

"Did you make this, Anna?"

"Yes," Anna said, tickled by his interest in her skills.

"Turn around and show everyone."

Anna stood up and turned around in a complete circle, like a child, laughing at the show.

"Did you sew the buttons?"

She giggled. "They are rhinestone. I've had them for a while."

Her suit had several types and colors of yarn. It was a remarkable outfit of blues and purple woven with gold threads that gave off light. It fit her form perfectly.

It was a delightful experience to see Anna transformed into a school girl of about six. The energy in the room went from serious to jovial. It was fun and lighthearted.

Robert commented, "Sometimes the group feels like Christmas regardless of the month of the year."

His expression then changed.

"All schools have a task. Gurdjieff's, Ouspensky's, and Collin's tasks were to present knowledge. Our school is a school of poetry and will produce two or three conscious poets."

He paused, then continued.

"Poetry reaches spaces that the language of the teaching cannot. A teaching points the way, but is not the spirit itself."

A hand went up.

"Poetry is allurement. How does one stay away from that?"

He thought before penning his reply.

"In a conscious poet, the state — third eye — observes and knows it is not the words. According to Whitman, the Self delights in words — like a word bath."

This made me smile. What a poetic way to express a simple pleasure that touches the heart.

A woman asked the following:

"What about conscious women?"

His reply came quickly.

"Queen Elizabeth the First was conscious, to my knowledge."

A male student raised his hand and just as quickly stood up before being called on.

"Saint Thomas said of Mary Magdalene, 'Banish her not. I will make a man of her and she will be worthy of the Kingdom of Heaven.' Meaning?"

Robert replied, "That is making her intellectual center in charge of her emotional center. In all humans, male or female, they each have a man and a woman in them."

A flurry of hands rose and rapid-fire questions came at Robert. This seemed like a hot topic.

"What saints are conscious?"

"Saint Augustine and Saint Benedict are conscious."

"Saint Francis?"

"No."

"How about Christ's disciples?"

"They may not have been as high as you think. Why? They all failed him. It does not speak high of their being to fail him. Yet it is their level — it is their play — they have to be at a level where they will fail Jesus. They fell asleep on him. Where were they when Jesus was crucified?"

Then Robert addressed the student who posed the question.

"If Yorgos were crucified, would you be there?"

The student answered yes.

"Then that is your level. Also, to have in his inner circle a student at a level of being to deliver his teacher to the local authorities is not good. I do not know anything about his disciples for sure; this is to my knowledge. I am pointing out weaknesses that a man the level of Christ should not have attracted in his inner circle. In an inner circle, there should be an unbreakable reliability. One of the reasons we discuss this is to show the many kinds of wounds — not just physical — that Christ had to transform."

The room took a deep breath.

Robert looked ahead and upward, as if beyond us.

"This is informational only. Nothing has to be verified."

And with that the first half of the meeting ended.

During the intermission, I used the opportunity of the full room to go to students who had yet to make their November teaching payments. There were only a few, so I prepared my list quickly and placed the funds in the envelope to give to Robert, who usually departs before the small groups begin. He, however, was mingling with Mac and Mary C. and did not seem to be in a hurry. Just then, Jim came through the kitchen door. He had returned from Carmel. I had expected at that point for Robert to depart with him, but he lingered still. It was time to reconvene.

We returned to our seats. Robert mentioned Mary had come back from Vancouver where she received acupuncture treatment for her physical malady, which he did not disclose. Robert asked her to describe the treatment briefly. He was pleased she felt better.

It was clear to me Robert had something to say.

"The teaching is leaving many of its students on their own now, with less help from me. Do you see the value in that?"

I imagined he was referring to Yorgos and Miles.

Looking straight at me, he said: "Remember, it is incredible luck and a gift to meet a conscious teaching. Such a teaching is for all in the age in which it exists, and yet each student must have luck. Democracy is intentional insincerity by higher forces. There is no justice in this world."

He stood up and left the room. It was too late to organize into small groups so we took this as the sign the meeting was over.

Refreshments were being served from the kitchen area. I quickly handed the envelope to Robert when he was leaving with Rose and Jim from the kitchen door. He thanked me, and I felt relieved I had completed my octave before he left.

Just as I took some crackers and cheese, Annette approached and said she had some news she wanted to share with me. I smiled, and she indicated it was private so we went into the bedroom I was occupying.

We both sat on the bed. Her eyes were full of happiness, which in turn made me feel happy. It was contagious. What could make her so happy?

"Jeff and I have decided to leave the Fellowship. We came here to tell our friends, and I especially wanted you to know since Robert mentioned we were so alike."

I stared at her in disbelief. I was utterly stunned. She continued speaking, providing some sort of explanation, but I was unable to process her words. The shock and horror of this decision left me not only speechless but deaf. All I could do was watch her movements, as she took my hands gently as if to thank me for something.

She waited for my response. I had none. This perplexed her and made her a bit uncomfortable.

"Nothing is wrong," she assured me. "I'm fine."

But she wasn't. Couldn't she see how difficult it was to awaken and how lucky we were to find this school? She tried to relieve my distress, so I realized I needed to say something.

"Okay. Well…good bye."

I did not want to hurt her, but try as I might, I couldn't share in her happiness. My abrupt response shocked her. She stood up and walked out of the room, closing the door behind her.

How could she not see what she was doing? Hadn't she verified C Influence? Hadn't she verified her sleep?

Unable to join the company of others in the state I was in, I stayed in the room quietly and prayed to the gods that this would not be my fate.

※

Do not be afraid; our fate cannot be taken from us; it is a gift.

Dante

CHAPTER 89

When the house became still, I emerged from the room to wash up and prepare for retiring. It was around midnight, and Rosemary was sitting alone at the kitchen table with a cigarette in one hand and a pencil in the other. She was putting together a list.

"Where did you go?" she asked.

I explained what had happened.

"Don't let that bother you. They were just passing through."

Her nonchalance surprised me. She saw it right away.

"Why are you surprised?"

I told her I thought Annette was a real student, who made efforts to be present and valued the school. Rose took a deep drag of her cigarette and said she was a nice person but that was her mechanics.

"You need to study people," she advised.

What does that mean? She saw my perplexed look, but ignored it.

"You better go to bed," she said. "We have an early morning tomorrow and a full day. We're leaving at seven."

As I retired, I pondered her suggestion to study people. I had thought I was studying people all these years, but the fact that I was repeatedly blindsided and suffering the consequences revealed that my observations were faulty. Why that was, I had no idea.

* * * *

I arose later than planned. Scurrying to keep up with Rosemary, a quick face wash, donning clothes and rolling up my sleeping bag was all I could accomplish. I hoped I could find time to shower at the farm.

"Let's go. We need to pick up the girls."

Her younger daughter was staying with her boyfriend. There they were in front of his pride and joy, a Ford 100 pickup truck that he had fixed and repainted. It had a large cabin and running board. When I told him his truck was cool, he smiled at me, happy that I appreciated it. I could see the daughter wasn't as impressed about the car as I was. She quickly turned to her sister and said, "Let's go." Her sudden abruptness startled me. What was that about?

With both girls now in the car, the energy level soared. I listened as they each recounted the events of the past few days to their mom. Rosemary enjoyed her daughters. They were spreading their wings properly, learning the intricacies and subtleties of living their lives on their own, while always having access to the mother bird who could correct their flight if needed. I envied them.

We arrived at the supermarket by 7:30 and the crowds had yet to appear. Rose divided her list among us, and we all managed to find the supplies for Thanksgiving, meeting at the designated check-out within thirty minutes.

While on the road, I thought, Who could have imagined this Thanksgiving? Here I was in a new family. I looked forward to the stuffing. It was my favorite part of the meal. My mother made a huge batch in a pan the size of the turkey and added a secret ingredient: Manischewitz wine. Because the small bottle of Manischewitz was too expensive according to Dad, the following year he replaced it with a gallon of "Red Wine" (that was what the label said). Together with plenty of poultry seasoning and sage, the dark stuffing had an earthy taste. Each year Dad would sneak in to add more wine to the mix. One year he splashed a bit too much and it was soupy. Mom became upset because she knew she had to toast more bread to soak it up, which meant more work for her. It didn't matter. We couldn't eat enough of it. I remember snatching a cold handful from the fridge at night. It was gone within two days.

Once we arrived at Via Del Sol, we each focused on bringing in the food before our personal items. Rosemary parked the car at the top of the dirt patio to make it easier for us all. After lugging in my first sacks of food, I quickly stopped to sign my name on the bathroom list, since I planned to shower immediately after lunch. I was number three. I then went back to the car to retrieve my stuff.

It was almost noon and fortunately lunch was waiting. I was starved so I ate quickly. Cooked greens and brown rice plus a squash soup and bread tasted delicious on this chilly day. I kept my eye both on the bathroom and the two students ahead of me on the list who were still chatting and taking their time eating. When the bathroom door opened, I quickly entered and locked it behind me.

That's how it worked. Timing was everything. If you weren't on time, you lost your place, and your name was crossed off by the next person on the list. If you still needed to use the bathroom, you had to put your name at the bottom of the list or plead your case to someone ready to enter. It was a crazy system. But those were the rules. For some of us, using a list formulated by the intellectual center to govern the instinctive center's need to urinate had become the perfect example of wrong work of centers.

* * * *

We spent the evening doing as much food preparation as possible for the next day. The plan was to have a Thanksgiving dinner for everyone at six. Certain students would arrive by four with their turkeys. It would be a buffet with long tables set up for dining.

It was a festive atmosphere with happy anticipation of being together amidst an abundance of traditional foods. I stood at the chopping counter with two others, cutting up yams and potatoes and carrots and onions and celery and mushrooms and green beans. The stuffing ingredients were ready for the early morning assembly under the direction of Rosemary. Kerrie decided to make apple and pumpkin pies, which went into the oven at ten. When I retired around midnight, the smell of freshly baked pastry perfumed the air and served as a culinary trumpet, heralding what was to come.

* * * *

I was awakened before dawn by the sounds of students entering the kitchen. Rosemary had already chosen her crew to complete the stuffing and prepare the three fifteen-pound turkeys we had purchased. Her strategy was to cook one after another. Each one took about three hours to cook; her schedule was 6 a.m. to 9 a.m., 9:30 a.m. to 12:30 p.m., and 1 p.m. to 4 p.m. The birds would rest and be sliced, then reheated just before serving. At least that was the plan.

After lunch, David and other gents set up long tables with a variety of chairs. A discussion ensued about whether to put the cutlery as place settings on the dining tables or leave them at the buffet table for persons to pick up with their plates. A more active type took over and the decision to place them on the buffet table won out.

As I stood there observing the bareness of the long tables, with their worn wooden tops exposed above the battered metal legs, Robert entered the room. He looked around and immediately focused on the tables. Quickly he wrote a few words on his pad to show Jim, who went directly upstairs. I waited to see what would happen next. Jim returned and said to Robert, "Anna said she would call others."

The afternoon moved on rapidly. The couple from Vacaville arrived with their turkey and a tablecloth at 4 p.m. Jan showed up next with her family members, each of whom pitched in to carry the foodstuffs and two tablecloths. Anna had yet to arrive, which was understandable since she was coming not from Vacaville, but Berkeley. Alice was scheduled to bring two large cooked turkeys with her famous stuffing, I was told.

I asked what was so special about Alice's, expecting them to say Manischewitz. Instead, they said, corn bread stuffing with Italian sausage. What?

Cornbread instead of toasted white bread? Sausage in a turkey? I couldn't imagine pig meat going into a bird. How weird. I never realized before how many "traditional" family recipes there were. I just assumed everyone prepared what my family did. It expanded my horizon.

As I entered the kitchen at 4:30 p.m., Rosemary had a man carry the final turkey from the oven to the main counter where all the chopping had occurred. It was now the resting place for the turkeys, which lined up like different models at a car lot. The birds' pimpled skin ranged from pale yellow, to dark roasted blotches, to crispy brown all over. It was not the fault of the cook. The oven was still notorious for its uneven temperatures, like the previous one that I had used with my barley buns.

The Saturn lady who decided on the buffet table arrangement entered the kitchen.

"We need help ironing the tablecloths and setting the tables," she said, a bit disgruntled that the teacher overrode her vision of a single buffet.

I immediately followed her since this seemed like a good octave for me. As a child, I enjoyed ironing my white shirts and gym clothes. I wasn't good at it but I liked the challenge of pressing the cloth perfectly without wrinkles. This was different than anything I had done before, however. The cloth size overwhelmed the board. Fortunately, another person gave me instructions on how to do it more efficiently. Folding it into sections was the key. It took me an hour to do. David and another fellow helped to carry my finished pressed cloth to the table. Another student joined me in the octave, and moved much faster. I was the first to start and the last to finish. The first shall be last, I thought. I'm okay with that.

The cloths were on the table and the utensils were in place, but something seemed missing. It was now past six and like magic, Marie, Don and Doris walked into the Lodge carrying not just the wine and pies from the Nut Tree, but vases. Following them was Anna wearing a colorful flowery blouse and dark pants, cradling a bouquet of her prized yellow and pink roses from her garden. The roses looked so jovial, like Anna, in their beauty and abundance.

Robert approached her immediately and gave her a big hug, which caused her to giggle. He was so pleased that she had thought of this.

When Mac arrived, he went directly into the kitchen, rolled up the sleeves of his blue-striped shirt, and donned an apron to do the honors carving the turkeys. Taking two long knives, he brushed their edges together rapidly. I had never seen anyone do this before so I asked him what he was doing. "Sharpening the knives," he said with a bright smile and loving blue eyes. He was clearly enjoying himself, as this role is generally reserved for the patriarch of the family. He worked quickly and skillfully. Turkey meat soon overflowed the platters, so we improvised and placed the extra on aluminum foil.

He then surprised me by turning to the stove, grabbing a big skillet, and adding the browned bits of meat and vegetables in the bottom of the roast pans to it. I watched as he stirred flour and wine gradually into the mix. What was he doing? Within minutes, this liquid became gravy! I'd never seen gravy made before. We always opened cans that read Turkey Gravy for our Thanksgiving. What magic.

It was now 7:30. Dinner was late. Alice and Richard had yet to arrive and couldn't be reached by the pay phone so we decided to begin. As we placed food on our plates, we were told to wait before eating until the toast was given. Mac was chosen to offer it.

His selection was from Walt Whitman, and its message resonated. It was the most special Thanksgiving of my life, because for the first time it wasn't all about the food. Listening to Mac's rich honey-toned voice, I breathed in the aroma of the moment. My life was now on track. This was my fate. I just needed never to forget it.

*

I dream'd in a dream, I saw a city invincible to the attacks
 of the whole of the rest of the earth;
I dream'd that was the new City of Friends;
Nothing was greater there than the quality of robust love – it led the rest;
It was seen every hour in the actions of the men of that city,
And in all their looks and words.

Walt Whitman

CHAPTER 90

Alice and Richard arrived with their clan of children at 10:30 p.m. Thanksgiving night. The reason they offered Robert for their tardiness was that they were also hosting a large family gathering. Robert accepted it.

I had already anticipated the arrival of the laudable stuffing so I volunteered for dishes. This way I was positioned to sample it. When Alice carried the large rectangular Pyrex dish brimming with the dressing into the kitchen, we had spoons ready for tasting. There were plenty of sausages sticking up amidst the corn stuffing. The temperature of the dish had cooled down considerably in travel, but I didn't care. I scooped a bite size portion containing a piece of sausage surrounded by cornbread and placed it into my mouth.

Holy cow, I was not expecting this. The heat from the spices blasted my tummy out of its comforting Thanksgiving stupor. I quickly drank water, but it had little effect on the burning in my mouth, esophagus and organs. Others were relishing it, and complimenting Alice for her extraordinary dressing. I smiled and nodded, not wanting to appear rude. I backed off looking for some remedy to neutralize the bomb that I swallowed. I found a bit of cranberry sauce to help extinguish the burn in my mouth, but the combination made me a bit nauseous. No accounting for taste, I thought afterwards. Next year, I think I'll pass on this.

* * * *

It was a late bedtime, and the Friday morning was late as well. We each arose from the crypt, as it were. Breakfast was an assortment of cold cereal placed on the counter. In my household, we wouldn't eat until noon the next day because of gorging ourselves the day before. Work octaves continued as usual, washing clothes, cleaning the Lodge, feeding the animals, etc.

I took the time in this late morning to write in my journal. I tried to set aims, and they centered around building will. And building will, for me, had to do with not overeating. It was traditional to forgive oneself for gluttony on Thanksgiving Day, but overindulgence was not an occasional habit I had. Sex and food were occupying my every thought. It was a stream of the many 'I's and their accompanying urges. Lack of control plagued me. Moderation was a goal I had dreamed of attaining since childhood because of all the excess I had witnessed around me.

How do I achieve moderation? By setting goals. This was the only activity that gave me a sense of structure and of control. To accomplish the aim required discipline and will, both of which I lacked, leaving nothing accomplished in the end. But did I give up? No. I would set another aim the next day. And then, chocolate cake would appear, and I was doomed to failure once again.

The setting of personal aims had become a bad habit — a drug, actually — that I was dependent upon to alleviate the anxiety of failure. I was addicted to it because it sustained the illusion that it was possible for me to accomplish whatever I set out to do. It was a buffer.

One thing about buffers is they are fine if you want to be lulled into the soothing sleep of wishful imaginings. But in the business of awakening, they are often ripped off or made unavailable, which leaves you raw and exposed. It is easier to live in a world of "Tomorrow's another day" than to control oneself in the moment.

Just as I was deep in thought, Robert found me huddled in the corner of the library with pen and paper. Standing above me, he wrote a message on his notepad and handed it to me.

"Please write your father for a car."

"Okay," I said, nodding in agreement. My heart, however, froze. That epic letter my father had sent me a couple of months ago included the promise of a car with the stipulation that I abandon this nonsense and return home.

Although I didn't want to comply, I obeyed Robert and began to compose a draft letter. It was a difficult endeavor since I had Dad's voice inside my head, rejecting every rationale I proposed for a car.

I ended up with this:

"Dear Dad, Things are going well. I've had some substitute teaching jobs in Vacaville, but it's clear I need a car to continue my career as a Secondary English Teacher. I enjoy living up north here, and hope you can help me by providing me with a car. Love, Linda."

I had no stationery except the 5-inch by 8.5-inch lined paper in my three-ring binder. It would have to do. After lunch, David drove me to the local post office, where I bought an envelope and stamp and mailed it. Task accomplished.

I worked in the kitchen preparing dinner that evening, and we were able to make a turkey stew out of the remains of our Thanksgiving feast. Before bedtime, I returned to the library corner and my journal entry.

But personal aims were no longer on my mind. The letter had been mailed and apprehension regarding Dad's response began to surface. Would he again require me to leave the school for a car? Would there be new and impossible requirements he would establish?

At this point, however, I've passed that River of No Return. I can't turn back to a synthetic life, for it is fool's gold. My outer life may not be improving, but my inner life has found tiny specks of real gold, however infinitesimal they may be.

THE DIVINE BEGINNING

Where there's memory, there are moments of presence. And my memory is filling up quickly, beyond my expectations. I have lived more in these past months than in all the years before. The school has given me this. I can easily die now knowing I have lived. The future, I guess you can say, is all gravy.

❖

Consider thyself to be dead, and to have completed thy life
up to the present time; and live according to nature the remainder
which is allowed thee.

Marcus Aurelius

CHAPTER 91

I awoke Saturday morning longing for a cigarette before breakfast. Outside was Alden, who was actively talking to David sitting next to him. Puffing on his pipe, David was focused on Alden, which was a bit unusual. The big Venusian would often listen to you without looking at you, as if he were mulling over what you were saying. My curiosity was strong, so I sat down on the dirt next to David.

"He asked them to leave after this weekend," said Alden.

Leave? Was someone else leaving the school? My heart sank.

"Did Robert say where they were supposed to stay?" asked David.

"According to Meg, Robert said they were to take a motel in Carmel along Ocean Avenue and operate out of it for the open meetings."

Meg and Harold were moving to CARMEL? I couldn't imagine that. After meeting the Esalen guy and Sheila, Meg with her big flouncy flowered dresses, floppy hat, and caricature makeup was the unlikeliest person to attract someone from Carmel, which was a rich person's enclave. Of course, I had never been there, so this was just my opinion.

There was talk throughout the day about these changes. Robert had mentioned we would be expanding to Big Sur and Tahoe, but I had no idea he would act so quickly. We had barely arrived here at the farm. And to move two of the oldest students away like this left me a bit shaken.

The last month or two we had settled into life here. It was true the chores were becoming increasingly monotonous and sleep-inducing. We all thought we were hunkered down in a retreat from life for life, and many had given their life savings to buy the property. It must be difficult for them.

Robert had indicated two months ago that we were near the end of an octave, and that we needed to be prepared for more difficulties. I could feel a pulling away from the farm, with new meetings held in other towns like Vacaville and Walnut Creek. But this new octave was much bigger than changing a meeting site. It was about forming new groups outside of the Bay Area. We were moving the school south and east.

I could hardly wait for tonight's meeting. What would Robert say about this new direction? Would I be asked to move? Is this why Robert wanted me to have a car?

* * * *

The Lodge living room was crowded. Mac began the meeting by reading from Robert's notes for the week.

"People in life know things, but they do not understand."

Mac paused to let each statement penetrate. Robert's face was solemn as his eyes looked upward upon hearing his words spoken. His hands were folded and his legs were crossed. Robert's posture was never haughty. It was relaxed and humble and contained.

"I have an acceptance….and acceptance is harder than questioning. It is not faith. It is seeing, receiving knowledge, and accepting it.

"It is good not to accept this knowledge. One must verify it for oneself. Whatever I am sharing with you, it has worked for me, as higher centers are present here. And I always try to tell the truth with all four centers at once."

A long pause followed. I peered around and saw a variety of expressions on students' faces — from smirking to confusion — as it seemed his statements contradicted themselves. Somehow, however, I understood what he meant. As you feel your life unfolding, and events have no rational origins or direction, all we can do is accept whatever occurs. They come from the gods. This I had verified.

"If you ever have a flash of consciousness, when higher centers wake up briefly, you will then know that humans literally are not real. It is an old statement, and Eastern and Western teachings say the same."

A Saturnine fellow from the Bay Area raised his hand, interrupting the reading of the notes. Robert nodded for him to speak.

"What I feel on this level is real to me, on this level, though."

Robert wrote on his pad and handed it to Mac to read.

"I know what you mean. It is an error. You are not real. It is the robot that dreams of not being mechanical. It is Pinocchio."

Robert continued his thoughts.

"What is real or not real? Only the Self is real. Man is asleep. What he perceives does not correspond to anything but brain patterns. To see something real, something more real has to see it. It is high to accept thoroughly that it is a machine. Few are allowed by higher forces to discover it. The Mormons, for example, are an interesting American phenomenon. Has anyone heard that the Mormons believe an atomic war is inevitable and that they keep in Utah a three-year supply of emergency food and that they have a shelter?"

A few members nodded in agreement. A hand went up.

"Maybe we should examine the Mormons," said the student, before being acknowledged to speak. "They work the earth and have music, literature, and beautiful buildings."

Robert replied, "This is a beautiful group. We also have been given problems for friction for higher centers. There needs to be an amount of degeneration in the group to provide friction for the group. If not, it is a sleeping nicety."

This stimulated the next question.

"What is the form of degeneration in this group?"

"Promiscuity, uncleanliness, lack of reliability. The Mormons don't have these. No friction. They are faithfully asleep."

Several questions were asked and Robert indicated others could offer angles. I must admit, I don't recall what these were. I was thinking too much about the practical issues of the outward growth of the school, which Robert did not address. I tried to find a moment in the meeting to ask, but it simply did not jive with the tone of the subject matter being discussed. The practical matters were often addressed outside the meetings. Before I knew it, the meeting was over.

* * * *

Tuesday was the next scheduled meeting in Vacaville. I was able to hitch a ride to Vacaville after Sunday breakfast with Rosemary and the girls. During the ride, I asked Rose if she had heard about Meg and Harold's relocation, and she said yes. She then read my mind.

"You need to focus on finding a job and making money to support yourself. Forget about Meg and Harold," she advised pointedly.

All the denying forces that could make this happen flew up and hit me in the face: transportation, location, money for gas and food — an overwhelming fear enveloped me. Where do I begin? How do I do this?

I sat there in the backseat feeling lost, helpless, and a bit angry. As we passed the Yolo Causeway outside of Sacramento, a heated discourse began in my head.

"My desire is to be around Robert. And Robert is making this difficult. He is elusive, walking to his own drum. Just when I think I recognize the rhythm, it vanishes, then reappears with a different beat and instrument," said the first group of 'I's.

Another group had this take on the situation: "In a school there are tests to pass and lessons to be learned. But how can you understand the lesson or pass the exam when the course keeps changing? I feel as if I signed up for a class in French romantic poetry (the *do*) and then the midterm exam (*mi-fa*) is given and the test is on nineteenth-century American history. So I decide to switch to this topic and study what is happening to me from that viewpoint, only to be faced with a final exam in microbiology. It is crazy! One is living blindly, not knowing from one moment to another what class I'm taking!"

A third chimed in: "Yes, but not only is the subject changing, the venue is as well. It's like finding yourself at USC when you enrolled at UCLA. Moving from the property with its rustic, natural impressions of World 24 to Carmel, the heart of A Influence with its rich people — I didn't sign up for this."

A fourth added, "I heard that Robert is now collecting gold coins, when he had refused to even touch money, wearing fine leather shoes, when he had refused to wear animal products, and eating high cuisine (fancy food, not organic raw vegetables). It is a definite about-face. His standards are changing."

As that last group of 'I's stepped down from my mental podium, an image appeared in my head. It was a carousel. I saw myself on a horse bouncing up and down, going round and round. It reminded me of my dream of jumping into the inner circle. But what was occurring now, based on this new image, was the carousel suddenly reversing direction, and I felt like I was going backward at high speed. The others on the carousel were flying off. It was chaos.

Then an 'I' from some other place entered my head, in its uniquely wordless way. It said, "Your job is to hold on tight and not be thrown by the ups and downs of the mannequin horse galloping backwards."

A smile appeared. This school is no ordinary carousel. It's run by the gods. Expect the unexpected. I've certainly had a taste of this, and I am still here. If I treat the journey more as an adventure than a dreadful experience, and watch out for expectations, I should be fine. Let's see what happens next.

❧

Hold on tight, for by such rungs as these, said my master, panting like a man exhausted, must we depart from so much evil.
Dante (Virgil speaking to Dante climbing upward, escaping Lucifer)

CHAPTER 92

After a restful Monday, Tuesday finally came. Everyone had left the house early for whatever reason. It was not for me to know. It was the last day of November. Four more weeks, and we would be entering a new year, 1972.

I arose around noon, ate a sandwich and small salad, and wrote in my journal, setting aims once again. My goals were to be honest (pay off my debts), to be sincere (follow my own way), and to be truthful (seek objective truth). These three goals did not come from me, but were borrowed from Rodney Collin, who had an inspiring approach that I found uplifting. Sometimes Ouspensky and Gurdjieff left me a bit depressed.

Around two I heard the mailman drive up. I walked to the box and, to my surprise, found a letter addressed to me. It was from a tenth-grade student I had taught last year named Julie. She was an earnest student. I would type her as Venusian-Mercury. She was round without being overweight and had dark curls that framed her face and fell to her shoulders.

Before opening the envelope, I held it in my hands, recalling the sweet card she handed me and the book that was my gift from the class. This act of kindness she had orchestrated, I was told later. The book was *The Giving Tree* by Shel Silverstein and her inscription was full of gratitude. That class was a joy. The students were open and eager to learn. We studied Shakespeare's *Julius Caesar,* taking the plot, characterizations, universality, theme and other elements and transporting them to a different place in time, which the students in each small group could select. They would rewrite the text to match the language of the period. It was fun.

During that final class hour, I had asked the students what they had learned in my class. Expecting them to talk about how to organize an essay, they described a totally different experience. "I liked how you played hangman to help us spell a word," or "I enjoyed the way you let us read for fifteen minutes." In some cases, a student would mention something that I clearly did not do. The impact of their comments upon me was powerful. I had no control over what they learned. What was the point of teaching?

Sitting at the kitchen table, I slit the seal. The letter was handwritten on ornamented stationery. Dear Miss Kaplan, it began. She asked if she could correspond with me since I had been her favorite teacher.

I was stunned and helpless. I could not reply to her. I knew this. The reason, however, would have surprised her. You see, I was myself a child when I taught her. I was only 21 and she was 15. That's a six-year difference. That time in my life was playacting. I only pretended to be a high school English teacher.

What can I offer her now? This thread of my past that yearned for some present-day continuity is a painful reminder that my hard-earned diploma is just a piece of paper. It is no longer a viable direction. It has become a dead end. This makes the search for meaningful employment in order to support myself financially weigh even more heavily upon me.

As I sat at the table, I remembered a moment in my acting class at UCLA when we had gathered together to assign roles and partners. We were each to play a scene from a different play and receive critiques from our fellow students. A pretty, petite blonde with a perfect complexion was paired with me. She was like honey in color and disposition. A sweet girl indeed.

We had spoken about our career paths. I told her I was studying to become a high school English and Drama teacher. "Really?" she said. "You're such a talented actress." I ignored that.

"And you?" I asked.

"I want to be famous," she said.

I was unexpectedly struck dumb by her comment. In a flash, the course of her desire appeared before my eyes: learning how to portray different roles, finding an agent, going to countless auditions, facing disappointment, securing bit parts, meeting an important director, being hired, years of struggle to make a name for herself, and finally success. Fame, where you live in Bel Air in a hidden-away mansion with millions of dollars, yet cannot go to the supermarket or a museum without being harassed by fans.

In that moment I knew Fame was imprisonment. It was a trap, and I wanted no part of it. And now, being a school teacher was not an alternative either, however altruistic it seemed in comparison.

I wished to live invisibly. I wished to taste my life fully and anonymously and leave this earth without a sound or a trace.

Pray tell, what career is that?

* * * *

The meeting I had so looked forward to attending came with a surprise. The insatiable Fourth Way student Linda, eager to learn, was replaced by a Linda whose mind swirled with 'I's about my life and my future. The notes were read and they sounded so banal to her. I was in a dark place inside and could hardly concentrate on anything outside. A struggle began in me to regain focus.

A student stood up to speak, which brought me back a little bit.

"When an individual wants something that false personality does not want, things one wants most may be the hardest to do. Why is that?"

Robert replies, "Most wants are in false personality. And when balance is reached, then there is a striving for the Self."

This topic interested me.

Another student asked, "When one has to do what one doesn't like to do, is that a task?"

"It may be irritating to the personality," answered Robert. "Gurdjieff said, 'Learn to love what it doesn't love.'"

A new student from Vacaville timidly raised her hand and was called on.

"How does one distinguish between a true want and a false want?"

"It is up to each being," wrote Robert. "Essentially, we don't need much. Existence is flavored by travel, food, books, and people. We could do without them, but existence may be found to be flat. What people in a teaching are working toward is simplicity. The highest level of needs are spiritual needs. Yet all can be had at the same time. Existence was not designed to be functional or communistic. It is a bridge to something."

At this point, an old Peanuts cartoon came to my mind, and I started to chuckle. I raised my hand and Robert called on me, somewhat reluctantly.

"Lucy asks, 'How are you ever going to accomplish anything, Charlie Brown?' He replies, 'Accomplish anything? I thought we're just supposed to keep busy!'"

Everyone laughed. Except Robert, who focused on the ceiling.

I started to feel badly about the timing of my joke. When the room stilled, Robert continued.

THE SEEDS OF

"We will cover the same subjects many times in our lives, adding and subtracting angles of thought.

"I would like to give you some observations that have been the result of my silence. I have been silent only 90 days, since September 4th. Seems longer, doesn't it?"

A hint of a sweet smile came upon his face. He appeared as that shy child I had seen peering from the shadows, watching the magic of Helga and John joyously dancing in the Lodge.

"My throat didn't like it for the first two weeks. Now I cannot speak naturally. Twice I made a mistake and spoke, but it was just a faint whisper that flowed out. In silence it has been easier not to identify with the many 'I's. People in life are extra kind. It is a pleasure."

He paused as he gathered his thoughts before proceeding to give his hand gestures to Jim, who had become Robert's voice.

"I am not concerned with the loss of my voice, if that comes about. Anna told me Meher Baba was unable to speak after his long silence. And I do not know if I will speak again. It is better presently for all of us if I do not.

"Some of you may remember my voice. I always spoke with an evenness, not fast or loud or with emphasis. Emphasis is lying, and it means that what the person said before was not worth listening to. Emphasis is the same problem as are the words 'get,' 'very,' 'really,' and 'a lot.'

"Also, remember that I was once a student and was afraid to speak to my teacher. I tried to serve. My teacher was a Martial type and he loved me, yet I never had one private meeting or a coffee with him. It was a form of payment for our gatherings at the Coffee Tree."

This insight from Robert stunned me. He was so open about his struggles and failures, without complaining. He found value in the friction he received.

As I entertained these thoughts, suddenly people stood up. The meeting was over. Refreshments were being served in the kitchen, so I moved in that direction. Meg was sitting in her chair and pulled out a handful of her journals. I took mine and was eager to read from Robert's notes, which she published from the prior week.

I took a small plate and placed some snacks on it and returned to a chair in the living room to read the journal. I came upon these thoughts from Robert.

"One of the things you have done is confronted boredom. You have nothing to tend to…fewer and fewer family responsibilities…no house to keep up. So you have time to 'think.' It is an existential process, from one angle.

"You need to be positive and create interests...things are meaningless...so, things are meaningless...then try to enjoy meaningless things...if something brings you joy, this is fine. Like enjoying a cup of coffee at the Coffee Tree. Try to create positive interests that can fill the flat spots of your life. Keep good householder wherever you are. This helps. Things are sometimes bad and a cheerful environment makes it better.

"I have been flattened this weekend also. Try to allow for being weary of the struggle. Sometimes we become weary...it will pass. It is necessary...I think things will go better for our group eventually. Remember: what bothers you now won't bother you later."

I felt he was talking to me, about me. This was exactly my life. I had nothing to do. All family responsibilities were stripped away, and I was forced to unveil what my existence was truly about. His encouragement penetrated deeply, and helped me to make sense of my current condition. Could it be I was forming a foundation upon which to build something in the future? If so, the shape and form of that something was a great unknown to me. The unknown is always scary. Whatever it was, I felt I would grow into it. For the time being, however, I must learn the importance of patience, and of bringing joy to whatever filled my day.

Although Robert wasn't often nearby, these notes proved once again that we were comrades, fighting the same battle side by side. His words comforted me, and helped me to rest a little easier that night.

*

> *The spirit that is engaged in the war against the passions*
> *does not see clearly the basic meaning of the war for it is*
> *something like a man fighting in the darkness of night.*
> *Once it has attained to purity of heart though,*
> *it distinctly makes out the designs of the enemy.*
>
> Philokalia, Evagrios the Solitary

CHAPTER 93

I was hoping to hitch a ride with Rosemary back to the farm on Wednesday but that was not to be. That morning, she received a call from Robert to join him at the Coffee Tree for lunch. I was becoming accustomed to bidding her adieu, as if I were the housewife and she was the man going off to work.

As I was settling in to my now familiar routine of housecleaning, reading, singing to Shirley Bassey records, and writing in my journal, I heard a car pull into the driveway. Rosemary quickly entered the kitchen and went directly to her bedroom to gather items because, as she described to me hurriedly, "Robert suddenly decided to go to Carmel and he wants me to come with him."

There's an old expression that we use in the Work: you must be able to turn on a dime. This means that one should not place more than ten cents of identification on any given moment. And so off she went.

It was like a tornado that entered and exited within five minutes, leaving a void of energy in its wake. I was stunned, as the depth of my solitude revealed itself. I felt like an empty chair.

That was Wednesday.

* * * *

Thursday, I awoke to an empty house once again. I took a walk, hugging the property perimeters of the neighboring homes since there were no sidewalks in her neighborhood. I found a *Vacaville Reporter* newspaper on someone's lawn. I hoped no one was home as I stole it. I needed a television to ease the pain of my loneliness. I thought maybe this paper could help me connect with the world.

Returning to the house, I lit a cigarette and started to read the paper from front to back. One student from Vacaville worked at this paper I was told. What would his life be like? I imagined how nice it would be to go to an office and sit behind the desk each day to a new event occurring in the world. What variety that would be! I turned to the classifieds and tried to find a possible job. Could I wash dishes? Be a secretary? Sell clothing? Everything I read came with a caveat: I would need to imagine first that I hadn't met a school, that I had the freedom to choose what I wanted to do with my life. I felt my hands were tied by an invisible rope. I couldn't explain this. But it was true.

So I returned to the records, the dust cloth, the waiting.

That was Thursday.

* * * *

Friday morning brought Rose's younger daughter home. She came to check on her horse. We walked together to the stall, and she asked me to help her feed the little palomino pony. She had her rubber boots on as she cleaned the manure and laid a fresh bed of hay in the stall. I asked if she planned to stay for lunch and she said No, her boyfriend was picking her up.

It was good to see him, and their interaction warmed my heart a bit. Off they went.

After scrambling two eggs and toasting slices of whole wheat bread for lunch, I heard the mailman's truck. In the box were bills for Rosemary and a handwritten business envelope with my name on it. It was from my father, and this time it was light as a feather.

"Dear Linda, come home. We are not giving you a car. Love, Dad."

Whoa. That was to the point. The response was not a surprise, and I was grateful that I did not have to wade through pages of his many 'I's.

Around six, Rosemary entered the house with Jim and Robert. I approached the teacher with the news from my father.

Robert replied, "They cannot admit you are right because then they would have to admit they were wrong."

With that insightful thought, Robert left quickly with Jim for the farm. Rosemary decided to retire and leave early in the morning. Yes, she said, I can come with her. I was grateful that I could return for the weekend meeting.

How to relate to my parents was on my mind as I lay in bed that night. I do not fault them for their reaction. It is hard for them to let me go. I was considered the Gullible One since childhood.

When I had read my B Influence books — from the Talmud and the Bible to Edgar Cayce as well as Kazantzakis' *The Last Temptation of Christ* — I had told my parents that I believed in Jesus' ability to be transformed into an immortal God. This spiritual path made sense to me and did not seem impossible.

My dad laughed, saying that he, too, had believed in this once. But hard facts of life — the Depression, to be exact — brought him back to earth with a thud. What I considered possible he considered impractical. For Dad to agree with me now would expose the possibility he may have made the wrong choice. That was Robert's point.

I would not, however, give up this belief. It was more than just a fancy. It was the answer to "Why am I here?" To evolve into a god is possible and could be realized in this lifetime with divine guidance and effort.

Our journey here is truly brief. Everything pointed to time's demise. I was born with a sense of urgency.

Everyone has a Jesus within him, waiting to be born.
Rumi

CHAPTER 94

When we arrived at Via Del Sol at noon on Saturday, Robert was speaking with Jim and Yorgos by the locust tree. The teacher looked serious while

Yorgos was speaking. My curiosity was piqued, but it was clearly a private conversation, so it wasn't like I could ask them what's going on. I had to let it go.

The Lodge was bustling with students actively cleaning and cooking. The whole area had apparently fallen into tramp while the teacher was travelling. Lunch was the usual simple fare of soup and salad with bread, yet the emotional nourishment was truly sustaining.

It was wonderful to be with students again.

"Where've you been?"

"Did you find work?"

Those were the first questions asked of me. My reply was, "In Vacaville looking for work, but nothing yet." The truth was far from this light optimistic response. It had been an exercise in patience, while fighting off the demons of depression.

The light energy that I always received from being in a circle of students with the teacher at the helm had to wait until Sunday morning. The meeting was postponed for some reason. We are given a change to the schedule with little notice and rarely told the rationale behind it.

The winter light of December days moved quickly into night. We were all pretty exhausted from the housecleaning octaves. After a solid Saturday rest and an early breakfast, the Sunday morning meeting finally arrived.

But not as expected. Robert was nowhere to be found. The message came that we were to begin with small groups.

I quickly positioned myself next to Meg and Harold. Meg was often entertaining in her angles of thought, and was a popular choice. It reminded me so much of elementary school, when at recess you tried to fit in with the most athletic kids to experience the thrill of victory, rather than the agony of defeat. In small groups, the agony of defeat was sitting with Lunars. The Lunar leader would ask, "Are there any questions?" and the remaining Lunars would start doing the looking exercise. No one would offer a thought or question. For anyone with a bit of Mercurial type, such as myself, it was excruciating. Once, I even asked a question and offered my own angles of thought.

Meg was perceptive and often would photograph students for their mechanics, including body type and center of gravity. Her specialty was determining chief feature. The first question was exactly that.

"I would like angles of thought," asked a Mercurial type, "on my center of gravity."

"Mercurial types often have power features, which you have," offered Meg. "You show it when you move and are in charge of an octave. Your moving center is active, much more so than your intellectual center or emotional center."

Harold chimed in, with a twinkle in his eye, "You're too thin to be emotionally centered."

Everyone laughed. I had never heard Harold give an angle before at a meeting. It was so off-handed, like a thought that suddenly escaped his lips. But it was pointed. The student who asked the question looked a bit stunned. It reminded me of that meeting when I stood up to represent the Venusian type and descriptions of lazy and slothful were thrown at me like rotten tomatoes.

Features were distasteful to talk about because they are weaknesses of the machine. Nobody likes their weaknesses discussed. Body type and center of gravity were more palatable — like your astrological sign. I'm a Pisces. I'm a Taurus. I'm a Saturn. I'm a Venusian. That was better than, I have Non-Existence, I have Tramp.

Still, we were reminded that this is the machine we're talking about, which is not who we are. We are talking about functions, not states. And yet, talking about being in the third state of consciousness through the effort to self-remember was not a topic of conversation among us. Others looked at you funny, like Who do you think you are? A conscious being? None of us were awake and to think that or intimate that publicly was considered the height of vanity, which is a feature. It was more comfortable to talk about the functions of the machine or the table of hydrogens.

These thoughts were circulating in me when we were told to end the small groups and to reassemble into a larger circle for the main meeting. It was wonderful to see Robert, and this was the first thing from his pen:

"How are efforts at self-remembering going?"

I felt so relieved. Just his mentioning the phrase self-remembering elevated my state. This was that trick of the machine Ouspensky spoke about: by asking someone if they are awake, presence is evoked for that moment. Then it disappears and the machine goes back to sleep.

A student from San Francisco raised her hand.

"I felt different when I returned to work in the city. I was inner considering less. Then by the end of the week, I felt overwhelmed because I saw I was just a small cog with all the other people in a big machine."

The teacher wrote, "Ouspensky called big cities big mechanical toys. How many of you have been stunned by the mechanicalness of people?"

Most of us raised our hands.

He continued.

"The city is a lovely place to visit; one needs to be selective."

Then Robert switched gears.

"How many people have 'I's that blame C Influence?"

No one raised their hands.

"The reason they have to take barbaric measures," explained Robert, "is the level of the seed. Remember, our human seed is trying to become another level, as a walnut seed becomes a tree. If you don't have them now, you will have 'I's that blame C Influence for stroking us awake."

A faint smile came on his face, as he continued to write.

"Enjoy the highs and separate from the lows. We do not have to suffer when Influence C is demonic. It is our present level if we do. What gives you trouble now will not later. How many have verified this?"

Several hands were raised, including mine.

"Your being has changed then."

He had Meg tell the tale of the missing hamburger in the bun. It was a fun moment.

"Was the full moon a problem?" he asked.

The moon had been full on Thursday. That was the day I was alone in the house. I guess so, I thought. I raised my hand when he polled us so that it would seem to others that I had much to deal with while looking for work. That I didn't have much of anything to deal with was the problem.

"Positive events can overcome negativity. Rosemary, Jim and I hopped up from coffee and drove to Carmel for two days and it was fun. Yet, we lost two students during this full moon."

A lady raised her hand, which he acknowledged.

"Why did Dennis leave the teaching?"

Who was Dennis? He must be from San Francisco.

"He cannot take responsibility. That is why he is single."

The lady then added, "There are more women students than male students."

Robert wrote, "This Christmas we have 75 students. Next Christmas we may have 150. Personality would like an equal amount so there could be couples to 'live happily ever after.' Also, I'm recording the possibility that C Influence may want more women to absorb the males' emanations. Too many males may be impossible. It doesn't matter….as long as Yorgos doesn't take up knitting."

We all laughed. I thought it was cute and looked over at Yorgos. He wasn't laughing.

"Yorgos is in charge of the farm," added Robert. "If we have trouble separating from another student who is negative during the full moon, the problem is within us, not them."

With that, the meeting ended.

*

Certainty only comes through work we do in the invisible world. Seeds planted there never disappoint.

Bahauddin

CHAPTER 95

Mac surprised me on Sunday morning.

"Are you coming to Vacaville this week? I want to introduce you to a new student."

As usual, I was scrambling to find a ride down to Vacaville after the weekend, so his comment was a relief. Maybe he can help me.

"I hope so. I don't have a ride yet."

With that, Mac went up to Trisha, who said she was driving there on Monday, but her car was full with her children. I watched him melt her resistance with his charming smile. It would be a tight squeeze, but she could drop me off at Rose's house around noon.

So that was the plan. After breakfast on Monday, Trisha and her teenage daughters and son crowded into the back of the car while I occupied the passenger seat. It was kind of Trisha to give me this space. I could look out the window quietly while the mother was addressing issues with her kids. Once we arrived at Rosemary's, I thanked her and entered the kitchen using the hidden key. I had taken some food from the Lodge kitchen with me in case the refrigerator was empty.

After settling in, I was about to take a nap when the front door opened. It was Mac with his girlfriend.

"Are you ready?" he asked.

"Where are we going?" I questioned.

"To Vallejo. You look fine." That's all he said, chuckling.

I sat behind the passenger seat during the half-hour drive. His girlfriend had her left arm positioned on the back of his seat, as her long fingers caressed his pockmarked neck and thinning hair. It was such an act of intimacy that I immediately looked away. Waves of self-pity drenched my heart. Images flashed in my mind's eye of me in the same posture with Miles as we drove to Mount Diablo for the picnic and on our way to Anna's house in spring. Was that this year? It seemed like a decade ago.

I snapped out of it when she returned her arm to its proper position at her side. We had exited the highway and wound our way through a quiet residential area, pulling into the driveway of a modern California ranch style home. The house occupied the end of the cul de sac, as if it were the crown of the street. It was larger than the other residences, and the landscaping was perfectly designed and immaculately maintained. The other houses paled in comparison.

Mac entered the home as if it were his own, with his girlfriend close by. I followed sheepishly.

The first person to greet us was Rosemary, who was standing there in the doorway. She must have heard his car pull up.

"You're late. The meeting is over," said Rose, as she led us into the living room. She ignored the woman accompanying him, who hid behind Mac.

There were my friends, the couple from Vacaville, sitting on a beautiful beige sofa, and Marie in an elegant chair enjoying tea served by a petite lady. She was actually tinier than Rosemary. In fact, she looked like a child.

The four students were leading the prospective student meeting. I could understand the couple leading the meeting with Rose, but I was actually startled to see Marie. Why wasn't I included? I had more to offer regarding the knowledge, I thought, than Marie. She had barely read the work books.

"Clare," said Mac, "I'd like to introduce you to Linda."

Gentle eyes and a sweet, generous smile adorned her round face. Lunar type was my first thought.

Rosemary was not pleased by Mac's actions. His entrance and tardiness, and his decision to bring his girlfriend and me, was another "in your face" act that was designed to push Rose's buttons. It clearly worked. I did not want to be aligned with this, as it may compromise her perception of my loyalty to her in the midst of her suffering. Suffering is a powerful bond that can link people together, and I needed her support.

Everyone stood to greet us. Mac then explained the connection.

"Clare's kids were part of our swim team." He went on to describe how he had been coaching a swim team in Vacaville, which was how he met not only Clare but Marie as well. What couldn't this man do?

THE DIVINE BEGINNING

While Mac continued speaking, Rosemary mechanically reached down and took the tea cups into the kitchen with Clare. I collected the napkins and Marie carried the plates, leaving the Vacaville couple with Mac and his girlfriend.

The kitchen was huge and modern. A large island was in the center of the room, and seated at the island were a young boy and a man, each eating a big slice of chocolate cake with thick chocolate frosting. I was formally introduced to Clare's son and husband.

"Dad, we have to get going or I'll be late for practice."

They left abruptly, kissing Clare on their way out.

"Clare's husband is a dentist," said Rosemary, "and she has two boys and two girls."

My ears were half-listening to Rose, while my eyes were fully focused on the cake.

"Would you like a piece of cake," offered Clare.

That woke me up a bit.

"Yes. Thank you."

The first bite was exquisite. The frosting was rich and creamy, with extra butter you could taste, and the cake was light and fresh. But the amazing part was the height and perfect symmetry. It wasn't lopsided, like my mother's. It looked like the picture on a box of Duncan Hines cake mix.

"Did you bake this?" I asked.

"Yes," she replied. "You know, I don't have a sweet tooth, but my kids and husband do, so I bake it for them."

A soft chuckle came from her as she continued.

"The only time I had the urge to eat cake was when I was pregnant. I baked it in the middle of the night and ate almost the whole thing. And I wasn't even hungry!" she exclaimed in wonder.

"Welcome to my world of being emotionally centered. This happens to me daily."

She stopped and stared at me.

"Really?"

Both Rosemary and I laughed as our hands flew up to photograph "really."

"Thank you," she said gratefully.

We chatted for a while about high school (Rosemary mentioned my profession) before we noticed the afternoon had rapidly slipped into the dinner hour. The only ones left were Rose and Marie so I travelled back to Vacaville with them.

Over a wonderful dinner of fried chicken and rice and vegetables, we spoke about the friendship and history they each had shared with Clare. As I listened to them, I realized more than ever how seemingly casual social interactions could miraculously reveal which friends shared a common interest in evolution and wanted more than just words. They wanted to experience the states the words described. Looking at Rose and Marie sharing tales of their children's swimming successes and memorable moments warmed my heart and made me happy. I felt my conscious family growing.

> O the blest eyes, the happy hearts, that see, that know the guiding thread so fine, Along the mighty labyrinth.
> Walt Whitman

CHAPTER 96

Once again, Rosemary had received a call in the morning to join Robert for lunch at the Coffee Tree. I was surprised to see how quickly my machine adapted to this familiar pattern with habits of my own.

When she returned from lunch, Rose was uplifted. As she walked into the kitchen, she didn't bother even to put her keys down.

"Would you like to come with me to pick up Clare?" she asked.

I was so delighted to be able to leave the house and travel to Vallejo. That little town reminded me so much of those quiet suburban communities of the North Valley of Los Angeles, where I spent my childhood. It truly resonated and I, too, felt uplifted.

During the drive, Rosemary told me about her lunch with Robert. Marie had joined them as well.

"I think his trips to Carmel are making Robert happy," she said.

"Where does he stay?" I asked her, knowing that Meg and Harold were still hanging out in an inn in the heart of Carmel. I wasn't sure if he was staying there also.

"He stays at Sheila's apartment. It's centrally located. I think being able to walk around and visit the shops is good for him. He doesn't belong on the farm. He's not a farmer."

I asked her if I could have a Marlboro, and she nodded. After the first few puffs, my head cleared.

"Why do we have to pick up Clare?" I suddenly found myself asking. That was bold, I thought. Where did that 'I' come from?

"Her husband isn't thrilled about her interest in the Fellowship."

I chuckled. "I know the feeling of being rescued," I replied. No comment came from Rose, who slowly sipped the last smoke from her cigarette before crushing it out.

As we pulled into Clare's driveway, she came out to greet us. She gave each of us a warm embrace.

"I'm almost ready," she said, leading us into the kitchen. "I am trying to finish preparing dinner for the family."

The smells assaulted my senses. Roasted meat in the oven with vegetables and potatoes. She was in the midst of making a big salad with her daughter, when I spotted it. It was the chocolate cake.

"Since you liked it so much, I baked another one to bring to the meeting."

It was such an act of generosity and kindness.

"Rosemary, would you like to see the finished shower I told you about?" Clare asked.

We went into the marital bedroom, and I was amazed at its elegance. Her bed was covered with a cloth of pure gold. It was perfectly fitted yet seamless and was smooth as silk. In fact, it was silk. I had only seen polyester copies in my life, so this was a real treat for my eyes.

"Where did you find this?" I asked.

Clare smiled and the most gentle, little girl giggle came forth.

"I made this ten years ago."

My jaw dropped.

"You made THAT?!"

She nodded.

Rosemary wasn't interested in that, perhaps because she was a seamstress herself. She was taken in by a huge structure in the bathroom. It was a shower the size of my small bedroom in Brentwood. You could fit a family in it. Dark moss-green glass tiles lined the back wall and floor; the other three walls were glass panels that reached the ceiling.

Clare showed Rosemary how the front glass moved to allow entrance. It was not intuitive. It seemed extravagant to me, and I wondered how she was able to keep it so clean. It was as if no one had used it.

The Fellowship was exposing me to people whom I would never have known, with such a vast range of standards of living. My standards had adapted to the farm, although I yearned for refinement. What would become my future standards? Coarse impressions or refined impressions?

This question sent adrenaline into my system as I sat in the backseat of Rose's car. The future's unknown face stared tauntingly at me, teasing me to guess its nature. Will it be easy or difficult? Will I be up to the challenges? Is it here or there? The future was the ever-shifting bogeyman that goaded me to come along into the world of imaginary scenarios.

Mechanically, my fingers tightened their grip on the cake container that held Clare's chocolate masterpiece. As I looked through the plastic, a sweet, kind voice inside my head said, "Linda, life is a piece of cake."

The gods were reminding me not to worry. I took a deep breath and nestled into the present moment.

* * * *

The meeting that night came as no surprise. It began with small groups. Miles assigned us numbers from one to four as he went row by row. I was number two, and joined that group of students. Rather than have assigned leaders, Miles instructed that someone from each group would volunteer to lead it. It was an interesting experiment, and it seemed to work well for me. My group had a mixture of active and passive types, and one of the active types naturally assumed the role of leader.

I tried to listen and share angles, but I was more curious about Robert's whereabouts. He wasn't in the house. Who's missing? It was Rosemary and Clare! How could I have missed this? They were probably with him at the Coffee Tree.

After thirty minutes we ended the small groups and went into the kitchen for refreshments. Crackers, cheese, salami and cookies were placed on the table with the wine bottles, but the cake was missing. I found it in a dark corner on the kitchen counter, untouched. Although I wanted a slice, it wasn't mine to cut. I had imagined Clare would present it, and we would all oooh and ahhh. That didn't happen.

Robert, Jim, Clare, and Rosemary entered the kitchen just as I was eating my fourth cheese and salami cracker. Clare was beaming. Miles approached Robert, and Rosemary introduced him to Clare. It was lovely to see Miles smile. I hadn't realized how rare this had become and how much I missed it.

As I watched this scene, someone tapped me on the shoulder. It was Mac, suggesting I help arrange the chairs in the living room for the main meeting. Grateful to be pulled out of a gawking state, I happily followed him.

As we took our seats, Robert indicated he wanted Clare to sit in the first row in front of him. Rosemary sat to Robert's right and next to her was Miles.

On Robert's left was Jim as always and another lady from Vacaville next to him.

After Miles led good householder, Robert began.

"The small group meetings are useful. We will continue to have them. It is an opportunity to teach, to empty one's vessel.

"We will continue with no required weekends at the farm, and see what we see. Also, due to the cost of food, anyone wishing to move to the farm will have to pay $60 a month for food. New students will pay $30."

I registered this information, and the pressure to find an income intensified.

"Donald, would you like to explain the group that is forming in Big Sur?"

Mac stood up to address us.

"There are three people that have been worked with by Robert, Klair, Mary, Jan, and Jim. Their background is from Esalen. Also working with these people will be Miles, Helga, and Rosemary."

I was puzzled. Are these the same people I met? Didn't Robert say to let it go? What is happening here?

"If a Big Sur group is formed from these people, Robert will spend two days a week there."

Robert asked if there were any questions.

"Will the Big Sur group be separate from ours?"

"Not separate. There will be interchange between us," clarified Robert.

"Will leaders of this group come from this group or the new one?"

"From this group."

There was an increasing tension in the room. I could certainly feel it in myself.

"We have cozily grown," responded Robert to the dense energy. After a pause, and with a sudden seriousness, he added, "Rosie has given permission to knock the bedroom wall out…." He turned to her, and we all witnessed Rosemary's face turn pale. "But we will wait ten minutes."

Everyone laughed at Robert's comic timing. He then turned his focus on Via Del Sol, the heart of our school.

"Since we have had that farmhouse, we have worked on frugality of space. It has entered our being. If we start a new group, it is a major step for us.

"Whatever we do, whether in life or at the farm, try to do it competently, but do not take it seriously or consider it important. Be sure to use common sense."

Richard raised his hand, and Robert acknowledged him.

"Meher Baba said that experiences in life are a good place to work on oneself." Many nodded in agreement.

I raised my hand to offer an angle of thought.

"Ouspensky describes the Fourth Way as a way to draw from life by using life's shocks. It is not a monastic system."

Robert replied, "Monastic is fine for some here, like Yorgos and Kerrie, or David and Bonita. It can be rich also. Others find what they wish in life. We will try to be balanced."

I felt Robert had shot my angle down. I wished I hadn't offered it.

Robert looked at me as he continued.

"One of C Influence's favorite tricks to stir up negative emotions is to arrange things that don't make sense, after we have worked hard to make sense of it all. Why? It makes the emotional center flip. Confusion is a high state. It allows us to find another, higher alternative."

He just described what happened to me, but what do I do with the rest of his photograph? I didn't think I was confused. He just gave me an opposite 'I.'

"Our second year is coming to a close. It has been a big growth year. Next year will bring more changes and more students."

The meeting ended on that note.

After students left, and the house was set back in order, I reflected on what a good day it had been, with friends, food, and conscious energy. Once alone in my bedroom, however, a dread of the future with its money and lodging uncertainties returned to fill a void in me. This lovely day quickly had become the past. What would tomorrow bring? Where will I live? How will I survive? As soon as I observed these many 'I's, they melted into an emotion that burned inside of me without words. I could not shake it.

When I awoke in the morning, for the briefest of moments my heart was light. But then, as soon as I realized where I was, my state quickly darkened. This fear patiently had been waiting for my eyes to open, like a devoted cat resting heavily on my chest, wishing to become my morning companion. The bogeyman emerged once again. But where were the gods?

❖

> *Depression has weakened your heart, but I am the one*
> *who has established good cheer for you. He will fix it forever*
> *as your lot that you shall lift your head high.*
>
> Sumerian Texts

CHAPTER 97

The phone rang in the kitchen late Wednesday morning. Rosemary had gone with Robert to Carmel (she left a note and a few Marlboros for me on the kitchen table), so it was up to me to answer it.

"Linda?"

"Yes," I said startled.

"It's Kerrie. I'm on my way back to the ranch, and Rosemary called me to say you need a ride."

She did?

"Well, yes, I do. That would be great."

"Good. I'm at my mom's house and can be there in fifteen minutes."

"Uh, okay."

Well, not actually. I hadn't showered yet, and so I scurried to be ready. She did arrive in fifteen minutes, but had to wait for me. We left almost an hour later.

As we headed east on Highway 80, I realized Kerrie hadn't been to the meeting the night before.

"Where've you been?" I asked.

"I was staying with my mom for a few days because we are planning to sell the Buck House."

Oh, no. Another landmark in my life is disappearing. "Here I am, how strange" was now becoming, "Here I am…No. HERE I am….Uh No. There I was….Where am I?"

She added, "My folks bought it for me as an investment."

You mean, this was just an investment and easily cashed in? This was never meant to be Kerrie's and Yorgos's home? There were so many memories in that house for me in such a short period of time, and now the set is being struck. I knew it was none of my business, but places that contain your conscious energy are part of the fabric of your soul. It was like a fragment of me ripped off.

She interrupted my soliloquy.

"So how was the meeting?"

"It was good. Robert talked about the new group forming in Big Sur."

She was quiet.

"He mentioned you, also," I added.

"Oh?"

"Yes, he said some students like you and Yorgos are more suited to a monastic life at the ranch than to Big Sur."

Her face froze. She then expelled a big breath of silent, agitated 'I's.

I thought I was complimenting her. She seemed upset for some reason.

We said nothing for the rest of the trip. Once at the Lodge, I helped Kerrie prepare dinner that night. I liked her, and still felt a kinship. After all, she was the first to teach me how to cook. I was grateful to her for that.

* * * *

After breakfast on Thursday, Small Jane approached me with a piece of paper.

"Oh, I forgot to give this to you yesterday. You received a call from the Marysville School District about a job."

What?!

She handed me the note with a phone number on it. Immediately I went upstairs to the pay phone and called it.

"Marysville Joint Unified School District," was the lady's response on the other end.

"Hello, my name is Linda Kaplan, and I was called yesterday about a job."

"One moment," she said.

The fear and panic that I had experienced in Rosemary's kitchen with Robert re-emerged.

"Oh, yes. That one was filled," she said casually.

Before I could say anything else, she added, "Oh, but we do have a need for a substitute tomorrow in a Home Economics class. It's at Marysville High School. It's not a full-time position like the other one. It's only a two-hour class, but you will be paid for a full day. Are you interested?"

"Oh, yes!" I said exuberantly.

She told me to come by at noon for paperwork and instructions. With that, the call ended.

I was elated and went downstairs quickly to let others know.

"I just landed a job substituting tomorrow!" I said to several students, who were standing in front of the fireplace.

"How ya gonna make it there?" asked one.

My jaw dropped. I had no idea.

"Who has a car I can borrow?" I asked them.

Two of them expressed ignorance by shaking their heads and shrugging.

I started to ask each student in the Lodge. Both Small and Tall Janes said I couldn't use their car. David was there, but his VW was not running well. Trisha explained she had other matters to attend to in Grass Valley.

I was sick to my stomach all day. I couldn't find anyone to help me. What was I going to do?

That evening, as I was preparing to retire, I had accepted the fact that I would have to call in the morning to cancel.

Then Jan walked into the Lodge. I had thought she was with Robert in Carmel, but apparently not. She had her two boys with her and was signaling to them where to put their sleeping bags. It was clear she was tired. I hesitated to approach her, but I was desperate.

I explained my plight to her, and that I needed it from 12 noon to 3. I was ready for the usual rejection, but to my utter astonishment she simply said, "You can use my car. We'll talk in the morning."

I thanked her and returned to my place on the floor. With a smile on my face, I snuggled next to the brick that encased the wood burning stove. It retained heat on a cold winter's night, and that Thursday evening was especially cold. Still feeling anything could go wrong, I had to content myself with a piece of hope.

* * * *

After breakfast, I showered and put on my purple coatdress. When I exited, Jan was up and sipping some tea while her boys were eating their cereal.

"Here are the keys. It's the beige sedan three cars down the hill. Just be sure you put gas in it."

"Thank you so much," I said to her with affection.

"You are welcome," she said, almost businesslike. I was surprised that this woman could be so generous to me without an overt display of emotion. Unlike the others, offering me her car she considered a natural response to the request.

I could see why Robert relied on her. She was a woman who would do the right thing when asked without fanfare. That was a virtue I wanted to have.

* * * *

As I arrived at Marysville High School that Friday, the day was cold and overcast. A white opaque sky held the light. I hadn't seen a sky like that before.

The clerk walked me to the classroom that was set up with a kitchen and a few rows of chairs.

"This is the Home Economics Class. You'll have both boys and girls in the class. The teacher's instructions are here," she said, pointing to a piece of paper on the counter.

As she walked out, I read the lesson plan for the day.

"Make an omelet."

The ingredients and cooking utensils were listed. That was all I was given.

Why there was a Home Economics class at the high school level was bizarre to me. I recall taking this class in middle school. In Los Angeles, Home Ec included cooking ("Chipped Beef" was a go-to recipe, involving a package of chopped deli meat mixed with a white sauce poured over triangle shaped toast) and sewing (aprons, then skirts with a zipper).

It was now almost one o'clock. As the kids came in, I was surprised to see that there were both black and white boys. The black boys were actually passive. The white boys were ranchers' sons: they wore jeans, had short hair, and cowboy hats. They turned out to be the bullies.

I had lined up the bowls, pans and whisks, and eggs. The smallest Martial-type cowboy didn't hesitate a moment to grab an egg and throw it at a black student. Of course, everyone laughed.

Here we go, I thought.

I put on my best adult face and said to the cowboy, "Take a towel and clean that up." We stared at each other for a moment, but I was bigger than he was so my serious face and ample figure won the competition.

"Look everyone, today we are making an omelet." I had memorized the instructions and guided them through the process, dividing the students into groups and assigning roles within each group: preparation, cooking, and cleaning.

That took about an hour. Now what?

This was not an academic class, where I could tell them to read their next assignment at their desks until the bell rang. I had to improvise.

I asked them what else they cooked in class, what kind of foods they prefer, what was the worst thing they ever tasted. That took about 30 minutes. We had another half hour to go.

They started to ask about me. Oh, dear.

I told them I was from Los Angeles, was born in Hollywood and went to UCLA to study film and English. Had I ever met a movie star? Well, yes. I told them I interviewed Robert Vaughn, who played *The Man From U.N.C.L.E,* when I was in high school. They had no idea who he was or what that was, even though it was the most popular television program at the time.

I realized we were all winging it as the clock hands moved ever so slowly. Finally, it was 2:45. The class was over at three. I couldn't bear another fifteen minutes of this, so I offered the following.

"Tell you what. Since you've been a good class, I will let you all go if you promise me you will be quiet when you leave and keep it a secret."

They couldn't believe I said this. Neither could I.

I grabbed my purse and slowly opened the door to see if the coast was clear.

"Okay. Now be quiet when you leave."

I led them through the empty hallway and had to shush a few girls who started giggling. We all escaped through the massive front doors and down the brick stairs, going our separate ways.

As I drove back to the farm after filling the tank, it became clear to me that I had a long way to go to emulate Jan's virtue of doing the right thing without fanfare. I was directionless in a classroom and easily tempted to talk about myself, which was a buffer to relieve the discomfort of new circumstances. It was an easy way out. I realized that would probably be my last experience at Marysville High School. Kids can't keep secrets.

To live a life of virtue, you have to become consistent, even when it isn't convenient, comfortable, or easy.

Epictetus

CHAPTER 98

Saturday was the coldest morning so far at the farm. Even the bricks around the woodstove were struggling to stay warm. Instead of the usual cold breakfast, Kerrie made cooked oats, and that was greatly appreciated.

We were asked not to smoke in the Lodge, so we would huddle closely together against the chimney stack outside to try to stay warm. The chill was bone-penetrating, however, and our effort was more the idea of something, as it did not prevent the shivers. That white opaque sky hovered over us ominously. Cold weather slows the blood, and it was a challenge to find any incentive to move. So we talked and rocked back and forth to keep the fluids circulating.

How was your substitute teaching experience? Fine, I replied, being careful not to elaborate.

Did you hear that there's no heat in the children's house? No! You're kidding. Yup. So that's why the kids are sleeping at the Lodge.

Where does Robert stay? Good question. I don't know. I heard he had a deluxe tent site with a special heater that keeps him warm at night. Really? Photograph "really." Oh, thanks. How can he have a heater when there's no electricity? I don't know. Where is his tent? It's up the hill. I've been up the hill and haven't seen it. No, I mean, WAY UP the hill. It's pretty well hidden. You mean he walks up and down the hill at night? I guess so. Well, I know I don't see him sleeping in the Lodge. He just magically appears in the morning for his breakfast.

Once the cigarettes are smoked down to the filters, conversations end. We then proceed to heat ourselves inside by the fireplace, and begin the conversations once again. That is a typical morning on a frigid December day when the teacher was not around.

* * * *

When Robert appeared in the afternoon, the morning sluggishness was immediately replaced with activity. He directed us to prepare the main room for the Saturday meeting, cleaning areas that we had not noticed were dirty or, according to some students, that did not even need cleaning.

The Saturday night meeting was normally the highlight of the weekend, and students would come up from the Bay Area late afternoon. There were not as many this time, however, and I think the weather had something to do with it. During the meeting, the children stayed quietly in the library with a parent attending.

There were about twenty of us. After good householder, Robert asked if there were any questions.

"I watched a cloud. It looked as though it was a dove landing."

"It is difficult to accept or verify," replied Robert, "but I have said C Influence controls the weather."

A mother raised her hand.

"There were 'I's that said, 'I don't care what C Influence does to me, but leave my children alone.' The next day my boy fell off a bike and split his lip and chipped his teeth."

"That was no accident," commented Robert.

She added, "There were no resentment 'I's."

"Those 'I's will not alter anything," Robert replied.

Alden raised his hand.

"It seems the instinctive center registers what is not good, like missing a meal, but the emotional center looks for something to be negative about."

Robert listened closely, paused, and then wrote:

"A strong piece of knowledge is to remember the emotional center is negative as a buffer. People can't remember themselves, so they become negative about the day's many subjects of negativity. To keep themselves from going mad, they select 'upsets over easy' or 'sad a la mode.' Keep trying to self-remember, and it will be better."

Nadia raised her hand to speak. I'd never seen her do this before at a meeting.

"How do we go about acquiring consciousness if we don't do things well?"

"You do things well. You're a good bookkeeper, a clean person, and a good cook," replied Robert kindly.

"I know, but it isn't enough. Some people think it's a joke."

"I was pointing out that you can do things well," explained Robert. "It is not a joke to anyone in the teaching, but we can allow for humor. No one here is a day-tripper. C Influence doesn't allow it."

Nadia continued the conversation, as if it were private.

"It's not about laughter. I like to laugh as well as the next person."

A Martial man turned to Nadia and said, "Why don't you say what is bothering you?"

Nadia blurted out, "When do we become responsible human beings? What about the chickens?"

Everyone laughed. That broke the tension in the room.

Jim chuckled before sharing Robert's response.

"Want to gather them up and take them to the auction?"

Another student joined in, "The coop under the house is almost finished."

That was in reference to the demise of the chickens last summer. I was enjoying the casualness of the moment. Then a thought occurred to me, and I offered it.

"Once the teacher said when something irritates us it might be false personality and our idea of the way things should be."

There was silence. I didn't mean to put an end to the fun; I just thought it was a useful angle. It was a stupid angle.

When Robert stood up it was clear the meeting was over. Why can't I ever say or do the right thing? The evening's chill and darkness quickly descended into my heart.

❖

The lower self tries to get the better of you and will not leave you alone. It says for example, "You are one of the losers!" Do not let its words disturb you or alarm you.

Darqawi

CHAPTER 99

"Quick! Come outside!"

It was dawn, and such a cry from a student standing over me could only be met with an immediate response. I wiggled out of my sleeping bag, put on my shoes and followed him.

It was snowing!

The entire landscape was pristine in the blanket of white. It was as if that ominous opaque sky had dropped to earth, and the state that it produced inside of me was magical. How could snow bring sun to my heart? It was uncanny.

Some tried to form snowballs, and I didn't want to have anything to do with a fight of that sort, so I stood under the roof eaves and just observed them have at it. The snowflakes had stopped falling after thirty minutes. The purity that graced the earth at dawn soon disappeared, as the frolicking mixed the soil with the ice. It had become brown slush.

We went inside to begin breakfast preparations and stoke the fires. Slowly people came down the hill to the Lodge. They had heavy boots that provided traction for the steep slope. These students were the "monastic type" that Robert had mentioned. To me, they were die-hard hippies that looked grungy and didn't care. The men wore woolen caps and had long, wet straggly beards when they arrived for breakfast.

I was waiting to see Robert and Jim. They came after the rest of us had dined. By that time, the snow and ice had melted so the route was less treacherous to navigate. Robert wore gray cotton corduroy pants and a wool Nordic sweater under a heavy 3/4 length wool coat. Jim was in his usual blue jeans, tee shirt and dark green plaid flannel shirt under his snug leather jacket.

THE DIVINE BEGINNING

Jim smiled at me as he entered, while Robert went straight to the bathroom without sharing eye contact with anyone.

Robert was definitely paradoxical: you can feel the power of his gentle emanations when you are looking at him, but when you're not looking, he can be right behind you and you would not know it. His energy was so fine and quiet that it made him virtually invisible. I wonder if that's how the gods are?

* * *

At 4 p.m. we were told that there would be an impromptu meeting. It was not the first time Robert would sense the need to gather together in the moment like this and act upon it. Those who left early missed it.

"The earth is more real today," began Robert.

His words penetrated deeply, returning me to the quality of presence I had experienced when first I saw the white snow silently falling.

"Remember last night I mentioned the gods control the weather? That was not an accident."

He looked around the room at us.

"Some people never stop from the moment they meet a teaching. It is what they have been wanting. When you are on the Way, you are off the ladder."

I had not read of this concept of ladder. My interest was aroused.

"Some are on the Way here, although their ladder fell."

He gave an example of two ladies that he thought were on the same ladder. One, however, recently left, to which he said she "fell off the ladder." He then said, to his knowledge, the other lady was safe.

I guessed "fell off the ladder" means "left the group," which that lady just did.

"Bonita, Meg, and Trisha are all on the same ladder. They are Venusian types, some entering the type and some leaving it."

A fellow raised his hand.

"Should we be able to know whose ladder we are on?"

"You do not need to know," replied Robert. "Yet, if your level of being can see it, then you may tell. You are Yorgos's replacement and Yorgos replaced Miles. You should have someone soon come to manage you over your final interval to being on the Way."

Someone asked, "Do you see or know who will fall from the teaching?"

Robert replied, "I see who is in trouble."

As Robert started to list the persons who occupied the same ladder and were on the Way, I couldn't help but think of Deuteronomy, with its "And so and so begat so and so...."

I also couldn't help but wonder when my name would be mentioned.

"And then we can't forget..." Robert paused with a serious face.

Linda?

"Pepper, Beatrice, Banjo, and Falstaff."

Huh?

These were the dogs owned by students. Everyone laughed, except me.

Robert then changed the subject.

"C Influence designs personalities according to one's task. We are born and bred for our roles. Task is a better word than role."

John asked, "What is my task or role?"

"You are playing the task or role of John Graham," Robert answered. "From one angle, you are the Lincoln figure for the group. Some have conscious roles, but their level this time is not meant to crystallize. They are most probably stepping-stone roles to a higher role. Remember that moments of self-remembering are said never to be lost, and may be carried from one life to the next."

Returning to the subject of ladders, he explained groupings of students, some who were in the room and others who were away. He had yet to mention me, so after the meeting, I went over to Robert to ask him whose ladder I was on and what my role, or task, was.

"You are probably on Kerrie's ladder. You may be living in Carmel soon. Perhaps to take care of a house is your future task."

That's all he wrote. The three lines were like insights from a palm reader. It produced many 'I's inside of me that wanted to question him further. But that was not possible. He looked past me to the next person standing there, wanting to know the same thing.

When I returned to my journal that evening, I wrote these three sentences down to record them and contemplate them. I could understand and accept the first two, as they were within the realm of possibility, but the third was a mystery. Where would this house be? How could I care for a house when I could barely take care of a tent?

The Linda who would have this future task is someone I wanted to meet one day. Maybe she rests deep inside me, like Sleeping Beauty, waiting for that right moment to awaken and assume the fullness of her fate. Robert seems to know her. Perhaps one day he will introduce her to me.

That was my last thought as the weight of this magical day came down upon my eyelids.

> *To make our way up to the upper air,*
> *this is our task, this is our labor.*
>
> Virgil

CHAPTER 100

Robert and Jim left early the next morning for Carmel, while other students who worked in life departed after the meeting for their homes to prepare for the work week ahead.

The magical energy had gone out of the Lodge. It wasn't a negative energy that circulated, but more a feeling of a boat adrift in the doldrums with neither a wind nor pilot to guide it.

After lunch, two male farm residents said they were going to town to buy some clothes and asked if I wanted to come.

"Where are you going?" I asked.

"There's an Army Surplus store in Marysville, and I need some new boots," one said. Looking down at my sneakers, he added, "You could use a pair of boots."

The store was on D Street in Marysville. I had never been in such a store before. It seemed to cater to outdoor and military men, with its camouflage fabric and masculine designs.

The guys thumbed through flannel shirts and jeans. I looked for women's clothes and was told that all clothes were unisex. I tried a shirt on and looked at myself in the mirror. Immediately I removed it. Who is THAT? Not the future Linda I had in mind.

The boots the store carried were too large for my feet. I tried the smallest size they had, with the thought that extra socks would fill the space; but when I tried to walk around, they felt like they were made of cement. Plus, they were sixteen dollars, which was a great deal of money for me. I had seven dollars in my pocket. Instead, I bought a pack of white cotton tube socks for a dollar. It didn't exactly go with my granny dresses and sneakers, but they were long and would keep my feet and calves warm.

On the way back to the farm, I asked them if they knew anyone who was going to Vacaville for the meeting on Tuesday.

"We're both going," said one of them. "You can come with us if you like, but we're leaving around five." It takes approximately two hours to drive to Vacaville and the meeting was to begin this week at seven-thirty. That meant I would arrive just in time for the meeting and would return to Via Del Sol immediately afterwards, without much interaction with students.

"Okay," I said.

I scouted around the next morning to see if anyone else was going, but the ride offered to me at the store was the best deal in town, because it was the only deal.

The ride to Vacaville was quiet. Conversation was not the strong suit of these two moving types. I spent time smoking a borrowed cigarette or two and looking out the window at the gray skies of December.

As we reached the Vacaville off-ramp, the student driving suddenly said, "I'm hungry. Let's stop in the Coffee Tree."

This detour was totally unexpected. These fellows were working on the side in Oregon House hauling wood for local residents. I knew they had cash to spend. I now had six dollars and it was already 6:45. The pressure to sit, be served during the busy dinner hour, and arrive at the meeting on time was stressing me out.

I approached the woman at the desk taking reservations and explained we needed to eat quickly.

"There's space at the counter. Just go right in," was her reply, so we were allowed to enter ahead of those families waiting for a booth.

The place was full. I looked around and sure enough, there was Robert sitting in a big red booth with Jim and Rosemary, Clare, and Mary C. I was surprised to see him at this hour. I wanted him to call out to me, "Hey Linda! Why don't you join us? My treat." That of course did not happen.

I positioned myself in a seat that would give the optimum view of the teacher. I tried not to stare, but would glance at him occasionally to see if they were still there. I ordered a basic burger and fries and a Coke for three dollars. That left me with four.

It was now seven. Robert and the group were still dining. Then our burgers came. I dressed my burger with mayonnaise, saving the ketchup for the fries. I sipped the Coke, which was sparkling and sweet, and took a bite of burger and two crispy, salty hot fries slathered in ketchup. I had been truly hungry, and it was wonderful to taste the grilled meat after so many vegetarian dishes. I repeated this several times.

Robert!

I looked over and the booth was empty.

My watch said 7:20. I had still to eat half my burger. There was no way we would make it in time.

* * * *

Mac's driveway was full with cars when we arrived, so we had to park straddling the main street pavement and grass. In the dark I followed the guys up the stone steps and through the front door.

The meeting had begun, but with small groups. There were four circles of eight or so students each. The leaders were Miles, Meg, Mac, and Yorgos. Miles shot a look at me as I entered. Meg glanced over with an "I'm not surprised" expression on her face. Mac was speaking and didn't see me. Yorgos's summer sky blue eyes met mine, and a gentle smile spread on his face.

I pulled out a folded chair from the corner and selected Yorgos's group. Students made room for me and I sat struggling to listen.

"Welcome," said Yorgos.

It was difficult to focus. I felt horrible that I was late, and the 'I's inside my head were brutal. Yorgos's forgiving energy helped to neutralize my negative 'I's. He was such a blessing. He's my friend, I thought. He's my brother.

At 8:15, Donald stood up to signal that this phase of the meeting was over. We each took our chairs and placed them in rows for the next phase with Robert. As we went to take refreshments, Robert was in the kitchen talking with Rosemary and Mary C. It seemed a serious discussion.

I hid behind a salami and cheese hors d'oeuvre. I wasn't hungry after the big burger, but I pretended to be so nobody would question my tardiness.

Just then, I felt a tap on my shoulder.

"Robert wants to talk with you," said Jim.

Oh no.

As I stood there waiting for him to finish writing his message to me, the many 'I's raced through my head: I am going to be punished for arriving late; he saw me staring at him at the Coffee Tree; he will ask me to leave the school; he doesn't like my tube socks.

The message read, "Mary is buying a new car and will give you her old one."

I stared at the paper in disbelief. The many 'I's departed. I looked up at Robert, Mary, and Rose. The ladies were not elated. Robert wrote a second note. It read, "Rosemary will help coordinate the transfer."

With that, Robert proceeded to the main room to lead the meeting. We followed. I sat as close to the front as I could in order to be present to Robert.

No more hiding in shame. I could not believe what had just happened to me. He was giving me an opportunity not to be late to a meeting again. The subjects of the meetings paled compared to the state I was in. It was wonderful just to be there.

It does not matter whether you are early in your life or late; draw close to presence and you will become better.

Bahauddin

CHAPTER 101

I did not return to Via Del Sol that Tuesday night. I would be staying the rest of the week in Vacaville to arrange for the transfer of the vehicle. This entailed registering it with the Department of Motor Vehicles. I had never owned a car before, so this process was completely new to me. Having Rosemary there to help was wonderful.

As I entered the kitchen the next morning, Rose came out of her bedroom in her bathrobe and said she had just spoken with Mary C. The new car would not be available until Monday. She would meet us for the exchange on Tuesday morning at the DMV in Concord.

I would miss the Saturday farm meeting, I thought. But to have a car would be wonderful. I imagined the kind it would be. I hoped it would be a four-door sedan so I could take friends with me. Rosemary said she didn't know and that I had to wait. She didn't share my joy, and I think it was because she had to do a great deal of work to make it happen.

The week went by fast. I did not have as many chores as I had at the farm, and so I was able to enjoy the company of Rose and her daughters.

Thursday morning, the sisters took me to a local fabric store that was having a sale, and we found a happy cotton cloth with blue flowers against a white background. It was 19 cents a yard. I could afford that. The sisters agreed it would make a nice dress for me since it matched my blue eyes.

"Let's look at patterns," the younger one suggested.

We found a simple dress pattern that only required elastic on the short sleeves, neckline and high waist. I could make this, I thought.

We returned home with the pattern and fabric. Once the sewing machine was set up, the younger seamstress brought out her shears to help me cut out the cloth pieces. The dress was made within two hours. It was nice to have something new to wear.

THE DIVINE BEGINNING

* * * *

Saturday afternoon, the elder sister decided the three of us should take the horses out for a ride. We saddled up. I rode Billy, that devilish quarter horse that almost bucked me. To be sure Billy behaved, the elder decided to take the lead on her thoroughbred, while the younger on her palomino pony pulled up the rear. Although Billy was striding in the middle, his ears continued to point backwards toward me, a sign he was not relaxed with his rider nor happy he was not dominating the situation.

The rhythmic percussive sound of the hooves on the pavement filled me with joy. This was the music of my childhood with the early television Westerns' theme songs. We proceeded along the narrow shoulder of Pleasant Valley Road. It was fortunate there was little traffic on the weekend. Also, not many people were out because the temperature was near freezing.

The elder sister crossed the road to turn on Gates Canyon. She clearly was familiar with the area. I wondered if we were heading toward a meadow where we could trot the horses a bit. The road she chose became dense with foliage as it paralleled Alamo Creek.

"Will we be able to trot a little?" I asked her.

"Probably not," she said.

I sat back in my saddle. The curiosity about where we were going, what we would see, what we could do was beginning to pull me away from just enjoying the movement of the horse's muscles and spine beneath me.

Billy was also a bit anxious to move. Several times he would try to begin a trot and pass her. He didn't like being constrained. It was an odd thing to experience: this horse and I were sharing the same impatience.

"Do you think animals experience the queen of hearts?" I asked my riding companions.

"That's interesting," said the elder. "I don't know."

"They seem to have emotional centers," the younger added, telling me how her little pony would know when she was upset or sad.

"Well, they definitely have body types," I said with confidence. "They remind me of people I know." I didn't elaborate on my observation that the horses they were riding were perfectly matched to their types. Billy, on the other hand, was not a Venusian like me.

"Remember that book by Berman on the endocrine system?" I asked. They did not respond, but I continued anyway. "It would stand to reason that if animals have glands like we do, they would be subject to planetary influences, and hence have a body type."

It felt good to articulate work knowledge to them in this manner, as I enjoyed sharing what I was learning with others. When I finished my statements, however, I realized my face was becoming numb from the cold temperature. My lips had difficulty forming the last six words.

As we continued along the path, I could not feel the reins in my hands. Although I was wearing gloves, my fingers were numb.

"I'm feeling cold. Are you?"

The girls said no.

Now my thigh muscles were becoming numb through my pants. How did the cowboys do it?

I was becoming concerned. What if Billy bolts?

"Um, I hate to say this, but I can't feel the reins, and my thigh muscles are losing their grip on the saddle."

Hearing this, they both agreed we should go back.

The elder was the active type, and I could see she loved her riding. How she managed to not feel the cold was a mystery to me. She stoically turned her thoroughbred around and we returned to the house.

Rosemary had prepared a pot of coffee and had placed store bought cookies on a plate for us to enjoy. We sat around the table, talking about the elder daughter's new apartment in San Francisco. She was excited about beginning her life there. The younger sister had now moved in with her boyfriend in Vacaville.

As I listened to these young ladies who were younger than I, it suddenly occurred to me that I was the only one living with their mom. I still wasn't on my own; I had gone from one parental home to another. I felt like an older hatchling that hadn't quite broken out of the egg and had to watch the younger fledglings take flight first. A sinking feeling hit me. I had left LA thinking I would soar like an eagle, and less than a year later I'm still flapping my wings, unable to leave the ground.

My life is stalled, I thought, puffing on a cigarette. Maybe this car will jump-start it.

* * * *

We four went shopping on Sunday at the Sun Valley Mall. I passed the Tinder Box where Miles used to work, and stopped to look in the window.

"You don't smoke pipes. Come on," urged Rosemary. She had no patience with my incessant longings.

I watched as both girls were finding accessories for their newly purchased clothes. Their fashion sense naturally evolved from their mother's good taste. Unlike these girls, my mother never took me shopping. She once confided in me that when she and Dad were first married, she went shopping for the groceries one day. When she returned home, Dad yelled at her for being reckless with spending, and that he was going to do the shopping from then on. Mom was a peacemaker. She acquiesced, and allowed him to rob her of a key role in their marriage.

This excursion was an eye-opener for me. I was studying the girls closely, trying to learn how to match patterns and colors and items, like scarves and jewelry, and shoes and purses. They asked if I was going to buy something, and I politely said I hadn't found anything particular that I liked.

I lied. There in a display case was a pair of the most beautiful, elegant brown leather shoes I had ever seen. I reached out my hand and caressed the softness of the calfskin. The curvature of the shoe and delicate stitching revealed the craftsmanship.

I immediately put it down and turned away. Something held me back, and it wasn't the fact I had no money to spend. The cause of the resistance I felt inside was the fact that I had never been given permission to spend any money on myself for beautiful things. They were for others, not for me. This was my programming, and I knew it. It was not a humble stance; it was a deeply rooted fear.

But something new was growing inside of me, something that could battle these lifelong feelings of inadequacy. I was learning to value myself.

> *Are not two sparrows sold for a cent? And yet not one of them will fall to the ground apart from God your Father. But the very hairs of your head are all numbered. So do not fear; you are more valuable than many sparrows.*
>
> Jesus

CHAPTER 102

After breakfast Monday morning, Rosemary and I departed for Concord.

"I used to live in Benicia," Rose mentioned casually as we drove across the Benicia-Martinez bridge on Highway 680.

As we were approaching Martinez, I asked Rosemary what Mary C. did for a living.

"She's a city planner. Her family is wealthy. They even have a street in Concord named after them."

This accounts for her generosity, I thought. She probably doesn't need another car and can easily give it away.

When we pulled into the Concord DMV, Mary saw us and exited her car. After greeting each other with a quick hug, I noticed a man was behind the wheel. I thought, why is a man driving my new car? Then I realized that was her new car and that she had parked her old car in another space.

Mary led the way to this white Buick Wildcat four-door sedan. She appeared nervous as she handed me the keys.

"Please take good care of this car. It takes premium gasoline." She continued to detail the maintenance, but I was overwhelmed by the moment and her words went right by me. Something about tune-ups, wheel sizes, type of oil. I smiled and tried to be present to her. I could see this car was precious to her and she didn't trust me.

She handed me the title of ownership ("pink slip") and I signed my name. We thanked her and she left quickly with the man in her new car. He was never introduced to us.

After we registered the car inside the office, I hopped into the Buick for the first time and could not believe how immaculate it was. It had red pleated upholstery and chrome not only on the dashboard, but also on the seat edges. It was an automatic transmission. The steering wheel diameter was large, yet the wheel itself delicate and narrow so that a female's hands could easily grasp it. No wonder Mary liked this car; it was super cool!

Once Rosemary verified I could start the car, she instructed me to follow her home.

"Here's 35 cents for the toll. I don't want to have to wait for you on the highway," she said firmly.

Heading toward Fairfield I could feel the power in this new car of mine. It must have a V8 engine, I thought. Wow! I was cruisin'.

When we arrived back at Rosemary's home, we learned that there would not be a meeting that night in Vacaville. It was Christmas week and Robert apparently was staying in Carmel. We had yet to hear about a group Christmas celebration. I guess this was understandable since many students still had strong life family commitments during the holidays.

Whether Robert would return to Via Del Sol for Christmas Day, which was Saturday, was anyone's guess. Do I stay in Vacaville or go up to the farm? The pleasure of driving decided it for me: early Wednesday morning I headed up the highway to Via Del Sol.

With both hands on the sleek wheel, I reminisced about the past year that began with the classic American Christmas in San Diego. This year was anything but traditional. It was like an emotional black hole. I could not rely on my parents for help. I'm without a job or relationship. This car showed me that the gods somehow provide what we need and I was grateful to them for this. I wondered what new roads lay ahead for me.

Remember, you have been given a gift superior to everything else.
Epictetus

CHAPTER 103

As I drove up the road to the Lodge, I carefully parked the car. It was lunch time and I spoke liberally about my new good fortune. Kerrie was thrilled for me and accompanied me to see it.

"Let's go to Grass Valley," she said, "and shop for dresses."

Although I had just made a new dress, it was Christmas, after all, and I would like to have something special for New Year's Eve to wear. Plus, I had just received my Marysville High substitute teaching check. Everything was coming together. It must be the magic of the Wildcat, I thought.

Once we arrived in Grass Valley, we walked the Christmas-lit streets, bopping into store after store. We hadn't quite found the dress shop we liked, so we drove to nearby Nevada City. It was Wednesday afternoon, and the rush of shoppers was evident. One storefront displayed Victorian-style dresses, with lace around the high neckline and long skirt lengths and sleeves.

"Oh, this is Laura Ashley," said Kerrie. "Let's go inside."

I hadn't heard of Laura Ashley. Kerrie explained she was a hot designer. What? Kerrie knows fashion?

"What's your size?" she asked.

I told her I had no idea.

She looked at me and said, "Here, try this on."

I looked at the label and it was not Laura Ashley, so I pointed it out to her.

"It's in the style of Laura Ashley. These prices are more reasonable."

I wasn't interested in the high neckline and earthy, rustic colors with lace trim. It reminded me too much of my flannel nightgown. But that didn't matter. I was quickly becoming Kerrie's mannequin, as she thumbed through the racks.

Because my size was big, my options were small. Just as I was giving up, my sight fell upon a long dress with a cream background and delicate blue flowers. Without thought, my hand reached out to it, as if to caress a lost lover.

I held it up and noticed it had a plunging v-neckline.

"I want to try this on," I said to Kerrie.

We went into the dressing room. Although it zipped up, the neckline revealed the front of my substantial bra.

"Hmm," said Kerrie. "Let's try it without the bra."

"I need my bra," I insisted. Kerrie was flat-chested. My breasts were weighty, and I knew this would not work. To please her, however, I submitted. The whole impression changed. Rather than Cinderella, I looked like the Fairy Godmother.

"Well, maybe we can sew up the neckline," she offered.

I pointed out there was not enough material to close the gap. I was so saddened by this, but my longing for the dress was strong.

"If you love it, you should buy it," Kerrie said.

She gave me permission. So I bought it. It cost half of my paycheck.

When we returned to the farm, I pulled out the dress to show people. I didn't try it on, knowing full well that it did not actually suit my figure. That Wednesday night I looked at it often, and the sunny fabric with beautiful blue flowers was the last image in my head before I drifted off to sleep.

* * * *

The dreariness of the late December skies weighed on us the next morning. We each moved slower and chatted more as we stood in front of the small fireplace of the Lodge. The topics usually began with the whereabouts of Robert, what students were doing, and whether or not we would celebrate Christmas here at Via Del Sol. In between, we would do our chores: milking cows; cooking meals; eating and then cleaning up; running the washer and dryer; and for me, reading work books. I wanted to finish the Berman book on glands before the weekend.

The possession of the Wildcat also attracted interest in taking a trip to Carmel. It was an additional topic of conversation. I had never been there before, and the thought of driving that distance by myself elicited in me a mixture of curiosity, excitement, fear, and resistance. I did not encourage this topic, and hoped my friends would not bring it up again.

Friday was Christmas Eve. Nothing had been said about celebrations, and for me, being Jewish, it was not such a big deal.

Klair, on the other hand, was sensitive to the needs of the children. She made sure a symbol of Christmas would be properly displayed. Midafternoon, she hauled in a six-foot tree by herself and placed it in the main room, equidistant from the fireplace and wood burning stove. It was a dark area of the room. I watched her unpack a large box filled with decorations. I had never decorated a Christmas tree before, but was eager to try my hand.

Approaching Klair to ask if she needed help, she said no. And added, "Don't touch anything." I persisted and asked if I could hang one ornament. She was adamant. This was her project. I watched how she stood before the tree and studied the way the limbs were spread. She cut some back so that the tree was symmetrical. Oh! That's why they call it trimming the Christmas tree. You actually do cut off the branches.

I stood there watching her for almost an hour. The way she strung the lights amazed me. She weaved each strand through branches and around the main trunk. She studied where to hang each ornament, as if she were a Leonardo or Rembrandt applying a stroke of color to their canvas. I never knew that was the method; I thought decorating a tree was done quickly and haphazardly. Her daughter, who had a strong artistic sense and moving center, was the only person she would allow to help her. She followed her mother's instructions and attached crimson velvet bows to the deep green limbs.

That day, the sense of being abandoned by the teacher was circulating within us. This unspoken gloomy state mirrored the overcast skies. By dinner time, the tree was fully decorated, although its beauty was barely visible since it stood in the darkest part of the room. The plan was to turn on the lights of the tree with everyone surrounding it after we ate our dinner.

We numbered no more than 25 people, including the children. Tall Jane read a Biblical passage describing the birth of Jesus. When she finished, Klair plugged in the lights and the tree magically came to life. A gasp of joy issued from each of us. Those many small bulbs when glowing in unison evoked conscious light within us out of the darkness of our previous state.

It was an intimate, quiet Christmas Eve that could have been treated like an ordinary day. The Lincoln Lodge, a rough-hewn log cabin, could easily have been the inn at Bethlehem, and Lord knows, we certainly had the cow and the donkey. In this modest place, the teacher may have been absent, but the gods did not forget us. They made a simple moment miraculous.

God, in his kindness to man, set over us a superior race of spirits who took charge of us with no less ease to themselves than convenience to us.

Plato

CHAPTER 104

On Christmas Day, Robert arrived late afternoon. He was immediately drawn to Klair's tree. The two stood together for some time as he studied various ornaments and asked her about their history.

I had a chance to speak with Jim about Robert's whereabouts, and he explained something astounding to me. Robert had asked Mary C. to fund a small airplane for him. They were looking at planes in Monterey.

"Who's going to pilot it?" I asked him.

He chuckled and replied, "I am. I'm taking pilot lessons."

He explained further that Robert put him on a fast track for this so he could begin to fly in six weeks.

"Ah, it's a crash course," I said, not realizing at first what I had said.

"I hope not!" was his immediate reply. We both laughed.

Robert then called to Jim, who immediately came. He was showing him the ornaments and had Klair explain each one. This is how it seemed. What it was instead was Robert pulling Jim away from me. He looked at us when we laughed. It was a photograph from the teacher, and it produced a conscious moment within me. When Jim walked away, my third state left with him and was replaced with feelings of inadequacy, judgment, and anger.

But something astute in me realized Robert was right there to catch that moment of sleep, which was his job. Robert was like a physician whose calling was to heal the sick. The illness is sleep. I would watch students immediately act noble whenever Robert suddenly entered the room. They stopped talking and would look away or down, as if they were dividing their attention. I wanted to be cured, so if I was unconsciously laughing or talking before he entered the room, I would continue this behavior when he appeared. Why? I figured, why hide your illness from your doctor if you want to be healed?

Anyway, that was my understanding. I could see how others thought I wanted his attention. I couldn't control myself without his help; this I knew for sure, and each photograph he gave me was a tool to help me in my struggles.

We gather our crumbs of consciousness as best we can.

* * * *

Sunday morning, we assembled in the Lodge main room for the Christmas meeting. The children had been sequestered upstairs. We could hear loud talking and laughter from them, and Robert had requested of the parents monitoring them to try to keep the noise down. Some kids had received gifts that included games, which they were playing. It was a challenging request.

During the good householder part of the meeting, Robert offered some practical items of his own, which was highly unusual.

"We will be selling the cows. Does this make the milkers happy?"

Nadia, who frequently complained about the octave, blurted out, "Why?"

"Some milkers did not like them. They cost money, and also limit mobility."

I could see Nadia was not happy about this either.

Robert then added, "One thing you may find is another negative emotion may pop up to fill its place."

He changed the subject.

"Last year, the Christmas donation was $7. This year I would like the same."

He asked us to please give our money to the Architect, because the money will be used to build a deck for the house.

"Do not give it to Nadia," he added, "as it is separate from our checking account."

This comment revealed to me how much Robert understood about the funds and their purposes.

He followed this money request with a joyful announcement.

"We will celebrate New Year's Eve at Rosemary's home on Friday night. This is also a celebration of our second year. Please try to attend."

I was so relieved that we would all be together. It was also incredible to think next weekend will be 1972. What a long, amazing year it has been. I wonder what the next year will bring? Where will I be? Carmel? Vacaville with a job? The farm? Will I find my soul mate? Is he waiting for…

The first question of the meeting came from Short Jane.

"What subjects should we teach the children here?"

"Useful subjects, like reading and the arts," replied Robert. "Blake was self-educated. His parents kept him out of public school. Shakespeare also. Perhaps Helga can teach the children."

I looked over at Helga and she appeared a bit surprised, but had a gentle, willing smile on her face.

Another hand rose. The student stood and asked whether the ten commandments were meant for Moses's disciples or life.

"Both for esoteric purposes and life. Remember we are born and created without our wishing it. We may be food for another level. It's not a pleasant idea, but it may be true. Higher centers are the only thing on the planet that is not eaten."

The students squirmed noticeably in the room. Robert took the subject in a different direction.

"To my knowledge, Miles and Yorgos have conscious roles. It is the highest hope students have. Each person is here to self-remember, and help each other if sleep sets in. Common sense says to make the most of this role of Bonita, or Linda, or Jim, etc. Information does not come unless your being is ready for it."

I raised my hand and was called upon.

"Does C Influence speak to you on different levels, and do some things seem clearer than others?"

Robert replied, "Most everything is generally clear, and I do my best to accept the puddles. I do not question C Influence."

A student stood up to share an experience he had at a séance where a table levitated.

Robert said it was a C Influence shock and that clairvoyants are not conscious but a tool of Influence C.

"Any other questions on how to save our souls in the next five minutes?"

A gentle laugh rippled through the room.

"Okay then," said Robert, "let's have a hug."

As we stood to hug one another, the Sunday noon sun revealed itself from behind a gray cloud and shone its rays within the little cabin for the first time in several days. The warm embraces, which mirrored the caress of the light, brought us back to earth, to this precious moment in time, to be a part of this family, this god-driven fellowship of friends.

❖

Someone who has the gods as friends would possess the best art of divination in his home.

Euripides

CHAPTER 105

Robert left after the Sunday meeting for Carmel. He was constantly on the move and expanding not only his horizons, but the school's as well.

Like a homing pigeon, I drove back to Vacaville on Tuesday morning. A pattern had set in. Staying at the farm depressed me in some way. The absence of Robert left a void in energy, and my own internal state could not trigger self-remembering. But these were 'I's. Living alone in Vacaville was just as bad. Meetings with Robert were like oxygen. The higher functions could breathe.

Rosemary was not at home when I arrived on Tuesday. I began the cleaning after eating lunch, and soon she arrived with a bouquet of flowers. She asked me to arrange it for the refreshments table. This raised my state. In addition, I wore my newly made dress for the meeting because it made me feel feminine and attractive. This also heightened my energy level. You never know who you're going to meet.

The lineup for the meeting up front was Mac, Jan, Robert, Jim, and Rosemary. Mac began with good householder items for the upcoming New Year's Eve party on Friday. After the preparation and cleanup assignments, Robert first wrote something on his pad to add to the list, and then passed the piece of paper to Mac to read.

"Robert would like the ladies to prepare their favorite cheesecake recipes. We will have a little contest."

A giggle circulated in the room.

The full moon was scheduled for New Year's Eve. This should be a fun evening, I thought.

Once Mac finished reading from Robert's notes, the teacher began the meeting.

"A recent edition of *Esquire* magazine had an article about Gertrude Stein. On her deathbed, she asked, 'What is the answer?' When no answer came, she laughed and said, 'In that case, what is the question?' Then, she died.

"To be or not to be — that is the question. All ideas revolve around one idea in this and in all systems: self-remembering. It is a state of To Be. There are many levels of self-remembering; it is not just one level or angle of thought. Different 'I's will think self-remembering is different angles, and they are all correct. The formatory center tries to make it one definition or one angle."

A new student from the Bay Area raised his hand.

"How can I maintain Observing 'I' when it can be pushed aside by the many 'I's?"

"That 'I' has to be stronger than the other 'I's," replied Robert. With that small twinkle in his eye and a straight face, he added. "I suggest eating Wheaties, the Breakfast of Champions."

Rose and I chortled. No one else did.

Robert continued, "It will become stronger and other Work 'I's will gather around it and form an Observing 'I.' An Observing 'I' is a single 'I' or a group of 'I's that observes other 'I's that are mechanical. Later they become Deputy Steward, later again Steward, and later the Self arrives. This is possible. Not probable, but possible."

He paused as he looked around the room at us.

"Deputy Steward is in a hot battle. Its advantage is it is not mechanical. It can only come about through each person's own effort to self-remember."

Mary from Vacaville raised her hand.

"What is the Work 'I' that does not speak but sees?"

"It is the child Jesus spoke of," replied Robert. " 'Lest ye be as a little child ye shall not enter the Kingdom of Heaven.' So when muteness is watching from you, it is all you have been working for — and in reality, all you have."

Another question.

"Do changes in consciousness cause changes in the physical brain?"

Robert nodded yes. "A chemical change does take place in self-remembering, and the latent pineal gland is activated. It is healthy in every person in the room."

Suddenly the kitchen phone started to ring.

"Did anyone have an 'I' that said 'telephone' or anything about it?"

Several of us raised our hands.

"That is mechanical," Robert explained. "The 'I' is produced automatically. Be Present is a good Work 'I' to handle that."

"It can be photographed that there are chains of 'I's, like on a telephone party line, that just watches the process," offered Miles.

Miles's angle confused me. I didn't know that a chain of 'I's can watch the process.

"If it is an 'I' that is watching the other 'I's," added Robert, "then it is part of Observing 'I.' Remember, Observing 'I' can be a single 'I' or a group of 'I's. Sometimes the Work 'I,' Be Present, has to be repeated several times to capture wandering attention."

"Does a Work 'I' become silent?" asked a student from the Bay Area. "There was no need here to say, Be Present."

Robert answered, "Your being is such you are not distracted, and so it does not need that Work 'I' anymore in that situation."

A long pause came as Robert looked up at the ceiling. This usually indicated there would be a change of subject.

"We will have open meetings in Carmel January 3, 6 and 10," said Robert, turning to Mac who nodded in agreement. "We will also have open meetings in Vacaville February 3, 7 and 10. Plan now and work with as many qualified people as you can.

"This is something I do not wish to bring up, but since there are many new students, it is necessary. If you leave this teaching, please do not return unless you have a minimum of $500, which you would give to Nadia before we speak. It is one way a teaching protects itself from 'casual' traffic."

A hand went up, "What about people who have left the teaching already. What do we do?"

"Please try to avoid the people," was Robert's response. "Are you starting to notice that you literally have no identity? People have become an act, a role. It is predictable; they cannot surprise you. They are like fruit that has fallen to the ground."

"What about people who are earnestly searching for something, but do not see the value of this teaching?"

Robert replied, "They cannot hear. They do not have eyes — Work 'I's — to see, or ears to hear. The Bible says, 'The harvest is great, but the laborers are few.' I will tell you this, but you probably will not accept it. Humanity may be food for the moon and the planets."

"How does the moon eat us?" asked a student.

"I'm not sure...there may be an invisible umbilical cord that eats the magnetic field that departs from a fleshy being when it meets death. When I cannot understand something, I simply nod, yes. I know it does not come from me. It is not my system or idea of anything. It comes from C Influence or higher mind on the planet. Man wants the truth as *he* sees it. I have not verified man is eaten by the moon; I am simply passing on what the system says about it."

Robert stood up, which signaled the meeting was over. Other topics along the same lines were discussed that I'm not mentioning. My head was spinning from the speed of changes and the amount of new information. Since so many ideas were unverifiable and doors were opening in so many places, it was all I could do to hold on, and as Robert advised, simply nod, yes.

❖

You road I enter upon and look around,
I believe you are not all that is here,
I believe that much unseen is also here.
Here the profound lesson of reception, nor preference nor denial.
                                                                          Walt Whitman

CHAPTER 106

In an octave, the *si-do* interval is like a river just before it enters the ocean; it becomes increasingly slow and narrow as it tries to overcome mountainous obstacles and often dense terrain. There's the sense that the new octave is about to come — right within reach — with its high waves; its saltiness in contrast to the sweet taste of fresh melted snowfall; and, of course, the tidal surges and retreats. But that river has to be patient and let nature take its course, as it finds that perfect opening that leads to the next phase of its existence. That's the difficulty. When the opening is found, it flows freely and is now consumed by what once was considered its future.

The last Wednesday and Thursday of the year 1971 flowed into one another naturally and quickly disappeared. During the past year, I had studied the law of octaves as it was occurring both within me and without me. The slowness of the pace these past couple of months indicated to me I was in a *si-do* interval. The *si-do* is sluggish with heavier hydrogens. The *do* contains energetic, lighter hydrogens. This pressure I was feeling indicated something new was about to enter in a rush. Was I ready for it?

Intellectual analysis always kept my emotions at bay. But what good is logic against fear of the unknown? The part in me that wants so desperately to know my future and have it run smoothly toward happily-ever-after is in my DNA, that is, intricately fixed within the mechanics of Linda Kaplan. Having a school with separate groups — the farm group, the Vacaville group, the Carmel group, and maybe even a Lake Tahoe group — confuses me. I want us to be one school, one family.

So I tried to focus on the Friday night party and not think about the open meetings in Carmel on Monday.

Early Friday morning what was closest at hand was my dust cloth. I told Rose I would focus on making sure every knick-knack would be cleaned and polished. That helped me to control my fear. She was in the kitchen with the girls planning to make the soon-to-be-announced winner of the Robert Burton Cheesecake Contest. They decided to use the New York cheesecake recipe from *The Joy of Cooking*, the preeminent cookbook of American housewives. It was an elaborate process that required it to be chilled for at least eight hours after baking, and the ladies were following the instructions to the letter. The smells coming from the oven were warm and sweet, which soothed my anxiety.

Robert wanted us to gather around 8 p.m. Trisha came over around five to arrange the flowers she brought. They were festive and fragrant. Don and Doris delivered the champagne glasses shortly thereafter. He suggested I rinse them and wipe each one clean before arranging them on the table. I couldn't figure out how to do it because these flutes, as these glasses were called, were so narrow. Don quickly demonstrated, by picking up the linen towel and twisting it so the cloth easily fit inside and could be moved around to absorb the water droplets. It was always a joy to learn something new.

At six I was scheduled to use the shower. Rose's elder daughter was staying overnight, so she and I would be sharing the bedroom. I had planned to wear my Nevada City dress. When I tried the dress on, she was shocked to see my bra showing, and we tried to conceal the plunge by using a scarf she had. The color and the patterns were not right.

Kerrie had arrived and she entered the bedroom to change as well. She told me to take my bra off, so I did. Rose's daughter clearly didn't agree, so a discussion ensued between them.

"You are so feminine and beautiful, don't worry about it," she said. The compliment was soothing, and for a moment I believed her, when suddenly someone knocked on the door. I went to open it, and there was John Graham. He looked at my face, and then at my large breasts loosely encased and exposed in the bodice of the dress. He shrieked. His hands flew up to cover his eyes, and with a pivot, he exited.

After closing the door, I, too, made an about-face and quickly unzipped my dress.

"I'm wearing my usual granny dress with shawl," I announced.

"But Linda, this was your special dress!" Kerrie said pleadingly.

"It still is a special dress," I replied, disappointed. "But it's something for me to look at, not wear."

This was such a common experience for me in my life, and it always left me painfully sad. Wanting to look like a beautiful young woman, and then having to contend with this matronly body.

After dressing, I went directly from the bedroom to the kitchen. The women were bringing in their cheesecakes and the refrigerator was becoming full. This was something Rosemary had not anticipated. She and the ladies spent time rearranging the items to accommodate their desserts.

Mac arrived with his girlfriend. Annabella would come shortly afterwards. Meg was there, too, with Harold. Richard and Alice arrived with their children, who went directly to the refreshment tables. Alice brought her famous cheesecake. All the ladies were waiting for her presentation, since she was considered a special cook.

Robert had yet to appear with Jim. Where he and Jim were staying was unknown to me. I tried to take a head count to discover who was missing, and it was Anna Gold. Perhaps he was staying with her in Berkeley. I imagined the traffic must be horrible, given that it was New Year's Eve. Maybe that was why he was delayed.

It was almost nine o'clock and we were becoming concerned about Robert. Anna showed up and we asked her if he had stayed in Berkeley, to which she responded, No. We learned Sheila was still in Carmel and would not be coming.

Since the fridge was full, some of the cheesecakes were laid out on the special table in the kitchen reserved for the contest. I was told it would be a blind tasting, so no names were attached to them.

At ten o'clock, the last cheesecake arrived with Clare. Her dessert was a simple circle of whiteness about an inch and a half high, with the mandatory graham cracker crust. It was almost lost among the larger, elaborate versions displayed on the table.

The house was packed with students. I maneuvered into the living room to find a chair in the corner. My plan was to wait out the next two hours until midnight. Everyone there was in all manner of garb: some of the farm group appeared in jeans; the men in the Vacaville and Bay Area groups wore suits and ties, and the ladies wore dresses with appropriate jewelry and scarves. I enjoyed how beautiful they looked. It reminded me of my senior prom in high school. Yes, I attended it, but not in a gown or with a boy. I was the one who volunteered to be the coat check girl.

A half hour passed and suddenly someone came in to say Robert had arrived. I stood up to see him, imagining he would be more formally dressed, like the Bay Area group. As I walked into the kitchen, I couldn't find him in the throng.

"Where's Robert?" I asked Tall Jane, thinking she may have a better perspective due to her height.

"In the corner there, talking to Annabella."

I looked and saw the back of a tall man with black hair wearing a pure white shirt with bright red fabric sewn across the shoulders and on the cuffs. Oh, my! It was a cowboy shirt.

He turned around with a shy look on his face to glance at the crowd of students. It indeed was Robert. His gaze immediately went down as he turned back to Annabella, who was thoroughly enjoying his exclusive attention. He looked like a big ten-year-old who went to his first dance with a girl that he had a crush on, and his mother dressed him.

Behind me I heard snickering, and turned to see Meg and Harold whispering to Alden. Marie and Anna and Rose as well commented about the odd apparel. It was a mystery why he chose this garment to wear, as it was not representative of any group: too fancy for the farm and too exotic for the city folk.

As Rosemary once noted about his wardrobe selections, he needed help. And so did I. There we both were, obviously not on the best dressed list of the evening. I felt sorry for him that he would be the object of ridicule, and wanted to go up to him and hug him long and hard, but his position in the room, and the energy circulating around him, prevented me from even approaching him. I tried not to stare.

Meanwhile, all of the cheesecakes were waiting on the table for Robert to pronounce the winner. Robert was handed a fork. He went down the line, looking at each and taking a small bite. He then pointed to the winner with his fork. He chose that simple white circle with the graham cracker crust.

"Clare!"

She was shocked, explaining it was nothing special, just a no-bake cheesecake. In other words, you make the crust and mix the filling ingredients, pour it into the pie pan and refrigerate it. Those who spent hours working on their masterpieces were upset. "Robert doesn't know cheesecake," was the common sentiment. The buzz of complaint lasted quite a while.

As midnight was quickly approaching, Mac went up to Robert with a book in his hand. Annabella's eyes beamed when he stood close to her, and I could feel the sex energy flow between them, like sticky honey. Robert handed a note to Mac, who nodded in agreement.

I was asked to help distribute the champagne glasses to one and all as we gathered in the living room for the New Year's Eve toast. Mac would be offering it, and Jim was checking his watch to let Robert know the time. With one minute to go, Robert nodded to Mac to begin.

"Robert wishes me to share this," he said. " 'Last New Year's Eve we celebrated our first year together. We were twenty-six students. This New Year's Eve we are eighty-two. Next year will bring more growth and more changes.' "

Putting the paper in his coat pocket, he lifted his glass and recited Whitman's poem, "I Dream'd in a Dream." We toasted one another, and the sound of glass on glass echoed in the room like church bells.

I stood as close to Robert as I could so that I could toast him. There was such love in my heart for this man, my teacher. His generosity and unrelenting support during this past year kept me afloat. When we looked into each other's eyes, I so wanted him to know what I felt. The clink of the glass lasted a second. It was quickly followed by outreached glasses from the students lined up behind me. That would have to do.

I turned around and there was Helga. We looked into one another's smiling eyes and saw the year in review. We chimed our glasses and warmly embraced. We had survived.

Now it was time to look for Miles. I went up to him and we toasted.

"You seem well," he said. I smiled and replied, almost boasting, "I AM well."

At that moment, Helga approached, and she and Miles smiled lovingly at one another. Out of nowhere, my heart pounded and this darkness tried to return. I had no control over the demon that wanted to ruin such a clean and beautiful exchange. Jealousy demanded attention. But not tonight, said a voice inside. Go away.

The new year of 1972, with all its hopes and mysteries, has now begun.

*

> *The vile, vicious demon mocks the true Self.*
> *The true Self's so gentle, what could it do?*
> *The gods lend their protection.*
> Journey to the West

THE DIVINE BEGINNING

CHAPTER 107

While we were restoring the house after midnight, Robert sent a message to us all that we would have a meeting at the farm on Saturday evening. He and Jim had left around 12:45 a.m., as did many other students, leaving the cleanup to a few of us. I retired at three in the morning, quietly entering the shared bedroom.

I awoke at nine and took a quick shower. When I was done, Rosemary was in her bathrobe making coffee in the kitchen. Her elder daughter came out in her pajamas. She joined in to make the toast, while I set the table for us and Rose quickly scrambled some eggs.

I was then surprised to see Anna emerge from the master bedroom. She apparently stayed over and shared Rosemary's bed. This enabled her to avoid driving back to Berkeley late at night.

"Good morning, Anna," I said, giving her a quick hug. I was delighted to see her.

She greeted me in the same way, and I put another place setting down for her.

The breakfast conversation centered around Robert's cowboy shirt. There were giggles all around. They also spoke about how Annabella was flirting with Robert, and how shameful it was. After we finished eating, Rosemary took her first puff from her cigarette and casually offered this statement.

"I'll be leaving for Carmel Sunday morning."

This surprised me, since she rarely shared her future whereabouts with me.

"What will you do in Carmel?" I asked.

"Robert is buying a Cessna airplane on Monday. Mary is putting up the money. He wants me to look over the agreement."

Anna let out a "WHAT?!"

Of course, I had heard about this briefly from Jim, but wanted to know her opinion.

"What's Robert going to do with an airplane?"

"It will save him travel time. It will only take 45 minutes to fly to Carmel and land in Vacaville. He can then fly to Lake Tahoe, and that takes about 40 minutes."

"But we don't have a group in Tahoe," I replied.

"That reminds me," said Rosemary. "Trisha has friends in Tahoe who might be interested in the school. She's going to give a prospective student meeting there. It would be good for you to go."

"Okay," I replied. "I'll talk with her."

Anna started to speak about Robert's money issues. He was beginning to spend too much on extravagant items, she said. It obviously distressed her, but I didn't know why.

After breakfast, we told Anna we would clean up since she had a longer drive back to Berkeley. Once she departed, Rosemary shared her story with me.

Anna was born in Russia and came from a distinguished musical family. Her father was the first flautist for the Russian Philharmonic, and she and her two sisters had formed a cello, violin, and piano trio that was world famous. She came to America and, against her father's wishes, left the trio to marry a jeweler who eventually ran off and left her with two young boys, a mortgage, and heavy debt. She gave piano lessons and rented rooms out to Berkeley students each fall to support herself and the boys.

"She also took them to Boy Scout retreats," said Rose's elder daughter, obviously impressed by Anna's self-sufficiency and motherly instincts.

"I can understand now why Anna is sensitive about money," I said. "It must have been quite a struggle."

"She has a chief feature of fear," added Rose quickly, by way of explanation.

I said nothing. I could understand Anna better now, with or without a fear feature. I don't have a chief feature of fear, but the thought of being left like that with kids and debt scared me. No wonder Robert loved her so much. She was a survivor.

As I drove to the farm, the thought of Anna resonated with me. She was a queen-of-hearts type and Robert liked to gently poke her in fun, much to the delight of us all, including Anna. But underneath was such a solid, remarkable, accomplished woman with the strength to do what simply needed to be done. Who knew?

The Jewish programming is strong. Anna also had to defy her father and leave a career behind for love. I recalled Chickie Bubbie, the four-foot eight-inch matriarch of our large family, refusing to go to my cousin's wedding because the young woman was marrying a goy, which was the first for our family. My uncle pleaded with his mother, until Bubbie finally consented to appear at the wedding reception. Everyone was delighted she agreed to this, since we all knew how rigid she was about adhering to her strict orthodox rules.

During the reception, I went up to Bubbie to hand her a plate of food while she sat in the corner of the room surveying the activities. It was there that she imparted this memorable edict to me.

"Linda, do you love me?" she began.

Looking down at her I said, "Of course I do."

"Well, if you love me," she instructed, measuring each word with a thick Yiddish accent, "you vill marry a Jewish man! Even though I am dead, and in my grave, I VILL KNOW! I VILL KNOW!"

This is what I have to contend with. It is so nice to learn my play has been played before.

* * * *

As I arrived at the Lodge, lunch was still being served. I took my plate and sat next to Trisha to find out more about this prospective student meeting in Tahoe.

"Oh, they're friends of mine from before the Fellowship. They study astrology and meditation, and I used to do yoga with some of them," she answered.

"Rosemary suggested I come along. Is that possible?" I asked.

"Well, I guess so. Mason and Marsha are coming, too. We're leaving tomorrow after lunch."

I learned from her also that the evening meeting would begin at five because Robert had plans to head out to Carmel afterwards. She was not too happy about this. It seemed to her that the farm was no longer a place of preference for him, whereas for her it was her home. These were not her words, but it was the gist of the matter.

* * * *

After good householder, which included information about the Carmel open meetings and the open meetings the following week in Vacaville, Robert began with this angle of thought.

"This is the beginning of a new octave, the year 1972."

I smiled immediately, because he was expressing my understanding as well. I felt relieved that we were on the same page.

He continued.

"It is many octaves, for the group as a whole as well as personally for each individual."

Robert asked if there were any questions. A long silence followed.

"Ouspensky and Gurdjieff used to rise and leave the room if there were no questions," said Robert. "We seldom have questions, but do well."

His comment did not trigger a response, so he continued.

"Every hair is counted. The true witness is mute. The Work 'I's are the seed it will grow out of."

He then changed the subject.

"Kerrie will teach the children at the children's house for income. She is tops in that area. She will speak to parents of children. It will be successful in this situation."

I was puzzled. I did not know Kerrie had this skill or training. I wondered what had happened to Helga teaching the children.

"Also, please hold your work in keeping the children's house clean. Train them and pick up after them as well. I have been picking up at the farm ever since July Fourth. And I never leave the bathroom empty-handed; I carry out two or three towels and put them in the bin for washing. For both men and women who are on duty there, keep looking for areas to clean. It should be like brushing your teeth."

Robert paused to see if anyone had a question or angle to offer. They did not so he continued.

"We will have two new exercises to strengthen self-remembering. First, make an effort to know all the names of everyone in the group. Try to be present when a new student gives you his or her name. Also, please do not use the word 'I' when ordering food in a restaurant. Usually we say 'I will have this or that.' This all seems simple, but halfway through your sandwich you will stop short and be surprised that you did not remember to avoid using 'I.' The first three times the students tried it with me, they forgot."

Another pause.

"This Tuesday is January fourth. We will have had the farm for six months already. Weeks turn into years, how quick they pass."

He was quoting Burt Bacharach's, "Do you know the way to San Jose?" I chuckled briefly, thinking weeks *appear* like years, how quick they pass.

Looking around the Lodge, he shared this observation. "This house is a little miracle. We had to pay for it with our labor. It is a strange example of receiving something for nothing."

I understood immediately. He was both referring to the usual example of wanting something for nothing, which is characteristic of the chief feature of tramp, and the fact that the Lodge was a nothing that we turned into a something.

"Sometimes C Influence scrapes not only the bottom of the barrel, but the sides, too."

I enjoyed Robert's insights like this. They were briefly stated, yet carried several meanings. It brought a lightness to the struggles we were experiencing. I looked around to see if others were as delighted and saw blank faces. It was odd to me.

A student raised his hand.

"How do you stop a chain of 'I's?"

"Chains of 'I's are one 'I' observing another 'I,' observing another 'I,' etc. It can be endless — and exhausting. It's good to do the looking exercise…or have a beer, or something."

A few students chuckled. The room had a heaviness to it, and I could tell Robert was trying to lighten us up.

"We are trying to keep useful, profitable 'I's in control. It's common sense. Life picks on one another. Consciousness serves. Existence can be brutal."

Another pause. Robert looked at his watch, and many of us imitated. It was 5:44.

He paused once again.

"We may change the name of the farm."

I could feel people bristle a bit.

With a straight face, he looked up at the ceiling and said, "From Via Del Sol to the Circle Bar S Double Get Along Little Doggie, hmmm."

This is too good! Few found it funny.

Robert stood up and we all followed his lead. Rather than stay for dinner, Robert departed for Carmel, while the rest of us put away the chairs and returned to our evening octaves.

Trisha and I were working side by side at the kitchen counter to finish dinner preparations. I asked her how she liked the meeting, and she said, she couldn't understand Robert's humor.

"Many of us gave up a lot to live here, thinking we would 'all be here together forever,' which is what he told us."

I photographed "a lot" by a wave of my hand. She didn't register it, so I mentioned she said it and she thanked me.

I then shared with her my image of the carousel and how it reverses course to throw people off. It is C Influence's design, and we have to learn to go with the flow. She didn't understand that either.

I wondered what else she didn't understand.

❧

*The secret of change is to focus all of your energy,
not on fighting the old, but on building the new.*

Socrates

CHAPTER 108

Sunday's drive to Lake Tahoe was magnificent. Leaving Oregon House, we drove to Highway 20 through Nevada City and entered the national forests with their densely populated pines and firs, which brought an inner stillness to me. There was not much talking other than giving the occasional direction. And as far as directions go, when I'm a passenger, I shut off my intellectual center's turn left/turn right capabilities and just settle in emotionally to observe the beauty of the colors and shapes. I become a child, once again, in the back seat.

Mason took on the driving responsibilities with Trisha in the passenger seat. Marsha sat quietly next to me. Mason and Marsha were Saturn types, which made them easygoing. Robert had recognized them as more suitable for the farm than the city. This young married couple was probably moving-centered and enjoyed the outdoors even though they joined in the Bay Area. They had what we called an "organic" essence, which is more comfortable with nature and simple, unsophisticated ways of life. Society referred to them as hippies.

Soon the Donner Pass appeared, with all of its infamous history. We stopped to read the placard, describing the Donner Family's tragic starvation that led to cannibalism during the relentless winter of 1848. As we continued driving, a lake appeared.

"Is this Lake Tahoe?" I asked, excitedly, having never seen it before.

Everyone laughed.

"That's Donner Lake," said Trisha.

We arrived in nearby Truckee and stopped for gas. The Truckee River was turbulent from the melting snow as we crossed over the bridge. But the town was rough. I thought it would be more like Marysville, but it was filled with mountain folk: bearded men and pony-tailed ladies in jeans, boots, plaid shirts, baseball caps, and leather jackets. These were not vegetarian flower-children. They were rugged hunters who cared more for basic needs and working trucks. They both fascinated me and scared me.

THE DIVINE BEGINNING

I wondered if these people we were meeting were more like them. As we wound our way along the streets of Truckee, we stopped in front of a narrow, two-story Victorian home with a porch, not unlike the Buck House in Vacaville.

It was at this moment I realized that I was not likely to see Lake Tahoe.

As we exited the car, a tall blond man with a generous smile and soft eyes came to greet us on the porch. He was joined by two ladies. We climbed the stairs, and Trisha embraced them. After introductions were made, we entered the house. Four other people were sitting in a small circle in the tiny, crowded living room, and we were introduced to them as well. They had set out four chairs for us, and we each took a seat.

We followed the leader, who was breathing deeply and seemed to be in a state of meditation. No one spoke.

Then the unexpected occurred. A sudden knock on the door startled everyone. One of the ladies stood up to answer. Who could it be? It was Miles.

I was in shock. What was he doing here? How did he know about this? So many questions entered my mind. I looked at Trisha and she apparently knew. She greeted him and introduced him to the prospective students.

As we rearranged our seats, it became clear that the blond Saturn was in charge. We were on his turf.

He asked one of the ladies to start the record player that was housed in a corner cabinet.

"Let's close our eyes and take a deep breath as we begin our journey," he said.

The music was weird. It was a modern piece with violins and synthesizers. It reminded me of an episode of the Twilight Zone.

"Our astral bodies are now releasing themselves from our physical bodies. They are hovering above us and can begin their journey through the solar system."

I peeked and saw Miles sitting there with eyes wide open, so I followed suit. Trisha, Mason and Marsha had their eyes shut.

"We are now passing Mars….Jupiter is in our sights….the astral projection is approaching Saturn's rings…."

Miles quietly stood up and lifted the needle from the record. The music stopped abruptly with a slight scratch.

Everyone opened their eyes, confused, as if their astral bodies suddenly became stranded in space. Now what?

"We're done here," said Miles, as he headed for the door.

Trisha quickly followed him, and they stood on the porch discussing the situation. Mason and Marsha were still sitting in their chairs, a bit stunned, as was I.

When the blond leader stood up to join Trish and Miles on the porch, I knew it was time for me to move as well, so I followed him. I listened to the three of them: Trisha was telling Miles how rude he was and Miles was saying they don't need anything we have to offer. The blond leader tried to bring them both inside the house, but Miles purposefully turned, walked down the stairs, entered his car, and drove off.

The man tried to persuade Trisha and me to return to the living room, but Trisha was torn and confused. He re-entered the house, leaving me alone with Trisha. I told her that Miles was right. We need to go. She was reluctant at first, but cooled down and understood that this was our only option at this point.

"Let me at least say goodbye," she stated.

We thanked the people, and Trisha even told them we would be back. They waved to us from the porch, with gracious smiles on their faces.

On the way home, Trisha couldn't stop talking about how formatory Miles was; there were many ways to approach awakening, she said. These were her friends. Astrology and astral projection were legitimate studies according to her. Mason and Marsha tried to support Trisha.

I simply looked out the window, grateful for the view.

Few see through the veil of illusion.
Bhagavad Gita

CHAPTER 109

Monday morning, I awoke with the sense of not knowing exactly where I was and where I was going. The farm suddenly took on a strange appearance, as if it were something old from my past that I was revisiting in the present. Put a different way, it was becoming clear that the farm didn't fit me anymore, like a garment, full of reminiscences, that has remained in the closet fondly for a year without being worn.

Do I go to Vacaville today? Do I stay at the farm? The urgency of finding a ride to the Tuesday meeting was no longer pressing since I now owned a car. But what will I do? Then this 'I' appeared that said, "Ah, perhaps this is the *si-do* interval. You will know what to do when it's no longer a question."

THE DIVINE BEGINNING

Tuesday morning I arose with a clear direction: Vacaville. After lunch I headed out and arrived at Rosemary's house around 2 p.m., thinking she was probably still in Carmel. I was surprised to see Rose's car parked in the driveway.

As I entered the kitchen, the house was quiet and the master bedroom door was closed. I went into the living room and selected a book of Shakespeare poetry from the bookshelf. My concentration was faltering, and that feeling I had at the farm returned. But this time, the location of my past was Vacaville. This didn't fit either.

I sat quietly in the stillness of the lavender and purple living room, and remembrances of the meetings and events returned, like watching clips of a recently released movie. The Presence that visited me in Bubbie's house returned. I was content with this location, this chair, this book.

My higher state began to wane when sounds came from the kitchen. It was now 3:30.

Entering the kitchen, I gave Rose a fright.

"I didn't hear you enter!" she said.

"Sorry to startle you," I replied apologetically.

She was making a pot of coffee. I went to pull down two cups and two saucers from the shelf.

"How was Carmel?" I asked as I opened the drawer for the spoon that Rose would need for her sugar and cream. I drank mine black.

As we sat down, she lit her cigarette and pushed the Marlboro pack and Bic lighter towards me.

After a few puffs, she opened up.

"Robert wants me and Klair to look for a residence in Carmel that we could use as a teaching house."

"A teaching house?" I asked, since I hadn't heard that expression before.

"Yes, a central place for the group in Carmel so that students could live together, like at the farm."

"Interesting," I said. "Sounds a little like the Buck House. Robert lived with several of us there, remember?"

She hadn't been part of that short-lived experiment so did not respond to the analogy.

"Did Robert purchase the plane?" I asked.

"Yes. Mary was not too happy. It cost more than she thought."

"How did the Carmel open meeting go?" I asked, since she was down there and would know.

"I don't know," she said. "Meg was leading it, I assume."

Then she dropped a bomb.

"I'm selling this house and moving to Carmel once we find the teaching house."

I took a deep draw of my cigarette and slowly let the smoke stream, trying to control my breath since this almost knocked the wind out of me. Where was I going to live now?

Before I could respond, the phone rang and Rose went to answer.

"Hello," she said in a sweet voice. "Oh! Hello Jim. Yes. Six? Okay."

I knew the conversation. Are you available for dinner at the Coffee Tree, Rosemary?

I told her I would wash the cups. She thanked me and entered her room to prepare for the evening. It was approaching five.

When she left, I went to the garage to bring in the chairs for the meeting, carrying one in each hand. As I carefully set up each chair in the living room, I observed that the slow process of preparing for the meeting somehow comforted me. I could focus my attention on the task at hand since it was all I knew for sure in this moment. This pace was in stark contrast to my life, which was now becoming a whirlwind. So many surprises were occurring at every turn that I could not keep up with them all. Nothing was going my way. It was no longer as tempting to indulge in presumptions, expectations, hopes, imaginings — they proved worthless. It was apparent that whatever I could wish for or imagine definitely would NOT occur. I could bank on that.

* * * *

Robert began the evening meeting with a statement.

"Unnecessary suffering requires identification. What is a problem now, won't be in six months. Why? The person has changed his level of being and can separate."

A new student from Vacaville raised her hand.

"When does voluntary suffering become unnecessary suffering? How long should one sustain voluntary suffering?"

"Stay with it as long as you can," advised Robert, "then stay ten minutes longer. Personality is such that it will give up its comfort in comfortable areas. It is tokenism."

Robert paused, and then smiled, adding, "One student said to me, 'Pain is my pillow; Sorrow is my blanket.' I told the little jewel to buy a new pillow and a new blanket."

The energy in the room suddenly shifted. It became lighter and gentler. Robert's humor spreads like fairy dust, I thought.

"Remember, all pain can be separated from. Mourning the death of a close one is understandable — and it is good not to let the emotional center go down as we talk about these subjects. Meher Baba would not mourn even the death of his brother, who was close to him. That is why C Influence arranges difficult shocks, because our personalities are too easy on themselves."

A Bay Area student asked, "How can we work with fear?"

"A passive way is to be like water and let it flow around fear. Fear is an 'I' or a group of 'I's and has its roots in the emotional center. You do not have to have a disease, like fear, to know about it. The emotional center looks for fear 'I's as subjects for negative emotions to buffer the reality of how difficult it is to remember oneself. Trying to control fear 'I's is real 'doing.' It takes self-remembering to control the 'I's because then you are not the 'I's."

He continued, "Fear is part of all people's journey. Remember that with each new octave, the same old problems will return."

This angle of thought hit me hard. I could not imagine replaying the same painful lessons of last year. Why would I have to go through this again when it was clear to me that my heart had become pure and was ready for the new direction and tests? I felt I had not only transformed but transcended weaknesses in myself to emerge with a new, loving being toward those who harmed me.

Hadn't I?

When you are riding a horse and you fall off, you must stand up, dust yourself off, and get back on the horse. If you fall off again, you must stand up, dust yourself off and get back on the horse. No matter how many times you fall off, you must stand up, dust yourself off, and get back on that horse. And one day, you will be like one who has never fallen.

Miguel de Cervantes

CHAPTER 110

Rosemary went back to Carmel the next morning, and I stayed in Vacaville that week looking for work. It was more something to do with my time rather than expecting any results. I still had been giving the occasional massage at the farm. I could fill up the Buick's 25-gallon tank with five dollars, which was what I charged for an hour of massage work.

It was strange knowing there was a great deal of activity to the north and to the south of me. Those on the farm had their daily chores, and new students were joining at the Carmel open meetings. Or so I imagined.

On Wednesday afternoon, I had a call about a permanent teaching position at Vanden High School in nearby Fairfield. They asked me if I was available for an interview, and I hesitated. It was like seeing something you once wanted, but that person who wanted it no longer exists. Again, the garment that didn't fit.

I thought about it in the evening, chastising myself for not stepping forward. The next morning, I called them, only to learn the position had been filled. I lost the job, but it wasn't mine to lose.

Thursday afternoon dragged on. As I was about to sit down to an early dinner, the phone rang. I slowly rose to answer, wondering who it could possibly be.

"Hello."

"Linda?"

"Uh, yes."

"It's Yorgos. I wondered if you would like to come to a party this evening at my parent's home?"

I was stunned. I thought he was at the farm.

"Sure," I replied.

He said it was at 7:30 and he gave me directions to their home. He further explained it was a Greek celebration honoring his parent's wedding anniversary.

I sat back down and finished my dinner, not wanting to arrive hungry. This would be the first time I could recall that I actually went to a party of any sort on my own without an escort. It scared me a bit because I had no idea who would be there and why I was even invited. I didn't know his parents or any of their friends for that matter.

Although I had showered in the morning, I decided to do it again so I could appear fresh, and I chose my handmade polyester dress since it seemed festive. I had been putting on weight so I wrapped my shawl around my waist in a Bohemian fashion and repaired my makeup.

His parents lived in Vacaville, so it was only a ten-minute trip. I pulled into the driveway at 7:30. There were not as many cars as I had anticipated. I knocked on the door and a young lady, whom I had not met before, opened it. She greeted me warmly, and I smiled, hoping that would secure my entrance. It did.

Yorgos was sitting on the couch with his father, laughing at something. As I entered, my friend immediately stood up to give me a warm hug. "Dad," he said, "I want you to meet Linda."

His father was a diminutive man with Mediterranean features and coloring: tan, balding, muscular, and robust. Yorgos shared these physical characteristics, but with an added golden beard with streaks of brown. Each had sparkling, full-of-life Zorba-the-Greek eyes. Yorgos's eyes were sky-blue, however, and his father's were jet black.

"WELCOME!" responded his father with a manly hug. He looked into my eyes and communicated his genuine liking for me. I was instantly made comfortable.

His mother had entered from the kitchen. She was less demonstrative, but equally happy to have me join their celebration.

I sat on the couch with Yorgos and his dad, listening to stories of their family. Yorgos's family was born in Greece and tonight would be a Greek celebration. His mother brought out some dishes to sample, food that I had never heard of nor seen, let alone tasted. Wrapped stuffed grape leaves called "dolmas" and a dip called "hummus." It was all homemade, his father explained, adding, "The best in California!"

As the hour went by, people started to arrive. They brought gifts. I hadn't had a thought about this and started to feel ashamed that I had come empty-handed. But no one noticed, so I let it go.

Until two people walked in.

Miles and Helga arrived with a gift.

My heart sank.

By this time, the music had started and I had tasted some Greek wine. His father made sure my glass was more than half full at all times. I was quickly feeling loose. A circle was forming in the living room and his father took my hand to dance with me. I had taken folk dancing at university so knew how to do Greek dancing. With each oopah! I followed the lead of his father with encouragement from the family. He did a Zorba solo and turned to me to improvise. I did a little belly dance that I learned from Bonita, to many more oopahs and a bit of delightful laughter. I looked over at Miles, expecting him to share in the enjoyment. His face was stone and he hurled it at my heart.

Instead of shrinking from his judging stare, the opposite occurred. By now the wine was circulating and I had lost control. But I didn't care. I was having fun! Take that Miles! If you don't like me or want me, other men do!

Those were my thoughts. And yet, something else inside my head had an internal projector on, filming it all.

The party wound down an hour or so later. Miles and Helga left after the dancing. I was able to bid my adieus shortly thereafter.

As I lay in bed that night, I replayed the reel from the evening's performance. I could see I was still identified with Miles. If this were a new octave for me, something old, indeed, has been dragged along with it.

The very remembrance of a former woe proves a new one to me.
Miguel de Cervantes

CHAPTER 111

I headed up to the farm Friday afternoon, looking forward to seeing my friends and, above all, Robert. The skies were gray in Vacaville, and as I turned left at the 76 gas station heading toward Oregon House, the atmosphere had changed considerably. By the time I arrived, dark clouds hovered over the Lodge and were pregnant with rain.

David and Trisha's son had just carried in wood for the stove and fireplace as I passed through the living room. Klair was directing the kids to set the table with flatware and plates.

As I entered the kitchen, the first lightning flashed, and seconds later a sonic boom of thunder rattled the house. The storm was making itself known.

"Whoa! That was a close one," I said to the dinner crew of Kerrie and Short Jane, who were inside chopping vegetables for the salad. The cooked rice was resting in its pot under a lid and the soup was exposed with steam rising. It was a comforting place to be until that first crack of thunder coursed through the timbers. Who knew what was coming?

I left the kitchen to see how the storm was brewing. Several of the younger boys, led by a teenager and David, excitedly positioned chairs outside under the honey locust tree to watch nature's fireworks on display. I went out to join them, curious myself about the spectacle. The air smelled of wet grass even though the rain was still in the distance.

"Have a seat," said David, pointing to one of three wooden director's chairs that was still empty.

"This reminds me of that moonless night," I said, "when we waited to see the August meteor showers."

"You left too early," replied David, with that twinkle in his eye. "The light show was at 3 a.m."

It was true. I was surprised how little patience I had with nature, until I realized I had been spoiled by television's time-lapse photography. In LA, I was fed on fast-food impressions.

"Oh!" I exclaimed, as the distant dark strata let loose a chain of white light. It was dusk now and the sky looked like a parfait: whatever natural light was left from the day filled the middle section, making it appear like vanilla cream between two layers of blueberry puree.

We counted seconds to see when the thunder would sound, and it was later than expected. It seemed the storm was moving past us.

Nothing was occurring for quite a while, so I lit a cigarette to pass away the time. David stoked his pipe. Two kids went inside for their coats because it was becoming colder.

And then it happened. A gust of wind came from behind us, hurtling down the hill, heralding the second wave of the storm and knocking over one of two aluminum chairs.

The kids returned wearing their coats and sat in the aluminum chairs. Within a minute, a bolt of lightning illuminated the patio. The loud boom of thunder followed in a heartbeat. A cloudburst fell upon us like dropped water balloons.

The kids screamed in delight as they were drenched. I ran for the door.

It was then that Short Jane, being of sound mind and motherhood, ran outside and called the kids in immediately, leaving us all with this warning: "Are you CRAZY? The lightning strikes metal chairs and trees. Do you want to be KILLED?"

Uh…oh yeah. I forgot about this.

It was a quick moving storm that brought excitement to the day. No one was killed. Her warning of our possible demise helped to make the dinner that night especially tasty.

* * * *

The next morning, I awoke to discover no one had arrived overnight from the Bay Area. This was unusual for a Saturday morning. I could imagine that perhaps the storm had dissuaded students from coming to the farm. Would this mean Robert would not show up to lead the meeting that night?

THE SEEDS OF

No one knew whether or not we would have a meeting, but it didn't seem to matter to most. Everyone just focused on their duties and socialized, discussing work ideas and sharing the latest gossip.

I was most interested to learn about Carmel. After lunch, I went outside to smoke a cigarette and saw Klair. Maybe she knew something.

"Robert wants us to find a big house as soon as possible — by February," she said, adding, "I may have found one."

I knew about the search for a house from Rosemary, but Klair's timeline shocked me. She said she had travelled to Carmel multiple times in the past weeks. I had thought it was Rosemary's job to look for the house. It sounded like Klair was leading the charge, not Rosemary.

"Who's going to live there?" I asked.

"For now, it's Rosemary, Marie, Nadia, and I who will be responsible for the lease on the house. That's the plan."

This blew my mind. Nadia? She was the most organic essence around, with her devotion to the cows and calves. I was amazed to think that she could "turn on a dime" like this and consider living in Carmel. And does this mean Rosemary's house will be gone in a week? Life continued to spin around me while I was standing still. It was distressing.

Saturday night before dinner we learned that Yorgos, who had been in Vacaville for a couple of days selling his olive oil, would lead the meeting. Apparently, Robert had asked him to do this. Whether or not it was true, I couldn't verify, but I was grateful that we would at least have a meeting.

Strangely, I could not focus on the questions or topics. We discussed body types and centers of gravity, but it did not carry the weight or energy that I experienced with Robert. I tried to contribute an angle or two, just to keep me interested. I was in a low place inside.

Sunday came and went. Students came and went. I was still in this holding pattern, waiting for the new octave to arrive. It was scary, and yet, it was clearly in the hands of the gods, and I trusted them. What exactly was to come I could not say. Whatever lay ahead, however, felt ascending.

❖

Your own positive future begins in this moment.
All you have is right now. Every goal is possible from here.
Lao Tzu

CHAPTER 112

I left Monday morning for Vacaville, hoping Rosemary's house was still accessible, and that she would be there so that I could learn more about this transition to Carmel.

The key was still under the mat at the kitchen door, but Rosemary was not home. It was quiet, which allowed me to study work books.

The phone rang late afternoon and it was the school district checking to see if I was available to substitute teach on Tuesday. I immediately said, "Yes!" The freedom the Wildcat gave me was glorious. I didn't have to ask about the location since I could simply drive there now.

* * * *

When I arrived at the Will C. Wood High School early Tuesday morning, I went to the office and learned I'd be teaching a ninth-grade class. The class was clean and the kids were cooperative. I brought my Berman book to finish and kept my purse close to me. It was an uneventful day of money-making.

Returning home, Rosemary's car was parked in the driveway. The hour was approaching four.

She was resting. I put my stuff in the elder daughter's bedroom as usual and decided not to change my clothes since I was meeting-ready. I took the dust cloth and began preparing the living room for the evening event.

I heard Rose come into the kitchen around five.

"Hi," I said, smiling. "How was your trip?"

She sat down at the table and pulled out a cigarette from the Marlboro pack, lit it, and took her first deep inhale. I had my own pack and mirrored her movements. I listened intently as she opened up about the newly formed Carmel group.

"Right now, meetings are at the Wayside Inn in downtown Carmel. This is where Meg and Harold are living. Her daughter found a job as a maid there, so she's with them. By the way, how is your job search going?"

I told her about my teaching this morning, and she was thrilled to hear about it. She wondered if it would result in a full-time job, and I told her they didn't mention that.

"Well, maybe you're not meant to be here," she said.

"Did you find a house?" I asked, not only to change the subject, but to find out if her information jived with Klair's.

"There's an adobe house in Carmel Valley, but I'm not sure if Robert wants us to be that far away from Sheila's apartment, which is in downtown Carmel."

I didn't know where Carmel Valley was so I asked. She said Carmel is a small tourist town to the west near the ocean and Carmel Valley, which is to the east, is primarily farmland.

"We're still looking for something closer, but the rent in Carmel is expensive."

This surprised me, since Klair had a different story to tell. Without thinking I said, "Klair mentioned to me that you found a house to rent in Carmel."

Rosemary paused.

"We found something, but it's too expensive. We need to talk to Robert first."

She left it at that.

I went back to the living room to finish the meeting setup. The familiar ring of the telephone at six from Jim inviting Rose to the Coffee Tree for dinner before the meeting came, and it freed me to search the refrigerator for leftovers. It had become my habit.

Students started to arrive for the meeting at seven. I was surprised to see Robert walk in early with Rosemary and Klair. As I set the refreshment plates out on the kitchen table, I pretended to occupy myself with napkins and wine glasses so I could eavesdrop on the conversation, which was occurring in the corner near Rosemary's bedroom. It was as I suspected. Jim, reading Robert's notes, communicated the involvement of Marie and Nadia to help pay the rent of the new house in Carmel, if the lease should go through. Meanwhile, we could still consider the adobe house in the Valley. The last comment from Robert was, "Let's see what C Influence wants."

There were faces unknown to me: a Saturnine woman from Vallejo named Jean; a couple from Oakland; and a man with a full head of hair, twinkling eyes, and a sweet engaging smile. His name was Jim Keahey, and I liked him at once. The four of them were introduced at the start of the meeting by the students that brought them to the school. This was the custom.

There was no news of the Carmel group. Instead, Robert asked for questions.

"Can you describe the difference between external and internal consideration?" asked a lady from the Bay Area.

Robert responded, "External consideration is a selfless act. It usually means giving up comfort, or 'me, mine and I.' Inner considering is negative;

external consideration is positive and is not a means to something else. It does not have a hidden motive. It is pretty simple, but big words cloud it."

Another student asked for clarification on buffers.

"The moving center quite often buffers when things are tight," Robert explained, "and I've noticed students do not seem to see it. They will take a drink of water, or there will be a flurry of cigarette lighting."

He paused and added, "I've also noticed that some people will give a pleasant-sounding laugh when they make an error. It can be okay, and it can also be a buffer."

His look changed slightly as he contemplated the next thought.

"One reason we do not see the horror of our situation is that there is so much to entertain us, which serves as a buffer to difficult circumstances."

"What do you mean by horror?" asked a lady from Vacaville.

"Everything is eating each other all the time on this planet."

People started squirming in their chairs, which made a noticeable noise.

"The subject of buffers is not a pleasant one," observed Robert, "so be careful not to allow the emotional center to go into negative parts. Buffers keep a person mechanical."

Robert then asked if there were other angles of thought on the subject.

Miles slowly raised his hand and added, "Opposite thinking is a buffer."

Robert turned to Miles and smiled in acknowledgment.

I raised my hand.

"Also, one center can buffer while other centers do not, which allows perceptions and a new understanding to enter a person's being. This happens when we receive a photograph and we react to it, although later we discover the observation that was given had actually penetrated, and we begin to see in a day or two the mechanicality that was being photographed despite our initial resistance."

There was a heavy silence when I sat down. The flow of the meeting had stopped. I thought the angle was comprehensive. I may have been talking too long. Maybe the angle was wrong in some way. I could feel the heat of inner considering clouding my mind.

Robert continued the subject, which interrupted the onslaught of my internal 'I's, for which I was grateful.

"If buffers fall too fast, a breakdown can occur. This is one of C Influence's well-used tools. They break students down so they can crystallize correctly. Trouble stops, in general, at a complete number five. A balanced school person is rid of buffers, but that is long work.

"Most of life cannot accept this system, because it is not naïve and rose-colored. It reveals man to be a machine. This group is the only real family. It is not mechanical. Because we are identified, our life families seem real. They are loyal but not real. It is fine to have both, but I would not trade one student on the Way for my own life family. That is what Christ said to his mother: these are my brothers and sisters who hear the word of God and do it — that is, to be present. You do not need to forsake your family, but it is necessary for it to be second to your Self."

This was a powerful moment. How to handle my family was still an issue for me. The time would come for me to address it, but not now.

What is renounced is of little value in comparison with what is received.
                                                                Al-Ghazali

CHAPTER 113

I remained in Vacaville on Wednesday. Why? You could say I was inert, but a greater truth was, I felt that was where the gods wanted me to be. How did I know this? The silence of the house produced a stillness inside. It was that "quiet place within" that Ouspensky spoke about. Everything was slowed down and it was easier to self-remember. I would dust an object and handle it with care, and the simple movements centered me.

When Thursday morning came, the school district once again called and I accepted another stint of substitute teaching at Will C. Wood for Friday. It was the same class; it seemed the teacher's health remained poor and she was unable to return. I was now making $137 this month, which was one hundred dollars more than last month. As long as I had my $30 for teaching payments, I knew I would be fine.

Friday evening something totally unexpected happened. When I arrived home from teaching, Rosemary was there packing her bags. It was close to four in the afternoon.

"Let's have some tea," she said.

She put the full kettle on the burner and turned on the fire before sitting down with me at the kitchen table.

"I'll be going to Carmel for a few days. Klair and I will be taking Robert to look at the houses we found that we can rent."

She asked me what I did today and I told her about my substitute teaching.

"That's wonderful. They like you. Maybe it will lead to something here."

I didn't like her answer. I wanted to go with her and be with Robert and discover the new center emerging. I wanted to be where the action was. It certainly wasn't in Vacaville.

The kettle blared its horn announcing the water had boiled.

I went to the cupboard for a box of Constant Comment, her tea of choice. After some sips and a few drags of our cigarettes, she said Jim will be staying overnight so he can take Marie to Carmel in the morning.

Rose went back to her packing. Robert and Jim arrived around six. It was good to see them. The best part was embracing Robert. His body was soft and his arms enfolded me. It was like being wrapped in a big down pillow.

While Jim was carrying Rosemary's bags to her car, Robert wrote, "How is your job search?" and I was able to reply that I worked today. He was pleased to hear this.

Jim and I stood on the kitchen porch waving to Robert and Rosemary, as she pulled the car out of the driveway and headed toward Klair's home. It was then that I realized Jim and I would be home alone, together.

"It's pretty cold in here," he mentioned as he stepped from the kitchen into the living room.

I hadn't noticed, but he was right. I just was used to being in a cold house. My father rarely turned on the heat in our home because of the cost. I was accustomed to bundling up.

"I can start a fire. There must be wood in the garage," he softly stated, as if assessing the situation and coming up with a solution independent of my opinion.

It was so odd that in all the long days and weeks I lived at Rosemary's home, I never realized the fireplace was functional.

He gathered some newspapers and began to build the fire. I was suddenly transported back over a year ago to that moment when Miles methodically built his four-story, log-cabin structure made of kindling in the barbecue pit. Jim, on the other hand, did something unexpected: he explained what he was doing. He was teaching me how to build a fire.

"A fire needs three things," he began, "fuel, a spark, and air. You must have all three in balance. Too much fuel and not enough air will put the spark out. So that's why you layer it. Air lets the flame breathe and when the fire grows, you keep adding more fuel."

I was fascinated that he was teaching me. He cared enough about me. This warmed my heart.

Just as he was instructing me, the fire went out. We both laughed. He was a little red in the face.

"Well, now we have to rebuild it," he stated.

I watched as he made a second attempt. The fire was weak because there were no larger pieces of wood in the garage, apparently. But it was a comfort, nonetheless, as we huddled together seeking a bit of warmth. He placed his arm around me and I leaned in. I hadn't had a comfort like this in a long, long time.

I realized neither had he, when he kissed me.

We played with this, exploring our particular ways of expressing such affection. It soon began to escalate. How far it would go quickly became a question. I had become eager to consummate. Let's do it!

But he was not. So when the fire relaxed, so did we. He helped me up, and we each retired to our respective rooms. But not without a final hug and a sweet departing kiss to acknowledge that two lonely people that night had made a much-needed connection.

* * * *

When I arose in the morning, Jim had already left for Carmel. It was Saturday, and I thought it would be good for me to go to Via Del Sol and not stay alone in the house. My queen of hearts had filled my head with images of Jim and me together. Maybe this is how Helga and Miles started. They were friends before it became a beautiful and lasting relationship. I had seen this script in movies and television many times, so wasn't it possible for me?

This type of thinking was driving me mad. It was like living at the foot of a dam that kept breaking. The 'I's gushed forth, knocking me off my feet. They found the biggest orifice to emit their excess energy and that, unfortunately, was my mouth. I couldn't eliminate images of sex, let alone romantic notions, from my head. And others would soon see it: Linda was in love.

When I arrived at Via Del Sol, there was a glow and grin on my face that wouldn't fade. People asked me what happened, and I pretended to attribute it to finding work. I didn't sell it well, as my friends' skepticism was immediately evident.

I learned that there would not be a meeting that weekend at the farm, but there would be one on Monday in Carmel at the Wayside Inn. Trisha expressed interest in going, as did others. Guess who had the big car?

The plan was to leave early Monday morning for Carmel in the Wildcat.

THE DIVINE BEGINNING

I was looking forward to seeing Jim. I missed him.

❖

Happiness cannot be consistent with a longing after what is not present.

Epictetus

CHAPTER 114

Trisha, Mason, Marsha, Nadia and I crowded into my Wildcat at eight in the morning to head toward Carmel. I was at the wheel, and Mason agreed to share the driving responsibility. It was a four-hour trip. The plan was to arrive by noon, have lunch, take a tour of the town, go to the meeting at 7:30 and be back to Via Del Sol around midnight. Because the cows were gone, Nadia was free to sleep in the next day rather than attend to the pre-dawn milking tasks she had so faithfully done for the past few months.

I was familiar with driving to Vacaville, but going beyond that through the Bay Area and south was unknown to me and a bit scary. As I pulled into the gas station off of Highway 80, where I normally filled up, the attendant recognized me, but had never seen me with friends. Usually he and I would flirt, but this time he was particularly businesslike.

Mason offered to drive to Carmel. He said he knew the way. He adjusted the driver's seat to accommodate his long Saturnine legs. The seats were electric and Nadia had the shortest legs, so she agreed to sit behind him next to Trisha in the middle, with me on the passenger side. Marsha was in front of me, in the shotgun position next to Mason. Even though it was my car, I was good with this since they were married.

We took 80 to 680 through Pleasant Hill, where I lived with Miles, south to Alamo, where I first met Robert. Soon we were entering new terrain for me — there were no associations from my past, which was refreshing. We passed through the town of San Jose to connect with Highway 101. I had never been there before, having taken Highway 5 north from LA last year with Miles. The beauty of the valleys and hills was stunning. It was so peaceful to see the farmlands with grazing cattle and acres of crops. The winter rains had turned the hillsides green. We came upon one valley after another. San Jose was predominately a rural town. It was nice to be away from the big city.

As we were coming closer to Carmel, we started to discuss what we would find there.

Trisha said she had visited before. "They have wonderful shops."

Mason and Marsha, too, had explored the area; they both enjoyed hiking. "Big Sur is south of Carmel, and you can go into the hills off the ocean."

Nadia said nothing. I asked her if she'd been there and she said, "Yes. Once."

I was more interested in seeing Robert and Jim, but didn't say it.

We were approaching the town of Gilroy with a big sign that said, "The Garlic Capitol of the World." What a strange claim to fame I thought. Trisha wanted to stop in to browse but Mason said, "Maybe on the way back." He quickly passed the exit, and Trisha's 'I's disappeared.

The next big town on the route was Castroville, with its large billboard proudly displaying it as "The Artichoke Center of the World." Merging onto Highway 156, which led to Castroville, had been tricky to navigate. We had to pay attention to the signs; we missed the exit the first time and continued south on 101. The four women became self-proclaimed navigators — turn right, no left. It was fortunate Mason was driving and a dominant Saturn type. He quietly corrected his initial mistake and brought us back on track, disregarding the squawks of the hens on board.

Once we had passed Castroville on 156, the road narrowed and the most remarkable impression appeared to our right and to our left: rolling fields stretched to the horizon with the strangest crop. They were hip-high, deep green, dense, fern-like bushes, in parallel rows that undulated as far as the eye could see with round bulbs erupting from the center of the plant. They looked otherworldly.

"Artichokes," said Mason.

"Wow!" said I.

Highway 156 merged into Highway 1, named Cabrillo Highway here. In Los Angeles, it was known as the Pacific Coast Highway, which meant we would be near the Pacific Ocean. I was looking forward to seeing the beach since it had been a long time and I missed it. When I lived in Brentwood, the beach was just down Sunset Boulevard and readily accessible.

It was wonderful not to have to navigate another exit; we were able to relax and enjoy the view as we simply followed the road. Vegetables of all sorts were populating fields that were now level with the horizon. With my window down, I sniffed to see if I could detect the salt air. I could not, but I did feel the cool humidity, which was an indication that we were approaching the coast.

When we reached the Marina Dunes, which were a strange impression of ten-foot-high desert sands next to a flat wet beach, a glimpse of glittering sea first appeared and my heart leapt.

"This is Monterey Bay," remarked Mason.

We were travelling rapidly now, passing Fort Ord, where I seem to recall my brother-in-law was once stationed early in his career, to little towns aptly named Seaside and Sand City. But then the highway swerved inland.

The terrain abruptly changed as we headed up a steep incline. It was becoming a dense forested area on both sides. Because of the shift in shapes, I began to fear we were lost.

"Are we almost there?" I asked, without realizing I was sounding like a six-year-old.

"Check the map," replied Mason.

Now I was really scared. He doesn't KNOW?

We stopped at a red light. The street said Carpenter. We were checking the map. It was a big map of California.

As we continued to drive, Nadia suddenly commanded, "TURN RIGHT!"

Huh? There wasn't a sign saying Welcome to Carmel, like we saw in Gilroy and Castroville, so this couldn't be right. Mason drove on, with confusion in the backseat.

"Stop! We passed it," said Nadia.

Clearly, we couldn't stop, but there was a traffic light approaching and luckily it was red.

"The sign says Carmel Valley Road," said Trisha, "and I think we need to turn left here to go back."

Mason did just that, and when we came back to the place on Highway 1 that Nadia had directed us to five minutes earlier, we made that turn. A few quaint cottages lined the narrow two-lane road. We travelled slowly since it had a steep descent. At the first stop sign, the most remarkable impression appeared before us that took my breath away. We could see the ocean in the distance, which rose to a horizon line that defied logic. The sea soared to a height comparable to that of a mountain, appearing higher than we were. How could this be? It was pure magic.

"Is this Carmel?" I asked Nadia, who ignored me. As we passed little shops, a sign indicated the street we were on was named Ocean Avenue, so we continued its full length until it ended at the beach. We found a parking spot and exited the car. There before us was the Pacific Ocean. Now this makes a bit more sense, I thought. Ocean Avenue should lead to the ocean. Yet, I could not understand why everyone made such a big deal about Carmel: it was basically a shop-lined street dotted with inns. Where do the residents live?

I looked at my watch and saw the journey took us five hours. It was now one o'clock. We all agreed it was time to find a place to eat. We ascended on foot toward the middle of town, and I was quite surprised how narrow and broken the pavement was, which made it laborious to climb. After fifteen more minutes we reached a street named Dolores, where a little café with outdoor dining beckoned us. It was named the Bistro.

"Let's eat here," I said, famished. It was a tough sell since Mason, Marsha, and Nadia were vegetarians. The Bistro offered tomato, avocado and alfalfa sprout sandwiches, which was a trendy hippie cuisine that was acceptable to them. Trisha and I ordered the roast beef sandwich au jus. Sandwiches came with fries.

After rapidly consuming my meal, I sat back to watch the people of Carmel stroll past. They were well-dressed, sporting jewelry and wearing nice shoes. I was in my granny dress, tube socks and sneakers. I admired what I saw, and was thankful that the attitude of the times was to "do your own thing," which helped to diminish my inner considering. However, I noticed my envy was still as strong as ever.

After lunch, Mason and Marsha wanted to walk the beach. Trisha and I wanted to hit the stores. Nadia wanted to do something else: she wanted to be alone. We all agreed to meet at five o'clock at the car since January sunsets occurred at that hour. It was already almost three.

As Trisha and I strolled along Dolores, I asked her if she knew where Sheila lived. I was still hoping to catch a glimpse of Robert and Jim.

"I heard she had an apartment around here," was her vague answer.

We saw a Royal Danish Bakery on the corner of Dolores and 7th. Trisha wanted a cup of coffee and pastry. We stopped inside. It was a cheerful place with high glass walls letting in the light. I decided not to order anything since the Bistro sandwich was more expensive than a Denny's hamburger with fries. I had to watch my pennies. Trisha took pity on me and let me taste her pastry. It was scrumptious.

It was just past four when we returned to Ocean Avenue. We came upon a colorful shop that was large by Carmel standards. It had all sorts of stuff in it, from clothing and coffee cups to books and fashion jewelry. There in the south corner of the shop, where the bookshelves rose from floor to ceiling, was Nadia, deeply engrossed in a paperback.

I quietly approached from behind and tapped her on the shoulder.

"Hello," I said, which startled her.

"What are you reading?" I asked.

She showed me the title and it was a B Influence book on health and wellness. I was not familiar with it. But looking up, I saw *The Fourth Way* by Peter Ouspensky. This bookstore had work books!

"Look!" I said to Trisha and Nadia. As I pulled the copy down, I saw *In Search of the Miraculous* close by. These books were so hard for me to find in Los Angeles. I was surprised and delighted to find them here.

Nadia went to the counter to purchase her book, since it was now 4:30. The middle-aged woman behind the counter was the most colorful character I had seen since leaving LA. She had rings on all of her fingers; the long oval-shaped nails were perfectly manicured in hot pink. Her elegant gestures had a flare that matched the yellow, orange, blue and purple geometric-patterned silk caftan she was wearing. With a bold multi-gemmed necklace and matching chandelier earrings, and blond soft curls that fell to her shoulders, she was a large Juno who reigned supreme in a gift shop.

She was clearly a Jovial type and emotionally centered, friendly, talkative, inquiring. She told me her name: Doris. I told her mine: Linda. We liked each other. She asked us where we were from, and I said, "North of Sacramento." We left it at that.

By the time we arrived at the car it was shortly after five, and the sunset was incredible to behold, with its primary colors of blue, red, and yellow and with the sounds of the waves rhythmically crashing on shore. Mason and Marsha were leaning against the car, taking it all in. The daytime was now in the books. The evening was yet to reveal itself. And the gods left everything to our imagination.

* * * *

The Wayside Inn was located at the entrance to downtown Carmel on the corner of 7th and Mission. I drove the car into the parking lot, and was stunned to see how small it was. The front desk said there were only 22 guest rooms. They called Meg and she said it was fine for us to come up to her room.

Meg greeted us at the door with a hug. As I entered, I saw a king-size bed and a couch. How is this a meeting room?

"We heard there was a meeting here tonight," I said, hoping for clarification as to where exactly it would be held and whether Robert and Jim would be there.

She looked puzzled, as if to say, Where did you hear that?

"We had a meeting this afternoon with Robert. Mary C. and I were there with three of our new Carmel students: Bob and the Laceys."

Their names sounded familiar. As I recalled, these were the three people from Esalen that I had met at Rosemary's house. How strange that they had decided to join.

"Where was the meeting?" I inquired, trying to form a picture of it in my head.

"Here," she said, "in the downstairs lounge." I recalled seeing some chairs and two couches at the front desk. I guess that would hold everybody.

"Well," said Mason, "I think we should head on back to the farm. We'll grab a bite to eat on the road."

No Robert. No Jim. No meeting. This was the play.

As we said goodbye to Meg, we entered my car and headed up Ocean Avenue. This time I was in the passenger seat next to Mason, who was the self-appointed driver. It was now dark. The exit from Carmel had no traffic lights, only a modest Stop sign. This made it difficult to merge with the fast-moving Highway 1 traffic, since we only saw a car's headlights as it approached, and it was hard to gauge its speed. We waited for minutes. Suddenly, my eyes peered straight ahead and it was then that I saw what was right in front of us: an illuminated wooden sign that read Carmel HIGH School.

"Look! It says Carmel HIGH School!" I exclaimed, but Mason had quickly turned left onto the Highway. It was too late for others to see it. I tried to explain how the circular sign had the word Carmel curved along the top perimeter and School along the bottom and the word HIGH in capital letters in the middle, but it carried no message for them. To me, it was significant. The Carmel group was to be a strong part of the Fellowship. We had come to the right place. It was literally a sign from above.

※

All work for the creation of groups on earth is concerned with the building of arks to be navigated from a higher level.
We are preparing for a great demonstration from Higher School.
                                                            Rodney Collin

CHAPTER 115

We made it back to the farm after midnight. The moon was new and the darkness brought out the Milky Way in all its majesty. Everyone was asleep by the time we entered the Lodge, and my designated spot by the woodstove across from the bathroom was already taken. I had to sleep in the coldest corner of the living room, which was near the front door.

Tuesday morning began quietly, and I was in no hurry to leave the warmth of my sleeping bag. My mind still had visions of Carmel, with the reality of our adventure, but it was becoming more and more mixed with the nagging curiosity of Where Were Robert and Jim. It had become a mantra that stuck in my brain. Like the soundtrack to a movie, it played incessantly in the background of my activities that morning.

I was asked at breakfast how the Carmel meeting was. I briefly mentioned the series of events, but I did not share the shock of the Carmel HIGH School sign. These shocks, which would occur to me throughout my life, were so intimate and precious, and produced moments of higher consciousness — yet were so often met with visual or verbal HUHs? by my friends — that I was used to keeping them to myself.

Since it was Tuesday, many of us would be going to Vacaville for the evening meeting. I decided to leave after lunch. Those I talked to wanted to wait until late afternoon since it is only an hour and a half drive. Unlike the Bay Area, there's nothing to do in Vacaville, so there is no incentive for them to leave early. My incentives were personal: enjoy a bit of solitude, prepare the house, and hope that Rosemary is there to let me know what's going on in Carmel and with her home in Vacaville.

When I arrived, the house was empty. It was three in the afternoon. The meeting wouldn't begin until 7:30. Perhaps I left too early, I thought. When I'm with people, I want to be alone. When I'm alone, I want to be with people. When I realized this, I shook my head and started to laugh a little. There's no pleasing the machine, I thought.

I sat down at five to eat the food I had packed from the farm. Rosemary hadn't come home. Maybe she's at the Coffee Tree with Robert and Jim.

I assembled the chairs after vacuuming and the first students arrived around seven. Mac and his girlfriend came from Vallejo, as did Jean and Clare, who brought refreshments. But almost no one arrived from the farm. Only Mason and Marsha. Anna showed up, driving her little VW Beetle, with several new students. I counted about twelve people in all.

At 7:20 Robert and Jim appeared. But still no Rosemary.

We gathered in the living room. I sat in the front row. Robert began the meeting.

"The Carmel group is off to a C Influence start. Sheila was in a car accident and broke five ribs."

We all gasped.

"Rosemary is taking care of her. She will be fine. This shock was given because we are too lazy — too easy on ourselves, which is why C Influence gives us this type of friction to awaken us."

The room had become still. This was powerful to hear.

"When things are rough, we are slaves to C Influence. When things are smooth, we are in the hands of C Influence....that's an advanced joke."

No one laughed. It was a subtle joke that seemed to go over the heads of most students. Basically, when the shocks are harsh, we view the gods as tyrants; when the shocks are pleasant, we view them as loving and caring parents. Anyway, Robert tried to lighten the meeting up with this observation. It didn't work.

"My jokes are never directed at anyone," he continued. "One reason for more joking is I am spending more time in life now. I'm also less concerned about being 'perfect.' There is no perfection.

"This shock is an opportunity to verify C Influence. Each of you has C Influence with you. A miracle of miracles for this planet. Remember: Many are called, few are chosen."

Robert paused a moment before continuing.

"Rodney Collin had seen a man dying in the street in front of him. Later Collin died in the street. This was no accident. He fell from a church tower when the railing failed. When they turned him over, he had a smile on his face. He left his body as it died. It was to show he had fate. His death was all planned by Influence C. His book, *The Theory of Celestial Influence*, was also written by Influence C through him, which he states in the book."

Robert then asked if anyone had a question.

A new student from the Bay Area raised his hand.

"Do drugs help self-remembering?"

Robert signaled his reply to Jim, who quickly relayed his response to us.

"It's possible to develop the nervous system to conscious potential. A physical change does occur in self-remembering; the nerves are used, heightened, worked.

"The average man does not use his brain. Acid does activate the nervous system. However, it is not good to take acid because it begins to deform the birth of the infant. The pineal gland, you see, produces a conscious child — an immaculate conception. And plastics in an organic process can, to my knowledge, poison the process.

"I am aware many have taken acid here, and many have stopped without being asked. I do not try to control people's lives. I make suggestions only when they reach an impasse and ask. It is best not to take acid. It opens the door on one level, and closes it on another.

"The same states can be earned and opened up without drugs. If they open up and fuse or crystallize, after years of hard work directed by C Influence, you can have a Leonardo da Vinci.

"Hashish and marijuana are good for some people to take, though it is a private matter. We do not use them in this school because of the country's harsh punishment if caught.

"Any states gained through drugs are temporary and should in the user accelerate a thirst to learn how to be there permanently. The only permanent way to awaken is through your own natural efforts."

Robert had finished that subject and asked if there were other questions.

I was surprised to see Mason raise his hand.

"Can you give us guidance about the work to be done on the farm?"

"We will not do much besides gardening and improvements on the Lodge," replied Robert, without hesitation. "Gradually people will build their private homes there. To my knowledge, C Influence wished it bought for a life preserver for us. As predictions approach, the farm will become bigger and bigger in our lives. We will try to have the farm paid for and be self-contained."

He looked at Mason when he said, "The farm also is a tool for those who wish that way of life. I think it will have more use in spring, summer and autumn. Presently, it doesn't have much use, and doesn't have to. To my knowledge, it's for the future and for those who wish. I don't think the work there is imperative, presently, though there is work to improve the impressions."

He paused, which he often did when he wanted us to focus on something else.

"Nothing we do is imperative, whether at the farm, Vacaville or Carmel. Nothing is real except self-remembering, so we try not to identify. Essentially, we have now what we need. Also, C Influence keeps moving us around… mixing us up…putting us in different homes…starting new branches of the teaching…separating husbands and wives. Some of you are more used to this by now."

I smiled, appreciating the fact he wasn't oblivious to my crazy life. He recognized what was going on, even though he wasn't around that much to observe it. It was comforting.

Robert changed the subject to the direction of the school, which interested me.

"Tonight is a step backward for the teaching," he commented, referring to the poor attendance. "A teaching goes two steps forward and one step back. We are used to it. Last night Carmel had a step back, too."

I assumed he was referring to Sheila's accident.

"Our sincerity will ensure a sound teaching. I work every day, all day, directing my energy to my students. About fifteen students are not here. The weather, jobs, etc. are factors — these are denying forces. All is well, however. There once were two 'dots'…"

He fondly called us "little dots."

"Then three, then thirty, now ninety. Next Christmas we should have 200. The more new people, the more older students must teach. Probably we will number 1000 one day. No hurry. This is our fate."

With that, Robert stood up to signal the end of the meeting. We retired to the kitchen to consume the delicious cake Clare had prepared and the cheese platters from Jean. We toasted each other with the wine that Mac brought. It was a cozy, intimate group, and the affection was flowing between us. Standing there, with Robert toasting us individually, all the identification I had struggled with in the past days evaporated. The glow from Robert's smile and his direct, loving eye contact brought me back to the present, back to my Self. This simple moment of presence, and the internal freedom of being in contact with something other than the many 'I's, reminded me of why I was in the school.

I was grateful to be counted as one of the "little dots."

So small, so next to nothingness, it shall seem strange that I was someone loved and cherished by a god.

Ovid

CHAPTER 116

I rested well that night in Vacaville, feeling I was indeed in the right place. Wednesday morning came and went, and that afternoon, I received another opportunity to substitute for the local school district on Thursday. There was now emerging, I believed, a rhythm in my life. I could see myself continuing like this: substituting one or two days a week, traveling to the farm and Carmel between jobs. I didn't need much: I had a sleeping bag, with which I could sleep on someone's floor, and enough money for gas and cigarettes, and the occasional Denny's burger and fries. I was happy knowing I could take care of myself.

When I arrived home Thursday afternoon, I was delighted to see Rosemary's younger daughter. She was there briefly, and commented that it looked like I had lost weight. It surprised me because I knew the opposite to be true. I was eating quite a bit and smoking more cigarettes. I was lamenting this, so her observation made me realize how distorted was my view of myself.

Around six o'clock, as I was beginning my dinner of bacon and eggs that I found in Rose's refrigerator, the phone rang. I stood up quickly to answer, hoping it was Rosemary checking up on me.

"Hello?" I said.

"Linda? This is Jim. Robert wanted me to tell you that there's a meeting tonight at Don's house. It's at 7:30."

A flash of heat gripped my throat, making me almost mute. After swallowing hard, I replied.

"Okay. Thanks." And with that we hung up.

JIM?

I had just lost my appetite. The many 'I's on the subject were unleashed like a disturbed swarm of bats in a pitch-black cave. Will he be there? What is he doing in Vacaville? Will Robert come too? Do I need to bring something? Should I shower first?

I finished my dinner to the cadence of the 'I's. I think better when I'm eating. Then I lit a cigarette to continue my thought processes. Finally, I turned to the dishwashing. The scenarios were forming in my head as I envisioned the evening to come. I was excited at the prospect of seeing Jim and Robert.

The drive was short, and yet I became lost in the dark. It was 7:25 when I rang the doorbell. Don answered and greeted me with a warm hug. He led me straight to a secluded outdoor patio, which I had never seen before, that was enclosed by a redwood fence. Along the fence were attached redwood benches with colorful cushions of red and orange and yellow for seating, that matched the ceramic art work hanging high on the fence above it all. I recognized the décor from the Nut Tree.

When Don and I entered, Doris and Robert and Jim were conversing. The couple with whom I had briefly stayed was there as well. This was the group for the meeting that night.

We sat quietly for a long time. Robert spoke of topics that we were all accustomed to hearing: body types and how two unrelated persons could look exactly alike (called "duplicate machines"), the necessity of self-remembering, etc. Nowadays, it was so unusual to be sitting so intimately like this with Robert in a meeting format; he seemed more like a student in a small group than the teacher. It brought me back to those early days in the Buck House, when there were just a few of us with him. Did I just say early days? It was not even a year ago, but it felt like that special period was placed in some timeless archive that was now part of my historical past.

The meeting reached a lull.

It was then that Don asked the unspoken question.

"Robert," Don quietly said, leaning forward, "are you the second coming of Christ?"

This question had been raised by some students privately in whispers, but I couldn't believe it would be Don who would ask this of Robert publicly.

What was Robert's answer?

Silence.

Don began to clarify.

"We wonder if that is your role?"

Robert was being pressed. He still said nothing.

Don stared at Robert, waiting for the response he wanted to hear.

What Robert did next was exactly that. He gave Don the answer Don wanted to hear.

"Thou sayest."

This was Christ's response to Pilate who asked if he was the King of the Jews. What did Jesus care about being the King of the Jews? That was a political issue that threatened Pilate's power. He was basically telling Pilate what he wanted to hear. Thou Sayest is the same as telling him, If you say so. In other words, you can call me whatever you like. It doesn't matter to me.

I looked at Don, who sat back with a big smile on his face. He appeared content, as if his Christian upbringing had been fulfilled and he had landed in this sacred company at last. It was a shock to me: I had never truly witnessed someone before who was that satisfied with an imaginary idea.

It produced immediate discomfort in me. I never believed in the "Christ's Second Coming as Savior" approach to evolution. As Robert had said at the

THE DIVINE BEGINNING

last meeting about drugs, it's laziness if you think awakening would come without efforts to be present on a moment-to-moment basis. Robert never professed before that he was the second coming of Christ. He referred to Jesus as a conscious being who had the role of Christ. He refers to himself as Robert, a conscious being who has the role of teacher, helping others to awaken.

The silence continued, and the state it produced was off the charts. Then, Robert offered this.

"I am not here to save anyone."

He stood up and motioned to Jim to follow. They both exited the house. We remained seated for a while, stunned. Finally, Doris tried to ease the tension by suggesting we bring the refreshments out onto the patio. The couple went to help her. We sat together, nibbling on the snacks. A discussion followed about Robert's role and how some had known in their hearts that they had met another Christ. I said nothing. It was a landmine conversation.

Being Jewish, I understood the denial side of the equation. Jesus was no one's idea of the Messiah (another word for Christ), being a common carpenter. And those Jews who looked for someone to create a better world on Earth for all Jews against tyranny and oppression wanted a political leader. And the remaining Jews, who wanted someone to explain the meaning of this difficult life and offer visions of Green Pastures — believing he could guarantee free entrance to Heaven — happily positioned him as their Savior.

We each have our own idea of the man, and see what we want to see. What do I see? Robert was a fourth-grade teacher when his higher centers started to emerge. I was in elementary school when my higher centers started to emerge. We have this in common. I can relate to this. This man is teaching me how to become conscious. He is clearly ahead of me in his evolution. This is good enough for me.

That evening, I was concerned for Robert. Students gossip, and I knew how tempting it was for some to idolize Robert — putting him up on the high pedestal of expectation, which could easily collapse — instead of seeing a man who is not perfect, and is here to help us. Positioning Robert as Savior is a dangerous game. It didn't go well for Christ, after all. But then again, that was His play.

❖

The most important of all, however lightly you take it at the moment, is to get the right ideas about the gods and so live a good life.
Plato

CHAPTER 117

Friday morning, I headed back up to the farm. I did not want to stay alone in Vacaville on the weekend, and going to Carmel to attend the Monday evening meeting was simply not part of my routine, not to mention there was no place for me to stay in Carmel. My options were limited.

It was now January 17. The winter days were definitely slowing down every function within me. Even though I had met the miraculous, I still had to contend with the monotony of the mundane. Breakfast, lunch and dinner preparations sprinkled with occasional conversations around the woodstove, and seven-minute cigarette smoking huddled on the bench against the chimney stack pretty much made up the day. I measured how long it took to smoke a cigarette, and yes it was seven minutes. It had come to that.

We were the caretakers of the property, while the growth spurts were happening in the Bay Area and Carmel. Saturday came and went, as did Sunday, as did Monday. We relied on gossip and Meg's *Via Del Sol Journal* for summaries of meetings and Robert's angles of the week. That Thursday meeting at Don's had somehow not made it to the farm. I didn't bring it up.

I continued to study the work books, and decided to re-read *In Search of the Miraculous*. It was not so much to learn anything new, as it was to reconnect with that hopeful and curious Linda who first read it, that girl who longed, like Ouspensky, to find a conscious teaching. What I discovered, however, was that that Linda did not exist anymore. I was no longer a seeker. I had become a finder. To extend Ouspensky's metaphor that we are on a train and the train is going somewhere, well, the train had left the station and I was on it.

What I was part of was different from those in Gurdjieff's group. We were not dodging bullets on our way to meetings. Our journey was not that kind of outward adventure. Ours was an internal exploit, combatting the onslaught of the many 'I's and dodging the slings and arrows of negative emotions. The danger we faced lay primarily within.

Sleep crept into my day like never before. The time with the teacher was hit or miss. I reflected on last year, and it seemed like I had been given a free sample of the most exquisite elixir. When the last drop was gone, I wanted more but was told that now I had to pay for it. The price was exorbitant. It was not monetary. It was laborious work that required distillation to capture a single drop of presence. That drop was quickly depleted. And so, the process of distillation had to be a continuous, moment-to-moment effort. Was it worth it?

It was then that I realized to awaken fully, and not just be content with a whiff of presence, you must want it badly enough, for a long, long time. No wonder many are called, and few are chosen.

* * * *

Tuesday I was planning to head out to Vacaville after lunch for the meeting. I saw Mason and Marsha eating their bowls of cereal by the fireplace and I joined them for breakfast.

"You guys going to the meeting tonight in Vacaville?" I asked them.

"We heard there wasn't one tonight."

"Who said that?" I asked, stunned.

"Yorgos," Mason said, pointing through the window at him.

Without thinking, I put my bowl down and went out there to speak with him.

"Hi," I said, and he responded with a nod and a smile, while continuing to clear some soil with his shovel.

I explained what I heard and he replied it was true. He had been in Vacaville visiting his family and learned from Kerrie that Robert was staying in Carmel over the weekend and through next week. Robert apparently wanted us to go to the Bay Area meeting this week instead. There was no communication to this effect, and I felt totally out of the loop. I felt a panic, as if my evolution was suddenly in jeopardy. Why would I feel like this? Because I was desperate to be around Robert; I needed his light to ignite my own.

I returned to my bowl of cereal, shoveling each spoonful in my mouth as I contemplated what the heck am I going to do now?

Yet, I did nothing. I spent the entire week at the farm, feeling more and more that Via Del Sol had become not the center of the school, as we originally were led to believe, but an abandoned island of hippies. It was as if invisible shackles were around my ankles, keeping me at the farm and keeping me asleep. Without Robert around, this group appeared to me to be nothing more than a B Influence commune.

To be around the teacher, I had to find a way to be useful to him, as Gurdjieff said. How to do this I could not even imagine. So I asked the gods for help. Surely, they would guide me in the right direction.

※

I am not ashamed, afraid, or averse to tell you what ought to be told: that I am under the direction of messengers from heaven, daily and nightly. But the nature of such things is not, as some suppose, without trouble or care. Temptations are on the right hand and on the left. Behind, the sea of time and space roars and follows swiftly.
He who keeps not right onwards is lost.

William Blake

PART IV
The Beginning of the End

CHAPTER 118

MY RHYTHMS WERE thrown off. It had been almost two weeks since I saw Robert. The news flowed up to the farm that there would indeed be a meeting in Vacaville with him on Tuesday, which brought renewed energy to me.

I headed to Vacaville right after lunch, bringing food supplies in case my stay would be longer. When I arrived close to 2 p.m., I was thrilled to see Rosemary's car in the driveway. Finally, I thought, I will learn what's going on.

When I entered the kitchen, the house was quiet. Rose's bedroom door was open, but there was no sign of her. I was confused, and felt my emotional center plummet from that momentary high to the bottom of the roller coaster track. Where could she be?

After stuffing the fridge with my bags of food, as usual I picked up the dust rag and went to the living room shelves to polish items that I had grown fond of — but they were not there. What's going on? I looked around, and near the front door was a shipping box. Oh, my.

I placed the dust rag on the shelf and heated up the kettle for tea to comfort myself. The cupboard had dishes, thank goodness, and an open Constant Comment box with a few teabags left.

It was after three when I heard a car pull into the driveway. Girlish giggles burst forth into the kitchen as the door opened. It was Rosemary and her younger daughter.

We were all glad to see one another.

"Help us bring in the groceries, will you dear?" asked Rose.

"Certainly," I replied.

Following Rose's girl out to her car, I asked where the two of them had been.

"Shopping," she answered.

I felt a bit stupid. That was the editor-in-chief of my internal *National Inquirer* speaking — the queen of hearts in me — that has to know everything, even if the answer is self-evident. It's one of my machine's great features.

As I placed the first grocery bag down, it occurred to me that my own food was occupying considerable space in the refrigerator, so I went directly there to push my stuff aside.

"It's our turn to bring refreshments," said Rosemary, "so why not help us?"

"Sure," I happily responded.

Her daughter was most creative, as it turned out, making canapés. She would give me the prototype and I would make six of them, using foodstuffs that my mother not only didn't have in her pantry, but had never heard of, like capers, and marinated mushroom caps, and artichoke hearts.

I was hoping Rosemary would join in so I could ask her questions about Carmel, but she retired to her room, and I could hear the shower running. It would have to wait.

We finished the canapés in an hour, and her daughter rearranged the shelves in the refrigerator to accommodate the platters.

We both sat down at the table for an afternoon smoke. Maybe she knows something.

"I was dusting the living room," I began, after exhaling my first puff, "and noticed some of the objects are missing from the shelves."

"Mom wants us to help her begin the packing," she said, "since we're selling the house."

"Do you know how soon that will be?" I prodded.

Just as the question came out of my mouth, Rosemary appeared, ready for the meeting. She sat down and took a cigarette from her daughter's pack.

"Why don't you ask Mom your question, Linda?"

"Ask me what?" said Rose, as she lit her cigarette.

"Klair said that we may have found a house in Carmel and that Robert wants you, Klair, Nadia, and Marie to move there by February first." I couldn't believe this came out of my mouth.

"Well," she began slowly, "YOU," she said emphatically, "need to focus on making a living and supporting yourself. You have a wonderful education and you're not using it." She went on a bit more, and I felt that I had failed her. While her two girls were securely on the road to adulthood, I was lagging farther and farther behind.

"This house will not be around much longer for you," she added. "Mac and I have put it up for sale and we may have an offer."

That was a gut punch.

"Okay," I said weakly. It was the only 'I' left in my head in that moment.

I stood up from the table, and went into what was now becoming my bedroom to prepare for the meeting. At least that's what I told them. I went there to cry.

* * * *

I emerged from the room at six after I heard the familiar sound of Rosemary's car pull out of the driveway. She was on her way to meet Robert and Jim at the Coffee Tree, no doubt.

I was hungry so I went into the kitchen to find my food stash. Rose's daughter passed through, saying she was going over to see her boyfriend before the meeting.

"You look nice," she offered, in sympathy for the Martial directness I received from her mom. When the kitchen door closed, I quietly prepared my go-to dinner of salad and sandwiches.

The first students arrived thirty minutes later, while I was washing my dishes. It was now approaching meeting time, and I had placed the platters and dishes, napkins and glasses on the kitchen table covered by the regular refreshment cotton tablecloth.

Students were chatting and hugging each other upon arrival. My emotional center, however, did not bubble up. It was hiding in a dark, remote corner inside, and the front door of my heart, my expression, had a smiley face on it.

Even seeing Jim didn't cheer me up. Fear was more powerful than romance, I guess. Could I take care of myself? Where would I live? And most of all, how distant would I be from Robert?

These questions circulated as I took my seat for the meeting. A new student next to me from the Bay Area said hello and introduced herself. I did not register her name. Instead, my eyes went right past her, to the dirty dust cloth hiding in a dark, remote corner of the bookshelf where I had left it. Oh, my God! Robert will notice it and point it out as an example of sleep!

I turned my attention to the front of the room, hoping no one else saw it. When Robert walked in to take his seat, with Rose and Klair flanking him, he looked noticeably different. The good householder was brief, with requests for volunteers to clean up after the meeting. Nothing was mentioned about Carmel. And, thank God, nothing about the rag on the shelf.

"In case you're wondering why I cut my hair," he began, "it's because I'm on a diet."

It was a fat joke. A few chuckles rippled through the room. I realized he had cleaned up, and now looked more suitable for Carmel than for the farm. I felt he had changed and I hadn't. How will I keep up with him?

"Has everyone seen Miles's duplicate machine?" he asked.

No, I hadn't.

He passed the picture around.

"I have seen three duplicates of my own machine," he commented, adding, "and they were all thinner."

Another fat joke. A few more chuckles. My mind was focused on the dust cloth.

The teacher continued.

"Do you feel the lightness of quietness in the room? We are collectively still. It is a state of nothingness, yet it is present. This is what the Eastern teachings mean when they speak of nothingness, or a great void. This state can crystallize in each person here. If it does, it is metaphysical and immortal. It is the light from the Self. It is still here…only less so. Did you feel it diminish?"

The energy in the room did grow heavier. I was trying as hard as I could to find a place within that was not obsessed with the dust cloth, which was a dirty flag taunting me about my sleep and what a bad student I was, not completing that octave.

"According to Gurdjieff, this state is always working in us, but can't make it through the mechanicalness of lower centers. As you observed, it is much finer than other energies."

My ears perked up. Robert was trying to reach me but it was as if my ears were full of wax.

The rest of the meeting was a blur. I couldn't concentrate. Robert ended the meeting and we broke into small groups. Before I could reach the rag on the shelf, someone found it and I immediately approached him and said, "I can take that." I went into the utility closet in the kitchen and tossed it in there.

When I returned, I was stunned to see the small group circles were filled, with no empty chair available. I returned to the kitchen for a stool and squeezed into the smallest group. It was led by a Lunar. We sat there waiting for someone to speak. For the first time, I was grateful there wasn't much conversation. I just wanted to sit and be free of the onslaught of 'I's, the incessant button-pushing. I settled in and my state improved, gradually.

As I retired to my room that night, I pondered what had occurred. The meeting was such a struggle for me. It was simply awful. Robert was talking about higher states and I certainly was not there. I had longed to be in his company, thinking that his presence would automatically generate my presence. I was shocked to see that it didn't happen this way. I could be fast asleep right in front of him. I could be negative right in front of him. It was shameful.

Pulling myself out of identification was HARD. The teacher can't help the student if the student can't help himself. It was a profound lesson.

❧

> A student asks the teacher, "I traveled to Mecca and did not find God there." The teacher replies, "Yes, God wasn't there. He was traveling with you."
>
> Attar

CHAPTER 119

When I awoke the next morning, my head had cleared and a thought appeared that did not result from any intellectual process on my part. It was just there, as a ribbon-wrapped present that magically unfurled itself as my eyelids opened.

"Focus first on the inner. Then the outer will take care of itself."

It was a voice of wisdom, soft and gentle and to the point. I lay there in bed, letting the words sink in. It was time to arise, and then I remembered something. When I lived with Robert at the Buck House, he privately shared with me that he always starts the day by removing the bedsheets intentionally. I had forgotten to do this all these months. It was my first conscious act of the day.

I took my clothes and went into the shower, thinking that I had no idea where I was in my development. I knew I had the ability to observe, which meant I had Observing 'I.' Where was I in relation to Deputy Steward and Steward? I knew the definitions but not the personal reality. Perhaps I will read that section of Ouspensky again in the afternoon for some insight. It felt good to have a thought-project.

I entered the kitchen for breakfast, and there was Rosemary scrambling eggs in the cast iron skillet.

"Good morning," she said. "I made enough eggs for both of us."

I was pleased, and may I say, a bit surprised at her overt kindness.

"Looks good," I commented.

I set the table for us both.

"Go take the ketchup from the fridge," she directed. "I like ketchup on my scrambled eggs."

I chuckled, shaking my head in disbelief. "So do I," I replied. "That was how we ate our eggs at home. I always felt it was uncouth. But it tastes good to me."

"It's American, you know."

"I guess it is."

The eggs were soft and fluffy, and the tang and slight sweetness of the ketchup brought immediate comfort to me. I started to relax.

"You wanted to know more about Carmel," she began, after taking a sip of coffee.

A smile came to my face. I looked into her blue eyes, which communicated more than the words she expressed. Her eyes said she was sorry.

"We found the house and will be signing the lease on Monday. The house is near Carmel High School."

What a shock! It was as if the gods had stamped the house with their approval. But the shock didn't stop with that.

"It's on a street named Whitman Circle Drive."

"That's a nice shock," I said to Rose, hoping she would agree.

"Yes, it is. Robert thought so too, which is why we are taking it."

A warmth of energy flowed through me, as I felt a connection from above us in the room. It was that third point in the pyramid. It made me present.

"When are you moving in?"

"He wants us to move in immediately," she said, adding, "and it looks like we have a buyer for this house."

"How soon?"

"Escrow would close in a month," she replied.

I didn't know what escrow was, and I didn't think it was important to ask.

I had started my second cigarette by this time. She joined me, and as she lit it and exhaled the first stream of smoke, she asked the leading question.

"What are your plans?"

I sighed deeply. This was not mine to figure out, I felt. I had no idea what would happen to me. But I answered anyway.

"I may go back to the farm."

She shook her head almost imperceptibly, but I caught it. She didn't like me hanging out with those students, and I had to admit, I didn't either. It felt like a dead end of sorts.

"Maybe you can find a job in Carmel," she said.

I told her about my trip to Carmel, and said I had no idea what kind of job would be there for me.

"There are many nice stores there. Maybe a salesgirl."

Me, a salesgirl? Not with my granny dress and tube socks and sneakers.

"I do want to be near Robert," I mentioned.

"Yes, that would be good. How's your money holding up?"

"I'm okay for now. At the farm, I'm able to still make five dollars for a massage, which fills up my gas tank. And the occasional substitute teaching job here. I guess that's not going to continue."

"Maybe Carmel High School has an opening," she suggested.

"Maybe. I can look into it," I said.

I flicked the ash from my cigarette into the tray. She followed suit.

We sat there together quietly. Much of what we talked about was hypothetical. Guessing about my future direction was an easy pastime. Images entered my head, picturing myself in that bookstore with the flamboyant Jovial lady. Maybe she would accept me.

Rose interrupted my reverie.

"You can help me pack some of my knick-knacks, if you have time this afternoon."

"Sure," I said, thinking it's the least I could do to help her.

That was the end of the conversation. In the afternoon, we packed up things that were hers and that contained many memories, some of which she shared. Other objects belonged to Mac; those went into a different box.

After an hour of sorting, I placed two more items into Mac's container, which was now almost full. Then it struck me. Mac's items were more numerous than hers. Rose's life had been intertwined with her husband for decades. Her marriage was all about supporting Mac. He was the star. There was little that spoke of Rosemary — who she was, what she wanted for her life. Her move to Carmel was not just relocation. It was a formal announcement of her separation. It was the beginning of a new life for her.

She hid her pain well. How she was able to carry on in the midst of having her life shredded was a marvel. I guess you can say, we had this in common.

Here we were, two courageous women, trying to carve out from years of expectations the real, authentic being we were fated to become. This endeared me to her forever.

※

Accept the things to which fate binds you, and love the people with whom fate brings you together, but do so with all your heart.
Marcus Aurelius

CHAPTER 120

Thursday morning, after a blueberry pancake breakfast, Rosemary headed out to Carmel. As I waved good-bye, I could feel something in me had changed. That old soul part of me was looking through my eyes at Rose. When I turned to re-enter the kitchen, the fragrance of the higher state accompanied me. Unfortunately, it lasted but a moment. The first 'I's appeared about what the course of my day would be. Would I stay in Vacaville for the small meeting that night? Would I drive back to the farm? What would I do this afternoon?

Why is my higher state always interrupted by a question?

I started to laugh at this thought. Excuse me dear. That's a question, too.

Then I remembered my thought-project. Studying the difference between Observing 'I,' Deputy Steward and Steward would be a nice activity.

I entered the living room to pull down *The Fourth Way* from the shelf, but the shelves were empty. I had forgotten. The books were all packed away. It was a shock to see that the 'I' desiring to read was an old one and had not participated in yesterday's activities. As the Work says, the 'I's are separate and do not know one another, yet all call themselves 'I.' It was a reverification of the many 'I's concept.

The next 'I' asked, where is my own copy? It took me a few moments to recall that my beat-up copy was in the trunk of my car, with my other belongings. The car had become a portable tent for me.

Once I retrieved the book, I sat on the couch in the living room and turned to the sections describing deputy steward. Last year I seemed to recall that the definitions were quite concise and that it would be easy for me to use them as guidelines for my evolution. Reading this section now, these definitions are pretty theoretical. In another section, he talks about not actually knowing what is meant by steward or master. I don't recall him saying this before. It's odd. How could I have missed that?

THE DIVINE BEGINNING

When I first read *The Fourth Way*, I felt it had all the answers, and now it feels like it leaves me with more questions. The primary distinctions he makes between these levels of development are valuation and efforts. Those I understand. I also understand that the 'I's are like buttons that are pushed by external circumstances, like my hysterical laughter. I've learned to control that much better this year. I may laugh, but then I see that I laughed, and that observation in itself disengages the trigger of hysteria. Maybe this is deputy steward.

As I was thinking about my mechanics and whether I've been able to control certain manifestations, I formulated the following understanding of Observing 'I', Deputy Steward, and Steward.

Imagine having a fist thrown at your face. Observing 'I' can only say, "I was just hit by a fist." It observes what happened after the fact. Deputy Steward sees the setup — the pattern — and the fist coming. It knows what's about to happen just before it occurs, but is not fast enough to avoid it. It says, "I'm about to be hit by a fist." It's helpless to do anything about it because it lacks will. Steward? It sees the setup and the fist coming and knows the outcome in advance, as if in slow motion. It has time to say, "Duck!" That's will.

We read, we process, we verify, and we explain our understanding based on our experience. My analogy suits me. After all, unlike Ouspensky, my father was a boxer.

* * * *

It was midafternoon when a strong 'I' suddenly appeared in my head: I need a meeting. I acted on that 'I' and called Don to see if he was hosting a meeting at his home that night.

"No, but Doris and I are going to Richard's house. Would you like to come with us?"

I was so happy to hear this that I immediately responded, Yes. Then he added something delightful.

"Doris wishes you to come for an early dinner at her place. Say, 5:30?"

"Of course," I replied, adding, "how sweet of her to invite me."

Don gave me the directions, and it was on Edgewood, which was a street off of Buck Avenue.

It had been an overcast day at the end of January, and that simple 'I' to call Don brought a ray of sunshine into my day. I must remember to act on these types of 'I's more often, I thought.

* * * *

I arrived on time and was proud that I could find the place in the darkness. Her residence wasn't a house but an apartment complex. This surprised me, as I thought for sure Doris, being of a certain age, had a house that she called home for many years. It was at that point that I realized I knew little about her.

Doris greeted me at the door with a smile and a hug and welcomed me inside. It was a small, compact apartment with minimal light in the living room. Another couple from Vacaville was there, but in the dimness, I could barely make them out. I recognized them when they stood up and we embraced. I was then told they also would be going with us to the meeting. We followed Doris to a square dining table off the kitchen area. She squeezed a chair in to accommodate me. It was clear that I was the odd man out.

Doris was gracious and lovely. She was a Saturnine lady with thick glasses that enlarged her blue eyes and a hairdo that was from my high school days of beehives and French twists. Her hair color was honey blond. Her nose looked more Jovial — bulging at the end — and not much like a narrow, straight one belonging to the Saturn type. She had a sweet, feminine voice, and suited Don in her traditional dress and appropriate manners. They made each other happy.

The first course was a special avocado and grapefruit salad, with a honey poppy seed dressing. What made it unusual was the plate she used: it was not a round salad plate or bowl but a crescent-shaped white porcelain one. I recognized it as part of the Nut Tree collection. Don proudly explained it was a Nut Tree recipe that Doris made to perfection. It was indeed tasty and exotic. I had no idea that you could serve fruit with lettuce. The chicken main course was delicious as well.

We helped Doris clear the table. She told us not to worry about the dishes for now, since it was late and we needed to make it to the meeting in Walnut Creek. Don suggested we all drive in his car, which could hold the five of us.

I positioned myself in the back seat behind the driver. Because Don had long legs, it was cramped, yet it was not a difficult thing for me since I appreciated it whenever anyone wanted to drive me somewhere. The conversations between Don and Doris extended to include the other couple, but left me out completely. I sat there silently as we crossed the Benicia-Martinez Bridge. While listening to their conversations, a most amazing thing happened.

THE DIVINE BEGINNING

Quietly, my eyesight landed on the door handle. That object came into perfect view with a clarity that went beyond my eyesight's normal capability. Its three-dimensionality popped out at me. It was HERE. And I was HERE looking at it. It was the same part of me that SAW the lace curtains when I was a child in Bubbie's house.

A higher state magically, and unexpectedly, emerged. It came from nowhere, and with its appearance, the many 'I's vanished for seconds. I tried to keep its clarity. As soon as I moved my gaze slightly to refocus, the first 'I' appeared ("why are you looking at that stupid thing?") and the rush of 'I's followed like a flood to engulf the state. The three-dimensionality was now gone and the object appeared flat and common.

I turned to look at Don and Doris in the front seats, talking away, mechanically. Their pleasantness was not presence. It wasn't a judgment, more a shocking, painful realization that being nice and polite in that way was the second, not the third, state. Wanting to be liked, wanting to be accepted, with good manners and all, was about changing external behavior. I wanted to change my inner state — to live in a three-dimensional world — more than live in a two-dimensional world and appear civilized and proper to others.

It was then that the light bulb went off inside of me. Oh, that's what the voice meant yesterday morning: "Focus first on the inner. Then the outer will take care of itself."

* * * *

We arrived at our destination. The meeting was in the wood-paneled room. The subjects were body types, features and centers of gravity. I gave a few angles. It was what we do.

The higher state I experienced crossing the bridge still resonated within me, but even if I lingered on the memory, I could not resurrect the real experience. Despite my efforts to self-remember and divide my attention, the state did not return that night. It had been an unexpected gift. I understood my work in a new way. I saw how awakening has setbacks, that higher states can be followed by lower states. Awakening was more like a roller coaster than a rocket ship.

Ah, yes. Didn't Robert just say this, that in a teaching, it's two steps forward, one step back? He was talking about the school. Now I see he was also talking about our personal evolution. Enjoying the highs and enduring the lows is the nature of the ascent. It tests valuation. To be or not to be? To sleep, perchance to dream? Ah, there's the rub!

Alas, two souls are living in my breast,
And one wants to separate itself from the other.
One holds fast to the world with earthy passion
And clings with twining tendrils:
The other lifts itself with forceful craving
To the very roof of heaven.
         Johann Goethe

CHAPTER 121

We arrived back in Vacaville well past midnight. It was now Friday, and I had no substitute teaching job that day, so I decided to sleep late. Rose's home was becoming a ghost house. It would not be a center of activity much longer. Monday was January 31, a big day for the school. We were sounding a new *do* as Carmel would now have a house for the students there.

 Where was I to go? The farm was where I could replenish my food supply, but I had to sleep in a public area and not see the teacher. Vacaville was where I had a private room, but little food and no teacher. Carmel was where the teacher was, but I had no room. These were the logistics of my situation.

 Although I wanted to be around Robert, and enjoyed having my own space, the teaching is practical. Ouspensky said a good householder has not lost the capacity for practical thinking. With that, I knew I had to go to the farm that weekend for food and possibly new massage customers to help me pay for gas. It was that basic.

 I left for the farm after a late breakfast of scrambled eggs (I used the last two in the fridge), toast (the last two slices in the loaf), and coffee. As I arrived at the Lodge, it was colder than I remembered. Valley temperatures were often warmer than the foothills. It was three in the afternoon, and the kitchen was quiet. I went into the cooler to see if supplies were plentiful and half the shelves were empty. I was hoping the food van would make its appearance by Monday at least. I grabbed some dates and nuts, which were still plentiful, as a snack.

 I entered the main room and decided to sit near the fading fire to read the latest copy of Meg's *Via Del Sol Journal*, which I had picked up at the meeting. The last time Robert was at the farm was the beginning of the year, which was

THE DIVINE BEGINNING

only four weeks ago. It was so hard to believe this, because it felt like a year had passed in that short period of time. Since Meg was in Carmel, she was able to provide notes from the Carmel meetings. The meetings were still being held at the Wayside Inn, and I read that a new student joined whose name was Sharon and that a person named Ken was to lead one of two meetings a week. It was odd not to know who was in the school.

My reading was interrupted by Yorgos, who entered carrying logs for the fire. I was both glad and surprised to see him.

We exchanged greetings and I asked him about the food van.

"Kerrie's coming back from Berkeley soon with the van."

I was relieved and watched as he added fuel to the fire.

"Where is everybody?" I asked.

"Oh, they're around."

He wasn't a communicative guy. Suddenly, this 'I' popped out of my mouth.

"I've decided I'm moving back here."

Did I really just say that?! Oops. Photograph "really."

Yorgos looked at me for further explanation. Other 'I's came out of my mouth. It was obvious to me that I hungered for conversation.

"Yes," I continued. "Rosemary's selling her home in Vacaville."

He probably knew this. But I went on about my logistics and other thoughts that had been swirling in my head while I was alone.

I hoped he would reply, and he did.

"It is common for a Venusian body type to sit around and wait for something to happen to him. It is Venusian mechanicalness. If you wanted to move back here badly enough, you would find a job in one day. I do not think you know what you want."

He was spot on. From one angle.

I agreed, furthering the verbal exchange by adding, "It is a slow process for the Venusian type to decide what it is 'I' want."

"Yes," he concurred, "it's the steadfastness of the Venusian."

I thanked him for his thoughts. Perhaps tomorrow morning, unless I receive a call to work as a substitute, I will scour the town of Marysville. Yet, as soon as that thought appeared, another 'I' said, "Didn't we already do that?"

I didn't listen to that 'I.' It was a time for initiative, a time for action.

* * * *

The van did arrive around five that evening, and I helped Kerrie prepare dinner. While dining, I learned that some students regularly attend the Bay Area meetings on Tuesdays and that next week will be open meetings. They suggested I go too, and I understood why: they needed someone to drive them. As long as they paid for the gas, it was a good possibility.

When the morning came, the incentive to go to Marysville simply disappeared. I didn't listen to that 'I' either, apparently. Was this Venusian? Dad called me lazy. It didn't feel like that. It felt more like I simply wasn't meant to do something. It was hard to explain to him, and I beat myself up about it for years when I was a child.

Everywhere I looked, I seemed to see people who were content with where they were and what they were doing. They had a focus in their external daily life. I had none. My focus was internal and cerebral, studying the system and developing the steward. Perhaps I belonged more in a monastery than a Fourth Way school.

I spent my time helping in the kitchen. There were no visitors this weekend. I tried to find massage customers, but the people who now lived at the farm were as poor as I was. My gas tank was still close to full so I was fine there, and I paid my February teaching payment at the last meeting so I was good with the Fellowship.

It was hard to leave my life family, and now I am finding it's hard to leave my school friends and spend hours of my day in a job with sleeping people. But I need to be responsible, yes? Perhaps, that's what my issue is. I still haven't grown up.

This way, that way.
I do not know what to do: I am of two minds.
Sappho

CHAPTER 122

Monday morning came, and it was particularly cold. I stayed in my sleeping bag near the woodstove as long as I could. The smell of coffee and toast beckoned me to rise. I popped up the moment the bathroom door opened and quickly snuck inside.

When I came out dressed, Mason was adding wood to the stove with Marsha nearby.

"We're thinking of going to Carmel for the meeting there tonight. Interested?" asked Mason.

"Are you driving?" I inquired.

"We could. Or we could go with you if you want."

They had an old car that was beat-up and dirty. I knew he liked to drive mine, but I had had no intention of going to Carmel. Or did I?

"I would want to be back tonight," I stipulated, knowing I didn't have money for an overnight accommodation, "so if you would drive us back that would work for me."

They were pleased with this and we decided to leave within the hour.

I packed up as much food as I could without appearing like I was stealing. I thought I could eat in the car, and this way minimize spending money on dining out.

As we prepared to leave, another student named Paul decided to go with us. Mason offered to drive, and I didn't resist. I sat in the front passenger seat this time. The route was pretty direct and becoming familiar to me now. The traffic all the way down to the Bay Area was light since it was Monday before three. I tried to memorize the route as we passed San Jose, and when we came to that tricky place on Highway 156, I studied it and correctly guessed where to take the exit. In that moment, I returned to my childhood: I would memorize routes in Los Angeles that my father would take to Bubbie's house, to the stores, etc. Why would I do this? I had an intense fear of being lost, and I learned to control it by being attentive to my surroundings.

The sun was shining as we reached Monterey Bay, which was a surprise. The blue sky reflected itself on the mirror of the ocean, and lifted my heart. As we ascended the hill toward Carmel, Mason spoke.

"We have time. Let's drive to Big Sur."

"Yes!" said Marsha and Paul from the back seat.

I didn't know what that meant, having never been there, so I just sat there passively. I'm just along for the ride, I guess.

As we drove on past the Carmel Valley entrance off of the highway and past the Carmel Highlands, with its beautiful homes tucked away under massive and majestic pine trees ("They're Monterey Pines," said Mason), the scenery opened up and the Pacific Ocean appeared. The clouds had now covered the sun, which made the view more somber. But the waves were not affected: they were playfully crashing on top of each other, destroying their forms until they slid, overlapping, along the narrow damp sand. Again and again and again they frolicked. Their joyfulness was contagious.

"This is beautiful!" I found myself saying out loud.

Mason took the curves in the road with great skill. As we rounded one bend, there, in front of us, was the famous arched bridge that I recalled seeing in iconic Hollywood films, where a motorcycle hero zoomed across the narrow lane, alone, with no traffic. It epitomized the freedom of the American Way, or, as the song said, "Get your motor runnin', head out on the highway, looking for adventure, in whatever comes our way."

We stopped at the lookout point to take in the impressions of the bridge and the expanse of cliffs and the wild waves pounding the rocks below.

The road took a turn inland and the terrain became dense with vegetation. Eventually, after over thirty minutes of driving from Carmel, we reached our destination, the Big Sur River Inn.

Mason and Marsha had made a big deal of this place, and I was stunned to see it looked like a weathered burger shack with a single gas pump. I might as well have been back in Oregon House.

As we entered the restaurant area, the low wooden ceiling and walls made it a bit claustrophobic for me. I was looking for light and it was a dark place. It made me uncomfortable. I realized I was an LA girl, and I liked more refined impressions. Carmel was more appealing to me. Would I ever be able to live there?

The time was around six. The food I brought had quickly disappeared during the drive, so I was hungry and the menu listed a burger with fries and a Coke. As we waited for our food to arrive, Mason and Marsha were talking about how they loved to come here to hike and swim in the river.

"There's a place down the highway where the river goes into the ocean," Marsha said, poking at her salad.

Mason was chewing his veggie sandwich when he added, "You can take a bridge to the small waterfall that empties onto the beach. It's cool."

There seemed to be magic to this inn for them. It did not shower down on me, however. I was becoming negative inside. I wanted to leave as soon as I could. The place kind of reeked of hippie-dippy B Influence.

While we were chatting and chomping, a man appeared at the table.

"Hey, Mason and Marsha!"

It was apparently an old friend of theirs. We were introduced, and, surprisingly, this guy also knew Paul.

I looked down at my Timex. It was almost seven.

"Shouldn't we be going?" I asked suddenly.

"Yeah, in a moment," replied Mason.

I stood up to use the restroom, and he continued to talk with this man.

When I returned, I received my bill and paid it. The others took their time, and we eventually entered the car to drive back to Carmel. This time, I was positioned in the back seat.

As we turned onto Ocean Avenue, Mason stunned me.

"Does anyone have the address to the meeting?"

Silence.

I thought he knew. I kind of knew.

"I heard it was near Dolores and the bakery there," I offered.

We turned on Dolores toward the bakery, and I leaned forward to direct him.

"Trisha said it was the next block on the corner."

We drove to Lincoln, and the two-story building on the corner was not a house or a standard apartment building. It looked like a place for businesses.

"Are you sure it's here?"

"Pretty sure," I replied.

The first thing we needed was to find a parking space, which was more difficult than anyone thought. We went several blocks to find a spot that was not in front of someone's driveway. Most were two-hour parking limits, and that was not good for us, since the meeting would last longer than that.

Once we found a space, which was on a side street several streets over, we began to hike back to the 7th and Dolores corner. It was now 7:55 and the meeting was to begin at 8. We entered a corridor of the building and immediately ran into Mary C., much to our delight.

We followed her up a staircase at the western corner of the building that led to Sheila's apartment on the second floor. As we entered, Meg and Don were talking to Robert and Jim. Don had a piece of paper in his hand and they were discussing its contents. They looked serious. Meanwhile, Nadia and Marie and Alden sat in a circle on folding chairs, together with other students I did not know.

The apartment was quite small, with a simple room and few pieces of furniture that were weird to me. One was a leather tufted bed with a roll at the end for a headrest and shiny chrome legs. You could see the bed was resting on straps. Who would ever want to sleep on that? It looked cold and uncomfortable. There were also two matching leather and chrome chairs next to it with straps for the seat and backrest. No one sat in these. That corner was like a tiny museum display.

As the three of us were standing there, Rosemary and Sheila appeared with water glasses from what I assumed was the kitchen. Rose was shocked to see me. She said nothing.

There were no extra chairs to be found, and no place to put them if we had them. Obviously, we were not expected.

The meeting was about to begin, and Mason, Marsha, and Paul gravitated to the floor. They each had on jeans. I was in my granny dress, and folded legs were not easily achievable, considering my Venusian type. I was perplexed what to do, and Robert motioned to a male student, who reluctantly gave up his chair for me. He sat on the floor.

We turned our attention to Robert. He began with the news of this day.

"We have a new meeting home in Carmel."

He gave the address and directions to it. I smiled at Nadia, Rosemary, Mary, and Marie but they were focusing on Robert.

"A party is planned for this Saturday, February 5, at the new house and the farm and Bay Area students are welcome. Buffet starts at 7:30."

That meant I needed to come back to Carmel in a few days, I thought.

Suddenly, a small child emerges from a hidden room and runs up to a woman sitting across from me. The kid is telling her mother she wants the lights in her room turned up. As this woman stands up and takes her daughter by the hand into the back room, the meeting pauses until she returns.

Robert then directs his comment to her.

"Linda, separate from the discussion we are going to have about your child, and see that the same has 'happened' to us."

I am shocked! Her name is Linda?

Robert continues.

"Do you all photograph the child is lying? What she is trying to know is if her mother is in the other room. She also wants Linda to be with her. She is lying already. A certain amount of lying is automatic."

Linda raises her hand.

"Can it be helped with the child?"

"It can be minimized," replies Robert, adding, "Later, like us, she will have to help herself. From what I observed, you are a good mother. You try to provide non-warping environments. That is the best we can do. You also do not live for your child, which is lovely."

Robert turns to Meg and asks her to explain about being identified and not knowing it.

"When I heard about the demise of the little white rooster at the farm, the emotional center went CLUNK."

We all chuckled when Meg said this. I felt the same way.

"I never thought I was identified with that chicken until I heard the news and photographed the reaction."

Robert clarified further. "People can think they are not identified with something, until the identification is tested."

This angle from the teacher hit me especially hard. That was the case with Miles and me. But I insisted on calling it love, not identification.

Alden raised his hand.

"From one angle, people believe something if it is in print."

"What Alden said about print being 'officially' true," commented Robert, "is a good point. Just about all of it is a lie. One reason it is a lie is that authors take their subject, whatever it is, as the most important subject there is. Immediately, that makes it a lie. The highest 'print' a person can struggle with is 'To be or not to be.' Six little words. 'To be' — World 6 and World 12 — 'or not to be' — World 48 and World 96."

With that, we took an intermission. We gathered around a table for refreshments and chatted. Robert sat talking to Rose, so I was not able to speak with her about the Vacaville house. I was tired, and was looking forward to returning to the farm. We were planning to leave after the intermission.

We hugged everyone and proceeded down the stairs toward the parked car. It was fortunate Mason remembered where it was, because I didn't.

He stopped by the driver's door and handed me the keys. This was not our arrangement. And then he said something that blew my mind.

"Marsha and I and Paul are hanging out in Carmel for a few days." He went on to say they were meeting his friend at a local bar on Ocean and would be staying with him. He handed me five dollars for the gas, and I watched them walk away, joyfully.

I stood there alone. It was an overwhelming moment. I had not brought my sleeping bag, and the thought of begging the ladies to allow me to stay on the floor of the new meeting house was more than I could consider. It was humiliating.

The air was clean and cold with a sprinkle of sea salt. That silent, three-dimensional clarity returned to me. It was the third state. Everything was perfectly delineated with energy that throbbed with life — the lamp posts, the uneven pavement, the bougainvillea hanging like tresses over the shoulder of a wall. From this place, I felt the presence of the gods, and was assured they would guide me, as they did on Mount Tamalpais that night in Marin.

I drove up Ocean and the Carmel HIGH School sign reminded me that this turn in the play was intended for my evolution. I checked my gas tank all the way home, and decided not to stop for gas, because being alone in a car at midnight pumping gas scared me. Hopefully, I had enough to make it to the farm.

As it happened, my tank took me as far as the Monte Verde exit in Vacaville. That would be my final destination. I pulled into Rose's driveway, praying the key was still there, under the mat. It was! I unlocked the kitchen door and turned on the light, which still worked. The clock showed 3 a.m. I thanked the gods for the safe journey home, wherever that home would be.

> *Know that your realm is a home, and a home sits on the four sides of its foundation. That home is you.*
>
> Ibn Arabi

CHAPTER 123

I awoke around eleven the next morning. Images of the long ride the night before — connecting from one highway to the next, battling my fears of being lost in the full-moon-lit wilderness of the mountains before reaching San Jose — played like a film in a movie theatre. A feeling of pride in my ability to continue the journey made me happy. I could manage what I thought I couldn't. It opened a door for me. Last night I became more independent, more grownup.

By noon my stomach's emptiness had me change the channel, and a big breakfast of eggs, bacon, hash browns, and toast and coffee appeared on the mental screen. There was basically no food in the house, so I decided to go to a local Denny's and place the order I had just envisioned. It should cost me about two dollars. That leaves enough money for gas to allow me to drive to the farm.

Upon my return from lunch, Rosemary's car was in the driveway. This was not totally unexpected since many of her items were still in the house. I was actually hoping to see her, not only for some company, but to find out more about the Carmel house.

I entered the kitchen as she was putting some food away in the refrigerator.

"Hi!" I said, pretending to be surprised to see her.

"Hello," she said, quickly turning her head in my direction to see who was speaking before placing the next item on the shelf.

I went to hand her a jar and she took it.

"It was good to see you last night," I said, mainly to evoke the same response from her. It didn't work.

"How are you doing?" I asked, trying to stimulate a conversation. It worked.

"There's a meeting tonight, and I could use your help."

I forgot it was Tuesday.

"Be happy to."

I was just at a meeting, and now this would be a second meeting in a row. I could feel the pace speeding up, and it was a bit disorienting.

"What would you like me to do?"

"Vacuum."

"Okay. I can dust, too, and bring in the chairs."

"That would be nice."

Rosemary had finished unpacking her groceries and went to sit down at the kitchen table with her Marlboros in hand. I joined her.

"The deal on the house fell through."

I looked at her stunned. Which house?

After a puff, she continued.

"Another couple is interested so we have another month at least here in Vacaville."

My cigarette plume rode the gentle air of a deep sigh rather than a controlled exhalation. What a relief, I thought. This may mean I could still use this house for a couple of weeks, perhaps finding more teaching jobs.

"The piano mover will be here tomorrow."

"Will the piano go in the new Carmel house?"

"Yes."

It was clear she had much on her mind.

"Does everyone have a bedroom?"

"Yes. It's a large house in the woods. Robert liked it immediately."

My next thought leaked from my head through the portal of my mouth.

"Will students be able to stay overnight?"

She took a deep draught of smoke before replying.

"Not right now."

That answer was not like Rose. She's usually far more direct, one way or the other. It almost felt like someone else answered my question.

The afternoon was passing quickly. I went to complete my chores while Rosemary retired to her room. She emerged looking ready for the meeting.

"I'm going to the Nut Tree Airport to pick up Robert, Jim, and Sheila."

"There's an airport at the Nut Tree?"

"It's a small strip."

As I stood on the kitchen step waving good-bye, I wished I were going with her. It was 5:30 and I was sure she would be heading to the Coffee Tree afterwards with Robert and Jim and Sheila.

I went into the kitchen and decided to make a sandwich from a loaf of bread she bought. I took slices from the center of the loaf so that it appeared nothing was missing. A few pieces of cheese and a leaf of lettuce with mayo would do the trick to take me through the meeting until refreshments.

Students began to arrive around seven, and it was nice to have more company. I had reserved my seat in front of Robert's chair before anyone showed up, and was helping with the hors d'oeuvres platters when Robert, Jim, Sheila and Rose entered the kitchen. Robert went to speak with Don, and it was nice to see the loving embrace and conversation they were having. Doris, who stood by Don, had a twinkle in her eye and would giggle softly every so often.

I was finishing the refreshment setup when Jim came up to me. My heart fluttered a bit, but I quickly learned he was a messenger and it was not personal.

"Robert would like you to sit up front with him."

I was speechless. This is an honor. I often thought Robert didn't see me anymore.

As we entered the room and took our seats, Robert paused before beginning. A slight smile could be seen on his face as he gestured his thoughts to Jim, who spoke.

"Much good news tonight. The first is that the moon is waning."

He waited for a response, and it came as a chuckle from a few of us. It had been a strong moon for me, with the Mason and Marsha play and the long drive home alone. It wasn't life as usual.

"We have a larger airplane. It's a Cessna 182 Skylane. It is in excellent condition…for a 1936."

He made a joke…I think.

"Ah, no. It's a 1971 model," he corrected.

Robert's sense of humor was like a ten-year-old's. It was kind of cute, but wouldn't make it in Vegas.

"Do not worry about the airplane. C Influence will fly it all the time, just as they now move my hand. William Blake said, 'My hand is moved against my will.' He also said, 'The authors of my poetry are in heaven.' "

I smiled. I felt my drive home in the dark was a similar experience. It would be hard to explain it to anyone, so it was good to hear Robert's comment. It validated my understanding.

"Also, we have a new house in Carmel."

This I knew. He gave specific directions and a phone number. I couldn't write it down since I was sitting up front, but I knew I could ask for it later from Rose or Jim.

"We are all new faces tonight. This is good. It means we have changed since we last met. Also, many faces are wise enough to know not to expect anything from the meetings. That means their being takes whatever C Influence serves through us, good or bad, up or down."

I had verified this.

"If we are not looking to the future, it is an indication we are in the present."

He looked around and then added, "It is also good to look to the future — both are true."

This relativity I needed. It was too scary not to know what I was supposed to do next.

"Remember, formatory mind will often think just the opposite of a statement."

He stopped, and I sat there looking out at my fellow students. All eyes were on Robert, with a few exceptions. There was a different quality of gaze, however. Some looked like they were watching television, with a glazed look, and the pauses were commercials. I wondered if Robert saw us this way.

"Any moonlight observations?"

A Bay Area student raised his hand.

"The City of Miami reports each month that there's more crime during a full moon."

Another hand was raised.

"During the full moon, there's usually many 'I's rattling around inside my head."

"Do you still feel the moon here tonight?" asked Robert. Many of us nodded. "Our body is 78% water, and, like the tides, it feels the pull of the moon's gravity. It is still dining. It will vary from person to person, and as a group, the effect of the moon can be overcome. Also, remember C Influence runs us roughly at times during moons as a form of payment for more pleasant times, like the party in Carmel this weekend. We are overdue a bit for this party."

On this note, we had our intermission. I went around to see if any students had teaching payments to give me. I collected a few and handed the envelope to Jim as he and Robert left with Rose and Sheila before the small groups began.

After the small groups, I asked a few guys to help me restore the living room, while several ladies cleaned up the kitchen area. Everyone had left by ten.

The evening was cool, and I stood by the kitchen porch railing to smoke a cigarette. I wondered where I would go tomorrow? I needed food, so that would be the ranch. I needed money, so that would mean staying in Vacaville. And now Carmel may be calling me to join in the fun down there. My instinctive, intellectual, and emotional centers were in a three-way split.

What day is it? Today is February first. Where was I a year ago? Ah yes, I had met the man of my dreams, and I was sure my future included love and romance, a secure job, and smooth sailing ahead. And then within a week, the Los Angeles earthquake came. From one angle, the shaking hasn't stopped since. My inner state is slowly appearing clearer while my outer life has no form or direction. How long can I live like this?

*

> To endure and to have patience (this is how one gains experiences),
> to expect no help but truly great, almost miraculous help:
> this is what allowed me to go on since childhood.
> Rainer Maria Rilke

CHAPTER 124

I did drive to the ranch the next morning. After lunch, a special thing happened. Tall Jane came up to me and asked if I could give her a massage. She had strained her back cleaning the children's house and had actually been waiting for me to appear.

At dinner, Jane said she felt so much better and suggested to Small Jane to have me give her one, too, since she was having neck issues. Small Jane was Martial and was not into it. I asked her if I could just check it out. She agreed, so I went to her neck and felt the tension. My fingers touched her with as much presence and care as I could. After about ten minutes, she could move her head from side to side. She handed me a five-dollar bill just for that. They both scheduled massages for the next day. I was delighted.

That night, as I rested in my sleeping bag on the floor next to the warmth of the wood burning stove, I thanked the gods for their generosity and expressed my gratitude that I did not have to play salesman with my friends. It was an odious act that I hoped could be avoided.

* * * *

Thursday night students were making plans for the weekend. It was clear Robert would not be at the farm, given the fact there was the big party in Carmel, not to mention the first of the Bay Area open meetings on Friday evening. It was funny to be in the position of having a car and not in the position of looking for a ride. Now I found myself in a new position: looking for riders who could share the cost of the drive.

After dinner, a few of us gathered in front of the fireplace to discuss our plans. One person said we could go to the Bay Area meeting, stay overnight with Anna in Berkeley, where the meeting was scheduled, and then go on to Carmel.

"I tried that once," offered another student, "but she doesn't want this because University students rent from her, and she doesn't like them seeing people sleeping on the floor of her living room." Well, that's out.

We spent over an hour talking about it because there were so many options: not going to the Bay Area open meeting but going directly to Carmel on Saturday morning; going to the Bay Area, staying in a Motel 6 (after all, it's only $6, which is why they call it Motel 6, and we could share rooms to make it less expensive) and then heading out to Carmel; going to the San Francisco meeting, staying with a student in Walnut Creek or Vallejo (but this is backtracking — going north instead of south). It was becoming too complicated.

Finally, it was David who offered us the best option: Let's sleep on it. Tomorrow's another day.

* * * *

During Friday morning's breakfast, the conversation resumed — and ended quickly. Nobody wanted to go to the Bay Area meeting or to Carmel. I was shocked to see how a completely different set of 'I's emerged in people. I read about it in the books, but to witness each person agree on not doing anything except keeping to their daily routine was actually disturbing.

It was now up to me to decide what I wanted, and it was clear: I was going directly on Saturday to Carmel. Whether or not anyone would accompany me was still a mystery, but not a determining factor. I had twenty dollars, an aim, and a car. That's all I needed.

* * * *

Friday evening just after dinner, Tall Jane approached me.

"I just arranged for my son to be looked after on Saturday and wondered if you had room in your car for me. I would need to return after the party, if that would be okay. I can share the driving and pay for gas."

"That would be great!" I replied, thinking how nice it would be to know her a bit better. She seemed like quite a sweet person. We arranged to leave after breakfast. That way we would arrive in the early afternoon, do some window shopping, watch the sunset and be at the buffet table by 7:30.

* * * *

In the morning, we found another lady who wished to accompany us. Her name was Tina, and she just joined from Vallejo. It surprised me how people would come up to the farm with someone and how little I would know of them. I just knew their first names, mainly. Students were mostly acquaintances. I did not feel close to anyone in particular. Funny, huh?

After breakfast we headed out according to plan. I actually drove directly to Carmel, stopping briefly for gas at a station in Gilroy since the price looked right at 19 cents a gallon (the same as Vacaville). As I turned on Ocean Avenue, I drove to Lincoln, the street of Sheila's apartment, to park and window shop. It was lunchtime, and we went to the Bistro to have a sandwich and fries. The jewelry shops on the main street of Ocean attracted me strongly, while Jane and Tina liked the craft stores.

We decided to return to the car and drive along the Scenic Road to see the ocean. It was a soothing impression, even though the temperature was cool. We were becoming a bit tired of walking around, so I offered a suggestion.

"What do you think about going to the Carmel house now? Maybe we could help out?"

There was no opposition. I must admit, however, my suggestion was based on finding the place before it was dark. I was more afraid of being lost than eager to clean or set up.

Jane was from Napa and told me she and her ex-husband used to come to Carmel, so she could navigate while I drove. We realized that the directions we received were based on arriving to Carmel, not being in Carmel, so we had to backtrack. It was confusing. It said to take Stewart Avenue to go to Flanders, but we turned directly onto Flanders, not Stewart, which connected to Whitman Circle. I assumed the house and house number

THE DIVINE BEGINNING

would be immediately visible. Not true. We found ourselves back on the highway, so we had to take Flanders again to Whitman Circle that then led back to the highway. Whitman Circle was well named: we were going around in circles.

A discussion ensued. Each house was hidden, so the numbers were not easily visible. Jane insisted we turn left onto a long driveway off of Whitman. She had a hunch and she was right. There stood the house with the number clearly marked.

It was late afternoon, and as we exited our car, Klair came out with a beautiful petite young woman with a blond ponytail and pastel capri pants and white shirt. We were introduced. Her name was Cheryl, and I was surprised to learn she was not a new student from Carmel. She was the landlady. She couldn't have been more than a few years my senior. Wow, I thought, how could she afford this house in Carmel? I hadn't met a rich young person before. It was a different world from mine.

She was polite yet looked a bit nervous. She quickly left in a nice car. Klair ushered us in, but no one else was in the house. I assumed it would be bustling with students preparing the food for the buffet, so I asked Klair about this.

"Robert wanted us to order food from the Mediterranean Market. Everyone will have to contribute a few dollars."

She gave us a quick tour of the house. The formal dining room had a large wooden table and enough chairs to accommodate a dozen people comfortably. Expansive windows and thick curtains, which were open, let in the light that filtered through the dense foliage of trees and shrubs. To the left of this room, we stepped down into the living room, where a meeting could hold as many people as Rosemary's house. There in the corner was Rosemary's piano. It was lovely and comforting to see, as it brought me a sense of continuity.

We moved on to the bedrooms.

"This is Nadia's room," said Klair, as we peeked inside. The room was small, with a mattress on the floor. It had a sliding glass door that led to a small, private balcony.

Next, she opened Marie's room. It was similar to Nadia's, but slightly larger with a nicely made bed and a few pieces of furniture. Between them was a bathroom.

We went into the kitchen that was off the entry way. It had a dinette set (small metal table with three chairs) pressed against the wall in the corner next to the long counter with sink and stove. On both sides of the kitchen was abundant cupboard space. Across from the sink was a large refrigerator.

Klair led us from the kitchen down a narrow hallway, with four closed doors. The first door on the left was Rosemary's room. She did not open the door for us to enter. Across from it was a full bathroom with tub and shower and next to the bathroom was Klair's room. It was dark with a small bed under the window. And at the end of the hall was the master bedroom. This is where Robert will stay when he is in town. We entered and saw a beautiful bed and a long balcony that extended toward Rosemary's room.

"There's nothing for you to do here," Klair said after the tour, adding, "so why not go down Ocean to see the sunset?"

It was a good idea.

As we arrived at the beach, we ran into a few students, and we gave them more specific directions to the meeting house so that they didn't go round and round Whitman Circle like we did.

We still had an hour or so after sunset before the evening's event began, so we ended up with those students who suggested we go to a local bar. It wasn't my idea. There, at the bar, however, was the actor Doug McClure. I had a crush on him when I was a kid, watching his Westerns on TV. But to see him smoking away with his right hand and holding a whisky in his left, while already clearly drunk, was a shock. He was talking to some guy who listened to him ramble on, complaining that he did not land the role he wanted. I couldn't take my eyes off of him. Here was a juxtaposition of images: the clean-cut character on the screen that I knew, and this mess of a man in real life. And here I was. In a conscious school, trying to awaken. How did I choose this life and how did he choose his? Or was there ever a choice?

"Ready?" asked a student, motioning that it was after seven and we needed to leave now. It interrupted my reverie. I mentioned the movie star at the bar, but no one knew who I was talking about. How could that be? I never realized there were people who didn't watch television.

* * * *

Students from the Bay Area and Via Del Sol showed up. I guess they left later in the day, and their change of heart was a nice surprise for me. It felt more like we were one school, not a bunch of groups. Robert looked happy. I met some of the new students, although I can't remember their names offhand.

With a plate on my lap, I sat in a corner of the living room close enough to Robert to listen to his conversation. He signaled to Rosemary, with Jim translating, "The farm was everything I wanted until I had it." At that point, I understood why he was in Carmel. It suited him. He tried it on like a garment and discovered the cowboy hat and blue jeans simply didn't fit. It so described where I was also. I'm not a hippy. I'm a city girl. But how am I going to make it in Carmel?

At one point, Robert stood up to introduce a new puppy that would be the house mascot. Her name was Toast, which was an affectionate moniker Robert began to use with his favorite students, like Hello, little Toast. It was a black Lhasa-Poo (Lhasa Apso and Poodle mix) with a white tummy. Robert turned to Jan, saying that she had Toast's brother. Robert then handed Toast to Klair. Perhaps Klair would be the official caretaker.

Robert then asked Anna to play "Clair de Lune." It was funny to see her resist. She wanted to play Bach, not the vapid Debussy. That was her argument. The Robert and Anna Show was always fun to watch, like an old married couple displaying the depth of their love and history together. Who won? Robert, of course. He had her play Bach first, and then Debussy.

It was almost eleven o'clock when we left Carmel. Jane offered to take the first leg of the drive back, which I greatly appreciated. I sat in the passenger seat. The buffet was so lavish that we did not need to stop for a snack. I asked Jane if she wanted me to drive, but she said she was good and could make it home. I fell asleep after we passed Sacramento, on that long, dark stretch of road toward Marysville.

"We're home," said Jane as she parked the car along the road to the Lodge.

I awoke, and thanked her for driving. My Timex said 2:44 am. Four hours for a direct route was good to record, since I knew visits to Carmel would become a necessary part of my evolution.

As I lay down in my sleeping bag, the film in my head was not showing the highlights of the evening with Robert. Instead, the camera was panning the meeting house for men as mates. I had never realized before that there were two cameras inside of me, shooting the same event, but from different angles. One was interested in the higher emotional content, and the other was looking for sexual opportunity. One was innocent and the other lecherous. I wished I didn't have these thoughts or tendencies, as it took so much energy and clouded my life. There was a purity in the Work that these 'I's wanted to sully. Self-remembering vs. instinctive urges. My aim to awaken was becoming stronger, but so was the desire for sex. A silent, secret struggle was on.

❖

It is provided in the essence of things, that from any
fruition of success, no matter what, shall come forth something
to make a greater struggle necessary.

Walt Whitman

THE SEEDS OF

CHAPTER 125

It was peaceful at the farm, and I was grateful to have the time to return to my books. The subject of sex interested me, and I was hoping the work books could explain the machine's preoccupation, other than the obvious fact of procreation. Of course, I could say I was simply horny, yet my intellectual element wanted to understand the aspect of sexual energy and its connection to awakening.

Going back to Ouspensky's *In Search of the Miraculous,* the subject of sex and the lower and higher centers revolved around ultra-detailed discussions of the table of hydrogens as it related to the food, air, and impressions octave of the human machine, and the transmutation or transformation of materials to refine energy suitable for the higher centers to awaken.

Some of this I could verify. For example, he talks about the food octave (*do re mi* kind of thing), and that the *mi-fa* interval is where the air octave enters to bridge it. At lunch, I was able to observe that when I was eating and became full, I'd find my machine taking a deep breath. Ah! That's the bridging of the interval with the air octave. More energy would kick in. But did I stop there? Usually not. I would keep eating until my tummy hurt. That must be wrong work of centers. My moving center kept shoveling and my emotional center found solace in the warm food in my mouth, again and again.

Regarding the impressions octave, Ouspensky talks about having finer energy (what he called *si-12* or hydrogen 12) that is suitable for higher emotional center (World 12) to operate. The first interval in the impressions octave is *mi-fa*. The shock needed to bridge the interval is self-remembering. The *si-do* interval is bridged by a second shock. He describes this as the transformation of suffering.

Okay. But what does this have to do with combatting my sexual thoughts?

Ouspensky relates in his book how Gurdjieff explained it. He says *si-12,* or sex energy, is the highest level of transformation within the human organism. This is the finest energy the machine can produce, in other words. This energy is like a seed from which something can grow. And if there's enough of this sex energy in the machine, and a shock, or spark, can energize it enough to go forward toward a new octave, it can produce another organism, or body.

He's talking about an orgasm as a shock and a baby resulting. Or, that's how I read it.

He goes on to say this is the normal and natural way to use sex energy. But there's another possibility. And that is, if you can manufacture *si-12*, or sex energy, without the male and female "principles," as he calls it, something new can develop that *remains* inside the organism. This is the birth of an astral body.

Someone had asked him a question closer to mine: Is sexual abstinence useful for the Work or not?

Gurdjieff says it's only useful if it involves all centers. "If there's abstinence in one center and full liberty of imagination in the others, then there could be nothing worse." Plus, one needs to know what to do with all that energy. It's not enough just to save it.

So, as I read it, what good is virginhood in a sacred chapel if you keep imagining having sex in an adjoining room with the next male you see? Sex energy is conserved in one place and leaking out in another.

But HOW do you stop the energy leaks? That's my real question.

I read on and found him describing the abuse of sex, which occurs when this energy is locked into coarse impressions or wandering imagination or extreme emotional responses such as cruelty or jealousy. The energy leak is caused by the flow of imagination in the four lower centers, an endless stream of unconscious 'I's.

Again, Gurdjieff basically describes the nature of the leaks and how they manifest, but not so much how to stop them.

I read this and struggled. Imagination had been such a positive aspect to my life, full of hopes, creativity, possibilities. As a child, I would spend my hours in the morning, lying in bed on hot summer days, creating imaginary scenarios, in which I was the star and people liked me. Or, a quiet hour at UCLA, imagining my future.

Ouspensky said imagination satisfies all centers. Since I've experienced the third state, imagination has become a kind of poison, not nourishment. It's no longer as satisfying as it used to be. But just because it's not as satisfying doesn't mean it stops.

I couldn't find a direct answer on how to stop sexual imagination and energy leaks other than remember yourself. Self-remembering is so hard, so hit or miss. It's like trying to siphon water from the Hoover Dam with a straw.

The upward channel to my third eye barely exists, which makes it far easier for the sex energy to go down instead of up. The only solution, I guess, is to keep working on raising consciousness and balancing functions. This is going to take forever. There is no magic pill.

❖

> *If you do not listen to what imagination says,*
> *your inner light will increase.*
> — Al-Darqawi

CHAPTER 126

Monday was a meeting in Carmel with Robert. This I heard, and I also heard that there would not be a meeting in Vacaville on Tuesdays anymore. The Vacaville group would have to go to the Bay Area, Carmel, or wait for their optional meeting on Thursdays. I also heard that the Bay Area open meetings were bringing in new students. We were approaching 100.

I stayed at Via Del Sol throughout the week. A heaviness had sunk in with the daily chores and routines. The animals were fewer so the caretaking was minimal. We did our best to keep the Lodge clean, as well as ourselves. We were looking pretty scruffy, which was reflected also in the upkeep of our property. It was more than we could handle, and Yorgos and his small crew did their best to prepare for the spring gardens, where fresh vegetables would be available to us. Theoretically.

Fortunately, Meg's *Via Del Sol Journal* kept me going. Because we were more spread out now, Meg was mailing these journals to those who subscribed monthly, just as she had done a year ago for me in LA. It was a lifeline then, and it was one now, too. The latest edition included Robert's comments from his notebooks. It was remarkable how timely Robert's thoughts were to my internal struggle. This edition included the subject with which I had been struggling.

"Sex has many angles, and people are in different parts of their being while having sex, and different parts afterwards. After you have sex, intellectual 'I's may appear that don't like it. They are not of the sex center, simply another brain. Remember, we have seven people in one body.

"The highest use of sex energy is transmutation, which is self-remembering. Also, sex energy sometimes is forced into different channels in the body and shaking or rapid acceleration is manifested."

The last thought spoke directly to me as I recalled how my body shook when I lost my virginity. He concluded with this thought on the subject.

"Remember, humans are not supposed to understand how to convert sex energy, or even hear the idea."

The understanding of how to control sex energy and how it manifests in an awakened being remains elusive to me. I know that energy is like money and we use it to support what we value. Isn't it funny I have so much sex energy and so little money? I've learned to conserve my pennies but not my energy. Laughter, sexual imagination, talking, etc. are expenditures. I wouldn't waste my money, but why do I waste my energy?

When days drag on, my mind exercises itself with intellectual gymnastics. I enjoy this. Robert also wrote that Orage was involved in "intellectual sex," another use of sex energy. Is it useful? Is it a waste? It seems useful. How else can I verify ideas and concepts, unless I think about them fully in order to formulate my understanding and then share it with others?

* * * *

This edition of the *Via Del Sol Journal* also announced a change to its format. A new publication by Don would replace Meg's two-column, manual typewriter newsletter. It would be typeset and printed on colored paper. And the price was higher. And it was not optional. The cost ranged from $2 to $5 a month. Small Jane and Meg would tell each of us what price to pay monthly, based on our ability to pay. It would be an amount separate from our monthly teaching payment.

I had glimpsed a copy of Don's publication last fall. He was a graphics man, and thought Meg's newsletter could be improved visually. Meg was more an editor, and had been sending out meeting notes from the beginning. She was not interested in visual impressions or refinement. "Just the facts, Ma'am," was her approach.

I realized only now that when I had entered Sheila's apartment for the Carmel meeting, Robert was in the process of working with Meg and Don to refine the newsletter. That was the piece of paper in Don's hand. It was an interesting step to take, because it meant this publication was the definitive one, replacing Meg's, and that Meg would no longer have this as a source of income. Also, it would no longer be her octave. Meg did not look too happy about having Don take it over. And Don did not look too happy having Robert decide what graphics to use.

Robert moves on, fearlessly, regardless of how we view his directions. Impressions are a key to bringing the right hydrogens to our higher centers, and this now seems to be his focus.

I'd been wanting to bring more beauty to my life since childhood, but felt stuck in the functional existence of my parents. I used to cut out pictures of art and landscapes and beautiful rooms that I would see in *Life* magazine each week and keep them in a drawer in my desk. One day, in a fit of rage, my sister took the stack and tore them all up. I stood there stunned. I'd spent years collecting them and would look at them whenever I felt depressed. It lifted my spirits. But now those images were gone. I knew back then, however, that a better and more lovely life was out there for me.

A few years ago, I told my parents I wanted to cook a dinner for our bubbies and wanted to use the fine silverware. My father liked the idea so he could brag to the relatives that Linda was a high-class girl. The recipe I used was chicken a l'orange that I found in *Life* magazine. It was a roast chicken with a sweet, syrupy sauce from canned orange juice and mandarin orange slices, which was served over white rice with broccoli. The recipe was actually an ad for Minute Maid orange juice, but the picture was so elegantly photographed — picture-perfect cooking — that I wanted to present a beautiful dish to them rather than the piles of food mixed on our plates, which was the norm in our household.

Dad went out to pick up the bubbies and bring them to our apartment. Everyone was thrilled about the dinner. Once they looked at it, however, nobody ate it. Dad insisted the bubbies at least taste it to proclaim the brilliant chef that was now in the family. They did. The next morning, Dad called his mother and she told him she was sick all night ("but don't tell Linda"). Of course, he did.

If I can learn to raise my standards, it will be most wonderful. I hope Robert will take me there.

But there are things that are hard to give up. Humor, for one. I like to tell jokes and make people laugh. Life to me is ironic. So many contradictions. Ouspensky described laughter as something hitting both the positive and the negative halves of centers simultaneously, and the result is this little explosion of energy that generates World 24, or essence. I don't do it to make people happy, though. It's not the reason I do it. I do it because it's the only time I can actually feel relief from inner considering. I don't read people well. A good joke or funny observation disarms them momentarily, and I feel safe and liked.

I'm too afraid to let this go.

Before you cure a man, ask him if he is willing to give up the things that make him sick.

Hippocrates

CHAPTER 127

"Robert is coming."

This was the lead headline of the morning. A week had passed. It was now Tuesday and Valentine's Day. Alden had returned from the Carmel meeting and was sharing the news.

This was exciting. It had been a while since we had a meeting with Robert here. We decided to focus on preparing the Lodge for his arrival, since the last time he came, he silently engaged us in a third-line marathon of cleaning. Robert had a different sense of time from us. It was a 24-hour octave for him, and he was not above initiating a cleanup at midnight.

I decided to help with the kitchen area. Of course, I wasn't the initiator of the octave; it was Kerrie. She assigned me the cooler, which would have been a lovely place in August, but dark, damp and freezing in February. I could observe many 'I's resisting, but I knew there were worse octaves, so I went in there with her instructions: consolidate like foods into one crate or container and remove the extra bins to be washed or tossed. I noticed the avocados had a few teeth marks, and I smiled. How funny this did not bother me anymore. I had a knife and cut away the bad areas and tossed them in a compost bucket to give to Yorgos.

Other students would focus on the fireplace and woodstove, the floors and the windows of the living room, and the bathroom. The regular octaves of laundry and meal preparation continued along with the cleaning octave.

Our pace was leisurely, knowing we had several days to put it in order. We were expecting Robert to come Saturday night, lead the Sunday morning meeting, and then leave early Monday for Carmel. That was his schedule. That was our expectation.

* * * *

Wednesday came and went, and the work octaves had stalled at the *si-do* — or was it the *mi-fa*? The person in charge of cleaning the fireplace started scrubbing the left side but the right side of the bricks was left undone. He still had time, reasoned the student. The bricks were blackened, and not as easy to clean as he had thought. The temperature had warmed enough for him to do it in the afternoon, but by the evening, we all needed to have the fireplace working to warm the room so the cleaning stopped.

Thursday began overcast, and it was clear the weather was becoming cooler. We had a slow start in the morning. Most of us thought we would focus on our octaves afterwards, but that didn't happen and we didn't accomplish much on our own. Lunchtime was approaching. Maybe the afternoon would be more favorable, suggested a student, as we sat down to eat. A third force was clearly lacking.

And then it arrived.

As we were eating lunch, Robert appeared with Jim, Rosemary and Marie. It took us all by surprise. Me, especially, since I had just told a joke and everyone had burst into laughter. Robert looked right at me and curled that index finger of his. I went to him.

"Please control your laughter," was the written note.

"Thank you," I said, meekly.

My first 'I' was from the Bible, something about You, too, must keep watch! For you don't know when the master of the household will return.

Robert immediately saw the fireplace and inquired about who was in charge. Jim found out and went up to the student with Robert's message. The student stopped eating, assembled his cleaning supplies, and began scrubbing away. Robert had another student help him.

Next, he focused on the windows. They, too, had yet to be cleaned. Two students were assigned to that. The vacuuming, the kitchen, the bathroom — it was as if Robert had been with us all along and was watching on some distant TV our goings on. It was uncanny.

My assignment was the library. The books were in disarray and Robert wanted them to be placed in order according to subject matter. He left that up to me. It was curious, to my knowledge, how few students used the library. It needed dusting, and Lord knows, I was good at that.

It was Thursday, not Sunday, and a message was circulated that we would have a meeting at seven followed by dinner. Our work octaves finished at six. I had already placed my name on the bathroom list, since I knew I would need to shower before the meeting. By the time I entered, there were at least fifteen names behind me. I took a quick shower (for me) and Robert was waiting as I exited.

He wrote, "Can you help Rosemary with the dinner preparation?"

I smiled and nodded, going directly into the kitchen. Robert wanted a roast chicken dinner with biscuits and gravy. Jan was there to help as well (she had arrived midafternoon with the supplies). I rolled out the biscuit dough, cut it into individual biscuits, and placed them on the baking sheet. They would be baked after the meeting.

Just before seven, the chairs were arranged in the living room and the meeting began promptly.

Robert pointed out the beautiful job that the two students did on the fireplace. He had been standing over them during the cleaning, indicating areas that needed more scrubbing. He did not mention my job, but extolled the virtuous efforts of others. I felt like a puppy waiting for a treat while watching my siblings in the pack receiving their rewards. Mine didn't come.

He began the meeting by speaking about the Carmel group, reiterating the address and its significance. Robert then asked if there were any questions.

We sat quietly. It was such a shock just to have Robert here. The stillness permeated the room. After about five minutes, an unexpected noise came from the walls and ceiling. You could hear the rats scurry about. I started to chuckle, and it was becoming a bit uncontrollable. Nobody moved. The thought that ignited my giggles was this: it was so quiet at Via Del Sol you could hear, not a pin drop, but rats scamper. This was our life in the wild. No wonder Robert wanted out of here.

Robert turned to Jim, who said, "Rats."

That did it. My 'I' apparently was contagious. A few of us started to shake, doing our best not to emit a sound.

Robert brought us back in line by asking what effects did students observe from the full moon?

"There's more laughter," said Alden.

Jan offered, "The many 'I's are more active."

"Yes," replied Robert, "like a wolf howling at the moon."

"The moving center wants to move more," said Mason.

"There are more negative emotions," observed Rosemary.

I raised my hand. "There's an increase in appetite."

"Yes," added Robert, "the moon is eating us, and the instinctive center will eat more to buffer this fact."

Yorgos raised his fingers slightly. Robert immediately called on him, with a smile.

"There's restlessness and lack of sleep."

Marie's hand went up. "There may be more natural disasters and crime."

Tall Jane mentioned an increase in inner considering.

Robert discussed the effects in more detail. I did verify before the school that the longest time I could stay on a diet was two weeks. I never knew why. Could it be that they were started on a moon and ended on a moon? The sway of the many 'I's? It's something for further observation, I thought.

After the meeting, we all enjoyed a wonderful chicken dinner. I was inspired and happy to help dry the dishes. Robert's presence rejuvenated me. The sluggishness of the past days was gone.

At midnight, I retired to my space on the floor and pondered the question of how do I find my own strength of purpose in his absence. It was not a question of aims. That, I see now, was merely replacing one 'I' for another. It was more a question of attaching my will to his. The strength of purpose comes from him. I do not have it yet for myself. I felt like a little chick who ran after the mother hen for its survival. To be so dependent on another human could be a negative thing. But it was not. Why? Because being dependent on a conscious teacher — not a B Influence lecturer — is going to result in the growth of my own consciousness. I was sure of this.

I can already observe I'm both more asleep and more awake. How can that be? I'm beginning to see my sleep, and that takes Observing 'I.' That's an achievement. But more importantly, I now know why I was born. It's no longer a question. And that's a relief.

Do not spend the numbered breaths which have been given to you just to wander around the face of this earth, without purpose, with actions of no consequence. Every action, every motion, must be for a divine purpose.

Ibn Arabi

CHAPTER 128

"A Solar type has joined the school."

It was Alden who broke the news at breakfast Friday morning.

"Sheila's daughter Sheilita and her husband joined, and Robert said Sheilita is a pure Solar type."

Of all the types, the Solar type was the rarest and most enigmatic. It had no place on the enneagram, as Rodney Collin described it. He referred to it as the Peter Pan type, and connected it to the thymus endocrine gland. All types are characterized by the predominating endocrine gland in a person's body. The Lunar type is governed by the pancreas; Venusian by the parathyroid; Mercurial, the thyroid; Saturnine, the anterior pituitary; Martial, the adrenals; and Jovial, the posterior pituitary. The Solar type is governed by the sun, and the influence is not planetary, but on another level altogether. It's also an active masculine type, yet positive, unlike the Martial, which is an active masculine type and negative.

That's the concept. What would a Solar type look like? None of us had ever seen one, to our knowledge. I envisioned a petite, delicately framed young lady with ethereal blond hair. She would be shy and introverted, but friendly and kind, with a little splash of naïveté.

"Have you met her?" I asked Alden.

"No, not yet. I just heard she was coming up for the weekend."

We continued our cleanup that day. The fireplace was still not done to Robert's standards, and had to be redone several times. Friday was especially chilly. We were wearing heavy clothing in the house, since the only source of heat now was the wood burning stove.

Students from the Vacaville and Bay Area had arrived slowly during the day, and by ten at night there was no floor space to be had for sleeping. Of course, I had secured my spot early, next to the wood burning stove, with a direct line to the bathroom. I snuggled into my sleeping bag wearing my long flannel nightgown with my tube socks pulled up high. The darkness of the new moon, which had been on Monday, still lingered, and I had no idea who was sleeping next to me by the time I retired.

In the middle of the night, I was awakened from a sound sleep by hushed voices around me.

"There's space here. Do you have the bags?"

"I'm bringing them in. Here, you take her."

It was clear that late arrivers were trying to squeeze into the corner next to the bathroom door, doing their best not to block the entrance. Then I heard an unusual sound.

"Waaaaah!"

Whaaaaat?

It sounded like a baby, but I dismissed this immediately. I knew of none in the school, and anyhow, this was not the children's house, where a baby would belong. I turned over, and waited for the noise to disappear. It didn't.

I was becoming a bit perturbed. Since the desire to return to sleep was stronger than my irritation, my centers eventually disengaged, returning me to the first state. My slumber lasted about thirty minutes, when the noise began again. This cycle continued until the break of dawn.

As the sun arose, I went to use the bathroom, barely finding foot space to get to the door. Before entering, I hovered over the two bodies stretched out in their sleeping bags. Both had long black hair and one, a magnificent long black beard. Between them was the source of the noise: a baby.

"Ah! There's the little culprit!"

This awoke the two adults. With bleary eyes, they looked up at me. Their exhaustion was evident on their faces. They said nothing. Nature's call was too strong for me to linger.

When I exited, they were sitting up. He took the baby in his arms as she readjusted herself, propping her back against the wall. He was clearly a Saturnine type, the midmost point of masculinity. He looked like a refined hippie, like Peter Fonda in *Easy Rider*. She was the most beautiful young woman I had ever seen. Tall and elegant with prima ballerina limbs. Her long, straight black hair knew its proper place, as it fell gracefully regardless of circumstance, just like Cher's. But, unlike Cher, her features were nature's perfection. Her skin was radiant and creamy, without flaws.

Who were they and where did they come from?

"Hi," I said. "My name is Linda."

She wasn't too welcoming, but that was totally understandable. Her little one was feeding and she clearly had her hands full.

Standing over her, I waited for her to respond. When her child's eyelids were drooping from the morning meal, she turned to answer.

"Hello. My name is Sheilita."

* * * *

How did Robert know she was a Solar type? How does Robert see these things? So much of what Robert teaches is a mystery to me. Still, there was something special about her. Her beauty certainly radiated, and I wanted to be friends. I hoped she would like me.

I watched how Robert that morning gave her special attention. He was not attracted to her baby, unlike most of the other students, who circled around the infant. In a way, she was his child. He was especially fond of her mother, Sheila, and it seemed this affection extended to her as well.

Saturday continued to be a work day. Robert found so many areas to improve. He directed us to clean the front patio, picking up stones, branches, and leaves. Then he moved to the side of the building, where he had two students disassemble and remove the hastily built barbecue pit, since it was no longer in use. But he didn't stop there. He went around the Lodge and discovered a rope tied to a tree that someone was using to hang their underwear to dry in the winter sun. He immediately requested the student take it down and not dry his clothes outside like this, stating it was a "poor impression" for us.

He had other students clean up the barn, since we had been rid of a number of animals. He assigned me to one of these projects. I was to clean an outdoor pen where one of the cows had stayed. Jim was in charge of the octave. He looked down at my white tennis shoes and told me to borrow rubber boots. "You'll thank me later," he said, with his impish grin.

I teamed up with Clark, who was pulled away from helping Yorgos with his farming octave. Yorgos was not too happy about it, as Clark was his right-hand man. The boots I got were a bit big on my feet since I borrowed them from a Saturn lady, so I wore two sets of tube socks. I found the shoes hard to walk in, and the wet manure was deep. It tried to suck my boots off my feet, which was accompanied by a farting sound with each step. It made me giggle.

"Stop that!" said Clark, repressing a laugh, and we both instantly recalled the stubborn donkey incident. I had to focus hard on controlling my emotional center, and this time after a few seconds of remembering myself, I was able not to trigger the hysteria. It was a wonderful moment for me to verify the growth of my small will.

We both returned to the task at hand. Quickly we established a rhythm of shoveling the droppings into the wheelbarrow. He carted it off to the nearby compost area that Yorgos had developed for his garden. After numerous trips, he announced we were done. While I smoked a cigarette, Clark raked the ground so the remaining muck would blend into the soil. My attention was drawn past Clark to the field where Yorgos was hoeing a row of rich soil. He worked alone, and did not stop his efforts. I thought how focused Yorgos is on his aims. I admired his tenacity.

We washed off our boots and headed toward the Lodge. Jim had just finished working with another crew to clean up the inside of the barn. This meant stacking hay bales, shoveling droppings from the stalls, and dismantling the chicken pens. He called to us to wait up. We stopped and were happy for his company.

"Do you know how long Robert will be here?" I asked.

"No," he replied. "I never know from one moment to another."

The romantic feelings I recently had toward him had disappeared, and it was easier to see him, not as a potential mate, but as a student and friend. This was another wonderful verification that perhaps my identification with men had diminished. Was this a new change in level of being for me?

When we arrived at the Lodge, I took my boots off in the boot room and walked inside in my socks. There in the living room was Robert, sitting in a rocking chair, watching the fireplace cleaning octave, which was still continuing. He realized that this fireplace, with such a small opening, was not adequate for the space. He wrote down, "In spring, we will need to rebuild this."

I stood there, watching others receive his message, but something more pressing was on my mind. Kneeling by his side, I asked him a question.

"Robert, if a situation does not come up at a new octave, does this indicate that it was worked on sufficiently?"

Turning to me, he indicated, Yes.

I was elated with his response. Maybe I had, after all, passed the test of sexual obsession.

I stood up and found the bathroom was, to my surprise, available. I took advantage of this. My items were close by, and I hopped in to take a much-needed shower. As I washed my hair, I thought about how men and laughter were my two major areas of identification. As long as situations recur, it means I still have work to do in that area, but that if they don't recur, I can move on to the next level of development. My evolution seems to be ascending.

Before the evening meal, I went to the library and found Miles in there, reading a book. It was a potentially awkward moment since we had not interacted for a long time. He looked up and smiled, and I reciprocated. I could feel my Self present. It was loving and could see him as separate from me. We had a caring, simple talk. I told him, "Isn't it fun to see each other grow?" I wanted to hug him, and did. We both saw respect and love in each other's eyes. I was in a blissful state. We had made it.

※

This world is a place of ambush, so, you who travel far, be careful.

Hafiz

CHAPTER 129

The Saturday night dinner was particularly festive. It was nice to have students from different groups — Bay Area and Carmel — come together with us residents of Via Del Sol. For the Bay Area new members, the rustic nature of our living accommodations was truly out of patterns. There was no motel in the area where anyone could stay. Robert was particularly delighted by the new members, and of course, was happy to have the older students around. Meg and Harold, Rose and Marie and Jan, Mac, Richard and Alice, Bonita and David, and Miles and Helga among them.

The Sunday morning meeting was at ten, and the sun was making its appearance between slow-moving clouds. The stream of light was beautiful, as it crossed the faces of those sitting up front.

The meeting began, after good householder, with Robert providing an observation.

"Yesterday a student asked me for a task. I explained that to want a task is like wanting a credential from the teacher. Remember, Christ's only credential was a crown of thorns. I told the student that C Influence would provide a shock soon. The student drove to Berkeley and inexplicably returned here that same night. C Influence drove the student up and down the highway, without reason, granting the wish."

A new student from the Bay Area raised her hand and asked, "How did life arrive on the Earth?"

Robert paused. One thing I know about Robert is he will respond to any question asked of him. I did not say answer, only respond. Sometimes his response was ignoring the question, and other times it's providing practical guidance. I was interested to see how he would address a question like this, since its scale was pretty large. It reminded me of Gurdjieff asking, "Who can formulate his own aim?" After his students gave several grandiose aims, like save the world, G. pronounced that the best one was to be master of oneself, for without that, nothing else was possible or of value.

"Life may have been transplanted here or may have been designed here. Ouspensky formulated an interesting angle, not a theory according to him. He states that humans are an experiment designed by conscious beings in a massive laboratory inside the sun.

"Ouspensky also pointed out that Darwin's theory of evolution was a theory that people now take as a fact.

"I know it is explainable — the origin of life — if we seek the higher in us long enough."

Miles then turned to Robert and said, "That is unusual for you to say — that you know something."

Robert smiled and replied, "Yes, it is unusual for me to say I know something, and it was good that a student picked it up."

"Please speak about how to work with absurd negative emotions," asked Richard.

"From one angle, they are all absurd," replied Robert.

We chuckled. Then I realized, it's easy to say, but when one's in it, it's harder to see.

Robert continued.

"A chain of negativity doesn't solve the problem and is a waste of energy. Negative emotions have their roots in vanity. They are selfish, thinking of 'I,' or 'my' way."

I raised my hand and was called on.

"One way to handle negative emotions is to photograph another brain at work. The Work 'I's can be saying 'Be present' to try to maintain control, while the emotional center continues to boil, even though the circumstances have changed. After a while the emotional center will settle down, maybe after a nap, and then even the 'I's cannot re-invoke the boiling negativity."

I sat down, content with my formulation.

Another student offered an angle, with a bit of firmness. "The negativity in life is so unnecessary."

"Your own expression," remarked Robert, "is a negative emotion. I try not to be bothered by anything, as 'bother' is a negative emotion and a waste of energy, which is not a good habit to allow. Higher states can be born out of the desire not to be bothered.

"A student was disturbed by another's cigarette smoke," continued Robert, "and I cautioned him to take it as long as he could for voluntary suffering. Then quietly remove himself when he could no longer separate. After you've done a good job, expect C Influence to arrange a follow-up shock to test the strength of your will."

This last comment shook me a bit. It was like being given a pop quiz after the final exam. It implied a level of vigilance in the Work that I was not expecting.

The meeting ended, followed by a big lunch, which was far more than just the soup and salad we residents were accustomed to eating. It was planned by the older ladies and included Robert's favorites: broccoli with cheese sauce, fried chicken and whipped potatoes, with apple crumble for dessert.

During the meal, I kept my eye on Robert, hoping for a moment with him. He moved so quickly and silently that you could look down at your plate, take a bite, only to find he had vanished from the place he was sitting. This is exactly what happened. He was walking out the front door. I jumped up to go after him.

"Robert," I called out. He stopped and turned. Approaching him, I posed my burning question: "Do you have an idea where I should live?"

"Do what you wish to do, not what you should do," was his reply.

"But, Robert, I don't know what I wish to do," I said, expecting him to guide me in some direction.

"I know, it's easier said than done. There's no hurry. A decision will come out of a need for a decision."

With that, he walked with Jim down the hill to the car. I watched as they drove off, heading to Carmel.

* * * *

By 4 p.m., the visitors from the Bay and Carmel had left Via Del Sol. We residents had a cleaner, yet emptier, place in which to live. The quiet that remained was filled with magic energy from our conscious teacher and the camaraderie of fellow students trying their best to be present.

By 8 p.m., as I walked outside for a cigarette, the evening skies had cleared and the stars had stepped out from behind the opaque clouds. I joined Alden and David, who each puffed their pipes. There was nothing to say.

The farm had a quality about it. There was no sound but the locals, who in this case were wild animals. An owl repeatedly uttered a fading trail of "Hoos," the crickets clapped a scraping castanet percussion, and the coyotes exchanged their yip-yaps with each other. You could hear the intermittent scampering of mice, and lizards, and bush-loving quail that would flutter in fear, flying from their nests upon the approach of some predator that roamed about unrecognized by us. It was far from the whiz of the cars and the sound of brakes or the blaring ruckus of rock music in a city music hall.

The stillness reached deep within me. This was a place that nourished something gentle and sweet inside, however primitive and poor. Essence was safe here. But essence needs to be fed, and the generous banquet we just experienced requires money. Would I ever be able to support myself, let alone treat others to such a feast? It looked bleak.

There was no determination in me. I was simply content to sit and enjoy the simple company of friends under a star-studded sky. The earth's sweet fragrance was enough for me. How can I move from this? Is this my Venusian mechanics? What could possibly come that would produce that "need for a decision"?

Too many questions. I bid my friends good night and retired that evening in a strange state of contentment and confusion. Two opposing forces were pulling at me. It was more than I could analyze, and besides, it had been a long day, and the chatter of the internal 'I's became as much background noise as the incessant drone of insects. Exhaustion rapidly overtook me.

The play of this day had come to an end. Curtain down.

❧

> *Night was upon his spirit, and it was long before he could distinguish his right hand from his left.*
>
> Arabian Nights

CHAPTER 130

For the next two weeks, I remained at the farm in this Push-Me-Pull-You state.

As a child, my favorite author was Hugh Lofting who created Dr. Doolittle. Dr. Doolittle's specialty was being able to talk to the animals. My favorite character was the Push-Me-Pull-You, which he spelled Pushmi-Pullyu, I guess, to make it more exotic. This almost extinct fantasy creature descended from Abyssinian gazelles, Asiatic chamois, and the last of the unicorns. Its design was perfect for warding off attackers since it could not be attacked from behind. Why? Because there was no behind. It was conjoined with heads at either end. One head could eat while the other would talk. For a child instructed not to talk with her mouth full, it was an ingenious solution. The two heads also allowed half of it to sleep, while the other remained wide awake and watching. This made it especially endearing to me, since I was always curious about what was going on around me, and frequently snuck out of bed to observe my parents talking and watching television.

The way Dr. Doolittle's animals captured the Push-Me-Pull-You was also ingenious: they encircled it. They didn't mean to harm it. They just wanted to convince it to come with them to help the good doctor earn a better income in the white man's land. This unique animal would be the star attraction, bringing in a pretty price. They insisted he would not be caged, only looked at during a show. This was hard for the Push-Me-Pull-You to consider, for you see, he was shy and he hated to be stared at. Finally, after three days, he agreed at least to speak to the good doctor.

When the Push-Me-Pull-You met Doctor Doolittle and the other animals, the little duck Dab-Dab mentioned to everyone that this weird beast must have a hard time making up his mind. Good observation.

Dr. Doolittle was curious but not particularly enthusiastic. Chee-Chee the monkey explained to him that he could earn a fortune by exhibiting this creature, to which he replied, "I don't want any money." This caused an uproar, as each animal explained why money was necessary, such as to buy food and a new boat for the sailor who brought them to Africa. The impractical doctor quietly said, "I could build a boat." Dab-Dab told him to try to be reasonable. Good advice.

After a big farewell party thrown by the monkeys and attended by the remaining animals of the jungle, the doctor and his troop were ready to leave the black world of Africa. Their passage through the jungle meant they had to go through the evil Black King's land, which contained a dense wilderness. Through a mishap (the animals got distracted), Dr. Doolittle and the less intelligent animals became lost. They turned left instead of right, whereupon they were captured and imprisoned for trespassing.

How did the good doctor and his troop escape? The king's son, Prince Bumpo, was strolling through the gardens, reading fairy tales and wishing, with all his heart, to be, not a black prince but a white prince so he could marry Sleeping Beauty, whom he met after reading all about her in a fairy tale book. He kissed her, she awoke and screamed, "You're a Black Prince!" and immediately moved away and went back to sleep.

Polynesia the parrot, who wasn't captured, overheard the prince's lament and convinced him, while hiding in the bushes, that she was the Queen of the Fairies, and knew a sorcerer who could fulfill his wish but who was a captive in his father's prison. The prince believed her. Polynesia flew away and told the good doctor about the plot she cooked up. He didn't think it possible to transform Bumpo in this way and was scared the young prince would hurt him. But he had no other option. He managed to create a potion, and it did indeed make the prince white — at least as long as it took for the doctor and crew to escape to the boat and sail away.

I could relate to each animal. That was the magic of the book. As I looked around Via Del Sol, it seemed to me that the farm was the jungle and the students were the menagerie. Who was the Pushmi-Pullyu? Dab-Dab? Chee-Chee? Polynesia? The evil king? The black prince? The good doctor? Good questions.

Students started to grumble about things. The person who had been told not to hang laundry from a line became willful, arguing with those who reminded him of Robert's request. He wanted his clothes to smell fresh from mountain air and not "chemical" from the clothes dryer. A reasonable preference, but that's not the point. Does he not understand he's in a school with a conscious teacher, and that learning to obey is intrinsic to awakening? Gurdjieff talks about this.

I went to the library and found this quote from Gurdjieff to show him:

"The fear of being subordinated to another man's will very often proves stronger than anything else. A man does not realize that a subordination to which he consciously agrees is the only way to acquire a will of his own."

He became even more negative. How silly to resist over underwear, I thought. But that was his test. I put the book back on the shelf.

The mothers also struggled with providing an education for their kids in the children's house. There was no curriculum that I heard of, and I was definitely staying out of the discussion after my controversial attempt to teach five- through fifteen-year-olds. I listened to these things, and realized I was not the only one who suffered feelings of being left in the lurch.

The more rustic types complained about the rich foods, new clothes, costly airplane — all the trappings of Influence A that they had renounced before coming to the Fellowship. We were going backwards, in their eyes ('I's).

We were a bunch of people pulled out of our daily grinds to live in this twentieth-century fairy tale. I had already lost my Prince Charming. My hair was becoming longer, my body was becoming bigger. Did I feel lost? Sometimes. Did I feel cheated? Sometimes. There was a spark in me that viewed my *current* circumstance as a *curious* circumstance, one that I would never have chosen. Yet it continuously revealed my sleep and conscious possibilities, for which I was grateful.

And then there's that other head that wishes to take control of its destiny and simply hop in the car to drive somewhere — anywhere — to escape.

Who, what, how, why, when? The answers depend on which head is asking.

One head says I'm Linda Kaplan and am trying to survive and need to get a job to support myself now.

The other head has a different view of existence:

Who am I? Not Linda Kaplan.

Why am I here? To wake up from this dream.

How do I do it? Remember myself, always and everywhere.

What do I do? Wait for the play to reveal itself.

When will it happen? In good time.

This is the struggle. This is my life.

❖

Fate leads those who follow and drags those who resist.

Epictetus

CHAPTER 131

My eyes opened quickly at dawn. It was now March 1, a Wednesday. Those were the first two thoughts in my head. The Lodge was quiet so I easily slipped into the bathroom to prepare for the day. Something in me found it odd that I was so awake so early for no reason.

As I rolled up my sleeping bag and went upstairs to store it, the pay phone rang.

"Hello," I said, curious about the timing of it all.

"Is this Linda Kaplan?"

"Yes."

"Are you available to substitute this morning?"

"Yes."

I wrote the information down on a pad located next to the phone. I was grateful the pencil was still hanging from the string.

My day just revealed itself.

* * * *

The 3:16 p.m. alarm announcing the end of the school day could not have come too soon. It was a simple assignment with seventh graders. I was given explicit written instructions from the teacher. Have them focus on reading and then ask them to put their books away before administering a quiz at the end of the period. Then collect all quiz papers, use a large paper clip to collate them from each class, place the papers in a folder, put the folder in a bottom drawer, and lock it before leaving the room. The teacher would correct the papers the next day.

As I drove back to the farm, I felt my day had been full of opportunities, and a sense of normalcy spread through me. It uplifted my state. I would have a nice dinner and rest, knowing a paycheck is in the mail.

When I got to the Lodge, I was surprised to see a few students dressed as if they were going to a meeting.

"Jim called to let us know Robert will lead the meeting tonight in Vacaville."

"What time?" I asked.

"Eight."

"Where?"

"Mac's farm."

This made no sense. Rose's house? I thought it was sold and unavailable. Apparently not. I took a deep breath. This was unexpected. What do I do? A part of me felt it had earned the right to rest after a hard day's work. It had already mapped out my evening. Now, the other part was so hungry for Robert's conscious light that I knew it would be an extra effort. What do I do?

While the internal battle raged inside of me, this came out of my mouth. "I'm going."

I went to the kitchen to grab some nuts and dried fruit and make a cheese sandwich, all of which I gobbled while standing. Meanwhile, those few students had already left. They had plans.

It was 4:15 when I drove away from Via Del Sol.

* * * *

I arrived at Rose's house just after six. When I entered through the kitchen door, which was my habit, the house was stunningly quiet. It seemed no one was there. I looked inside the living room and saw chairs positioned along the wall but not set up. Instinctively, I started to arrange them.

Suddenly, a bedroom door opened and who should be standing there? Robert.

He smiled. We hugged. He wrote on his pad, "Rosemary and I are going to the Coffee Tree. You may come if you like."

My heart pounded with joy. He and I walked into the kitchen. We both sat down at the table. He asked me how things were going.

"I taught today in Yuba City," I said beaming.

"Good," he wrote.

Just then Rose emerged from her room. She had been resting, apparently. I turned to Robert and noticed he looked a bit forlorn. It was odd to see him this way. Something had occurred.

Robert sat in the passenger seat while I sat right behind him. Rose knew the quickest way to the Coffee Tree, and we were there within five minutes. Inside were people standing around, some sitting on the banquettes along the wall, waiting to be called. Rose had apparently phoned ahead, and our names were already on the list. Robert and Rose were frequent customers and well known, so the waitress knew where he preferred to sit.

As we stood there waiting, Rose turned to me.

"Let's wash our hands," she said, guiding me into the ladies' room.

By the sinks, she explained Robert's mood.

"He just came back from visiting his mother in the hospital. She had a heart attack."

"Oh, no!"

"He did not break his silence. This was hard for him."

We went out and Robert was waiting for us. The server had the menus in her hand, ready to show us to the table.

We followed her through the busy restaurant to our booth. Robert took his seat across from us. After ordering, I looked at Robert, and he was looking down at his napkin. He appeared gray, and it was the saddest thing to see. Rosemary broke the tension by asking me about my week. I told her I taught in the morning, explained the grade level after she inquired, and also the assignments.

There was a distance between Robert and us. He easily could have been in another booth.

Our food came, and we ate in silence.

Then Rosemary began to tell a story.

"Anna invited me to go to a recital by a young violinist. Her teacher was an old acquaintance of Anna's and she never liked this woman, but she felt she had to go. Anna said she needed my support, so I went along. We decided to sit in the back row of the auditorium."

Robert looked past us, so Rose turned to me. I was rapt.

"The first piece was Bach, and she played it HORRIBLY! Totally off pitch. She may have hit only three right notes. It was excruciating. Anna and I stared at the ceiling, but I could see her trying not to laugh. We both looked at each other, and totally lost control."

Rosemary started to laugh, just telling the story.

"We tried to contain ourselves through the whole performance, but it only got worse! People turned around glaring at us, shushing us, but each time we were able not to laugh, the student would hit a sour note or screech the bow, and we lost it again."

I was laughing with her. It was so Anna and Rosemary. They could be like naughty little school children.

"When it was over, we knew we had to go backstage to congratulate the girl. Her teacher was standing by her, receiving the accolades. Anna whispered to me, 'I don't know what I'm going to tell her.' I told her, 'You have to commend her performance.' But she said, 'I CAN'T do that! It was TERRIBLE. I can't lie to her.'"

With this I started to shake with giggles, knowing full well that both Anna and Rosemary, being Martials, suffered greatly from bluntness.

"Meanwhile the line was getting shorter and shorter. When it was our turn, Anna shook the young girl's hand and blurted out, 'Isn't Bach WONDERFUL?' She nodded, and we headed toward the door. We held our smiles until we were outside, and then totally lost it!"

We both had tears in our eyes from laughing. The story, however, was over, and our giggles slowly simmered down. Robert took out his pad and began to write a note. I thought for sure he would be photographing us for laughing. He passed it to Rosemary. She handed it to me.

"I appreciate you both trying to cheer me up."

It was endearing. He was a little boy, after all. So tender, so exposed. It reminded me of Rosemary's comment last year, "Linda, Robert needs a friend." It made me love him even more.

* * * *

Robert had Rose and me sit up front at the meeting. He began slowly, telling students what had transpired during his day, mentioning the task he kept in the face of his dying mother.

"It was a milestone for us all. We broke through feminine dominance."

A new student from the Bay Area raised her hand.

"Could you explain what feminine dominance is?"

He paused, looking up, with a serious look on his face. "It's what keeps the planets in their orbits."

I thought he would speak about the trips people place on one another, like "you should do this." Instead, his response blew my mind. It was both succinct and cosmic. This law we are under is larger and more powerful than I realized. It made me see that this is what keeps society in order too. I offered this as an angle of thought.

"Yes," Robert replied. "Its purpose is to prevent barbarism."

I must say the rest of the meeting was a blur. This new formulation of feminine dominance — that it's not just a "woman's thing" — made me ponder what other forces impact the human machine to which we are totally unaware.

When the meeting ended, Robert turned to me and Rose. He wrote, "Linda can stay at the Whitman House when she visits Carmel."

I was happy to hear this. I looked at Rose, who nodded, yet I knew the logistics may be more complicated. I would simply have to face this. His offer was the missing piece for me to visit Carmel.

I decided to drive back to Via Del Sol that night. It was an unusual move for me, but something had changed and the solitude of the drive gave me time to think. Something familiar inside came to the forefront. It was connected to that conscious moment in Bubbie's house, but it was far more informed. It could process and fathom subtle meanings from simple, abstract concepts. It had relativity and scale and could relate cosmic order to social order. It was the Work, and it was alive and growing within me.

Robert called the incident with his mother a "milestone for us all." He used the words "us and we," not "me and I," intentionally. His conscious evolution and my conscious evolution were intrinsically tied together. It was not just about him or just about me. And the fact that he shared a painfully private and personal event so openly and so quickly with us was remarkable. It was a teaching moment, and he used it for the benefit of us all. He was ahead of us, yet beckoned us to take the next step and keep climbing.

Who are the companions? They are rungs on your ladder.
Use them! With company you quicken your ascent.

Rumi

CHAPTER 132

Back at the ranch, the topic of the week was Robert's experience with his dying mother.

"I can't understand how he could be so formatory, when his mother just wants to hear his voice."

"It's cruel, and not loving."

"A bit lunatic to me."

These were some of the comments. I tried to offer my view that he was holding to his aim in order to strengthen his will, and he's the teacher, and he serves as an example to us all. He put his work on himself first. I talked about feminine dominance, mothers putting their children first instead of themselves, and Robert trying to bring this to our attention last year with his request for all adults to eat before the children. It fell on deaf ears.

It had never occurred to me before that there could be such a difference in understanding between students that remained in the school, and not just those who decided to leave. What was obvious to me was not obvious to others. Wasn't reality supposed to be objective? It raised issues about subjectivity, morality, and universal understanding among students.

Ouspensky talked about the morality of men number one, two, and three as being subjective. I could understand this as the difference in expression between right and wrong, and principles and priorities. What I experienced last night from Robert, however, was a different level. It was breaking free of one of the cosmic laws that bind man the machine in sleep. This applies to everyone on earth. This is objective.

The weekend slipped by quickly. Yorgos led a meeting on Saturday night, taking questions and sharing angles. It was a pretty normal Fourth Way knowledge exchange. I enjoy this, as it is stimulating intellectually for me.

My main focus, however, was receiving my paycheck. Mail delivery did not come directly to the Lodge. It was an octave, and I volunteered for the week to go and retrieve the mail from the Dobbins Post Office. We had one box for the residents. The library had a tray for the mail, and we went through it individually. It was a simple system, and seemed to work.

My plan was to check the post office every day, and hopefully receive it by Wednesday. Then I would go to Carmel on Friday. Why Friday? It was March 10, my birthday, and all I wanted was to spend some time with Robert. It was my birthday wish to the gods, for only they could arrange our schedules for it to manifest.

Wednesday came, and as I thumbed through the letters and bills while sitting in my car, there was nothing from the school district for me. But there was something else for me. I was stunned to find my name on a letter with a postmark from Los Angeles. The script was all too familiar. Bold blue ink in large cursive shouted at me. It was my father's.

I swallowed audibly before opening it. It was a birthday card. On the opposite side of the printed greeting, was a handwritten message that was deceptively simple: "Happy Birthday Linda. Please call. Dad and Mom." They were still out there. The message was clear to me. My turn was coming to address feminine dominance.

This was my birthday gift from the gods.

* * * *

The check arrived late Friday morning. I cannot begin to tell you my anxiety, as I had no money to drive to Carmel without it. I left for Carmel at noon, stopping in Marysville to cash it and buy gas.

THE DIVINE BEGINNING

I arrived at the Carmel Whitman House around five. There was a car in the driveway, which was a relief. I knocked on the door, but no one answered. I tried the door, and it opened.

"Hello, anybody home?"

I walked in to look around, and found Nadia. She had just come out of her small bedroom.

We greeted each other, but she looked surprised to see me. I handed her my March teaching payment, since she was the bookkeeper in charge of the Fellowship checking account. A sense of relief that my membership was secure for another month permeated my being.

"Is Rosemary here?" I asked, wanting to speak directly with her, instead of Nadia, about my overnight accommodation.

"She left with Robert around lunchtime."

We stood there for a moment. I didn't know what to do or say.

"How are you enjoying the house?"

"It's fine," she said.

She was Lunar, so I knew I couldn't ask to see her room. They are private people.

I opened my bag to look for a cigarette to buffer the tension.

"There's no meeting tonight. Why are you here?"

Lunars can be blunt, too.

"Robert said I could stay at the house." There it is. It's out.

"Where would you stay? There's no room for you."

"I brought my sleeping bag."

"This is not the farm."

The conversation was rapidly descending.

"I know. I'll keep it in my car until bedtime."

She was not happy. She turned and went into her room and closed the door.

I went to the couch to sit and recover a bit. The cigarette was still in my hand unlit, so I went out onto the back deck to smoke it. The house was nestled in a forested area, with thick foliage and the fresh smell of pine.

After two cigarettes, I heard a car drive up. It was approaching 5:30.

Rosemary and Marie entered and they, also, were surprised to see me. I explained to her that I came down to Carmel for my birthday.

"When is your birthday?" Rose asked.

"Today. I'm 23."

"That's nice, dear. We are going to a Mexican restaurant in Monterey for dinner. We just came back to freshen up. Why not come? Robert will be glad to see you."

We took Marie's car and drove to Monterey. I'd never been there before, so this was quite exciting. I'd read John Steinbeck's book about Cannery Row (well, actually I just saw the movie), and it was filled with California history. I imagined a quaint cantina — a small, quiet place with Mexican flags hanging on the walls, plenty of chips and salsa, and waitresses wearing white blouses off the shoulders with colorful embroidered full skirts and long braided black hair. A Mexican guitarist with a sombrero would be sitting in the corner, strumming softly. The Venusian bartender would be wiping the glasses pretending to clean them, while scanning the room for customers.

We parked and walked across the street to a two-story building made of pale-yellow clay with tile roof and wrought-iron banisters and wide terraces. It looked like a rich hacienda. The place shouted expensive. I shrunk as we entered.

Robert was sitting by the small reservation entry with Jim and Sheila and Don and Doris and Mary C. I felt quite out of place. These were grown-ups who could pay for their meal. I only had eight dollars.

Robert stood immediately to embrace the three of us. Rosemary then mentioned to Robert that today was my birthday. He asked how old I was, and I replied. Then he communicated something that put a smile on my face.

"You can be my guest for dinner."

"Thank you!" I replied profusely.

We went to our table, and it was a long one, seating the nine of us. Don was placed at the head of the table, and Sheila and Rosemary were on either side of Robert. To my surprise, Robert put me across from him with Jim to my right and Doris to my left. Mary was next to Rose and Marie was next to Jim. We placed our orders, which included an alcoholic drink known as a Margarita. I was unfamiliar with this so I just asked for a beer.

Don had brought a copy of his latest *Via Del Sol Journal* with him for Robert to review. I could see the back contained one of Harold's work cartoons. He would take a subject, like considering (internal and external) and describe its meaning and illustrate examples, sometimes using caricatures of students. Robert liked Harold's work cartoons, which used to be handouts to new students, saying they appealed to essence.

The journal was passed around, and when it came to me, immediately I noticed something odd: It was Volume I but the number on it was 26. This implied there were 25 other journals that had been printed and distributed. How could that be?

I turned to Jim and asked him quietly when the waitress appeared with our plates.

"Robert was still working with Don on them," he quickly replied, "and some people received them but most didn't."

I had to be satisfied with this, since my dish arrived. I ordered the chicken enchiladas, which was Robert's recommendation.

I began to combine my beans and rice, cut up my enchiladas and add them to the mix. As I was doing this, Robert stared at me and my plate. He motioned, "Do you do that often?"

"Uh-huh, yes," I replied sheepishly.

"Well," he advised firmly, "never do it again."

There was silence as everyone looked at my plate. The dish had become unrecognizable. My father used to do this to his food. My sister would express her disgust, but he would retort, "Well, it mixes in the stomach anyway." I just accepted it. Robert's comment made me realize I didn't have to see my father's stomach.

It was embarrassing. I couldn't undo it. And he had bought my dinner. I lost my appetite.

But I continued to eat because that's what everyone else was doing. And because I was still hungry. I was inner considering with each bite.

We ordered dessert and Robert recommended something I had never heard of before: Mexican flan. "Oh, you'll like it," whispered Doris, whose taste was more cosmopolitan than mine. There was a chocolate cake on the dessert menu, which would have been my choice. We each ordered the flan, however. Mine came with a little candle, which I blew out. My wish? To find love this year. When I cracked the crust with my spoon and tasted it, it was a custard pudding that was a bit rubbery, but the burnt sugar on top made up for it. It was yummy.

After dinner, we all embraced and I returned to the Whitman House with Rosemary and Marie. There was a little turmoil when we got back. Rose had to talk with Nadia, who was not happy about it, complaining that she was paying a lot for her tiny room when I got to stay for free. Once Nadia understood it was Robert's request, she had no viable position in the discussion. It was what the teacher wished.

I slept on the couch, unzipping my sleeping bag all the way so it served as a blanket. As I lay there, I reviewed the events of my special day. Receiving my paycheck. Driving to Carmel on my own. Making my teaching payment. Dining with Robert and friends, and finally sleeping in a luxury home in Carmel.

But what I considered the best news may surprise you: I still had my eight dollars. It was not much, but it was enough for me to stay in Carmel for the Monday meeting. I would return to the farm broke. That didn't bother me. Somehow, I knew I would survive. I was paying for something priceless: a life of conscious moments. I can feel myself living more in the past year than in all the years combined. That is a happy birthday, indeed.

How happy is that happy-faced pawn who is pushed by the king to checkmate every moment.

Rumi

CHAPTER 133

I spent Saturday and Sunday walking around Carmel and going to the beach just to look at the ocean. The cool wind that blew across the salty waves was invigorating and woke up my senses. I couldn't believe I was here.

Each morning I would have coffee at the house and a bowl of cereal with milk. Rosemary said it was okay to share her items. Then I would drive down Ocean Avenue and park on Lincoln near 10th or 11th, which was close to Sheila's apartment on 7th. I heard that Robert and Jim were staying there sometimes, and I was hoping I could catch a glimpse of them. I wouldn't dare go up to her apartment without an invitation.

From Lincoln, I walked to Ocean Avenue, where the main stores were, window shopping on both sides of the street. I would then explore Mission, San Carlos, and Dolores streets, which ran perpendicular to Ocean, finding alleyways that hid unique craft shops and small specialty dining spaces that sold ice cream, candy, or cookies only.

On Saturday around lunchtime, I went to the Mediterranean Market on Ocean and Mission. It was an extravagant shop, full of the most exotic foods and imported items from all over the world, including napkins and tablecloths from Italy and spoons and decorative tiles from Greece. I could buy a sandwich for two dollars that would tide me over until dinner time. On Sunday, my lunch was at the Village Corner. It was far less expensive, and attracted more hippies.

I also found myself browsing the books at that little shop where I met the Jovial lady named Doris. Sequestered in the back, I pulled the work books down to look at them. I found that particular spot in the store contained a special energy. It was almost like Ouspensky and Gurdjieff had personally placed these books there, beckoning those with a true magnetic center to reach for them from the shelf, buy them, and receive an exclusive ticket to enter a conscious universe that the other books on the shelf only pretended to offer.

On Saturday evening, Rosemary was with Robert, which left me at home with Marie and Nadia. The three of us had a simple dinner. It was a big California salad, with lettuce, alfalfa sprouts, red onions and avocado. Nadia was vegetarian and on a strict diet. I was hungry still, but the walking and light fare made me realize my stomach was shrinking, which is a good sign I would lose weight. That thought made me happy.

On Sunday, after the Village Corner lunch, I stopped to buy some bread and cheese at the Nielsen Brothers Market. I thought I could contribute to the evening meal. When I got back to the house, Rosemary was preparing chicken, vegetables and rice. She was a believer in animal protein, for which I was grateful. Robert was dining with Marie and Sheila. Nadia had fled the kitchen when she smelled the oven aromas of roasted chicken skin.

"What did you do today?" Rose asked, as we sat to dine at the intimate kitchen table.

I mentioned my explorations.

"Why don't you use tomorrow to drop by some of the restaurants and fill out job applications? You're a good cook and have experience at the farm."

I was shocked to hear this. I did not consider myself a good cook. True, I did have experience at the farm. Maybe this is not a far-fetched idea. I told her I would do it.

The next day, after breakfast, I went down Dolores to fill out job applications.

"Excuse me," I would begin, "I wondered if there are any job openings here."

Every place replied, "Sorry, not at this time. But you can fill out an application if you like, and we'll contact you if something opens up."

One of the first places had a surprising comment to give me. "You graduated UCLA. Why are you looking for a short-order cook's job?" I was overqualified. I couldn't explain it, not to them. The answer was simple but not acceptable to anyone but myself. I needed to be near my conscious teacher. I would give up everything for this, including a career.

THE SEEDS OF

I began to eliminate college education on the form. I still looked pretty young. I had to create a rationale to satisfy their curiosity: I moved up from Los Angeles, and want to stay in the beautiful town of Carmel. This explanation fit in with the times. Many young people were doing this, so why not me?

The Monday evening meeting was small and held in Sheila's apartment. It was curious how we have this huge place in Carmel, yet Robert was more comfortable in smaller spaces. I did not ask where exactly he was staying; I just knew he was not yet in the Whitman House.

There was a sweetness in the air, but it was not a manufactured fragrance. It was a joy of being with him. The ease with which I rested there with him in front of me, as he clarified concepts that we all had read in the work books, stilled the wheels of my mind and made that quiet place within me more accessible.

"Each student here has verified it is possible to be closer to consciousness or further from it," he said.

Yes. It is true.

"When a person is on the Way, his or her center of gravity is in Self-remembering, and as a student stated, you start to fit your life into the Work instead of the Work into your life."

It was Klair who had given this angle. It was so precise and poetic.

"If the teacher is eaten, it is called 'crime.' It is one of the ways C Influence works. Crime can make other students stronger who see and do not make the same mistake. One area where a student eats the teacher is when the student wastes the teacher's work, for example, by not doing a task."

Robert had given this angle before. This was a somber reminder that we must be diligent in our actions. It is difficult to know what inside of one is making decisions. This, for me, is the reason I need a teacher to guide me. He alone has recognized the lower and can let me know if my actions come from there.

I left the meeting feeling encouraged and inspired. This new *do* of my life seems impending, I thought, if not already here. I can imagine it. Perhaps within a week or two I can find a job, make money, and live here in Carmel. My future appears bright.

The past is an interpretation. The future is an illusion.
If you want to experience eternal illumination, put the past and
the future out of your mind and remain within the present moment.

Shams

CHAPTER 134

I drove back to Via Del Sol on Tuesday with a dollar to my name. A quarter tank of gas grounded me for a while, but I had the solace of food and a roof over my head.

It was a strange feeling to know that Carmel should by all accounts be my home now, and yet I was living in the past by being at the farm. Have I mentioned this? Perhaps I did. The many 'I's are like a broken record, for sure. They fill the space with their song, which, in my case, was the unrelenting childhood refrain in the backseat of my father's car, "Are we there yet?"

My favorite movie has now become replaying the memories created from last year. Friday marked the one-year anniversary of meeting Robert. Yet 1971 could easily be ten years ago. Its memories are locked in some cosmic time vault. This year, so far, has been a strange movie indeed. Certainly not a boy-meets-girl script, nor a heroine that succeeds beyond anyone's expectations. The plot line has been uneventful, and, dare I say, boring.

Time is indifferent to boredom, however. It moves ahead regardless of my opinion about its content's worthiness. This is the hardest part of awakening. Robert reminds us that every hair is counted, meaning each moment not remembering myself is wasted time. But most moments are not full of action and drama. The desire for entertainment was bred into me from childhood. What I have verified so far, from that first moment of higher centers manifesting in me, was that the Self does not need to be entertained. It's happy just to be.

* * * *

The month of March became a verb. The days progressed steadily forward, each containing a morning, an afternoon and an evening that mirrored the previous and the subsequent. They were ordinary.

Nevertheless, I tried to find the magic in them. And there was magic to be found. It was a quiet time at Via Del Sol. I would sit outside, smoking a cigarette between octaves, and feel the Spring warmth stretching over the land. The manzanita blossoms silently fed the hungry air with perfume, as the bees and the ants built their homes anew. I walked up the hillside that had green stubble from winter rains and spring sun, and saw snow on the distant mountains cringing its way up the peaks from the slap of heat on the rocky terrain.

Even the little fig tree that had once provided my early refuge had an extraordinary resurrection. I had no idea that when you eat a fig, you are consuming both fruit and blossom. Little green balls protruded from the new stems. One day, I pointed it out to David, and he explained that wasps pollinate the small buds of fruit, while dropping their eggs in it.

"Eww!" I replied.

His belly shook with laughter. He often likes to give me simple tidbits of information in a way that's shocking and a bit revolting.

"You mean I'm eating baby wasps?"

He puffed a while before explaining that the fig has an enzyme that dissolves the wasps, which in turn feeds the fig.

"It's nature."

"How do you know these things?"

"I read."

He was such an unassuming fellow. There was a lot there that was easily missed.

These moments with friends nourished my heart. Whether they nourished my soul — that is, produced conscious moments — required a level of effort from me that seemed, unlike last year, to be unachievable. The commands to "divide attention" or "remember yourself" often had no force of conviction. And most of the time, I simply forgot to evoke them, being content, instead, to enjoy the camaraderie of fellow students — laughing, teasing, joking when Robert was away. To photograph others when this was going on was not a popular approach to take. Sometimes, one would be ridiculed. At least, that was my experience. It was more harmonious to let it go and join in.

It was hard to sense the gods during these ordinary days. I wasn't sure why. Had the gods abandoned me? Or, perhaps, distributed their help to others, and would return to me when they could? I missed sensing their presence. How they worked to awaken us oftentimes was a great mystery. They were elusive and, in their absence, we were left to our own devices. Or so it seemed.

Ah, as we prayed for human help: angels soundlessly,
with single strides, climbed over our prostrate hearts.
Rainer Maria Rilke

CHAPTER 135

The morning of Saturday April 1st was full of light. Many students had appeared from the Bay Area and Carmel on Friday. This was the herald of Robert's coming.

I slept until eight since I had a late-night octave washing dishes, and waited in my sleeping bag for the student to leave the bathroom. As soon as the door opened, I grabbed my clothes, towel and toiletries, and almost tripped over the person in front of me to enter. Once inside, I disrobed and showered. When I had dried off, I reached for my underwear.

Oh my God! Where's my bra?

I searched over and over and over again but it wasn't there. I couldn't possibly leave without having it on. What do I do? What do I do? I sat on the toilet seat totally frozen with indecision. Someone knocked on the door.

"Are you done?"

I opened it slightly. "Can you find Helga? I need Helga."

Why Helga? She alone shared my bra size. Maybe she has an extra bra.

I waited for quite some time. A knock came, and Helga was there.

"I need your help," I said, as I hid behind the door to let her inside.

I explained the situation and she did indeed have an extra bra I could use, although she said it was a bit worn. I didn't care.

"You can use it as long as you like," she said generously.

I knew I needed to buy one for myself, since bras, once gone, never reappear.

"It's fine," I replied. "I will go to town and buy a new bra at J.C. Penny."

After hurriedly eating a bowl of cereal, I drove to Marysville. The Playtex bra was on sale for $3.99. I had made five dollars from a massage that week, but had no idea that's what I would spend it on. Oh, well.

When I returned midafternoon, Robert was there and asked me where I had been. I explained the situation, and he pointed upward, while shaking his head and grinning broadly.

He wasn't the only one grinning. Several other students snickered as I passed by. They were focused on my chest. It was humiliating. I guess news spread while I was in town. Of course, no one would inform Robert, which is why he asked me directly. It would be considered gossiping if they did, and students generally avoided being photographed by the teacher. They saw photographs as reprimands; I saw them as remedies.

By early evening, a mother approached me, asking to speak with me privately. We went to the far corner of the living room, whereupon she opened the paper bag she held.

"Is this your bra?" she asked, pulling it out discreetly.

Yes, that's my bra. She returned it to the bag and handed it to me.

"One of the older boys found it in his sleeping bag in the morning. Perhaps it was an April Fool's joke the kids played on him last night."

Neither of us knew how it was taken from my pile of clothes without waking me and stuffed into the boy's bag without him realizing it. The Lodge floors were crowded last night. There was hardly a space for a foot to fall. My clothes were between me and the next person sleeping and those kids were huddled downstairs with their parents. It was an impossible act. How it was done forever perplexed me.

* * * *

While I was in town shopping for bras, there had been a big work octave to plant 500 cedar seedlings around the property. Yorgos coordinated the effort. It was not a small task, and even Robert participated briefly I was told. I had wondered why there were so few students in the Lodge when I returned. I was only attracted to nature poetically. I was not fit for hard physical labor.

At Sunday breakfast, Jim circulated an announcement that the tree planting would continue before the meeting and after lunch, and that Robert requested everyone to participate for at least one hour.

Does this mean me? I was hoping I would be considered a vital member of the kitchen crew. I had arisen at first light to set up the breakfast and decided to focus on preparing lunch, washing dishes, then helping to cook dinner. I would use the apron trick, and leave it on all day. It would be my uniform. I watched students, who were dressed in their work clothes, mount the back of two trucks and then were carried away to the planting sites up the hill. I felt exempt and safe, and thought the planting octave would be over by dinnertime. I was sure I had dodged a bullet.

When the meeting time came, Robert allowed everyone to stay in their work clothes, since he considered it a third-line work day. Yorgos began the meeting with the following comment.

"When a large number of people in the teaching are engaged in a common effort, there is enough collective energy there so as to help us all. It serves as a third force. Also, there is a quality of work involved in determining where the seedlings are planted."

Robert smiled and added, "The little trees are grateful for their new home, and they need external care and love. In the same way, Work 'I's — those that want to self-remember — go against nature: the 'I's in false personality, the mechanicalness of life, and laziness. To grow and become strong, Work 'I's need external care and love, too. This is where C Influence shocks come in."

A hand was raised, and Robert nodded for her to speak.

"May we have some angles on 'planning ahead' and living in the present?"

Meg motioned to Robert that she wished to speak.

"It does no harm to plan ahead as long as you do not identify with the outcome. To be not identified means to be able to adapt to an outcome different from the one expected."

Mac contributed an angle.

"Planning is useful as long as it is actualized — that's creative imagination. When it is not actualized, it is known as negative imagination."

This angle confused me.

Another question.

"What is it when one thinks about repairing something, but doesn't do it?"

Robert replied, "Imagination frequently takes the place of actualizing something. That is why it is best not to speak about things you are going to do as it drains their possibilities of becoming realities."

This I understood.

A student from the East Bay raised his hand. Instead of offering an angle, he offered a question.

"How does C Influence manifest to you?"

This question interested me.

"Well," began Robert, "like the time I met Don in the middle of Vallejo, it was C Influence that had said, 'I am going to Vallejo,' meaning, they instructed me to go. Also, C Influence does speak to the higher centers within this being of Robert Burton.

"I hardly speak to them because they bring so much friction. I'm tired of being around them many times, but I carry on. They also appreciate themselves through us, meaning they appreciate it when we express gratitude toward them. Everything here is their work, happy or sad.

"Yet, I pretend they aren't around. Pretend you do everything, even if you meet Don in England by chance in May, for example. They want it that way."

What? What was Robert talking about? England in May?

"They wish to keep an individual spark within each of us. They don't want us to lean on them.

"Someday they will raise a table for us, just as they raised a piano for Lincoln. It is in the United States records and was reported in the newspapers a few weeks ago that Lincoln had levitated atop the piano when it rose."

Miles signaled to Robert to speak. Once acknowledged, he offered this.

"An angle of thought on C Influence controlling us: No matter how it tries, C Influence cannot put swear words in our speech, since our level of being is above that."

Robert and Jim looked at each other, with a big grin. Jim read Robert's note aloud.

"Robert had written this," stated Jim, "before Miles began speaking: 'An "I" just said, I sure as HELL can't raise a table.' It wasn't a table, but it was pretty good," said Jim chuckling.

Indeed. Amazing timing.

"Starting the group on Lincoln and Seventh and then moving to Whitman Circle should be enough to verify C Influence. Also," continued Robert, "Miles's chief feature is grayness, and today we passed two streets in Los Gatos that crossed each other named Gray Street and Miles Street."

Miles's face was stoic. Maybe he did not see the magic in this.

Robert paused before communicating this next angle.

"According to George Gurdjieff, when large amounts of knowledge are available, a disaster is imminent. C Influence has given certain dates, one being the California earthquake — the Big One — with the date of 1998. I have to keep sounding that note until 1998 to keep it from being too much of a shock IF it happens. We will be well prepared, and history is full of false alarms, as ours may be."

Another question came from a Bay Area student.

"Did you receive this information from C Influence?"

"Yes," Robert replied. "They keep sounding it over and over to keep me realizing it may happen."

The meeting ended on that note. It was almost noon and lunchtime. I was able to keep to the kitchen octave for the rest of the day, leaving the tree planting to those with jeans and boots. I was grateful I did not have to be included in that outdoor octave. Thank the gods.

※

*The harvest is indeed great, but the laborers are few;
but beg the Lord to send laborers into the harvest.*

Jesus

CHAPTER 136

"Robert would like you to join us to plant some trees."

I was awakened at 6:30 Monday morning with this personal invitation from the teacher. My heart soared and my body sank.

Grabbing my glasses, first, as always, I recognized the student. It was Clark standing over me with a big smile. He seemed to take particular delight in this. Perhaps my apron trick didn't trick anyone after all.

No time for a shower or makeup. A few pieces of bread and cheese carried to the truck was all that was allowed. After squeezing my way into the cab, we headed up the hill.

There were only three of us. It was odd that we were so few and we had so many seedlings to plant.

We pulled the truck over against an embankment on a hill above the Lodge. Our mission was to plant the seedlings on this hillside. It was steep and rugged. The other student was a Martial type. He was eager to tackle the terrain and started giving directions to us both.

"This is the best place to plant them," he directed, "away from the pine trees so they can get plenty of sun."

I carried the shovel while the guys carried the plants up the hill.

"Dig here," said the Martial type to me.

What? I had never used a shovel before.

I tried to position the shovel on the slope. My small foot could not press down with enough force to get the shovel tip to penetrate the dry earth.

"Wait," said Clark, "let me do this."

I felt useless.

Clark dug the small holes and I would place the seedlings in them. I checked my watch, wondering when the hour would be over. I was only supposed to work an hour, right?

Wrong.

We were supposed to work for several hours, until lunch time at noon. Our energy levels had subsided with each passing hour. It was clear we would not finish the octave.

The Martial type had started to complain about how ridiculous this octave was.

"This makes no sense," he said. "I mean, look at this situation. These are not going to survive without water."

I hadn't thought about that. There was no water supply. Our assignment was to dig a hole and plant a tree, not to ensure it would grow. It was a bit strange.

"Well," I offered, "maybe you can speak with Yorgos about this. Maybe this is a test."

"A test?" asked the Martial type.

"You know, we are in a school, and Gurdjieff used to create all sorts of tasks that lacked common sense. Maybe that's what this is."

"You have to use common sense," he replied. "This is a stupid octave. It's a waste of time and money."

I could not convince him to see it differently, especially since he made a good point. My esoteric interpretation fell on deaf ears. Clark said nothing. No one was there to watch us, so we hurriedly stuck the seedlings into the shallowest of holes just to finish the job. Afterwards, the three of us sat on the hillside taking in the view, and waiting for the noon hour to announce we could return to the Lodge.

Who cares how well we did. The seedlings hadn't a chance to survive.

Or maybe, one would. Nature is funny that way.

❧

A sower went forth to sow; And when he sowed, some seeds fell upon stony places, where they had not much earth: and they sprung up, but because they had no deepness of earth they withered away.

Matthew 13:4

CHAPTER 137

Robert surprised us all at the farm by staying through the week. There was a pressure, an intensity that one could feel when the teacher was around. It was exhilarating to the higher parts in me and oppressive to the lower. A student has a love-hate relationship with his teacher, I thought. Of course, I wouldn't offer this at a meeting. But I did appreciate Robert's honesty when he described how he related to the gods. This was often how I related to him.

One new exercise he gave us was to eat our meals in silence. Afterwards, we would go outside and smoke and discuss what we observed. Some felt it prevented us from socializing; others felt it helped us to focus on tasting the food. Whatever our views, it definitely generated many 'I's. It was as if the lid had been placed on the emotional boiler and the contents spewed out once the heat was raised. Again, an internal pressure cooker for us to control.

Wednesday morning after breakfast, I went outside to smoke a cigarette and watched Miles and Yorgos speaking with Robert and Jim on the front patio away from other students. It looked like something was cooking, since the conversation lasted a while.

At lunch, a messenger was sent around to each table to let us know that we would have an impromptu meeting at 2 p.m. No other information was provided. Because of the silence exercise, we had to hold the questions inside, which was almost excruciating for some types. My mind, in particular, was racing, as I was trying mentally to complete the scenario that would be fully explained at the meeting.

When that time arrived, we rearranged the room so that chairs were facing Robert in a circle.

It was Yorgos, however, who spoke.

"We will be slaughtering chickens this week, beginning tomorrow morning early. Robert wishes each student to participate in the experience. The barn will be used to gut the birds and the shed will be prepared as a plucking station."

He went on to appoint various students as the octave leaders of each phase of the process.

Robert signaled to Jim, who began to speak his words.

"When I was in Alex Horn's group, I was given the task of slaughtering a lamb. I wished not to make it suffer so I swiftly dispatched it with a sharp knife quickly across its throat. It was a real experience for me."

The image was shocking to me. The thought of hurting an animal sent shivers through my body. I had heard Bubbie talk about the kosher butcher preparing the chicken we ate every Sunday. It was important how the blood drained, to make it kosher, I was told. I didn't inquire further.

"Another reason we are doing this," continued Robert, "is to help us manage our food costs. These chickens we will eat throughout the months ahead."

Robert stood and the others followed. That was the end of our impromptu meeting.

* * * *

The next day, after setting up the breakfast table and preparing tea and coffee, I learned that the octave leaders had selected the students to assist them. I was not among them. I prayed I would somehow find a way not to be asked to slaughter a chicken. Still, I was curious. I walked down the hill to the barn and saw Yorgos standing by a post. Yorgos smiled when he saw me.

"This is the slaughtering post," he explained. A nail was positioned at the top of it and fresh red blood drippings were visible.

Behind him was a pile of wood. Then I realized it was not. It was a pile of live chickens, whose feet were bound. They quietly nestled against each other. I stared in disbelief.

"Why aren't they flying away?" I asked Yorgos. "I mean, don't they realize their fate?"

"No. Once their legs are bound, they are resigned to their fate, I guess. They become passive."

He brought one to the slaughter post and positioned the string that held its legs together on the nail. At this point I turned to go. And at this point he swung the ax. No fowl sound was heard, only the thwack of the metal blade into the wood.

I walked up the hill to the Lodge in a state of shock. Each step I took was intentionally placed, and I could tell my higher centers were jarred awake. The internal camera was on.

The sudden leap from a lower world to a higher world was a momentous shift in scale. From this rarified perspective, my consciousness had seen something significant about this moment, this episode in my life. It was metaphoric. I needed quiet to decipher the deeper meaning.

I sat on a big rock on the patio and pulled out a cigarette from my pack. I lit it and took a big inhalation. A few students passed me by, as they grinned and shook their heads. They were busy working.

How could these chickens remain so passive when one of its own was being slaughtered close by? Do chickens have buffers? Their wings still worked, but they refused to use them. Not even a squawk was uttered, no alarms sounding to alert their comrades, "Hey, guys. Something's not right here."

It was not a surrender, because where was the fight? It was pure acquiescence, an unquestioning acceptance of their fate. Do we shake the chicken awake? Would that even help? What do they imagine is happening to them, or will happen to them? They are being led to their deaths and to their destiny of being consumed by a higher order of creation.

I could see the analogy. Why this work is not popular, how people think they have the capacity to be in control of their lives when sleep shrouds the truth from them. They, too, enjoy the calm comfort of comradery, while bound hand and foot by invisible threads.

I find myself a chicken run free, given the opportunity to learn an almost impossible feat: to use the feathers not for preening or display but for flight. That is the offer the gods have given to me. Am I able to do this work? Am I able to fly with bound feet?

For once you have tasted flight you will walk the earth with your eyes turned skywards, for there you have been and there you will long to return.

Leonardo da Vinci

CHAPTER 138

We focused on the chicken octave during the week. Over the following weekend, I joined the crew in the shed, plucking the pin feathers out of the dead birds. We used tweezers to take them out. I sat on a small stool next to Anna Gold, who seemed to be an old hand at this type of thing, extracting them with a single movement. I struggled.

"Look how skinny they are," she observed, with her characteristic bubbly laugh that tickled Robert every time he heard it. "It's ridiculous! They are not worth the effort."

I hadn't noticed this until she said it. It was true, there was not much meat on the bones. Anna was famous for her juicy roast chicken and rich chicken soup, and it was clear she understood, like all Jewish women, how to choose the best for the table. She wouldn't use these birds even if the kosher butcher gave them to her for free.

At one point, she brought up a subject I totally forgot to ask about from last weekend's meeting.

"Rosemary is excited about her trip with Robert to Europe."

"Robert mentioned something about meeting Don in England in May. I wondered about this. Is Don going?"

"No, he's working."

I asked her who else is going, and she listed the names: Mary C., Rose, Jan, Helga, Miles, Sheila, and Jim. They all seemed to be the closest students to the teacher. They also seemed to have money to spend. I envied them.

"Rosemary has wanted to go to Europe for a long time. She's always been interested in art."

Europe seemed so distant, so inaccessible an experience. I could not imagine myself travelling to exotic lands.

"Why aren't you going?" I asked.

"I'm not interested."

It was a short response and I felt it may also have to do with money. I didn't pursue it, so the subject dropped.

My back began to hurt, so I decided to leave the shed and go to the kitchen for my dinner octave. Anna remained, chatting with Klair, who took my seat to help out. Klair was one of the octave leaders, of course. As I rose, Klair said, in her no-nonsense voice, "Be sure to come back."

I smiled and nodded, knowing full well that the answer was, "Probably not."

* * * *

After the first week, Robert had left with Rosemary to return to Carmel. Going into the second week of poultry processing, fewer students came up from the Bay Area and Carmel. It was a gruesome octave that held little attraction.

The farm work was hard and wore on us over time. We were looking scruffier. Miles was resembling someone from Truckee. His curly hair and beard looked like they hadn't been cut or washed all year. I, too, was looking worse. I washed my hair once a week, parted it down the middle and let it air dry. The thickness overpowered my small head, and with my glasses on my face I was so camouflaged that it was difficult for me to recognize the Linda in the mirror that existed over a year ago.

We had become, officially, hippies. It reminded me of the scene in Disney's *Pinocchio*, when Pinocchio went to Pleasure Island with his friends and became a donkey with his ears protruding through his cap. Had I become like this? The outside certainly did not match the changes I was experiencing inside. My higher states were more delicate and refined but invisible to others. The lower was becoming more apparent, being unfocused, uncaring, and lax in its ways. It was always a challenge not to be pulled down by this.

* * * *

Here's a question: What could possibly draw students here without the presence of the teacher? Answer: It was the magic of springtime. How can you not love baby-blue skies, the bite of crisp morning air succumbing to the warmth of the welcoming noon sun, and the joyous, quiet proof of nature's renewals? It made the daily chores lighter.

Perhaps this is what attracted Don and Doris to the farm, as well as Clare and the Vallejo student Jean that Saturday, April 15th. I registered this date because it was associated with Tax Day, which reminded me of my dire financial situation. Money continued to restrict me from travel, so it was lovely to have an infusion of positive energy from these people.

Clare and Jean joined us in the kitchen to prepare the evening meal. Clare was remarkably adept at chopping and slicing food. I still hadn't figured out how to use a kitchen knife effectively. We all took direction from Kerrie. I thought Jean would ask questions about the Work, being a new student, but we did not bring up any topics. There was such a simple pleasure in the company of these ladies that my work-related thoughts got impatient from lack of attention and voluntarily departed.

At around five in the afternoon, when the sun was lowering itself in the sky, Clark came into the kitchen excitedly.

"Everyone, come outside!"

That was all he said. I thought something serious had occurred, or at least odd, like finding a mountain lion taking a bath in the pond.

We followed, and instead found a gathering of students positioned on the embankment above the fig tree. Don was directing us with one hand while holding his professional camera in the other.

He had instructed Clare and three children to sit on the ground in the front row. Then Miles and Clark brought a bench for the second row. Jan's 14-year-old son, who had begun to work alongside Clark, sat first, followed by Small Jane, Miles, Jean, Clark, and Tall Jane. I was told to stand in the back between Bonita's teenage daughter, and Kerrie, with Helga, Doris, the Architect's son, Klair, and Laura completing the row.

Don took his time to focus. As I stood there, the 'I's that circulated in my head were numerous. I hadn't fixed my makeup or hair and felt totally unprepared for this impromptu moment. I did, however, manage to grab my shawl to cover my plumpness. Why is he doing this? What memory is there to capture? This is a ho-hum, nothing kind of day. Robert isn't even around. The 'I' that said, "Don't worry, no one will ever see this photo," calmed me down.

"Everyone, smile! This is a happy moment!" he insisted.

That worked. We all started smiling and giggling. Click, click, click. Done.

As I turned to go back to the kitchen, I was suddenly aware of the light filtering through the delicate young green leaves of the fig tree on that April day. Its beauty astonished me. I stood there for a moment, entranced. But something else inside me dismissively acknowledged the impression before insisting I move on to the dinner octave. I heeded the third-line call, reluctantly.

That night, before sleep came upon me, it was not the group photo that lingered in my mind, but the impression of the magical fig tree. My own third eye had captured that singular moment of beauty when time stood still. It found a place in my heart, preserved itself there for eternity, and would be what was left of my day.

❖

Then might I say, that moment seeing: Oh, linger on, thou art so fair!
The traces of my earthly being can perish not in eons. They are there.
                                    Johann Goethe, Faust's last words

CHAPTER 139

Robert had been mentioning that this would be a school of poetry, and I thought he was speaking of the future until I picked up the latest edition of the *Via Del Sol Journal*. It included a poem by Yorgos, titled "Sunflowers." I had no idea he wrote poetry. It had a simple structure and was not filled with multisyllabic words or scholarly references. It was refreshing. When I read it, I realized how little we truly know of one another. That this poem emerged from a quiet, hard-working friend with the dazzling smile, warm azure eyes and open heart stunned me. What else do I not know about him?

That curiosity I played with, but did not pursue. Instead, I thought about poetry writing. I enjoyed painting with language. Poetry had begun to flow inside lately, but for some reason, the words evaporated from my mind before they hit the page, lodging, instead, in the objects as I beheld them. I felt I was living my life now, so I guess no more need for two-dimensional scribbles.

Nevertheless, the fondness for poetry remained, having served me well in the past. I was awarded a scholarship to UCLA because of a poem I wrote and recited upon request at the interview. It was a simple poem, too.

As a freshman, I had submitted a few poems to the English department and had been accepted into a graduate seminar led by the poet laureate of the United States, James Dickey, who also happened to be the writer of the novel

Deliverance. That became a movie. A poet, a professor, a novelist and screenwriter. That was my career dream at the age of eighteen.

The freshman year, however, had taken an unexpected turn. I started to experience higher states. It derailed me. Also, the class was filled with sophisticated young people, one of whom proudly expressing to me that he could decipher Ezra Pound's works. This meant the reader needed to be a scholar who could know obscure references in Latin or Greek that Pound loved to drop between words to challenge (mock, actually) the reader's level of intelligence and education.

We were expected to pump out poems weekly. I had nothing to say. My poems were inspirations that would drop in my head at the oddest moments of presence. They were not manufactured to satisfy a writing assignment. Dickey had us reading and commenting on each other's recent poems. It was not just competitive and arrogant. It was brutal. Students were tearing each other's poems apart. It was like ripping open someone's heart. Because I was forced to generate a poem, I came up with this one, titled "What's Donne is Donne," out of a sense of rebellion.

> "Donne come save your poetry!
> This butchering, carving of connotations taken from your drawn notations
> Evokes a blandsome monotation of the entire verse.
> The slicing, slashing of your phrase no singular feeling does it raise.
> It's a mixture of madness that may amaze, perhaps will daze your mind.
> Oh, only if you could be among us to tell us of your rightful meaning.
> Your 'theme,' your 'mood,' your 'attitude' are all careening in mid-air.
> Which interpreter is correct?
> The straightforward or the indirect?
> The symbolist with knife in hand dissecting lines — Just let it stand!
> Poems are the man himself expressing his personal thoughts and feelings.
> You left a trail of words behind so mankind may attempt to find your meaning.
> But in my quest my thoughts were stunned by interpreters of every kind.
> But never mind, you did your best.
> What's Donne is Donne."

They were not amused.

I was attracted to poetry that unlocked a higher state within me, not something that would serve merely to impress others or criticize society. Still, there remained in me a deep need to find words to capture the uncapturable. I knew it was a futile task. Words intrinsically fail because they are units that live in a subjective world — the world of the machine — and will always be subject to interpretation. It was like building the Taj Mahal to capture the highest experience of ethereal love using cold, impenetrable white stones. What could be more paradoxical than this effort? Good try, nonetheless.

But this is the nature of art: the attempt to communicate to others what we consider of value to us. Gurdjieff spoke about objective art as being understood by all in the same way as intended. It was an ungraspable concept to his listeners, however. How could I speak about my higher states to those who had never experienced them? Can you understand the frustration? Experiencing higher states of consciousness sounds crazy… unless, it isn't.

My university experience was not wasteful, however. The class on John Milton was one of my favorites. It was a grueling pace for me; we had to comprehend two books a week of *Paradise Lost* and *Paradise Regained*. These so-called books were chapters actually. Milton's language was complex, and yet, if you focused your attention on it, the images he created were remarkably cinematic. What I learned about his life is that his blindness forced him to dictate to his daughters and friends the entire epic. The Greeks had muses that breathed their inspiration into humans, so this must have been true for him, too.

This connection with a higher level was happening to me. But to have it, like Milton, where your job is to listen and record without opinion, was beyond my ability to imagine. What a gift this must be to experience. To be so close, so obedient to the gods while overcoming even the obstacle of blindness to complete his work is astounding. Yet, what other choice had he? None, which he so eloquently expressed in the four words of his opening line: "Of man's first disobedience." He would not dare disobey them.

And his reference to his muse, "Sing heavenly muse," would eventually lead to the request to the gods, invoking their aid to complete his task: "What in me is dark, illumine, what is low, raise and support, that to the height of this great Argument, I may assert Eternal Providence, and justify the ways of God to man."

THE DIVINE BEGINNING

This is my invocation, too. Help me, gods, to awaken and serve you.

❧

Muse! Be thou mine oracle, and I shall be thine interpreter.

Pindar

CHAPTER 140

It was the last week of April and the full moon was scheduled to appear on Friday when Robert was to arrive at the farm. I had become accustomed to being distant from him for a week or two, and then to have his energy return to nourish me. The days of living with him in a familial way were so brief. Many 'I's longed for last year, and the sweet hope it brought. This year was a harsher reality.

Nothing made this clearer than what occurred to me that Friday morning. It was after breakfast. I joined two guys on the patio, who were smiling broadly between puffs of their cigarettes.

"What's up?" I asked as I approached them.

"We were just talking about the good news. We're having a wedding here!"

"Wow. Who's being married?"

"Helga and Miles."

The shock stopped all thought. That pressure in my forehead struck once again. A bullet between my eyes. I stood stunned.

The fellow who spoke suddenly realized to whom he spoke. They looked at one another with the same understanding, that they had each forgotten about my play with Miles and were sorry. They stood up and exited, stage left.

My legs had to move, and I found myself fleeing, climbing the hill rapidly from the Lodge. The state had me in its grip. I was beyond tears. Why did this shock me so? They were a couple. Everyone knew that.

Sitting on the hillside, pondering this circumstance, I waited for some 'I's to inform me. I was not alone inside this state. The gods, who know all, exposed what I had so secretly stashed away in my Pandora's box: that Helga and Miles would inevitably end their relationship and he would return to me. And that tiny bit of hope with its longing and the scenes of unconscious imaginings had both been murdered with a single shot to the heart and the head.

I had asked the gods for help to awaken. They did not disappoint.

* * * *

My appetite did not return for lunch. I had gone to Lake Francis to be alone. Still, no tears were shed. I could see so many dreams dashed within a year's time. Yeats had written a poem that came to mind as I looked at the sun's rays glimmer on the lake: "Things fall apart. The center cannot hold." That center in me, the quiet place within, is so undeveloped that nothing certain can reside nearby. What do I want? I don't know. Where do I go? I don't know. Why don't I know anything? Because to know is to imagine the future. Haven't I done this enough in my life, only to have my dreams dashed? Knowing is a dangerous endeavor.

I drove back to the Lodge. It was late afternoon when I saw Robert sitting alone in a chair on the patio. This was most odd. He watched me approach. For some strange reason I was compelled to pull up a chair and sit next to him. We did not exchange a word for several minutes. Then he wrote on his pad and handed it to me.

"C Influence controls the 'I's."

I read it and looked into his saucer-shaped deep blue eyes.

"Yes. And the heart."

He looked sorrowfully at me, as if he did not want to tell me it was true. He then nodded.

"It is a hard lesson to learn," I said.

Another note.

"It is a hard lesson for a loyal love."

We sat quietly together for a while.

He put his pencil to paper.

"Perhaps it's best for you to contact your parents for help. Maybe even visit LA."

I knew this was coming, and it may indeed be time to face this part of my play. Work on feminine dominance is not easy. Yet, I had reached a dead end financially. Robert and I both knew this.

"I will write to them."

"Maybe call them."

I nodded. My teacher was my guide, and this was his instruction. It made sense that now I must act.

* * * *

I placed that call, collect. My father answered and I could hear his excitement when he told the operator, "Yes! I will accept the call."

"Hey, Lil," I heard him say, speaking to my mother, "Linda's on the phone."

He asked me how I was doing. I told him, well. It was actually, "Well…"

I mentioned I wanted to visit. And I also mentioned that I wondered if it were possible for him to give me $100.

"Of course, honey! Whatever you need or want. We just want to see you. When are you coming?"

I did not have money for the May teaching payment, which was a first for me. This impacted my answer.

"Tuesday." The 'T' popped into my head and out of my mouth. I was thinking of May 15th a second before this word was uttered. Guess not.

"Great. See you soon."

And with that, the call ended. He did not even think to hand the phone to my mother, whom I was sure wanted to hear my voice at least. I knew he was counting the minutes that he had to pay for the call.

Returning to my parents' home after eleven months would have been inconceivable last week. The events of today have given me strength to venture forth, knowing full well the den of negativity I will be entering. What I will receive from my parents will be up to the gods. What I will transform will be both my payment and reward.

Work not for a reward; but never cease to do thy work.
Bhagavad Gita

CHAPTER 141

Before Sunday's breakfast, Robert approached me to ask if I had called my father. I told him how it went, and he had these suggestions: stay overnight in Carmel at the house and drive to LA from there; and contact Vija, who is in LA.

He saw my questioning look about Vija and he wrote, "Ask Jim for her address and phone number."

Who was Vija? I think I saw her at the Carmel meeting once, but I wasn't sure. Her name was unusual, and I do recall a young lady with a slight accent. She was not from California. The school was growing and I had given up trying to know everyone. We just stayed within our particular comfort zone of friends. Mine was at the farm, for the most part.

I looked for Jim but couldn't find him. I learned he had been working with Yorgos early in the morning so was not around when I arose. Thirty minutes before the meeting, I saw him standing in line for the bathroom to shower.

When I approached him for her address and phone number, I had to ask him who she was.

"She's an artist who lives in Los Angeles. You'll like her."

"Is she from California?"

"She was born in Latvia."

Because my grandmother came from Lithuania, I knew Latvia was a country nearby. I looked at her address and saw she lived in Venice. That place is like an artist colony. I had heard of its Muscle Beach, where guys build their bodies using the equipment on the sand. Beatniks lived there, too. I knew Santa Monica, which was more family-friendly, but was warned to stay out of Venice when I was at UCLA. Strange people lived there, I was told.

"Okay. Thanks."

He entered the bathroom and I went back into the living room to help with the chairs. I saw Rosemary and realized I needed to let her know what was going on, since I will be staying over in Carmel tomorrow. I filled her in and she said I could use her bedroom, since she will be staying in Vacaville on Monday night in preparation for the trip to Europe. It was truly generous of her.

There was a strong sense that a new *do* was sounding. Finally. My energy had spiked with a clarity and calmness of state.

The meeting began with the usual good householder followed by Robert making a timely comment.

"In the teaching, we have had many problems during the full moon, but fewer and fewer as the months go by. C Influence often uses this period to bring shocks as a special time to make will, so that, eventually, we can avoid being affected by the full moon. Some moons can be overcome also if we are in an especially joyful situation."

I had verified what he said about bringing shocks, but I could not understand its connection to making will. It did not feel like I was controlling anything consciously. Or was I?

"C Influence gives only as much help as is valued. The more it is valued, the more help you are given — often painful help. You have fate, and a decision is all made for you, yet you must play the role and feel out your path."

He looked at me when he gave this angle. It penetrated deeply.

A hand was raised.

"Is it correct second line of work to help someone who is having difficulty?"

"Whenever you help someone in difficulty, save a space inside yourself that accepts they may leave the teaching, as C Influence arranges such shocks for people on the Way to test their valuation."

He paused for a few moments before continuing.

THE DIVINE BEGINNING

"We all have had 'I's about leaving the teaching. Let them pack up and leave. They are only hot air. Nothing makes sense but the teaching."

The student asking the question had a look of shock on her face. I wasn't sure why she asked the question. She was from the Bay Area, and I had little contact with this group so did not know her.

But Robert was sensitive to her. He changed the subject.

"The group in Carmel is now balanced. There is about the same male-female ratio. C Influence also has a good sense of humor. They started this group with women of thirty-five to fifty-five years of age, and men mostly in their twenties."

There was a wave of giggles throughout the room. That was funny.

"It is an honor to be among the first students in a group. You will see why when this group reaches sixty students. It will be a large group over the years and all who come are fated to come to it."

Turning toward Bonita, who sat near the window, he said, "It is wise to accept that we are not the same people we were a year ago. Bonita is a different person than she was two years ago. Try to relate to each other as fresh, and allow and give credit to people who have changed their being."

I could feel my own change inside, and was grateful to him for this angle.

A young woman from Oakland raised her hand.

"Is Baba Ram Dass a conscious being?"

Robert replied, "No, he is a tool for C Influence and is in imagination. He is after the right values but can't stop talking. Talking is a buffer for him. Yoga students claiming conscious experiences are also in imagination. If an American takes a deep breath, he will feel a rise in his chest and think he's on a trip. It is imagination in the moving center. A year after I met this teaching, an 'I' thought it had crystallized and was in eternal bliss — at a pool table, no less."

A few chuckles could be heard. How did he know it was just an 'I'? That's remarkable.

Another question was asked by a Bay Area student named Richard. He was a black person.

"How does separation of 'I's and true Self relate to false personality?"

Meg raised her fingers to reply and Robert acknowledged her.

"Every 'I' is seen as personality at first, simply because a new student has no way of knowing one 'I' from another. Many of the 'I's are wolves in sheep's clothing. Later he will have a Work 'I' in control. In a school, another student will help by making photographs for him."

Robert added, "Yes. 'I's that are friendly toward the teaching and your development are in true personality and useful. Those not friendly to the teaching are in false personality."

Addressing Richard directly, Robert said, "Richard, you are luckier and more precious than many people know. You represent a pinnacle for black people, but few will ever know it. Your Self is playing the role of a black man. The world is hard on black seeds. If blacks were on top, it wouldn't make much difference as someone else would be suffering. Humans need a pecking order."

A silence filled the room. Robert stood to signal the end of the meeting. Students sitting with Robert rose also, exiting through the front door, as was the formal protocol.

I sat there for a few minutes before moving. Robert's comments were so direct and yet objective and kind. There was so much for me in this meeting. My state was heightened, and gratitude filled my heart for Robert's guidance.

This coming week, I had to do everything possible to sustain my work while dealing with the attitudes of my parents on their turf. They gave birth to me and yet, I do not want to lose my Self to them. This is my greatest fear. How can I remain present in the face of the most mechanical of all relationships?

The most important hour is always the present.
The most significant person is precisely the one sitting across from you right now. The most necessary work is always love.
Meister Eckhart

CHAPTER 142

The way to Carmel had become a familiar route. I had enough money for a one-way trip to LA, little more. After eating a hearty breakfast at the farm and preparing sandwiches for later, I left, and arrived in midafternoon. I drove down Ocean Avenue to the beach, parked, and found an empty bench near a weathered picnic table to sit and enjoy the sandwiches I had made.

As I sat there, taking in everything around me, I was particularly drawn to the brutality of the waves. The image was symbolic. I had more in common with the passive sand, that by nature's design submits to the relentless pounding.

A welling up of words entered my heart. I took a pencil and paper out of my bag and wrote it down.

THE DIVINE BEGINNING

"Ceaseless thing you are, O Sea:
Tripping phosphorescent upon a level, plain.
Battering rams of foam
Continuously charging and discharging whitened sand.
The grains silently acknowledge the process.
(Rocky forms were they before reduction:
Crevassed, sharp,
Lying low beneath the waves,
Upon a lower level, plain;
Surfacing for atmosphere to face this Process of Reduction.)
I, too, acknowledge the process.
I, too, am made pure by such thunderous attacks."

Intentionally folding the paper in quarters, I placed it and the pencil back in my bag. Returning to my car, I drove up to Lincoln to window shop. There, in one of the secret alleyways, was a small gift store crowded with items, from jewelry to handkerchiefs. I entered, and behind the counter was a little Chinese lady. In the cabinet in front of her was a big crucifix necklace of turquoise blue. I was immediately drawn to it by its color. Appearing in LA with this around my neck I knew would rile my dad. Maybe it would serve as a leverage to throw him off balance.

As I put it on, the blueness stood out against my purple cotton turtleneck. I liked it. Perhaps this would protect me, like an amulet with hidden powers. How much? Five dollars, she said, adding with a twinkle in her eyes, "It's not real, you know."

I didn't care if the turquoise was just painted on and not actual stones. It cheered me up, so I bought it.

* * * *

Dinner that night with the ladies at the house was simple. I had to explain to them that Rosemary had given me permission to stay overnight in her room and that the idea of me staying was Robert's. Despite the explanations, Nadia did not look pleased with this. Oh, well.

I decided to use my sleeping bag on Rosemary's bed. It would be strange I felt to get under the sheets, knowing this was her space. I could barely sleep, however. Images of the entrance to that apartment unit on Sunset Boulevard kept popping up in my head. Dad did agree without an argument to give me the money. That was a relief.

It's so difficult not to think about the future. The pull of imagination was powerful, and the many 'I's swirled inside of me endlessly. The future is the unknown. It is like standing on a narrow precipice staring into a dark chasm that had no bottom. Treacherous and unfathomable.

And then I thought of the gods. I smiled, content with the fact that the gods know what will happen to me tomorrow. It was a comfort indeed. And with that, I was able to close this final scene of my day.

* * * *

The sun filtered into Rosemary's room and landed on my face. For a moment, I forgot where I was. There were no 'I's. Then, as if the script were handed to me, I recognized I was in such-and-such scene of this-and-that act. In Carmel. Preparing for the trip to LA, take one.

I went into the bathroom to prepare for the five-hour trip. At dinner, Klair and I had gone over the map, and she suggested I take Highway 68 through Salinas to reach Highway 101 rather than Highway 1 through Big Sur and the coast. It was a faster route, she said, although not as scenic. Faster was better, gas-wise, so I was grateful for her suggestion.

After a bowl of cereal and a cup of coffee, I put my things in the trunk and the map in the passenger seat. With a deep breath, I turned on the ignition. The tank was full. The journey has begun.

* * * *

Highway 68 went through the Salinas Valley. It was a rich and quiet impression of green rows patiently waiting to mature. I smiled, knowing the feeling exactly. Instead of taking the road through Salinas itself, I followed Klair's suggestion to turn off of 68 to Spreckels Avenue, which was renamed Harris Road, before connecting south to Highway 101.

The name Spreckels brought up a childhood memory of a bag of sugar. This was the family that made sugar for Californians. Their house was grand. It was the first time I realized that a bag of sugar could make a mansion.

There was a sense of relief once I turned onto 101. I could relax without having to confront my fear of being lost. The highway signs announced towns that I had not heard of — until I came upon Soledad, and immediately recognized its name. It was the setting of John Steinbeck's book *Of Mice and Men*. The entire Salinas Valley was his backdrop for stories, including *East of Eden*.

To read a book and to visit the place that inspired the author went deep. My life was no longer locked in some classroom or library. Stories were based on actual places and the lives of people who struggled on this planet. It was bringing me a sense of relativity and scale, removing me from the sheltered life I had been living.

I did not stop in Soledad, but continued on, hoping I would arrive at the apartment in time for lunch. The junction at Paso Robles was the tricky part of the drive, and I could feel my adrenaline pump into my head, heart, and hands. I would be going east now to move from the southbound 101 over to the southbound 5. The map referred to it as State Route (SR) 46, but it was also labeled SR 41. At a certain point this road diverged and I needed to take 46, which connected to 5 far below the 41 connector in Kettleman. In other words, if I missed this turnoff, I would be heading north and then have to travel south, which would cost both time and gas money.

My attention had to be acute for 25 miles. Never before had I truly understood how difficult it was to be present for an extended period of time. The muscle of my king of hearts repeatedly failed to hold my focus on my surroundings. I was easily distracted by outside impressions that stimulated internal commentary. Presence is not just a pretty word. It's a formidable task.

Once I merged onto Highway 5, I settled in and could feel my body relax from that effort. At this point, I was sixty miles to the Grapevine, where a year ago I was thinking my life had just begun as I travelled north. Now, travelling south, could I actually say my life had begun on that day?

I thought about that person — that Linda — who had definite ideas about the future. A year later I can say that the future is so full of uncertainties, whatever I imagine will happen most certainly will not. It's the unimaginable — the unexpected — that dictates future moments. And when that moment appears, we adjust our thinking and attitudes accordingly, making believe it was our original intent. This bad habit is how the machine lies to itself to buffer its powerlessness.

Had I changed? I did feel I am more open and affectionate than the Linda who had just graduated UCLA. My childhood was not one of warmth and affection, especially from my mother. The only time I could remember her caressing me was when Dad threw a shoe at me as I was lying on the floor watching television, and it was a direct hit. I ran to Mom's lap crying, and she chastised Dad while she slowly stroked my head. I didn't want her to stop so I kept sniveling. Now I want to be able to show affection to her. I want to express my love.

I also wanted to show Dad that I was responsible now. I had survived a year without their sheltering. True, I was asking for money, but I was able to drive down by myself and clothe myself. Hopefully, he'll see that.

Just as these 'I's were circulating, I passed the truck stop café where Miles and I had had lunch on our way up. That Linda would find it hard to believe that I was returning to LA on my own, without a man to drive me.

The exits came quickly. Castaic…Santa Clarita…San Fernando Valley, where the 5 became the 405. And finally, the Sunset Boulevard exit.

As I approached the white apartment building, I turned onto Stonehaven, the side street, to park the car. Switching off the ignition, I sat for a few minutes to collect myself. Here I am. How strange. The moments are about to reveal themselves. I am ready.

The art of life is more like the wrestler's art than the dancer's, in respect of this, that it should stand ready and firm to meet onsets which are sudden and unexpected.
                                                         Marcus Aurelius

CHAPTER 143

The stairwell was much smaller than I recalled. I wondered for a moment if I would have to knock. I did know from experience that you could hear each step made because the material was a type of white marble that caused sounds to resonate.

They heard me coming. The door opened and the smell of coffee grounds and fried onions and bacon presented themselves along with Dad and Mom. This was home.

Dad's smile was extinguished quickly.

"What are you wearing?!"

I smiled. I had always been the dutiful, quiet daughter and now I'm branching out, shall we say.

"You're not coming in with THAT on!"

"Dave," spoke up Mom, softly, "just leave her alone. If she wants to wear this, let her. She's home."

I entered. There were no embraces.

The three of us sat down in the living room. There were two couches. One was Dad's, which was discolored and threadbare. He spent almost his entire day sprawled out lengthwise, reading the stock market reports while watching television. He only left the apartment to shop for food and go to the banks. The other couch was for Mom. I joined her on this one. Mom was excited to hear about my life and adventures. But Dad would begin the interrogation.

"So did you find a job yet?"

I explained that I had been substitute teaching in Marysville and Vacaville, and that I was considering extending my search to Carmel, since some of my friends lived there. I did not mention my massage work.

"Where did you get the car?"

Of course, I didn't tell him about Robert. I just mentioned a friend had arranged for me to have it.

"Well, you'll find out what kind of friends you have when you ask them for money."

That was his reply.

There was a silence, since I did not respond. I only looked at them with as much presence as I could muster.

I could tell they were uneasy. My mother spoke up.

"Are you hungry?"

I said I hadn't had lunch. She replied that I could make something for myself from the fridge, if I wanted.

I stood up to enter the small kitchen, and as I opened the cabinet to look for a box of raisins, which were a staple in the family and easy to eat, Dad appeared next to me.

"Did you lose your virginity?"

The question was so amusing, I almost laughed out loud. I just looked right at him and smiled broadly. I had broken through a fear.

"OH, MY GOD!" he screamed melodramatically, and repeated it several more times.

I opened the refrigerator and could not find any lettuce to make a salad. Mom tried to help me but said they were out of a lot of fresh vegetables.

"We need to go to the grocery store but Dave hasn't done it yet," she said.

It was at that moment, I told her I could go and that she could come with me.

Mom told Dad she was going with me to the store.

She took her purse and we left Dad behind.

When we exited the building and turned the corner to Stonehaven, she saw my car and remarked how big it was. I opened the door for her, and as she sat down in the leather seat, I could see how uncomfortable she felt in its luxury.

We arrived at the local Von's grocery store and started to walk the aisles. I didn't need much, just some vegetables. There was cooked chicken in the fridge and eggs and bacon, and cans of tuna fish. I bought two types of lettuce, romaine and a round iceberg. I also bought a loaf of Roman Meal whole wheat bread, which I knew was my mother's favorite.

I rarely had been alone with my mother in a store before. Usually, Dad would have us stay in the car while he did all the shopping for the family.

It was such a pleasure to be with her, finally. As we walked the aisles, she offered to pay for the purchases. I accepted her generosity.

While standing in the checkout line, my hand gravitated to her back and gently caressed her. It felt so good to be able to express my love for her physically like this. I was thinking she was enjoying it.

She turned her head and looked up at me. But it wasn't love I saw.

"What are you doing? Feeling me like a piece of meat?!" she growled.

I was stunned. I withdrew my hand and kept it to my side, looking away from the cashier as Mom paid with cash.

But what had occurred inside of me was even more surprising. For the first time I realized this was her problem, not mine. I was suddenly set free. I had learned to express my love. She had not. It was sad, but there was nothing I could do about it.

When we arrived back at the apartment, I put my items away and Mom heated up the chicken soup with chicken pieces floating in it. We ate around four, so that was the meal of the day.

I did what I had done all my years in college. I washed the dishes and Dad turned to the couch to rest and watch television. Mom quietly took her position on her couch, staring at the screen.

After cleaning up the kitchen, I excused myself and retired to my bedroom. It was an acceptable thing to do because it was my habit that they had become accustomed to during all those years. They now could settle in to their evening routine of watching TV together, and at the sound of Dad's snoring, Mom would shake him to say, "Dave, let's go to bed."

Linda was home. Invisibly so.

* * * *

Wednesday morning, I awoke in a bed with sheets. The sound of traffic whizzing by shocked my senses. Here I was, back in this place that for years I vowed to flee.

The bathroom was still in need of cleaning. It was my job in the past to keep the place clean because Mom had given up long ago, when she concluded, "Why bother? It only gets dirty again." I found some Ajax cleanser under the sink and began to scrub the shower before bathing.

I had slept in late, and by the time I entered the kitchen it was almost eleven. I heated up the coffee and poured a cup. Bread went into the toaster and two eggs were fried with slices of bacon.

I sat at the kitchen table after wiping it off first. Mom sat down with me while Dad was watching the news.

"What is Carmel like?" she asked. I told her about the shops and she smiled. I looked in her eyes and I realized she was happy that I was happy. The incident at the store was not her nature, and I did not understand why she said what she said. It was a bit uncharacteristic of her, but I let it go.

After brunch, Dad called me over. He did not rise from the couch, but scooted over to make room for me to sit. This was his custom since I was a child, and there was little room for me now as an adult. He could see I was almost falling off.

"You've gotten fat."

I said nothing.

"I've been thinking about the money," he began, "and decided I'm gonna give you $50 now and then if you need more, you can let me know and I'll send you the other $50."

I could hear shackles snap shut.

With Dad, he was not the negotiator, but the deal closer. We had no say in the matter.

"When are you leaving?"

I told him Friday morning.

"Good to know. I'll go to the bank tomorrow to take out the money."

The rest of the day was spent watching television together.

* * * *

Thursday morning, I followed my customary routine. As I entered the living room, Dad was waiting for me.

"Come here," he commanded, heading to the kitchen. As he opened the refrigerator, he reached down and pulled out the romaine and iceberg, slamming them on the counter.

"Do you see this?!" he yelled. "You bought it and never touched it. They're still here! You're wasting food. You have no sense of money. Forget about getting the $50."

He walked back into the living room and began to rail about my circumstances.

"I'm not giving you ANYTHING because you're just gonna give it to that Hitler of yours…what's his name?"

I softly said Robert.

"Robert? Robert! The Hitler!"

"Dad, I need gas money to return," I explained, almost pleading, with tears welling in my eyes.

He continued for fifteen minutes, telling me he was saving me and didn't want me to go back, calling me a "stupid idiot" and reminding me of how "gullible" I was. These were among his favorite descriptors of me. He was, above all, doing me a favor that I'll thank him for later.

I felt trapped. What am I going to do now?

I returned to my bedroom and sat on the bed. How many of my tears has this bed absorbed? Fear was spreading throughout my body. What do I do? I was bound, once again, in this ivory tower of concrete.

After an hour, there was a knock on my door.

"Your Mom and I are going out to run errands. We'll be back soon."

I closed the door. It was then that I remembered I still had Vija's phone number and address in my purse. She was the only Fellowship member living in Los Angeles. I waited to hear the front door shut before going out and picking up the yellow phone and dialing her number.

"Hello Vija."

"Yes?"

"My name is Linda Kaplan and I'm a student in the Fellowship." At that moment I started to cry. I told her my situation and she immediately told me to come over.

She gave me instructions to head down the 405 to Venice Boulevard and stay right at the split. I wrote down the cross streets, and she said she would wait for me in the parking lot. It would take about 30 minutes. I told her I was driving a white Buick Wildcat.

I grabbed my purse and rushed downstairs, with my adrenaline pumping. I felt the clock had started, for I had no idea when my parents would return. I drove as quickly as possible to Venice.

Vija was waving to me and indicating where to park. I followed her into a small commercial building that seemed to be part of a strip mall. It did not look like an apartment complex. Through a small door we climbed narrow steps that were made of beautiful, shiny blond wood. It opened to a split-level tiny residence. The first level was a charmingly cozy living space with solid, blond-wood furniture and green and beige upholstered chairs. Original paintings were on the wall. It was tidy and clean. There was a stillness that resonated within me.

We sat on those beautiful chairs. After explaining the whole story to her, she stood up and climbed a few steps to her loft that accommodated her bed, dresser, a tiny bathroom and a window that let the light shine in down the steps. She opened the bottom drawer of the dresser that contained her lingerie and pulled out an envelope.

"Is this enough?" she asked, handing me a fifty-dollar bill.

I was speechless for a moment.

"I can't take this," I said, shaking my head. "I have no way to pay you back."

She dismissed all of this, saying, "Don't worry, Linda. You don't need to pay me back." She hugged me, and then asked, "Are you sure you don't need a hundred?"

"Oh, no. The fifty is enough." I replied, staring at a fifty-dollar bill, which I had never seen before in my life. "Thank you so much."

"What are you going to do now?" she asked, holding my hand.

"I guess I'll go back for the rest of my stuff and wait for them to return to say good-by before driving up north."

"Linda, NO!" she said emphatically. "Don't wait for them to come home. Go back, pack your bags and leave!"

She was right. And so I did.

* * * *

Returning to the apartment, an overpowering fear shook me as I hurriedly grabbed my clothes and supplies. I was hungry but dared not take food, as it had already been an hour and a half since they had left. They were never gone long on their errands, and a confrontation, should they encounter me, was beyond my capacity to handle.

As I drove the car onto Sunset, I realized I had to stop for gas. I pulled into a station less than a mile away and imagined they would be shopping nearby and see me. I was paranoid. It took so long to fill the huge tank, but these moments could not be rushed. I had to endure this state of absolute terror.

Finally, I entered the 405 heading north. It was not until I reached the long stretch of highway beyond the Grapevine that I felt any sense of relief. I thought about the origins of my life with these people, and asked the gods, how was it possible to have survived such an upbringing?

And then, I saw it. In the middle of the road. There ahead was a little orange California poppy emerging from a crack in the concrete. My sight captured it as the car rolled on. In its singleness, the courage, the resilience, the love of the light of the sun drove it upward, piercing stone. That's how.

This is the miraculous.

Stand up, my heart! Look toward the direction where light is born.
There you will find the power and the kingdom, the beautiful flower.

Toltec Wisdom

CHAPTER 144

That image of the flower remained with me. It had become an emblem of my journey and a source of comfort whenever I felt afraid. It was the reminder that the gods designed my life, and as long as I proved grateful and obedient to them, all would go well in the end.

I found myself retracing my steps. My hunger had gotten the best of me, and I stopped in Paso Robles at a Denny's to order a hamburger and fries with a Coke and a green salad. I ate slowly, savoring each bite. To be at a restaurant alone like this was also a little act of courage. No one bothered me, which was nice.

My plan was to land in Carmel for the overnight, not knowing whether I would be welcomed. The goal was to hand over my May teaching payment to Nadia. The rest I would accept.

When I arrived, Marie was home. Because Rosemary was still in Europe, Marie thought it was fine for me to stay in Rose's room since she had given me permission before. As we were speaking in the kitchen, Nadia entered the house and greeted us briefly before going to her room.

Marie told me Nadia has a bookkeeping job in Monterey.

"Have you found a job?" I asked Marie.

She stood up and led me to her room. There on the floor were pieces of driftwood and paint brushes and cans of shellac.

"This is what I'm working on," she said, handing me a polished slab of driftwood with a saying written on it in italics, from Meher Baba: "There is nothing that love cannot achieve, and there is nothing that love cannot sacrifice." It was beautifully crafted.

She told me she finds the driftwood on Carmel beaches, and already she has a shop that wants to sell her items. I was quite impressed by her creativity. This is how she is going to survive here.

I joined in to help with the dinner. Nadia entered the kitchen to prepare her own meal, and I took the opportunity to hand her my teaching payment.

The three of us sat down at the dining table to eat. I listened as they spoke about the new Carmel students.

"Doris called me this morning," said Marie to Nadia, "and she's going to carry my first plaque in her store. She also mentioned there were other people she knew who were interested in joining."

Doris? Store?

"Who is Doris?" I asked.

It turned out she was the flamboyant jovial woman I had met on my first visit to Carmel in that shop on Ocean. How amazing! It was like watching puzzle pieces coming together.

We could hear the heavy front door open. It was Klair with grocery bags. I rose to help her and went back out to her car for more.

Klair put her items away in the refrigerator, as I set the last two bags down on the counter.

The phone in the kitchen rang.

Klair picked it up. She listened a few moments before saying, "You're kidding!"

Our attention was drawn to her. She listened more than spoke. The conversation ended with her saying, "Okay."

She turned to us.

"It was Mac. Robert and the group are coming back tomorrow from Europe. He and James and Rosemary and Sheila will be flying into the Monterey airport and want us to pick them up."

She then turned to me.

"Linda, I have a doctor's appointment and can't go. Maybe you can pick them up since your car is big enough for their luggage."

ME?

"Their plane lands at three. You need to leave here around 2:30. Take highway 68 and follow the signs."

"You may want to wash your car and clean it out first," advised Marie.

I had not even considered this, so was grateful she mentioned it. It actually became a topic of conversation when I said I didn't have the materials to do it. Marie stepped in and said she had car washing soap and rags in the garage. She recommended newspapers and ammonia to clean the windows and told me how to clean the inside.

Of course, I agreed. I considered it an honor to be asked.

* * * *

It was Friday morning and I arose around eleven. I was more tired than I thought. The day before had been filled with unusual events, from fearing I may be stuck forever in LA with my parents, to receiving money from a stranger, to learning I would be picking up the teacher in my car. No wonder I needed to sleep late.

By the time I started cleaning my car, it was almost one. I figured I could do it in an hour. I was wrong. The car was big and the inside was filthy, with gunk in the tiny crevices of the dashboard. I had not cleaned the car before, just put gas in and drove it, so what did I know? The clock inside the car was ticking down the minutes, and the anxiety of having Robert inside a less-than-pristine auto was causing my heart to race.

It was now 2:30, and I had to let it go. I emptied the bucket of dirty water and put it and the rags and cleaner inside the garage where I found them. By the time I pulled out of the driveway, it was 2:44.

The anxiety commingled with happiness at the thought of seeing and being with Robert. I followed the signs and did not know whether to park or pick up. A decision had to be made quickly. I did not see them on the curb under the Arrivals sign so I parked the car. It was now 3:10.

By the time I came back to the Arrivals door, they were waiting there with their luggage. Oops.

I was expecting an embrace but that didn't happen. They were clearly exhausted. I went back to my car and pulled it up to the curb. Jim handled all the bags, and they did indeed fit. Robert sat in the passenger seat, while Jim opened the back door for the ladies. I looked carefully as I pulled out into the traffic, for I had precious cargo onboard.

During the drive, Robert was quiet. I was inner considering. Jim leaned forward and gave me instructions from the middle seat. I was to drop Robert, Jim, and Sheila at her apartment. Rosemary would go with me back to the Whitman House.

Once alone with Rosemary, I tried to speak with her about the journey to Europe, but she was only interested in going to her room, which I had quickly tidied up in the morning. It was, after all, around midnight London time for her, she said. I thanked her for the use of her room. She told me I could stay in the extra room reserved for the teacher since he was staying with Sheila.

I carried her bags in, while she greeted Klair, Marie, and Nadia. She explained to them that she had jet lag and needed to retire. I stayed up with the other ladies, talking about what could possibly have brought Robert and his group back so early. It was speculation.

What was discussed was a plan to celebrate Robert's birthday at the Tuesday Carmel meeting. This was the second message from Mac to Klair. Robert wanted it to be at the Whitman House, and perhaps this was one reason he returned early, although his birthday was actually on Friday the 12th. It was a curious, last-minute request.

After dinner, I went to the garage to return my personal items to my trunk and retrieve those I would need for the night. It had been a whirlwind 24 hours. We were now into the weekend, and I knew Tuesday would be a festive time in Carmel. I had enough money left to stay.

It felt wonderful finally to have something to look forward to after such a harsh week filled with future fears. Joy, at last, was returning. It would be easier now to be present.

*
> *Now is the moment, now,*
> *To take what happiness the gods allow.*
> Alcaeus

CHAPTER 145

I sat at the kitchen table, nursing my third cup of coffee in hopes that Rosemary would appear. The other ladies went about their business: Nadia went to work, Marie took her finished plaque to Doris's store, and Klair had left before any of us arose. She was active for a Lunar type.

After all that coffee, I needed to use the bathroom and discovered Rose was in there. I used another one, but was glad to see she was up. It was Saturday midmorning and I was in Carmel. This alone made me happy, although it was overcast outside and cool.

By the time I made a fresh pot of coffee for Rosemary, she entered the kitchen. She scrambled some eggs quickly and toasted some bread. We sat down together for a meal.

"Tell me about Europe. Where did you go?"

"We landed in London, checked in to the hotel and immediately went to the National Gallery, where the Leonardo da Vinci paintings are. Sheila recommended we see the Wallace Collection and the Tate Museum. It was a whirlwind, and I was exhausted."

"What was your favorite painting?"

"I love the Turner landscapes and wanted to see them at the Tate, but Robert came up to me and said, 'We're going. Don't waste your time on this.' It made me mad. I came all this way to see his works, and Robert told us what to see and what not to see."

She took out her pack of cigarettes and offered me one, which I accepted, since we both enjoyed the same brand.

"I have some brochures I'll share with you," she offered, after the first deep inhalation.

"That would be great."

She paused for a moment, as if pondering whether or not to share the next thought.

"Robert was so much like Mac. I would go to the Legion of Honor in San Francisco with Mac. I was the one pushing the kids in the carriage and dealing with their needs, while he just went freely to the paintings he wanted to see. He never helped me. I felt trapped, when I wanted to enjoy the art myself. I thought this time I'm on my own, and was excited about going."

I listened sympathetically.

"We spent three days in London, and then flew to Amsterdam. I was looking forward to seeing the Van Goghs and Rembrandts. Then suddenly Robert said we are going home."

"Did he say why?"

"No, he didn't say why. But it looked like he was in shock. He's American. He's from Arkansas, you know. That's his essence."

That explanation suited me. I would be scared to go, too.

She asked me how my visit with my parents went, and I told her the whole story. When I mentioned the flower, it had no effect on her.

"What are you going to do today?" asked Rose, changing the subject.

"I hadn't thought about it."

"Why don't you distribute bookmarks in the bookstores?"

I had heard about these but hadn't seen them. Apparently, Don designed bookmarks to put in Fourth Way books saying Gurdjieff-Ouspensky School Now Accepting Students with the phone numbers of Carmel (the Whitman House) and San Francisco (Anna Gold's house).

"Do you have any?" I asked.

"There's a bunch in the drawer in the hallway cabinet."

I stood up and brought back a package of them. They were made of heavy colored paper.

"Why not start with the Pilgrim's Way bookstore on Dolores between 5th and 6th?"

So that was my assignment for the day.

* * * *

Once again, I parked near Sheila's apartment, hoping to catch a glimpse of Robert. It had become a habit, almost a reflex. I walked to Dolores Street and decided to stop by the shop on Ocean to see if Doris was there. When I turned the corner, the window display showed Marie's plaque. It was wonderful to see it there. As I entered, Doris was busy talking to customers so I went to the back where the books were and checked each volume of Gurdjieff, Ouspensky, Collin and others of their circle to see if bookmarks were missing. None were lacking.

I had nothing to buy, so I pretended to browse. Finally, going up to the counter where jewelry was displayed, I said hello to Doris, and explained I was a member of the Fellowship. She responded by reaching out and enwrapping me in her jovial bosom that was as soft as down.

"Well, how ARE you?"

I said fine and that I was checking the bookmarks. She told me to go to Pilgrim's Way bookstore and gave me the names of other stores in the area where I could place them.

The bookmarking octave took me a few hours. It was nice to stroll around Carmel. This town fed my soul with such beautiful impressions. It was no wonder Robert liked to be here.

* * * *

Sunday and Monday rolled by quickly. We were preparing for the Tuesday meeting and the celebration of Robert's birthday. Ordering food, organizing the furniture, cleaning the house made this a busy time.

Students started to arrive Tuesday morning to help out. Klair was in charge of the decorations. She seemed to be the intellectual part of the moving center (king of spades) and had a great sense of design. But then again, that Christmas tree she ornamented last year already demonstrated her abilities, didn't it?

The food had arrived around six with the meeting to begin at seven. It would be a short meeting, and then we would party. Robert requested it that way.

The living room was packed with students when the meeting began. I was able to secure a seat, but so many gents had to sit on the floor that it looked like a sea of them extending into the dining area. Students came from the farm, Vacaville, the Bay Area, and Carmel. We were all one group. It was a lovely feeling.

After good householder, we waited for Robert to begin the meeting. He stared up at the ceiling with the most serious look on his face. Everyone was focused on him. He had written something down for Jim to read.

"I am not sure how my voice will sound after the many months of silence. I have searched many volumes of writings for the best advice I could give any human being."

And then, the most unexpected thing happened.

He spoke for the first time in eight months.

"And this above all, to thine own Self be true."

Ten words.

I had forgotten the sound of his voice. It has a gentle feminine quality, as soft as velour, as smooth as silk satin, not high pitched or rough, but even-toned.

There was not much else to say. We sat there in silence for a minute or so. Robert then turned to Don who presented the next issue of the *Via Del Sol Journal*. Don mentioned it was Volume I Number 33, and it was no accident that this was published the week of the teacher's thirty-third birthday. The edition was on melon-colored paper, and as he held it up, I could see there was a picture on the cover. Suddenly, I realized, it was that group photo he took at the farm that ordinary day! So much for keeping it a private moment; now it was part of our public history. Had I known, I would have fixed myself up. Oh, well.

Mac then announced we would have a toast to Robert for his thirty-third birthday. Champagne was poured and some glasses and small plastic cups were passed around. There were not enough glasses for everyone apparently. As I received my cup, I thought how last year, when we bought the property, we had real champagne glasses for everyone to celebrate the occasion. We were fewer then.

We gathered around the dining table with its rich bounty of foods from the Mediterranean Market. As the evening went on, students were approaching Robert to speak with him. I waited, looking at my copy of the journal and that photo of me. I felt so different inside from the picture. I've never reconciled the anomaly of my internal being and external appearance.

THE DIVINE BEGINNING

Thumbing through the journal, which I heard had been assembled quickly in the last few days, I came upon a statement under Teacher's Notes. It read, "Being awake requires energy. Being awake means creating memory and evokes the astral body or Self. Thus, we are supporting two bodies with our energy and tire more easily, that is, traveling in a foreign country."

Perhaps that is why Robert returned so quickly. It may have simply been too overwhelming for him to secure his higher state, which is the explanation he had given us for his entering silence.

As dishes were being taken to the kitchen, the line to talk with Robert had diminished. I saw my opportunity, so went up to greet him. He embraced me, and I held him tight.

He whispered, stumbling at first: "He...Hello, Noble Effort."

I broke down and cried in his arms.

"It has been such a rough week," I said softly, through my tears, "like Milton's darkness visible — both light and blackness. I am so grateful."

"We have help," he replied.

"I know. That is why I am grateful."

This moment with Robert validated all my efforts to transform the pain of being reduced. His words of support, love and comfort lifted me to that higher level. It was plain. I was on an ascending path.

❖

With the help of a god, one man can sharpen another who is born for excellence, and encourage him to tremendous achievement.

Pindar

CHAPTER 146

The high that I experienced on Tuesday night plummeted by the time Wednesday afternoon came. The ladies of the house (actually, Nadia) informed me that I needed to pay for my lodging at the Whitman House if I planned to stay the week. My cash was running out, and so this request for good householder was a bit frightening, to say the least. Regardless of how much I wished to remain in Carmel for my internal work, my more practical, instinctive nature forced me, within an hour of notice, to pack my bags and head up to the farm.

The farm had indeed lost its charm. It was dirty and wild. People at the Oregon House store hadn't bathed in a week it seemed. Then I realized these 'I's were coming from a different part of me. It was helpless and angry. Observing 'I' had kicked in, and was able to observe it was self-pity, a form of vanity. The pull of wanting to be a responsible adult, and the habits of being taken care of by another person, was a type of suffering that seemed unresolvable. Being stuck, being helpless is a horrible state of mind. How can I emerge from this place? Why hasn't Carmel opened its doors to me?

The days at the farm were tediously long and yet the weeks of May passed rapidly. Time was so distorted since I joined the school. The Memorial Day weekend was a marker of sorts, because following this, on June 3, was Miles and Helga's wedding, an event I dreaded. I had free food and lodging but no money for independent travel. There was no escape.

Where was Robert? That was the question. He hadn't come to the farm, and we all supposed he would be here for the wedding, since it would be a big school affair. So I waited. And read the journals that were sent to us. The meetings we had over the weekends led by fellow students lacked the conscious energy of the teacher, although they were sincere and full of useful information about mechanics.

The Saturday of the three-day weekend was a full moon, and it hit me hard. I had been away from Robert's influence for over two weeks. I was caught in an internal centrifuge, with the spinning of the many 'I's. But instead of the lighter elements separating themselves from the coarser and floating up, I had been dragged down by the weight of my mechanics.

There was one angle in the recent journal that helped me, however. It was from Robert, and I could hear him saying it to me as I read it, now that I recalled the sound of his sweet voice: "You already may have verified that C Influence does not hold back anything to wake us up. The means justifies the end. So much of the time, it's 'grin and bear it.' "

* * * *

After the three-day weekend, on Wednesday, May 31, at lunchtime, I overheard the conversation.

"What's the plan?"

"Miles wants it in the meadow."

I had successfully compartmentalized my brain, focusing only on each octave and leaving emotional areas alone. I was doing laundry again, plus helping in the kitchen preparing dinners. The wedding was days away now. Kerrie was thrilled about the wedding; I nodded to each expression of her excitement. I had taken Robert's advice. I had a plastered smile on my face with a heart that had turned to concrete. Basically, I was numb.

Friday arrived with many students pouring into the Lodge, since the invitation had been open to everyone. Helga and Miles showed up, of course, and the weekend belonged to them. I was handling it pretty well, I thought. Until the afternoon.

Miles appeared with a grin as radiant as the summer sunrise. Everyone gasped upon seeing him. He had shaved his beard off and cut his hair short, so that his golden curls danced atop his head. No one had ever seen his face, and it was indeed the Paul Newman I had known and loved. My heavy heart sank deeper inside my chest.

Robert arrived by dinner time. Even Robert was surprised to see the clean-faced Miles. Robert rarely spent time with him, and he gave him much of his energy that night. I watched from the corner of the Lodge living room. I decided to cut my dining short, to help with dinner plates. Of course, that was not the reason. I could not articulate it. I was a walking camera by now. A bi-pod, with my two legs supporting a head with a lens.

The morning of Saturday, June 3 had come, and I arose early as usual to prepare the large coffee urn for breakfast. I went to the laundry room and looked in the bin, but there were no more clothes to wash. I had done the loads the day before. The wedding was around noon, and then we would have a celebratory lunch. That was what I was told. Many of the foods were prepared the night before. Helga had not been seen. She was preparing, I guess, with a few close friends as her assistants.

At 11:30, students left for the meadow. I hid in the cooler. But not for long. Rosemary found me.

"Let's go," she commanded.

I walked up the hill with her and Anna, who wore sturdy leather beige shoes and was remarkably agile. Standing near the back of the crowd, in the vastness of this meadow surrounded by trees, we remained there, waiting for the ceremony to begin. Signals were given, and we saw Miles emerge from one side of the wooded area wearing beige pants and a casual open shirt that exposed his chest, and Helga from the other, adorned with a wreath of delicate flowers. They walked toward each other, like their paths were destined to meet. And they were.

The ceremony was short. And then they kissed. I had never seen them kiss like this before. Everyone burst into applause. Those gathered made a natural path for them as they joyously scampered down the hill. I looked down as they passed, keeping that smiling mask on. Others followed them, but I could not move. My legs had locked.

"Come on," said Rose firmly yet kindly.

I tried to follow her, but my Tin-Man legs faltered, and I collapsed on my knees. THAT WAS SUPPOSED TO BE ME! screamed a voice inside. With that, my heart ruptured. Gasps of pain that had been stored up for a year triggered a flood of violent tears.

"STAND UP!!" ordered Anna, reaching down to grab my arm that was used to steady my body on the ground.

"Leave her alone," repeated Rose twice, taking hold of Anna's arm in turn and leading her away from me.

People passed me. Some looked, some didn't. Amidst the anguish, the smallest part of me sat still, unperturbed inside, watching…watching… watching.

> *Study the devotion of the bride. With what a vigilant eye she watches for the Bridegroom's coming. Happy for her that the Lord finds her watching.*
>
> Bernard of Clairvaux

CHAPTER 147

I was broken. I felt small and insignificant, like a second thought that is easily dismissed. The joyous celebration still resonated in the days that followed, and its echo diminished me further. What to do? Where to go? Why am I not worthy to be loved? These questions entered my bloodstream, circulating, searching for answers deep inside. They had become the rhythm of my daily heartbeat.

It was also humiliating to know that others saw my breakdown and subsequent reactions. It appeared as a queen-of-hearts attack, which is the greatest example of loss of control and sleep in the Work. I had been branded once again. To be this emotionally exposed in public showed others how weak was my will and low my level of being.

At one point of glumness, a sweet Lunar-Venusian approached me in the kitchen. Her boyfriend was a Martial type, and they had been speaking of going to Lake Tahoe with other students to visit friends who were interested in joining the school. They had a truck, and were looking for a car.

"We were thinking of going tomorrow," he asked, "and wondered if you would like to come with us?"

"It would be good for you," she added, "to see Tahoe in the spring. It will cheer you up."

I told them I had no money.

"We'll chip in for the gas," he said, as she nodded in agreement.

The plan was to leave in the morning after breakfast. I agreed, since they seemed to be interested in my welfare, and they said I wouldn't have to drive. We could return the same day, since Tahoe was only three hours away, like going to San Francisco.

It was now Thursday, June 8. Before leaving for Tahoe, we gathered in the kitchen after an early breakfast to prepare snacks of sandwiches and cut vegetables and fruit. There were eight of us. Three in the truck and five in my car. I had never been to Tahoe before, and was excited finally to see it.

Unlike the trip to Truckee, when we went through Grass Valley from Highway 20, this time we took the backroads from Dobbins to Highway 49 through Camptonville and Downieville. It was beautiful and more isolated, with towering pine trees closely bundled together lining the two-lane stretch of road. The forest was dense.

At one point, we passed the most pristine meadow. It had a single homestead nestled against the forest with the vast expanse of green pasture in front of it. What a view this family must have each day, I thought. It was idyllic. I had only seen paintings of such retreats, and had never considered these paintings to be taken from real-life. I had always considered them fantasies. This place had special energy.

"We're stopping here." The guy driving my car had apparently coordinated this with the Martial student in the truck.

We pulled to the side of the road that faced the meadow. Some of us had a snack, while others just walked around, stretching their legs, and picking some white, pink, purple and yellow wildflowers that colorfully speckled the spring-green pasture.

After twenty minutes or so, we continued toward Truckee and beyond.

Heading along the highway, Lake Tahoe finally came into view. It was beautiful and serene, with the sun's rays dancing upon it. It was much larger than I imagined. We were now in Nevada and drove along the shoreline for a considerable distance to the south. I was told we would stop at the Sahara Tahoe, where Harold was working in the lobby, drawing his caricatures of tourists.

When we arrived, I was surprised that the carload of friends dispersed to a café nearby where the prospective student meeting would be held. I was not invited to attend. It was okay.

When I entered the main lobby of the Sahara Tahoe, Harold was sitting against a wall near the front entrance, facing his easel that held a large drawing pad. He was rapidly sketching a lady sitting on the stool near him. Her companion was delighted at how quickly and accurately he was able to depict both her outward and inward characteristics. He was done in a few minutes. They paid him and gave him a generous tip to boot.

I stood there while he was working, and he knew I was there, yet he focused on the job at hand. He closed his big drawing pad, folded his two stools and easel, and put them in a hidden closet nearby.

"Let's go to the coffee shop," he said.

He treated me to a cup of coffee and a piece of cake. I told him how wonderful it was to see him work. He stuffed his pipe instead of replying.

"Where is Meg living now?" I asked because I heard while in Carmel that she was no longer staying at the inn.

"She found a place in Seaside."

The waitress came by to refill my cup and I focused on the cake.

"Bonita is here," he suddenly said.

This stunned me. I then realized I hadn't seen her at the farm for a while. Apparently, she had moved to Tahoe and was working in this casino as a masseuse. He gave me the floor number and said I could visit her if I liked. After his break, he returned to his business, while I took the elevator up to the place where she worked.

A receptionist greeted me, and I explained I was a friend of Bonita.

"Yes, Bonita is here in a room working."

I misunderstood the receptionist, thinking she was simply confirming she worked here, so I insisted I wanted to see her. She misunderstood me, thinking it must be life or death. I walked into this small room, and there was Bonita massaging a naked man. Oops.

She ushered me out, but gently, telling me it was inappropriate. I apologized. We embraced as friends.

When I returned downstairs, I saw another student talking to Harold, who was waiting for his next customer. It had been an hour since we arrived, and the rest of the students soon showed up in the main lobby to greet Harold. It was time to go. We went to the parking lot and entered the vehicles that brought us to Tahoe.

It was now approaching two in the afternoon. We would arrive back in time for dinner, I thought. As we drove up the shoreline toward home, we shared the events of our day's adventure. I did not mention the naked man.

The big meadow made its appearance around the bend when it happened. A loud noise suddenly came from the engine.

THE DIVINE BEGINNING

"Pull over!" said one fellow in the back, but the driver had already done this. The truck was following behind and stopped as well. The Martial and the driver of my car looked under the hood, consulting each other. My throat was burning up in fear. I can't afford this.

"I can haul the car in. I know a garage nearby," said the Martial.

I sat on a log, staring at the ground, with my head in my hands. Tears flowed and darkness was overtaking me. I felt I had truly hit rock bottom. How did that feel? The past was dead and the future was non-existent and the present was dire.

"Don't worry," said the sweet Lunar, as she hugged me, "it will get fixed."

"But I have no money to pay for it," I replied with tears streaming.

She said nothing.

After an hour had passed, we were surprised to see them return with the car.

"It was a fan belt that almost busted. It's minor. Only cost six dollars. It's fixed now."

"I can't afford to repay you six dollars!" I said, in an emotional meltdown.

"Don't worry about it," he said, "it'll work out."

How could it? I had no job. No money. No hope. I was vanquished.

* * * *

"You have a message," said a student, handing me a piece of paper as I entered the Lodge.

It was from a middle-eastern lady at a small sandwich shop on Dolores Street in Carmel, where I had filled out an application months ago. She was looking to hire me as a cook. Was I available?

My life was about to change.

When you are down to nothing, God is up to something.
Benjamin Franklin

PART V
The End

CHAPTER 148

THE WOMAN'S NAME was Latifa and she spoke quickly, with an accent. She wanted me to come in on Monday, June 12 at 7:30 a.m. to work with her current full-time cook, who would be leaving in two weeks and would train me. Was this fine with me? Of course it was fine with me. The hourly wage she offered was $1.60. That meant I could make around $60 a week.

I left Sunday to go to the Whitman house, and when I arrived, I was surprised to learn from Nadia that Robert said I could stay there for $20 a month. How did he learn about my new job? I thought the information remained at the farm. I didn't talk to many students. Or, maybe I did.

I had borrowed an alarm clock from Marie because I would need to leave early to be on time for work. When the hour came on Monday morning to arise, I needed no clock. The energy in my machine was high-pitched. It was the sound of a new octave, a new *do* and the vibration was electric.

When I arrived at the little café, the door was locked. It was a tiny place sandwiched between two larger shops. That thought made me chuckle. Of course, it is. It's a sandwich shop.

I peered inside and saw it had six tables, three on either side of the room. The room itself was quite dark with no natural light other than the glass-paned entry door. I stood waiting outside, doing a little dance with my arms wrapped around my body to protect me from the chill of the morning fog. After about fifteen minutes, a dark-haired, black-eyed petite woman appeared with keys rattling.

"I'm sorry I'm late," she said, hurriedly fumbling with the keys, until she found the one that opened the door. "You must be Linda."

"Yes," I said to her back, as she swung the door open and entered.

We went directly to the kitchen area in the rear of the café. She showed me where to put my purse. It was a hook in a deep closet that served as a large pantry.

"Jennie is coming at eight to prep."

I assumed this was the head cook I was replacing.

"We have some forms to fill out first."

I sat down at one of the tables to complete the necessary legal documents for employment. I was glad I had the information about the Whitman House address and phone number. I never had a job like this before, so this form was a new experience. I did not want her to know this, so I pretended I understood what I was doing.

She showed me the menu and described each item that I would be preparing. They were all open-faced sandwiches with exotic names and ingredients. It would be my job to memorize them all and learn from Jennie how to make them. That shouldn't be too difficult, I thought.

Jennie did come at eight. She was a soft Saturn-Mars type, tall with long blond wavy hair. She wore a bright smile with no makeup and bell-bottom jeans and a loose cotton blouse. She had a kerchief to pull back her hair. I didn't have one so she handed me a hairnet that the owner had originally given to her. She also handed me a white apron.

Guiding me to the pantry, she and I brought out the necessary ingredients that were the basis for most of the sandwiches. She showed me how to slice the meats and cheeses thin, using different settings on the large metal food slicer, making sure to clean the blades between cheese and meat. We put the foods — like mushrooms, chopped onion, sliced green peppers, olives — into metal bins that could easily be lifted up from the prep table to replenish them.

The kitchen space could barely handle the two of us. The food bins and small counter where we would assemble the sandwiches faced the dining room and behind us was a stove and refrigerator. It could not have been more than three feet of space in which to work. There was the noise of a fan over the stove but not much air. It was claustrophobic.

The doors opened at 11:30 and by noon, the place was full. Jennie did all the work, while I watched. I tried to keep up. She had so much fluid motion. All I could do was observe and hand her items. It was more a cerebral experience for me than a hands-on training for my moving center.

I took my break at two. I had eaten my sandwich in the back (I was not to eat at the tables) and then took a stroll outside to smoke a cigarette or two. When I returned, there was a big kettle of boiled eggs with a note from Jennie that I was to peel them to prepare them for the next day. Sounded simple enough.

I took the first one and cracked it. The shell stubbornly clung to the egg membrane. I tried to peel off the jagged bits of shell but clumps of white came off with them. When all the shell was finally removed, I looked at the little egg that was left. It was disfigured. So I ate it.

The same happened with the next two. I tried to run it under hot water. At that point, Jennie showed up and she saw my dilemma. She kindly said, "This happens. Don't worry. I'll take care of it."

We spent the end of our day cleaning the kitchen. She showed me how to use a square brick made of steel wool material to scrape the grill surface after all the bacon we fried. It was quite a revelation. The sweeping and washing of the floor, the cleaning of bins and replenishing for the next day were the final acts before we untied our aprons.

As I drove back to the house, the fact I couldn't even peel an egg left me quite concerned about this job. Perhaps it's beyond my level of being. I feel like a failure. Learning to do simple things is not so simple, at least not for me. Tomorrow would be another day. I prayed that magically all the instruction would penetrate my brain overnight and that tomorrow would go smoother.

* * * *

The next day I made my first sandwich, following Jennie's instruction. We also discussed how to peel an egg, although it was not expressed this way. I watched her take a hardboiled egg from the refrigerator and gently crack it all over before peeling. I tried it, and it seemed to work better. We had a manual slicer that I remembered from childhood, so I already knew how to use it.

The owner arrived at noon and grabbed a number of menus. She greeted the diners who entered, some of whom were her friends. She gave them warm hugs. Jennie saw me looking and smiled.

"Latifa's divorced. She decided to open the café because her friends loved the sandwiches she made in her home. This is her first restaurant experience," she explained.

I smiled and nodded, as if I, too, were as experienced as Jennie, when in fact I had more in common with Latifa.

Latifa would deliver the plates, and it was sweet of Jennie to mention I had made the one she took to her lady friend. Latifa smiled and said, looking at it, "Very nice." Each day that week became better, as I learned another sandwich and then another. I was in a comfort zone, and it felt good.

I also watched Jennie give the list of supplies to order to Latifa for her approval. Would this be part of my responsibility? How would I know the amounts to order? I wasn't sure I was equipped to manage the kitchen like this.

When I arrived back home that day, the ladies asked me how the job was going, and I told them it was going well. I almost hated to tell them about my insecurities.

I was scared almost every day that I worked, wondering if Latifa would find out I was a fraud with no real experience in a commercial kitchen.

The head of cabbage appeared one night in my dreams, laughing at the thought that I could run a kitchen. I prayed to the gods that I would be able to keep this job and succeed, yet the time of Jennie's departure was rapidly approaching and my anxiety level was ever-increasing. I just needed to take it a day at a time, I told myself, and try to learn quickly how to do this job while Jennie was still around. That was my new aim.

If you pursue worldly deeds your body, speech and mind will run wild in worldly experience.
Padmasambhava

CHAPTER 149

What shocked me the most about my life here in Carmel was the absence of the teacher. Where was Robert? We had a Thursday meeting at the Whitman House, but he didn't show. With the plane and Jim as the pilot, Robert would magically appear, I guess, at any of several "centers" (as we began to call them now, instead of groups) — from Lake Tahoe, which was beginning to form, to Berkeley, Vacaville and, of course, Carmel. That's what I imagined, anyway. Although the question was in my head each day, no one spoke of it.

Despite the difficulties, it had been a good week for me. I finally had a real job where money came each Friday in a paycheck. I had a beautiful place to live and the impressions were civilized. When Saturday came, I was expecting a small turnout at the Whitman House, like Thursday, but students kept arriving. I found out Robert was coming, even though it was considered an optional meeting, and we had some new students attending as well. I was elated.

It was good to see Anna, who brought new students from the Bay Area with her. Richard was there, and a guy named James, who was married (I think) to Millicent. It was not easy to know who was married and who was not. People often hung out with each other and were considered simply a couple.

Millicent was a Mercury type, with curly black hair and a childlike face. What made her so interesting was what she brought to show Robert. I sat with her before the meeting, and she showed me three photos of James. The first was the regular full-face portrait. The other two looked distorted.

"It shows James' face as essence — the left side — and as personality — the right side."

"Cool," I said, as others gathered around.

She explained how she did it. She took the regular portrait and cut it lengthwise, down the nose, so there was a right side and a left side. Then she flipped the negative so that the right side could also be the left side. Then she put the two right sides together to form another face.

It was a clever experiment. She said she was doing this for students in the Bay Area for $10. My curiosity had the best of me in the moment, so I asked if she could do this for me, too. Sure, was her reply. She had brought her camera, and we could do it now. Others were interested, so we went to the deck off of my bedroom, where the light was natural, and she took care of it quickly. She said that it may take a few weeks to put it together. I asked if I could pay her then, and she hesitated. We agreed on a five-dollar deposit, which I could handle.

The energy in the room was high, and made higher when Robert and Jim entered with Sheila and Rosemary. I saw Anna approach them to introduce Millicent, who showed Robert the photographs. I tried to listen in on the conversation, but the noise in the room prevented me from hearing it. He smiled at Millicent and gave her a hug, so it seemed to go well.

The chairs were arranged already around the perimeter of the room. We found our places, since the meeting was about to begin.

After good householder, new students were introduced. One new student from Carmel was named Susan, who was the sister of another student who had joined here recently. Like her sister, Susan was quiet and sat there observing. It made me smile to see that.

Robert began the meeting by asking if there were any questions.

One of the new students from the Bay Area raised his hand. "What are the exercises we need to follow? Is there a list?"

Robert turned to Meg, who gave the first angle of thought.

"We try not to express negative emotions."

Jim read from Robert's notes, since the teacher had continued his silence.

"We do not keep lists, as this would make us too institutionalized. One can observe that the 'I's that are negative can fizzle in five minutes if we don't give them attention. The main reason they fizzle is that there are so many other 'I's that wish to replace them and take control."

He paused for a moment to allow this angle to penetrate. Then he added, "Allow for defeats. They are a part of all struggles. And remember, C Influence sets up failures for friction."

I smiled, as the cabbage and boiled egg appeared in my head, taunting me. Mac offered an angle.

"The ability to follow rules is part of all esoteric teachings and requires self-remembering."

We spoke about formatory mind, unnecessary talk, the word exercises, and being on time. It was nice to see what we now call "older students" give angles. I even offered one about not putting your hands on your hips, and other postures that make the body appear larger. Robert had mentioned that whoever is speaking, offering angles, is the teacher. He had told us that he wanted others to begin to take on this level of responsibility, because it would enable their being to grow faster. This reminded me of Rodney Collin's comment that we have to teach to learn. These 'I's were circulating in my head when Robert gave this thought.

"We subordinate our will to C Influence here, often through the teacher, who is the vehicle for C Influence. In a group of two or three students, maybe all are not self-remembering. Sometimes a person has to take a stand and self-remember. C Influence provides situations for students to make being. One of the reasons it is difficult to self-remember among certain people is that some want to be liked. People have 'I's that would rather be liked than BE."

With that, Robert signaled the end of the meeting. I was shocked it was over. I looked at my watch, and forty-five minutes had passed since it began. It went quickly.

A lot of energy was generated from the meeting. I found myself talking to several students about Robert's comment regarding failure and confessed to them my issues with the egg. We laughed and one of them reminded me of the cabbage. It was pretty hysterical that they remembered this. I was feeling wonderful, being able to relax among friends like this, sharing my funny plays with them.

I stepped out on the balcony off the dining room to smoke a cigarette. Several other students joined me, and we caught up on the news about the people at the farm, Vacaville, and Berkeley. There's another wedding scheduled with two students from Vacaville. For some reason, I was good with this, accepting that my life was now on a solo path, and with money in my pocket, a new-found freedom emboldened me.

When we entered the living room, the classical music that was playing during refreshments had changed. Someone had put on rock music, and there was laughter that released tension in the room. Students began to dance. Robert had left before refreshments and was not around for this. It reminded me of the time at the farm when a festivity descended into unbridled behavior. It shocked me that this was happening again. But the greater shock was to witness how I joined in on the revelry, finding it fun and lighthearted.

It was later that night, while I lay in bed reviewing the events of my day, that I could see the missed opportunity. What seemed so joyful and fun in the moment left a bitter aftertaste. Something was off. That's the best way to describe it. Was I feeling guilty? I don't know exactly. I do know that something deep inside recorded the fact that the sweet state I had experienced in Robert's presence had been gobbled up by something lower. That higher state was so hard to hold and so easy to drop.

Wait a minute. Didn't Robert end the meeting talking about this? He spoke about taking a stand for self-remembering in the midst of a crowd and attaching your will to the gods. I could do neither in that moment. What would it have looked like if I had stood up and, like Miles did in Truckee, removed the needle from the record? I didn't have the courage. I would be branded as a killjoy. I couldn't bear that. I had few friends as it was.

The teacher's angle was prophetic, as if he knew what would occur when he left the house. How Robert could hold his work in the midst of other's opinions of him astounded me. Could I ever be that strong? He was not imprisoned by the hell of inner considering. Wherever he resided — his inner location — was where I wanted to be within myself.

Forget the cook's routines. That state of freedom is the only aim that mattered to me now.

❖

> *I do not worry how others see me, rather how I appear to myself. In all antiquity, it is hard to pick out a dozen men who set their lives to one certain and constant course, which is the principal goal of wisdom. One must be allowed by the Gods to formulate the right aim.*
>
> Michel de Montaigne

CHAPTER 150

Sunday morning was a day off from work so I slept in late. I came into the kitchen around noon to find Marie and Rosemary drinking coffee at the small kitchen table. As soon as they greeted me, Rose stood up, saying she needed to meet Robert at Sheila's.

"Take my seat," she said, as I poured a cup of coffee.

Marie was smoking a cigarette and offered me one, which I declined. I could afford to have my own pack and preferences now. A cup of coffee and a cigarette had become my normal breakfast.

We sat for a while in silence. It made me uncomfortable, so I told her the story of the egg. She didn't laugh. Then I mentioned the next wedding at the farm. I had no idea whether or not she had heard about this, or even cared, but believed this may trigger her to open up and share. Instead, she offered this.

"I remember you quieter when we first met."

It was as if she ripped off my garments, exposing my weaknesses.

"When we met, my vanity manifested inwardly," I replied softly.

"Perhaps," she said, snuffing out her cigarette, and saying she had work to do.

I was left alone at the table. I knew she was referring to how loud I was after the meeting last night. The secretive 'I's that felt better than others had found room to demonstrate their superiority. It's like having a big pimple on your nose. You know people are not looking at your eyes when they talk to you. You know it's there because you can feel it, even though you cannot exactly see it without a mirror. It's ugly and is not you, but try to convince others of this.

Thoughts about chief feature began to circulate inside, so I went to my room to retrieve my journal to jot those thoughts down. Chief feature is well hidden until self-remembering begins to stir the pot, as it were. One's chief weakness begins to fester under circumstances arranged by C Influence. It comes to the surface for all to see. At a certain point, it ruptures and one is free for a moment from the poisons it carries, as it is wiped clean.

Something like that.

I could not exactly express it with satisfaction. Understanding is such a strange experience. It is a wordless circulation of newborn emotion that rushes through the intellectual center's narrow pipeline, looking for the right words to clothe it. Most of us must be content with a wardrobe of fancy phrasings and worn-out clichés. Rarely do we find something that truly fits the understanding we paid dearly for with our tears.

* * * *

The afternoon was free and the house was empty. I had a member directory so decided to call around to see if anyone was available. To my surprise Meg answered and said she was going to a place named the Chopstix restaurant with Alden. I could join them if I liked.

This was the first time I visited Seaside, where Meg and her daughter, and Harold, and Alden all lived. The restaurant was on Fremont Street, a main thoroughfare, so it was easy to find. When I entered, Meg and Alden were there with another student that I saw Saturday night, but had yet to meet. He was a bit muscular and tall, with a black mustache and black straight short hair. The leather jacket told me he was a biker, and there was, indeed, one parked outside the restaurant. I assumed it was his. Also at the table was Trisha. I hadn't seen her for some time. She was sitting so close to the guy that it looked like she was snuggling. I learned that she and her daughter had moved down here as well. I guessed she and her husband had separated.

The waitress approached, and I learned she was also the owner. Her name was Ling. She was a diminutive gray-haired Asian in her early fifties. That would be my guess.

"Here menu," she said, thrusting it into my hand. "You like tea?"

I said yes, and ordered the cashew chicken. It came with white rice.

Taking a sip of tea, Alden casually said, "Robert's been here."

"REALLY?" I replied, and the hands of everyone at the table flew up to photograph my using that word.

"Yes, he came last week with Jim," said Meg. "I told Jim about the place and I guess Robert decided to tag along." We all chuckled.

Alden then added, "Yeah, Ling handed Robert his plate and said, 'For Robot.'"

We all laughed.

"Did Robert laugh?" I asked Alden.

"Not exactly. He smiled and pointed upward."

Ling came back quickly with her daughter, each carrying several plates. The others at the table had ordered before me. Everyone grabbed a dish and used the big spoons provided to shovel food onto their plates. No one offered me food, so I just waited for my order to arrive.

The new guy, who was known as JT, was demonstrating how to use chopsticks. I had never mastered this so followed his example. He let me taste his food, which he said was Kung Pao chicken.

Just as the first piece landed on my tongue, he said, "I hope you like spicy."

"It's good," I replied with a mouthful. About two seconds later, the heat pierced my taste buds and my eyes started to water. He burst out laughing. Meg's stomach shook a bit in quiet amusement. She seemed to enjoy his sense of humor. She then took a cigarette, lit it, inhaled and blew out a puff, and then positioned it in her portable ash tray that was a signature item of hers. She took a few bites, then a few puffs.

By the time my plate came, they had finished dining, leaving half of their food untouched.

Approaching Meg, Ling said, "You have call."

JT, Judith and I had to vacate the booth to let her out. When she returned, we let her back in.

The call was from her daughter, who said she couldn't come. She signaled to Ling for takeout containers. While the rest of the meal was bundled up, I was still trying to place food in my mouth with the chopsticks. It wasn't going well.

"Just use the fork. It'll go faster," Alden suggested.

"Let her learn," insisted JT. "She needs to learn."

Meg found it amusing, but said nothing.

It was clear others were ready to leave, so I asked for a takeout container too.

The bill came, and it was nice mine was separate since I arrived late. It took about fifteen minutes for everyone to figure out what they owed. By the time we left the restaurant it was almost four. The bike was indeed JT's and Trisha mounted it behind him. They had come together.

I arrived at the house to finish the rest of my meal. Sitting at the kitchen table, I pulled out a fresh pack of wooden chopsticks that came with the takeout, and began to practice feeding myself with two thin rods. I had to concentrate on each movement, positioning my fingers correctly, keeping one stick straight and immovable, while the other moved up and down to secure the size perfectly with the right pressure. My focus had to be pure and undistracted. If I thought of the food in my mouth before it was inserted, the morsel would land instead on the plate.

This effort continued for thirty minutes until, finally, a solitary grain of rice remained. As I stared at it, poised to pick it up, suddenly I froze. It stared back at me. A higher state was emerging within me, without reason or cause, and the grain of rice had a message for it. Waiting for words to manifest, none came. Instead, an 'I' inside shouted, "Don't be ridiculous!" With that, I quickly inserted the rice into my mouth. The state withdrew, leaving me with an empty plate that needed washing.

That night I thought about the single grain. How strange that it held my attention like that. And then I remembered something from my past.

In my second year at UCLA, during the English History final exam that would represent 100% of my grade, I saw through the required action of test-taking. It was a beautiful day, full of sunlight and warmth, a day to be outside instead of locked indoors focusing on an empty pamphlet that would contain my responses to questions.

The professor stood in front of the assembly and announced, "Open your books." That was the signal to begin the exam. The sound of turned pages rippled throughout the hall. Rather than follow that command, however, a voice inside stated, You don't have to take the test, just enjoy this moment.

The moment suddenly had become the most important thing to me. I followed this instruction. The Now was replaced by another Now and another. I stared at the clock, watching patiently for the longer hand to click into place signaling the end of a minute.

With fifteen minutes left in the two-hour session, I stood up and handed an empty blue book to my professor. He was in shock and wanted to help me, but I dismissed him by saying, "No thank you."

As I walked out of the large classroom, I looked at those people, without judgment, scribbling and simply doing what they were told to do.

Heading toward the bus stop, I passed many students rushing to their classes. I looked at them but they did not look at me. I saw they did not know my state, which moved invisibly among them. They were asleep, kept cozy and warm by their imaginary importances.

The trees along the pathway, however, called out to me. They were bursting with life, swaying freely in the gentle, warm breeze. They were more alive than the students who were oblivious to them. From this higher state, the trees and I acknowledged each other.

When I made it home after the exam, a panic seized me. How would I describe my actions to my parents? I could not tell them of my higher state. To say nothing was wrong would be incomprehensible to them. I failed the test. It was the panic — not the state — that caused me to shake. My sister labeled it a nervous breakdown, and they agreed. I agreed too, and kept the real experience of piercing a new level of existence a secret.

The tiny grain of rice knew me also, like the trees. We met in that place of reality. Without sanctifying these simple moments, the part that screams how ridiculous such thinking is, will always be ready to dispose of the truth.

❖

> In one small particle of time, little as it is,
> heaven can be won and lost.
> Anonymous English Monk

CHAPTER 151

The week at work was stable for the first few days. Jennie was talked into staying through Friday, which began a long weekend, culminating in July 4th on Tuesday. A flock of tourists was expected in Carmel, and Latifa wanted to take advantage of this.

Jennie told me a new girl was starting on Wednesday, and Latifa wanted Jennie, not me, to train her. I said nothing, as I stood there a bit surprised. Surprised at what? That Latifa did not feel comfortable with me doing the training. Of course, I knew I wasn't capable of it, but what surprised me was that she knew it, too. I guess my inexperience was that obvious to everyone.

When the new girl arrived Wednesday morning, she was nice but did not seem like a short-order cook. Her name was Nancy. She was short in stature with a thickset body. This would indicate, according to the system, that she is instinctively centered. Jennie was lean, which is a sign of a moving type. I was a fleshy, emotional type. It would be an interesting day, I thought, for observation.

It was obvious that Nancy felt comfortable in the small space of the kitchen. With the three of us maneuvering, it seemed I had boarded a crowded bus for eight hours. She took quickly to Jennie's instructions, and whipped out the sandwiches. I was shocked how well she did. She did not seem that intelligent. Her language was rough at times. At the end of that first day, she said she had no problem preparing the supply order list, too, which was crucial for Latifa. I could see the relief on the owner's face. I began to fade in the background.

At the end of Friday's shift, we had a little cake brought in to celebrate Jennie's departure. I still felt out of place and just sat and listened, with my smile on my face. I tried my best not to let the fear rise up to my heart. The thought of working with Nancy, who had clearly been anointed the new team leader, was difficult to accept.

THE DIVINE BEGINNING

Saturday, Nancy and I arrived at 8 a.m. to do the prep. Whenever she entered the pantry, she had a mouthful of something. I said nothing, even though it irritated me. It wasn't until the end of the day that I realized it reminded me of myself in the cooler at the farm. It had never occurred to me that my snacking was actually depleting the food supply and costing the Fellowship money. What a clever position Nancy occupied. She was playing both Kerrie, who ordered the supplies, and Linda, who ate the supplies. I could not complain to Latifa, however, since I was not prepared to replace Nancy.

We worked on Sunday as well, hoping to entice the crowds with our posted menu. It seemed to work. Four of the six tables were occupied in a steady flow, although there was no line of customers outside the front door waiting to enter. I was able to keep pace with Nancy as we alternated fulfilling the orders that we received from Latifa, who was the only waitress and was naturally quick on her feet.

Monday and Tuesday, which was July 4th, were equally busy, but by Wednesday the 5th, the tourist crowd almost vanished. It was surprising how slow it had become. We did not attract repeat customers. At least, I didn't recognize the same people returning.

After work on Wednesday, I drove to Carmel beach to be alone before returning to an empty house. The ladies had gone to the farm, I presumed. There must be some kind of celebration at the farm with Robert to honor our arrival a year ago. I had no way to confirm this. It didn't matter anyway, I thought. I was stuck in Carmel working in a dark, cramped kitchen.

The Thursday meeting in Carmel had been cancelled. It was a strange time, working as a short-order cook a year after graduating UCLA. My state took a dip that whole week. I needed help, but students weren't around. Were the gods still helping me? I did not know. I had lost the sense of their presence.

* * * *

Friday morning, I arrived at work to discover Nancy had called in sick. It would be me and Latifa managing the day's orders, and the first time just the two of us would be working together.

I started by doing the prep and filling the containers. I discovered that we were short of some items, and worse, that the avocados were too soft to use. This was a big problem. Some of the most popular sandwiches had sliced avocados on top. I went to the front to mention this to Latifa. She went through the pantry and saw the influx of customers early in the week had depleted the supply. We didn't have enough food to last until Monday, when the next supply order would be made. Nancy apparently had screwed up the order on July 3, misjudging the amount of food we would need for the week. We were left with half a dozen old avocados.

"What do I do with the avocados?" I asked her.

"Use what you can."

"Can I eliminate it?"

"No. It's part of the sandwich."

"Okay."

That would be my instruction. That would not be my experience. Once an avocado goes bad inside, you cannot cut away the bad stuff and expect the slice to be presentable.

At noon, a woman entered the café, much to Latifa's delight. She was an old friend, and I watched as Latifa sat with her for a while. This old friend was the only customer, so it was like watching Latifa entertain at home.

They began to talk about the décor. Her friend seemed to like it, but to me, the café's décor was noticeably odd. A part of the left wall jutted out and was designed to look like the side of a cottage, with two windows that were mirrored and a shingled roof on top that slanted at an angle over one of the tables. Above this roof was a painted skyline. The intent, I guess, was to make you feel like you were dining on a rooftop, enjoying the open air. This was far from the truth. You were actually locked in a closet of powerful kitchen smells. The whole café was inside out. I felt like Alice through the looking glass.

Latifa called me over to meet her friend. After the cordial greeting, Latifa handed me the order, which was one of the house specialties. It included avocado.

I started to assemble the sandwich. I cut open the avocado and it was brown-black inside. I tossed it. The next one, too, was unusable. And the next. I tried to cut around it, but it was not possible to find something that did not have discoloration. I did my best piecing together chunks of green with gray edges.

While I was finishing the sandwich, two other customers entered for lunch. They were also her friends. The sandwich was ready and, noticing Latifa was busy with them, I decided to help by taking the plate to her old friend.

Latifa was smiling, and in a good mood. She went to her old friend to find out how she enjoyed the sandwich. The lady pointed out the inedible avocado that lie on top of the layers of meat, cheeses, and tomatoes like a dirty green blanket.

"Linda!"

I immediately came.

"What happened here?! This is unacceptable."

Confused for a moment, I looked at her and uttered a defensive comment: "I did what you told me to do."

It slipped out of my mouth. I failed to see the customer sitting there. She took me by the elbow into the pantry, and closed the door before beginning a tirade of angry corrections. It was quite a blast of negativity, and I could feel it penetrate my chest.

She left me there. Returning to the kitchen, I watched my hands mechanically put together the other two sandwiches. There were no thoughts circulating in me. I was in a state of shock.

When the sandwiches were done, I hit the little bell to indicate it was ready for pickup. I looked up and watched her old friend give her a quick hug before exiting, mentioning she should not be bothered by this. It was kind of her to try to neutralize Latifa's reaction.

It was tense between us for the rest of the day. I cleaned up and finished the shift. I could only hope that Nancy would show up tomorrow.

* * * *

Nancy did not show up on Saturday, but did on Sunday. She had a bad cough, but worked through the day. She needed the money as much as I did.

"I have a young daughter and mother to take care of," she explained, adding that her no-good boyfriend had left her without support. She hadn't finished high school, and had worked these types of jobs for quite a while to survive.

Sunday was a good day financially for Latifa. She sat down with Nancy to work out the supply list, which would be ordered on Monday. I could see she was able to work with Nancy, so I studied their interaction. Nancy was able to provide the comfort Latifa needed. She had worked in various places and not only knew how to cook and prepare the supply list, but more importantly, how to be trusted by the owner. She stood her ground with Latifa and was not intimidated by her. I, on the other hand, was too unsure of myself. Latifa scared me.

Monday at 3 p.m. the food supplies arrived, and Nancy and I were able to clean out the pantry and restock while Latifa went to the bank.

"How do you handle Latifa?" I asked Nancy.

"Oh, she's just scared and panics. I've seen it before. The business is slow and she panics. The business is booming, and she panics. I ignore it."

It was surprisingly perceptive. My first thought that Nancy wasn't intelligent made me see I was using an academic yardstick. This girl had street smarts, which I sorely lacked. It gave her a freedom I longed for. I misjudged her.

Before the day ended, Latifa asked to speak with me.

"I'm going to have to cut your hours. I cannot afford to have two full-time cooks. Take tomorrow off and start again on Wednesday. You can take the morning shifts."

The morning shift was prep work, which was the hardest part physically. Assembling was easier. But my stomach sank. I felt rich with this full-time steady job, and now everything is uncertain again. More concerning, however, was the fact she didn't trust me. I lost to Nancy, said an 'I' inside my head, the rough, uncouth girl without the college education. So much for a higher degree. Street smarts were worth far more, and I was impoverished. Watching others succeed so easily in simple tasks baffled me.

Why is doing so difficult? Where are the gods when I need them?

The difficulties of all men are about external things,
their helplessness is externals. "What shall I do, how will it be,
how will it turn out, will this happen, will that?" All these
are the words of those who are turning themselves to things
which are not within the power of the will.

Epictetus

CHAPTER 152

When I arrived home from work on Monday, the ladies had returned. They each had tasks to accomplish in Berkeley and Vacaville. They were not at the farm, nor did they know where Robert was. They had not heard of any celebration. I thought of the students there and felt badly for them, imagining they must feel truly abandoned. Last year, Robert claimed we would be together forever. The first anniversary of the farm went unheralded. It was just another day at the farm, so to speak.

As dinnertime approached, I offered to make the salad. Rosemary made chicken, Klair roasted russet potatoes in the oven, and Nadia prepared a variety of vegetables. Marie set the table and arranged flowers in a lovely vase.

"How's the job going?" asked Rosemary as we sat down.

It was the last topic I wanted to discuss.

THE DIVINE BEGINNING

"I was cut in hours."

She made an obvious comment, that, strangely enough, I hadn't considered. "Well, you need to find another job."

Because of the struggle to find this one, I felt overwhelmed with the prospect of job hunting. It took me so long just to find this menial job. Where do I begin?

As if hearing my thought, Klair mentioned the latest *Pine Cone,* Carmel's newspaper, was in the hallway and it had a Help Wanted section.

"I'm not sure what you're looking for," added Marie, "but I think I saw a Help Wanted poster in the window of the bakery. The baker just died of a heart attack, and his wife now has to run it."

"I'm so sorry to hear this," I replied, recalling his bright face and soft demeanor. "He was such a lovely jovial man."

Rosemary responded in her direct Martial way. "You better go down in the morning and apply."

I nodded in agreement. The subject changed to household issues, to which I turned a deaf ear.

During the dishwashing, I felt a sudden exhaustion and started to cough. Klair looked at me.

"You didn't touch your food. Let me feel your forehead." She reached over. "You're burning up!"

She exited quickly and brought back a thermometer.

The ladies took over the dishwashing, as I was guided to a chair. After three minutes, Klair looked at the number. It was 105.

Rosemary took a look at it and couldn't believe the number. "You need to go to bed. NOW!"

"But I feel fine," I answered, "and want to finish the dishes."

Klair had a no-nonsense way of thinking. Her response was, "You're gonna fry your brain."

It was clear what my next action would be: go to bed.

* * * *

During the night, a chill spread throughout my body. My lungs had pressure like I experienced in childhood with asthma. It felt like an elephant had stepped on my chest, and breathing was like lifting the weight of its big foot to allow space enough for oxygen to flow. Each breath that normally would be a mechanical instinct required a conscious effort now. It only increased my exhaustion.

In the morning, I could not find enough energy to make it to the kitchen for coffee. Klair had given me the thermometer, and my temperature had dropped to 103. I simply lay there, unable to move.

Around noon, Klair opened the door.

"How are you doing?"

I told her my temperature and exhaustion level.

"Stay in bed. I'll bring you some food."

I told her I wanted toast and coffee, and within fifteen minutes she obliged.

But she did not stay with me. She had things to do that day and did not want to expose herself, apparently, which I could understand.

I lay in bed most of the afternoon. I managed to go to the toilet once by holding on to the furniture and leaning against the walls. When I opened the bathroom door to exit, Nadia was there.

"Here's a book you should read," she said, handing me a small paperback.

The title was *Dr. Ehret's Mucusless Diet*. I thanked her and hobbled back to bed.

In the evening, Klair asked if I wanted something to eat. I told her a salad. I had been reading Nadia's book, and it focused on eating raw vegetables to be healthy.

When Klair brought in the dish, she took my temperature.

"It's 101. You cannot go to work tomorrow. I'll call to let them know."

I hadn't planned on this.

* * * *

Through the night, the coughing increased in violence. After many long hours struggling to breathe, I finally drifted off to sleep.

Waking in the depth of darkness. With clarity and calmness, yet confused. Pitch black, except for a faint, red light far in the distance. Where is this? The red light begins to pulse. Pulsing. Pulsing. Pulsing. What is this? Pulsing. Pulsing. The faint sound of a siren can be heard. It grows louder.

A voice says, You must act NOW. And repeats, You must ACT NOW!

I bolted upright in bed.

KKKAAAACH...KKKAAACH...

My lungs convulsed in wet coughing. Repeatedly I expelled the contents into tissue for almost an hour, until the airways began to clear.

What just happened to me?

It was a vivid dream that I experienced fully awake. How could I be awake in the middle of sleep? How could the third state of consciousness exist within the first state of consciousness?

Still struggling to breathe, I replayed the dream over and over again to understand the strangeness of it all. This is the telling of my experience.

In the dream, I was a mere pinpoint in the midst of vast darkness. I was reduced to who I truly am, my conscious being: mild, whole, unharmed, and bodiless within my body. This is no metaphor. It was, and is, a simple reality. The pulsing red light and sound in the distance was from my body, which was signaling an emergency. What was the emergency? It had stopped breathing. It was about to die. Without an immediate conscious act, life would be over in my sleep.

That's what happened to me.

My God. How close is extinction. Merely a breath away.

> *This life has many dangers; it is more unstable than a bubble blown about by the wind. With breath coming and going, it is the greatest miracle that one ever awakens from sleep.*
>
> Gampopa

CHAPTER 153

I did not tell anyone about my dream. It was too fantastical. How can you possibly use words to describe a state to anyone? The experience was real for me. That was enough.

As the days passed, the exhaustion and coughing did not stop. Each time I tried to prepare to go outside the house, I found myself pulled back to bed. It was a helplessness, as if I wore invisible fetters that kept me in the place the gods dictated. This time it was not mental restraints that bound me. It had become physical.

How did I occupy my time? I read work books as well as journals again and again. I could feel the relentless pull of the practical part of my nature that daily harassed me for my laziness and lack of householder. It had a voice. It was parental in tone. It was best to ignore it.

There was another side to my nature now that I had come to know as a result of the dream, or, should I say, the reality within the dream. That side was a state, and that state was true identity. I tried to recapture it, and the best way was to remember it existed.

How could I reconnect myself to its qualities? It was small, sweet, silent and serene with a childlike joy of simply being where it was, even in the midst of darkness.

Then I recalled in one *Via Del Sol Journal* this angle from the teacher:

"I have entered silence again for an indefinite period. I seem to be happier in silence."

I could hear his voice when I read it, even though he was still in silence. I would lie in bed, trying to find that space of internal happiness, that space of silence. I had time to practice. I wasn't going anywhere or doing anything. It was a useful time to focus on consciousness and bear the difficult circumstances of my functions.

* * * *

Another week had passed, and another. It was now July 27. That morning, Dr. Mac stopped in to check on me (I'm sure Rosemary had told him to do so).

"You have viral pneumonia," he said, after listening to my chest and hearing about my symptoms.

"Why am I still so exhausted?"

"It comes with the territory," he said with a chuckle. "You need to rest as much as you can."

"But that's all I've been doing."

"Be patient. Otherwise, you'll have a relapse."

I took his advice for about four hours. I had been without income for almost the whole month. Worries about paying rent and making my teaching payment finally pushed me out of bed and to the telephone. I couldn't wait any longer. The cough had lessened considerably, but I tired easily. I would have to make a super effort, I thought, as I dialed the café's number. Latifa was not there, so I left a message with Nancy. She asked how I was and I lied. She called back within an hour to let me know I could report to work on Saturday, the 29th. I was so relieved to still have a job.

* * * *

Latifa met me as I arrived that morning. I learned that another person had just been hired as a full-time chef, but could not begin until August 15 because of a previous commitment.

"I can employ you until then," she said, "but I'm not sure yet if I will still need you."

"That's fine." I was in no position to negotiate.

I managed that Saturday to be on time and to make it to noon. I had just removed my apron when Nancy arrived to take over the afternoon shift. We greeted each other fondly.

"I have something to tell you," she said, "but it's a secret." She quickly peeked into the dining room to make sure Latifa was occupied with a customer. Escorting me into the pantry and closing the door, she opened up.

"I got another job and I'm quitting, but I haven't told Latifa yet. She's been working me like a dog. I was the only cook. I asked her for a raise and she flat out refused. She needs two people here."

"Maybe she would let me work full time?"

"Why would you want to do that?"

"I could use the money."

"There are a lot of jobs around."

Just then, Latifa opened the pantry door and found us both whispering.

"We have two orders! Nancy, you're responsible now. Get going!"

Nancy walked right past her saying nothing. I had my hand on my purse and quickly left through the front door.

I stood outside the café for a moment, trying to collect myself. I felt like I had just left a lion's den, like Daniel in the Bible. I would soon be the only chef until the new one arrived and would have to deal with the lioness from the Middle East. What choice did I have but to continue?

I took a step to the right to go to my car, and in front of me was the bakery across the street. There in the window was the Help Wanted sign stating "Bakery clerk position available" that Marie had spoken about weeks ago. I walked inside and asked about the job.

A sales girl behind the counter introduced me to the owner, who had a strong accent, which, I presumed, was Danish. She was like Latifa but much older, with pin-curled short orange hair that looked as if it could not decide between brown, red, or yellow. She said the position had been filled. She just forgot to remove the poster. I could, however, fill out an application and if something came up, she would call me. We had a pleasant conversation, which was important. I completed the form and left with the wonderful aromas of pastries and coffee comforting each breath I took. It was the smell of happiness.

* * * *

The next day Nancy came in early to tell Latifa she was quitting. Unlike Jennie, she would not be easily swayed. No matter how much Latifa pleaded for her to stay until the new girl started, it was a done deal. I now had the full-day shift, since I was the only cook on hand. It was more than I could handle, energy-wise, but again, what choice did I have? I needed the money.

I continued through the week, and my coughing had gotten worse. Each day was becoming more and more difficult. My work day at the café relied mainly on my jacks, or mechanical parts of centers. In other words, I simply went through the motions, half asleep, cutting up the vegetables and frying the bacon and assembling the sandwiches. I spent the evenings resting. This had now become my life. My light was flickering. I was definitely more asleep and mechanical than last year. I did not plan on this, either.

It was clear that I could not do this much longer. Do I have the courage to quit?

* * * *

On Wednesday, August 9, I arrived at work fifteen minutes late. Latifa was waiting for me, expressing her unhappiness about my tardiness. I held onto the counter as she pounded me with her negativity. The struggle to breathe and to withstand her tongue lashings pushed me to a higher state. Without hesitation, right action presented itself.

"I quit."

"You can't do that! I need you!"

I quietly, and intentionally, placed my hand on the pantry locker door to open it, untied my apron, removed it, and hung it on the hook, and reached for my handbag.

"You can mail me my check," I said softly.

As I walked to my car, a serene feeling entered me. Gone were the confused emotions surrounding What should I do? It was apparent. It was no longer a question. Right action was simply reality and reality could only be found in the moment.

Wait a minute. Today is August 9th. It is my mother's 55th birthday. Her life appeared before me, with all of her struggles to exist in the face of my father's strong demands. It penetrated deeply. I am my mother's daughter. That part of me that easily succumbs to others' opinions of what is right belongs to her. That's feminine dominance.

But unlike her, I have been given a chance to break through the chains of childhood. That's the struggle. That's the lesson. And today, I passed a test. Turning on the ignition, I smiled as I headed home.

> *Heaven lies about us in our infancy!*
> *Shades of the prison-house begin to close*
> *Upon the growing Boy,*
> *But he beholds the light, and whence it flows,*
> *He sees it in his joy.*
>
> William Wordsworth

CHAPTER 154

I spent several days sleeping. The Thursday meeting occurred without me. I could hear the sounds of students chatting, and the quietness that accompanied a meeting with the teacher. All of this I supposed since I was not able to exit my bed to verify it.

Late Saturday morning, my energy returned, and I finally showered. The house was silent, and it felt good to have that much space to myself. I wandered around the living room and saw the record player hidden away in an alcove off the entry. The equipment belonged to Rosemary, and it brought memories of Vacaville where I would play her records in the seclusion of her home. There were also albums that did not belong to her. Thumbing through them I came upon several from my favorite singer, Barbra Streisand. I was delighted! These were albums I once owned myself, but left behind when I travelled north from Los Angeles.

I put the first one on, and that sweet voice caressing each note soothed my heart. I knew each word and sang with full voice, as if I were still alone in my bedroom in LA. I had a voracious appetite for this music, and played through the list for two hours straight, crooning to the tunes as I pictured a large audience enthralled by my emotional and vocal delivery.

In the middle of a phrase the music abruptly stopped.

There was Robert lifting the needle off the record.

He handed me this note: "Please dear. That's enough."

"Okay. Sorry."

He must have been napping. When he went back to his room, I put the records away, with a big smile on my face. That personal connection we had last year had not been lost after all, it seems. The gods were still using me as friction against him.

* * * *

Jim came back within the hour of the music incident and found me drinking coffee and smoking a cigarette in the kitchen.

"Hey," he said, surprised to see me, "I heard you were sick."

"Yeah, I had viral pneumonia. I'm feeling better. Need help?"

"No, I have this."

He had brought in several bags of groceries.

"Robert wants to have an early meeting tonight and then a dinner. Sheila's cooking."

"That sounds wonderful. What time's the meeting?"

He looked at his watch. "In about an hour."

It was three, so that meant the meeting would be at four. That was quite odd. Most people would still be at work.

He sat down across from me, pulling out a packet of cigarette papers and a small tobacco pouch from his shirt pocket. He preferred sometimes to roll his own.

"Did you hear Robert rented a house in Carmel Highlands?"

"No!" I guess that meant he would not be staying at the Whitman House anymore.

"It's parallel to Point Lobos and has its own private beach."

"Cool."

He starts to chuckle. His whole body moves up and down, and he has an impish grin that's endearing.

"What's up?"

"There was a weird shock when we first walked inside the place. It was totally empty except for a poster of the Mona Lisa under a light switch just outside the master bedroom."

"That IS weird."

"Yeah, it was the only thing there. No furniture or anything. Just that poster."

"You can't make this stuff up. Did Robert say anything about it?"

"Yes. He said it was a gift from his guardian angel, Leonardo da Vinci."

"Oh. I didn't know that. That's pretty special. What's the place like?"

"It's got a big picture window looking out over Big Sur. Dark wooden floors — pretty neat."

He snuffed his cigarette and took to rolling another.

"You know," he continued, "the owner of this house is now a student."

"What house?"

"Whitman."

"You're kidding! He joined?"

"Yes. Our lease is good for a year, so in January we have to move out of this place."

That struck me like a lead pipe.

"Wow."

"That's one reason Robert thought about renting another."

Looking at his watch, he stood up quickly. "Hey, I need to shower for the meeting."

I returned to my room to prepare. Sitting on my bed, I thought, "Oh, great! Not only do I need a job. Now I need a place to live." Nothing I can do about this now, another 'I' said in response, adding There's a meeting with Robert today.

That thought was enough to make me happy.

* * * *

The meeting at 4 p.m. was sparse. Jim, of course, was there to deliver Robert's thoughts, but only seven or eight students showed up. Rose wasn't there, nor Marie, Nadia, nor Klair. Sheila hadn't come either to prepare the dinner. The light was still strong, however, as it filtered into the living room. It was not an evening meeting or a morning meeting. It was an afternoon meeting. This in itself was so out of patterns that it heightened my state.

The students who showed up must be new, since I did not know any of them. We sat in a small circle in the living room. A Saturn man with a beard and shoulder-length black hair was slumped in his chair, with his long legs extended and his arms crossed.

He lifted his hand and Robert acknowledged him to speak.

"You say the king of clubs is the mind behind the machine. Why is this a bad thing? I mean, if this is true, then it's right work of centers, right? Isn't that what we're after?"

Robert looked to the ceiling for a few moments. Then he wrote the following for Jim to read.

"C Influence cannot control the third state in us, as it is not mechanical and needs to be shocked awake by suffering, which is a form of payment for the gift."

Huh?

Robert didn't answer his question. That was unusual for him.

We sat there for a while. I looked around the room and I saw that the students were uncomfortably squirming in their chairs. The fellow tried again.

"Aren't men number one, two, and three trying to balance their centers? Isn't that the main aim for us?"

Robert's reply: "The Self is a being of the third state of consciousness. It must be able to collect enough moments back-to-back to stay awake and gain intelligence and being."

Again, this was unrelated to the question.

I looked at the guy's face and could practically read it: "How can Robert be conscious if he cannot even answer a question directly? Is he not listening?"

Then I realized something: I don't recall hearing these angles from Robert before. It is new information to me. Ahh. Perhaps the gods are releasing knowledge. This is now becoming interesting.

The meeting continued in this fashion. One of the ladies asked Robert a question about children and he gave another unrelated response. It was a miracle I saw what was going on, and it was wondrous. It was like looking for food on the ground when manna was falling from heaven.

After thirty minutes the meeting ended. The man stood up and took his coat and left the house. Two of the ladies followed him.

The other four ladies stayed for dinner. Sheila arrived at 6:30 with the food that she had prepared at her home. Marie and Rose showed up with her. Others came at seven, including Nadia, Mary C., and several new Carmel students.

I retired early since my energy level was still low. While lying in bed, I thought about that Saturn guy who came to have his questions answered. He did not come to listen. It sounds like a simple difference, but it was huge. I learned an important lesson today: humans want their ideas validated, not verified. Growth begins with listening, not formulating. I must remember this.

❖

The main part of philosophy is not to impart some new knowledge, but to help it to remember. Ignorance is oblivion. Knowledge is remembering. Learning is simply remembering.

Plato

CHAPTER 155

It was a time of transition.

Although the lease had been signed, the new Carmel Highlands house was not ready for Robert to occupy since it did not come with a stick of furniture, only the enigmatic smile of Mona Lisa welcoming Robert to his new abode. Robert asked Sheila to decorate it with furnishings by the weekend so he could have the first meeting on Monday, August 21. She pushed back and said that was not possible. Robert stayed in Carmel to supervise her selections and help her to actualize his request.

THE DIVINE BEGINNING

Meanwhile, on Thursday, August 17 a call came for me at the Whitman House while I was out, and it was fortunate Marie was home to take it. It was from the bakery! The bakery clerk position opened up again and the owner wondered if I was available. Of course, I was, and this time my salary was $1.85 an hour. I was moving up in the world, I thought.

I met the owner the next afternoon. Her first name was Freya and I was to call her Madame. This was an old-world Danish bakery, and she was certainly from the old world. I would be working with Debbie, who had called to let me know about the job.

"Debbie will explain to you what you need to know," said Madame, in her Danish accent. She quickly disappeared into the bakery office, which was upstairs behind the ovens.

"She's strict but don't worry about it. She's actually quite sweet," said Debbie in a hushed tone, "and relies on us to help her out."

I smiled.

"You're gonna need to buy a uniform. Here's the address."

As she handed me the card of a janitorial supply store in Carmel, I was concerned about the cost since I was almost out of money.

"You'll need a white baker's clerk outfit. Just tell them where you'll be working."

"Are they expensive?"

"Oh, no. About fifteen dollars."

I had sixteen left.

"Okay," I said, a bit shocked. But I kept the smile on since I did not want her to know my circumstances.

Debbie showed me the trays of cookies and pastries and cakes and how to present them beautifully in the glass display cabinets, which I needed to keep spotless. She then taught me how to make the coffee and use the cash register.

"You'll also be serving customers. We make sure they have enough coffee."

Debbie gave me the employment forms, which this time didn't take me long to complete.

"See you in the morning," she said, brightly.

"6:30 yes?" I replied.

"Yes."

After heading down to the store, which was only a few blocks away, I found a nice-fitting white outfit that they said would do the job. It wasn't until then that I realized I must have lost weight. I actually felt pretty as I looked in the mirror.

When I arrived back at the house, I was surprised to see several cars in the driveway, including Anna's little VW beetle. How wonderful! Maybe Robert's here.

As I walked in, I could hear laughter erupt from the kitchen.

Rosemary, Robert and Anna were sitting at the kitchen table. Anna was talking quickly, in an emotional tone of denial.

"What's going on?" I asked, wanting to join the fun.

"Linda," replied Rose, "Pepper just pooped on the floor after Anna said he was housebroken."

"He didn't poop!" exclaimed Anna, defending her stance.

Robert and Rose started laughing again, each in their own manner. Rose with her loud, joyous giggle, and Robert with his big grin, his head shaking in disbelief at the utter ridiculousness of the whole affair, and his long fingers wiping the wetness from his eyes.

"Anna," Robert wrote, "we just saw him do it."

"But he never does it. He did not do that."

"Who's going to clean it up?" I asked, adding a bit of gasoline to her queen-of-hearts fire.

"I'm not!" said Anna. "It's NOT from Pepper."

Klair heard the ruckus and came out of her room. She was told what happened, and then quickly went over and cleaned it up. That silenced us. She poured some coffee and returned to her room.

Robert wrote another note to Anna.

"Anna, it would be good if we all went to Mexico and smoked some marijuana. I will go with you. It will help remove some buffers."

This shocked all of us.

Robert added: "We could not do it here since it's illegal."

"I don't want to smoke marijuana," said Anna, tears welling in her eyes.

Rosemary calmed her down and glared at Robert.

Robert, picking up the cue, jotted, "It was only a suggestion."

His last note was to Rosemary. Her reply to him was, "I'll call her."

She picked up the kitchen phone and spoke with Sheila.

"She said she can prepare dinner." They stood up to leave, and I remained there, hoping for an invitation. It did not come.

I was on my own and prepared a sandwich from a few slices of bread and a can of tuna fish I still had in the pantry.

Nadia came home just as I finished eating, and we spoke briefly. She had read a book she highly recommended. It was titled *Bury My Heart at Wounded*

Knee, and it was a best seller. She offered it to me, and I took it since I didn't have television or magazines to entertain me. It was about the American Indians and their struggles. Sounded interesting, although I wasn't into that kind of civil rights thing anymore. I put it on the side table next to my bed.

After dishes, I went to the utility closet and pulled out the iron and ironing board to press my new uniform. My energies were returning. Tomorrow is a big day, full of new possibilities. I longed for a happy working environment, and it seems the gods may have granted my wish. Given my previous play — the near-death experience and squalid conditions of the place with a mean lady — I was sure I had made the payment for a pleasant reward. The bakery was clean, open and I particularly enjoyed Debbie, plus I would be making more money.

The future looked brighter to me. A chance to be in good householder, to be near the teacher and school, and to achieve conscious harmonious development. What more can one wish? My heart was filled with gratitude to the gods that I survived the trials and passed the tests.

※

Do you think you shall enter Paradise without such trials as came to those who passed before you?
                                                              Mohammed

CHAPTER 156

When I arrived the next morning at the bakery, Debbie greeted me at the door.

"Come in! I want you to meet the baker."

Immediately the sweet warm smells of sugar, cinnamon and baked dough enveloped me like a maternal hug. As she led me to the bakery area, there stood the baker removing long trays of cinnamon buns from the rotating shelves of this huge oven that rose beyond the first story of the two-story space. It was massive in dimension, ten feet high and eight feet long, would be my guess. I had never seen anything like it. Nor had I seen anything like the baker.

He was a Venusian-Mercury type with black curly hair and a short, well-trimmed mustache. He would not have been particularly attractive were it not for the twinkle in his eyes and the where-have-you-been-all-my-life seductive smile. I detected a Spanish accent as he was introduced to me. His name was Miguel, and I watched his tan arms strain under the weight of each tray as he slid them quickly into the cooling racks.

"We have to work fast," said Debbie, pulling me out of my trance.

She took a tray of warm buns to a table and placed it next to a big bowl of white icing that the baker had made. Then she demonstrated the maneuver to apply the right amount to each roll.

"Put your four fingers into the icing, and with this motion," she indicated, with a sweep of her hand, "gently wipe each bun so they are iced enough to see a bit of the roll underneath. Don't cover them with a thick layer."

She moved so quickly that it was like watching a ballet dancer gesticulate.

I tried my hand and immediately a glop of sticky stuff landed on the first one.

"No, not so much. You should be able to cover the two dozen on the tray with one scoop of icing."

I tried again and she announced, "Much better."

"Once the buns are cold, the icing doesn't stick, so we have to hurry. You'll get the hang of it. It took me a while, too."

We both worked the trays and I could see it did require a lighter touch. I appreciated the fact she was non-judgmental.

Once she saw I had the hang of it, she thumbed through the orders.

"These are going to all the inns in Carmel and we need to box them by 7:45. That's when the inns send their delivery guys over for the pickup."

She showed me how to put together the pink bakery box. I focused on assembling the boxes as she began to fill them with the proper number of rolls requested by each inn.

It was rapidly approaching 7:45 when we managed to complete them all. But there was no time to rest. The bakery opened for customers at eight, and the first two, a man and a woman, were already at the door as she went to unlock it.

"Hi, George," she said to the old man, who had a stilted walk and half a smile.

"Good mornin' to you, Debbie."

"Hi Adele, let me help you," offered Debbie, as she carefully took the woman by the arm and slowly walked her inside.

The two customers sat separately in their accustomed seats. As she filled their coffee cups, she introduced me to each of them.

"Linda will be working here now."

The man didn't look at me, but the lady's face lit up with a childlike expression of joy, as if I were a long-lost friend.

"Well, helloooo," replied Adele.

Debbie went behind the counter and I followed her.

"George likes the cheese Danish and Adele likes two cinnamon rolls. They order the same thing every day, so just bring it to them after you pour their coffees."

I smiled at Debbie's consideration. She truly was an angel.

By ten, the place was full of customers. George and Adele each left when the place became busy and loud.

I cleared the tables and Debbie showed me how to run the little dishwasher next to the big, deep sink where we first stacked the dirty dishes, after disposing of the uneaten pieces and rinsing the plates of crumbs. It was unbelievable how she was able to stuff that tiny dishwasher with the plates, cups, and utensils and a glass coffee pot.

"Madame doesn't want the dishwasher run unless it's full."

We kept busy throughout the day, from the peak of the morning rush to the cake orders that came in during the afternoon. I watched her personalize a round chocolate cake with white icing. She scripted "Happy 6th Birthday Suzy" by filling a piping bag made of parchment paper with the end cut off. She had me do another cake from an order that wanted "Happy Birthday Sonny."

"Miguel knows how to make pastry roses. We can ask him to show us tomorrow when he's here."

"That would be wonderful!"

The bakery job was becoming fun and creative. I left that first day filled with happiness and assured in my heart that the gods were smiling upon me.

* * * *

The next morning was Saturday, and when I arrived at the bakery, Miguel said he was willing to show us how to create roses from the pastry cream. Debbie and I received this "rose nail" — a flat circle of metal attached to a metal skewer — and our own filled pastry bag that had a metal tip at the end.

Miguel began by squirting the cream into an upright tight cylinder in the center of the nail. Then he squeezed the bag as he moved in small half-circles while rotating the platform, once, twice, and three times so that the edges of one petal touched the edges of the other. It happened so quickly that I could barely follow it, but this is what he did. He asked us to try it. Debbie did well with the first petal but didn't connect it to the second, and the third was too small because there wasn't enough room on the platform to complete it. I tried and my first petal was a blob. I squeezed the bag too hard.

Miguel, laughing, took our nails and wiped them clean. "Try again," he said encouragingly.

We tried several times, rather unsuccessfully, giggling as Miguel wiped our attempts off with his towel. I could feel he was flirting with us. Debbie had a nice figure, and I guessed she was around twenty. I could see an attraction between them. I wanted to be found worthy of his affection, too. That was my last 'I,' when suddenly Madame entered the room.

"No time for this!" she said.

We scattered like mice when the cat appears. Madame scolded the baker and he absorbed it with a straight face. Debbie and I went directly to caressing the buns with sweet icing. We boxed the rolls quickly and by the time I finished the last order, Miguel had left.

It was exciting to have my sex energy flowing once more. It made me feel alive.

* * * *

This was the first time I worked with the Saturday crowd, and it was bustling during the morning and early afternoon. By 4 p.m., there was only one customer. I was already sweeping the backroom when I heard familiar voices. I put my broom down to see who it was. Trisha and Nadia had taken a table and Debbie was pouring their coffees.

I went up to them.

"Debbie, these are my friends, Trisha and Nadia."

"Nice to meet you," she said, smiling. Then turning to me, "You can take the orders. I'll finish up in the back."

Trisha ordered the cheesecake, which I highly recommended, having sampled this and other pastries as part of my job. Nadia did not order. I knew she had given up sugar so I wasn't surprised.

There was one last slice, and when I brought it to her, Trisha asked when I was done.

"I usually leave at five. Why?"

"We're picking up some food at the Mediterranean Market for dinner and then going back to the house to watch an episode of *Elizabeth R*. Wanna join us?"

"Sure!"

They hung around until five, which wasn't hard to do. It was common for customers to linger. When the time came, I took my purse and went with them to the market a few blocks away.

Trisha took the lead, and when she entered, she went right to the cheese and meat displays. Behind the counter was a young man who stood out from the rest. He had golden hair, blue eyes, a gentle countenance, was six feet tall, and a build that looked like an Adonis. I was smitten.

"John, this is Linda and Nadia," said Trisha. Then, turning to me, she added, "He just joined the school."

I couldn't believe it. Maybe he's the one, I thought. So much was going right in my life, why shouldn't the gods reward me with something like this?

He also was planning to come over to watch *Elizabeth R* after his shift. The PBS Masterpiece Theatre program began at 8 p.m. It would be a full day, but my energy was soaring, so no problem staying awake for this.

At home, a number of students gathered to watch the show. The television wasn't large, but we all managed to see the screen. It was a magnificent performance. I could feel, however, my queen of hearts pulling me away from the episode, as I frequently would look at John to see if he was enjoying it.

When the program ended and we cleaned up, we hugged each other good night. Hugging John did not disappoint. I could feel the firmness of his frame and it was definitely squeezable. I wondered what it would be like to be with him.

That would be the fantasy that lulled me to sleep that night.

> *You make yourself stupid with false imaginings,*
> *and so you do not see what you would see*
> *if you discarded them.*
>
> Dante

CHAPTER 157

I learned on Sunday that Sheila had indeed accomplished the impossible and decorated the Carmel Highlands house. The Monday evening meeting was scheduled for 7:30.

The summer crowd had swarmed the bakery that morning. I was kept quite busy. Whether pouring coffee, serving pastries or taking phone orders, all my thoughts revolved around seeing John at the meeting. When five came, I went home to shower and beautify myself. I had eaten enough pastry during the day to not have an appetite for dinner. I decided to drive to the new house early, and Nadia said she wanted to join me.

As we headed down Highway 1, the road became narrow and curvy.
"It's here!" Nadia exclaimed.
"That's nuts!" I answered.

There was no "here." The directions said the house was past the entry of Point Lobos Natural Reserve and across from the small Carmel Highlands gas station, but the only thing on that side of the road was a long, weathered redwood fence. There was no indication that a house existed anywhere.

I circled around and stopped at the gas station. They were ready to close. I asked the attendant, and he said there was a sign with a number and that must be it. He did not know but was guessing. My agitation, fueled by the fear of being lost, was rising. At that point, another car pulled in and in it were students. We spoke with them and one of them crossed the street, which was dangerous given the quick flow of oncoming traffic. He ran back to let us know there was a gate with the numbers on it corresponding to the address we had been given.

We had received instructions that we were not to park inside the gate. There was no shoulder on the highway for the cars. We made U-turns, and parked the cars as close to the fence as we could while still allowing students to exit their vehicles. It was a scary situation. I was grateful that we arrived early. I had no idea where the others would park, and did not envy the difficult trek they would need to make in the dark to find the place.

Inside the gate, a paved road led to a multi-level redwood home that was both rustic and elegant. The front door opened to a narrow hallway with beautifully polished dark wood floors. At the end of the hall on the right was the spacious living room that also included a large dining table close to the eastern wall. Large picture windows faced west, and they framed the crashing waves and majestic expanse of the Pacific Ocean. Near the dining table was the entrance to the kitchen. I peeked inside and saw Sheila, who was instructing students on how to arrange trays of hors d'oeuvres for the intermission. I joined in to help. It was now approaching seven.

When I returned to the living room, Robert had entered and went to the window to watch the setting of the sun. The declining orange disk sent miles of shimmering streaks of light out upon the deep blue waters as a last offering of the day. We gathered to watch with him, in silence, until the sun itself melted into darkness.

The room was crowded with chairs. Sofas were pushed against the back wall. As students began to take their seats, I looked around for John. He wasn't there. Perhaps he had to work late, I reasoned. He was on my mind as I took a front row seat. My legs were less than a yard from those sitting with Robert.

It was time for the meeting to start. After good householder, Robert waited before sharing his thoughts.

"The school is moving quickly. We are on a painful schedule. Sheila has decorated this house in one week after saying it could not be done. We are trying to do the impossible — to remember our Selves. You have discovered the highest mystery a human can discover in his existence: the secret of self-remembering. It is against nature. We are supposed to naïvely live and die like sheep. The Self remembering is a miracle that few people are fated to discover. Humans are not intended to be twice born."

Robert asked for questions, and a lady raised her hand.

"What does C Influence mean?"

"It has several meanings," answered Robert. "Celestial Influence. Conscious Influence, and direct communication with the angels. We are so lucky we have the painful help of C Influence. As your level increases, you will see we are totally dependent upon C Influence.

"Are there other angles of thought on C Influence?"

No one raised a hand.

In that moment, we heard a powerful noise, like a sonic boom. What could that be?

Robert turned to Jim and asked him to check it out. He took two others with him and went outside the house with a flashlight.

The meeting continued.

"Is there another question?"

A tall man from the Bay Area asked, "Can you talk about the use of sex energy?"

"Sex energy is the same energy used for higher centers. This idea is hidden from humanity. Humans are seeds that are designed to enjoy the feeling of sex and spend it outwardly instead of inwardly for an immaculate conception, an inner second birth."

Robert then asked for other angles.

Alden raised his hand.

"We lose sex energy through imagination."

"Yes," said Robert. "The machine, specifically the queen of clubs, wants to uncover the mystery of another person."

He looked at me when he said it. It was as if he knew my night imaginings. I had never heard this thought before. These imaginings were simply a byproduct of a function known as the queen of clubs. It was a new understanding.

"I do not expect you to abstain from sex. Try not to have sex or abstain from sex out of form, form meaning to do things because we should.

"I go over the same ideas so they will enter your being. Do not expect a perfect teacher. One does not exist. Students wish a teacher to have a magnetic center like theirs, yet a man number five embraces all the magnetic centers in the teaching because they are all within him. I place few rules on anyone so that they might be my master. If I am your teacher, then I am your student."

The three students returned and Jim went up to Robert. It was an odd scene. Quietly, Jim told him there was an accident. A woman had fallen asleep at the wheel and ran off the road, crashing into other cars. She died.

Robert repeated it, although we all heard it. It was so strange that my first thought was, "I hope my car is okay." There was no thought about the woman. I felt a little guilty.

"It was no accident that we had just spoken about C Influence. This is a World 6, higher intellectual, shock from them. She fell asleep behind the wheel. That is the condition of life. They are asleep at the wheel. It is also meant to let us know how serious C Influence is about our evolution. Nothing is sacred to them except your desire to awaken."

The energy had dramatically changed in the room. We adjourned and gathered around the large dining table laden with trays of treats. The "coincidence" of that car accident with Robert's statements jarred some students more than others. Some buffered by eating and drinking. Others wanted to do something to help the woman. A few went to check their cars for damage.

I sat on a sofa, quietly watching the others in the room. Jim saw me and brought me a plate.

"Do you want to see the poster?"

I nodded. He took me into the hallway and turned on the light in the tiny alcove. There under the switch was Mona Lisa staring at me. I could feel the third state of consciousness emerge easily within, and it was accompanied by the sense that an invisible being was hovering nearby. I looked at Jim and we both smiled.

"Don't worry," he said softly, "your car's all right."

He returned to the living room while I remained with the Mona Lisa.

As I stared into her face, I recalled Robert's words: Nothing is sacred to them except your desire to awaken. I could still feel and hear the impact of the collision. The presence of the gods was still palpable. A strange emotion filled me as I returned to the sofa — a mixture of fear and comfort.

I think it's called "awe."

❖

> *The Gods know all things, our words and deeds and secret purposes; they are present everywhere and grant signs to men of all that concerns men.*
> Socrates

CHAPTER 158

Tuesday and Wednesday were long days at the bakery. Repeat customers from the summer throng kept us busy. There was, however, a strange man who appeared that did not look like any of the locals who frequented our place. He was thin and short, brown-skinned and had an intelligent face with a ready smile. He first approached me when I was bringing freshly baked cookies to arrange in the display cases.

"Hello," he said, with an accent.

"May I help you?"

"I would like to buy a dozen cookies."

I quickly assembled an appropriately sized pink box and grabbed the tongs to select the ones he wanted.

"Could you describe these?" he asked, pointing to plain sugar cookies.

"These are plain sugar cookies."

"And these?"

"These are sugar cookies with chocolate swirls."

"And these?"

"These are sugar cookies with raspberry swirls."

It continued like this down the display case.

"I'll let you think about it," I said, walking away.

He left the shop.

The next day, he reappeared in the morning.

"There's the guy I told you about," I said to Debbie.

"Don't worry. I'll take his order."

I went to clean the counter tops, and could see him eyeing me while she poured his coffee.

"He wondered what the best pastry was in the bakery," whispered Debbie, as she placed the pot back on the burner.

"What did you tell him?"

"Bear claws."

I turned around quickly to hide my laughter.

She proceeded to pull one out of the case for him and put it on a plate, which she carried over to his table.

She came back with it.

"He wants it warmed up with butter."

"See what I mean?"

"Yeah. But that's okay."

She heated the pastry and grabbed a knife and fork, which was unusual, but she explained.

"He's the kind of guy that would ask for this."

After she took it to him, she said, "He told me I was reading his mind."

"Maybe you should go out with him."

"I'm fine," she replied automatically, with a shocked stare.

I continued to clean the displays and make a new pot of coffee just to keep busy.

He stayed around as the morning customers filled the room. Around noon, when I took my lunch break, I saw that he was gone. I scampered to the Mediterranean Market to pick up a sandwich at the cheese and deli counter. Of course, I hoped to see John there. I learned on Tuesday he would be working, so I was excited to see him.

We exchanged greetings, and I gave him my order of ham and Swiss cheese on rye with mustard and a dill pickle on the side and a Coke.

"Are you planning to go to the Thursday meeting?" I asked.

"This Thursday? No, I have other plans."

That surprised me. He seemed to be a good student.

That was our only interchange, as it was lunchtime and he was busy.

I took my sandwich to the nearby park across the street. As I sat there on a bench hidden under a tree, I was thinking about how to bring John closer to the school. Popping the last bite into my mouth, I saw I was not alone. The strange man was there on another bench eating a sandwich. Oh, God.

I turned my back and quickly placed the sandwich wrappings and napkins into the bag. I scurried back to the bakery, hoping he did not see me.

He did not show up that afternoon, so I assumed it was a coincidence we both appeared in the park eating sandwiches. It proved to me it was a chance situation. I could let it go.

* * * *

Thursday morning, crowds had magically disappeared. I asked Debbie what was going on.

"The summer is over. People are going back to work and to school."

"So suddenly?"

"Oh, yes. It happens like this every year."

And then she added something that stunned me.

"By the way, my last day is Sunday August 27th. I go back to school on Monday."

"You're leaving the job?"

"Yes. I thought Madame had told you when she hired you. You'll be replacing me."

We talked a bit more, and I learned this was her summer job. She was attending Monterey Peninsula College studying biology. I never spoke to her about my background. I preferred to keep this a secret.

We concluded the conversation and went back to work laying out the cookies, and cleaning the cabinets and the area in the back where we had quickly boxed the buns for the inns. The bell attached to the front door chimed, indicating a new customer had entered.

"I'll take this," I said to her.

It was the strange man.

After our conversation, seeing this man was not so strange. I was already put off-balance by Debbie's news regarding my future here at the bakery.

I took the coffee pot to him and asked if he would like the usual.

"Yes, please!" he replied, with joy in his eyes.

I brought him his warm pastry and butter, with the knife and fork.

"Ah, miss?"

"Yes?"

"Excuse me. I am rather new here, and I wondered if there's any chance you would like to have dinner with me tonight."

He could see the fear in my eyes, so he clarified.

"I mean…in a restaurant. I mean…I would like to take you out to a restaurant."

I breathed a deep sigh. "Let me think about it. Please enjoy your pastry."

I returned to the back and told Debbie.

"He seems nice," she said, "and you'll be in a public place. You should be fine."

She was right. I had almost no money. Payday was Friday, and it turned out there was no meeting since Robert had led one on Monday. I was free and I was hungry. I returned with the pot of coffee.

"Yes," I told him.

"My name is Sandy."

"My name is Linda. Where shall we meet?"

"I'm staying at the Pine Inn. I can meet you in the lobby at seven?"

I agreed. He paid and left, giving me a five-dollar bill as a tip, which I pocketed.

As I watched him leave, I thought, "Well, Linda. You wanted adventure." Maybe he has a magnetic center, I thought. Who knew what was to come?

Only consider at what price you sell your freedom and will.

Epictetus

CHAPTER 159

It was the purple dress of graduation that I wore as I walked up the elegant stairs of the Pine Inn. This was one of the most exclusive inns in Carmel. Who is this guy? How can he afford such accommodations?

We met in the lobby. He was nicely dressed in a dark gray jacket, perfectly pressed light gray trousers, and a white shirt that was tieless. I felt so poor in my purple dress, as he escorted me to the dining area. The maître d' had taken us to a small table-for-two by the window, and Sandy pulled out the chair for me. The white tablecloth and folded napkins and clean, crystal glasses put me in a higher state. But this state was not comfortable. I felt awkward.

I was handed the menu, and my eyes read from right to left, like a Jew reading Hebrew. The prices were more than I made in a week. I decided to pick something that was not that expensive. I did not want to feel obligated to this guy.

"What do you recommend?" he asked the waiter.

I breathed a sigh of relief.

"The Catch of the Day is very special," replied the waiter. And very expensive, replied Linda to herself.

We ordered the Catch of the Day, which was grilled halibut, my mother's favorite.

"Would you like wine?"

THE DIVINE BEGINNING

"No, thank you," I said. I was not a drinker.

After the menus were removed, he leaned forward to ask, "Tell me about yourself."

I was struck dumb, as I rearranged the napkin on my lap, keeping my smile on my face, and my eyes down.

"Not much to say, really." OH. I said REALLY.

He started to ask me about where I was born. He was digging into my private life, and I felt so uncomfortable. How could I explain the school and my interest in awakening? I had to flip this.

I told him I was from Los Angeles and asked where he was born.

"I'm from India," he said. "My name is actually Sanjay, but people here kept calling me Sandy, so I just accepted it."

"How come you're in America?"

He then began to tell me about his parents, who were wealthy and traditional, his education, his aspirations, his this, his that. You have the picture.

He talked about himself the entire evening, while I ate the halibut, which was sweet and fresh, dabbing my mouth and smiling and nodding between bites.

As I listened, I was studying him. He was looking for adventure, and I fit the bill. A bakery girl. What could be more outlandish for a fellow from his upper class than to hook up with a simple bakery girl. I wasn't interested in playing that role.

What could I tell him that would make it clear we were on separate paths?

When the chocolate dessert came, I told him how appreciative I was for the dinner invitation.

"It feels to me that we are on separate paths," I said to him.

"What do you mean?" he asked seriously.

"I'm not interested in being with anyone at this point in my life. You are a wonderful person and I'm sure you'll find the right person that pleases you and your parents."

"I see," he said, folding his napkin. He called for the bill.

We parted in front of the Pine Inn door after a sincere "Thank you" from me. No hug, no handshake. I walked at a brisk pace to my car.

I wondered what it was in me that attracted him. He had definite problems with his parents and was imagining a life outside of his heritage that would challenge this. I could not relate to this man. We had nothing in common.

* * * *

After work on Friday night, I went to the Chopstix, hoping to see Meg and Alden there. They were, along with Trisha, JT, and John, which was a pleasant surprise.

The six of us squeezed into a big booth. I ended up sitting next to John, much to my delight.

They had yet to order, so we all decided to share food (it was JT's idea). The owner and her daughter carried the plates three-on-the-arm style. With my paycheck, I had enough money to splurge on more than one dish.

"It's a full moon, you know," said Alden, who kept track of the celestial events for the Fellowship. His articles appeared regularly in the *Via Del Sol Journal*. He's a queen-of-diamonds type and a tall Lunar. His mathematical explanations about the progression of the enneagram from Gurdjieff were too intellectual even for me.

"It's been pretty wacky," I replied. And then I described my date last night in detail, while everyone was passing around the dishes. I couldn't stop talking.

"That doesn't sound nice," commented JT, while passing me the plate of broccoli beef.

"What do you mean?" I asked.

"I mean, you said you weren't interested in him, so why did you let him spend all that money on a fancy dinner? You took advantage of him."

That was not why I shared my experience. Deep inside, I wanted to show everyone, especially John, that someone considered me attractive enough to ask me out. Making fun of the guy was never my intent. They didn't understand.

"It's what he wanted," I replied, defensively.

JT responded, "He wanted to come to know you. He was interested in you. But if you already knew you couldn't care less about him, why did you lead him on like this?"

"It's true," I agreed, "I wasn't interested in him. I thought I was satisfying this need of his to know me. How can he know me? Our lives are too different."

Trisha stood up for me. "I don't think she did anything wrong. When a guy asks you out, you owe him nothing other than to enjoy the dinner and his company."

"But it doesn't sound like you enjoyed his company, that's all I'm saying," added JT.

John surprised me with this comment. "But she knew she wasn't interested in him in the first place. I agree with JT." My heart sank.

"Sounds like tramp to me," added Alden, as he was pouring me a cup of tea.

"How could this be tramp?" I questioned. "Tramp doesn't know what to value. It has too much relativity. How does that relate to this?"

"You're not valuing him," he replied.

"What does that mean? He was after me and by going out with him, I was valuing him. I was giving him what he wanted, Alden."

This whole conversation was disturbing to me. My queen of hearts flipped into negative territory. Meg said nothing. She was poking at her food with a fork in one hand and her cigarette perched in the other.

"Meg," asked Alden, "what do you think?"

All eyes were on her. She swallowed, took a sip of coffee, inhaled and exhaled some smoke, before speaking.

"It's her vanity."

That went through me like a bullet. I stared at my plate.

"That's what it is!" burst out Alden.

"That sounds right," agreed JT.

It was now my turn to poke at my food. I took out a cigarette from my pack and lit it.

"Now, she's buffering."

I had lost my appetite, and signaled for a takeout container. After a while, Trisha spoke.

"Tomorrow night we're watching the next episode of *Elizabeth R.* at John's place."

John smiled and provided the location, which we all wrote down.

More subjects changed after that, and I just sat there quietly, trying to digest what had happened. I said nothing. The bill came and we paid it. When we left the booth, we embraced one another. I tried to smile, but tears were ready to appear, so I looked away with each quick, half-hearted hug.

Meg and Alden stayed to buy more cigarettes from the vending machine in the restaurant. Going outside, I saw Trisha and JT zoom away on his bike. John had just turned the key to his motorcycle and scooted off as well. I walked slowly to my car, entered, and drove home.

Later that night, I still grappled with how a lovely evening could turn into something so hurtful. It was necessary suffering, I guess. They didn't mean it. They were sharing their observations and trying to help me awaken. Seeing chief feature of vanity is not a pleasant thing, and I should be grateful. I should not have talked so much about my experiences. It was vanity.

A nice aim would be to bring more intentionality to conversations instead of talking about myself.

But how do I do that?

※

Speaking is harder than all other work.
He who understands speech, makes it serve.
Egyptian Texts, Wisdom of Ptah-hotep

CHAPTER 160

Saturday's crowds were fewer than the week before at the bakery. When five o'clock came, I returned home to prepare for the evening at John's. I had considered not attending, after the comment he made, but curiosity won over.

It was such an interesting thing for me to observe in myself. I'm drawn so much to handsome men that I lose myself in the attraction. What is this attraction? Are they thoughts, or 'I's, or sensations of the instinctive center, as Robert mentioned? Can they be stopped? Why does my heart race so when I'm around John? Why do I talk so much? How should I act? What are proper subjects to use in conversation?

As I drove over, I decided to keep as quiet as I could. This silence, however, was not a high state. It was sullen. It was self-absorbed. It was what the Fourth Way system calls inner considering. I could see this, I could know this, and yet could do nothing to change it.

When I arrived, some of the people, I learned, were not students but friends of John. He shared a large two-bedroom apartment with another fellow. They had a good-sized television positioned in the living room next to a fireplace. Two sofas and chairs, some from the dining room, were assembled for us. John, of course, had an assortment of snacks and beverages on the table from the Mediterranean Market.

We watched the program, which was aired live from Great Britain, and I was trying to focus on it. The stream of thoughts regarding social etiquette played in my head like background noise. This diminished as I became more engulfed in the characters on the TV.

When the program ended, interest in John flooded inside of me, involving not just the head but the heart. I went to the kitchen to help with the cleanup. I wanted to stay there as long as I could, to be close to him. John did not detect my ulterior motive. Or, maybe he did. I finished the glasses, wiping each one many times to be sure there were no spots or fingerprints.

THE DIVINE BEGINNING

People left slowly. I could not leave. This part in me that was so focused on John was like a phantom that took control. It had patience and waited until we were finally alone.

"Would you like some wine?" he asked, while pouring himself a glass.

"Sure," I replied. But you hate wine, Linda, a small voice inside said.

We sat on the couch.

"I didn't mean to hurt you last night," he whispered, after a few sips.

You mean he was inner considering, too?

"Oh, that's all right. I'm fine."

"It's just that I've been shut down before, and it touched a nerve."

I couldn't believe it. He seemed like a dreamboat. Who would do that to him?

"Me, too," I said sympathetically.

And then I couldn't resist. I told him about my play with Miles and Helga. A tiny voice inside said, Stop! But the saga was too dramatic to drop. The movie reel was out of its can and projected on a big screen of self-pity, with its nuances of hurt, surprise, and bearing unbearable wrongs.

He put his arm around my shoulders to comfort me. The tale of woe was working, smiled the phantom.

That night I received comfort from him.

I left in the early hours of the morning for home to change into my bakery uniform before heading to work. Before leaving, he mentioned he had friends coming over Sunday evening, and I was invited. No one in the Whitman House knew what I was doing. The comfort of John was addictive, and I wanted more.

* * * *

Sunday was Debbie's last day at the bakery. Miguel had created a special cake for her with dark chocolate and fresh whole raspberries on top. Madame was pleased. It was clear how much she had relied on Debbie and valued her. We would party at the end of the day, said Madame, and then instructed us to go back to work.

Debbie's farewell celebration occurred at four. Miguel returned with his girlfriend, who was gorgeous and considerably younger than he. It was a festive time, as Madame placed a candle on the cake for Debbie to blow out. I smiled and enjoyed the cake, but in the back of my mind, it was not a joyous time for me.

For most of the day, I felt split in two, each side of me in a different location. Half of me was back at John's, as the events of the night kept replaying in my mind, and the other half was going about its business at the bakery, pouring coffee and placing pastries on plates, and cookies and cakes in boxes. My machine was functioning. I was living my life, but there was no real life in it. There was no third dimension in my vision. It was flat. I was sleepwalking.

When I arrived at John's that evening, Trisha and her daughter were there, as well as two people named Wanda and Ed. It was not a casual evening. It was a gathering on the subject of Selective Awareness that Wanda and Ed were into. It was weird. I felt uncomfortable, because it was clearly imagination. Trisha was open to what they were saying. She had the chief feature of tramp, which has too much relativity, I thought, but said nothing.

I then remembered how the previous night John talked about how tired he was of intellectualism. I guess he viewed Ouspensky that way. He was clearly struggling, and still searching. I excused myself after an hour, saying I was tired and had to be at work early. John and I exchanged glances, smiling at our shared secret.

As I drove home, I questioned myself. Why was I with John? Was I there to help him strengthen his work? Was he still meant to be an eventual partner? Were my interests in him honorable? It was hard to make sense of it. I could not see where this was going. Perhaps tomorrow it will be made clearer.

❖

Your most subtle and deadly adversary is
the sexual energy in your loins.

Saadi

CHAPTER 161

The last few days of August flew by, as I poured my energy into the job. Since Debbie's departure, I was working over ten hours a day, making good money. The icing of the rolls I had mastered, and I would challenge myself to complete them in record time. I learned the names and preferences of the customers who enjoyed their first meal of the day, a cup of coffee and pastry of their choice at their favorite tables. They struck up conversations and extended friendships to one another, which made it a pleasant environment.

Madame would show up in the late morning and stay until 1 p.m., covering me for the lunch hour. She returned at the end of the day to add up the revenues. This was not something she trusted anyone else to do. It was her livelihood. I understood.

She chastised me if something did not suit her standards. I would wipe the bottom of the glass cabinets of cookie crumbs, but that wasn't good enough. She instructed me to remove all trays and racks at the end of the day, reach into the cases and clean the slanted windows from the inside. It was hard work.

I went to the Mediterranean Market each day at noon for my sandwich and Coke. John was there on Tuesday and Wednesday. His greeting was lukewarm, treating me like an ordinary customer. On Thursday, he didn't show up. I was told he switched his shift to later in the day. Okay. I still ordered the sandwich and Coke.

I had found a new place to enjoy my lunch. It was closer to the bakery and not on the main thoroughfare of Ocean Avenue. In fact, it was between the bakery and Sheila's apartment. It was the Church of the Wayfarer, and it had a bench in the midst of flowers and green shrubs. It was the perfect place to practice self-remembering.

I would initiate divided attention with, "Here I am. How strange." That located me in the space. Then I would taste a bite and focus on a yellow or purple flower in the garden. Those were the first two elements of divided attention. The third element that brought the present forth was remembering C Influence was with me. Some efforts succeeded and some failed. I could feel my master appear briefly before the strain of the effort collapsed the triad. This often happened when I shifted my eyes to another object, or when I forgot about the third point and was fascinated by the object. So many ways to lose the state. Yet, effort was the key. Practice, practice, practice.

* * * *

Friday was the first day of September. When I arrived home, a luxury car was in the driveway. It did not belong to anyone I knew. As I approached the front door, Klair was standing there talking with a tall strawberry-blond gentleman.

"Anthony, I'd like you to meet Linda."

"Hello," I said, shaking his hand. He had a lot of freckles. Must be a Saturn-Mars type, I thought.

"Anthony is our landlord. He just joined the school."

"Wow!" I exclaimed. Although I had learned this from Jim, I had forgotten. "Nice to meet you. Welcome."

After a brief, cordial conversation, he left in his fancy car and Klair and I entered the house.

"Did his wife join, too?" I asked.

"No. They're divorcing."

Klair changed the subject.

"Robert will be leading a meeting tomorrow night."

"Where?" I asked.

"At the Carmel Highlands house."

I was hoping she would say Whitman Circle because I truly did not want to deal with that tough parking situation. It was a lovely house once you arrived. It was the arriving that was difficult and scary.

"We will have some guests staying overnight tonight. They will take Robert's room."

I was okay with this since I still had my sleeping bag and the living room couch was comfortable; this option was considered acceptable given the circumstances. I smiled when I learned it was the couple from Vacaville with whom I had stayed that would be occupying the room. I hadn't seen them for a long time. It sounded like tomorrow night's meeting would be a big one. I wondered if Yorgos and Kerrie would show up.

"Anyone from the farm coming?"

"I don't know," she said curtly.

I asked if the couple from Vacaville would be staying for dinner, since it would be nice to spend time with them again.

"No, they're going to dinner with Robert. I've been invited, too, and need to prepare."

As she headed toward her room, I stood there in the kitchen, alone. A flash of self-pity swept over me from being excluded.

A voice behind me said, "Are you having dinner?"

It was Nadia.

"I thought I'd make a sandwich," I replied.

"I'm preparing some vegetables, if you want to join me."

I could not believe how kind she was. Usually, she is unemotional and distant.

"Sure," I smiled.

She offered me raw vegetables and I ate them with my tuna fish sandwich. We spoke about our respective jobs. Hers seemed to be going well. It was a typical 9 to 5, Monday through Friday bookkeeping position. She told me she was happy I was making money to support myself.

"Oh! I have the teaching payment check to give you," I said, suddenly remembering.

"It's fine. You can give it to me tomorrow."

THE DIVINE BEGINNING

It had not occurred to me before that Nadia may be as lonely as I was. She did not have a husband or children to my knowledge. I was too afraid to pry into the life she had before joining the school. I also did not want to disturb this pleasant time together.

As we removed the plates from the table, she said she wanted to show me something.

She went to her room and came back wearing a beige shirt dress with delicate blue flowers that matched her eyes.

"How lovely!" I exclaimed.

"I made this," she said beaming.

"No kidding! I did not know you had a sewing machine."

"I do not. I sewed this by hand."

I was incredulous. She lifted the hem to show me the seams and the tiny stitches that allowed each piece of material to come together.

"I can't believe you did this! When did you learn to do this?"

"When I was a child. I thought I would try."

She told me this was how women in her family made their clothes.

"Where was this?"

"In Russia."

"Were you ever married?" I asked, a bit shocked that this question came out of my mouth. I did not want to offend her.

"Yes. I left my husband and came to the States."

"That must have taken courage."

She nodded. Her smile disappeared.

"Well," I added, "this is such a remarkable dress. It fits you perfectly. Are you going to wear it to the meeting tomorrow night?"

"I could, I guess," she replied, modestly.

"Oh, please do."

We hugged and said good-night.

Upon retiring, I remembered the incident of the tiles, the first octave we worked on together at the farm. How could anyone escape Communist Russia? I could not imagine what harrowing situations she faced and survived.

I was glad she was my friend.

❖

This world is but a thoroughfare of woe,
and we are pilgrims passing to and fro.
                                    Geoffrey Chaucer

CHAPTER 162

Saturday began with sunshine. When I unlocked the bakery door, George, our usual first customer, was waiting for me. After pouring his coffee, he and I were alone in the place. He told me that Adele, who usually accompanied him, was not well so wouldn't be coming. He looked a little sad, so I talked about the beautiful weather.

"This is our secret in Carmel. The best weather is in the fall," he commented in a gentle voice.

I went back to my daily chores: wiping counters, bringing out the pastries, placing the freshly baked bread on the counter. That kind of thing. It was a slow morning and the start of the Labor Day weekend, which announced the end of summer. The summer throngs of people had already fled back to the big city, it seemed.

Then, at ten o'clock, the most unexpected thing occurred. Robert and Jim walked in. I brought the coffee cups and coffee pot to their table by the window. I placed each cup intentionally on its saucer and watched as the pot I was holding tilted to fill them. Robert's presence ignited my own. It was as if we were on a stage set, and I was playing the role of bakery girl. I had never worn my outfit in front of the teacher. He and Jim were playing the role of customers. It brought up a childhood memory of kindergarten, when I wore an apron to serve my two friends invisible tea from a teapot in an imaginary kitchen that was part of the playroom.

Jim ordered several pastries for the table (bear claw, prune Danish, cheese Danish, cinnamon roll and butterfly) as well as a to-go box of napoleons and eclairs for Sheila as a treat.

I went back to the counter to put together their selections and then returned to place them on their table. Two other new customers arrived and sat at the table next to them. It was distracting emotionally. I wanted to be intentional, especially with Robert and Jim around. The customers, who were loud, called out to me.

"Miss, we'll have some coffee."

"Sure. One moment."

I went to retrieve the cups and saucers. Pouring their coffee, I glanced up and saw Madame appearing at the cash register. She was early. The door opened again.

Miles and Helga came in. I was both happy and distraught. They were my friends, but I had to keep this purely business with Madame around.

I quickly went to retrieve two more coffee cups and saucers and placed them on Miles and Helga's table. We greeted each other as I poured their coffee. I hadn't seen them in a long time, and they looked well. We exchanged pleasantries.

"Miss?"

It was the rude customers. I had forgotten to take their orders.

"I have to go," I said rather abruptly to Miles and Helga.

The rude customers wanted two hot cinnamon rolls with butter and two hot bear claws, which was the bakery's specialty. I placed them in the warmer that was near the coffee area.

"You need to be faster!" screamed Madame in a whisper.

"Yes, Madame."

Then I realized I forgot to take Miles and Helga's order. And Robert was watching it all from a few feet away.

I returned with the sweets for the customers and turned to Miles and Helga.

"I'm sorry to make you wait."

"Oh, that's okay," said Helga, kindly.

I took their pastry orders and packaged a box of cookies as well for them. When I returned to their table, I noticed Robert and Jim had left. I hadn't even heard the door open.

During my lunch break, I ate my sandwich at the church and reflected on what had happened that morning. I was flustered, not because I was slow, but because it felt like two worlds collided within me: the world of life on the planet, the life of a machine, and the world of school on the planet, the possibility of man's conscious evolution. It was difficult to operate my machine while being present. That was it in a nutshell. I hoped the evening meeting would shed light on this.

* * * *

My car was full of students, since we had visitors from Vacaville. I parked behind four other cars on the shoulder on the side of the main gate entrance to the Carmel Highlands house. Using a flashlight, we walked down the narrow road leading to the house.

The hallway was crowded with visitors from the Bay Area, who had just arrived. Among them was Millicent, who handed me an envelope containing my photos. I was delighted to receive it, and instantly had an imaginary idea of how my face would appear. I handed her the remaining sum owed, and took the pictures into the living room. The room was almost filled, since it was approaching the meeting time. I located a small chair in the corner. I needed privacy to view this.

I pulled out the three photos. The first was my face as if I were staring in the mirror. This I recognized. The second was my right-side face, which represented my personality side. It pleased me. It was thin and had angular features, showing the Mercurial part of my nature. The third was my left-side face, which displayed my essence. It was broad and fleshy, with a thick nose and no bone structure revealed. This was a pure Venusian face. That's my essence? I was horrified. I was fat by nature.

"Let me see," asked a male student from the farm, who had watched me thumb through the photos.

"No, it's fine," I replied quickly, while stuffing them back into the envelope.

"Come on," he insisted.

"The meeting's about to begin. I'll show you later." Of course, I had no intention of doing so.

The meeting was indeed about to begin. I looked up and Robert had just taken his seat in the front. I would be watching the meeting in the far back corner of the room.

After good householder, Robert began to teach.

"We appear to be a major school manifesting in a major time of humanity, and more conscious beings should come from our school than any other time since the Renaissance. This is a theory, and not a fact, and relentless time will verify this at one level or another. A theory is a theory until it is verified and becomes fact."

He paused for this to sink in.

"It requires a strong magnetic center, fate, and luck to meet a conscious teaching and remain. One of the tools C Influence uses is to have their students work with prospective students simply for shocks, when the persons are not fated to join the Fellowship of Friends. It also allows students to teach and not to identify with the result of their efforts."

He took a sip of water before continuing.

"When we meet a teaching, we begin an ascending octave that will last our whole life, for those who penetrate the inner circle. It is often two steps forward and one step back, which can be depressing. This occurs because our being at that time is inadequate in its ability to separate."

There was a pause. Robert, who had been signing his words to Jim, instead wrote this note for Jim to read.

"Robert underlined this sentence," began Jim. "DO NOT TAKE ANY 'I' FOR THE WHOLE." He paused before reading the last part of the note. "This is advice that is difficult for any of us to be. Please remember at these times I love you more than ever."

It was a powerful statement.

Robert resumed signing to Jim.

"The farther we go, the more it is seen C Influence does everything significant in humanity and around each of us in our daily lives. They even 'think' our positive and negative emotions, and do the looking exercise for us. We are truly noble vegetables."

He then asked for questions.

"When one is able to stop thoughts and just be, is one looking through the Self?"

"If the state that watches from you is silence," responded Robert, "then it is the Self."

Another hand was raised.

"How can my being work against self-pity?"

"Try to do the looking and listening exercises," Robert replied. "Look, read, walk, listen to positive music — classical is best — or be with friends. Keep trying to cut off the self-pity 'I's, even though they are justified on a mechanical level, yet not on an astral level, as self-pity 'I's are food for the Self. Allow for failures, remembering in the lives of the best of humans, rain must fall.

"One of the most useful tools C Influence has is to arrange a shock that does not make sense. A common shock they use for a number four being is to arrange something negative while the student is attempting to do something kind. This is about all an emotional center can take, as it fumes, and we attempt to separate. The queen of hearts has no soul and yet it creates one."

These were the angles I was looking for, although they were not in the words I expected. This is practical and helpful advice.

Other questions and angles came, but I was focused on these little gems I received. I let them go deeper into me and hoped to preserve them for later use.

The meeting concluded, and we gathered around the big table laden with snacks. I noticed a stack of the latest *Via Del Sol Journal,* and took my copy.

Thumbing through it, I saw angles from Yorgos. One in particular resonated with me. He described how to regulate the feeding of the wolf, which was a concept Robert had introduced. Yorgos observed that it was good to feed the wolf — the lower self — occasionally so that it would not threaten one's work on nourishing the Higher Self. Yorgos added that a properly fed wolf does not increase in size, permitting one's level of being to grow and strengthen, and that problems themselves will diminish over time.

"Can I see your photos?"

This was the male student that asked me earlier.

"Oh, you have your photos!" said a woman. She added that Millicent did hers as well.

She reached out for it and I mechanically handed it to her, while reading the other four angles from Yorgos that were printed.

"Boy, this is interesting! You have a real different personality and essence. Mine was pretty much the same."

She was a beautiful woman. Didn't surprise me.

"Wow, you really do have Venusian," remarked the male student, looking over her shoulder.

"Photograph REALLY," I replied, a bit irritated at this observation.

"Oh! Thanks."

Putting down my journal, I turned to this fellow.

"How is Yorgos?" I asked.

"Oh, he's fine. Working the fields, you know," he said chuckling. "He's a farmer in his essence."

"Let me look at these!" said a third student, peering over the shoulder at my photos.

It had become a topic of conversation. Millicent approached and began her sales pitch. I was not pleased. In fact, I was ready to go. Taking my photos back, I went to those students who rode with me to inform them I was leaving. All said they were not ready to leave and agreed they would find a ride back to Whitman Circle.

The flashlight we used to arrive didn't belong to me so I walked slowly in the dark to my car. Each step required acute attention. While sitting in the driver's seat, waiting for the traffic flow to stop, an inner quietness emerged that was glad to be where it was, in this moment. The 'I's were background murmurs. No button-pushing here.

At the house, the fresh cool breeze heightened my senses as I stepped out of the car. The many 'I's wanted to be heard, but not even images from the meeting gained permission to enter. Near the outdoor lamp illuminating the driveway was a bougainvillea bush clinging to the side of the house. Its intense magenta shone quietly under the spotlight. It greeted me and held me in its enchanting simplicity for minutes.

Could there be a better ending to a tumultuous day?

❖

"When the sun has set, and the moon has set and the fire has gone out and speech has stopped, what serves as light for a man?"
"The self, indeed, is his light, for with the self as light he sits, goes out, works and returns."

Upanishads

CHAPTER 163

The streets of Carmel had a different feel once the Labor Day weekend was over. They were quieter. It was an interesting thing to observe. During summer, Carmel along Ocean Avenue shouted opulence and refinement and charm, with its boutique shops and quaint inns. The bakery was part of this illusion, giving visitors a taste of old Denmark. But if you walk the blocks away from the main drag of Ocean Avenue, you will find the true heart of Carmel. In September, the residents of Carmel took back their town.

Madame surprised me one morning by introducing me to a young girl named Camille, who would be a bakery clerk. It was odd timing, since the crowds were smaller. I had the sense she did not trust in my abilities. Oh, well.

Camille was a gentle girl, around my age. She was demure, with soft long blond hair and doe-like blue eyes, and her figure was petite. I would guess a Lunar type, which was the midpoint of femininity. We liked each other immediately.

It was my turn to teach her how to caress the morning buns, how to load the dishwasher, and how to clean the display cases. She was a natural and did not need second instructions. It was interesting to me that Miguel did not flirt with her. In fact, I noticed he was less social in the morning, and as soon as everything was done, he left. Madame no longer covered a particular time now that a second bakery girl was hired. Instead, Madame was making her appearance at various times of the day. We never knew when she would appear.

The days at the bakery were becoming routine, and I looked forward to my evenings with students, either at the Whitman Circle house with the ladies or at the Chopstix with Meg and her motley entourage.

THE SEEDS OF

By Friday night, Klair informed me that Robert was in town and we would have another meeting at the Carmel Highlands house Saturday evening. The pleasant weather suited him. His presence was bringing emotional stability to me, and conscious momentum, although I seem to recall Ouspensky claimed there was no such thing. Regardless, a meeting with the teacher resulted in an opportunity to string more conscious moments on my pearl-of-great-price invisible necklace. This was fact, not theory.

Rosemary had informed me Saturday morning that she was having lunch at Sheila's with Robert regularly and that he used the time there to select the graphic ornaments, called "dingbats," that would appear on the pages of next week's journal. I had no idea he was working when he was there. I thought he was socializing and resting.

Around 3 p.m., Madame said she would return at six to tally the receipts and lock up for the evening. She had a dinner party to attend and was going to the hairdresser for an appointment. We were to stay until she returned.

At four, Camille was serving the only customer, when a bold thought entered my head. I acted on it.

Debbie had informed me when I started that we could take home any broken cookies. Knowing this, I went in the back and broke a few of the expensive ones that were still on trays and put them in a bag and took the bag downstairs to the garage that stored not only bakery supplies and Madame's car, but was the place of our toilet, too. I then grabbed a broom resting against the wall there and returned to the bakery counter.

"Camille, I'm going to sweep the sidewalk in front of the shop. This will make Madame happy. I'll be back soon."

"Okay," she replied without hesitation.

I started to sweep along 7th Avenue, heading toward Lincoln. Popping into the garage space, which was left open, I grabbed the bag of cookies with one hand and held the broom in the other. I gleefully and quickly headed toward Sheila's apartment a block away.

Climbing the stairs, I knocked on the door and when Jim opened it, I said, "Special delivery!"

I entered and saw Robert quietly cutting a dingbat with a small, sharp pair of scissors. He didn't look up. Jim, instead, ushered me into the kitchen, where I showed him the fragments of cookies. I told him they were delicious, and he thanked me before escorting me out the door.

Happy I saw Robert, at least, I rushed back to the bakery and entered through the front door. I must have been gone fifteen minutes or so.

THE DIVINE BEGINNING

"Where were you?" asked Camille.

"Oh, I just kept sweeping. Anyway, here I am. I'll start cleaning the cases," I said, changing the subject.

At the end of my work day, while walking to my car, the quiet image of Robert came to my mind. There he was, focusing on the simple task at hand. And there I was, spewing my emotional energy throughout the room. That was not my expectation. I thought I would be greeted with open arms. Instead, it was a photograph for me. I had no control of centers. How do I go from that to living within that silent space where Robert resides?

A soft voice in my head answered, "Stay the course."

* * * *

By the time I arrived home, the house was empty. I quickly showered and hopped into the car to drive to the Highlands. There were no parking spaces on the gate-side of the highway, so I turned into the gas station and parked nearby, which meant I had to cross the lanes of fast-moving traffic on foot. It was crazy. I had to time the traffic flow perfectly.

It was dusk when I entered the house. The hallway was empty. As I went into the living room, students were already seated and a splendid ruby and sapphire sunset could be seen through the large windows. A student motioned to me to sit with her on the crowded couch against the back wall. Adrenaline was flowing inside, which fueled my focus.

The meeting was about to begin. After good householder, Robert waited for the room to settle down before starting.

"Students are here to gain as many moments of Self-consciousness as possible from their play. This is what death will not take. Christ informed us every hair is counted, meaning moments of self-remembering are not lost, and pass from one ascending life to another.

" 'Choice' or 'will' is a naïve Western idea. Choice or will can come only from a complete number five, six or seven being at the death of the physical body. They know they are in a play, so how can there be choice? There can be the 'play' of choice, yet this is not choice. The conscious Egyptian priests said they were slaves to the deity, in gratitude.

"We have the play of choice until our being reaches a level where we see we have fate, and do not have choice. If we have fate, then we can realize we can be nowhere else but in our school, and what a gift, and what luck!"

Miles, who was sitting up front with Robert, raised his hand slightly to be called upon. Robert acknowledged him to proceed.

With a serious face, Miles offered, "In our plays, we don't know our lines ahead of time, so we don't have to worry about forgetting them."

One, two, three. The room burst out laughing. Even Robert had a big grin on his face. It was so refreshing to see Miles with a sense of humor.

"That was a good joke," responded Robert.

I looked at Miles. He wasn't laughing. Maybe it wasn't a joke to him. Hmmm.

A Saturnine student from the Bay Area raised his hand.

"Don't we have some form of will?"

"What I presently observe as our machines' biggest drawback is willfulness," replied Robert. "I do not think it can be completely overcome, yet we can attempt to minimize willfulness. One way willfulness manifests is through personality in us that wants to be the 'doer' in situations. That is identification.

"This is a theory for Fellowship students, yet a fact for me," he continued, "that neither you nor I do anything. C Influence controls every word that is uttered here."

"But will is the force behind our efforts, right?" added the Bay Area student.

Robert paused, looking up before speaking. I wondered how he would address this.

"What you wish is a lie, instead of the truth, to fit your imagination. Man wishes the truth as he sees it, not as it is; he prefers allurement. Remember, Peter Ouspensky formulated correctly that humans can only receive the truth in the form of a lie, primarily because existence is simple. In Zen, before enlightenment, a student was told to eat his food and wash his dish. After enlightenment, he ate his food and washed his dish."

Robert stood up, which signaled the first half of the meeting was over. I went to the dining table for some snacks and stood next to Miles.

"It was nice to see you at the bakery," I said.

"It looks like you're doing well," he replied.

"I'm surviving, I guess."

Helga approached us. "We are moving to Carmel," she said.

I was stunned.

"Yes," Miles clarified, "the job came through at the Marble Ranch."

I had only heard briefly about this but didn't want to know more. I smiled and offered congratulations, then took my full plate and sat down on the couch from where I had watched the meeting. I had no idea why this affected me so, but my heart sank. Somehow, I felt I was free from having to see them regularly together, like the mornings at the ranch when I would find them cuddled under the fig tree. It was difficult. I was identified. The wound began to weep anew.

When I went to leave, I walked out with several students, and one of them, a sweet fellow, told me to give him my car keys and he would gladly bring my car around so I wouldn't have to cross the highway. We watched as he did this. It was so gentlemanly of him. Why couldn't I find someone like this? He was married. And I was alone.

> *Lady, be so kind as to purify this heart and this life that I place in your hands. For only you are favored with the gift to cleanse all stains.*
>
> Quetzalcoatl

CHAPTER 164

My head was swimming the next morning when I arose. It was Sunday, September 10, my half-birthday. Twenty-three and a half years old.

I was quiet throughout my shift, which was strange not only to Camille but also to my regular customers. I lived in a glass house, emotionally, and could never hide the hundreds of subtle shades of my disposition. Why did this hang over me so? Seeing Miles and Helga frequently in Carmel would be a constant reminder of the intense need I had for the comfort of a man, and the gods' deprivation of it.

The gods provided shocks that day, half-birthday presents I guess you can say. Madame was yelling at me to focus more on the customers. I was sleepwalking to be sure. A man sat at one of the tables reading a book with the title, *You Haven't Slept*. I went back to the dishwasher with a tray of coffee cups, but instead of rinsing them out at the sink, I took one cup that was half-full of mocha-colored liquid and tossed it into the machine. It flew back at Madame and drenched her perfectly white uniform. She screamed and punched me. I deserved it.

When I arrived home, a letter was waiting on my bed, with my name on it. It was from UCLA and had the Dobbins address. It was a big shock. It meant the university now had my Carmel address and was after me for student loan payments. I'm sure my father gave it to them. He turned me in.

That was all I needed. I was emotionally distraught. Who could I talk with? Maybe John, who had provided the comfort I longed for before. Perhaps he's home. I showered and fixed my face, but the mirror slipped in my hand and shattered. Oh, perfect. Seven years of bad luck.

But that did not deter me. I went to my car and drove to John's house. His bike was outside. I knocked on the door. I rang the bell. But no one answered. I sat on the steps, head in hands, crying. I need to talk with someone. Why isn't he there? I peered through the windows even though the curtains were pulled down, and tried knocking again and again. After an hour, I knew it was futile. Where can I go? I decided to drive to the Highlands house, hoping Jim would be there. He wasn't. No one was there. No one was home.

No one was home.

Oh, my. I sat in the car and saw the frenetic energy of the queen of hearts chasing one illusion after another, one craving after another craving. When I'm in that state, the higher in me is absent. It's not home. That is the lesson.

The depth of the pain of solitude penetrated not only my soul but my body. I felt sick to my stomach. These feelings and thoughts were not new to me. They were as old as childhood. I cannot rely on anyone. No one is there to help me. I alone have to help myself. Even having the school in my life did not bring me the type of joy and harmony I longed for. In fact, it was the opposite experience since meeting the Fellowship. Through middle school, high school, and university, there was no companion. Here, at least, were people of my own persuasion, with similar values, interests, and insights. But no one here to love me, to be faithful to me.

With tears in my eyes, I drove back to the Whitman House and went directly to my room. The internal tempest had finally passed when the last teardrop dried upon my cheek. I was in a higher state, it seemed, but it was not joyful. I was numb emotionally. I was spent.

Looking up at the ceiling, I asked the gods, Is this what you wish for me? Why am I being punished? I'm a good person. Why am I attracting this play? Why are you not giving me love?

I sat at the edge of my bed, waiting for a divine response.

They did not answer.

In the end, these things matter most: How well did you love? How fully did you live? How deeply did you learn to let go?
Buddha

PART VI
The Next Beginning

CHAPTER 165

TWO WEEKS HAD gone by. I was in a perpetual fog. A deep anger was building up inside of me. The object of my negativity? The gods.

One morning, Camille and I were chatting as we slathered the cinnamon rolls and boxed them.

"I'm getting married," she said.

"No kidding!"

"Jeff and I have finally set a date. I'd like you to come."

It was so thoughtful that she would ask me to attend her wedding, which is one of the milestones of life.

"Sure. I'd be honored."

"We're having a bridal reception on Saturday at seven. I wondered if you would have time to help me prepare for it."

"What time?"

"After work on Friday. I need help making the hors d'oeuvres. Could you come?"

"I'd be happy to help, Camille."

"That's really nice of you. Cool."

"No problem. My pleasure."

I smiled as I completed the final order. It was a different feeling inside, and I liked it. The thought of going to her house and helping was a welcome break from my circumstances and state. There was a part of me that felt a little guilty that I was hanging out with someone who was not in the school, but I felt this was okay for once. I just wouldn't tell the house ladies.

* * * *

After work, I drove to her home in Carmel Valley. It was a modest house and she lived there with her mother, who was of Greek origin. I had no idea that Camille was traditional like this, not living with her boyfriend until they were married.

The kitchen was small and filled with foodstuffs, some already cooked, some in preparation mode, and others simply ingredients for use. Her aunt and mother were large, and they worked at the stove and sink as if they were conjoined twins. There was a harmony in their movements.

"We'll be making the mini spanakopita on the dining table," Camille said. The table was within eyesight of the kitchen, although it was not part of it.

I sat at the table, just observing her mother and aunt working together. It was going to be a lavish buffet. Her mother was happy that her daughter was able to find a friend to help her. She thanked me profusely. It was a large family, and many women would be attending.

"Have you made this before?" asked her mother, as she brought the items to the table.

"No."

She began to show me how to unfold the phyllo dough that came in sheets and cut it into squares using a ruler and small knife. You had to place a small amount of the mixture (spinach and cheese) in just the right place before folding it over to make a triangle.

"You must work fast because the dough dries up quickly and becomes brittle. Camille, why not show her?"

It was nice to see the respect between Camille and her mother. Camille was wearing bell bottoms with colors of green and purple and pink flowers and a tie-dyed shirt with streaks of red and orange and blue. Her mother had on an old-fashioned apron that covered her chest as well as her lap. Two different generations without discord. I admired that.

We worked for two hours, chatting about her wedding plans, how she met Jeff, her desire for children. She asked me if I had a boyfriend.

"Not at this time," I said smiling. This was no place to play my album of sad songs.

There was a different Linda here. It was such a relief to be above the self-pity 'I's that were so addictive. It was also healing to be helping. Yet, something was missing in this picture.

Before I knew it, it was approaching nine o'clock. I was feeling quite tired. We had completed 72 of the 100 triangles she had planned to make. She noticed my exhaustion. The next day was her day off but for me it was a work day.

"It's fine if you want to go," she said.

"Oh. Are you sure?"

"Yes. You have to get up early."

She walked me to my car that was parked in a crowded driveway illuminated by the garage's single beam of light. Her mother and aunt joined us and they each hugged me, in sweet gratitude.

As I drove home, that missing piece of the picture came into view. Camille had a pleasant home, and I could feel the affection, the connection, the traditional path to happiness. But there was no presence. It was clear their hands operated independently from the rest of their bodies, their eyes were not looking at me when they spoke, but gazing past me, unfocused, while their mouths moved. They were automatons with no light inside, however pleasant they were. It was not judgment. It was what it was.

And it made me sad. Another part inside longed deeply for this illusory happiness. The craving would not go away. It would be my struggle, and I hated the gods for putting me in this no-man's-land of wanting to awaken and not achieving it and wanting to sleep yet being unable to slumber with sweet, hopeful dreams. My sleep had forever been disturbed. I knew too much and verified too much. I was living a nightmare no matter where I turned.

Would the gods leave me stuck here forever? It seemed so.

Who never ate his bread in sorrow,
Who never spent the darksome hours weeping,
And watching for the morrow,
He knows you not, ye heavenly Powers.

Johann Goethe

CHAPTER 166

The next day at work was difficult, not from any external pressure from Madame or customers, but from an inner one. The negativity that lodged in my heart was like a fuel leak in my car. I had little energy to complete the tasks that already had become so mechanical. I could barely cross the finish line of five o'clock.

I called Camille and cancelled the bridal shower that evening, with my apologies. There was a meeting with Robert, but my body would not permit me to prepare to leave the house. Something was wrong. I felt as if my pneumonia was returning, because the ache in my heart and lungs was profound. Sunday was my day off and I took advantage of it. I stayed in bed most of the day, and slept.

By Wednesday, I was increasingly weaker, and my symptoms were strange. It was like no kind of sickness I had ever had, and there was no label to it. Mucus came out of my eyes, my nose, my throat and my urine that morning. I made it to work, but excused myself to use the toilet within two hours of arriving. I rested my head against the wall and could not move. Something dire was happening to me, and for the first time I was scared. Should I call an ambulance? That would cost money. I had no money. It was clear I could not complete my shift. How would I explain this to Camille and Madame?

I went to lunch and decided on a root beer float at a local hamburger place. It always cheered me up and was a treat since childhood. One sip of it and I wanted to throw up. It was clearly the wrong direction. I had no choice. I went back to the bakery and explained to Camille I was sick and needed to go home.

"Take care of yourself!"

I waved as I exited.

Marie and Klair were home when I arrived and were surprised to see me. I explained I felt ill and was going straight to bed. That was the last I saw them that day.

When I awoke the next morning, I remembered I had that book from Nadia about mucusless diets. As I was reading it in earnest, Klair knocked on the door to check on me.

"Do you want something to eat?"

"Maybe a salad."

About an hour later she brought it to me.

"How are you feeling?" she said, checking my temperature. It was almost normal.

"Still feeling weird."

I tried to put a fork filled with salad in my mouth. My hand would not complete the insert. This was STRANGE. It was like a child that turned its head from the food the mother tried to feed it, knowing full well this was the wrong food to eat. The body was now in control. That is the king of clubs, the mind behind the organism, I thought. It is in survival-mode.

"I think I'll have some apple juice," it said to Klair.

"Apple juice?"

"Yes."

"I don't have any. I'll have to buy it. It will be later in the day."

"That's okay."

She left me alone with the book. It was strange that the book had proposed eating raw vegetables, like a salad, to cure a person of mucus, which Dr. Ehret claimed was a source of illness. But my king of clubs wouldn't allow me to eat what the good doctor swore was healthy for it. How could that be? Who

THE DIVINE BEGINNING

is this guy? I turned to the back cover and read this was a system to cleanse and heal the body. I saw a picture of him. His beady eyes and thin frame suggested he was instinctively centered with an intellectual element. He was 55 years old when he died. That doesn't seem like a long life to me.

I put the book away.

Instead, I was left to my thoughts and a weakened body and a pack of cigarettes. Oh, yes, I was still smoking through it all, even the pneumonia. It gave me something to do.

* * * *

Around 2 p.m., I decided to take a shower. It felt good to soap my body, but when I toweled off, my skin began to itch. I looked at my legs and they were blotchy. How strange. The more I scratched, the itchier it was.

I returned to bed. I put the pack of cigarettes away. Scratching became my new occupation.

* * * *

Klair returned with the apple juice. She left two quarts. I drank the first one immediately, as if I were stranded in the Sahara.

I didn't see her until the next day.

* * * *

Klair appeared around noon. I told her to buy a gallon of apple juice. And a box of Kleenex. The mucus was intensifying.

She left me to my scratching.

* * * *

Another day passed. Another gallon of apple juice. And an overflowing basket of Kleenex. Klair was now dropping in whenever she could. Sometimes she would skip a day.

* * * *

Weighed myself today. I've lost twenty pounds in the last six weeks. Looking in the mirror, I noticed the whites of my eyes were becoming golden against my baby blues. UCLA colors. Go Bruins.

* * * *

Rosemary came to see me. She was in shock.

"You look awful. I'm bringing Mac."

"Okay," I said softly, thinking, I'm not going anywhere soon anyway.

* * * *

The next day, Mac stopped by.

"What day is it?" I asked.

"Monday."

"I mean, what's the date?"

"October second."

What? September is gone?

After a quick medical check, and a few questions, Mac made his pronouncement.

"You have infectious hepatitis. Stay in bed, rest, and quarantine yourself."

"I'm doing that."

"Good. I'll be back to check on you."

When he left, I went to use the bathroom and Marie met me at the door.

"You're NOT to use this bathroom. I don't want to come down with infectious hepatitis. Mac said you're in quarantine."

"But I have to use the toilet," I pleaded.

Klair heard the commotion and came to my aid.

"Marie, she needs to use the bathroom. Let her in."

The two went back and forth, and Klair won. I entered and noticed for the first time how thin and jaundiced I was. I did look scary. I'm sorry, Marie. I did not mean to upset you. She did not hear me.

She was on the other side of the door, with gloves and bleach, ready to erase the source of her discomfort.

I returned to my room. The scratching was now removing scabs that had formed all over my legs, and orange ooze was appearing instead of blood. Deep scars were visible in other places. My legs would be marred for years to come, I thought, and hard to hide. Like a leper.

* * * *

The next afternoon, there was a knock on the door.

"Yes? Come in." I grabbed my glasses to see who it was.

It opened slowly. There was Robert.

"Hi Robert!" I said, waving at him. My voice was weak, but my heart was strong and elated. My teacher came to visit!

But he did not respond equally. Instead, he gasped, threw his hand over his mouth, as tears welled in his eyes, and his head shook in dismay. He turned and left, gently closing the door behind him.

My heart sank. Why did he leave so abruptly? I was hoping he would come in, write a few kind words while sitting on the side of my bed. I needed comfort more than ever now. Was I that disfigured? I am fine, Robert. Here I am. I am here. Nothing has changed. It's still me. Linda.

* * * *

THE DIVINE BEGINNING

Another week went by without visitors, and Klair was losing patience with her tending, or so it seemed, since she would come when it fit her schedule, not my needs.

I started to read that book on my nightstand, *Bury My Heart at Wounded Knee*. It penetrated me as I read about the fate of those Indians who had no choice but to submit to their destiny. It was brutal, and destructive, and full of injustice.

The appearance of this book was no accident. Something inside of me, too, was brutally and unjustly being destroyed. I could feel it deeply. The gods are fond of metaphors. This one was not lost upon me.

* * * *

One afternoon, the door opened. It was not Klair. It was a man. He was a mercurial type. He greeted me and introduced himself as a new student.

"I have infectious hepatitis, and am quarantined," I explained, thinking he would be driven away by that. But he wasn't.

He approached my bed and sat on the edge.

"Aren't you afraid you'll catch it?"

"No," he smiled.

He held my hand and we spoke a bit about the book that lay open upon my breasts. He removed it to thumb through the pages and placed it on the nightstand. He then reached over and his soft lips pressed against mine. The human contact that had been so missing was finally sent. He caressed my face and hair, looking into my eyes without fear, but with affection and compassion.

He slithered his body next to mine and I welcomed it as he pressed himself against my withered frame. The weight of another human, and the gentle touches, nourished that aching need for connection.

The kisses came and I was focused on them, as his hand followed the curve of my body.

And then disappeared below.

Wait…wait… something's not right.

He's doing something else.

He reappeared…he entered

I did not see it

Until I felt it

I did not believe it

Until he was done

What just happened? No. That could not be.

It doesn't matter now. It's over and he's withdrawn.

I lay still. Raising my eyes from the reclined position, I watched him approach the door. He turned and looked at me, with a satisfied, sinister expression, as he exited.

It is done.

It is done.

It is done.

༺

Divine Providence permits these trials to assail us for the great benefit of our soul; from them we acquire a contrite and humble heart which God will not despise.

Philokalia, Bishop Ignatii

CHAPTER 167

Mac returned a week later.

"I'm feeling much better now, and the eye discharges have stopped. But I'm still itchy. When can I leave this room?"

"Oh, you could have left the room a week ago."

"A week ago?"

"Yes. But you need to go to a doctor first to be tested. You're not contagious anymore."

"I don't have a doctor."

"I'll find one for you and give the information to Marie."

He left the room. I went to shower, hoping I could finally be out in the sun and fresh air that day. Marie stopped at the doorframe shortly thereafter and told me that because I did not have any insurance, the doctor that Mac recommended would not see me.

"They said you need to go to the county hospital. It's a public one, and they will take you there. But it's in Salinas."

"Will you drive me?"

"No. I do not want to be in the same car with you, because you still may be contagious until I know for sure from the doctor."

"But Mac said I wasn't contagious."

She wouldn't listen to this. She said both Klair and Rose were not around either.

I had to drive myself if I wanted to be released from this bedroom prison. I accepted it.

* * * *

I decided to leave the next morning. When I turned on the ignition, the Wildcat groaned from misuse. Finally, the engine engaged as if the memory of how it functioned came back to it suddenly. I could relate. I pulled out of the driveway slowly, both hands on the wheel. I was frail and a bit shaky, yet determined to drive the forty-five minutes or so to the county hospital.

I knew this road. It was Highway 68, the same one I took at the start of my trip to Los Angeles. I could see the Linda who had travelled there, trying with all her might to focus on each sign so that she would not become lost. The effort to divide attention was massive then. This was only five months ago.

This Linda had no such struggle. There was no energy for anxiety or anger. Through bodily illness, the gods had reduced me to a tiny dot of a person. It was quiet in the cab. There was a gentle energy inside of me, measured, yet flowing. Fall was that type of season, too. The exhausted landscape that flew by my window, having yielded its harvest, mirrored my state.

I turned right onto East Blanco Road, then left on San Juan Drive, and right on San Jose Drive. A sign appeared leading me to the hospital and parking. As I shut off the engine, I sat still. My body did not want to move. It, like the car, had come to a rest, as if the parking lot were its destination. The effort this time was not a mental one, but a physical one. I had to move.

Walking through the front door, the waiting room was filled with poor Mexican farmers and their families. Children ran around while parents let them. I could see another Linda would have wasted energy on judgment. That was not the case here, now. From this state, it simply was what it was: children running around while parents let them.

I went to the registry and told them my condition and reason for coming.

"Take a seat. We'll call you."

I found a chair facing the door that would open when a nurse would call out a name. I waited for my name to be called. I waited a long time.

When my name was called, I was led to a room by a woman who clearly was not a nurse. She pointed to a chair for me to occupy. She sat across from me, with her papers on a square table.

"I need to ask you some questions to see if you're able to pay for your treatment."

"Okay." I smiled weakly.

"Do you own a car?"

"Yes."

"Do you have a job?"

I thought for a moment. Madame said it may not be there when I recovered, so I answered No.

She went down a list: bank accounts (No), real estate (No), furniture (No). When she finally asked me if I owned a radio, and my reply was No, she put her pen down and looked at me with a sweet smile of compassion.

"Don't worry. You qualify for state medical assistance as well as food stamps."

"I don't know what that is."

She looked at me in wonder. Perhaps I was the only person who spoke native English who had said this to her. Once she explained the help I could receive, she steadied me as I rose and took me into a large, open room filled with single beds with long curtains separating them.

"Sit here," she said, motioning for me to place myself at the edge of one of the beds, "while I get the doctor."

I could barely sit straight. My body hunched over within a few minutes. The doctor did not arrive for thirty minutes. I looked at my watch, and simply waited. It reminded me of the final exam at UCLA. Time moved. I did not. There were no thoughts circulating within me. It was peaceful.

"Hello...Linda?"

"Yes."

"I'm Doctor White."

"How do you do?" I said, mechanically.

He checked my pulse, and looked into my eyes.

"You clearly have jaundice. I will need to run some tests."

He left and brought a nurse with him.

She began to draw blood from my left arm. The floor started to spin and my body collapsed forward. I heard the doctor say "Whoa!!" as he steadied me.

"Go get some orange juice," he ordered the nurse, adding, "I'm going to run these tests now."

She came back quickly with a plastic cup.

"Drink this."

I felt much better. I laid down and waited for my test results. The nurse had closed the curtain, and I fell asleep.

Another hour had passed when the sound of the curtain ripping open awakened me. It was the doctor with papers in his hands. He helped me to sit up.

"You have the highest bilirubin count of anyone I've ever treated."

"What does that mean?"

"It's an indicator of jaundice and perhaps liver disease."

"Do I have liver disease?"

"Not necessarily."

He began to explain things. I did not understand it. He assured me my other vital signs were good and that this would pass, but I needed to be sure I ate nutritious food. I did not know what he meant by nutritious food. He handed me a pamphlet.

"You're no longer contagious and do not have to quarantine."

That's all I wanted to know.

I drove back to the Whitman Circle house. I immediately announced to everyone that I was no longer contagious. I went straight to my room and collapsed on my bed. Glasses off and eyes closed. Sleep was waiting for me there.

*A gem cannot be polished without friction,
nor a man perfected without trials.*

Seneca

CHAPTER 168

It was noon by the time my eyes opened. I was still tired, but more hungry than tired. I dreamt of a steak and baked potato with sour cream and cooked vegetables. It was my king of clubs commanding this menu. I no longer questioned its demands. After showering and dressing, I planned to drive to a restaurant and order it.

As I entered the kitchen, Rosemary and Marie were having lunch at the table.

"How do you feel?" asked Rose.

"I'm still quite tired but I finally slept well."

"You're less yellow," observed Marie.

I put some makeup on, trying to hide it. I thanked her.

"What's the date?"

They looked at each other, a bit bewildered.

"It's October 23rd," said Rose.

"Monday," chimed in Marie.

They saw the shocked look on my face. My first thought was my teaching payment. I wanted to go to the restaurant, but I'll need to pay my donation. I need to call the bakery. I need to work.

Klair walked in and went to the coffee maker.

"How are you feeling?"

I told her what I told Rose and Marie.

"Maybe you should go to the ranch for a month to recuperate."

Rose and Marie said nothing. Back to the good ol' womb, I thought. I did not like this idea. I wanted to be settled, and Carmel is the place where I could at least find a job that would take care of my basic needs.

"I'm going out," I said. "I need some sunshine."

The ladies wished me a good day, each in their own way.

As I pulled out of the driveway, I was surprised that I did not go to a restaurant, but headed toward Ocean Avenue. Something was waiting for me there.

* * * *

The ocean. It was magnificent. I parked at the end of the avenue and walked along the beach. There was a bench, unoccupied. I sat there, legs crossed, a gentle breeze moving my tresses across my face. My hand gently pushed them aside. The warmth of the sun was soaking into me, revitalizing and replenishing what had been lost over these weeks of isolation. The roar of the crashing waves reminded me of my poem. Now I see I only understood it poetically. The sand was not brutalized at all. It was grateful to the waves. Its existence and true identity depended on them.

I sat and watched. And was content just to be there. Time passed, but I had no place to go. How long could I support this state? It was so pure.

"May I sit here?"

It was a man. He was attractive and looked like a gentleman.

"I have infectious hepatitis," I replied, not so much to protect him as to protect myself from him.

"That's okay. I've had it."

It was a public bench and I did not feel I could tell him to leave.

"Beautiful, isn't it?"

I nodded and smiled, not taking my eyes off the horizon.

"It's a beautiful day. Would you like to take a drive with me?"

"No, I'm fine. I prefer to stay here."

"Big Sur is more beautiful. Come on," he said enticingly, "I have a convertible MG. It'll be fun."

An MG is a rare sports car, and expensive.

"No, it's…it's fine."

"Come on…," he coaxed, attempting to put his arm around my shoulders.

THE DIVINE BEGINNING

"NO!" I replied emphatically, standing up and leaving.

He did not follow me, although I did look back a few times. I was saddened that my state was disturbed like that. It was time, however, to feed my machine. I drove to the Del Monte shopping center, thinking I'd find a steakhouse, and I did. I placed the order, and insisted on a bottle of ketchup, which they brought. The first bite pleased my body as much as that first sip of apple juice. It was the right food, and the five dollars spent was well worth it.

When I returned home, I wondered why I was attracting the wrong attention. I decided to weigh myself. I had lost 32 pounds since these illnesses began. I had become attractive, despite my yellowing. Men take advantage of vulnerable women. I had to learn to protect myself.

* * * *

The next day, my energy did not return. I slept late again, and managed to shower and dress by eleven. I entered the kitchen, and found an unknown man sitting at the table having coffee.

I went to pour coffee without acknowledging him, and he greeted me anyway.

"I heard you were sick. I'm Jim Keahey, and we met in Vacaville when I joined the school. I just moved here."

I looked at him, and suddenly remembered. It was his bright blue eyes and happy smile and curly dark hair that brought me back to the memory of his first meeting. He stood out.

"Oh, my, yes! You joined with Jean."

"Jean?"

Then I realized he may not have known Jean. People are introduced together at their first meeting with Robert, even though they may have joined separately at different centers.

"The tall Saturn lady. Anyway, it's nice to see you."

"Would you like to go on the porch for some sun?"

"Sounds nice. Yes."

We went out on the deck and Jim moved two chairs for us to sit, chat, and sip our coffees together.

"I got a job as a waiter at the Sardine Factory," he explained.

"You said 'got.'"

"Oh! Thank you."

"You're welcome."

I smiled. "Wow, the Sardine Factory is very high class."

"You said 'very.'"

We both giggled.

We chatted a bit more before he needed to leave. What a lovely man. He didn't want anything from me. In fact, his energy nourished my heart. He could be my friend for the rest of my life, I thought.

※

> *Find the right friend, who will be a support for you,*
> *a good traveling companion on the path of truth.*
>
> Ibn Arabi

CHAPTER 169

By Thursday, October 26, I knew I needed to return to work, if Madame would accept me even part time. I called her, and she was reluctant, but I pressed her, letting her know how well I knew the bakery job.

"How are you feeling?"

"Oh, I'm fully recovered."

I lied.

She agreed for me to return for the afternoon shift the next day.

When I arrived on Friday afternoon, I could not hide the fact that my dress floated on me, that the whites of my eyes were still stained yellow and that I wore black long socks to hide my scars. She barely recognized me. She questioned the socks, and I had to tell her I was cold. She did not approve of the look.

Trisha came into the bakery toward closing. Madame had left and would return around five to total the receipts for the day, so I had some time to sit with her.

"There's a meeting tonight with Robert at Richard's house in Walnut Creek. Some of us are going and we have room for you if you want to go."

I was tired, but more truthfully, tired of being tired. I longed to go to a meeting with Robert.

"Do we have time for me to change?"

"Yes. We're leaving at 5:30. The meeting starts at eight."

It was 4:30. We closed at five but I couldn't miss this opportunity.

"Could you pick me up at Whitman Circle at 5:30?"

"Sure."

She left and I left a lot of the work undone. I knew Madame would be upset, but my time and energy were paramount to me. I did run the dishwasher, wipe down the tops of the counters, and sweep the floors. When Madame returned, I apologized to her that my energies are not up to normal yet, and played the wounded animal card. I was shocked how it worked. She thanked me for coming and said she would see me the next day, same shift. It was so unexpected to hear that. It was as if an angel was speaking through her mouthpiece.

* * * *

Trisha drove with JT and myself in her car. I learned another Carmel student had planned to go but cancelled. I was so pleased to be able to stretch out in the backseat, and sleep a bit, waking up periodically to attend to a random itch that still plagued me.

The conversation centered on the latest news from the ranch. I caught snippets of it as I dozed, until I heard Trisha talking about a baby.

"I wonder if Mason and Marsha will be there with their baby," pondered Trisha, to no one in particular.

"Mason and Marsha had a baby?" I asked, totally shocked by the news.

"You didn't know?"

"No."

"Their picture was on the cover of the journal about six weeks ago."

It was at that moment I realized that I had missed more than meetings. I had missed issues of the journal. It had not occurred to me how fast time had passed and how disconnected I had become to the circumstances of everyone's life in the school. I didn't even know that Marsha was pregnant. How is that possible? We had just been together earlier this year. It was now almost the eleventh month of the year, said an 'I' inside. Yes. Now I see how that's possible.

"Tell me more," I begged, hoping she would include other vital bits of information regarding other friends there.

She explained that the baby is a girl. The labor was difficult, especially since they decided to have a midwife and not use a hospital. The birth occurred on the floor of the Lincoln Lodge living room. It was pretty messy.

"That sounds scary," I said, with a shudder. "Why would they do this?"

"They wanted an organic, natural childbirth."

"They sure had one, didn't they," quickly replied JT. We all laughed.

"Robert said the birth signified the birth of Miles's and Yorgos's higher centers, which he said should be near," explained Trisha.

"Six to twelve months away," added JT.

Wow, I thought. I was so looking forward to seeing Yorgos. I had not seen him for many months and imagined his smile and softness and the loving twinkle in his eyes directed at me once again. He moves so fast, I thought. And I'm stuck in my many 'I's.

When we arrived at Richard's house, it was close to meeting time and the driveway was almost full of cars. We went to the wood-paneled room, and took seats in the back. There in the third row was Yorgos. I wanted to go up to him but he was not easily accessible, plus he was leaning forward to talk to Richard. I did not want to interrupt.

Robert had just arrived and immediately went to the front dais. This elevated platform held five chairs. Robert was in the center, with Jim, Rose, Mac, and Mary C. on the sides.

The meeting began with this request from Robert.

"Please do your best to spend time in Carmel. We are strengthening the group there, and lovely students are joining. Weekend meetings are at the Carmel Highlands house. Please speak with Meg about the schedule."

After Alice secured help with restoration, signaling the last of good householder, Yorgos raised his hand. Robert acknowledged him.

"Please do your best to come to the farm on weekends. We are preparing the garden for spring crops."

There was immediate silence in the room.

Robert's face changed. It was firm and not the soft look he brought to meetings. Then, looking directly at Yorgos, Robert signed to Jim, who spoke his words.

"Do not identify with the farm. We may even sell it."

The tension in the room was palpable. This was a confrontation. Yorgos's face was equally firm. Gone was the sweetness. I did not recognize him.

The meeting had taken a turn. Robert tried to recover from it and asked for questions. We sat there for quite some time. No one raised their hand. Robert finally broke the silence.

" 'I's can be evoked by subtle external circumstances, such as a scene, seating arrangements, anything. All 'I's are automatic. What is not automatic is controlling and letting only certain one's manifest.

"When 'I's say 'no' to an earlier perception, it is the lower eating the higher.

"Also, observe when you do ask for someone's opinion, observe who it is and why you may ask that particular person and not someone else. We have 'I's that want to keep their idea of things, and sometimes we seek out people who will agree with those 'I's."

Yorgos raised his hand. Robert ignored him.

He asked again if there were any questions.

THE DIVINE BEGINNING

A lady student who was new to me raised her hand. It was clear she did not know what was going on behind the scenes.

"I heard the idea of mechanical goodness. Can you explain this?"

He asked Mac to offer an angle.

"The machine wants to be liked. It tries to be good, like being a good student by following all the rules. This type of goodness is mechanical."

I tried to think of an angle to help Robert keep the meeting rolling. He smiled and nodded in my direction.

"Mechanical goodness often has inner considering as its basis."

I slowly sat down after speaking, trying to catch a glimpse of Yorgos's face. He was looking away from me, towards the floor.

The meeting continued from there, with several angles from others, as well as other questions. The tension relaxed and we made it to the intermission.

I stayed in my chair while others moved to the table of snacks. I watched Robert approach Yorgos, guiding him to a corner of the room. He wrote a note and handed it to Yorgos, whose lips were tightly pressed, clearly trying as hard as possible to prevent his words from escaping.

Robert left the room and the rest of the meeting, heading back to a destination unknown to us. It was time for small groups. Trisha, JT, and I decided to skip small groups and head back to Carmel.

On the way home, we did not speak about the incident for the first hour or so. Then Trisha, who seemed to know what was occurring everywhere in the school, brought up the subject.

"I found out from Alice that Robert asked Yorgos to go into silence."

"That's one way to shut someone up," added JT.

"What happened to him?" I asked.

"Oh, you know. First, Robert puts him in charge of the farm, and then Robert takes all the people who could help him away. Yorgos has to do everything himself. I feel sorry for him."

"Boy, that's a Catch-22," offered JT, sympathetically.

"Maybe it's a test," I proposed.

"A test?"

"You know, the gods are testing him before he crystallizes."

"A test on what? He just wants to plant his vegetables, and Robert isn't providing any support."

Trisha did not understand the concept. I let it go.

When I arrived home, I was both exhausted and replenished. My physical body had reached its limit. My state was renewed, just seeing Robert.

I did not sleep much that night, however, thinking about the weirdness of that moment between Robert and Yorgos. I hoped that silence would help Yorgos recognize something low in him was challenging the teacher. It smacked too much of Paradise Lost to me. God and Satan. The higher and lower in conflict.

We all know how that ended.

*

> That which rules within, makes a material for itself out of that which opposes it, as fire lays hold of what falls into it. And when the fire is strong it consumes it, and rises higher by means of this very material.
>
> Marcus Aurelius

CHAPTER 170

Lack of sleep made me a mess the next day. The 'I's were swarming. The incident with Yorgos actually shook me to the core more than I realized. It did not seem to affect others the way it was affecting me, and I had no idea why this was the case. Something in the school was brewing, and try as I might, I could not dismiss the feeling of foreboding.

My time in the school seemed to be characterized by loss. And to lose Yorgos's friendship now would be a devastating blow. He was my first friend in the school. He stood up for me. He counseled me. But who is he now? What has happened to him? I could not reach him last night. It was as if an invisible barrier had been placed around him, which I could not surmount. Others were comforting him when we left. They felt sorry for him. I just wanted to hug him and talk to him. Now I couldn't. In silence, he could no longer speak to me.

* * * *

I needed to focus my energy on the job, since the first of the month was rapidly coming. I worked Saturday and Sunday and through the next week, too. Sleeping in the morning and arising for the four-hour shift in the afternoon, and then returning to bed exhausted. This had become my daily routine.

I had lost touch with meetings, as well. It was hard to figure out Robert's schedule. Robert rarely kept to a schedule, even though one was printed. He would pop up at the last minute somewhere, and if you came for Robert, you were frequently disappointed. It wasn't the same meeting without him, despite his encouragements for the older students to take on conscious responsibilities.

No one was speaking about Yorgos, either. I tried to poll the ladies in the house, but they were not talking. We had an exercise of not gossiping, so they had a justification for remaining silent. Rosemary spent her days more and more with Robert at Sheila's. I rarely saw her anymore. She had been the best source of information, Trisha being second. My emotional center was drying up and I longed for a good, juicy conversation. That would have to wait.

* * * *

On Tuesday, November 7, I learned that the Bay Area had a new gathering place, and there would be a big meeting scheduled there that evening. I had enough money to attend, since I had made my teaching payment and paid my rent for the month from the week of work. I still, however, needed someone to drive me because my energies were low. Fortunately, I found a ride with two married students, who happened to be visiting Carmel for a week from Berkeley. They didn't mind a round trip to be with Robert. I appreciated their valuation.

We took our time arriving at Berkeley and ate in a restaurant on Telegraph Avenue that we heard Robert enjoyed. We hoped to see him. He wasn't there.

"Do you know where the new meeting place is?" the lady asked, as she finished her meal.

"I don't," I replied, although she was actually asking her husband.

"The map I have says it's a new real estate development named Hiller Highlands. It's in Oakland."

After paying the bill, we headed out to this new development that apparently was quite swanky. We went along Ashby, which turned into Tunnel Road. The exit was new and we became lost and had to double back around. Finally, we found Hiller Drive. We drove in circles along the road. All we saw were large townhouses. There was no building that was not residential. We had to stop for directions. It was confusing.

Other students were also in a muddle, as we found them stopped along the drive. We rolled down our windows to talk with them. Together, we figured out that the "auditorium" (as someone called it) was at the top of the hill.

When we exited our cars, the skies were black with the last streak of blood-red sunset in the distance overlooking the city lights. The development was so new that street lamps had yet to be installed. It was dark and felt ominous. I did not like this place.

THE SEEDS OF

I followed them, like a child, toward the building. We opened the door and recognized friends, which eased my anxiety. The lights were all on and the room was bright. There was Kerrie, whom I had not seen in a long time, chatting with her new boyfriend, I was told. He was quite handsome and a masculine type. She looked happy. Meg was there, and Alden, and Richard and Alice. Rosemary and Anna were there with Mac. The chairs had been arranged in a semi-circle. I found a seat in the fourth row.

I looked around for Yorgos and spotted him sitting on the aisle in the fourth row. I put my purse on my seat and went to him.

"Hi," I said, beaming with joy to see him.

He stood up and did not smile. I reached out for a hug, and he embraced me half-heartedly. My friend. Where did you go?

I went back to my seat a bit stunned. The place had a vaulted ceiling, and behind the platform where Robert would sit were four floor-to-ceiling glass doors. It looked a bit like a cathedral, but without the stained glass.

Robert had entered with Jim and went up to Kerrie, indicating to her she would sit next to him up front. It was good to see him giving her a well-earned respect, after all she has done for the school, I thought.

We were told to take our seats. Robert walked to his position with those who were chosen to accompany him. While I focused on the teacher, the person next to me tapped my shoulder, and handed me a folded piece of paper.

"Pass this along."

I looked at it and it said, "For Richard."

Richard was six chairs away from me. I passed it along.

After good householder, Robert sat there in silence, his hands folded quietly in his lap, with his legs crossed. Kerrie beamed. I sat upright on the edge of my seat, as I had that first meeting with the teacher last year. I yearned for Robert's words.

Just then, without any permission, Richard rose, and read from the piece of paper in his hands.

"This teaching is over. All those who wish can follow me."

Yorgos stood up and headed toward Robert, but exited through one of the glass doors behind him. Slowly, one, two, three, four and more students began to stand up and follow Yorgos out. I could not believe how many there were. People I thought I knew, who were strongly supportive of Robert, left.

There was an awestruck, deafening silence. I was more present than I had a right to be. This was more than just a state of self-remembering. This was the crystal clarity of a higher dimension, a higher reality. The palpable presence

THE DIVINE BEGINNING

of the almighty gods themselves circulated in the room, and the state they brought incinerated our sleep. Time did not just stand still. It vaporized.

I looked at Robert and Kerrie. Kerrie froze in suspended animation. Robert sat silently and humbly. He had a look on his face — it was both shock and immediate acceptance. With eyes directed forward, in an eternal gaze, was the face of the Sphinx.

We stared at Robert, waiting for him to respond.

When time returned, Robert signaled to James, who spoke.

"Yorgos will be under heavy shocks for the next two to three years as he prepares for his own teaching."

I was relieved that Robert was encouraging. Yes, that's what it was. Yorgos is on his own now, and his evolution is secure. Robert said this. He would know.

Robert ended the meeting. We all dispersed.

On the drive back to Carmel, my companions spoke of other things. I remained silent. I was still trying to formulate what had just happened. Although Robert was supportive, what occurred was still disturbing. I tossed and turned all night.

The next morning, I was able to formulate what shook me so much the evening before. The departures were a random act, and made no sense. It was as if the angels had swooped into the room and selected people who happened to be sitting in a chair that had no mark, like the angel of death during Passover, who struck dead the first-born child within the households that failed to put an X on their doors. There was no rhyme nor reason for those students to leave like that. They did nothing that would have indicated their destiny was to disconnect from the school, thereby ending their conscious possibilities. This arbitrariness put the fear of God in me.

Why were they selected to leave? Why was I selected to stay?

I felt I would never know.

* * * *

A few days after the students' departure, Robert had a different take on Yorgos's actions. The negativity toward the teacher from those who left made Robert realize that this was not a healthy situation. In fact, he referred to it as a Play of Crime, where the lower eats the higher — where a student robs from his teacher to establish his own group.

Once he understood this, Robert acted swiftly. He placed Mac in charge of the school in his absence, and he put the farm up for sale. He asked that we not dwell on the event, but move on with our work, which included Carmel students to attend San Francisco meetings, and vice versa. There was a healing energy that came from this. Someone called it "circulation."

At one such meeting, a petite student from San Francisco named Lucretia, with long wavy flaxen hair, approached me during intermission with a sincere question.

"You were such good friends with Yorgos, I'm surprised that you did not go with him. Why did you stay?"

I was shocked at first to think she did not know my commitment to Robert, the gods, and awakening. But then, I had never thought about it. It was a good question.

"Well," I replied slowly, "as long as I keep learning from Robert, I'm staying."

That was an honest reply. This response would become the North Star of my journey of awakening.

For the journey of the soul, gather those supplies which will go with you here and hereafter. These are obtained from the Perfect Guru, when God bestows His Glance of Grace.

Guru Nanak

PART VII
The Divine Continuance

CHAPTER 0000

ROBERT ENDED HIS silence on Christmas Day 1972, uttering these words:
"Struggling to awaken, even when our weary efforts fail."

The learning has yet to cease. The chapters of my life in the Fellowship have continued to unfold for over 52 years, and counting. The young Linda met with even more difficult tests that not only matured her as a woman, but also transformed her into an increasingly conscious loving being. Each day would bring its challenges, and through the grace of the gods and their guidance, the narrow path would be found again and again to continue the ascent. The personal tales are too numerous to share. But I can say, with relative certainty, knowing the members as I do, that my story is, indeed, their story.

As for the Fellowship, after the school lost approximately a third of its membership from the 1972 play of crime, the beginning of a great expansion out of California began the following year and continued into the 1980s. More seeds were flung across great oceans through the next decades, which resulted in centers of teaching around the globe.

As time passed, these centers expanded and contracted, people joined and left, and some, with good fortune, rejoined to pursue the quest of full, not partial, awakening. The angels' instructions, which they communicate through the conscious conduit of the teacher and fellow students, have taken many forms. It, and we, have become simpler. The teacher's loving connection to each one of his students has increased beyond measure, encouraging the continuance of their individual efforts.

Robert's and the gods' direct, divine assistance still serves to distil our being, like that pounding ocean, making it lighter and more compact, so that it readily can fit into each present moment. The journey of awakening does not end. It follows the path of its true destination. It continues upward.

❦

Beginners.
How they are provided for upon the earth, (appearing at intervals);
How dear and dreadful they are to the earth;

THE SEEDS OF

How they inure to themselves as much as to any —
    what a paradox appears their age;
How people respond to them, yet know them not;
How there is something relentless in their fate all times;
How all times mischoose the objects of their adulation and reward,
And how the same inexorable price must still be paid
    for the same great purchase.

Walt Whitman

Acknowledgments

This book would not exist without Robert Burton, whose conscious love is unwavering, and the guidance of those invisible beings who daily put me in the chair, placed my fingers on the keyboard, and insisted I sit back, relax and become conscious on the way while the text revealed itself.

I am indebted as well to my readers — Jeanne Chapman and Maria Kalliopi — whose suggestions helped to bring clarity to the text. To the photographers: Engelbert Goethals, who captured the double lotus in its moment of perfection and generously allowed the photo to be used for the front cover; Leonid Novoselov, who expertly provided the back cover image of the log cabin painting; and Susan Schofield, who offered this photo of me that reflects how her joyous conscious company and longstanding loving friendship easily evokes the highest within me, for which I am grateful. To William Bentley, whose design and layout brought integrity to the manuscript. A special thank you to Robert MacIsaac — editor, historian, and publisher extraordinaire — whose friendship and gentle prodding over the decades led to the book you have in your hands.

www.ingramcontent.com/pod-product-compliance
Lightning Source LLC
Chambersburg PA
CBHW022203090526
44583CB00012BA/205